D0983882

Buying Whiteness

Signs of Race

General Editors Philip D. Beidler, Tony Bolden, and Gary Taylor

Volumes Already Published:

Writing Race across the Atlantic World, Medieval to Modern
ed. Philip D. Beidler and Gary Taylor
Buying Whiteness: Race, Culture, and Identity from Columbus to Hip Hop
Gary Taylor

Future Volumes:

English and Ethnicity
ed. Janina Brutt-Griffler, Catherine Davies, and Lucy Pickering
Women and Others: Racial and Gender Difference in Anglo-American Literature and Culture
ed. Celia R. Daileader, Rhoda Johnson, and Amilcar Shabazz
Race, Nationality, and National Literatures: The Institutionalization of English
Postcolonial Otherness and Transnational Capitalism: Contexts, Contests, and Contradictions
Perspectives on African-American Vernacular Culture

Buying Whiteness

Race, Culture, and Identity from Columbus to Hip Hop

Gary Taylor

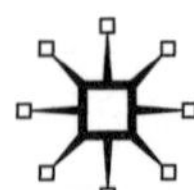

BUYING WHITENESS

First published 2005 by
PALGRAVE MACMILLAN™
175 Fifth Avenue, New York, N.Y. 10010 and
Houndmills, Basingstoke, Hampshire, England RG21 6XS.
Companies and representatives throughout the world.

PALGRAVE MACMILLAN IS THE GLOBAL ACADEMIC IMPRINT OF THE PALGRAVE MACMILLAN division of St. Martin's Press, LLC and of Palgrave Macmillan Ltd. Macmillan® is a registered trademark in the United States, United Kingdom and other countries. Palgrave is a registered trademark in the European Union and other countries.

ISBN 1-4039-6071-2

Library of Congress Cataloging-in-Publication Data

Taylor, Gary, 1953-
Buying whiteness : race, culture, and identity from Columbus to hip-hop / Gary Taylor.
p. cm.
Includes bibliographical references (p.) and index.
ISBN 1-4039-6071-2
1. English literature—History and criticism. 2. Race in literature. 3. American literature—History and criticism. 4. Race awareness—English-speaking countries. 5. Slavery—English-speaking countries. 6. Racism—English-speaking countries. 7. African Americans in literature. 8. Human skin color in literature. 9. Slavery in literature. 10. Racism in literature. 11. Whites in literature. 12. Blacks in literature. I. Title.

PR408.R34T389 2004
305.8—dc22

2004050646

A catalogue record for this book is available from the British Library.

Design by Letra Libre, Inc.

First edition: January 2005
10 9 8 7 6 5 4 3 2 1

Printed in the United States of America.

This work is dedicated to
the Coalition for Diversity and Inclusiveness
at the University of Alabama

Contents

List of Illustrations

Color Plates

Illustrations

GENERAL EDITORS' PREFACE

SIGNS OF RACE

> I have never been to Alabama before, but it is and will forever remain seared in my memory as the place where black Americans challenged America to live up to the meaning of her creed so as not to make a mockery of her ideals.
>
> —August Wilson, September 26, 2001

THE FIRST THING YOU SEE WHEN YOU ENTER the permanent exhibits at the Birmingham Civil Rights Institute is a pair of drinking fountains. Over one hangs a sign that says "White." Over the other hangs a sign that says "Colored."

As an inquiry into the cultural history of race, the series "Signs of Race" has its own obvious historical origins. It springs from a series of symposiums at the University of Alabama—the place where George Wallace made segregation's last stand. But the series finds its larger cultural and intellectual impulses in a deeper and wider history that surrounds us here. Black, brown, red, and white; African American and Afro-Caribbean; English, French, and Spanish; Celtic and Jewish; native American and northern European, creole and mestizo: such cultural categories, wherever they are found, in whatever combinations, and in whatever arrangements of historical interaction and transmission, constitute the legacy of the oceanic intercultures of race in the early modern era. In Alabama, the very landscape is steeped in such history. Twenty miles to the south of the town of Tuscaloosa, the home of the University, is a vast city of pre-Columbian mounds, the capital of a Mississippian empire that flourished at the time of the Norman Conquest and then disappeared two centuries later. The town of Tuscaloosa itself is named for a great Chief of the Alabamas, known as the Black Warrior, who engaged the Spanish explorer DeSoto in the 1540 battle of Maubila, to this day thought to be the largest single combat ever fought by native Americans against Europeans. The European settlement of the Gulf Coast pitted English, French, Spanish, and American colonizers against each other well into the nineteenth century. The Revolutionary War found native tribes, their ruling families frequently intermarried with Scots-Irish traders, allied with loyalists against American nationalists. The early nineteenth-century wars of extermination and removal against native peoples—Creeks, Choctaws, Cherokees, Chickasaws, and Seminoles—and the filling up of the rich agricultural lands thereby opened to a vast slave empire, were determining events in the southward and westward expansion of slavery eventuating in civil war.

In more recent historical memory, particular words and phrases constitute a litany of particular racial struggle. Jim Crow. Ku Klux Klan. Separate but Equal. The Scottsboro Boys. Autherine Lucy. Rosa Parks. The Schoolhouse Door. The names of major cities and towns ring forth as the Stations of the Cross of the Civil Rights Era: Selma, Montgomery, Birmingham, Tuscaloosa. Most recently, Alabama, like much of America, finds itself newly Hispanic, with large influxes of population from Mexico and the Caribbean, South and Central America.

To the extent that every social identity is to some degree local, the meanings of race in Alabama necessarily differ, in some demographic and historical particulars, from the meanings of race in North Dakota and Northern Ireland, New York and New South Wales, Cape Town and Calcutta. But the same questions can be asked everywhere in the English-speaking world.

How do people signal a racial identity?

What does that racial identity signify?

This series examines the complex relationships between race, ethnicity, and culture in the English-speaking world from the early modern period (when the English language first began to move from its home island into the wider world) until the postcolonial present, when it has become the dominant language of an increasingly globalized culture. English is now the medium of a great variety of literatures, spoken and written by many ethnic groups. The racial and ethnic divisions between (and within) such groups are not only reflected in, but also shaped by, the language we share and contest. Indeed, such conflicts in part determine what counts as "literature" or "culture."

Every volume in the series approaches race from a global, interdisciplinary, intercultural perspective. Each volume in the series focuses on one aspect of the cross-cultural performance of race, exploring the ways in which "race" remains stubbornly local, personal, and present.

We no longer hang racial signs over drinking fountains. But the fact that the signs of race have become less obvious does not mean that they have disappeared, or that we can or do ignore them. It is the purpose of this series to make us more conscious, and more critical, readers of the signs that separate one group of human beings from another.

Philip D. Beidler and Gary Taylor

CHAPTER I

INTRODUCTION: WHITE FICTIONS

Men formed a language—and that language, men.

—John Ford (1625)[1]

I'M WHAT'S CALLED WHITE. I LIVE, NOWADAYS, a block from the Black Warrior River, about a mile from where a white man named George Wallace stood in "the schoolhouse door," forty years ago, trying to preserve the segregated South. But I've lived lots of places, on both sides of the North Atlantic, and I've always been white, wherever I went. Whiteness was there, waiting, in 1953, when I popped from my white mom's womb into the hands of that nice white doctor, who passed me to a smiling white nurse and then went to congratulate my proud white dad. I was born into whiteness, as I was born into air. I inhaled it. So whiteness seems to me, as to other white people, not only as invisible, but as natural and necessary, as oxygen. As natural, as inescapable, as skin.

The largest and most sensitive human organ, skin is our first functioning perceptual system, responding to stimuli in an eight-week-old embryo less than an inch long.[2] Skin, though, has always been, for us, more than a thin organic membrane. For *Homo sapiens sapiens,* skin is a signed facade. The superb writing surface called parchment, used to record official documents for more than a thousand years, is the skin flayed from a dead sheep or goat. But animal skins can also be marked with signs while the animals are still kicking. Domesticated livestock are branded to identify their owners. And what we do to the skins of other animals we also do to our own skins. Slaves were branded, too, not only to identify their owners but to signal that they were just another form of livestock. The relative hairlessness of humans makes it easier to mark our skins and easier to see the marks thus made. We probably began making deliberate and artificial signs on our own skins—coloring, tattooing, scarring—long before we began engraving geometric designs in ochre, in Africa, 77,000 years ago.[3] That is why curator Michel Thévoz says that, for humans, "there is no body but the painted body."[4]

Once we began painting and marking our skins, then *not* to paint one's skin became a deliberate choice, an artistic statement (like not shaving, when everyone else shaves). In a world of painted bodies, any unpainted body—anybody who is unpainted—becomes as conspicuously and specifically meaningful as nakedness in a clothed world. For the clothed and unpainted European men who voyaged south and west across the Atlantic in the fifteenth and sixteenth centuries, the unclothed skins and painted skins of the people they encountered were spectacularly meaningful signs of social difference. Starting with Columbus, Europeans were fascinated by the Amerindian, deeply un-Christian custom of painting the skin. "This one thing was observed to be general amongst them all"—according to an eyewitness of Sir Francis Drake's landing in what is now California, halfway through the first English circumnavigation of the globe—"that every one had his face painted, some with white, some black, and some with other colors."[5]

But say we ignore for the moment the significance of such artificial skin-supplements as painting and tattooing and clothing. We still cannot help but interpret skin as a signed surface. Upon that surface birthmarks are signs; wrinkles, beards, scars, blushes are signs; beads of sweat are signs. Skin is the first sign system that we learn to read. I read my mother's face for years before I could read a single word of English. What is true of autobiography is true too of history. From ancient Egypt to imperial Rome, our earliest medical texts were pervasively dermatological. The easiest diseases to diagnose were those that signed their names on the body's outer envelope.[6]

Because members of our species routinely read skin, it would be hard for us not to notice its color. No human community has ever been monochromatic. Moreover, any departure from the pigment range to which a child or adult has grown accustomed will immediately register as a variation from the norm. Most academics now claim that the concept of race, and its association with skin color, is "socially constructed."[7] This intellectual orthodoxy is meant to challenge racist claims that certain human beings are biologically distinct from others. But epidermis is not socially constructed; melanin is not socially constructed; the spectrum of light is not socially constructed. Melanin, which makes skin darker, reduces its ability to synthesize previtamin D3 but protects it from ultraviolet radiation; the amount of melanin in human skin is related, in statistically significant ways, to the geographical homeland of a population group.[8] In layman's language: people come in different colors, and those colors in large part depend on where those people come from. Such physical phenomena exist and persist outside the language we use to describe them.

This does not mean people of different colors belong to different "races." Genetically, humans are astonishingly homogeneous, and individual variety within populations is greater than the differences between them.[9] "Races," or even "populations," are statistical fictions. Human beings can be divided into an infinite number of possible groupings. For example, without invoking racist categories, the superset of all human beings who have ever lived can be broken down into smaller sets of (a) "humans living in certain places" or (b) "humans living at certain times," and where two such sets overlap we get subsets of (ab) "humans living in certain places at certain times." The "races" of modern racist ideologies are neither geographically nor temporally limited: an "African" retains that putative biological identity, even if she is moved to Maryland, and from the perspective of racist theory a native African in the fifteenth century does not differ in any essential or significant way from an African American in the twenty-first. By contrast, the phrase "people living on the island of Britain in the fourteenth century" refers not to a "race" or even an "ethnicity," but simply to a "geotemporal population set," defined by precise regional and chronological limits. We do not have a word for such geotemporal population sets; I propose to call them "genres" of humanity.[10] The word *genre* derives from the same Latin root as the biological term *genus,* but genres are cultural categories. Genres may be clearly or loosely defined; they persist, but also change over time, and they are sometimes deliberately mixed, in ways that create new genres with their own rules of definition.[11]

The variant color of human skin is a biological reality, and the geographical distribution of relatively isolated, differently pigmented human genres until 1400 is a biological, historical and statistical reality. Nevertheless, the structures of the human brain, hand, and larynx are also physical phenomena, and *Homo sapiens sapiens* is distinguished from other primates in part by a capacity to create and exchange the extraordinarily complicated signals we call language. The language we use to describe physical reality affects how we understand variations in the pigment of human skin. We are creatures addicted to semiotics, to the interpretation of signs. H. Rap Brown was right to insist that "In and of itself, color has no meaning"; but he was wrong to claim that only "the white world" has imposed significance on the neutrality of the spectrum.[12] Having no intrinsic meaning, color can be given any meaning; it is a free-floating balloon of possibility, and it was inflated with particular meanings long before "the white world" existed. In fact, color terms have been the most frequently cited examples of the founding dictum of modern semiotics, "*the linguistic sign is arbitrary.*"[13] Color belongs to a continuous spectrum, which different languages cut up into different (artificial) segments. We could divide the spectrum of skin pigments into any number of different categories, and we could read the resulting categories in as many different ways. For instance, many citizens of the Roman empire harbored a nasty prejudice against eunuchs. Eunuchs—human males castrated before puberty—are biologically identifiable by the appearance of their skin: soft and very pale. Two thousand years ago, white skin was read as the sign of membership in a despised genre of humanity.[14] Like other sign systems, the language of skin changes across time and place.

Skin signifies. Skin means. For Americans, skin means race. But *racism* is a twentieth-century word, first recorded in 1936; its immediate predecessor, the British word *racialism,* is only a little older (1907). Those words come trailing clouds of concepts drawn from a white "racial science" that was not fully developed until the middle of the nineteenth century. The relevance of those concepts to earlier societies is, to say the least, debatable. William Wells Brown, a former slave who wrote the first African American novel, did not describe America as a "racist" society or slavery as an expression of "racism." Returning to America in 1854, Brown wrote of the "rampant" and "unnatural" "colorphobia" that pervaded northern cities.[15] The word *colorphobia* was used at least as early as 1838 in an African American newspaper, *The Colored American,* and it remained part of the African American vocabulary until at least 1926.[16] In 1849 Frederick Douglass described the "disease" of "colorphobia" as an "epidemic."[17] Douglass claimed that New Yorkers afflicted by "this wide-spread plague" suffered the same delusion as Brabanzio, a character in Shakespeare's play *Othello* (1603). Brabanzio thought it impossible "for nature so preposterously to err" (1.3.62) by making his white daughter "fall in love with what she feared to look on" (1.3.98).[18] Brabanzio regarded such "fear" to look upon a man of Othello's color as natural; Douglass, instead, treated that "fear" as a contagious illness, what medical science since the sixteenth century had defined as a phobia, "an abnormal or irrational fear."[19]

By his citation of *Othello,* Douglass asserted that colorphobia was at least as old as Shakespeare. Douglass was right: Shakespeare repeatedly associated the color black with fear, dread, terror, and the devil.[20] The normality of that phobia was assumed by the explorer Pieter de Marees, whose account of the Gold Coast of Africa was published in Dutch at about the time Shakespeare was writing *Othello:* "the peasants of the Interior did not at first dare to come to the Portuguese to trade with them, because they were unacquainted with other nations and it was something frightful for them to see white people. . . . And so it also happens to many of our nation: they too are at first frightened when they see Moors or Black people for the first time."[21] Colorphobia could and did affect blacks (afraid of whiteness) as well as whites (afraid of blackness). Moreover, black people could themselves harbor phobias about blackness. In 1917 the African American journalist W. Calvin Chase criticized the "colorphobia" of elite blacks, observing that "There is as much color prejudice among certain classes of colored people as there is among certain classes of white people."[22] Long before then, in 1853, William Wells Brown had observed "a great amount of prejudice against color amongst the negroes themselves. The nearer the negro or mulatto approaches to the white, the more he seems to feel his superiority over those of a darker hue."[23]

Nevertheless, despite its long-lived utility, the term *colorphobia* has been replaced by the term *racism.* Why? In part, because *colorphobia* belonged to the marginalized vernacular of African Americans, whereas *racism* developed out of the dominant and authoritative white scientific discourse of *race;* in part, because colorphobia eventually turned into racism. By the end of the seventeenth century, the term *race* was being used in something like its modern sense. But the first recorded use of the English word *racism* occurs in a book advocating American fascism, modeled on Nazi Germany's; more specifically, it occurs in a passage considering the merits of the proposition that "one of our values should be a type of racism which excludes certain races from citizenship," which might be implemented by "the annihilation, deportation, or sterilization of the excluded races."[24] The word *racism* presupposes the existence of races, just as *Marxism* presupposes the existence of Karl Marx. The word *racism* dignifies bigotry by elevating it to the status of an -ism, like feminism or capitalism or environmentalism; we might disagree with an -ism, but by granting it that suffix, we recognize it as an organized body of thought. By contrast, *colorphobia* treats skin-bigotry as a contagious neurosis, a devastating eruption of pigment panic. For commentators on the twentieth century, *racism* is an unavoidably necessary term. But the African American term *colorphobia* lets us analyze prejudices about skin color in Elizabethan London or antebellum Mobile, without assuming that they carry with them all the conceptual baggage of modern racist theory. We need not presume the existence, or presume that earlier people presumed the existence, of separate "races" (which do not exist); we need only presume the existence of different fractions of the spectrum of light, different pigments of skin, and different phobias about those pigments (which all exist). The word *racism* forces us into anachronistic debates about the fictitious categories of race. The word *colorphobia* forces us to focus instead—as Douglass, Brown, and nine decades of African American writers did—on the real colors of real skin and on the artificial meanings and irrational fears (or desires) projected onto skin by a particular society.

The pigmentation of human skin is a biological fact, but the significance of skin color varies. Demonstrably, the desirability or undesirability of white skin is arbitrary. What Douglass called "the Skin Aristocracy of America" associates white skin with certain virtues.[25] I am an automatic beneficiary of that assumption—and to that extent my whiteness is indeed, counterintuitively, "socially constructed." But if something has been constructed, then we should be able to pinpoint who built it.

This Book: The Argument

This book tracks the origin of the complex of notions that coalesced to form the modern idea of Anglo-Saxon whiteness. That history can be summed up in one paragraph. First, people living in what is now England had to decide that they were white and that whiteness was something to be proud of (part I). They had not always considered themselves white, in part because a white complexion was traditionally considered inappropriate for men (chapter 2). The evolution of modern whiteness was therefore, in large part, an evolution in definitions of manhood. It began with the third voyage of Columbus (1498), which—bolstered by other Spanish and Portuguese discoveries in the following five decades—undermined classical and medieval theories about the relationship between geography and color (chapter 3). For half a century after 1555, English elites struggled to assimilate the resulting European intellectual debates (chapter 4). Between 1584 and 1623 those complex debates were simplified and resolved by a growing number of contact experiences outside of Europe, where Englishmen repeatedly found themselves being called "white" by other men (chapter 5). This emergent sense of generic whiteness was consolidated during the seventeenth century (part II). Between 1613 and 1624, it was transformed into a trope of popular London culture (chapter 6). However, slavery had not yet been cemented to a particular human genre (or "race"), and in the early seventeenth century European servants and laborers were still subjected to many of the same prejudices that later focused on African slaves (chapter 7). Nevertheless, by the 1660s race/genre had become the key variable in distinguishing slavery from labor, and by 1691 generic whiteness had been written into law by most colonial legislatures (chapter 8). As whiteness became a significant social and legal category, it began to acquire a range of new meanings (part III). The collapse of climatic explanations for human diversity encouraged the development of biblical and moral explanations (chapter 9). Beginning in the 1660s, the scientific revolution decisively redefined whiteness (chapter 10). In the 1680s a new theory of the social contract installed whiteness at the foundation of modern political thought (chapter 11). Many of the assumptions about whiteness born in the seventeenth century are still kicking in the twenty-first (chapter 12).

By 1700 most Englishmen—perhaps all Englishmen—considered themselves "white" in a sense that we would recognize today. After 1700 lawyers, preachers, doctors, and philosophers continued to argue about the relationship between "whites" and other people. Even in the heyday of scientific colorphobia, from the middle of the nineteenth to the middle of the twentieth century, plenty of people contested the political and ethical significance of the alleged differences between the alleged races. But from the eighteenth century to the present, such arguments have all taken for granted the self-evident reality of the population category "white." They have all assumed that a relatively new intellectual classification represented a relatively permanent biological reality.

Identity, personal and social, depends on memory—which is to say, identity depends on what we forget as well as what we remember.[26] After 1700 Anglos *remembered* that they were white and *forgot* that whiteness was a recent invention. Upon that shared belief in permanent generic whiteness was built antebellum slavery, Indian reservations, American and South African apartheid, and the concentration camp. Nor are the consequences of that idea comfortably confined to the past. As I write this book, the Anglo belief in generic whiteness underlies racial profiling, the epidemically disproportionate incarceration and execution of African American males, the growth of the Christian right and of white supremacist groups, the electoral success of conservative Republicans, the racialized pattern of housing throughout the United States and Britain, and the arrogant self-righteousness of Anglo-American foreign policy.

This Book: The Proof

If you are willing to take my word for it—I'm white, after all, so you should—then you need read no further. But I assume that most people will need convincing and/or will be interested in the ways that this centuries-long evolution of white identity changed the recipes for law, literature, art, science, philosophy, music, and daily life throughout the North Atlantic world.

The argument depends on a variety of evidence. An important element in the evolution of generic whiteness was played by European travel narratives—by Columbus (chapter 3) and those who followed him in the sixteenth-century global expansion of European power (chapters 4 and 5). But those narratives themselves can be understood only in relation to the history of natural philosophy (chapters 3 and 4). Chapter 2, by contrast, looks at European art (from prehistoric cave paintings to Stuart royal portraits), at proclamations by Queen Elizabeth, and at Shakespeare's *Othello.* Chapter 7 concentrates almost entirely on literary texts, but chapter 8 reads seventeenth-century statutes and parliamentary debates, and chapter 9 switches to biblical commentary, ending with John Bunyan and books written specifically for children. Chapter 10, by contrast, brings together the fathers of modern secular science: chemistry (Robert Boyle) and physics (Isaac Newton). The strange bedfellows of chapter 11 are the first professional woman author (Aphra Behn) and the founding theorist of philosophical empiricism and liberal democracy (John Locke). In the epilogue I measure the distance traveled in the three centuries between Locke's death and the present by looking at whiteness in the work of the American hip hop artist Eminem.

I did not anticipate this diversity of materials when I naively began this project. The texts were forced on me by their relevance to the historical evolution of whiteness—an evolution much messier than the categories that determine which works get taught in which university departments or shelved in one part of the library rather than another. As I started asking questions, dominoes started falling in unpredictable directions. I followed the chain reaction as it raced and split and redirected me.

I have tried to frame this flux of materials by means of three constants: the word *white,* the city of London, and the perspective of early African American writers.

White Words

White is, first and foremost, a word. Words are tools that help us construct and communicate to others certain concepts, which would be difficult or impossible to think if we did not have the right word. To take a famous example, a small Amazonian tribe, the Piraha, has only three words for numerals: the equivalents of "one-ish, "two-ish," and "more than two-ish." Consequently, the Piraha find it hard to describe accurately or to think precisely about quantities greater than two. Without the word *white,* we would find it hard to construct a category that meaningfully links together a German-speaking lesbian welder living in Chicago, a married Londoner working for an international bank in Barbados, and a divorced retired New Zealand sheep farmer. As the French philosopher Jacques Derrida insisted:

> there's no racism without a language. The point is not that acts of racial violence are only words but rather that they have to have a word. Even though it offers the excuse of blood, color, birth—or, rather, *because* it uses this naturalist and sometimes creationist discourse—racism always betrays the perversion of a man, the "talking animal." It institutes, declares, writes, inscribes, prescribes. A system of marks, it outlines space in order to assign forced residence or to close off borders.[27]

Sticks and stones may break your bones, but words will really kill you.[28] Words will convince your killers they have a right, indeed an obligation, to kill you—kill you literally, or (as a special favor) merely subject you to what sociologist Orlando Patterson calls the "social death" of slavery.[29] Although all words have that destructive potential, some are more powerful than others, and *white* belongs to the category of "Keywords."[30] For centuries, to open certain doors, you had to be "white," and the word *white* is the key to understanding that locked racial culture. Legally and socially, white identity depends on how the word *white* is defined and used. Therefore, to "abolish the white race," we must track the history of that English word.[31]

That word began to be popularly used in a specific, figurative, physical, ideological, positive, popular, and recognizably modern "racial"—or, as I prefer to call it, "generic"—sense in London in 1613. Since then that local trope has been globalized and internalized, so that now it hardly seems figurative at all. But whiteness *is* figurative, as figurative as blackness. Film critic Richard Dyer points out that, "White people are not literally . . . white. We are not the color of snow or bleached linen."[32] Like "time is money," the generic term *white* is a metaphor. Specifically, it's an example of what linguist George Lakoff and philosopher Mark Turner call "metaphors we live by." Such metaphors "structure our everyday activities," and consequently "metaphors can create realities."[33] The metaphor of generic whiteness has been a part of everyday English for more than three centuries; like "up and down," it has organized our conceptions of social space.[34] Through constant repetition and authoritative endorsement (by parents, schools, governments), the word has become an integral part of what the sociologist Pierre Bourdieu calls our linguistic *habitus.* Not simply a habit but a collection of interrelated habits of speech and thought, the linguistic *habitus* is, for each of us, our "second nature," a pattern of mental and physical action so ingrained that for the most part we are not even aware of its operations. But any such "durably installed generative principle of regulated improvisations," according to Bourdieu, "produces practices."[35] The word *white,* construed as a generic identity, helps to produce practical colorphobia.

In saying this, I do not mean to portray individuals as helpless automatons, hypnotized by a collective *habitus.* I would instead endorse the view of sociolinguists like Jay Lemke, who argues that "the role of discourse in society is active; it not only reconfirms and re-enacts existing social relationships and patterns of behavior, it also renegotiates social relationships and introduces new meanings and new behaviors."[36] My only objection to Lemke's formulation is its impersonality: the grammatical subject of his first sentence is *discourse,* an "it" that in turn governs the active verbs of his subsequent sentences. But a discourse exists only in and through the speech acts of individual speakers; it is speakers who take on and modify a "role," constituted by a series of individual speech events.[37] Perhaps because I have spent so many years editing the work of several playwrights, I am particularly conscious of the differences between individual writers—even when they lived at the same time in the same city, working for the same company of actors performing in the same commercial and court theaters, and sometimes even co-writing the same play.[38] Drama depends on the interaction of distinct voices, and it is best understood through an analysis of the protocols of dialogue.[39]

Through dialogues between very different individuals emerged a new discourse, which changed the meaning of such English words as *white* and *slave.* This book attempts to define *what it means* to be "white"—or rather, to delineate how "being white" *came to mean what it means now.* I am trying to track semantic change. Seen as an apparently stable large-scale structure, a language will eventually predictably split and diverge and merge into new formations; that fact allows linguists to group languages into families, linked by a shared ancestor, such as Indo-European. But because of the degrees of freedom of individual agents operating within a speech community, the small-scale specifics of each new language formation will be chaotically unpredictable. "Linguistic change," James Milroy reminds us, "is speaker-based."[40] Individuals not only maintain a linguistic system; they also tinker with it; indeed, tinkering is one of the ways they keep it running. We cannot predict which individual act of linguistic tinkering will be repeated by other individuals and eventually lead to major transformations of the whole system.[41] Shakespeare could not have predicted which of his many neologisms would (like *invitation*) be accepted and turned into the common coin of global English, or which would (like *invised*) die on the vine.[42] I therefore prefer to install, as the subject of my own sentences, a speech community of individuals (not an "it") who are engaged in a conversation (not a "discourse"). If individuals in conversation can coalesce and construct racist practice, then through conversation individuals can coalesce to construct antiracist practices.

So, my method in this book will be to identify which specific individuals in which specific contexts first used the word *white* in something like its modern generic sense. Having identified them, I try to explain what they were doing or trying to describe, why they felt they needed this new sense of the word, who they were, whom they were addressing, how they changed the meaning of that monosyllable within a particular conversation among a social group to which they belonged. When was this new generic sense of the word *white* first imported into English, in translations from other European languages? When did it first appear in original works? in popular works? in legal statutes? When did it debut as an adjective (as in "white people") and when as a noun (as in "whites")? Who was the first scientist, the first philosopher, the first bureaucrat, to identify himself as "white"?

I can hope to answer these questions thanks in part to the digital revolution of the last two decades. For example, suppose I want to know when the generic word *whites* first appeared on an English title page. Because they were posted as advertisements all around London, title pages were much more widely read than the books they prefaced, and therefore serve as a useful index of the familiarity of vocabulary.[43] Twentieth-century bibliographers invested decades of collective labor to produce accurate catalogs of all English printed books from 1473 to 1700; those catalogs have recently been digitized as the Electronic Short Title

Catalogue (or ESTC). I can search this entire database, looking for the word *whites,* and within a few seconds the computer generates a short list of titles; I can then read those works, using another database (Early English Books Online), which lets me access from my desk photographs of every printed page. Reading those selected texts makes it possible to throw out cases where the word refers to egg whites, whites of eyes, and laundry. I can then declare, with absolute confidence, that the generic plural noun first appeared on an English title page in 1676, in a 22-page pamphlet called *Gospel Family-Order: Being a Short Discourse Concerning the Ordering of Families, both whites and blacks and Indians.* That pamphlet was written by George Fox, the founder of the Quakers, and it specifically reflects his missionary visit to the island colony of Barbados. It took two centuries of printing (1473–1676) for the generic word *whites* to reach an English title page, and it finally did so in the context of an English colony dependent on the labor of thousands of African slaves.

Unfortunately, title pages represent only a fraction of the text of a printed book, and printed books are only a fraction of the written record. But virtually all of early English drama is available in a digitally searchable database.[44] I can therefore pinpoint with absolute precision, in chapter 6, the first appearance of generic *white* in an English dramatic text (in 1613), and in general I can trace with reasonable confidence the early literary evolution of whiteness. Likewise, because the canonical texts of western philosophy are widely available in digitized databases, I can, in chapter 11, identify John Locke as the first white philosopher and show that he used *white* in a generic sense as early as 1671. But other important sources for the history of whiteness have not been digitized; indeed, in some cases—many of the colonial legal statutes surveyed in chapter 8, for instance, or the bureaucratic memos in chapter 10—they have never even been printed. Like any other historian laboring in the uneven light of the predigital age, I might have missed something.

But I can at least promise you that I have not added anything. I will cite only those texts that actually contain in them the word *white.* It may seem an elementary and obvious rule that one should not claim to find whiteness in texts that do not contain it. But distinguished modern historians of slavery and racism routinely use *white* to describe Englishmen or Europeans, even when their sources do not.[45] A reference work as indispensable and seemingly objective as *The Calendar of State Papers* interpolates the word *white* into archival records that do not contain it.[46] "It is frequently so tempting to read the past backwards," Winthrop D. Jordan wrote in 1968, "and so dangerous."[47] But Jordan himself (like most other scholars trying to understand the origin of America's racial hang-ups) found it fatally easy to assume that *white* is a transhistorical, biological category, rather than a word. Any reader of our most authoritative secondary works on slavery, race, or European voyages of exploration and exploitation would come away convinced that early modern Englishmen routinely used the generic word *white* to describe themselves. In researching this book I have, again and again, traced reputable modern references to whiteness back to their sources, only to discover that the alleged whiteness is a figment of the modern scholar's own racial assumptions. In innumerable treatments of the sixteenth- and seventeenth-century Anglo-Atlantic world, what scholarship anachronistically calls "white" is—as the African American literary critic Arthur L. Little Jr. has written—"more accurately, non-black."[48]

We shouldn't put words in other people's mouths. We shouldn't attribute generic white identities to people who would have been confused or insulted by that category.

White City

This book is the linguistic equivalent of local history—the locality in this case being not a single neighborhood, but a single word or, more precisely, a "lexeme" (since *white* can be adjective or noun, singular or plural).[49] Linguistic history is always local history. The history of a word belongs to the history of the speech community that uses it, and speech communities are always initially local. Various technologies may extend a local speech community into an empire of discourse, but even an empire of discourse will consist of a patchwork of related but distinct communities of speakers, each with its own idiosyncratic habits. My focus on individual speakers necessarily entails attention to the setting of their interactions. Every *who* implies a *where.*

Where is London, which provides the second constant in this history. That 1676 pamphlet by George Fox, which boasts the first example of generic *whites* on an English title page, may have been *about* Barbados, but it was printed *in* London. The many different kinds of texts I examine here were written, published, or read (and usually all three) in metropolitan London; the plays and pageants were all performed there. The genres of humanity those texts represent inhabited different parts of the planet, but representative samples were brought back to London; as early as 1555 English voyagers returned from Africa with three black passengers, and by 1768 some contemporaries estimated the number of black servants in London at 20,000.[50] Whether or not the natives of other continents came to London, always the experience of encountering them was sent back to be digested there. During the centuries covered by this book, London became western Europe's most populous city and the center of a white global empire; global English evolved from a dialect spoken in and around London.

This emphasis on London may seem misguided to many experts in the history of race. Recent scholarship on whiteness has been "framed almost exclusively within North American terms."[51] It is widely assumed that colonial slave plantations spawned the virulent prejudices that developed into the myth of a superior "white race." This assumption satisfies the belief in "American exceptionalism" embraced by most Americans, including historians: for good or ill, we tell ourselves, the US of A is unique. Blaming racism on Americans also suits British historians, although for different reasons: Brits have enjoyed their moral superiority over Yanks since the eighteenth century, and especially as American global hegemony has replaced its British progenitor.

Nevertheless, we should resist this institutionalized temptation to confine the nastiness of slavery and colorphobia to the colonial margin. That hygenic separation of England from its colonies duplicates, and helped to create, the systems of segregation and apartheid that allowed white elites to insulate themselves psychologically from the horrific exploitation upon which their own prosperity depended (and still depends). The generic sense of whiteness emerged in London before a single slave plantation had been created in an English colony. During the historical period when *white* acquired its full range of modern meanings—from 1498 (the third voyage of Columbus) to 1704 (the publication of Isaac Newton's *Optics*)—London virtually monopolized English book production, and was also the engine of English linguistic evolution.[52] London's ability to generate capital was crucial to Britain's colonial expansion.[53] The generic whiteness that eventually would permeate the Anglophone world radiated outward from an imperial linguistic base on the Thames.

Black Observer

In 1998 the distinguished British actor Hugh Quarshie—Oxford graduate, son of a Ghanian diplomat, the first black actor to break through the color barrier in the Royal Shakespeare Company—claimed that in writing *Othello* Shakespeare "was endorsing a racist convention."[54] More than one of Quarshie's white listeners objected that Quarshie's view of the play was "biased," because he was "black." It did not occur to them that *they* might be biased, because they were *white*. It did not occur to them that, in a dispute between two ethnic groups about the portrayal of those two ethnic groups, no member of either group can claim to be an entirely disinterested observer. Quarshie himself, like most other black observers, instantly recognizes this fact. Why then were so many whites so oblivious to this elementary logical point? Why, even when it was explained to them, did they have so much trouble seeing the irony of their complaint? And why do incidents like this happen so frequently?

Let us assume, for the sake of argument, that whites are not genetically inferior, intellectually, to blacks. If so, there must be some other explanation for the stubborn stupidity of these white people who insisted that their own bias was unbiased. If they were not born stupid, they must have learned to be so. They must have been taught to be obtuse about this particular issue. In fact, for centuries whites have been systematically taught to believe in their own (unique) objectivity. This myth of white disinterestedness began in the 1660s, with the scientific revolution; I analyze its emergence in chapters 10 and 11.

White people, you might say, all suffer from snow blindness. But I, too, am "white." Before I could write those chapters on white objectivity, before I could think them, I had to escape the mind-numbing assumptions that had shaped my own generic identity for five decades. By definition, I could not do that by myself. To see ourselves we need something or someone outside ourselves. To glimpse the outlines of my whitehood I needed the perspective of someone who was not white.[55] And if I needed a nonwhite guide, so would my white readers. Beginning this project, I realized that any attempt to track the evolution of white identity could succeed only if it incorporated the perspective of a nonwhite observer. Ideally, that observer should be as close as possible to the process I would be studying. What I needed was a brown or black writer, living in London, whose mother tongue was English, an observer of white behavior on both sides of the Atlantic who was also energetically interested in the Anglophone literary tradition.

As it happens, the first novel by an African American was published not in Africa or America, but in London. It belongs, then, to the local history of London and to the literary and linguistic history of English. It also belongs to the history of whiteness. It begins with a demographic fact: "With the growing population of slaves in the Southern States of America, there is a fearful increase of half whites, most of whose fathers are slaveowners, and their mothers slaves" (81). The novel's 16-year-old heroine is one of these "half whites." Actually, more than half white: her mother was a "quadroon" (one-fourth black), her father Thomas Jefferson (all white), making the heroine what would come to be called an octoroon (one-eighth black).[56] These fractions are, of course, absurd. But such fictions of generic identity were enshrined in the very first article of the Constitution of the United States of America, which counted a black slave as three-fifths of a white man.[57] Legally, in the case of octoroons, the one-eighth black erased the seven-eighths white. Because her mother was a slave, so is she. Nevertheless, her appearance "on the auction block created a deep sensation amongst the crowd. There she stood, with a complexion as white as most of those who were waiting with a wish to become her purchasers; her features as finely defined as any of her sex of pure Anglo-Saxon . . ." (87). African American fiction begins by challenging white assumptions about whiteness.

The novel I have been quoting is William Wells Brown's *Clotel, or The President's Daughter: A Narrative of Slave Life in The United States.* I quote *Clotel* throughout this book, using it as my fixed point of reference, my North Star.[58] Written in 1853, it was printed in London because its author had fled America four years before, a political refugee. The final sentence of Brown's novel returns from fiction to fact, lamenting the consequences of the Fugitive Slave Act: although "fugitives from American slavery, can receive protection from any of the governments of Europe, they cannot return to their native land without becoming slaves" (225). But this seemingly fortuitous explanation for *Clotel*'s place of artistic birth belongs to a larger pattern of modern black identity, a literal and cultural back-and-forth across the Atlantic. James Gronniosaw, Olaudah Equiano, Phillis Wheatley, Ignatius Sancho, and Mary Prince—they were all first printed, and first appreciated as literature, in London.[59] In the decade before publication of *Clotel,* Frederick Douglass had lectured in London as part of the 21-month tour of England, Scotland, and Ireland promoting the abolitionist message of his autobiography, an international best-seller published first in Boston but soon afterward in London. By the end of 1849 the Boston edition of William Wells Brown's own autobiography had sold 8,000 copies—but the London edition had sold 11,000.[60] The origins of Anglophone generic whiteness and the black backlash against white colorphobia both belong to the history of London.

Equally important, London is part of the history of black consciousness. First as the undisputed center of white political and cultural authority, then as an alternative to the tyranny of white America, London became part of the identity constructed for themselves by culturally and politically ambitious blacks whose first language was English. Although W. E. B. DuBois did not say so, idealized white London was one pole of the "twoness" he described in *The Souls of Black Folk* ("two souls, two thoughts, two unreconciled strivings; two warring ideals in one dark body whose dogged strength alone keeps it from being torn asunder"); London was one focus of the "double vision" that Richard Wright attributed to negroes, "both *inside* and *outside* of our culture at the same time."[61] This modern "double consciousness"—the result of "striving to be both European and black"—has been theorized by Paul Gilroy as a consequence of the diasporic experience of peoples of African descent within the black Atlantic world.[62] Born in America, William Wells Brown had "a dream" of making "a visit to the Old World." After five years in Europe—most of it spent in London—Brown wrote that "he had begun to fancy [him]self an Englishman," and "felt more clearly [his] identity with the English people." He had "sat in Westminster Abbey," spent "days in the British Museum and National Gallery," and "dined at the same table" with Charles Dickens and Alfred Tennyson.[63] Like other works by Brown (and Douglass), *Clotel* repeatedly quotes Shakespeare.[64] More surprisingly to us, Brown also quotes Shakespeare's younger contemporary, Thomas

Middleton (who plays a significant role in the history of English whiteness).[65] The first African American novelist, travel writer, and playwright believed that he belonged on both sides of the Atlantic. Newly arrived in the British Isles, Brown watched Queen Victoria parading through Dublin. *Clotel* is not simply an African American novel, but also a Victorian one.

We are used to keeping *Clotel* segregated from *David Copperfield.* In a lecture at the University of Alabama in September 2001, inaugurating the series in which this book appears, the Pulitzer Prize–winning black American playwright August Wilson lamented the sick absurdity of such distinctions.

> If you go into a Borders bookstore, as I did in downtown Chicago, you will not find Toni Morrison in American Literature. You will not find Ralph Ellison, Richard Wright, James Baldwin, Maya Angelou, Albert Murray or Ishmael Reed. They are not there. They are excluded from American Literature. Not having their books in American Literature says we are an appendage to American society, despite the fact that our excellence is beyond reproach. . . . We are removed from American literature and segregated into a hodgepodge of cookbooks, self-help books, and photo books in the African American section, delegated to the briar patch of American culture.[66]

When bookstores, libraries, and universities insist on the division between American and African American literature, or between English and African American literature, we reinforce generic ("national" and "racial") boundaries we should be breaking down.

What has been called "the Afro-American Literary Renaissance" can teach us something about the English Renaissance.[67] Like Paul Gilroy, I believe we need to harness the "ethical resources that can be drawn from histories of suffering" without succumbing to "unanimist fantasies," national or racial, and without letting the "frozen past" restrain our political imaginations.[68] Segregating the literary canon aint any healthier than segregating the classroom or the neighborhood. That's why I'm proud to teach at the University where, four decades ago, Governor George Wallace failed to inoculate white education against black infiltration. I prefer edgy, partially integrated Alabama to politically correct, utterly segregated Massachusetts.

White Slave

As an example of what the African American Renaissance might teach us about the English Renaissance, consider the phrase "white slave." According to the *Oxford English Dictionary* (*OED*), the first use of that phrase—meaning "a white person who is, or is treated as, a slave"—occurred in 1789, the year that slave owner George Washington was inaugurated as the first President of the United

States.[69] Both *white slave* and *white slavery* are what linguists would call a "marked form."[70] The unmarked form would be *slave* or *slavery* without an adjective indicating color, but with some other color (black) always actually implied. By 1789 *white* had been written into an immense body of American statutory law, and in 1790 it would be written into the new nation's first immigration statute.[71] By 1789 the color "black" was implicit in the word *slave.* Slaves were black, so "black slave" would be redundant. Slaves were black, so "white slave" was a paradox, an oxymoron.

Brown forced his white readers to imagine the sale, at a slave auction, of a white woman. The first scene's climactic horror is focused, rhetorically, on the whiteness of the woman being sold. "Miss Clotel had been reserved for the last," the auctioneer says, "because she was the most valuable." Why most valuable? Because she is a "Real Albino."[72] Of course, Clotel is no such thing. The auctioneer uses *albino* euphemistically: readers have already been told that Clotel's father was white, but it would be indecorous for the auctioneer to acknowledge her white ancestry. "Real" is a colloquial intensifier, not a claim to veracity; "Albino" testifies not to a medical condition, but to the extreme whiteness of the woman's complexion. Clotel's status as a "negro" is a legal fiction. She is as white as the people bidding for her, as white as the people reading about her. Indeed, "Albino" suggests she may even be whiter than those bidders and readers.

Contrast the literary treatment of white slavery in *Clotel* with its treatment in a scene from the play *A Very Woman,* written by John Fletcher between 1613 and 1625. In a Sicilian port city, a slave master and the captain of a slave ship enter with "diverse Slaves," and the master harangues his slaves. Imagine the manager of a department store, addressing the staff two minutes before the doors open for the big annual sale; or a director, backstage, fine-tuning a cast of male dancers just before the curtain rises on an underrehearsed flesh-spectacle.

> Come rank yourselves, and stand out handsomely.—
> Now ring the bell, that they may know my market.—
> Stand you two here: you are personable men
> And apt to yield good sums, if women cheapen.—
> Put me that pig-complexioned fellow behind;
> He will spoil my sale else. The slave looks like famine.
> Sure he was got in a cheese-press; the whey runs out on's nose yet.
> He will not yield above a peck of oysters . . . (3.1.1–8)[73]

John Fletcher observed the human meat market without much expenditure of indignation. There is laughter in both scenes, but in *Clotel* the crowd is "Laughing, joking, swearing, smoking, spitting, and talking . . . while the slave-girl stood with tears in her eyes." Her tears condemn their laughter. No one in Fletcher's scene is crying. The slaves are the butts of all his jokes. The people on sale include an Englishman, who inspires more comedy than anyone else. Indeed, since pigs have pinkish white complexions, the English slave may be mocked in the very first speech. Satirical comparisons between pigs and Englishmen have a long history, including George Orwell's *Animal Farm* ("Some animals are more equal than others") and the Beatles' *White Album* ("Look at all the little piggies living piggy lives").[74] As early as 1694, the white man's cemetery in the slave-trading port of Whidaw was being called, by local blacks, the "hog-yard."[75] But whether or not he compared people to pigs, Fletcher did not assign to pale pink skin, or Anglo-Saxon origin, the value it has in *Clotel.* Here's how the slave master describes the English slave to a customer:

> The finest thing in all the world, sir,
> The punctuallest and the perfectest: an English mettle,
> But coined in France. Your servant's servant, sir.
> Do you understand that? or your shadow's servant.
> Will you buy him to carry in a box?—Kiss your hand, sirrah;
> Let fall your cloak on one shoulder; face to your left hand;
> Feather your hat; slope your hat; now charge your honor . . .
> (3.1.105–11)

The actor who plays the English slave must mime a succession of rapid changes, demanded by the slave master, his director. English actors thus epitomize the English as a people epitomized by actors.[76] In this episode displaying the sale of an English slave, Fletcher not only calls the English "apes," he enacts a demonstration of the apishness of a nation of slavish imitators, taking direction from others, worshipping the idols of fashion, "God Tailor, and God Mercer" (3.1.132).[77]

These jokes—characterizing an Englishman as heathen, ape, obedient performing animal with a gift for mimicry—uncannily resemble later colorphobic depictions of African Americans. But the more important point may be that Fletcher supplies such jokes to make the scene theatrically compelling. He does not consider the sale of a white person into slavery intrinsically shocking.

The seller and the buyers are all Christians. At least two slaves are Europeans, and the Englishman is presumably, according to modern terminology, "white." Nevertheless, the English slave's pallor—if it is noticed at all—does not increase his value.[78] More generally, Fletcher seems not to assume that the Moors belong to a different genre of humanity than Europeans. He does not use the word *race;* he does not use *race* in its modern sense, or *white* in its generic sense, anywhere in his dozens of plays.[79] But the word and the concept of race are unavoidable for Brown, despite his hostility to slavery; even in defending his "race," Brown uses the noun elsewhere used to justify the "deadly antagonism between the white and coloured races."[80] Brown assumes, or expects his readers to assume, that "coloured" people belong to a distinct "race" from "white" people. Fletcher does not.

Between 1613 and 1853, between Fletcher's London play and Brown's London novel, the relationships of skin color to capitalism and slavery changed dramatically. Those contrasts prompt certain questions. When did "black" become implicit in the word *slave?* When did "white slavery" become a tragic oxymoron? When did emotional responses to human slavery change so profoundly, within the same city, among the sorts of ordinary people who went to plays in 1613 and read novels in 1853? When did certain ideas about slavery and about the genres of humanity become so widely internalized that a literary artist could count on what had once provoked spontaneous laughter to evoke, instead, spontaneous tears?

As Aristotle realized 24 centuries ago, in the earliest surviving example of literary theory, a literary genre can be defined by the emotions it attempts to produce. Literary texts testify to feelings: the feelings of those who produced such texts, and the feelings of those who responded to them. Literary genres presuppose and reflect certain genres of humanity. The history of literature is therefore the affective history of a civilization. Literary critics are, among other things, archaeologists of affect.[81] Changes in affect signal changes in "ways of thinking and acting, forms of life." As historian David Harris Sacks has written, at the conclusion of his prize-winning account of the rise of Atlantic capitalism,

> Forms of life have origins just as species do. They connect with past forms. Even though they live in environments different from those of their forebears, they use many of the characteristic features of their ancestors, if for quite unexpected ends. Moreover, just as with the origin of species, the rise of forms of life is unpredictable, contingent both on the nature of their surroundings and on the kind of adaptations they have been able to make.[82]

The contrasts between Fletcher's play and Brown's novel index a transformation of forms of life in the English-speaking world.

If the questions posed by those contrasts are so obvious and so profound, why have they not been asked before?—In part because the two texts have never been juxtaposed. To connect two events in the past, you have to remember them both; to connect two events that happened before you were born, both have to be part of the collective memory of your society, a collective memory that each of us acquires during the course of our childhood and education.[83] Fletcher was the most popular English playwright of the seventeenth century—more popular than Shakespeare among playgoers and readers for at least eight decades; John Dryden was influenced by this slave-selling scene from *A Very Woman,* and John Keats quoted it.[84] But Fletcher has been completely eclipsed by Shakespeare in more recent times.[85] Likewise, Brown disappeared from Anglo-American memory for a century. Before we could start making comparisons between an African American novel and a Renaissance play, African American literature had to enter the curriculum, the collective memory, of whites as well as blacks. Only then could white readers begin to see their history through the eyes of black observers.

Given the scale and urgency of the human problems caused by fictions of whiteness in our time, it is not surprising that the origin of whiteness has been sidelined.[86] The start-up White Studies industry has been industriously unpacking and exposing the current network of privilege invisible to most whites but all too obvious to people of color, inside and outside the United States. The little that has been written on the history of whitehood turns out to be unreliable.[87] The one work that claims to describe "The Invention of the White Race" is actually a two-volume history of "the origin of racial oppression in Anglo-America," which spares only a single (inaccurate) sentence to when and why those oppressors began calling themselves "white."[88]

Having written this book, I now know why the people who birthed me thought, mistakenly, that I was white. I hope that reading it helps other "white" people to understand and correct the mistakes in the maternity ward that have shaped their sense of personal identity. By tracking the specific development of generic whiteness, we can all turn what seems now to be "nature" back into "history." And perhaps, by doing so, we can vaccinate ourselves against a twisted fiction of identity that has, for centuries, been getting under our skin.

Part I

Initiation

Chapter 2

The Absence of Whiteness

One of the literary inspirations for *Clotel* was "The Quadroons" (1842), by the white abolitionist and feminist Lydia Maria Child. Child's heroine did not even know she was a slave's daughter until she was "ruthlessly seized by a sheriff, and placed on the public auction-stand in Savannah," where "she stood, trembling, blushing, and weeping; compelled to listen to the grossest language, and shrinking from the rude hands that examined the graceful proportions of her beautiful frame."[1] This inaugural moment of racial subjectivity—the traumatic event that forces an individual to realize that his social identity is racially defined—recurs in much subsequent African American literature. But Brown's development of this theme is specifically and explicitly indebted to Child. Passages in three chapters of Brown's novel incorporate, almost verbatim, most of Child's short story, and he acknowledges his use of it in a concluding note on his sources (226).

However, Brown fundamentally changes the complexion of the material he copied. The enslaved quadroons of Child's story are of a "brown color" or "a lighter brown" or with a complexion "rich and glowing as an autumn leaf" or as "the sunny side of a golden pear."[2] They are never "white." Brown insists on their whiteness. Clotel escapes from her last master because, being "much fairer than many of the white women of the South," she succeeds in passing as a "free white" man (167).[3] And Brown's titular heroine is not the only enslaved "white" in *Clotel.* So is its male hero, George Green, Clotel's daughter Mary, her younger sister Althesa, and Salome, a German immigrant woman "perfectly white" who had been illegally enslaved. Brown compelled his white readers to contemplate the image of a white slave auction, the image of a white child artificially blackened, the image of an enslaved white woman treated as breeding stock, forced to mate with a black male, forced to bear black slave children. He did so because his primary purpose, in 1853, was to persuade whites to abolish slavery, which he could do only by persuading them that slavery was abhorrent.

Brown's literary and political shock tactics depend on, and exploit, the prevailing assumption that Whites enslave Blacks. In *Clotel,* the people called "black" are really just as "white" as the people called "white." What is labeled "black" is in practice indistinguishable from what is labeled "white," because "black" and "white" are continually mixing in and through the bodies of real persons. This deconstruction of the black/white binary complements Brown's exploitation of that binary. If white readers were horrified *only* by the image of "white" people accidentally enslaved, they might *only* reform slavery, policing more carefully the legal definition of enslavable persons. Brown, who wants them to abolish slavery not reform it, demonstrates that the law cannot successfully discriminate between black and white. Black and white are not solid states, but illusions in flux. Having horrified his readers with images of enslaved whites, he expands their imaginative sympathies by breaking down the generic barriers that inhibit sympathy. The black/white binary is arbitrary. All of us are white, in the same way and to the same extent that all of us are black.

If we are to respect Brown's insistence that the black/white binary is arbitrary, then we should not reproduce that binary in exploring the history of generic mythologies.[4] An early, persistent English-language color prejudice against "black" peoples has been lavishly documented by four decades of modern scholarship.[5] But—unless we presume the permanent and universal validity of the generic binary that Brown goes to such lengths to invalidate—we cannot take attitudes to blackness as evidence of attitudes to whiteness. A prejudice against black bodies proves that English speakers did not consider themselves "black," but it does not prove that they considered themselves "white." In Ben Jonson's 1605 *Masque of Blackness*—one of the literary texts most frequently cited in recent discussions of early modern colorphobia—the word *white* is not once spoken.[6] Brown or yellow or red or chartreuse or orange or pink peoples might harbor prejudices against black ones (or against people of any and every color but their own). An ethnocentric island tribe might prefer its own skin color, without assuming that its own skin color was the "opposite" of some despised skin color.

The first colorphobic documents in English legal history demonstrate just such asymmetry. Between 1596 and 1601 Queen Elizabeth I issued three proclamations commanding the expulsion of "Negroes and blackamoors" from her kingdom. All three proclamations applied sanctions to individuals who were targeted on the basis of their color. Those proclamations have often been cited by historians of racism or the African diaspora. But Elizabeth, in singling out "those kind of people," did not contrast them with "whites." Instead, "blackamoors" were contrasted with "people of our nation," or with "her own natural subjects" or her "own countrymen," or with "her own liege people."[7] For Elizabeth, the antonym of the word *black* was not the word *white,* but a phrase ("our people" or "our nation"). In Elizabethan English, the opposite of *black* was *us.*

But what should we call Queen Elizabeth's ethnocentric island tribe, if not *white?* Part of our difficulty in escaping from the black-white binary, and thereby investigating the historical evolution of generic whiteness, is that we possess no other term to describe the people who would eventually learn to call themselves white. Neither did they.[8] In 1623 the English colony in Bermuda passed "An Act to restrain the insolencies of the Negroes," but the law did not use the word *white;* instead, it contrasted "the Negroes" with the English "inhabitants" (as if the imported Negroes did not have as much right as the imported English to be called "inhabitants").[9] By 1636 in Barbados, by 1638 on Providence Island, "Negroes" were being officially and explicitly enslaved for life, and a series of statutes passed by the colonial assembly in Virginia between 1660 and 1668 institutionalized the enslavement of "Negroes": like Queen Elizabeth's colorphobic proclamations decades before, these first colorphobic colonial documents and laws did not use the word *white,* but unlike Elizabeth's proclamations, they did use the word *English.*[10] In those seventeenth-century texts, *English* was describing the inhabitants of a territory thousands of miles from England; in Virginia in the 1660s, some of the so-called English had never seen England, and never would. Perhaps for that reason, early colonists did not consistently describe themselves as *English,* sometimes using *Christian* instead, or in addition.[11]

Their lexical difficulty, and our own, should not surprise us. If the word *white* constructed and defined a new social category, then that category did not exist before the word *white* created it, and therefore the constituents of that new category had no preexisting collective name. Moreover, once it became a legal and political category, the exact meaning of *white* would be contested by various population groups, seeking to restrict or expand the social privileges attached to whiteness. Therefore, any demographic definition of whiteness lends to the population so described a specious unity, which may be entirely anachronistic. And similar difficulties beset other identity categories. If I ask "how did the English become white?," I not only presuppose a natural relationship between whiteness and Englishness, race and nation; I also presuppose the historical continuity of a population that can plausibly be called "English." But the Englishness of the English is as problematic as their whiteness.

Englishness

Both race and nation are what political scientist Benedict Anderson calls "imagined communities," generic categories that join an individual to thousands or millions of other individuals he or she has never met and does not know. One characteristic of such communities is that they create genealogies for themselves, a collective "autobiography" establishing their historical longevity and importance.[12] "The integrity of imperial nations," Paul Gilroy reminds us, "was actively re-imagined to derive from the primordial particularity of premodern tribes."[13] If we step back from the categories created and perpetuated by our politicians, textbooks, curriculums, and library catalogs, it should be immediately obvious that no real biological or political continuity unites the various peoples who have inhabited the geographical locales we call "England" or "Britain." The invading Romans, who provide our earliest written descriptions of "the first inhabitants," suspected that even they belonged to different ethnic groups. Nineteen hundred years ago Tacitus noted that "Their complexions are different," and conjectured that the curly-haired and "colored" or "swarthy" southwestern population came from Spain, the "red-haired" northerners from Germany, while those nearest to France belonged to the same (undescribed) people as their neighbors directly across the Channel.[14] Eight hundred years ago Gerald of Wales contrasted the "fairness" of the English with the "brown complexion" of the Britons.[15] In the first 11 centuries of its written history, the largest island off the northwest coast of the Eurasian landmass was invaded by waves of inhabitants of the Roman empire, waves of Germanic peoples, waves of Scandinavian peoples, and finally the Normans in 1066. No invader subdued the whole island. In the 730s the Venerable Bede recorded that "This island at present . . . contains five nations, the Angles, Britons, Scots, Picts and Latins," each speaking "its own language."[16] That multiplicity was only intensified by the subsequent Danish and Norman immigrants. For five centuries after the Norman invasion, the southern and eastern parts of the island belonged to a kingdom with shifting boundaries and territories on both sides of the Channel. Not until the loss of Calais in 1558—shortly before Elizabeth Tudor was proclaimed queen—was an "English" monarch again confined to an entirely islanded realm.

On the islands she claimed to rule, her subjects spoke multiple mother tongues: Cornish, Irish, English, Scottish English, Highland Scots, and Welsh, to name only the varieties most widely recognized. But even these "languages" were and are less stable, homogeneous, and continuous than we tend to assume. Like nation-states, standard languages acquire what linguist R. A. Lodge terms "retrospective historicity"; they "are given, after the event, a glorious past which helps set them apart from less prestigious varieties."[17] But that alleged continuity is a myth. In 1596 the preface to a new edition of William Caxton's 1473–74 translation of *The Recuyell of the Historyes of Troy* complained that the "Translator William Caxton, being (as it seemeth) no English man, had left very many words mere French, and sundry sentences so improperly Englished, that it was hard to understand." The publisher had therefore hired a second author, to translate Caxton into "plainer English."[18] Caxton was born in Kent, a county as English as they come, and a recent poll identified him as one of the five most important Englishmen "of the millennium"—but four centuries earlier he had been judged "no English man," because he lived on the far side of the radical linguistic changes of the sixteenth century.

The language we call "English" is a relatively recent development.[19] If Anglo-Saxon is a form of English, then so are several other ancient Germanic languages once spoken on the continent, which have equal claims to linguistic continuity with the language I am writing and you are reading. What is now usually called "Middle English" (an amalgamation of Anglo-Saxon and Norman French) became the official language of courts of law only in 1362 and became the most common written language only in the late 1490s.[20] The first rudimentary history of "English literature," or the literature written in various languages by people born or resident in the British isles, was written by a Protestant nationalist and first published in 1548 (in Latin).[21]

As these facts and dates suggest, the rise of standard English—and histories of the rise of standard English—cannot be separated from the development of a particular political system. What linguist Jim Milroy calls the "ideology of the standard language" is itself intertwined with "an ideology of nationhood and sometimes race."[22] Like other languages, "English" was a collection of related languages (later pejoratively labeled "dialects"), shading over at its borders into versions of what would later be canonized as other national languages. A sixteenth-century author claimed that differences of speech not only separated "one nation . . . from another, but also" distinguished "one county, one city, one village, and (which is more) one street from another."[23] If "one street from another" seems absurd to us, we should remember that, until the 1640s, many people in England still annually ritually marked the borders of the *parish* most of them lived and died in.[24] Only after the arrival of the printing press in 1473 did one particular version of "English" start to become dominant and standardized within the literate population, and only with the increase of literacy did that dominant print language also become the dominant oral form.

The dialect that triumphed was that spoken in and around London. London triumphed because it was the largest city on the island, and print capitalism depended on a market big enough to absorb the many copies of a book that the new machines could produce; in the second half of the sixteenth century, London's population more than doubled, to at least 150,000 in 1600.[25] In 1557 the London Company of Stationers was given a royal monopoly on the right to own printing presses. By 1589 *The Art of English Poesy* recommended that "English" poets should use the language spoken in "London and the shires lying about

London within sixty miles."[26] This was good advice; the canon of English literature would be drawn almost entirely from texts written in that dialect.

This linguistic unification transformed cultural and social life during the sixteenth century, and was itself related to the Reformation. Since the early third century, a fluctuating proportion of the inhabitants of the island had consciously identified themselves as Christians, members of an ideological community dispersed over many territories and language groups, but centered in Rome (the center also of a political empire, of which the island was a distant periphery). In 1534 the Act of Supremacy created a separate English church, one among many new Protestant sects in northern Europe. From the beginning, London was more Protestant than most of the rest of the kingdom.

As an independent and relatively unified political, genomic, territorial, linguistic, and religious entity, "England" as we know it did not exist until the sixteenth century. In that century's last four decades, the histories of John Foxe, Raphael Holinshed, and a generation of Elizabethan playwrights and poets constructed a long and vivid genealogy of that newly imagined community. What Richard Helgerson has called "the Elizabethan writing of England"—the creation of canonical founding works of poetry, drama, history, theology, law, and imperial exploration—was the work of a single generation of men, born between 1551 and 1564.[27] At the same time, economic changes were making the inhabitants of that political space increasingly mobile; London in particular became a great melting pot of populations drawn from villages and towns all over the realm. Even so, local allegiances remained strong; the word *country* could still be used in senses equivalent to the modern *county.* The official divorce from the rest of Catholic Christendom would be contested by large sections of the island's population throughout the sixteenth century, and religious divisions still dominated political and intellectual debate for another hundred years. Thus, even in the seventeenth century many people living within the kingdom centered their personal sense of identity on communities smaller or larger than England. But by the second or third decade of the Stuart dynasty, almost all the spectators in a London theater who watched the slave market scene in *A Very Woman* probably considered themselves members of an imagined community called "England," inhabited by "the English," who—whatever else they might be—were not Jewish, not Irish, and not black.[28]

Those spectators also probably believed that the "England" to which they belonged had a long, glorious, and continuous history. But few—if any—would have called themselves "Anglo-Saxon," a compound epithet William Wells Brown uses to describe the appearance of Clotel. That compound first appeared in the 1580s.[29] William Camden's *Britannia,* published in Latin in 1586, used the compound to describe all the "Old English" peoples; Camden's English translator, in 1610, retained the Latin, thereby putting the English noun "Anglo Saxon" into print. Interest in the language and people of England before 1066 had revived in the 1550s, as part of the campaign to invent a distinguished pedigree for the new English church.[30] But those studies were written and read by a tiny intellectual elite. "Anglo-Saxon" did not appear in English fiction, poetry, or drama until 1735.[31] It took even longer for the original historical sense to expand to include "all descendants of the original inhabitants of Britain," including those in America. In that expanded modern generic sense, "Anglo-Saxon" is first recorded in 1832, only two decades before the publication of *Clotel.*[32]

Painted Europeans

Although English people at the beginning of the seventeenth century did not consider themselves "Anglo-Saxon," did they already consider themselves "white"? Did a sense of generic identity precede or follow the sense of political identity? After all, differences in pigmentation existed long before nation-states. A sense of generic whiteness might therefore have helped constitute an imagined community that—like Roman Christendom—preceded and exceeded the identity boundaries of the new English nation. Whenever and wherever it originated, the generic concept does not depend on a biological reality, but on a particular misapplication or redefinition of the word *white.* The bodies of the inhabitants of early modern England were, of course, not actually lily white. As Shakespeare reported of his mistress, "If snow be white, why then her breasts are dun."[33] In 1611 a French-English dictionary equated "flesh-color" with "pale pink."[34] The English could not look at themselves and see that they were white; someone had to tell them to *imagine that they were white.*

That imaginative injunction might have come from visual artists. The first sentence of Richard Dyer's *White* speaks of the representation of white people in "Western culture," and later in the book he claims that "Painters and photographers have often rendered white people entirely or in large part literally white."[35] But Dyer's visual evidence clusters within decades of *Clotel* (1853). Only two years before Brown published his novel, the British sculptor Owen Jones had scandalized the Great Exhibition by painting his model of the Parthenon in "bold, bright colors"; most English critics refused to believe or endorse the archaeological evidence that ancient Greek sculptures had been painted, preferring instead "the purity of whiteness."[36] In the heyday of a global empire justified by generic mythologies, the dominant European artistic conventions did, unsurprisingly, emphasize or imagine the literally white bodies of the European master class.

But for most of the history of western culture, artists have not represented "white people" as "literally white." Prehistoric European cave paintings use brown, black, or red-ocher for hands and bodies (Plate 1).[37] Some archaic Greek vases depict everyone as black; other vases make everyone red; whiteness was not an option (Plate 2).[38] Greek painters used a mixture of several colors (according to Plato) or red-ocher (according to Theophrastus) to represent flesh.[39] Early inhabitants of the Italian peninsula also used red-ocher.[40] The scores of mosaics and wall paintings preserved under volcanic ash in Pompei and Herculaneum demonstrate that Roman men, in the heyday of *their* empire, did not see themselves as "white," but represented themselves with the same dark pigments the Greeks and the Etruscans favored.[41]

In the earliest Christian art, from the third to the fifth centuries, the complexions are reddish brown (Plate 3) or olive (Plate 4).[42] In illustrations in the ninth-century *Gospel Book of Charlemagne* and the *Gospel Book of Archbishop Ebbo of Reims,* the evangelists are red and brown; on the binding of the *Lindau Gospels* (ca. 870), Christ is gold; in *The Gero Crucifix* in the Cathedral at Cologne (ca. 975–1000), he is a dark brown, his color emphasized by the contrasting gold of the cross. In the *Gospel Book of Otto III* (ca. 1000), the Jesus who washes Peter's feet is a light reddish brown, with black hair, his skin indistinguishable from that of the eleven human figures in the illustration. In Duccio's *Madonna Enthroned* for the Siena Cathedral (1308–11), Madonna and child—like the dozens of saints who surround them—are depicted with green and red flesh, highlighted by the gold halos that surround every head; likewise, in the Bohemian Master's *Death of the Virgin* (1355–60), golden halos emphasize reddish brown faces.[43] These conventions continue in other paintings of the fourteenth and fifteenth centuries (Plates 5–7).

When Dyer claims that "increasingly," Christ and the Virgin Mary "are rendered as paler, whiter than everyone else," he must mean "increasingly" during the late Italian Renaissance. His first example of this phenomenon—Giovanni Bellini's *Madonna and Child with John the Baptist and Ste. Elizabeth*—was painted at the very end of the fifteenth century (ca. 1490–95).[44] But Black Madonnas are far more common. The earliest representation of Mary, in the catacombs of Priscilla at Rome, is cocoa-colored, as are several paintings of Mary attributed to Saint Luke the Evangelist. Black or at least dark madonnas decorate churches or shrines in Bavaria, Belgium, France, Hungary, Italy, and Spain (to name only those European countries dominated by Latin Christianity); the exact number is impossible to determine, because so many were subsequently whitened.[45] Bellini's *Madonna and Child* is the earliest work of art Dyer cites in any connection as evidence of the pervasive representation of "whiteness" in "Western culture." Even that example could be contradicted by later religious paintings, such as the court painter Dosso Dossi's *Virgin and Child* (ca. 1513–14), which pictures a mother Mary and baby Jesus so brown that they were later mistaken for gypsies.[46] The whitening of European bodies in Renaissance Italian painting was not universal, even in the sixteenth century. Counterexamples are as easy to find as the Sistine Chapel, where varities of red, umber, ocher, violet, and yellow dominate Michelangelo's panorama of the history of human and divine flesh.[47] Rubens painted notoriously rubicund portraits.

Nevertheless, an artificial, idealized corporeal whiteness did enter Italian painting in the second half of the fifteenth century, suggesting that the physical self-image of some Europeans was beginning to change. The earliest example of this whitening that I have found is Piero della Francesca's *Battesimo di Cristo* (ca. 1460). Francesca visited Rome in 1459, and his painting (Plate 8) was visibly influenced by the classical statuary unearthed and displayed there.[48] Ancient Greek and Roman statues had been painted to reproduce Mediterranean flesh tones.[49] But stone lasts longer than paint, and by the Renaissance, when those statues were rediscovered (literally and imaginatively), the pigments had eroded away. Consequently, when Francesca painted his immobile statuesque white image of Christ, he did not realize he was radically changing the conventions of European visual representation; he believed he was simply imitating and restoring ancient sculpture's uncluttered purity of line and mass.

That emergent celebration of statuesque, excessively white bodies may also be related to significant changes in the Mediterranean slave trade. In the early fifteenth century Italians bought and sold tens of thousands of eastern European slaves ("Slavs"), shipped from the Black Sea to markets in Venice and Genoa. But in 1441 Portuguese ships, sailing south along the Atlantic coastline of Africa, began abducting and buying black slaves to sell in Europe. Then, in 1453, the Ottoman capture of Constantinople closed Italian access to the Black Sea suppliers of pale slaves.[50] In combination these developments shifted the focus of European slave trading to sub-Saharan Africa, initiating the color-coded system of slavery that would dominate the Atlantic world for more than four centuries: pale Europeans enslaved black Africans.[51] Italian seamen and financiers were instrumental in developing the African slave trade. The earliest surviving eyewitness accounts of the exploration of the sub-Saharan coast of west Africa were written down by two Italian merchants and slave traders, Alvise da Ca' da Mosto and Antoniotto Usodimare, after voyages in 1455; in both texts, "blacks" are contrasted with "white men" (*homini bianchi*).[52] By 1528 generic whiteness had entered the vocabulary of canonical Italian literature.[53] Castiglione's best-selling *Book of the Courtier* contrasts *bianco* ("white") and "*negro.*"[54]

The appearance of hyperbolically white complexions is not typical of the long history of European or Christian painting, but instead arises at a particular moment, in circumstances particular to Quattrocento Italy: the intensified Renaissance interest in unearthing and imitating classical statuary combined with shifts in the long-distance shipping of human cargoes. Neither of those circumstances had much immediate relevance to speakers of English. The Hundred Years War with France and the civil wars between Lancastrians and Yorkists left them no time or energy, in the fifteenth century, for archaeology or African exploration—or collecting Italian art.

English Complexions

Generalizations about "Western culture" do not tell us much about attitudes or art in the islands off the western coast of Europe.[55] Richard Dyer's earliest specifically *English* example of a painting idealizing white skin dates from the 1760s. But a tradition of portraiture had begun in Angle-land 1,000 years earlier. The image of the Crucifixion in the Lindisfarne Gospels (ca. 700) presents a Christ whose face is much darker than the white halo behind his head; in the Vespasian Psalter (ca. 750), King David is reddish brown; so is St. Matthew in the Trier Gospels (ca. 750). In the tapestries from the tomb of St. Cuthbert (ca. 934), the Anglo-Saxon faces are an even darker cocoa.[56]

These conventions for the representation of flesh continued after manuscript miniatures and tapestries had given way to stained glass (Plate 9) and modern canvases. Looking at a likeness of Henry VIII (Plate 10), one immediately sees why the complexions of both men and women were so often described as *ruddy.* The adjective was used for faces and complexions "naturally suffused with a fresh or healthy redness" from the beginning of the twelfth century; even earlier, the noun *rud* (meaning "red") had been so used. The fourteenth-century poet John Gower specifically contrasted the healthiness of a reddish complexion with the sickliness of a whitish one ("the discolored pale hue is now become a ruddy cheek"). Both *rud* and *ruddy*—and *red,* too—were being used to describe individuals, not just their faces.[57]

In the sixteenth century these words for the red region of the spectrum were supplemented by *carnation,* imported from French or Italian; originally derived from the Latin word for "flesh," by 1535 the English word was being used to describe "the color of man's body" and "a light rosy pink, but sometimes used for a deeper crimson color as in the carnation flower." It referred not only to human flesh but to cherries, and was pointedly distinguished from *white.*[58] The same distinction was made by Nicholas Hilliard (1547–1619), the most admired portrait painter of Elizabethan England, in his manuscript treatise *The Art of Limning,* probably written at the end of the sixteenth century. Hilliard recommended different types of white pigment for different functions: the brightest for satin, the next brightest for linens, and "the last and coarsest" for "the flesh color properly called carnations, which in no sort ought to have any glistening; that with a very little red lead only added maketh the fairest carnations" [that is, "the lightest, palest, most beautiful carnations"]. "If the party be a little paler," he recommended "less red lead and a little massicot among; if yet browner, more of each and a little ocher de ruse withal." Thus, for "paler" faces Hilliard reduced the amount of red, but did not eliminate it entirely, and supplemented it with massicot (yellow protoxide of lead). Even in unfinished portraits, Hilliard has added pinks to the cheeks and jaw line. He also made use of *russet* (another word new to English in the sixteenth century). In addition to these reds and yellows, he recommended litmus and indigo as "shadowing blues" around the temples, and warned against making the face "too red, or too brown"—thereby implying that redness and brownness were naturally parts of an English face, but that they should not be exaggerated.[59] As we would expect from his prescriptions, the complexions of Hilliard's portraits vary, as did presumably the complexions of his sitters.

Not everyone living in a society embodies its ideals. In the case of cave paintings, or Greek vases, or a horde of images randomly preserved by volcanic ash, the sheer number of portraits that employ the same pigments is compelling testimony to the uniformity of ancient norms. There is no comparably extensive or comparably random collection of Christian art, but any tourist to the Musée National du Moyen Age, at Thermes de Cluny in Paris, will notice that white faces are rare in its collection of medieval Christian art and artifacts. It contains, for instance, a stone altarpiece from Île-de-France, created between 1350 and 1360, with the white stone base overpainted in order to give Christ a reddish-brown complexion.[60] Images of Christ are not transcriptions of the actual features of an ancient Galilean carpenter, but materializations of an ideal. Likewise, although Archbishop Becket and Henry VIII were real enough, they also embodied ideals—of medieval piety, or Renaissance magnificence—that the inhabitants of England would all have recognized and that many would have aspired to imitate. By contrast, the commercial appeal of Hilliard's miniatures did not depend on their uniformity, but on the painter's ability to individuate each portrait: they are miniatures not only because they are small, but because they represent only one particular person, a tiny fraction of the social whole—and not necessarily an important or typical specimen.[61] Whatever he thought of other people, Hilliard did not see himself as white (Plate 11).

Before the English could comfortably imagine that they were white, someone had to tell them that *it was good to be white.* "What on earth is whiteness," W. E. B. DuBois asked in 1920, "that one should so desire it?"[62] Three centuries earlier, Pierre Charron's influential 1601 treatise *Of Wisdom,* describing "the skin" of the ideal human body, specified "the color vermillion."[63] Across the English Channel, at about the same time, the equally influential Thomas Walkington celebrated the ideal of a "purple sanguine complexion."[64] Charron and Walkington were summarizing an ancient preference. For one thing, abnormally pale skin is a conspicuous side effect of castration, and eunuchs were common in the Middle East and the Mediterranean from about 4000 B.C.E.; because eunuchs were generally despised, men in societies with eunuchs did not aspire to whiteness.[65] Likewise, leprosy produces shiny white scales on the skin. Accordingly, the God of the ancient Hebrews punished a woman by making her skin "like snow" (Numbers 12:10). In ancient Greek, the very word for leprosy contains the word *white,* because in humans the disease makes "skin turn partially white"—implying that it was not white before the disease. Perhaps for that reason, the Aristotelian tradition could equate "pallor" with "a corruption of the flesh."[66] Familiar to biblical and classical writers, leprosy became epidemic in western Europe in the twelfth and thirteenth centuries. Only after the unexplained decline of the disease, in the second half of the fourteenth century, could white skin have been regarded by most European men with anything other than ambivalence.[67] Even then, memories of the disease haunted European imaginations. As late as the early seventeenth century, a dramatic character could exclaim, "like leprosy: The whiter, the fowler."[68] From the Norman Conquest to the fifteenth century, the Anglo-Norman word *whit* did not have a generic sense, but could be used of a person or face "having an unnaturally pale or white color or complexion due to illness, weakness, emotional distress, etc."; *whit* identified a complexion that was "unhealthily pale."[69]

Such associations were based on the immemorial human experience of sickness, and did not require a scientific hypothesis about corporeal whiteness. But the western medical tradition had long situated white skin within a comprehensive theory of the human body.[70] Aristotelian physics recognized four elements (earth, water, air, and fire), and for 2,000 years physicians believed that bodies were composed of four corresponding humors: choler (fire), blood (air), phlegm (water), and melancholy (earth). Each of these humors was linked to a color, and phlegm—what we would generally call mucus—was white. A body would be white to the degree that it was dominated by the phlegmatic humor.[71] But snot and spit seldom inspire ecstatic praise, and phlegm was always the least appreciated of the four humors. Corporeal whiteness was a symptom of excess phlegm, and phlegmatic people were short, fat, slothful, sleepy, idle, dull, heavy, slow voluptuaries.[72] This theory, with its negative characterization of whiteness, dominated western medicine until the seventeenth century. There is nothing universal, within the western tradition, about an enthusiasm for white bodies.

The Anglo-Saxon word *hwit* had been used of skin color, in texts representing the Germanic dialects commonly spoken in the southern kingdoms of the island, as early as about 900. But that original usage—common for many centuries, as spelling and pronunciation of the word changed gradually to its modern form—differentiated one individual from another, just as portrait painters like Hilliard recognized the variety of individual complexions.[73] By contrast, the modern meaning differentiates one population group from other population groups. Most modern readers of early texts will be unfamiliar with use of the adjective *white* to describe an individual, simply because that sense has been obsolete for more than three centuries; therefore, a modern reader can easily misinterpret the early use of *white* to describe a particular individual as an example of our modern use of *white* to describe a genre of humanity.[74] Once whiteness has a collective meaning, then calling an individual "white" is an act of generic identification; but if the word does not already possess a collective meaning, then applying it to an individual does *not* invoke a generic category. References to "white" individuals are therefore, in themselves, intrinsically ambiguous. For the adjective (or the pigment) to signal a generic identity, it must be in widespread use with collective nouns: "white" men, folks, groups, nations, peoples, populations, communities, audiences.

It must, for instance, be used of both the upper and lower classes. Dyer recognizes that "Working-class and peasant whites are" literally "darker than middle-class and aristocratic whites," because those who "work outside the home" are "exposed to the elements, especially the sun and the wind, which darken white skin."[75] Early modern English writers took for granted the relative darkness of manual laborers and other poor people.[76] When Shakespeare wrote in *Cymbeline* (1609–10) that "Golden girls and lads all must Like chimney sweepers come to dust" (4.2.263–64), he contrasted the dusty complexions of chimney sweepers with the "golden" complexion of the young, wealthy, and carefree.[77] Similarly, in the anonymous Jacobean play *The Telltale,* the Duchess of Florence "umbers her face" to disguise herself, and by means of being thus "tanned" she can plausibly represent herself as a "cook and laundress."[78] Thomas Heywood and Thomas Dekker both describe gypsies as "umbered."[79] One of the favorite adjectives coupled with *slave* in early modern plays is *muddy,* literally "covered or spattered with mud."[80] People who do dirty work get dirty.

Dyer recognizes even these darker persons as still belonging to a "white" race, because modern notions of race transcend class differences; indeed, it has been argued that the fictional concept of race was deliberately fabricated by the ruling class, to obscure the shared interests of all oppressed peoples. Consequently, it does not seem paradoxical to us to speak of a "white auto mechanic" or "white roofer." Indeed, such workers are often most aggressively insistent on their own racial whiteness. But I have not found, the dictionaries do not cite, and to my knowledge no scholar has quoted examples of medieval, Elizabethan, or Jacobean English chimney sweepers, smiths, farmers, cooks, mechanics, laundresses, laborers, or peasants described as "white." Instead, in sixteenth-century literature and art, white (or "fair") complexions are reserved for the aristocratic, landowning elite.[81] To work as a generic sign, whiteness must be attributed even to the lowest classes of the population, those whose work makes it difficult or impossible for them to stay pale.

It must also be used of both sexes within a given population group. Modern readers are particularly liable to misinterpret a gender marker as a race marker.[82] The individuals most often described in early texts as having a particular "white" feature, or as being "white and red" or "fair," are women. According to classical, medieval, and Renaissance medical tradition, women were dominated by phlegm and therefore symptomatically cold, weak, inconstant, imperfect—and white.[83] As far back as classical Greece, paintings differentiated men from women by making the women lighter.[84] That distinction has been maintained throughout almost the whole history of European painting, and it continued in the Renaissance.[85] In the miniatures of Nicholas Hilliard and his protégé Isaac Oliver, women are consistently whiter than men. Likewise, in the plays of Shakespeare and his contemporaries, a brown complexion was "manly," and brown-faced men were described as "handsome" and "honest."[86] Of course, we cannot be sure that such images accurately reproduce the actual flesh tones of early modern men and women; they might represent, instead, ideologically inflected ideals or conventions—just as modern photography and cinematography artificially heighten the whiteness of Euro-American bodies, especially if they are female. But adult males faces do seem to be, in general, darker than adult female faces. Males tend to be hairier, and even clean-shaven men often have visible hair follicles or beard "shadow."[87] Globally, women tend to be paler than men of the same ethnic group "because women tend to have less hemoglobin in their blood and less melanin in their skin."[88]

This biological difference was exacerbated and exaggerated by the deliberate seclusion, often amounting to virtual imprisonment, of women.[89] A "good" woman was supposed to stay at home, indoors; women who did venture out were supposed to wear masks—which protected them from the male gaze and the sun's rays. The higher a woman's social status, the more likely she was to be shielded from activities that exposed her to skin-darkening sunlight or skin-dirtying labor.[90] The lighter a woman's complexion, the higher her apparent ranking on the index of modesty or the index of status, or both. That is why Nicholas Hilliard's portraits of women display such pale complexions: those who could afford one of his expensive miniatures belonged, by definition, to the upper classes. Queen Elizabeth, at the pinnacle of the pyramid, was naturally—artificially—the palest of all.[91] In one of his most famous songs Thomas Campion opposed "these Ladies" (upper-class women, belonging to the gentry or the aristocracy) to "the nut-brown lass" Amarillis; she is "nut-brown" because she is a "country maid," who spends her time outdoors. But "country" also puns on "cunt," and "wanton" Amarillis—unlike the coy, modest, respectable, inhibited, or cunning "Ladies" with whom she is consistently contrasted—is willing to make love outdoors, and "never will say no."[92] Campion does not say whether the coy "Ladies" were white, but they were obviously not "nut-brown." A "brown wench" was always, in literary texts, a cheap sexual commodity.[93] The noun *wench* often specified a woman "of the rustic or working class" (*OED* 1.b), and a brown complexion confirmed that she was too poor or too wanton to cover her body. About the "brown wench" in Shakespeare and Fletcher's *All Is True* (1613) we know nothing but the fact that she "Lay kissing in" Cardinal Wolsey's arms (3.2.296–97).[94]

An honest man could be unequivocally praised for a brown complexion, but *brown* was incompatible with female sexual honor. Men might occasionally use "brown" women, but they did not respect them, or marry them. As literary critic Kim F. Hall has demonstrated, the English tirelessly praised women for "white and red" or "fair" or "light" complexions; they favored and praised faces that were "fairer" or "lighter" or "whiter."[95] If women did not have such complexions naturally, they simulated them by the use of cosmetics. Male actors, in particular, seem to have needed "whiteface" makeup to impersonate women.[96]

Color coding was profoundly classed and gendered. The earlier class and gender significance of whiteness must be clearly differentiated from the modern generic significance of whiteness. It is misleading for Richard Dyer to claim that "For much of history, many white people have sought to make themselves look white of hue," then to cite as evidence "the legend of Cleopatra bathing in asses' milk to whiten her skin."[97] It may be true that "Much of the history of Western make-up is a history of whitening the face," but much of the history of western makeup is also a history of hyperbolizing sexual difference.[98] Like modern breast implants or traditional Chinese foot-binding, white lead makeup artificially enhanced the putative femininity of women whose bodies did not satisfy the criteria of the reigning female ideal. Because that reigning ideal was defined by a binary system of differentiated genders, what was ideal for women was diametrically opposed to the ideal for men. Traditional Chinese culture did not bind men's feet, and American cosmetic surgeons do not give men silicon tits. Cleopatra may have bathed in asses' milk, but Julius Caesar and Mark Antony did not. In classical times, the white soft flesh of eunuchs was despised precisely because it signaled their effeminate similarity to women; a pale male was not a manly man.[99] As literary critic Debora Shuger reminds us—typically, it takes a woman to point this out—every classical and early modern cultural ideal is "also an ideal of manhood."[100] So long as whiteness was idealized only in women, it had not yet become the generic standard it would represent once men appropriated it for themselves and gave it a positive male meaning.

Shakespeare, who used *white* to praise women's complexions dozens of times, never once used it to praise an adult male. When admirable, the male body is instead "silver" (for an old man) or "golden" or "brown" (for a young one).[101] Applied to men, *white* describes a corpse or a coward.[102] Fears are "by pale white shown," white cheeks are "signs of fear."[103] Macbeth relentlessly berates a messenger for being "cream-faced" and "lily-livered" with a "goose look" and "linen cheeks" and a "whey-face" because of his (twice repeated) "fear" (5.3.11–19). If white is the color of cowardice, men do not want to be "white." Lady Macbeth can therefore berate her husband by inverting the gender of color: "My hands are of your color, but I shame to wear a heart so white" (2.2.62–63). She has bloodied her own hands, so that they are red instead of the "white" appropriate to a woman, and her husband's terror has made him as white as women conventionally were supposed to be.

The very praise of women for pallor meant that, in early modern England, a pale male was likely to be thought effeminate, whether or not he was a eunuch.[104] In 1628 the undergraduate John Milton was nicknamed "the Lady of Christ's College" because of his "exceedingly" fair complexion.[105] Hence, the compound "white boy" described "a favorite, pet, or darling boy," as in "The Pope was loath to adventure his darlings into danger; those white boys were to stay at home with his Holiness their tender father."[106] Given the universal Protestant association of the Pope with sodomy, this passage suggests that his attention to his "darlings" is more than paternal; certainly, their unmanly whiteness avoids danger, staying at home like a woman.[107] In the anonymous play *Timon* (ca. 1602–03?), a young city gallant with very little beard, who is introduced to the audience admiring himself in a mirror, asks what "the Virgins" say about him, and is told "They term you 'the delight of men, white boy'"—an ambiguous commendation, suggesting that he pleases men more than women.[108] Sometimes the idiom seems to suggest the modern "spoiled brat" or "mamma's boy"—as in Richard Brome's *New Academy,* where a doting mother denies that her 19-year-old "white boy" is a man yet ("Alack, a child"), describing the "fright he took," because of which he "stayed at home." I have not found a single positive instance of the idiom. It describes the clueless Michael in Beaumont's *The Knight of the Burning Pestle,* the fool Bergetto in Ford's *'Tis Pity She's a Whore,* the clown in Heywood's *Love's Mistress,* two treacherous ingrates in Dekker's *The Virgin Martyr.* In a sermon of 1613 Judas is the Devil's "white boy."[109]

Because the white complexion praised in women was—in the same period and by the same authors—condemned in men, it can hardly have characterized what we would now call a "race." Nor did whiteness characterize the dominant group. Men were almost always more powerful than the women they called white. To locate the origin of whiteness as a modern generic trope, we need to find cases where it is used, collectively and positively, to describe male as well as female flesh. An attribute is racial only when it is routinely attributed to whole populations, rather than to one individual, one gender, or one class. Once a racial idiom has been established, it will almost inevitably infiltrate registers of class and gender (or it may arise from existing registers of class and gender). But we cannot be sure that an idiom expresses a specifically racial consciousness until it appears independently of other variables.

That modern generic usage—"applied to those of ethnic types (usually European or of European extraction) characterized by light complexion, as distinguished from *black, red, yellow,* etc."—did not become common until the seventeenth century, in English or French.[110] It is not recorded in Anglo-Norman ("Middle English") or in the Helsinki database of Early English Correspondence. Chaucer never used it; nor did Langland, Skelton, Wyatt, Surrey, Spenser, Sidney, Marlowe, or any other poet who died before 1600.[111] It does not appear in many poets and playwrights born in the sixteenth century who lived on into the seventeenth. John Fletcher, for instance—the author of that slave market scene so different from the first chapter of *Clotel*—never used *white* in the modern sense. Most conspicuously, in terms of our own canonical preferences, there is not a single unequivocal example in Shakespeare.

Othello

Before I proceed with the other evidence for the absence of racial whiteness in Elizabethan English, I must stop and pay some particular attention to Shakespeare, because my claim—that he did not use *white* in a generic sense—might seem outrageous to anyone familiar with the prominence of Shakespeare in recent studies of the history of colorphobia. *Othello* is undoubtedly the most widely read and performed color-coded text in English literature. In an influential essay on the representation of race in *Othello,* published in 1987, Karen Newman refers to "the white Cassio," to "the white male characters of the play," its representation of the "white male," the "white male sexual norm," a "white male hegemony" (twice), "the white male norms the play encodes through Iago, Roderigo, Brabantio," and "a white, elitist male ethos" shared by "the white male audience."[112] But in all these phrases *white* is the critic's adjective, not the playwright's. Cassio, Iago, Roderigo, and Brabanzio are never called "white" in either early text of the play. No male is called "white." The word *white,* in various grammatical uses, occurs much more frequently in Newman's short essay than in Shakespeare's long play.[113] This imbalance is not peculiar to Newman; the same thing happens in almost every recent essay on the play's "racial" politics.[114]

We need to look carefully at the language of Shakespeare, not the language of his modern critics. The Italian word for "white"—*bianco* or *bianca*—is not used to describe a person in Shakespeare's source for the story.[115] In *Othello* itself the adjective *white* appears only twice.[116] Both times it refers explicitly, not to Italian men, but to a particularly prized and idealized woman, Desdemona. At the end of the play, Othello is reluctant to "scar that whiter skin of hers than snow" (5.2.4). At its beginning, when Iago tells Brabanzio that "an old black ram Is tupping your white ewe" (1.1.88–89), the "old black ram" is Othello and the "white ewe" Desdemona. This line in particular—with its contrast between black and white, its reduction of persons to animals, and its expression of anti-sexual moral condemnation in color terms—seems to imagine miscegenation in a fully modern, fully racist idiom.[117] But of course Othello is not literally a ram and Desdemona is not literally a ewe; the color attributed to them in this line may be equally figurative and hyperbolic, equally indicative of Iago's desire to denigrate and shock. More important, *white* here again describes a woman, expressing the gendered color coding typical of its time. Beautiful women may be white, but men are not.

To resolve the ambiguity of these words, we have to consider who speaks them and who hears them. The correct perspective on an image is determined, literally and figuratively, by the point of view of the person viewing that image. When Iago plants in Brabanzio's mind the image of "an old black ram . . . tupping your white ewe," he puts himself and Brabanzio in the position of a farmer, watching the copulation of livestock; at least one of those animals belongs to Brabanzio ("your white ewe"). The literal position of the viewer of this tupping scene is the subject position of a European adult male, in this case specifically an upper-class European male patriarch, a senator, a father, an owner of property, both real (the house from which he emerges and speaks) and chattel (the livestock being tupped). He is also a widower, roused from his bed but not paired with a wife or lover in this scene or anywhere else in the play; he is presented as a desexualized center of consciousness. Unlike the farmer/viewer, neither the ram nor the ewe is human, and neither owns anything, and both are at this moment mating. Because the viewer differs in every other respect from both the ram and the ewe, we cannot assume—indeed, we have every reason to doubt—that he resembles either in the color of his flesh. *The image implies that the viewer of the image is neither ram nor ewe, neither black nor white.*

Shakespeare, the author of *Othello,* the author of this line, the creator of this image of black ram and white ewe, resembled Brabanzio and Iago: he was not a black man or a white woman. The acting company that first performed the play, that presented to audiences this image of a black ram and a white ewe, resembled Shakespeare, Brabanzio, and Iago: no member of that company was either a black man or a white woman. To portray Othello, one of Shakespeare's fellow actors had to alter his complexion by applying black makeup; to portray Desdemona, one of Shakespeare's fellow actors had to alter his complexion by applying white makeup. What is true of the imagined picture of black ram and white ewe is true of the stage spectacle, later in Shakespeare's play, of black man and white woman. At every level, the image presents a coupling of opposites that could be represented only by artificially modifying the normative male English body.

The opposition that *Othello* constructs and displays was also visualized in a tradition of European portraiture that paired an aristocratic white woman with a black male slave. That tradition began, in the 1520s, with Titian's portrait entitled *Laura dei Dianti* (Plate 12).[118] The deep black flesh of the servant boy in the lower right quarter of the painting is made more remarkable by contrast with Laura's adjacent white sleeve and also by contrast with her left hand, resting on his right shoulder. Laura's own flesh is not absolutely white: the triangle of white ruffles of her underblouse, the single pearl in her right ear, the many pearls in her headdress, all glisten with a startling whiteness against the softer tones of her fair complexion. Nevertheless, the painting organizes itself around the contrast between woman and servant: her hand on his shoulder, his face tilted to gaze up at hers, the expanse of her bright white sleeve in the lower left balancing his black face in the lower right.

Who is looking at this image? Like Shakespeare, Titian was neither a white woman nor a black slave. Nor was the patron who commissioned this painting. Laura was the mistress of Alfonso I d'Este, Duke of Ferrara.[119] Ferrara was one of the most important city-states of sixteenth-century Italy, and Titian's painting demonstrates the duke's great wealth and exquisite taste by displaying two of his most remarkable acquisitions: a black slave and a fair mistress. Alfonso apparently never married Laura, and certainly had not married her when this portrait was painted. The slave's black complexion indicates that he came from sub-Saharan Africa—making him an exotic and expensive commodity.[120] The fair complexion of the mistress indicates that she has spent her life indoors, guarded by the notorious jealousy of Italian men, shielded from the Italian sun and from unauthorized male gazes, as delicate and rare as the materials of her headdress. The intended viewer of the painting, its original owner, also owned both its subjects, the enslaved African and the kept fair mistress, who gazes out of the painting directly at him. The duke enjoyed looking at them despite, or because of, their difference from himself. We can be sure that, like the observing Senator Brabanzio, the observing Duke of Ferrara prided himself on being neither a woman nor a slave.

We can also be sure that Shakespeare never saw Titian's painting. But the author of Shakespeare's source for *Othello,* Giambattista Cinzio Giraldi, might have seen it. His *Gli Ecatommiti* (1565) was written and published in Ferrara and dedicated to Giraldi's patron, Alfonso I's son and ducal heir, Ercole II.[121] Shakespeare's patron in 1603–04, when *Othello* was probably written, was the newly crowned Scottish king of England, James I; that new king's wife, Queen Anne of Denmark, was a remarkably pale woman, in a royal family that had been acquiring black slaves for a century (Plate 13).[122] In the same Christmas season that featured the first known performance of *Othello,* Anne commissioned Jonson's *Masque of Blackness,* which begins with the entrance of a black male, Niger. Anne also performed in the masque. Thus, when he wrote *Othello,* Shakespeare, like Titian, was working for a male sovereign whose female consort was a young woman (even whiter than Laura dei Dianti) apparently fascinated by black male servants. Titian, Giraldi, and Shakespeare all represented a white woman in conjunction with a black man; in each case, neither the artist nor the patron was either female or black. For both artist and patron, both the white woman and the black man were radically Other. These three interlocked artistic works—Titian's painting, Giraldi's story, Shakespeare's play—are among the earliest examples of the axiom, articulated by bell hooks, that "racism and sexism are interlocking systems of domination which uphold and sustain one another."[123]

Writing at the end of the twentieth century, hooks assumes that the racist-sexist compound reflects the perspective of men who consider themselves white. But in these early examples the male gaze is not necessarily a white gaze. On the available visual evidence, neither Titian (Plate 14) nor Shakespeare (Plate 15) would have identified with the whiteness of Desdemona or the blackness of Othello.[124]

If the presumed male observer of these Renaissance images did not consider himself white, how did he imagine himself? We can see the origins of Titian's *Diana,* and of the artistic tradition it inaugurated, in Albrecht Dürer's *Virgin and Child with the Monkey* (Illus. 1). Dürer contrasted the conventionally idealized image of the Virgin Mother of God, the infant Christ in her arms, with an astonishingly realistic portrait of an African monkey, in the lower left. The human viewer stands in a conceptual space between divine and simian. Titian replaced the diminutive dark monkey with a diminutive African male. Associating Africans with apes would, of course, become one of the standard tropes of modern racism. (See chapter 11.) But for now the important point is that, in Dürer and Titian, the viewer does not identify with either extreme. European men occupied a space between the "black devils" of Africa and the "white devils" called women.[125]

The paired extremes in Titian's painting and Shakespeare's play put the male artist/patron/spectator in a position celebrated by the male authorities of both classical and Renaissance culture: in the middle. The "via media" was the declared justification for the English church, rejecting the Charybdis of Catholicism and

Illustration 1. Dürer's *Virgin and Child with the Monkey* (c. 1498) situates the human observer between the extremes of divine and bestial, represented by the white woman and child of the Holy Family and a black-faced animal. Courtesy of the Chrysler Museum of Art, Norfolk, Virginia.

the Scylla of Puritanism.[126] Proverbially, "the merry mean" (or simply "the mean") was best, and "the middle way of measure is ever golden," and man should "observe the golden mean." That last phrase occurs in the Elizabethan translations of the Latin *Oedipus* and *Hippolytus,* by the Stoic philosopher Seneca; in *Agamemnon,* translated Seneca had argued that "The things of middle sort, and of a mean degree, Endure above the rest and longest days do see."[127] Characteristically, Seneca illustrates the wisdom of the middle way by representing extremists, characters who seem barely to qualify as human. Shakespeare often uses the same dramatic technique: "The middle of humanity thou never knew'st," a character says of one of his protagonists, "but the extremity of both ends."[128] Horace had expressed the same idea as Seneca with the phrase *aurea mediocritas;* Jonson, who fancied himself the English Horace, translated this as "the golden mediocrity."[129] The difference between Jonson's and the modern meaning of *mediocrity* itself illustrates the decline of this Stoic commitment to moderation, the arithmetic mean, the middle position. (I will return to that larger change of values in chapter 9.)

We should pay attention to the color attributed to that ideal state. It is not white. It is golden. *Golden* may of course be used figuratively, but so could *white,* and the choice of symbolic color is hardly random. The phrase "golden mean" is ubiquitous in English literature from the middle of the sixteenth to the middle of the seventeenth century.[130] Within the western medical tradition, perfect health produced "a golden temperature," a balance of the four humors that resulted in a "golden" temperament.[131] Classical, medieval, and Renaissance art often used gold to represent idealized human or divine figures.[132] Likewise, in literary texts human or anthropomorphic figures are described as golden.[133] The male gods and ideals of the Renaissance imagination are more often golden than white. The "golden mean" was the preferred stance of authority, centrally positioned to evaluate the extremes represented by femininity and servility, white and black.

Of course, in the centuries since Shakespeare wrote the play readers and spectators of *Othello* have understood "an old black ram is tupping your white ewe" as a racial characterization. That is hardly surprising, given the later generic meaning of the word *white,* combined with the play's amenability to appropriation by colorphobic ideologies. Although critics continue to disagree about whether the play criticizes or endorses prejudices about black men, no one denies the play's preoccupation with the problem of black ethnicity. Throughout the seventeenth century the play was usually called *The Moor of Venice* and the protagonist simply "the Moor"—and because the play insists that Othello is Christian, the word *moor* here has nothing to do with Islam and everything to do with dark flesh. Various forms of the word *black* occur 11 times and *moor* 59 times. But these very figures demonstrate that the invocation of *black* as a generic marker need not entail a symmetrical invocation of *white* as a generic marker. Shakespeare did use *black* to modify collective nouns in the modern racial sense;[134] he never used *white* to modify a collective noun in the modern racial sense. Although *The Moor of Venice* was one of Shakespeare's most admired plays in the second half of the seventeenth century, although we have separate eyewitness reports of performances in 1610 in London and in Oxford, although it was quoted by Robert Burton and singled out for specific praise by Leonard Digges, although Samuel Pepys saw it repeatedly and Dryden wrote of it three times, although vicar Abraham Wright and playwright Aphra Behn and scholar Gerald Langbaine all discussed it, no one used the generic word *white* in relation to the play until 1693—nine decades after it was written.[135]

Words, Words, Words

We cannot find generic "whiteness" in early English literature, even in works that directly represent ethnic issues. We cannot find it in early nonfiction, either. Captain John Hawkins led three voyages to Africa and the West Indies between 1562 and 1569, initiating English involvement in the transatlantic slave trade; none of the accounts of those voyages used the word *white.*[136] The Englishmen who circumnavigated the globe in Sir Francis Drake's famous voyage of 1578 to 1580 do not seem to have considered themselves white; in none of the 10 different eyewitness texts describing that voyage is the word *white* ever used as a generic adjective, or to describe any of the English[137] Nor is *white* used as a generic adjective or to describe any of the English in Sir Walter Ralegh's account of his expedition to Trinidad and the Oroonoko basin in 1595.[138] It does not appear in any of the original writings of the two Richard Hakluyts, who from the 1560s to 1609 were the most influential propagandists for English colonies overseas.[139] One of the foundational texts in the evolution of the modern myth of a "pure" and superior Aryan race—Richard Verstegan's influential *Restitution of Decayed Intelligence,* published in 1605—claims that "Englishmen are descended of German race," but Verstegan does not call either the Germans or the English "white" people.[140] In 1607—three years after *Othello* was performed at court—two English ships spent 38 days in the Sierra Leone estuary; five English eyewitness accounts of that extended encounter survive, and are full of references to the "negroes," "negers," and "negars." But they never use the word *white* to describe themselves or other Europeans.[141] These contexts—of slavery, European imperialism, contact with tropical peoples, genealogical collective history—are precisely where we would expect an insistence on English whiteness. In later decades, narratives like these would be full of the word *white.* But it never shows up in these early texts.

In fact, the *Oxford English Dictionary*'s first citation of the compound noun *White man,* referring to "A man belonging to a race having naturally light-colored skin or complexion" (2.a), dates from 1695—and refers to Muslims in Morocco.[142] Its first recorded example of *white* as a generic noun dates from 1671—and refers to a North African Muslim.[143] In both cases, these earliest examples come from English translations of continental texts and do not refer to Europeans. The dictionary's first example of the adjective *white* defined in a generic sense (1604) is another translation—and again does not refer to Europeans.[144] More embarrassingly, the dictionary's only other seventeenth-century example of the generic adjective is simply wrong.[145] Like the Victorian *Calendar of State Papers,* the *Oxford English Dictionary*—originally dedicated to Queen Victoria—interpolated modern generic whiteness into texts where it did not exist.[146] Our chief reference work for the historical development of English meanings does not cite a single accurate example of the noun or adjective *white* as a generic characterization of Europeans before the eighteenth century. The Victorian lexicographers tried to find earlier examples of the idiom, and all four of their seventeenth-century examples come from nonliterary, noncanonical sources. But all four turn out, on even cursory inspection, to be bogus.

It may help, at this point, to situate the problem of the word *white* in terms of the more general field of semasiology (the historical study of semantic change).[147] To acquire its modern generic meaning, the adjective *white* was both "ameliorated" and "generalized." That is to say: it became a positive attribute (rather than a negative one) and a global referrent (rather than a local one). Within the larger context of semantic change, there is nothing implausible about this trajectory. Meaning slips and slides. That is why modern textbooks have to tell students what Shakespeare meant; even *Clotel,* much closer to us in time, has to be glossed to supply obsolete lexical information. The structural changes in the sense of the adjective *white* also occur, for instance, to the adjective *sophisticated,* which at the beginning of the seventeenth century was a specific and negative word ("adulterated by undesirable additives"), but by the nineteenth had become general and positive ("discriminating, cultured"), and in its new sense gave birth to a positive noun, *sophisticate* ("a person with sophisticated tastes"). A parallel evolution has extended the range and improved the connotations of the noun *enthusiasm.*[148] In all such cases—and there are many more of them—readers who apply the modern definition to an early modern text will take away exactly the wrong meaning. In the case of *enthusiasm* or *sophisticated,* such misapplication of anachronistic definitions creates only a local difficulty; in the case of *white,* it leads to a fundamental misunderstanding of our collective history.

Between the ninth and the seventeenth centuries, the use of the adjective *white* to describe human complexions went through six semantically distinct, chronologically overlapping stages of development.

Stage 1: *White* refers to the pigmentation of some part of the body of a specified individual (positively in relation to women, negatively in relation to men). This is the original sense found in Anglo-Saxon and related early Germanic languages (and discussed in this chapter).

Stage 2: *White* refers, negatively, to the complexion of a population in a specific region. This meaning, which originated in classical texts, was perpetuated by medieval and humanist translators and scholars (discussed in chapters 3 and 4).

Stage 3: *White* refers, neutrally, to the complexion of both European and non-European peoples. This meaning debuts in 1553 (discussed in chapters 3 and 4).

Stage 4: *White* refers, neutrally, exclusively to the complexion of Europeans. This meaning debuts in 1589 (discussed in chapters 4 and 5).

Stage 5: *White* refers, positively and exclusively, to Europeans. This meaning debuts between 1606 and 1613 (discussed in chapters 5 through 11).

Stage 6: The generic adjective *white* (defined as in stage 5) becomes a generic noun, usually in the plural form *whites.* This meaning debuts in 1661 (discussed in chapters 8, 10 and 11).

(The confusions of the *Oxford English Dictionary* result from its failure to differentiate stages 2 through 5.)

Although such changes to the meaning of words are common enough, the specific transformation of the word *white* does violate an otherwise apparently universal rule of linguistic evolution. With the passage of time the number of color terms in a language increases, and the meaning of any single color term therefore shrinks. As languages evolve, they divide the spectrum into smaller and smaller semantic segments.[149] For example, the color of English faces might now be described as "beige" or "tan" or "flesh" rather than "white." But *beige* first appeared in English in 1856, as an imported French word to describe an imported fine French woolen fabric, and then—in 1879—as an adjective referring to the characteristic color of unbleached wool. *Flesh-colour* is first recorded in 1611, *flesh-coloured* in 1703, *flesh* as a noun indicating the color in 1852; *tan* was not used to describe a color until 1665, and not attributed to "tanned" or bronzed bodies until 1749. Before the invention or adoption of these more specific color words, their place in the spectrum was occupied by more general words, such as *red* or *brown.* I have already noted the introduction of *carnation* and *russet* in the sixteenth century, occupying some of the space previously covered by *red* or *ruddy; rose* is another sixteenth-century addition to the linguistic palette, which like the others refers to colors and human complexions within the red spectrum. If we ignore for a moment the generic senses, the meaning of the adjective *white* has similarly contracted, as over the centuries other words have entered the language to indicate its specific hues. Thus, in its earliest recorded uses Anglo-Saxon "huitum" and "hwitne" and "huito"—regarded as the ancestors of English *white*—referred to things "of the color of snow and milk"; but in the same earliest texts the same word could indicate "a light or pale color, applied to things of various indefinite hues approaching white, especially dull or pale shades of yellow"; it was also used to describe silver, iron, and steel.[150] This swathe of tints would eventually be broken down as particular shades were siphoned off by new words like *whitish* (from the fourteenth century), *silver* (from the fifteenth), *iron* (seventeenth), *metallic* (eighteenth), and *off-white* (twentieth).

In other respects, then, the evolution of *white* fits the general pattern of color terms, contracting over time as newer, more specific words colonized some of its former semantic territory. But during those same centuries the word developed a generic sense that, by contrast, expanded its field of reference, so that by the nineteenth century *white* applied not only to artificially secluded aristocratic Englishwomen but to any member of the native population of England, to northern Europeans generally, and to Americans of English or northern European ancestry. In 1853 even southern Europeans could qualify. Clotel, so insistently described as "white," at one point passes for "an Italian or Spanish gentleman" (186). The popular adoption of this expanded generic sense was anything but inevitable; from a purely linguistic perspective, it was actually abnormal and counterintuitive. Normal language evolution will not account for it. Something abnormal happened.

It happened in English between the death of Elizabeth I (1603) and the revolt in Scotland that began the British civil wars (1639). In Thomas Heywood's play *The Fair Maid of the West, Part Two* (1631), a captive Englishman contrasts "we white men" with his captors, the Moors, who are consistently called "black."[151] Six years later, in Richard Brome's play *The English Moor* (1637), an Englishman is identified as "a white Man," and we are told that "'tis no better than a prodigy To have white Children in a black country."[152] In both these texts, *white* modifies a collective noun (men, children); in both, whiteness is specifically, explicitly, and positively attributed to English *men.* Moreover, the appearance of *white* in both plays highlights its absence from a parallel text written 30 years before. In the original play *The Fair Maid of the West* [Part One], apparently performed in the first few years of the century, Thomas Heywood had used *fair* rather than *white* as a marker of Englishness; but by 1631, when he wrote *Part Two,* the same English characters in the same un-English setting get characterized as "white." Brome had been a personal servant and literary apprentice of Ben Jonson, and *The English Moor* explicitly alludes to Jonson's 1605 *Masque of Blackness;* but Jonson had not used the generic idiom in that masque. Heywood and Brome were both recycling older dramatic materials, but in doing so they added the word *white.*

Neither playwright was inventing an idiom. In 1630 the Bishop of Exeter (Joseph Hall) meditated that, if we went to the distant lands populated by black people, "our whiteness" would be as "unpleasing" to them as their blackness was in England.[153] Hall, like Heywood, had changed his vocabulary during the preceding quarter century. At about the time that Jonson's *Masque of Blackness* was performed, Hall's satirical travelogue *Mundus Alter et Idem* was published, imagining just such a voyage to distant lands in the southern hemisphere; Hall had written (in Latin) that a certain cannibal ate "Ethiopians in the place of thrush, and us, in truth, in the place of quail" ("*AEthiopes illi turdorum loci, nostri vero coturnicum*").[154] Like Queen Elizabeth, Hall contrasted Africans with "us." A later translator would render this binary as "He likens a Negro to a Thrush, and a white man to a Quail."[155] But Hall, in 1605, did not describe "us" as "white"—and was apparently not thinking white either, since quails are reddish brown. Nevertheless, by 1630 Hall was writing of "our whiteness."

In Heywood and Hall (both born in 1574), we see an Englishman in his 50s apparently changing his vocabulary; in Brome (born ca. 1590), we witness a writer in his 40s changing the vocabulary of his mentor in the previous generation. Six other texts published between the accession of Charles I (1625) and the Bishops' War (1639) confirm the growing familiarity of *white* in a generic sense. In 1637 a colonist in New England contrasted native Amerindians with the English, whom he described as "white men."[156] The next year a London merchant's guide to international trade contrasted African blacks with "Christians"—including specifically the Portuguese and English—whom he described as "white men."[157] In two other texts the context establishes the same meaning. In 1634 a masque performed at Oxford assumed that members of the audience were "white."[158] In 1637 a London lawyer who had spent a decade in America referred to "our nation" as "white."[159] In both these authors—as in Hall, Heywood, and Brome—the whiteness is plural, and specifically refers to the English. In two other cases the whiteness is singular, but clearly implies a male plural. In 1627 the septuagenarian London cartographer John Speed described Prester John—the mythical medieval Christian who allegedly founded an empire in Abyssinia—as "the only white man" in his African domain.[160] Speed implies that there are other white men outside Africa; he associates white flesh with Christianity, and contrasts it with

"Negroes." In 1638 a groundbreaking treatise on painting contrasted "a white man" (generic) with others who are "tawny" or "black."[161]

White was not at all common in this new generic, positive, male sense: these nine examples are the only ones I have found, in hundreds of texts from the years 1627 to 1639. Nine examples in 12 years do not suggest that the idea of English male whiteness was yet universal. Furthermore, one of these texts was published in Amsterdam, one was never printed at all (and performed only once, before a small academic audience), and one was written by an immigrant Dutchman.[162] Nevertheless, the idiom cannot have been brand new either: between 1627 and 1638 it shows up in the work of two playwrights, two New England colonists, a bishop, a merchant, an academic, a mapmaker, and an art historian living since 1621 in the household of an influential courtier. None of these men, except the two playwrights, can be linked to any of the others. But at least six of the nine were longtime residents of London. Moreover, during this same period the Dutch portrait artist Daniel Mytens painted Charles I alongside his wife in the company of a black servant (Plate 16).[163] The male master was no longer, as in Titian, an outside observer of the contrast between extreme female whiteness and extreme male blackness: he had entered the picture on the side of whiteness.

Where did this new verbal and visual identity originate? What happened to turn Englishmen white?

To answer those questions I must move backward from the 1630s to the late fifteenth century. The next three chapters retrace the tentative, confused, slowly coalescing emergence of the modern generic meaning from 1498 to the early seventeenth century. Only then can I return—in chapter 6—to explain what happened to the literary treatment of whitehood in the decades after Shakespeare had imagined himself in a golden world somewhere between black and white.

CHAPTER 3

THE SHOCK OF WHITENESS

ON JULY 18, 1849, WILLIAM WELLS BROWN left North America for the first time, sailing east from Boston across the Atlantic to the "Old World." He transcribed his first impressions of Britain in a "Sketch of the Author's Life" that prefaced the first edition of *Clotel.*

> No person of my complexion can visit this country without being struck with the marked difference between the English and the Americans. The prejudice which I have experienced on all and every occasion in the United States . . . vanished as soon as I set foot on the soil of Britain . . . no sooner was I on British soil than I was recognised as a man and an equal. The very dogs in the streets appeared conscious of my manhood. Such is the difference, and such is the change that is brought about by a trip of nine days in an Atlantic steamer. (73)

It was his "complexion" that made the transatlantic voyage so momentous. "Colourphobia" reigned on the other side of "the broad Atlantic;" there, "They were white" but "my face was not white," and "that was enough." By contrast, in England he felt his "identity with the English people."[1] On the alien side of the Atlantic, astonishingly, he was treated *as if he were white.*

The difference an ocean can make to the meaning of color also informs *Clotel.* Late in the novel, Brown imagines a series of voyagers crossing "the length and breadth of the vast intervening solitudes, from the melancholy wilds of Labrador and New England's iron-bound shores, to the western coasts of Ireland and the rock-defended Hebrides." First, "Columbus found a continent," and then—almost equal "in moral grandeur" to "the great discoverer"—the "May-flower brought the seed-wheat of states and empire." Brown contrasts these with "a low rakish ship hastening from the tropics," freighted with rattling chains, carrying "the first cargo of slaves" to Virginia, initiating the American entanglement with the African slave trade, "the greatest crime ever perpetrated against humanity" (180–81). But in fact the only black characters who end the novel free, secure, and happy—Clotel's daughter Mary and her husband, George—have both "quit the American continent for ever" (217) and emigrated to Europe.

For English-speaking peoples, the meaning of body color, and of whiteness in particular, has always been bound up with the divisions and identities created by the Atlantic and by the consequences of crossing it, both east-west and north-south.[2] In all the examples of generic *white* in texts from the reign of Charles I (quoted at the end of the previous chapter), a positive sense of group whiteness arises in the context of a comparison with non-European peoples. The complexions of natives of England were probably even lighter in the 1620s and 1630s than they are now (after centuries of interbreeding between colonizing and colonized peoples), and their complexions are still generally of a lighter color than those generally found among the indigenous inhabitants of other continents. But for such comparisons to be relevant to the English sense of identity, inhabitants of Europe's largest island had to become familiar with non-European peoples. In particular, the positive generic myth of "white" bodies became plausible only after English *men* began regularly encountering much darker *men.*

I emphasize this gender distinction because it explains a striking linguistic anomaly in the history of the word *white.* Generally, women, not men, spearhead language change. For reasons more social than biological, women tend to be more open to innovation, more flexible stylistically, more sensitive to social contexts, more adept at multitasking and multiple role-playing. They also tend to be better listeners, which means they are likelier to notice when a speaker uses a new idiom. Moreover, the adults from whom children learn a language are primarily female. Women set the standard for every mother tongue, and they are more likely than men to create and adopt innovations that will eventually come to dominate a language.[3] For instance, between 1417 and 1681 Englishwomen preceded Englishmen in favoring the modern -s form of the third person singular present indicative (*does, has, knows*) rather than the older form in -th (*doth, hath, knoweth*).[4]

However, the evolution of the modern generic meaning of *white* massively contradicts this general rule. The first collective uses of *white* I have found, where the word apparently refers exclusively to Europeans (stage 4), occur in two texts, written by Arthur Barlow and Ralph Lane, printed in 1589.[5] By contrast, the first woman to use *white* in anything approaching the modern generic sense was the Duchess of Newcastle, Margaret Cavendish, in 1666—and Cavendish had clearly picked it up from a man, whose work she was quoting and contesting. Actually, both Cavendish phrases are ambiguous; for indisputable examples in a woman writer we must wait for Aphra Behn's *Oroonoko* (1688).[6] Men usually lag a generation behind women in adopting linguistic innovations.[7] But in the case of *white,* women followed at least three generations, and probably a century, behind men.

Why? Because women were systematically excluded from the social contexts where the new meaning emerged. The encounters between pale English people and darker people from other continents were made possible by a technology developed in coastal western Europe in the fourteenth and fifteenth centuries: wind-driven oceangoing ships. The "proximity engines" that breached the massive geological barrier of the Atlantic Ocean enabled regular contact between "geotemporal population groups" that had been, until then, relatively or totally isolated from each other.[8] Those machines were "manned" entirely by males, and accounts of their voyages were accordingly written by men and about men; so far as we can tell, they were also read almost entirely by men. Aphra Behn is the exception that proves this rule. Behn lived in the English colony of Surinam in the early 1660s; one of the few Englishwomen of her time with firsthand experience of an emergent interoceanic culture, she belongs to an even smaller fraction of women who survived, were literate, returned to England, then became a writer. In the century and a half before *Oroonoko,* almost all the English voyagers who satisfied those four conditions (survival, literacy, return, and publication) were men.

If one reason for male priority in this case is practical, another is ideological. Pallor was already desirable in women. Hence the development of generic whiteness depended on adoption of a new white ideal by and for men. Because calling a male "white" would traditionally have called his virility into question, a woman's use of the word inevitably gendered it; the new meaning had to emerge in conversations between heterosexual men who considered themselves, at some level, equals—and certainly equally male. The emergence of the generic meaning thus engaged, and altered, the English sense of what it meant to be male. That is why Brown's arrival in England immediately transformed the status of his "manhood," and why the turning point in the best-selling *Narrative of the Life of Frederick Douglass* was the moment that revived within him "a sense of [his] own manhood."[9]

Because the whiteness of English males was, between 1627 and 1638, repeatedly articulated in contrast to the darkness of men on other continents, we should expect English whiteness to have originated in accounts of the encounters of European males with non-Europeans. The earliest English examples I have found of stage 3 (where *white* describes a whole population in a manner not demonstrably negative) occur in works about Spanish and Portuguese exploration, translated in the mid-1550s by an alchemist and civil servant named Richard Eden. From a family of successful overseas merchants and early Protestants, Cambridge-educated Eden belonged to the first generation of English humanists with a serious interest in mathematics, geography, and colonization.[10] His few uses of *white* are worth analyzing at some length, as they establish the context for all subsequent developments.

In 1553 Eden published a translation of part of the vast *Cosmographia* by the German Protestant humanist Sebastian Münster. Münster reported that the king of the eastern Indian city of Tammesseri "doth not commit his wife to the Priests to be deflowered (as doth the king of Calicut), but to white men, as are the Christians and Turks. For this office is not committed to the Idolaters." A marginal note reiterates that the queen was deflowered by "white men."[11] Münster copied this information from a very popular account by the Italian traveler Ludovico Varthema, who spent six years in the Orient (1503–08).[12] In India Varthema joined the Portuguese, busy establishing their military superiority in the decade that followed Vasca da Gama's 1498 circumnavigation of Africa.[13] This example originated in an Italian author who had worked alongside the Portuguese in India. Another example comes directly from the Portuguese: Eden's 1555 description of the equatorial African island of São Tomé, discovered and colonized by the Portuguese, contrasts "the white merchants which dwell in that island" with the "black slaves of Guinea, Benin and Manicongo" they import to work their sugar plantations. The "white inhabitants" are equated with the "Portuguese," and Eden's source for information about São Tomé was "a certain pilot of Portugal."[14] It is no accident that these early examples come, directly or indirectly, from Portugal, the first European power to explore what Ca da' Mosto in 1555 called the "new world" of sub-Saharan Africa.[15] Nor is the presence of Italians like Ca da' Mosto and Varthema surprising: the Portuguese alliance with Italian voyagers, merchants, and financiers had begun early in the fifteenth century. Cristofero Colombo, although he sailed in Spanish ships, was an Italian with a Portuguese wife.

In both these passages translated by Eden, *white* describes a population group in a manner not demonstrably negative (stage 3). But the word did not yet differentiate Europeans from Asians, or "Christians" from "Turks." Islam had, of course, reached India long before the Portuguese. In the sixteenth century, the idea of "white . . . Turks" was no more paradoxical or oxymoronic than the idiom "white Moors," which distinguished Muslims native to the Mediterranean and Middle East from the "black moors" of Ethiopia and Guinea.[16] It has been plausibly argued that European colorphobia originated in Islamic demographic distinctions and prejudices.[17] If so, then we would expect the transfer of those ideas to occur in the contact zones where Islamic and western Christian civilization met and melded.[18] Italy was one of those zones. But the largest and longest-lasting was Iberia, and as early as 1332 Christians on Europe's southwestern peninsula were using *branco* or *blanco* ("white") as an ethnic term.[19]

European whiteness was almost certainly first articulated as an ethnic ideal and identity marker on the Iberian peninsula.[20] In 1332 Spanish and Portuguese idioms would have had no effect in the British isles, but in the sixteenth century Spanish became for the first time an important influence on English usage. Eden's other uses of *white* all originated in Spain. English adopted and naturalized only 13 Spanish words in the fifteenth century, but in the sixteenth century it borrowed some 260 (including *negro, mulatto, mestizo, cannibal, caste*) and in the seventeenth more than 300 (including *pickaninny*).[21] This linguistic mimicry belongs to a much larger process of political and cultural imitation. England's inaugural 1553 trading voyage to sub-Saharan Africa was inspired and led by a Portuguese pilot. Individual renegade Spaniards and Portuguese assisted and enabled English transatlantic ventures throughout the second half of the sixteenth century, as the English tried belatedly to duplicate the imperial economic miracle of their southern rivals.[22] How could England negotiate the passage—preferably overnight—from ordinary European kingdom to bejeweled world power?

Passages

Eden's 1555 translation included material written earlier than his 1553 translation, and that earlier material marks a crucial transition in European attitudes toward whiteness. Of the three relevant passages in *The Decades of the New World,* the most important is the first: the one written first, and the one likely to be read first, because it is closest to the front of Eden's huge book. The earliest historical work on the New World, *De Orbe Novo,* was composed in Latin by the Italian humanist Pietro Martire d'Anghiera (1457–1526), known in English as Peter Martyr.[23] In the 1490s Martyr resided at the court of King Ferdinand and Queen Isabella, and his account of the early Spanish voyages across the Atlantic was originally written as a series of letters to Italy; each letter was dispatched soon after Martyr received news of the latest discoveries from eyewitnesses, but Martyr kept copies of the letters. Ten such letters constituted a "Decade," and Martyr's "Decades" accumulated over more than thirty years. They continued to be reprinted, plagiarized, and translated for a century. Eden's 1555 translation of the first three Decades was reprinted in 1577, then again in 1612 (with the remaining five decades translated by Michael Lok); in 1587 Martyr's complete Latin text was reprinted in Paris, edited by Richard Hakluyt, the influential advocate of English colonization. For readers of English or Latin living in Tudor and Jacobean England, Martyr was a key authority for the geography and ethnology of the New World and for the history of Spanish discovery and conquest.

The generic sense of *white* occurs in Martyr's description of the third voyage of Columbus, in a passage almost never cited by modern historians or biographers and certainly never discussed in chronicles of the white race. Perhaps the passage has been overlooked because it cannot be easily accommodated by traditional narratives about European superiority or by newer narratives about European depredation. By 1498 the Portuguese had been shipping African slaves to Europe for more than half a century, and the Spanish were already brutally plundering the Caribbean; Columbus was sailing across the Atlantic for a third time to further a European conquest that cannot be excused legally or morally. Nevertheless, the 1498 discovery of whiteness did not spring from any discernible economic motive. Rather the reverse: Europeans had every motive to justify their conquest by maximizing differences between themselves and their victims. Instead, by accident, Columbus discovered similarity where he expected difference.

On July 31, 1498, Columbus sighted the island he christened Trinidad (here mistakenly called "Puta," presumably by confusion with a cape on the island); he soon encountered a group of the island's inhabitants, in canoes, and was particularly interested in the color of their bodies. Here is the key sentence in the 1555 English translation:

> For the Ethiopians are all black, having their hair curled more like wool than hair; but these people of the island of Puta (being, as I have said, under the clime of Ethiope) are white, with long hair, and of yellow color.[24]

Eden's English accurately renders the Latin's contrast between *nigri* ("black") and *albi* ("white").[25] Eden unambiguously uses the adjective *white* in a collective sense to describe an entire population on the basis of their physical pallor: "these people . . . are white." Collective whiteness arises here out of a contrast with collective African blackness.

Modern whiteness began on July 31, 1498. That claim probably seems absurd. Everyone can immediately recognize the significance of the first contact on October 12, 1492; but it is hard for us to see what was so remarkable about the later encounter off Trinidad. In particular, it seems absurd to link that Trinidadian moment to modern whiteness, because this passage does not attribute collective whiteness to Europeans. It attributes it, instead, to some of the Caribbean peoples who rapidly became extinct as a result of the very European contact that produced this record.[26] But although we are retrospectively disturbed by those millions of deaths, the European explorers were immediately disturbed by something else. To understand what bothered Columbus, and why modern whiteness can be traced back to this inaugural moment, we need to look at the paragraph surrounding this sentence. Because it inaugurates the historical evolution of modern Anglo identity, I will reproduce this passage in two forms, beginning with a photograph of the text printed in London in 1555 (Illus. 2).

> The higher the coulder.
>
> Here the Admirall consideringe with hym selfe the corporature of this people and nature of the lande, he beleaued the same to bee soo muche the nerer heauen then other Regions of the same paralelle, and further remoued from the grosse vapours of the vales and marysshes, howe muche the hyghest toppes of the byggest mountaynes are distante from the deepe vales. For he ernestly affirmeth, that in all that nauigation, he neuer wente owte of the paralelles of Ethiope: So greate difference is there betwene the nature of thinhabitantes and of the soyles of dyuers Regions all vnder one clyme or paralelle: as is to see betwene the people and regions being in the firme lande of Ethiope, and theym of the Ilandes vnder the same clime, hauinge the pole starre eleuate in the same degree.
>
> Difference betwene people of one clime. Ethiopia.
>
> For the Ethiopians are all blacke, hauinge theyr heare curld more lyke wulle then heare. But these people of the Iland of Puta (beinge as I haue sayde vnder the clyme of Ethiope) are whyte, with longe heare, and of yelowe colour. Wherfore it is apparente, the cause of this soo greate difference, to bee rather by the disposition of the earthe, then constitucion of heauen.
>
> Note the cause of difference.
>
> For wee knowe, that snowe fauleth on the mountaynes of the Equinoctiall or burnte lyne, and the same to endure there continually: We knowe lykewyse that thinhabitantes of the Regions farre distante frome that lyne towarde the northe, are molested with greate heate.

I assume that most readers of this book will find the original printing difficult to read and will want to skip immediately from the photo-quotation to the "modernized" version on page 58. But I ask you to suppress that impulse and endure for a moment the irritating obstacle of the original text; for my part, I promise not to do this to you again. Think of this illustrated excerpt as an artifact, a fragment of physical evidence from an alien culture: something unexpectedly hard and stubborn that the amateur archaeologist's trowel encounters as it slides through otherwise-unresisting sand. The artifact's curious illegibility forces us to recognize a gap we have all been conditioned to ignore. Most people who read sixteenth-century literature at all encounter it in modernized editions, which make the texts more accessible by removing from them, as much as possible, the texture of their differences; even academic specialists in Renaissance literature normally read and teach and cite it in modernized texts.[27] The unfamiliar typography, spelling, and punctuation of the original text remind us that "English" in 1555 was not exactly the "English" we recognize now. Our sense of linguistic identity across time is, like so many other aspects of nationalistic mythology, retrospectively constructed, imposed on the past by our own needs and beliefs. Two of those beliefs have been the assumption that English people have always been white and that the word *white* has always had its modern generic meaning.

That is why I am forcing on you, this once, a sense of the more general strangeness of early modern English. It is not just the word *white* that operated differently, in 1555, from how it does now. Because old orthography and typography are likely to distract readers from an argument already complicated enough, in the rest of this book I have routinely modernized quotations. Here is the same passage, with its spelling, punctuation, and typography modernized—but with a few words highlighted by bold type.

> Here **the Admiral**—considering with himself the corporature of this people and nature of the land—**he** believed the same to be so much the nearer heaven than other regions of the same parallel, and further removed from the gross vapors of the vales and marshes, **how much** the highest tops of the biggest mountains are distant from the deep vales. For he earnestly affirmeth that in all that navigation he never went out of the parallels of **Ethiope**. So great difference is there between the nature of th'inhabitants and of the soils of diverse regions all under one **clime** or parallel—as is to see between the people and regions being in the firm land of **Ethiope** and them of the islands under the same clime, having the pole star elevate in the same degree. For the **Ethiopians** are all black, having their hair curled more like wool than hair; but these people of the island of Puta (being, as I have said, under the **clime** of **Ethiope**) are **white**, with long hair, and of yellow color. Wherefore it is apparent the cause of this so great difference to be rather by the disposition of the earth than constitution of **heaven**. For we know that snow falleth on the mountains of the equinoctial or burnt line, and the same to endure there continually . . .

As the words printed in bold type indicate, even this modernized text does not remove all our trouble understanding this passage. Early modern grammar was in important respects different from our own.[28] In the first sentence "the Admiral . . . he" would now be stigmatized as redundant, while later in the same sentence we would require *by* before "how much." In this alien linguistic environment, simple words—such as *white*—that we think we recognize may be what linguists call "false cognates," or *falsi amici*.[29] Like false friends, words that we think we know can betray us. The French word *pain* ("bread") does not mean the same thing as the English word *pain,* even though they look exactly the same and are both nouns that could occupy the same grammatical position in a sentence ("give us this day our daily *pain*"). Likewise, in this passage *heaven* did not mean what it means to us: in 1555 it was not just a "poetic" synonym for *sky,* as it has been since the seventeenth century.[30] Martyr's text was pre-Copernican, and it presupposes a geocentric universe surrounded by fixed spheres—and a world where "Eden" was as real a place as Portugal, and "Paradise" had not yet become extraterrestrial.[31] *Ethiope* did not mean modern "Ethiopia," but sub-Saharan Africa more generally. *Clime* did not mean "climate," in its modern sense; Columbus and later European voyagers were in fact repeatedly astonished by the difference between the climate at one latitude on the eastern side of the Atlantic and the climate at the same latitude on the western side. *Clime* here refers to one of the seven latitudinal bands or regions into which classical astronomers and geographers had divided the earth. All these false cognates are relevant to the problem of whiteness.

Five things are apparent from the larger context of this early claim about "white" people.

1. Martyr's source for this information was Columbus himself.
2. Columbus did not expect to find white people where he found them.
3. Finding white people where he found them forced Columbus to reimagine the universe.
4. Columbus was right.
5. Columbus's astonished discovery of white people in 1498 initiated an intellectual chain reaction that eventually produced the modern racial world.

Columbus

1. Martyr's source was Columbus ("the Admiral considering with himself . . . he believed . . . he earnestly affirmeth . . .").

Earlier in the *Decades* Martyr had reported that "the Admiral himself (whom I use familiarly as my very friend) hath promised me by his letters that he will give me knowledge of all such things as shall chance."[32] Martyr's attribution is confirmed by the letter Columbus wrote to King Ferdinand and Queen Isabella and dispatched from Española on October 18, 1498, describing his third voyage. Columbus explained that Trinidad's inhabitants were "not negroes, but whiter than the others who have been seen in the Indies" (*no negros, salvo más blancos que otros que aya visto en las Yndias*).[33] That letter (not printed in the sixteenth century) establishes the veracity of Martyr's claim—evident to any reader of his Latin text or its English translation—that Columbus himself supplied this account of a "white" population in the New World.

Indeed, Columbus encountered whiteness throughout the third voyage, not only in Trinidad but also along the coast of what is now Venezuela (which he christened "Paria"). Where the river Oronoco empties into the sea, Columbus found the natives "of the same color as the others before" (*de la misma color que los otros de antes*);[34] this must refer to the "white" Trinidadians, since he had encountered no others in the interim. Columbus subsequently specified that "the color of this people is more white than any other seen in the Indies" (*la color d'esta gente es más blanca que otra que aya visto en las Yndias*).[35] In Martyr's account of these people—in the same chapter as his account of the Trinidadians—he reported that "they are white"—in the Latin, *albi*—"even as our men are, saving such as are much conversant in the sun."[36] Here, in Martyr, the whiteness of the Amerindians was explicitly likened to the whiteness of "our men" (*nostrates*)—that is, inhabitants of Spain; in fact, the Amerindians were whiter than sunburned Spaniards. A side note, apparently added by the English editor/translator, indicated that this fact merited special attention: "White men near the equinoctial." The men in canoes off Trinidad were not an isolated anomaly; all the inhabitants of this area seemed to be white. Moreover, this second passage, unlike the first, was not explicitly attributed to Columbus; in fact, this passage follows a sentence in which Martyr attributed his information to "the Admiral himself, and they which were his companions in the voyage, being men of good credit." What Martyr attributed specifically to Columbus is, then, not the fact of pallor in that New World population, but the explanation for that pallor.

A Surprise

2. Columbus did not expect to find white people where he found them.

The whole passage presumes that their complexion was a problem, a counterintuitive claim requiring emphatic confirmation, a puzzle to be explained. The letter in which Columbus reported the whiteness of the Trinidadians is the same one in which he realized that he had not reached Asia, as he had originally expected and believed; instead he had discovered what he called (quoting Isaiah 65:17) "new heaven, and a new earth." The discovery of whiteness coincided with the recognition of a new world. Trinidadian whiteness contrasted both with the blackness of the Ethiopians and with the characteristic darkness of other natives of the (West) Indies. On October 12, 1492, the day of his famous first encounter with the inhabitants of what we now call the western hemisphere, Columbus had recorded that "they are of the color of the Canarians, neither black nor white" (*ellos son dla color dlos Canarios ni negros ni blancos*).[37] That fact did not seem in itself surprising; it did not constitute a problem requiring further comment or explanation. On the first voyage, having left the Canary Islands and sailed west, Columbus encountered other islands, inhabited by people whose color resembled that of the Canary islanders; he was not surprised. By contrast, on the third voyage Columbus sailed south until he reached "the parallel which passed through Sierra Leone" (where the heat was "great" and the inhabitants were "black"), and sailed almost due west to Trinidad and northern Venezuela (where the temperature was "very mild" and the inhabitants were "white").[38] He was nonplussed. As the side note to the English translation emphasized, the problem posed by this new information was the "difference between people of one clime" (or as we would say, "one latitude").

A New Universe

3. Finding white people where he found them forced Columbus to reimagine the universe.

As the key paragraph makes clear, that whiteness is somehow related to latitudes ("parallels"), to distance from the equator ("equinoctial"), to astronomy ("pole star . . . constitution of heaven"), and to geography, especially in relation to the relative elevation of terrain ("so much the nearer heaven"). Thus, the side note to the later passage called attention to "White men near the equinoctial," even though "the equinoctial" is not mentioned in the adjoining sentences or anywhere else on that page; the antecedent to the side note's reference must be the first passage, where Columbus/Martyr had puzzled over the whiteness of the Trinidadians. But the logic that interrelates these terms is likely to elude a modern reader, because it is assumed rather than explained by Martyr's text (or Martyr's transcription of Columbus's report). Indeed, it is not only modern readers who found difficulty here. Near the conclusion of this chapter, Martyr himself became incredulous. He reported that the Admiral of the Ocean Sea had said

> that he hereby conjectured that the earth is not perfectly round, but that when it was created there was a certain heap raised thereon, much higher than the other parts of the same. So that (as he saith) it is not round after the form of an apple or a ball (as others think) but rather like a pear as it hangeth on the tree, and that Paria [northern Venezuela] is the region which possesseth the supereminent or highest part thereof nearest unto heaven. Insomuch that he earnestly contendeth the earthly paradise to be situate in the tops of those three hills. . . . [39]

Martyr was not misunderstanding Columbus. In his letter describing these discoveries, Columbus had indeed proposed that the world "is not round as they describe it, but that it is the shape of a pear which is everywhere very round except where the stalk is, for there it is very prominent, or that it is like a very round ball, and on one part of it is placed something like a woman's nipple, and that this part, where the protuberance is found, is the highest and nearest to the sky."[40]

But although Martyr accurately reported Columbus's hypothesis, he explicitly disassociated himself from it. He did not "understand" the astronomical observations that allegedly supported it, and the other "reasons which he bringeth" did not "in any point satisfy" him.[41] Martyr was not alone. Not one globe-maker or cartographer accepted this bizarre image of a global pear or of "something like a woman's nipple" protruding upward from the planetary sphere.[42] Even Ferdinand Columbus, in his biography of his father Christopher, ignored the planetary theory Dad had articulated so passionately in 1498.[43] The hypothesis was an embarrassment, and scholars now cite it—when they do—only for its eccentricity. In a recent book Kirkpatrick Sale describes the theory as "a very long and muddled mishmash of theology and astronomy and geography and fantastic lore, rambling, repetitive, illogical, confusing, at times incoherent, self-serving, servile and vainglorious all at once—and quite loony."[44] The "new earth" of 1498 has shrunk to the status of an amusing anecdote, something to liven up a dull lecture. (Undergraduates always perk up at the word *nipple.*)

Real Whiteness

4. Columbus was right.

The nipple hypothesis was wrong, but Columbus was right about all the facts that prompted his theory. The anomalous compass readings he reported, on that third voyage across the Atlantic, have been confirmed by subsequent observations of irregularities in the magnetosphere.[45] And our planet is, in fact, not perfectly spherical. Classical and medieval astronomers assumed it must be, for the same reason that the Catholic church initially rejected Galileo's observation of sunspots: God would not create something imperfect, like a misshapen planet or an off-center magnetic pole or a fluctuating spotty sun. Columbus just picked the wrong fruit: Mother Earth is not like an Old World pear but a New World pumpkin, a slightly squashed sphere, fatter horizontally than it is vertically (an unexciting belly-roll, rather than a divine breast).[46] NASA instrumentation has also confirmed Columbus's seemingly ridiculous claim that, as they crossed the Atlantic, "in passing thence to the westward, the ships went rising gently toward the sky."[47] As Martyr put it, in his account of the Atlantic passage, "The Admiral also affirmeth that . . . he ever ascended by the back of the sea, as it were by a high mountain toward heaven."[48] It is not simply that the land is higher; sea level is also higher. Nobody believed him, but Columbus was right. As oceanographers discovered only late in the twentieth century, using instruments unimaginable in the fifteenth, the surface of the Atlantic does rise as it moves from west Africa to the Caribbean. The water piles up, creating the pressure that drives the Gulf Stream.[49] Today scientists do not believe that those changes in sea surface height, or the fluctuations in the earth's magnetic field, or its variations in diameter, have any bearing on the color of human bodies. Nevertheless, in each case Columbus reported something that his contemporaries found incredible, something that has been absolutely confirmed and verified by subsequent men and machines. There was nothing "loony" about what Columbus reported in 1498.

There seems no reason to doubt those reports about body color either. Unlike the reports of wave height, planetary diameter, and magnetic fluctuation, the observations about body color cannot be confirmed, because the human genres Columbus was describing have all been exterminated.[50] Nevertheless, the native populations of Sierra Leone almost certainly had darker bodies in 1498 than the extinct native peoples of tropical America. Dark pigmentation is a responsive adaptation to high ultraviolet radiation; because our species originated in equatorial or tropical Africa, the human populations there have had longer to adapt to the higher UV levels than the corresponding human populations of equatorial and tropical America.[51] Humans apparently did not arrive in the western hemisphere until between 12,000 and 25,000 years ago, moving southward from a land bridge across the Bering Strait.[52] Coming from northern Eurasia, the people who crossed into North America were almost certainly much paler than Africans. In geological or generational time, the native human genres of the southern Caribbean had had much less time (6,000 years?) to evolve epidermal defenses against the tropical sun than their African cousins (9 million years of hominid evolution; 160,000 years of *Homo sapiens sapiens*).[53]

Some Amerindians may have been shockingly pale. When Europeans arrived, the Caribbean contained many different ethnic groups. In the 1630s a Spanish missionary in the province of Panama (which then included parts of what is now Colombia) described Indians who were "white and blonde as Flemings" [that is, Belgians]. In 1681 an Englishman spent several months with a group of "white" Indians in the same region.[54] In 1924 an expedition from the Smithsonian Institute encountered, in the village of Portogandi, another member of this distinct human genre: "His hair was a light golden yellow. His skin was as white as a Swede's." Subsequently they met others with "white skin, blonde hair, blue-green to brown eyes." Unlike the explorers of 1498, those of 1924 carried a camera (Illus. 3). The complexion of these Amerindians so disturbed racist American anthropologists that they invented for them a special category: they were said to be "imperfect" or "partial" albinos (that is, peoples who, although they show none of the physiological characteristics of albinos, must be genetic freaks because they are non-Europeans with European complexions).[55] Whatever the real genetic explanation for their pallor, indigenous people with white skin and yellow hair—just like those described by Columbus—survived into the twentieth century along the southern coast of the Caribbean. Their numbers may have been much greater—and more widely distributed geographically—in the fifteenth century, before the devastating depopulation wrought by European military and bacteriological invasion. Moreover, since Europeans treated Amerindians so harshly, such pale people would have had strong incentives and opportunities to "pass" as Europeans, and many might have been invisibly absorbed into the European population. Columbus and his men were not hallucinating when they saw white people in Trinidad and west of the Oronooko basin.[56]

What matters now, for the history of racism, is why the encounter with those white people drove Columbus to deduce the series of extraordinary claims reported by Martyr: that the earth was pear-shaped, that he had discovered not only "new earth" but also a "new heaven." He must have realized such a radical theory would be greeted with skepticism. His letter to his royal patrons, after first articulating the hypothesis, reiterated and summarized the evidence for it. Sailing south down the west coast of Africa, he noted that the inhabitants were first "black," then "blacker," until finally in Sierra Leone "the people are black to an extreme degree." But when he sailed westward from Sierra Leone,

> when I reached the island of Trinidad . . . both there and in the land of Gracia I found a very mild climate. . . . And the people there I found to be of very fair stature and whiter than the others who have been seen in the Indies, and their hair long and smooth. . . . The sun was then in Virgo, above our heads and theirs. Thus all this must proceed from the very mild climate that is there, and this in turn from the fact that the land is the highest in the world, nearest to the sky, as I conceive.

He does not mean that the mountains are taller than any other mountains, but that in this region the surface of the earth itself is farther from the center of the earth (and the center of the universe, in the Ptolemaic cosmography that he and his contemporaries credited).

About the alleged bulge in the earth's surface near Trinidad, Columbus was wrong. But he was driven to this conclusion because he needed an explanation for the "white" bodies and "smooth hair" of the inhabitants, which contrasted with the complexions and hair of Africans due east of them. The white Trinidadians were so astonishing to Columbus that they prompted him to propose not only a new geography and a new oceanography, but a new cosmography. The discovery of whiteness in 1498 challenged, and changed, the entire medieval understanding of the world.

Marvels

5. Columbus's astonished discovery of white people in Trinidad in 1498 initiated an intellectual chain-reaction that eventually produced the modern racial world.

Why was Columbus so astonished? Wonder, according to cultural historians Mary Baines Campbell and Stephen Greenblatt, is the decisive emotional and intellectual experience in the initial European responses to the New World: "a challenge, a disruption, a catalyst of discontinuities" produces a "failure of categories."[57] Some of the categories that organized the worldview

Illustration 3. Richard Oglesby Marsh, *White Indians of Darien* (New York: Putnam, 1934). Courtesy of the British Library

of Columbus failed when disrupted by the "white" men he found in Trinidad and northern Venezuela. Therefore, to understand his reaction, we have to identify those endangered categories. That should be easy to do, because the categories must have been assumed by Columbus and his crew and by Martyr and his readers; Columbus could be so elliptical because he expected everyone to share his assumptions.

The presence of "white" people outside Europe did not, in itself, disorient fifteenth- and sixteenth-century Europeans. On two other occasions in the 1550s Richard Eden translated works that described "white" people native to faraway places, but the emotional register in those other passages radically contrasts with the bewildered amazement of Columbus and Martyr here. Later in his 1555 volume, Eden translated Antonio Pigafetta's account of Magellan's circumnavigation of the globe (1518–1520), which calmly reported that "These people of China are white men."[58] In 1553 Eden had translated Münster's account of "the great empire of . . . the great Khan," which nonchalantly reported that "The inhabitants are white men"—and "vtterly void of all godly knowledge." Münster identified "this people of Cathay" with "the nation" formerly "called Scythians."[59] He copied this claim from his favorite source, the 1520 cosmography of another German humanist and Hebraist, Johann Boemus.[60] Between 1544 and 1650 Münster's book appeared in 46 editions in six languages; another English translation of extracts appeared in 1572, repeating the information that the Chinese were "a white kind of people."[61] In 1577 another Englishman translated Galeote Pereira's Italian account of the Orient, which testified that "The Tartars are men very white."[62] Both Hakluyt's famous collections entitled *Principal Voyages,* in 1589 and 1598, included Richard Johnson's account of his trip to eastern Russia, where a Tartarian merchant told him that "in Cathay . . . are people white and of fair complexion."[63] In 1612 Londoners could read the first English eyewitness report of India's "great white King," the Mogul, who was "a white man and of the Race of the Tartars."[64] Attitudes toward such peoples ranged from negative (stage 2) to neutral (stage 3). Boemus and Münster condemned the heathen people of Cathay they called white, and "the barbarous Scythian" did not have a good reputation among ancient historians or Renaissance humanists.[65]

But Boemus, Münster, Pigafetta, Pereira, and Johnson express no surprise at the presence of white populations outside Europe. The location of these white men did not need explaining. As the allusion to Scythians suggests, medieval explanations for the color of human bodies had a classical pedigree. That pedigree also shaped medieval Arabic geographers, who knew more about Asia but shared the climatic assumptions of Europeans.[66] Alexander the Great, after all, had reached India long before Islam did. The eastward explorations of William of

Rubruck and Marco Polo were "unthreatening" to medieval geographers, Christian or Arabic.[67]

The geographic theory they shared was articulated by—among others—Ptolemy (100–178 C.E.). Columbus could not easily dismiss Ptolemy, the most august authority for his conviction that the earth was round (and small enough that China should have been where the Americas are). But in 1498 he felt compelled to reject Ptolemy's conclusion that the world was perfectly round. He was driven to this heresy by observing "white" people in Trinidad. But if "Cathay" contained "white men," and Columbus believed that by sailing west he would reach Cathay, why should he have been so astonished to find white people in Trinidad?

The location of those "white" people contradicted Ptolemy's description "Of the Characteristics of the Inhabitants of the General Climes." Ptolemy had explained the "black bodies" (μέλανες τὰ οω´ματα) of "Ethiopians" as a consequence of their being closer to the equator, and hence closer to the sun, which burned them black. By contrast, "Those who live under the more northern parallels" were, according to Ptolemy, "white in color" (νευκοί τε τὰ χρώματά), like the "Scythians" (122–23).[68] In both these claims Ptolemy's authority was apparently backed by Aristotle's. In the *Problems*—in the Middle Ages and the Renaissance attributed to Aristotle—it is claimed that "the eyes of those who live towards the north are blue, because they are themselves white (for blue is akin to white)."[69] These ideas about the relationship between climate and body color originated in even earlier Greek texts. Unlike the ancient Egyptians and Hebrews, the ancient Greeks sometimes identified peoples on the basis of color; in particular the Greek word Αἶθίοψ ("Aithiops," the source of English *Ethiopia*) literally means "burnt-face."[70]

These classical Greek theories about the relationship between latitude and body color were repeated in the classical Latin of works as influential as Pliny's *Natural History* and Vitruvius's *On Architecture.*[71] From such authorities, they migrated to the medieval Latin of encyclopediasts like Albertus Magnus and Bartolomæus Anglicus.[72] Thus, the presence of "white" people in Cathay was perfectly predictable. But the 1498 discovery of "white" people in the same latitudes as the Ethiopians disproved an explanation of human corporeal diversity that had dominated European thought for a millennium and a half.

How then was the variety of human genres to be explained? It has taken five centuries to answer the questions raised by that encounter off Trinidad. The solution eventually required Hutton's replacement of a biblical with a geological time scale, Darwin's theory of human evolution, Mendel's analysis of the mathematics of genetic inheritance, Watson and Crick's discovery of DNA, Brown and Wallace's work on mitochrondrial DNA, and NASA's mapping of the planetary magnetosphere and its affect on the amount of ultraviolet radiation that reaches different areas of the earth's surface. But all those later developments themselves depended on a fundamental change in descriptions of the problem to be solved. Our own scientific explanations limit the problem of human color to the pigmentation of skin. But Columbus did not say that the inhabitants of Trinidad *had* white *skin.* He said, "these *people . . . are* white."

Columbus and Martyr were writing decades before Andreas Vesalius violated the traditional western taboo against dissection, publicly investigating and displaying for the first time the internal "fabric of the human body" (*De fabrica corporis humani,* 1543).[73] Our own perception of skin as a thin membrane itself derives from Vesalius and other anatomists (and eventually dermatologists) who followed where he led. I will return to the revolutionary consequences of dissection in chapter 10. But for now we need only recognize the difference between medieval and modern views of the body. Within the Ptolemaic paradigm, color was not simply an external or epidermal feature; it reflected the balance of humors within the body. Each of the four key humors had a characteristic color, and color therefore permeated the entire body and soul. The English word *complexion,* which we now use to describe the appearance of one's skin, originally referred to this whole intertwined ensemble of physical characteristics; it was synonymous with *constitution,* a general term for one's natural physiological being.[74] Thus the problem Columbus confronted was not simply "skin-deep." It affected every existing theory of the cosmos and every existing theory of the microcosmic human body.

Because the contradiction between classical theory and modern observations was first experienced in the New World, Spanish intellectuals reacted to it before their counterparts elsewhere in Europe. For decades some European geographers simply denied the existence of the New World altogether.[75] But the Spanish could not indulge in such denials. Gonzalo Fernándes de Oviedo, in his digest *De la natural hystoria de las Indias* (1526), compared the tigers of India, described by various authorities, with the "tigers" of the "Indies" he had seen himself (what we now call the "jaguars" of the "Americas"); he recognized the differences, but considered the similarities more important. To explain his position, he offered this analogy: "Men likewise which in some countries are black, are in other places white: and yet are both these and they men."[76] Oviedo's eyewitness statement was echoed, in 1552, by a Spanish writer who had never been to the New World, Francisco López de Gómara, whose account of the conquest of Mexico included a chapter entitled "Of the color of the Indians." "One of the marvelous things that God useth in the composition of man," he wrote, "is color—which doubtless cannot be considered without great admiration in beholding one to be white and another black, being colors utterly contrary."[77] Like Columbus, Gómara found the color of the Indians literally marvelous, a marvel, a subject of what he calls "admiration" and what we would call "astonishment."[78]

Black and white are only the extremes of color possibility; between and within them (as Gómara went on to explain) is an equally extraordinary profusion of pigments. Some men

> be yellow, which is between black and white: and other of other colors as it were of diverse liveries. And as these colors are to be marvelled at, even so is it to be considered how they differ one from another as it were by degrees, forasmuch as some men are white after diverse sorts of whiteness, yellow after diverse manners of yellow, and black after diverse sorts of blackness: and how from white they go to yellow by discoloring to brown and red, and to black by ash color, and murrey somewhat lighter than black, and tawny (like unto the West Indians, which are altogether in general either purple, or tawny . . .) Therefore in like manner and with such diversity as men are commonly white in Europe and black in Afric, even with like variety are they tawny in these Indies, with diverse degrees diversely inclining more or less to black or white.

In another sign of his dependence on Oviedo, all Gómara's West Indians were, for the moment, tawny (although some were a tawny that was "inclining more . . . to . . . white"). Whiteness was here primarily associated—by a writer who had never left Europe—with Europe, Europe alone, and Europe as a whole. This translated passage is, so far as I can determine, the first example of such a use of *white* in English (stage 4). Richard Eden—who included all these passages from Oviedo and Gómara in his 1555 anthology—found a generic sense of whiteness in three of the most authoritative early accounts of the Spanish New World, and he transplanted that borrowed generic sense into the English word that was the closest equivalent of *blanco* in its literal sense: "white."[79]

But Eden also brought into English the disorientation and ambiguity of his Spanish sources, struggling to cope with a contradiction they could not explain. Gómara's use of *blanco* was surrounded by qualifications. White was the color that "commonly" appeared in European men, along a spectrum of diverse degrees diversely inclining to black or white. European whiteness was here cited not for its uniformity, but for its variety. The association of whiteness with Europe was triply qualified ("in like manner," "with such diversity," "commonly"). Both syntactically and logically, the varieties of European whiteness were subordinated to a description of the varieties of color found in Caribbean and South American peoples. For six decades after Columbus sighted Trinidad, the newly discovered variety of human genres could not be explained; it could only be wondered at.

> No less marvel is it to consider that men are white in Seville and black at the cape of Buena Speranza, and of chestnut color at the river of Plata, being all in

> equal degrees from the Equinoctial line. Likewise that the men of Afric and Asia that live under the burnt line (called *Zona Torrida*) are black: and not they that live beneath or on this side the same line as in Mexico, Yucatan, Quauhtema, Lian [*sic:* Guatemalia], Nicaragua, Panama, Santo Domingo, Paria, Cape Saint Augustine, Lima, Quito, and other lands of Peru which touch in the same Equinoctial. . . . By reason whereof it may seem that such variety of colors proceedeth of man, and not of the earth: which may well be, although we be all born of Adam and Eve . . .

The evident variety of human colors seemed to contradict the biblical claim that all humans descended from a single couple. That diversity could no longer be explained by its geographical distribution, because color was not consistently aligned along gradients of latitude: as Eden's marginal note emphasized, there was "Difference of color in the same clime." That phrase echoed the marginal note in Martyr's chapter on the Trinidadians ("Difference between people of one clime"). But the problem, for Columbus isolated to Trinidad and "Paria," had in subsequent decades deepened; Gómara cited "Paria" among a host of other apparent contradictions (including Panama, where "white" Indians would be reported by many observers from the 1630s on). Unlike Columbus, he did not attempt to offer any explanation except divine caprice: Christians "know not the cause why God hath so ordained it, otherwise than to consider that his divine majesty hath done this (as infinite other) to declare his omnipotency and wisdom in such diversities of colors as appear not only in the nature of man, but the like also in beasts, birds, and flowers, where diverse and contrary colors are seen in one little feather, or the leaves grown out of one little stalk."

This seems to be the end of the matter: God created diversity to demonstrate that he could create diversity. What could not be explained by climate could be attributed instead to God. But Gómara did not stop at this logical dead end. For Gómara as for Columbus, hair compounded color, contradicting the hypothesis that human variety results from climate: "Another thing is also greatly to be noted as touching these Indians. And this is: that their hair is not curled as is the Moors' and Ethiopians' that inhabit the same clime: neither are they bald except very seldom, and that but little. All which things may give further occasion to philosophers to search the secrets of nature and complexions of men with the novelties of the new world."

Instead of leaving his readers with a catchall theological explanation, Gómara commended these "secrets of nature" to the attention of "philosophers." Since the fifteenth century, intellectuals who pondered such curiosities of "nature" had been called "natural philosophers"—a title they retained until the nineteenth century, when we began calling them "scientists." The problem of whiteness confronted by Columbus and his successors was handed over to Europe's professional intellectuals, who would eventually forge the categorical chains taken for granted by William Wells Brown, Frederick Douglass, and all the other pioneers of African American literature.

Chapter 4

Confounded Whiteness

The Europeans who found white people in Trinidad were disturbed for the same reason that William Wells Brown expected readers of *Clotel* to be disturbed by its opening scene. Clotel's whiteness is shocking because it is out of place. In 1853 it must have seemed obvious to all readers of English that no *white* woman should stand on an auction block. In 1498 it must have seemed equally obvious to any educated European that no *white* people should be living where Columbus found them. Like the early readers of *Clotel,* Columbus was confronted by something that contradicted his assumptions about the stability of the relationship between pigmentation and location. In both cases an aberrant whiteness broke the expected link between peoples and places.

For Brown, as for other free blacks, such expectations reeked of colorphobia. On the steamship that carried him from Boston to Liverpool, Brown overheard white passengers complaining "That nigger had better be on his master's farm"; at a soirée in Paris hosted by the French foreign minister, he noticed the American consul and "many of [his] own countrymen" staring at him, knowing that "Had I been in America, where color is considered a crime, I would not have been seen at such a gathering, unless as a servant"; at the Crystal Palace in London, "some of our Virginia neighbors" eyed him with "sneering looks," particularly outraged to see "an English lady . . . leaning on [his] arm"; freshly returned to America after five years in Europe, and trying to board an omnibus in Philadelphia, he was immediately reminded of the change in his social status when told "We don't allow niggers to ride in here."[1] In *Clotel,* the black man who helps the heroine escape from slavery is named (like the author) William, and (like the author) in Ohio he "took his seat in one of the train's first-class carriages"—only to be evicted (171–72); "colored people were not allowed to take seats in the cars with whites," and accordingly "blacks were generally made to ride in the baggage-car."[2] Dark people were, in America, barred from places of privilege, or permitted to enter them only as silent servants. As sociologist Pierre

Bourdieu argues, by such policing of space and speech a society teaches individuals "a fundamental dimension of the sense of knowing the place which one occupies in the social space."[3] Blacks, displaced by the slave trade, had to be kept firmly "in their place" in America. Or—according to the American Colonization Society—they had no place at all in white America, and should be sent back to Africa, where blacks belonged.

Space is never innocent.[4] It is always defined by a point of observation, which is always occupied by one person rather than another. Language begins at a point occupied by a speaking observer, whose position defines *I* ("this" person "here") against *her* ("that" person "over there"). Language is local, and local is social. American slavery tried to constrict "black space," to confine black experience to an intellectually and socially impoverished local knowledge; Brown had escaped from the local only to discover that the North was as colorphobic as the South. (It still is.) Over and over Brown witnessed the effect on whites of the appearance of a black man "in the wrong place," the place of a free man, the place of a white. In *Clotel,* he subjected white readers to a fantasy of the inverse violation of expectation: a white woman—a series of white women—"in the wrong place," the place of a slave, the place of a black. *Clotel* enacts the clash, in attitudes toward the color of slavery, between a black observer and a white one.

The intellectual crisis created by the contrast between the New World and an old worldview usually is constructed as a clash between ancient speculative philosophy ("authority") and modern empiricism ("observation"). That is how I constructed it, too, in early drafts of this book. But the more I read and reread *Clotel,* the more unsatisfactory that traditional interpretation seemed. What Columbus and Martyr and Gómara record, in their demographics of whiteness, is a problem created by *a clash between two different sets of observers.* By the Middle Ages, ancient philosophy had become an "authority," but it had originated in acts of "observation." The two sets of observers/authorities, ancient and modern, clashed because they occupied different positions, geographically and socially and linguistically.

That clash created more than a century of intellectual confusion for some of the best-educated minds in Europe. To avoid becoming as confused as they were, we need to begin with a few simple questions. What did the classical observers say? What did the words they used to describe skin color mean: to what part of the visible spectrum did they refer? And at what latitude did they think that "north" began?

Classical Observers

The racial assumptions in part assumed and in part attacked by *Clotel* are now usually traced to the "scientific racism" of the eighteenth century. The foundational text often is said to be *Systema Naturae* (1735, 10th ed. 1758), in which the great Swedish biologist Carolus Linnaeus divided "homo sapiens" (his coinage) into four separate varieties: *Europaeus albus* ("white"), *Americanus rubesceus* ("red"), *Asiaticus luridus* ("yellowish"), and *Afer niger* ("black"). But the problem of categories and origins posed by different genres of humanity had already begun to preoccupy European intellectuals in the second half of the sixteenth century. Sixteenth-century astronomers had a simple binary choice between earth-centered (Ptolemy) and sun-centered (Copernicus), but natural philosophers had no simple alternative to Ptolemy's explanation of human colors. Consequently the formulation of a new set of simple categories (Linnaeus) to replace the old set of simple categories (Ptolemy) took more than two centuries.

The sixteenth-century response to the shock of whiteness was not a single, simple theory, or even a contest between two simple theories, but a profusion of confused speculation. As happens with every paradigm shift, conservatives stubbornly resisted the new evidence, while moderates tried to adapt the old theory to fit new facts; new data and new hypotheses accumulated randomly. Because this intellectual ferment was confused and confusing, it does not look very "scientific" to us, and it lacks the sharp outlines of the initial encounter between Columbus and the Trinidadians. Nevertheless, the earliest English texts to invoke the idea of whole populations with "white" bodies all do so within the discourses we would call ethnography, geography, anthropology, and medicine, an interdisciplinary mix that cultural historian Mary Floyd-Wilson usefully christens "geohumoralism."[5]

But demographic whiteness, in the sixteenth century, was also a linguistic problem. Color terms are notoriously difficult to translate. To arbitrate between ancient texts and new observations, one first had to translate the ancient texts into the language of the new observers. Although some modern translators interpret the Greek word used by Ptolemy and pseudo-Aristotle as *white,* other modern translators prefer *fair.*[6] The most authoritative modern English lexicon of ancient Greek claims that Aristotle's word can refer to the color *white,* noting that Homer often used it of snow; but, as the Inuit know, snow comes in many colors. The same dictionary entry cites multiple uses and senses of the Greek word, and *bright* might be a better translation, since it would fit the largest number of contexts.[7] The standard *Greek-English Lexicon* was completed in the early 1840s, and revised between 1911 and 1938, a century when notions of northern European "whiteness" were firmly entrenched; both the original and the revision were heavily indebted to German classical scholarship. Anachronistic racial assumptions probably affected some modern scholarly glosses and translations of νευκοί as *white.*[8]

Similar uncertainties affect most Latin discussions of pale populations. Pliny and Vitruvius both used the adjective *candidus* to describe northern peoples.[9] Their modern translators, working in the same series in the same decade, in one case render the word as *white* and in the other as *fair.*[10] Its primary meaning refers to light or light sources, and the whole complex of senses is closer to *bright* than to modern *white.*[11] Although ancient writers used *candidus* to describe Germans, Gauls, and Saxons, the modern word *albino* derives (through Portuguese) from the Latin adjective *albus;* but scholars dispute whether *albus* meant "white" or "pale brown."[12] In both ancient Greek and Latin, the problem arises from the way the human nervous system processes the spectrum of visible light: the greater the "brightness" of a color, the more difficult it becomes to identify the hue itself.[13] If the definition of ancient color words is uncertain even among modern scholars (who have access to much more evidence), then we can hardly assume that medieval and early modern Europeans all understood those words the same way, or that the meaning of the Latin words remained constant over the course of more than 1500 years.

Such distinctions seem—and are—pedantic. But much of the intellectual energy of what we call "the Re-naissance" ("rebirth") was devoted to the translation, adaptation, and internalization of ancient Mediterranean literature and culture. Beyond the technical linguistic problem of how to translate νευκοί or *albus* was the much larger problem that critic Robert Miola calls "cultural drift," caused by "the clashing historicities of the signifier and the signified."[14] Even if we were absolutely confident about the referent for certain Greek and Latin words, the social values attached to that referent might have shifted radically. For English-speaking peoples in the modern north Atlantic world, whiteness is a privileged and valued generic category. But Ptolemy, who distinguished black southerners from white northerners, lived in Alexandria, Egypt, among "the inhabitants of the region between" those two climatic and epidermal extremes. He was writing from the perspective of a population self-described as "medium in coloring" (χρωμασι μέσοι).[15] Ptolemy belonged to the same civilization as Horace and Seneca, with their admiration for "the golden mean," and Ptolemy described people like himself, living around the Medi-terranean ("middle of the earth"), as "moderate in stature, in nature equable . . . civilized in their habits." The middle is the ideal.[16] Within the "Mediterranean-centered" medical theory of four humors, ideal health resulted from a balance of humors, and an excessively white or black appearance was symptomatic of corporeal imbalance.[17]

Ptolemy was a pagan living in the Roman empire, and similar attitudes can be found in other Roman authors.[18] But that prejudice does not belong to a particular religion or civilization. It reflects a geography. Ptolemy's contemporary, Rabbi Ishmael, compared Jewish skin color to "the boxwood tree, neither black nor white, but in between." Papyri from Ptolemaic Egypt described Jews as "honey-colored" (a term the Greeks also used of themselves).[19] In the early tenth century, the Islamic geographer Ibn al-Faqīh al-Hamadhānī contrasted the properly "pale brown" people of Iraq with the defective inhabitants of Europe and Africa; "the Iraqis are neither unbaked dough" (like "the Slavs") nor "overcooked" and "burnt" (like "the Ethiopians"), "but between the two" in color and temperament, like "well-baked" bread.[20] From the "here" of a speaker/observer like Ptolemy, Rabbi Ismael, or al-Hamadhānī, from the geographical perspective of their civilizations, excessively pale peoples were as barbarous as excessively dark ones. In that respect, the color values of Mediterranean pagans and Jews were much closer to those of Mediterranean Muslims than to those of northern European Protestants.[21]

Traditional Observers

That ancient antiwhite prejudice was the tradition transmitted by two northern European monks in the thirteenth century. Albertus Magnus, a Dominican friar born in southwest Germany who became Regent of Studies at Cologne, between 1248 and 1252 wrote *De Natura Locorum*[22]; Bartolomæus Anglicus, a Minorite friar born in England who became professor of theology at Paris, between 1230 and 1250 wrote *De Proprietatibus Rerum.* For centuries scholars throughout Europe cited these Latin treatises as authoritative summaries of what we would call science.[23] They encapsulated the tradition that would be challenged by the new evidence brought back by European voyagers, summarized by Martyr and Gómara. Thus, *De Natura Locorum* attributed every distinctive physical feature of "the Ethiopians"—color, teeth, tongues, and eyes, their "curly" hair and "thick lips"—to their tropical habitat: Ethiopians are "very black on account of their heat," and "their bodies grow dark on account of the scorching" African sun. Immediately following this description of the physical effect of one climatic extreme came a (briefer) description of the effect of the other extreme: "Conversely," the Goths, Dacians, and Slavs "are white on account of the cold"[24]—for the same reason that "Bears in cold and moist places . . . are white, while in other climates, they tend toward blackness."[25] The whiteness of the human inhabitants of northern regions was associated with the whiteness of polar bears. Although vague about where the Slavs lived, the German Albertus Magnus located Dacia and Gothia—inhabited by people who are "white"—somewhere north of Germany. He was also vague about exactly what constituted "cold," but the Orkney Islands, north of Scotland, were specifically described as "cold and dark."[26] Moreover, having contrasted the extremes of Ethiopian blackness and Gothic whiteness, he concluded his chapter on "predetermined diversities" by praising the "laudable middle properties" of the temperate regions and peoples who lay between the extreme. For German Albertus Magnus as for Alexandrian Ptolemy, *white* was not a term of self-definition. It described other people, inhabitants of an inhospitable climate north of the speaker's own "here."

Similar attitudes animated Bartolomæus Anglicus, who was better known in sixteenth-century England than Magus. Although *De Natura Locorum* circulated in Latin editions until the mid-seventeenth century, it did not migrate into English until 1971. By contrast, *De Proprietatibus Rerum* was translated by a contemporary of Chaucer. John Trevisa's translation (ca. 1394–98)—a big, expensive manuscript, "which cannot easily be lifted by one man"—for a century perhaps never existed in more than 40 copies. However, it was printed about 1498, then again in the 1530s, and finally in a version edited by Oxford scholar Steven Batman in 1582.[27] Its medieval geography was thus still being published in English almost a century after Columbus destroyed the medieval worldview.

Trevisa's translation contains the earliest example I know of the English phrase "white men" (stage 2). It occurs in a context that describes white-bodied people, dominated by phlegm, as "thick and sad," "heavy-going and slow," "dull of wit, and of thought forgetful," "fearful of heart," "full of sloth and of sleeping," "fat" and "short." Not surprisingly, therefore, it locates these "white men" somewhere else.

> Also cold is the mother of whiteness and of paleness, as heat is the mother of blackness and of redness. And so in hot lands cometh forth black men and brown, as among the Moors; in cold lands white men, as among the Slavs. So saith Aristotle's *in libro de celo et mundo*. . . .
>
> And the contrary is of men of the north land: for . . . cold that is mother of whiteness maketh them the more white. . . .
>
> Iceland is the last region in Europa in the north beyond Norway. . . . Also in that region be white bears most huge and most fierce . . . The men be full large of body and strong and full white . . . [28]

The belief that "cold is the mother of whiteness" derives from the Aristotelian tradition.[29] But, as these passages demonstrate, late medieval Christians knew much more about northern and western Europe than their Mediterranean pagan or early Christian predecessors.[30] That increased geographical knowledge transformed and perplexed the referent for concepts adopted from classical authorities.[31] Whiteness within the classical tradition had always been "over there," not "here"; medieval philosophers retained that deictic "over there," but because they were themselves living in lands that Ptolemy and Aristotle would have considered northern, "there" could shift hundreds of miles closer to the pole. White bodies, attributed to vague "northern" lands within the classical tradition, by the thirteenth century could be assigned to specific locations (Norway and Iceland) and specific populations (i.e., the Slavs) unknown to Ptolemy or Pliny. In Iceland white men cohabited with white bears, which were also native to Norway.[32] White bodies were not simply a northern trait, but an arctic one. No wonder Columbus was surprised to find white men in Trinidad.

But Trevisa's text of *De Proprietatibus Rerum* also illustrates the problem of translation. Barthomæus had cited a pivotal incident recounted by the Venerable Bede in his *Historia Ecclesiastica Gentis Anglorum* (ca. 731): "saint Gregor seeth Inglish children to-selling at Rome in time of paynims and heard that they were Inglish and he accorded with the name of the country and answered, 'Trulich they ben Inglish for they shinen in face right as angels. It needeth to send to them message with words of salvation.'"[33] The same incident was described, at greater length, in the first English translation of Bede, published in 1565:

> on a certain day when many merchants came to Rome and brought into the marketplace diverse wares to be sold, and many also came thither to buy, that amongst them Gregory himself came to cheapen and view the market. Where, when amongst other things he had spied young men set to be sold of white skin and comely countenance, with decent order and color of their hair. . . . "Alas," quoth he, "it is a piteous case, that the author of darkness should possess such bright beautied people, and men of so fair a face should inwardly bear so foul a soul." . . . "Truly not without cause," quoth he, "they be called Angles, for they have an angel's face."[34]

Bede's story is, to my knowledge, the first description of the complexion of the Germanic peoples who began invading Britain in the sixth century, who gave "Angleland" its name and what would eventually come to be called its Anglo-Saxon identity. In Rome, displayed as slaves, their Baltic complexions would certainly have been strikingly pale, surrounded by that city's darker Mediterranean inhabitants. But exactly how Saint Gregory or Saint Bede described that complexion depends on our understanding of several Latin words.

First, what color are angels? Modern white Christians tend to assume that angels are white, but in the Bible the whiteness of angels always refers to their clothing, not their complexion.[35] Medieval artists often gave good angels dark complexions (see Plate 17). So a comparison of Angles to angels need not imply that either was "white." Barthomæus had compressed the episode, so Trevisa's word "shinen" might be a translation of Bede's *candidi* (interpreted in 1565 as "white") or *lucidi* (1565's "bright").[36] The 1565 translation was printed in Catholic Antwerp, in the Spanish Netherlands; it used Bede to validate Catholic theology and historiography; it was never reprinted.[37] By contrast, John Foxe's rival official Protestant history of the English church, the *Book of Martyrs,* was printed in London and often reprinted and abridged; its antipapal polemic naturally omitted this story of the missionary activity of a sainted pope.[38] But Raphael Holinshed could not ignore the incident in his 1577 *Chronicles;* there the key phrases were translated as "fair skins" and "brightsome countenances."[39] Bede's Latin text was also quoted in William Camden's admired Latin *Britannia* (1586); Camden himself translated Bede's description, in 1605, as "fair."[40] When Philemon Holland translated *Britannia* in 1610, he offered English readers "bodies faire and white" and "bright and lightsome faces."[41] Verstegan's 1605 history of the English "race," citing the same episode, gave the slaves "a very fair complexion, ruddy and white."[42]

Depending on how the Latin was translated, Bede was describing skin, or complexion, or bodies. Within ancient and early modern medical theory, the three terms were interchangeable, because "skin" was symptomatic of the "complexion" (constitution) of the whole "body." The body/complexion/skin equation began to be untangled in the late seventeenth century, but until then the three words were effectively synonymous. The same cannot be said of color terms. Depending on the translator, the original Angle complexion was shining, or bright, or brightsome, or lightsome, or fair, or very fair, or white, or ruddy-and-white, or white-and-fair. Of all these variants, the one least familiar in England would have been the Catholic Antwerp "white" of 1565.

Nevertheless, the 1565 translation demonstrates that some sixteenth-century speakers of English did describe ancient Anglos as "white." Holinshed's 1577 *Chronicles* had begun with William Harrison's "Historical Description of the Island of Britain," which includes a chapter entitled "Of the general constitution of the bodies of the Britons."[43] (Notice here that we have shifted from the Angles/English, inhabiting the southern part of the island, to the whole of Britain, including Scotland.) According to Harrison, "Such as are bred in this island are men for the most part of a good complexion, tall of stature, strong in body, white of color." Harrison echoed and quoted from a lost manuscript by John Leland ("the Britons are white in color, strong of body, and full of blood"), an opinion grounded "upon Aristotle, who writeth that such as dwell near the North are of more courage and strength of body than skillfulness or wisdom." Leland's description predated English publication of Martyr and Gómara. Harrison also cited the thirteenth-century Byzantine historian Pachymeres, who affirmed that "the people inhabiting in the north parts are white of color, blockish, uncivil, fierce, and warlike." Here again, as in Trevisa, *white* is collective but negative (stage 2). Harrison qualified both authors by specifying that "white in color" was accurate only "for the most part" of the inhabitants; he did not claim that all Britons, or all Englishmen, were white. Nevertheless, "for the most part" Harrison reiterated the classical and Byzantine tradition, a tradition that also had been accepted earlier in the century by the humanist John Leland and by Leland's humanist contemporary Sir Thomas Elyot.[44] But although Harrison apparently accepted the traditional ascription of epidermal pallor to northern peoples, he spent most of the chapter contesting that tradition's defamation of the character and culture of white northerners.[45]

To the English humanist reiteration of classical prejudices against whiteness, from Eliot (1539) to Harrison (1577), belongs the first English poem inspired by an actual voyage to Africa. In 1562 Robert Baker sailed to "Guinea land, to seek for gold" (not slaves), and his poem describing his adventures was printed by Hakluyt in 1589. When Baker and others rowed toward shore, they were attacked by a party of blacks: six of the nine European crewmen were wounded, a seventh was killed, and the badly beaten crew retreated to save their lives. Baker immediately set this battle in a classical context: he dreamed of a quarrel between two Olympian gods, with "the great black smith Vulcan" defending "his burnt black men" of Guinea, while Mars champions "those white men," the defeated English. Mars and Vulcan were often at odds in classical mythology, and this latest dispute between them is mediated by Jove "in his great royal throne." Jove sends winds to drive the English back to "Albion," where they belong, with a warning that, if they dare return to Guinea, he will do nothing to help them.[46] The poem—written in prison in France, after Baker was abandoned on a second disastrous voyage to Guinea—does not assume the superiority of "white men." Instead, within the poem's traditional classical framework "white men" belong to one of two opposed and undesirable extremes, governed by a greater power that mediates between them and rebukes the defeated English for straying out of their natural geographical niche.

This classical attitude toward whiteness was reiterated yet again in an influential medical text that would soon be translated into 6 languages (including English) and that would appear in 70 editions by 1700. In a paragraph that cited Galen and Aristotle, Juan Huarte's *Examen de ingenios para las sciencias* (1575) claimed that the Flemish, Dutch, English, and French had wits "like those of drunkards," as demonstrated "by the whiteness of the face"—in contrast to Spaniards, with their admirably "somewhat brown" complexions.[47] This praise of Spanish complexions was written by a Spanish physician. But from Aristotle on, those who attributed whiteness to another people never intended it as a compliment, and the brownish Spanish in fact inhabited the ideal center of the climate spectrum defined by classical authorities. Those classical authorities were venerated by Renaissance humanists even more than they had been by medieval monks; in the sixteenth century, when humanism transformed English education, classical authors became the indisputable core of the school curriculum.

Humanists like Leland, Elyot, and Harrison could hardly ignore the classical assertion that northerners were white and that—from the perspective of a classical observer—England was a northern country. Some sixteenth-century English humanists accepted the badge of whiteness assigned them by classical texts, but no sixteenth-century Englishman bragged about being white.

Harrison's defensiveness represents the beginning of a prolonged English campaign, analyzed by Mary Floyd-Wilson, to reinterpret classical geohumoralism: the phlegmatic constitutions of northern Europeans were declared to be signs of innate civility rather than innate barbarism.[48] This campaign consisted of transparently self-interested rhetorical games (what an ancient writer calls "savagery," a modern writer can describe as "courage") played within the arena of a medical and geographical theory that would, soon enough, completely collapse. That tradition did not disintegrate because it offended English pride; English pride could have been satisfied by reinterpreting its moral implications (as Harrison and others did). It did not disintegrate because it was incompatible with the Atlantic slave trade, which had begun a century before Columbus discovered whiteness in Trinidad.[49] It disintegrated because it could not explain the global distribution of human colors—and hence could not explain the causes of human difference.

Modern Observers

Harrison ignored, or simply was ignorant of, the challenges to classical geohumoralism posed by modern explorers. But the challenges could not be ignored forever. Between 1580 and 1620, 28 books of descriptive geography were translated from Spanish, French, Italian, and Dutch sources.[50] The incoming tide began in 1577, the same year as Harrison's "Description," when the troublemaking texts of Martyr and Gómara were republished. In 1555 Gómara's meditation on human colors had been buried among miscellaneous items near the end of Eden's long *Decades;* in 1577 it was placed near the very beginning of the expanded reprint.[51] One year later an educated English voyager reiterated and emphasized the intellectual problem posed by variant complexions, and—like Columbus and Gómara—he rejected geography as an explanation.

George Best was not translating someone else's account of someone else's voyages. He wrote the first firsthand English narrative of an oceanic expedition that encountered peoples hitherto unknown in England, and he directly engaged the debate among natural philosophers on the issue of color. Best was a major participant in Martin Frobisher's Arctic voyages of 1577–78, and on the basis of his own experience he knew that the classical theory was wrong. Tropical Americans were lighter than philosophers had predicted (despite being close to the equator), and Arctic Americans were darker than they should be (despite being close to the pole). The Inuit people encountered by Best and the other English voyagers were "of the color of a ripe olive, which how it may come to pass, being born in so cold a climate, I refer to the judgment of others." We now know that the higher melanin count among Arctic peoples is an adaptation to the fact that, in high latitudes, the magnetosphere provides less protection from ultraviolet radiation. Without that twentieth-century knowledge, Best (and other sixteenth-century observers) dismissed geographical explanations for Inuit color. Best noted that the Inuit captives "that were brought this last year into England were all generally of the same color that many nations be, lying in the midst of the middle zone . . . which thing cannot proceed by reason of the clime, for that they are at least ten degrees [of latitude] more towards the North than we in England are . . . they are within three or four degrees of that, which they call the frozen zone."[52] Likewise, the fact that "the people of Africa" were "coal black, and their hair like wool curled short" could not be due to "the parching heat of the sun"; in refutation, Best noted that "even under the Equinoctial in America, and in the East Indies, and in the islands Molucca, the people are not black, but white, with long hair uncurled as we have."[53]

In this passage Best uses the word *white* to describe native inhabitants of South America and southeast Asia (stage 3).[54] Best himself had not visited all those places; indeed, in 1578 no Englishman had. So he must have been relying on Iberian sources: in 1578 only the Spanish and Portuguese were experts on equatorial America *and* Africa *and* the East Indies. Martin Frobisher—Best's leader and hero—had already voyaged to the Portuguese-controlled coast of western Africa at least twice, and as a young man in the 1550s he had spent time in Portuguese captivity; Frobisher took with him across the Atlantic various books and maps of continental manufacture, including texts in Spanish and French.[55] One of Frobisher's key advisors and investors, Michael Lok, had learned about Africa from his brother's voyages there in 1553–54 and knew Portugal and the Islamic world firsthand; during years of European and Mediterranean travel he had acquired what was probably at the time the most impressive collection of continental texts on geography and travel owned by any Englishman.[56] Although Best and Frobisher voyaged to North America themselves, to make sense of what they found there they used artifacts and concepts constructed by Iberian voyagers to other places. Those concepts included a generic categorization of peoples by categories of color. We have already seen *white* used in the way Best uses it in texts by Columbus, Martyr, Gómara, and Oviedo. Similar uses of the word can be found in other sixteenth-century Iberian sources.

Among the most influential would be Duarte Lopes, a Portuguese who spent more than a decade in southwest Africa. When he returned to Europe, his papers and conversations were edited by Filippo Pigafetta, who published them in an

Italian text (1591); Abraham Hartwell translated them as *A Report of the Kingdom of Congo* (1597). One chapter was devoted entirely to the problem of color, and promised to explain "the true cause of white and black in the bodies of the inhabitants of these countries."[57]

> All the ancient writers have certainly believed, that the cause of black color in men is from the heat of the Sun. . . . Notwithstanding it is as certain a thing as may be, that under the equinoctial, there are people which are born almost all white, as in the kingdom of Melinde and Mombaza situate under the equinoctial, and in the Isle of San Thomas which lieth also under the same climate, and was at the first inhabited by the Portugals . . . and for the space of a hundred years and upwards their children were continually white, yea and every day still become whiter and whiter. And so likewise the children of the Portugals, which are borne of the women of Congo, do incline somewhat towards white. So that Signor Odoardo was of opinion that the black color did not spring from the heat of the sun but from the nature of the seed, being induced thereunto by the reasons above mentioned.[58]

The English translation emphasized this attack on classical geographical theory much more strongly than the Italian original. To begin with, the English title page added four numbered statements, advertising the significance of the book. The first two are geographical:

1. Wherein is also showed that the two Zones Torrida and Frigida are not only habitable, but inhabited, and very temperate, contrary to the opinion of the old Philosophers.
2. That the black color which is in the skins of the Ethiopians and Negroes etc. proceedeth not from the sun.

Hartwell's prefatory epistle to his English readers expanded on these points and added his personal endorsement of the Portuguese arguments.

> Another paradox is: "That the heat of the sun is not the cause of whiteness or blackness *in the skin* of men." This position in the negative he may safely defend against all philosophers, by virtue of the reasons that he hath vouched in this report, which indeed do utterly overthrow their affirmative. But because neither any ancient Writer before this age, nor he himself, hath ever been able to declare the true cause of these colors *in human bodies,* very honestly and modestly he leaveth it undecided and referreth it to some secret of nature, which hitherto hath been known to God alone, and never as yet revealed to man. And therefore I do wish that some sound natural philosopher . . . would enter into the closet of contemplation to find out the true natural cause thereof. (Italics added.)

(Although Hartwell radically challenges traditional explanations of color, he still treats "skin" and "bodies" as synonymous.)

Hartwell wanted this refutation of the traditional geographical hypothesis to be "more publicly known" among his countrymen.[59] He quickly got his wish, with the first English translation of the influential continental cosmographer and map-maker Abraham Ortelius.[60] Ortelius had rejected the classical explanation in Latin as early as 1570—because "very white" natives of South America lived at the same latitude as "black" people in Africa—and since then his work had been often reprinted, revised, and translated into every important European language.[61] In 1598 Londoners could also buy an English translation of the first important Dutch voyage to Africa and Asia, which provided further damning evidence against the geographical theory. Describing southernmost Africa, near the Cape of Good Hope, John Huighen Van Linschoten reported that "the people dwelling about this river are black (although the pole Antarctic is there at 35 degrees) as also those that dwell in the cold hills . . . so that it is not the heat of the sun but the nature of the country that maketh them black."[62] Two years later, in 1600, part of Best's 1578 account of the Frobisher voyages was reprinted in the second edition of Hakluyt's *Principal Navigations.*[63] But Hakluyt retitled the excerpt "Experiences and reasons of the Sphere to prove all parts of the worlds habitable, and thereby to confute the position of the five Zones." Hakluyt's editing—both the new title and the abridgment—emphasized Best's "broader scientific pretensions."[64] Also in 1600, the first English translation of Leo Africanus included an introduction by the translator, John Pory, who cited the presence of "white people" in climates as hot as those inhabited by black Africans.[65] Between 1596 and 1600 the cracks in the classical theory, first opened by Columbus a century before, finally began to reach England in a wave of authoritative texts that could no longer be ignored by anyone seriously interested in geography or human variety—and that used *white* to refer to many peoples outside Europe (stage 3).

Hartwell's preface had recommended that readers unconvinced by Lopes should read the recent Latin translation of José De Acosta's *Historia Natural y Moral de las Indias,* published in Spanish in 1590.[66] By 1604 they could read it in Edward Grimestone's English version. Acosta's book has been described as "the most original and influential of all histories of the New World" and as "a more thoughtful and a more thorough account of the Indian world than anything then available," providing "the first systematic attempt to distinguish between the various Indian cultures in the new world."[67] An early and influential champion of empirical ethnography, Acosta repeatedly insisted that what he had himself experienced outweighed the authority of even the most canonical classical authors, including Aristotle. Many ancient writers "held the heat of the burning Zone to be insupportable," but Acosta knew that they were wrong, and therefore felt compelled to explain why they were wrong: the old theory was contradicted by his own observations, standing in places where Aristotle had never stood, and therefore Acosta needed to formulate a new theory consonant with his own experience.[68] In the course of that argument Acosta explained that there are a variety of climates near the equator: on the east and west coast of Africa, "they endure excessive heat, and the men are all black," but at about the same latitude "lies a part of *Peru,* and of the new kingdom of *Grenado*" (now northern Venezuela and Colombia), "which notwithstanding are very temperate Countries, inclining rather to cold than heat, and the inhabitants are white" (stage 3). Like Columbus, Acosta claimed that the original inhabitants of the southern Caribbean coastline were white. Like Gómara and Best, Acosta was not primarily interested in color; color belonged to a larger debate about the origins of difference. "I say then, that whosoever would consider these differences, and give a reason thereof, cannot content himself with these general rules before specified": existing theories were inadequate to explain the distribution of color.[69]

In Acosta, as elsewhere, *white* did not refer to Europeans at all, but to the native inhabitants of equatorial regions in the New World.[70] Tropical regions in Asia also contained varieties of white people, according to Linschoten. The inhabitants of Ormuz (at the mouth of the Persian Gulf) were "white like the Persians"; those of Bengal "somewhat whiter than the Chingalas"; in turn, the natives of Aracan, Pegu, and Sian (what is now Burma and Thailand) were "somewhat whiter than the Bengalon."[71] Rather than establishing the modern generic sense of European whiteness, all these texts demonstrate that, as late as the beginning of the seventeenth century, the apparent geographical distribution of whiteness not only challenged classical philosophy, but also contradicted any possible European claim to uniqueness.[72]

Secondhand Observations

The observations of men like Acosta and Linschoten continue to be valued by modern historians, because they represent firsthand accounts of early European contact with non-Europeans. But men like Acosta and Linschoten were the exception. Most Europeans stayed home. However, a lack of direct experience did not lessen men's appetite for learned gossip about the implications of the new discoveries. Uninhibited by any excess of facts, the observations of stay-at-home pundits were constrained only by their desire somehow to reconcile the strange new reports with the venerated theories of antiquity. Their speculations further muddled the already muddied waters of sixteenth-century whiteness.

White had first been identified as the color of Europeans in a home-bound Englishman's translation of a text by a home-bound Spaniard. Gómara's tentative and qualified attribution of whiteness to Europeans eventually showed up, in less qualified forms, in the observations of other home-bound authors. Once again, the earliest English examples I have found translate texts in other European languages.

Philippe de Mornay (1549–1623) was the principle leader of French Protestants; his polemic *De la verité de la religion Chrestienne* (Antwerp, 1581), translated by Arthur Golding and Sir Philip Sidney, was published in London in 1587 and reprinted in 1592 and 1604. Mornay's 854-page treatise defended "the trueness of the Christian religion" against the doubts raised by sixteenth-century discoveries, material and intellectual. Like the Catholic Gómara, the Protestant Mornay celebrates human diversity as a proof of God's infinite creativity, and compares the variety of human colors to the variety of plants. But unlike Gómara, Mornay does not encourage "philosophers" to investigate and explain such differences. Instead, he complains that "forasmuch as there is diversity, yea and contrariety in worldly things; some have gathered upon this diversity, that there be diverse Gods." Mornay answers this objection by asking such skeptics to "consider the sun: he maketh plants to grow all at one time, diverse one from another, and as diverse in themselves. He maketh some of them to shoot forth, some to ripen, and some to wither . . . he giveth summer, daylight, and fair weather to some, and winter, night, and foul weather unto othersome. He maketh some folks white, some black, some red, and some tawny, and yet is he but one selfsame sun . . ."[73] The English translation significantly misrepresents Mornay's treatment of the variety of human coloring: "il en fait de blancs, de noirs, de roux, d'olivastres, &c."[74] By omitting Mornay's "et cetera," the translation seems to suggest that humans come in only four colors. But on the very next page Mornay supplies a fifth: "And he that should say that it is any other than one selfsame sun that maketh the Ethiopian black, and the Scot yellowish, were not worthy to be answered."[75]

Mornay initially did not specify which "folks" were which colors; when he did link black to Ethiopians, he attached yellow to Scots (the only Europeans he specified). Mornay himself did not anticipate the modern generic use of *white.* But in attributing human variation solely to the operation of the sun, he defended Christian orthodoxy by disregarding the contrary evidence that had been accumulating since the beginning of the sixteenth century. Like the enemies of Galileo, Mornay set Christianity against science.

Mornay, in turn, was a major influence on *Nosce Teipsum* (1599), a verse treatise by Sir John Davies. Davies had attended universities in Italy and the Netherlands, as well as one of London's elite law schools (the Middle Temple); he was later Attorney General for the English colony in Ireland.[76]

> But as this world's sun doth effects beget
> 	Diverse, in diverse places every day:

Here autumn's temperature, there summer's heat,
    Here flow'ry spring-tide and there winter gray,

Here even, there morn, here noon, there day, there night;
    Melts wax, dries clay; makes flow'rs some quick, some dead;
Makes the Moor black, and th'European white,
    Th'American tawny, and th'East Indian red . . . [77]

In both Mornay and Davies, the argument about color is a simile, subordinated to a larger argument in defense of Christian orthodoxy. Versifying the passage, probably from the English translation, Davies missed Mornay's "&c.," ignored the fifth color (yellow), and attached the four initial pigments to four geographies. This fits his poetic form and contributes to the overwhelming and comforting sense of neoclassical tidiness that is, aesthetically, the most remarkable feature of *Nosce Teipsum. White* contrasts with *black,* as Moor contrasts with Christian European, as *day* contrasts with *night; white* simultaneously rhymes and contrasts with *night;* America (often called the West Indies) contrasts with the East Indies, thus supplying an east - west contrast to complement the north - south contrast of the previous line. By misconstruing the reactionary Mornay, Davies created a sense of comprehensive geographical closure.

But the tidiness of Davies's couplet makes complete nonsense of the argument about climate and color. When Mornay specifically contradicts the observations and arguments of Martyr and Gómara and Best, he does so by contrasting a black (equatorial) Ethiopian with a yellow (northern) Scot, thus lending some specious plausibility to the solar explanation for color difference. But when Davies adds geographies to all four colors, he destroys even the appearance of plausibility. The East Indies are as equatorial as Africa, and America stretches through almost every latitude. If unqualified European whiteness (stage 4) makes its debut in English literature in *Nosce Teipsum,* it does so in an incoherent passage of reactionary Christian verse, in a trope botched as it moved from French into English, by a man less influential as a poet than as an architect of "legal imperialism."[78]

Similar confusion attends another English translation from French. In 1605 Josuah Sylvester in London published a poem that contains the couplet: "The northern man is fair, the southern foul; That's white, this black; that smiles, and this doth scowl."[79] Sylvester was translating an enormously popular and admired poem published in 1584 by the Calvinist French poet Du Bartas: "L'homme du Nort est beau, celuy du Midy laid; L'un blanc, l'autre tanné; l'un fort, l'autre foiblet."[80] Both versions are bigoted; in both, this couplet is followed by a long list of contrasts between northern and southern peoples. Sylvester's "black" is darker than the French *tanné,* but "white" is an accurate translation of *blanc.*

However, these prejudices are not as simple as they seem. Du Bartas himself is transferring into verse the prose of the influential French jurist, philosopher, and witch-hunter Jean Bodin, an important figure in the evolution of modern theories about the genres of humanity.[81] Bodin has a paragraph filled with exactly the same contrasts between "them of the South" and "them of the North," including the statement that (as his English translator puts it) "the one hath a flaxen hair and a fair skin, the other hath both hair and skin black."[82] But Bodin alerts us to the fact that North and South do not have quite the meanings we might expect. He is not dividing the world into northern and southern hemispheres. Instead, like classical and medieval philosophers, he divides each hemisphere into three regions. The French—including both Bodin and Du Bartas—inhabit the middle region of the northern hemisphere. They belong to Bodin's category of "Middler," what Du Bartas calls "celuy du midy" (567), what Sylvester translates as "middling folk, who their abiding make Between these two" (593–94), avoiding the extremes of north (white) and south (black).

Where, in all this, is England? Du Bartas gives no clear indication. What is confusing in Du Bartas is made more so by Sylvester's adaptation, which substitutes England for France in the poem's final peroration and substitutes London for "la Cité du monde"—which, in Du Bartas, is transparently modeled on Paris. Thus, even the most careful scrutiny of Sylvester would not have informed English readers whether they should consider themselves "white" or whether that descriptor more properly belonged to the Germans, Scythians, and Danes. After all, Mornay called the Scots yellow, so you would expect whiteness to inhabit regions farther north. Scythians, according to Camden, were Scandinavians.[83]

In fact, according to Bodin's division, England belonged, like France, in the "middle" region. That is why Sylvester felt no qualms about substituting London for Paris. After all, London (51^0 30′) is only three and a half degrees of latitude farther north than Paris and only 30 seconds of latitude farther north than Louvaine.[84] Given these geographical realities, if the French are not northerners, neither should the English be. Indeed, Bodin at one point acknowledged that "the climate" in England "is milder than in France."[85] He divides

> all the nations that inhabit . . . this side the equator into three parts: the first shall be of thirty degrees on this side the equator, which we will attribute to the burning regions, and people of the south; and the thirty degrees next, to those that inhabit the temperate regions unto the sixtieth degree towards the pole; and from thence unto the pole shall be the thirty degrees of the nations of the north, and the regions that be exceeding cold.

In case your memory of latitudes is hazy, Bodin identifies the regions that belong to "the nations of the North." According to his scheme, the North begins with "the sixtieth parallel," which "touches the boundary of the Goths, Livonia, Muscovy, the Orkneys." The "people of the North" include "Sweden, Denmark, Norway, Poland, Bohemia, and Tartary"; elsewhere he takes examples of the "North" from Germany, Greenland, Moscow, Sweden, Denmark, and Latvia. These are the places whose inhabitants—the "Septentrionales," living under northern stars—can be described as "white" (*colore candido*). Bodin insists that "the statement of Hippocrates that men in the northland are ugly because they are pale and thin would be absurd unless he were referring to the furthest places of the north."[86]

All this was clear enough to George Best, whose 1578 map of the Frobisher voyages locates the "Septentrional" lands in the Arctic, clearly separated from Britain.[87] It was also clear to Louis Leroy, John Ashley, and John Norden. Leroy's *De La Vicissitude ou Variété des Choses en L'Univers* (1575) had been translated into English by Ashley (1594) and then versified and plagiarized by Norton (1600).[88] All three agree in specifying the countries of "the uttermost part of the North" as Lithuania, Latvia, Muscovy, Norway, Sweden, and Lapland; Norden adds Finland and Iceland. None of them included Britain among "Septentrional" countries.[89] All three contrasted Ethiopians (who "are black") with the inhabitants of "countries cold and icy," who "have softer skin, and white" (or "have their skin white and soft" or "*ont la peau blance & deliee*"). But none of them considers England northern, or white. All three contrast these undesirable "extremes" of black and white, heat and cold, with "the regions of the mean temperature" whose people are "well tempered of color."[90] The word *mean* here means "middle," and *tempered* means "mixed, compounded, intermediate." Referring to the medical theory that described health as an ideal mixture and balance of different physical humors, *tempered* is related to *temperate* (moderate climate or personality) and *temperance* (moderation).

The air of Britain, according to William Camden, was "most temperate and wholesome," because the island was "sited in the midst of the temperate Zone, subject to no storms and tempests as the more Southern and Northern are."[91] In 1601 in French and in 1608 in English translation, Pierre Charron concisely summarized Bodin's climatic theory in a brief chapter and chart, identifying "the middle and temperate regions" as "all Europe" (excluding Scandinavia) and describing the "middle" people as "temperate." He located the northern region in the "thirty degrees which are next to the two Poles on both sides, which are the cold and icy countries, the Septentrional people," whose bodies are "white, and yellow" (whereas southern people are "black").[92] Likewise, the English physician Thomas Walkington (1607) went out of his way to differentiate "our happy Island" from the regions "under the Pole, near the frozen zone, and in the septentrional climate," whose inhabitants all suffered from "dwarfish wits" because their brains were "stuffed with . . . phlegmatic matter."[93] Finally, in 1637 Thomas Morton, a member of one of London's law schools (the Inns of Court) who had spent 10 years in Massachusetts, began his account of New England with the statement that "The wise Creator of the universal globe hath placed a golden mean betwixt two extremes," a golden mean Morton located in the regions around 45 degrees latitude, halfway between equator and pole; that climatic "golden mean, most apt and fit for habitation," was to be found in both New England and England.[94] The philosophical and medical ideal of the golden mean corresponded to a climatic ideal. All three found their natural habitat in Europe, and particularly—for early modern French and English intellectuals—in the temperate kingdoms of France and England. By contrast, whiteness belonged to the intemperate climate of the far north, to the Arctic extremes of a summer without nightfall and a winter without sunrise.

But none of that would have been very clear to readers of Du Bartas or Sylvester, unless they already knew their geography. Even those who could read French and Latin would have to sift through Bodin carefully to extract his views about whiteness and geography. Color was not Bodin's primary concern. He focused on the relationship between climate and humors, and the impact of those on political life. Therefore, his "chief discussion is about the peoples who dwell from the thirtieth parallel to the sixtieth" latitudes of the northern hemisphere, "because we know their history." But all those nations belonged to the middle region, as defined by his own scheme. In order to relate climate to political history within that region, Bodin devoted much of his discussion to the *relative* northernness or southernness of peoples within his "middling" category. Thus, "the southerners nearer to" Frenchmen include the Spanish, Sicilians, Arabs, Egyptians, Libyans, Moors, and the Americans who inhabit Florida; likewise, "the northerners"—that is, those "nearer to" France, but slightly north of it within the temperate zone—"are those who inhabit the land from the fiftieth parallel to the sixtieth," including "Britain, Ireland, Denmark . . . Lower Germany." According to this logic, northern "Germany, Flanders, and England" could be contrasted with Spain and Italy to the south. Depending on whether Bodin was talking absolutely or relatively, "northern" could refer to peoples from the sixtieth to the ninetieth parallels, or to people from the fiftieth to the sixtieth—or to people from the forty-fifth to the sixtieth.[95] The case of England was further complicated by the fact that the country had at various times been invaded from the south (Romans, Normans) and from the north (Danes, Norwegians, and Germans).[96] Indeed, Verstegan berated Bodin for failing to distinguish between Caesar's ancient "Britons" and the "Englishmen" (who did not enter Britain until five centuries after Caesar's death).[97]

As if all this were not complicated enough, Bodin combined the Ptolemaic system, which related color to latitude, with the Hippocratic system, which related color to the microclimate of temperature, humidity, and prevalent winds. Hippocrates had argued that each microclimate was influenced not only by latitude and longitude, but by specific geographical features such as altitude, forests or plains, and adjacent mountain ranges or bodies of water. Of course, Europe contains many such microclimates, and not surprisingly Hippocrates concluded that "There exist in Europe . . . people differing among themselves in size, appearance and courage"; specifically, in regions "where there is a light waterless soil devoid of trees and where the seasons occasion but small changes in climate, the people usually . . . are fair rather than dark."[98] The Hippocratic treatise (written between 430 and 330 B.C.E.) is earlier than Ptolemy but more complicated; because of the authority of the Hippocratic corpus, it remained influential until the twentieth century, although authors tended to repeat its most general claims, ignoring the specificity and contingency of most of the text.[99] However, although he did not cite Hippocrates, Albertus Magnus made similar allowances for the qualifying effects of "accidents" such as "mountains, seas, woods, swamps"; hence, "Men born in rocky places, level areas, and cold dry places . . . are white or flaxen colored."[100] This is one of the few original features of *De natura locorum.* It provided Columbus with a framework in which to attempt to solve the problem created by the white Trinidadians. According to Martyr, Columbus had conjectured that the anomaly resulted from the high altitude of the land and sea: the area was "so much the nearer heaven . . . and further removed from the gross vapors of the vales and marshes," as high above other areas in the tropics "as the highest tops of the biggest mountains are distant from the deep vales."

Columbus did not cite Hippocrates or Albertus Magnus, but Bodin cited both. Bodin also cited the new data that had disturbed Columbus and Gómara: "About this body of knowledge the ancients could write nothing, since they were ignorant of regions and places which not so long ago were opened up."[101] Bodin repeated several of the Spanish examples disproving the classical explanation of complexion.[102] To account for this new data, Bodin insisted that "not only the nature of the heavens and regions in general are to be considered, but also the particularities of the regions . . . the air, water, winds, hills and valleys."[103] But unlike Hippocrates or Albertus Magnus, Bodin could give examples of the effects of difference of terrain upon color.

> The people on this side [of] mount Atlas are far less ingenious than the Numidians, and other nations which are on the other side mount Atlas: for the one are very white, and the other exceeding black.[104]

> Those who dwell near the Carpathians on the south are tanned [*retorridi*], those on the opposite side are white [*candidi*].[105]

> *Leo* of Afric hath no cause to wonder, why the inhabitants of the high mountain of Megeza in Afric are white [*blancs*], tall, and strong; and those of the valley are little, weak, and black [*noirs*]: for generally both the men, beasts, and the trees of the mountain, are of a stronger constitution than the others.[106]

It has been said that Bodin summarizes and synthesizes "the results of over two thousand years of speculation" on the relationship between environment, nature, and culture. But the result of that attempt at synthesis is often "painfully garbled."[107] Ptolemaic geography, with its correlations between complexion and latitude, resembled Ptolemaic astronomy (which Bodin preferred, rejecting the revolutionary clarity of Copernicus). By the sixteenth century both Ptolemaic systems could be sustained only by a profusion of epicycles so complex as to be incomprehensible.

Confused Observers

What should be clear to us is that whiteness was not yet clear to them. Bodin never specifically called the English "white," and when he did discuss complexion, his geographical scheme indicated that whiteness should characterize people farther north; in Du Bartas and Sylvester, *white* is ambiguous, but both authors probably thought they were referring to people farther north than either France or England. Charron's concise, lucid, and influential summary of Bodin made it absolutely clear that the English were *not* "white." In the half century between 1555 and 1608, texts printed in England attributed whiteness to a bewildering array of populations: Baltic peoples, Arctic peoples (or not), all Europeans, only some Europeans, no Europeans, some Americans, everyone except Africans—and even some Africans. Wherever whiteness was found, when it was attributed to an entire population, that characterization was at worst negative (stage 2), at best neutral (stage 3).

The English belatedly adopted whiteness from other Europeans, just as they belatedly followed other Europeans to Africa, Asia, and America (and as they belatedly wrote sonnets).[108] Until at least the beginning of the seventeenth century, generic whiteness was a confused and disparaged category in an imported discourse, made more confusing by the efforts of Englishmen to appropriate it. Such confusions were still swirling in 1612, when John Selden's notes to Michael Drayton's epic *Poly-Olbion* found it impossible to explain "why about the Magellanic straits they are so white, about the Cape *de buon speranza* so black, yet both under the same" latitude.[109] Things were no better in 1613, when Londoners could buy

Purchas his Pilgrimage, which promised "A Theological and Geographical History of Asia, Africa, and America." For his description of the peoples of Angola and Congo, Purchas was able, for the first time, to draw on the experience of Andrew Battel, an Englishman who had sailed away in 1589, been captured by the Portuguese, and spent close to 20 years in southwest Africa. Battel reported that in Angola, "There be certain persons . . . which are born of Negro parents, and yet are, by some unknown cause, white."[110] Given such new evidence of "white children" in tropical Africa, in addition to all the other evidence accumulated by more than a century of exploration, the classical theory of complexion was demonstrably untenable.

Purchas, like every other serious thinker since Columbus in 1498, could not avoid, and could not convincingly solve, the problem of explaining the diversity of human pigmentation. "Some allege the heat of this torrid region, proceeding from the direct beams of the sun—and why then should all the West Indies, which stretch from the one Tropic to the other, have no [black] people? . . . And if this were the cause, why should Africa yield white people in Melinda?" Once again white is set against black, in refutation of classic climate theory; once again *white* refers to non-Europeans. But later in the same paragraph, the same word does refer to European stock: refuting "the soil" as a causative explanation for blackness, Purchas cites the "white, or . . . tawny" Portuguese children born in Africa. Finally, Purchas imagines a time when "the tawny Moor, black Negro, dusky Libyan, ash-colored Indian, olive-colored American, should with the whiter European become one sheepfold under one great shepherd."[111] Like Davies, Purchas here associates colors with places. But even in this final image of global religious unity, Europeans are not "white," but simply "whiter."

Whiteness was still confused and confusing eight years later, in 1621, when the Oxford scholar Robert Burton published the first edition of his masterpiece, *The Anatomy of Melancholy.* Some peoples, he noted, were "soft, and some hardy, barbarous, civil"—these are what we would call cultural differences, but Burton immediately followed them with differences of color, which we would define as biological: "black, dun, white." The classical tradition had been confident of its explanation for this variety, but Burton was not. "Is it from the air, or from the soil, or influence of stars, or some other secret cause? . . . Whence comes this variety of complexions, colors, plants, birds, beasts, metals, peculiar almost to every place?" He had no satisfying answers, and in 1624 he added more questions: "How comes it to pass that in the same place, in the same latitude . . . there should be such difference of soil, complexion, color, metal, air, etc.?" In 1638 he piled the confusion higher: "The Spaniards are white, and so are Italians, whereas the Inhabitants about *Caput bonae spei* [the Cape of Good Hope] are Blackamoors, and yet both alike distant from the Equator. Nay, they that dwell in the same parallel line [of latitude] with these Negroes (as about the Straits of Magellan), are white-colored—and yet some in Presbyter John's country in Ethiopia are dun."[112] On and on Burton rambled, citing Martyr, Acosta, Bodin, Ortellius, and many others, worrying about the "opposite" complexions of equatorial inhabitants of Africa and Peru.[113] A modern scholar can complain about Burton's incoherence, but the chaos proliferates because he and his contemporaries lacked a theory that would satisfactorily explain, rein in, and organize the accumulating clutter of discordant facts.[114] Burton was as confounded by the global distribution of whiteness as Columbus had been. Unlike Columbus, Burton could not imagine a nipple that would soothe his anxieties.

But not everyone was anxious. In 1621, the year that Burton published the first version of his worrying, inconclusive anatomy, another Englishman was writing a confident, original, serious, nonfictional ethnographic text that routinely invoked whiteness as a generic category in a wholly unambiguous modern sense. He did so by abandoning the authoritative discourse of elite intellectuals from Hippocrates to Burton—and replacing it with the least authoritative discourse imaginable.

Chapter 5

White after Black

Clotel does not speak in the first chapter of the novel that bears her name. The chapter contains quotations from white politicians and white newspapers, speeches by the white auctioneer who sells her and the white gentleman who buys her. Clotel, her mother, and her sister are looked at, spoken to, and spoken about, but they live in a speech community that does not authorize them to speak. Nevertheless, the chapter does directly transcribe the voice of one black American. In 1847, in "A Lecture Delivered before the Female Anti-Slavery Society of Salem," William Wells Brown recalled seeing a young black woman auctioned off in the South; he recounted the progress of the bidding for her, summing it up with the observation that "her body and mind were sold for $400, and her religion was sold for $300."[1] That remembered auction, and its summation, is elaborated in *Clotel:* "This was a Southern auction, at which the bones, muscles, sinews, blood, and nerves of a young lady of sixteen were sold for five hundred dollars; her moral character for two hundred; her improved intellect for one hundred; her Christianity for three hundred" (88).

Brown had been lecturing almost constantly during the six years that intervened between his performance in Salem and the publication of *Clotel* in London; in Britain he gave more than 1,000 public speeches.[2] Like every good storyteller, he had learned, from the reactions of his audiences, which narratives interested them most, what details to dwell on, how long to suspend a sentence or an episode before bringing it to closure. *Clotel* embellishes the original "body and mind" (bones, muscles, sinews, blood, and nerves . . . moral character . . . improved intellect) and by raising the price of those items increases the original contrast. But the clinching point remains almost identical: "her religion was sold for $300" becomes "her Christianity for three hundred." Reading the words of the narrator of *Clotel,* we are attending to the voice of William Wells Brown, speaking to an audience of white women.

I do not mean to discount the difference between speech and writing, or the (at least theoretical) difference between a narrative voice and its author. Indeed, those differences haunted African Americans: the title page of Brown's autobiographical *Narrative* might declare that it had been "written by himself," but skeptics could always discount such claims, could always postulate the existence of a (white) ghostwriter, could always assert or insinuate that blacks were incapable of the intelligence and eloquence of any given written text.[3] It was much harder to dismiss as ventriloquism the active wit emanating from a black body addressing a crowd. Brown, like Frederick Douglass, became a writer after years of experience as an orator in an oratorical political culture.[4] He remembered Douglass as an "overpowering voice"; leaving England, he recalled "the deep, bass voice of the Bishop of London, in St. Paul's Cathedral"; he analyzed the "style of speaking" of various famous Members of Parliament, "the unadorned eloquence" of one, another "painful to listen to," the "lofty pitch of oratory" of Gladstone, the "fascinating eloquence" of Disraeli, whose "ringlets shake as he gesticulates," who "wrings applause even from his political opponents."[5] *Clotel* is a novel written by a professional orator, a black Lincoln. Not surprisingly, one chapter consists of a political speech by the white "True Democrat," Henry Morton, who had rescued Clotel's sister from slavery and married her (176–79). Brown belonged to a society where politics was a speech-act.

But Brown also belonged to a people whose every speech-act was political. For American blacks, bell hooks has said, "Coming to voice is an act of resistance. Speaking becomes both a way to engage in active self-transformation and a rite of passage where one moves from being object to being subject. Only as subjects can we speak."[6] African American oratory has been traced back to the centrality of formal oratory and debate in many African cultures[7]; it has been described as "the totalization of the Afrocentric experience."[8] But Brown himself was born in Kentucky, and his voice emerged, more particularly and more certainly, from an oratorical tradition that began with black preachers in the middle of the eighteenth century. For hooks, "talking black" is "talking back." For Brown and other black abolitionists, black speech challenged the white discourse that ruled their lives. It was thus profoundly dialogic.[9]

What "dialogic" means is dramatically evident in one of Brown's most compelling speeches. On September 27, 1849, Brown was introduced to a London audience by abolitionist George Thompson, who remarked that colorphobia in the northern states of America was "quite as galling" as slavery in the southern states. A Bostonian in the audience objected. Beginning by saying he was "really glad that this meeting has produced this discussion, for I think it will do all good," Brown then proceeded to "reply to our friend here." Concluding, Brown recalled another occasion when he had faced a hostile auditor, who asked, "Had

I not enough to eat when I was in slavery? Was I not well clothed while in the Southern states? Was I ever whipped?" The heckler then rose and made a speech.

> A portion of the assembly for a moment really thought his plea for slavery was a good one. I saw that the meeting was anxious to break up, in consequence of the lateness of the hour, and therefore that it would not do for me to reply at any length, and I accordingly rose and made a single remark in answer to this pro-slavery speech. I said, the gentleman has praised up the situation I left, and made it appear quite another thing to what it ever appeared to me when I was there; but however that may be, I have to inform him that that situation is still vacant, and as far as I have any thing voluntary to do with it, it shall remain so; but, nevertheless, if that gentleman likes to go into Missouri and fill it, I will give him a recommendation to my old master, and I doubt not that he would receive him with open arms, and give him enough to eat, enough to wear, and flog him whenever he thought he required it.

At this point, according to the published report of the speech, Brown's audience responded with "Loud cheers and laughter." Indeed, the whole report is punctuated by audience reactions: "Hear, hear," and "cheers" and "laughter" and "Cries of Oh, Oh!"[10] A member of the audience provokes the speech; the reactions of the audience are part of the speech event; the speech itself describes Brown observing an audience's response to another speech, and shaping his reply with an awareness of the crowd's impatience ("in consequence of the lateness of the hour"). His short retort does exactly what *Clotel* would do: put a white American in the position normally occupied by a black slave. A black speaker silences a white man.

Black Speakers

Of course, for centuries the white speakers had effectively silenced the black ones. It is therefore easy to imagine the linguistic relationship between early modern Europeans and early modern Africans as a one-way channel, in which whites spoke and blacks listened. The early modern texts I have been examining look like a closed loop, the transcript of a conversation in an exclusive private club. Whether they are using Greek, Latin, Italian, French, Spanish, Portuguese, Dutch, or English, they all speak the same language. Ptolemy and Albertus Magnus, Bodin and Gómara, Duarte Lopes and Huighen Van Linschoten all speak the educated language of privileged European men. We will not hear, in any of those texts, the voices of "poor whites" like those in Chapter VII of *Clotel,* the illiterate and indigent ("I 'spose you aint never bin in these parts afore? . . . Is you gwine to stay here long?"). And if even poor whites are excluded, we will certainly never hear, in such authoritative texts, a voice like Sam's in *Clotel* ("I don't like to see dis malgemation of blacks and mulattoes, no how"), or conversations like the one that takes place between the slaves at night in the parson's kitchen, where "the whole company joined in the conversation about color" (136–37).

But blacks—and Amerindians—did speak.[11] They spoke to thousands of Europeans in the fifteenth century, and the sixteenth, and the seventeenth. Some learned European languages. Some spoke through interpreters—who, more often than not, were non-Europeans who had learned European languages. When we read Ca' da Mosto's report of 75 to 90 blacks who, in 1455, "remained for a while gazing upon a thing which neither they nor their fathers had ever seen before, that is ships and white men in that river," we are actually hearing the voice of a black slave. The Venetian Ca' da Mosto can have known that those particular Africans had never seen white men only if he had spoken with them. But he did not speak their language. Someone else must have translated for him. "Each of our ships," he tells us, "had Negro interpreters on board brought from Portugal, who had been sold by the lords of Senega to the first Portuguese to discover this land of the Blacks." Ca' da Mosto had hired "these slaves" from their owners, and much of what he tells us about Africa is an Italian translation of a black interpreter's Portuguese translation of an African's native language.[12]

But not all the interpreters were slaves. In the summer of 1607—a century and a half after Ca' da Mosto's voyages—two bedraggled English ships on their way to India stopped in Sierra Leone to restock their supplies of water and food. The leader of the English expedition described the black interpreter, sent to him by the local African king, as "a man of marvelous ready wit" who "speaks in eloquent Portuguese." The interpreter's name was Lucas Fernandez, and he watched a performance of *Hamlet* put on by the English ship's crew.[13] The king that Lucas Fernandez represented (his brother-in-law) also understood Portuguese; as a Jesuit missionary reported, after years in the region, "some of them, such as the nobles and those who have been brought up among our people, understand Portuguese, and these listen without saying anything" in order to deceive the Europeans, who assume that the Africans do not understand their words.[14]

Thus in Sierra Leone in 1607, the English encountered not just one African who spoke eloquently a European language, but a class of "nobles" and other Africans who had learned that language. In the period following European contact, many of the contacted cultures in sub-Saharan Africa (and America and Asia) embarked on a process that sociolinguist Janina Brutt-Griffler calls "macroacquisition." We normally think of acquiring a second language in terms of an individual—me, or Lucas Fernandez—memorizing new words, new phonemes, new grammatical rules. But language learning fundamentally changes when a whole speech community, or a significant fraction of one, acquires a second language. A group tends not only to adopt, but to adapt, the new language to its own needs; a bilingual community more actively and aggressively reshapes the linguistic field, significantly transforming both languages in the process.[15] Thus, for example, the macroacquisition of Latin by English elites in the sixteenth century, as a direct result of the humanist educational revolution, led to an explosion of new Latinate loan words in English.[16]

No one supposes that dead Romans violently imposed Latin on Renaissance Englishmen; the macroacquisition of Latin was driven by an English agenda. The same is true of the African macroacquisition first of Portuguese and eventually of other European languages. As the noun *acquisition* reminds us, languages are goods, goods with a real market value. The Latin-speaking minority was not the oppressed, but the dominant fraction of society in early modern England. The same tended to be true of the minority of Africans who learned European languages, men like Lucas Fernandez, who belonged to an emergent class of cosmopolitan, multilingual, socially and geographically mobile Atlantic creoles. "The special needs of European traders placed Atlantic creoles in a powerful bargaining position, which they learned to employ to their own advantage," according to historian Ira Berlin. "The most successful became principals and traded independently. They played one merchant against another, one captain against another, and one mercantile bureaucrat against another. . . . Success evoked a sense of confidence that observers described as impertinence, insolence, and arrogance."[17] The acquisition of extra languages gave such multilinguals a crucial advantage over monolinguals, whether African or European. Perhaps for that reason, early-seventeenth-century "natives" in Sierra Leone, according to the resident Jesuit, "regularly and commonly say that the whites are like flies: despite the danger of falling in, they are always attracted by honey."[18]

The sentence I just quoted is an English translation of a Portuguese manuscript, and it is always possible that "whites" (Portuguese *brancos*) was not the word actually spoken by "the natives," but interpolated by the Portuguese observer recording what the natives "regularly and commonly say." But the natives must have used some collective noun in the sentence, and there is no obvious reason why the Jesuit should have substituted *brancos* for whatever noun the natives used.

By itself this single piece of recorded speech would be of little significance. But the same thing happens repeatedly in another text from the early seventeenth century, written in another language about natives from a different part of the west African coast. Richard Jobson's *The Golden Trade* (1623) describes his own experience as an English merchant on the river Gambia in the first months of 1621 (at about the same time *The Anatomy of Melancholy* was published). Visiting the same river Ca' da Mosto had explored 166 years earlier, Jobson used *white* to describe himself and other Europeans 18 times in 170 quarto pages. In no earlier English text does the word cluster, in that sense, anywhere near so frequently. And Jobson used it without any of the confusions or complications I surveyed in the previous chapter:

. . . the Blacks . . . made answer, they had considered amongst themselves, the white man, shine [sic] more in the water, than they did.

. . . the Black people, do not stick to say, that since the white men have had to do in the River, the Crocodile is not so dangerous, as in former times.

. . . others of them are mulattoes [*Molatoes*], between black and white.

The place where we had houses built . . . by the people of the Country, called *Tobabo Condo,* the whiteman's town . . . [with a marginal note, "They called our dwelling the white men's town"]

. . . amongst themselves a prophecy remains, that they shall be subdued, and remain subject to a white people: And what know we, but that determinate time of God is at hand, and that it shall be his Almighty pleasure, to make our nation his instruments.

. . . a people came down unto me, who had never seen white men before . . .

I shot off three such guns as I had to welcome [Buckor Sano, a great black merchant], at the noise whereof he seemed much to rejoice, calling the report of the powder, by the name of the white men's thunder.

[The black Merchant] told us . . . that [black slaves] were sold there to white men, who earnestly desired them, especially such young women, as he had brought for us.

These people had never seen white men before . . . [with marginal note "A people that never saw white men before"]

Buckor Sano . . . spoke that he might be called by the name of the white men's *Alchade* [with a marginal note: "Buckor Sano made the white men's Alchade"]

. . . it is apparent never white men either by land or water were up this country so far but we . . .

. . . diverse times they will not forget in our presence to sing in the praise of us white men . . .

[A black interpreter's] absence with the white people, which was some of our company . . .

[A black musician] told him that Ho-re [an African demon] acquainted him, that the next morning, and at such an hour, there would be so many white men at Pompetane, naming the number that were in our boats . . .

. . . we are now the first white people they have seen.[19]

In 1625, in the huge collection of travel narratives called *Hakluytus Posthumus,* Samuel Purchas published a few pages of extracts from Jobson's own "large journal," written during the actual expedition.[20] These included four additional examples of the same idiom:

> We being ten white men . . .
>
> . . . now were ten white and four black . . .
>
> Buckor Sano would needs be styled the white man's Alcaid.
>
> [Buckor Sano] made a speech . . . to entreat his kind usage to the white men.

In a manuscript petition written several years later, Jobson described himself as "the first white man" who had traded with the natives in that part of Africa.[21]

Jobson was the first Englishman to use *white* in its modern generic sense (stage 5) so frequently, casually, and unselfconsciously. He did not think that the idiom required explanation. But that idiom was attributed—12 times explicitly—to African speakers. Even when there is no attribution for the statement, its speaker is implicitly African: for instance, Jobson can have known that a particular group had never seen white men before only after that information got relayed to him by his bilingual black interpreter Sangully.[22] Jobson twice acknowledged his utter dependence on his black interpreter.[23] It was, according to Jobson, "the Blacks" or "the Black people" who called Jobson and other Europeans "white men"—or, as a collective singular, "the white man." On the other hand, although Jobson used *English* or *Englishmen* 15 times, he never attributed those words to an African speaker.[24] That contrast makes sense.[25] According to Ca' da Mosto, Africans living along that river had been calling Europeans "white men" since at least 1455, but few of them had ever encountered "Englishmen"—and none of them had any reason to suppose that "Englishmen" were different from other "white men."

Speech Communities

The English began confidently calling themselves white after they were called white by some darker peoples they encountered in other parts of the world. If this hypothesis is correct, not simply for Jobson but for other Englishmen, then the evolution of the generic sense of *white* would belong to a recognizable category of linguistic change. Etymologists have noted the influx of loan words that entered English from indigenous languages of western and southern Atlantic cultures (*hammock,* for instance, and *banana*). English was transformed by the need to accommodate new objects and new relations created by the encounter with unfamiliar civilizations.

English was not the only language being affected in this way. Dutch—another northern European Germanic language, spoken by another set of latecomers to the imperial enterprise—dealt with the problem of discriminating between Europeans and others by importing a new word. In his account of one of the early Dutch voyages to west Africa, Pieter de Marees contrasted "the Blacks" with "*de Blancken ofte Witten.*" This phrase is difficult to translate: it means, literally, "the Whites or Whites." To explain what he must have known was a new idiom (which might therefore be confusing to readers back home), the Dutch sailor used two words of the same meaning, one Germanic (*Witten*), the other adopted from a Romance language (*de Blancken*). In modern Dutch, *witte* usually denotes the color ("white"); the loan word *blanke* usually means "white man."[26] The Dutch preserved the original specificity of their own word *witte* and used the foreign word *blanke* as a new generic noun.

The English could have done the same. At least once they did do so. In 1591 Richard Rainolds and Thomas Dassel led an English expedition to the Senegal and Gambia rivers. An interpreter told them how friendly a particular king was to "Christians . . . whom they called *Blancos,* that is, white men."[27] This English sentence produces the same linguistic effect as the Dutch "*de Blancken ofte Witten.*" In both, the imported and unfamiliar Iberian word is immediately followed by its Germanic equivalent. Moreover, like Jobson's account of a visit to the same region 30 years later, this narrative attributes the idiom to the Africans themselves: "*they* called" Christians *blancos.*

Normally, though, English texts do not include words like *blancos.* This 1591 account was first published in 1599, in Richard Hakluyt's enormous second collection of *Principal Navigations.* The same volume also printed for the first time another eyewitness report, written in 1594 aboard an English convoy that attacked and sank a large Portuguese carrack. The survivors "told" the English that their ship "had not now above 150 white men, but Negroes a great many." This information must have come either from the rescued Portuguese or from "two or three Negroes" the English also picked up ("whereof one was born in Mozambique, and another in the East Indies").[28] In either case, "white men" occurs in a transcript and translation of foreign speech. The same thing happens repeatedly elsewhere in Hakluyt's collection. According to Hernando Alarcón's account of his 1540 discovery of California, the natives immediately interpreted the Europeans' arrival as a vindication of their own traditions ("Their ancestors told them that there were bearded and white men in the world").[29] Likewise, in 1535 Jacques Cartier attributed to Iroquois leader "Lord Donnacona" news of a country, farther inland, where "there are white men, who clothe themselves with woolen cloth," just like those in France. Donnacona's words were translated by two Iroquois men whom Cartier had abducted on his first voyage, taken to France, and taught French.[30] Although Hakluyt's narratives originated in reports of speech in one or more African communities and at least two widely separated Amerindian communities, he did not record the words in those native languages, and—with the one exception from 1591—he did not even reproduce the Portuguese, Spanish, French, or Italian words first used to translate those non-European languages. Instead, he simply translated the Romance word (*blanco, branco, blanc*) into the English *white.*

Languages can be transformed not only by importing completely new words, but by importing new senses into old words. "Influence on meaning," according to semanticist R. A. Waldron, "is sometimes discernible even when there is no similarity of form between the English and the foreign word." The new shades of meaning are taken into the English words, "which are regarded as their translation-equivalents."[31] Rather than import a word from one of the many Amerindian or African languages that meant "pale people" or import the word *branco* that the Africans had learned in the century and a half of their interactions with the Portuguese, Englishmen simply started using their own word *white* in the collective sense conveyed by the equivalent African or Portuguese or Amerindian word.[32] Or rather—because language contact takes place in the mind of a bilingual speaker—a native interpreter like Sangully, who had learned English, would use the English word *white* to convey a collective sense already present in the equivalent word in his mother tongue or in another language that had already been assimilated by his culture. The English listener might regard this new sense as somewhat odd—like the slightly unidiomatic speech characteristic of someone just learning a new language—but the new sense would be immediately comprehensible, in context, and in that context it would also prove useful.

It would prove useful because Europeans and non-Europeans alike needed a word that would differentiate all Europeans from all non-Europeans. In fact, *European* is first recorded in English in 1599, in that same couplet from *Nosce Teipsum* I quoted in chapter 4: "Makes the Moor black, and th'European white, Th'American tawny."[33] *European,* in the sense "a native of Europe," seems to be formed by analogy with the older nouns *African, Indian,* and *American.*[34] A language changes in response to changes in the environment in which users of the language live. Obviously, English speakers did not need the word *America* until they became aware of the existence of that large, inhabited, hitherto unknown and unnamed landmass. Likewise, until ships from other European tribes followed the Iberians to sub-Saharan Africa, India, and America, Europeans did not need to distinguish themselves, as a continental cultural whole, from other continental cultural wholes.[35]

In places like the East Indies or the west coast of Africa, the English belonged to an already important category of nonnative people, and speakers needed a way to refer to that larger population. By contrast, in a place like Barbados, which had no human inhabitants before it was colonized by the English in 1627, there were no other Europeans, and the colonists could be distinguished from their imported black and Amerindian slaves by using the existing word *English;* there was not much need for a new word, like *European,* or a new sense, like generic *white,* because non-English Europeans were not a significant presence. Consequently, although by the early 1640s Barbados had more English settlers than any other North American colony, the first important and extended account of the island never used the word *white* in a generic sense. Richard Ligon's *True and Exact History of the Island of Barbados* was based on his stay there from 1647 to 1650; it had a great deal to say about the Negroes, but (like Queen Elizabeth) Ligon did not use the black/white binary, even when he was contrasting Negroes with his fellow English citizens.[36] Only when other Europeans preceded them (as in Africa, or the East Indies) would speakers need a word other than *English.* Moreover, in contrast to the Spanish and the Portuguese in Africa and America, the English in Barbados would not allow their slaves to become Christians.[37] Only after a significant number of blacks had been converted to the religion of their masters would the word *Christian* fail to work in opposition to *Negroes.* The earliest generic use of *white* I have found in a text from Barbados was not written until 1652, 25 years after English settlement of the island, 30 years after Jobson's Gambian journal, 60 years after the Senegambian encounter reported by Hakluyt.[38]

The use of a new idiom among Englishmen in West Africa in 1591 or 1621 did not guarantee that it would be used promptly by Englishmen elsewhere. The English in West Africa and the English in Barbados belonged to related but distinct speech communities, and the two different social environments produced slightly different vocabularies. We can see here the beginning of a process that would lead, over the course of centuries, to the development of such subvarieties as American English, Nigerian English, Indian English, Jamaican English, and others. The generic sense of *white* did not instantly enter the vocabulary of all speakers of English just because one Englishman had used it (once) to translate the word *blancos* in Senegambia in 1591, or just because one Englishman traveling up the Gambia River in 1621 used it routinely. It would start to saturate the language (and the worldview) of the English only when large numbers of English speakers needed a way to conceptualize the same set of relationships. In this context, it is important to remember the pathetically small number of Englishmen in the early colonial speech communities: in 1625, at a time when the population of London may already have reached 200,000, only about 1,300 Englishmen lived in Virginia.[39]

The invention of the noun *European* in 1599 testifies to a change in the social environment, the opening up of a new conceptual niche, for which some convenient signifier needed to be found. But *European* was obviously not the only word that attempted to fill that new semantic niche. Derived from an ancient Greek noun, the new English word *European* originated at home, in England, in a learned poem written by a young man in the all-male early modern equivalent of law school; part of the word's appeal to such men was its linguistic cosmopolitanism, its reference to recondite geographical and mythological knowledge, its polysyllabic difficulty, which made it unlikely to be tainted by contact with uneducated tongues. But given the fact that so many of the peoples the English encountered on other continents were darker than themselves, the newly opened semantic niche that was filled by the learned new *European* could also be filled by common old *white.*

We could say that the two words were competing for the same linguistic space. However, it would be more accurate to say that one set of speakers was competing with another set of speakers. A language is, as linguist Salikoko Mufwene argues, not an organism but a species. Each of us speaks our own language (an "idiolect"), with certain features that distinguish it from every other, and what we call a "language" (English, French, Spanish) is just a collection of related idiolects with certain shared features. We should therefore take "a population genetics approach to language evolution," identifying why certain features of certain idiolects get reproduced more often than others. "Why," Mufwene asks, "do linguistic choices made by individual speakers translate into changes in the communal language?" In a language, as in a species, reproduction is everything, and reproduction in both cases depends on choice, on a preference for one feature rather than another. Feature selection drives linguistic change. To understand linguistic change we have to discover why, in a given historical environment, certain metapopulations tended, statistically, to choose one feature (*white*) rather than another (*European*).[40]

European was a more accurate description than *white* of the human genre that both words labeled: the native inhabitants of the geographical space were not literally corporeally white. But, as we have seen in the history of the competing words *colorphobia* and *racism,* semantic accuracy does not necessarily determine the fate of competing synonyms. More important is the relative social strength of the two speech communities most likely to use one word or the other. In the case of *racism* and *colorphobia,* the word preferred by American whites predictably replaced the word preferred by American blacks. Applying the same model, we might have expected the elite coinage *European* to have triumphed over the new generic sense given to *white,* a usage that apparently originated in encounters between sailors and "savages." But sociolinguists have shown that language change can come either from above or from below.[41] In fact, *European* has never disappeared, because elites have continued to use it. But the need for a new word had been generated, and remained greatest, in the contact zones inhabited by sailors and savages, servants and slaves. Although despised by European elites, statistically those groups overwhelmingly dominated the contact zones and therefore could strongly affect norms of speech within that habitat patch.[42] For native English speakers in the contact zones, the simple familiar monosyllable *white* would have taken less energy and less precise articulation than the polysyllabic neologism *European* (Illus. 4). Africans or Amerindians learning English as a second language would have had even more reason to prefer *white* (or *branco* or *blanco* or *blanke*) to the mouthful of foreign phonemes required to articulate *Eu-ro-pe-an* (four different vowels, three different consonants, no sound repeated, no obvious indication of which syllable to stress). For the English, too, *white* would have been easier to use than an utterly foreign combination of sounds like the equivalent Mandingo/Wolof term *tobabo* or *toubabes.*[43]

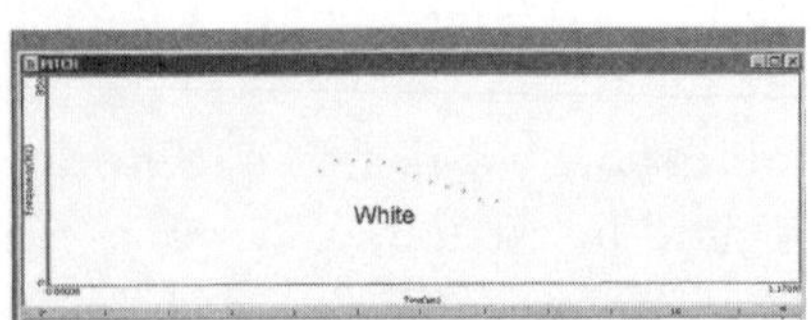

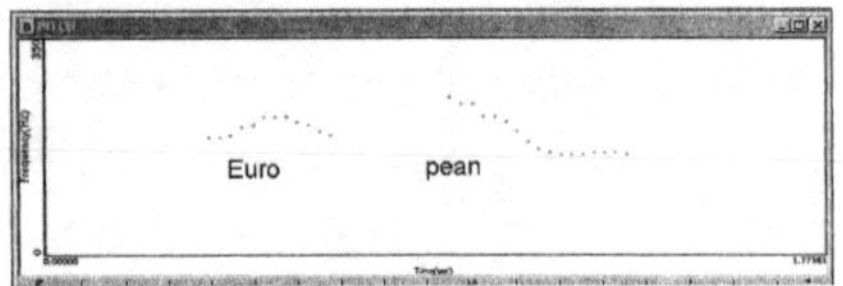

Illustration 4. Lucy Pickering's graphs (Computerized Speech Lab, Model 43008) illustrate how much more complicated to articulate is the word *European* (in duration, pitch range, number of pitch shifts, and combination of voiced and unvoiced phonemes) than the word *white.* The horizontal axis is duration, the vertical is pitch.

A great deal of language change is driven by the simple but compelling imperative of laziness. The English eventually started calling themselves "white" because doing so required less work than the alternatives.

Dialogues

Because Jobson and other English voyagers were encountering Africans who had been interacting for more than a century with the Portuguese, it is impossible to tell whether the African sense of European whiteness was original to their own languages or adopted from Portuguese.[44] The 1591 account makes it clear that the Africans were saying *blancos* or *brancos* (the difference between the Spanish and Portuguese pronunciations being very difficult for many non-Europeans to hear or reproduce). But they might have been using the Iberian word because it was the only way they could communicate with a new group of Europeans. The Portuguese had opened up sub-Saharan Africa to European contact, remained the only significant European trading partners of West African elites for almost a century and a half, and fathered the first mixed Afro-European populations in the Atlantic world. The Portuguese first taught a European language to significant numbers of West African interpreters, thereby eventually making Portuguese the coastal lingua franca and the European element in various African creoles.[45] Jobson knew "a black man called Sandie, who in regard he had some small knowledge of the Portugal tongue had great recourse amongst us," and he also described a larger group of Afro-Portuguese mulattoes in the area, who preserved "carefully the use of the Portugal tongue."[46] But from the English perspective, where the idiom originated (in indigenous African languages or in Portuguese words adopted by the Africans) would hardly have mattered. What the English experienced was a dialogue—or what Jobson called "familiar conversation"—with black people, in which those black people called the English "white" and referred to all other Europeans as "white."[47]

This hypothesis rests on the testimony of Jobson's breakthrough texts of 1621. The idiom Jobson used so often and casually had begun, tentatively and self-consciously, at the end of the sixteenth century. Thirty years before, in 1591, the English were called *blancos;* what separates the *blancos* of 1591 from the "white" of 1621 was the fact that, by the time Jobson arrived, one local speaker had learned English. In the other examples published by Hakluyt in 1599 cited earlier, "white" referred to other Europeans (not the English) and was in any case a translation of some other language.

But Hakluyt's volume also contained reports of the word *white* being addressed to Englishmen. Arthur Barlow's account of the 1584 exploratory voyage that discovered Roanoke island had been published in Hakluyt's first collection, in 1589, and he reprinted it in 1599.[48] Barlow did not use *white* as insistently as Jobson, or as positively, but he did explicitly attribute whiteness to Englishmen and implicitly limited it to Europeans. Barlow's narrative, written between 1584 and 1589, is apparently the first original English example—the first not translated from another language—of what I have called stage 4 (where *white* is used to describe populations neutrally, but refers only to Europeans). Barlow recorded that

> six and twenty years past, there was a ship cast away, whereof some of the people were saved, and those were white people, whom the country people preserved . . . other than these, there was never any people appareled, or white of color, either seen, or heard of amongst these people, and these aforesaid were seen only of the inhabitants of Sequotan: which appeared to be very true, for they wondered marvelously when we were amongst them, at the whiteness of our skins, ever coveting to touch our breasts, and to view the same.

Although early modern writers did not use quotation marks in the way we do, it seems clear that "white people" and "white of color" occur in a passage quoting

Amerindian informants.[49] Only they can have known of the ship wrecked on their coast 26 years before. At "which appeared to be very true," Barlow the listener/narrator responded to, and judged, his interlocutor's statement. What followed was an account of the natives' own fascination with the strangeness of English skin. The English noticed their own skin, as it were, for the first time, precisely because other people were astounded by it.

Like the English in South America with Ralegh in 1595, like the English in Sierra Leone in 1607, Barlow in North America established some form of communication with the native inhabitants, who directly confirmed their recent contact with other Europeans. But unlike the English voyagers in the Oronooko basin or the Sierra Leone estuary, Barlow put *white* into the mouths of native speakers. His attribution of the word to the Roanokes was seconded by another account, by another witness, of another dialogue with an Algonquin speaker a year later. Ralph Lane's account was also published in 1589, and like Barlow's seems to be an example of stage 4. After reporting the exceptional usefulness of his long conversation with "Menatonon," especially in relation to a native king on the Chesapeake, Lane concluded, "It seemed to me by his speech, that the said king had traffic with white men that had clothes as we have."[50] Again, *white* shows up—on its only occurrence in this text—in a report of Algonquin speech about previous encounters with Europeans (almost certainly Spanish).[51]

The source of the word *white* is more ambiguous in Lane's than in Barlow's account, because *white* occurs in the summary of Menatonon's speech rather than as direct quotation of Algonquin speakers. In both cases, non-European speech is transmitted through the consciousness and in the language of a European speaker, and therefore might well reflect European (not Algonquin) concepts. I say "European" deliberately here, because the 1584 expedition to Roanoke was in fact led, not by an Englishman, but by the Portuguese Azorean Simon Fernandez, pilot and ship's master, and the only one of the expedition's leaders known to have previously visited the coast of North America.[52] Fernandez returned to Roanoke in 1585 with the second expedition. According to the testimony of an English castaway to the Spanish authorities, it was Fernandez who spoke to the Indians.[53] The two examples of a generic use of the word *white* in Roanoke in 1584–85 may in fact be examples of the imposition of Portuguese concepts on a dialogue between a Roanoke and an Englishman.

That transfer of concepts could have occurred whether or not Fernandez was acting as interpreter. Linguist Yakov Malkiel has pointed out that European images of America were not formed at the moment of direct contact, but "during the long voyage from the port of embarkment," or even in "the long periods of waiting and preparation . . . which the prospective sailor or settler would spend in the unique environment of sea ports."[54] A ship at sea is a self-contained and often cosmopolitan speech community.[55] Speakers with little linguistic authority in the larger landed world may wield great authority in that small and vulnerable seaborne community. Every English member of the expedition was dependent on Fernandez to get them where they were going. He was not only personally more experienced than most of them; he came from a culture immeasurably more experienced in the business of oceanic exploration and alien contact. In fact, the hostility some of them later expressed toward Fernandez may itself reflect their ship-borne dependence on him, a felt inferiority galling to people inflated with a sense of their social and national superiority ashore. Whether it was the Algonquins or their own Portuguese pilot who called them white, Englishmen were responding to the way they were perceived by people they simultaneously needed and despised.

Generic Distinctions

Whiteness was, for the English, an imported idiom: imported from authoritative classical and continental texts, imported from African and Amerindian responses to English pallor. But the value of the import changed, depending on the exporter's point of view. Early modern European peoples were aware of, and sensitive to, innumerable little dissimilarities—physical, linguistic, religious, political, cultural—between different genres of European. The relationships between these different genres were often driven by what Sigmund Freud called "the narcissism of minor differences."[56] Epidermally, Europeans found significant many minor differences of complexion between themselves (women vs. men, gentry vs. peasants, Scandinavians vs. Spaniards). Because the English were paler than most southern Europeans, and because until the seventeenth century almost all of the most authoritative European texts were written by southern Europeans, descriptions of the English in such texts tended to emphasize their pallor; but, as we saw in chapter 4, those authoritative European texts did not value English pallor or consistently identify it as absolute white.

By contrast, for Africans and Amerindians it made sense to lump all those oceangoing, gun-toting Europeans into the catchall category "white." For the same reason that whites often could not tell one dark person from another, people of other human genres often could not tell one pale person from another.[57] Europeans regularly wanted indigenous people to make such distinctions—by trading with one nation, for instance, but not its commercial rivals—but the distinctions served the interests of the colonizer, not the colonized. From the perspective of other human genres on the Atlantic littoral, the differences between European genres were insignificant, measured against all that they had in common, including the appalling or appealing pallor of their bodies. The word

European—even if they had taken the trouble to learn to pronounce it—would have been of little use to native peoples, referring as it did to an abstract geocultural entity completely unknown to them. By contrast, the color of bodies was something anyone could see, and something noticeably different about Europeans, from a non-European point of view.[58] Moreover, although many of those indigenous languages had very few color terms, they all had the polar contrast between black and white.[59]

The color of European bodies astonished non-Europeans who saw it for the first time. Fifty years before the Roanokes marveled "at the whiteness" of Barlow and his fellow voyagers, Giovanni da Verrazzano led a French expedition to Florida, where the indigenous inhabitants stood "marveling at the whiteness of his flesh."[60] Seventy years before Verrazzano, Ca' da Mosto had reported that Africans who had never seen Europeans were fascinated by "my whiteness," assuming at first that it was dye or paint, and astonished when they discovered that it was "white flesh." Not white skin, but white *flesh.*[61] Ca' da Mosto—like Ptolemy before him, Columbus and Verrazzano after him—did not consider the color of human bodies something superficial.

All the accounts I have been considering in this chapter record *white* as an indigenous erasure of or indifference to the generic (or "ethnic") divisions between Europeans. In eastern North America in 1584–85 and in West Africa between 1591 and 1621, the English were dealing with indigenous peoples who had already encountered other Europeans. In both cases, the English desperately wanted to distinguish themselves from their European competitors; in both cases, the indigenes found it hard to *see* (literally or figuratively) the difference.[62] The English encountered a similar lack of discrimination in South America and southeast Asia. They justified their attacks on Spanish colonies with the claim that they were Protestant liberators, helping abused natives to shake off Catholic tyranny and superstition. But, as they discovered during Drake's circumnavigation of the globe (1577–80), not all the natives welcomed their putative liberators. Confronted by the hostility of Brazilian Indians, Drake's chaplain noted their "miserable bondage and slavery" and "intolerable bondage" to the Portuguese, and conjectured that "they suppos[ed] us to be Portugals, and therefore their deadly enemies." An attack by natives in what is now Argentina was attributed to revenge for "the Spanish cruelties there used" when Magellan had visited the same spot on his circumnavigation of the globe, six decades earlier; the Indians "could make no difference of nations, being, as it is likely, never acquainted with any before Magellanus, nor never after till our coming." Finally, when part of Drake's crew was ambushed by Indians on an island off the coast of Chile, "the cause of this force and injury by these islanders was no other but the deadly hatred which they bear against their cruel enemies the Spaniards, for the bloody and most tyrannous oppression which they had used towards them."

We cannot tell, from these accounts, whether the South American natives considered the English "white." In the first incident, the English did not even speak to the natives, but simply supposed that the Indians believed that "no other" but the Portuguese "had used travel by sea in ships," and so mistook the English ships for Portuguese ones; in the second incident, just before the attack "one of the Indians cried to them, and said: *'Magallanese, Esta he minha Terra'* (that is, 'Magellanites, this is my country')" explicitly comparing the English crew to Magellan's; in the third, the misidentification occurred "because they [the Indians] were never acquainted with any other nation but the Spaniards in those parts of the world," and therefore allegedly "persuad[ed] themselves that we were the same, and the rather because one of our men rashly spoke in the Spanish tongue."[63] The ability to cross the ocean in large sailing ships, or the ability to speak and understand Iberian languages, led natives to equate English expeditions with Spanish ones. From the perspective of Elizabethan Englishmen conjecturing about the conjectures of the natives, Europeans were united by the similarities of their technology and language rather than by their color.

"We can be certain," Stephen Greenblatt insists, "only that European representations of the New World tell us something about the European practice of representation."[64] In terms of English self-representation, the native attacks on Drake's crew created a rhetorical problem—or, rather, two problems: either they demonstrated the unremitting hostility and barbarism of all Indians, or they cast doubt on the idea that Indians would be grateful to the English for liberating them from the Spanish and Portuguese. Neither explanation was comforting. But both problems could be solved by attributing the attacks to an understandable mistake, which could be rectified by more prolonged contact between the English and the natives. The English therefore invented an explanation for Indian behavior that suited them better than the alternative explanations. That explanation may or may not be correct. But if the English were simply inventing an explanation that suited them, why did they base the case for mistaken identity on culture, not color?

Either there had been a significant change in English attitudes between Drake's voyage and Barlow's, or Barlow and his men encountered a significantly different native response to Europeans. I know of nothing that happened between 1580 and 1584 that would explain a change in English attitudes. Drake had kidnapped a Portuguese pilot, so the difference between Drake and Barlow cannot be attributed to Portuguese influence alone. Barlow was a member of Sir Walter Ralegh's household, and the fact that Ralegh did not use *white* in his own account of Amerindians, more than a decade later, suggests that the difference in these representations may have originated on the ground in America, not simply in the minds of Englishmen. All Englishmen did not respond to all Amerindians in exactly the same way, and all the genres of North and South American humanity need not have responded to Europeans in exactly the same way, either.

Such differences in Native American reactions are strongly suggested in William Wood's account of New England, based on his experiences there from 1629 to 1633. Wood used *English* or *Englishman* 129 times, and on two occasions he put the word *Englishman* into quotations from members of tribes belonging to the Algonquin language group, living in eastern New England.[65] But Wood gave a different account of the speech of the Mohawks, an Iroquois tribe living farther west than all the other peoples he described. The Mohawks, according to Wood, preyed on all the more easterly Indians, who looked to "the English" for protection, because "these inhuman homicides" [the Mohawks] "confess that they dare not meddle with a white-faced man, accompanied with his hot-mouthed weapon." Wood explicitly attributed this image of the English as "white-faced" to the Mohawks. Certainly, *white-faced* did not represent Wood's own view of the English complexion. "In New England," Wood bragged, "both men and women keep their natural complexions, in so much as seamen wonder when they arrive in those parts to see their countrymen so fresh and ruddy." For Wood, the "natural" complexion of the English was *ruddy;* he still belonged to a world that would have been recognizable to Henry VIII. Wood attributed this ruddy health to the New England climate, contrasting it with the "extreme hot summers" and "pesteriferous diseases" of Virginia, which had disastrous effects on the appearance of English colonists, "changing their complexion not into swarthiness but into paleness, so that whenas they come for trading into our parts we can know many of them by their faces." Naturally ruddy English colonists in New England could immediately spot English colonists from Virginia by the unnatural and unhealthy "paleness" of Virginians.[66]

The Mohawk description of the English as "white-faced" thus differed from Wood's own descriptions of his fellow countrymen and from the language used by Native Americans in eastern New England.[67] It came from a source that Wood described in unequivocally negative terms: "a cruel bloody people" of "more than brutish savageness . . . yea very cannibals they were." For Wood, *white-faced* was clearly a negative epithet from a hostile witness. Moreover, that witness probably was responding to other European faces, not just English ones. After recounting several anecdotes of Mohawk brutality, Wood concluded, "of the rest of their inhuman cruelty let the Dutchmen (who live among them) testify." By the early 1630s Mohawk peoples had regular contact with the Dutch in New Netherland as well as the English in New England (and the French in what is now Quebec); all those Europeans had equally "white" faces and equally "hot-mouthed" weapons. Like blacks on the river Gambia, the Mohawks confronted a multinational European presence, and *white-faced* could be used to lump all those different European tribes into one category. Moreover, the Dutch—with whom the Mohawks had most contact—described themselves as "white" (*blancken*). We have no way of knowing whether Mohawks invented the term *white-faced* themselves, or adopted and adapted it from the Dutch, or inherited it from their Iroquois cousins along the St. Lawrence, who had encountered Cartier's Frenchmen in 1535 (and who were extinct by 1600). But *white-faced* was, for Wood, an alien, distinctively Mohawk characterization of himself and Europeans, remarkable enough to be worth recording.

Speaker Location

The Dutch also may be responsible for the appearance of generic *white,* in an account—published in London after May 1606—of the founding in 1603 of the East India Company's trading post in Bantam in Java. As in Africa, the English arrived after their competitors, and were dismayed to discover that "the common people knew us not from the Hollanders." But in this case the Englishmen's desire to distinguish themselves from the natives soon overwhelmed their desire to distinguish themselves from other Europeans. A dark Asian, whom they employed as a servant, was accused of murder and condemned to execution; a large indigenous crowd gathered, having heard "that there was an Englishman to be executed." Since we have already been told that "the common people" did not distinguish between the English and the Dutch, presumably what excited them was the prospect of seeing a *European* (or a *white*) executed: even if they could tell the difference, why should they care whether the victim was English or Dutch? The national specificity here probably reflects the preoccupations of an English writer and his English readers. In any case, when the crowd saw the victim, the English "might hear them tell one another it was a black man." Americans tend to assume that *black* does, or should, apply to Africans only, but here—as often elsewhere in early modern English—it refers to the people of tropical Asia. Overhearing the crowd's reaction and seizing the opportunity to proclaim their moral superiority, the English told the Javans that the condemned man "was just of their own color and condition and that an Englishman or white man would not do such a bloody deed."[68] Once again the color distinction in this exchange allegedly originated with the natives, who recognized that the victim was not "an Englishman" (or "European" or "white"), because he was "black."

The English reply accepted the binary, treating "Englishman" and "white man" as synonymous. Perhaps the doublet "Englishman or white man"—like the Dutch "*de Blancken ofte Witten*"—was a concession to readers in London, a translation of the colonial shorthand "white man" into the more particular verbal formula favored back home. Or perhaps it was a concession to the Javan failure to discriminate between English and Dutch, a translation of "Englishman" into terms more readily understood by the crowd. In either case, the word *or* equates, rather than separates, the two identities. At the same time it demonstrates that one or the other was unfamiliar to one audience or another. "Englishman or white man" is a classic example of what linguists call "code-switching," in which someone who speaks two languages (or two dialects) switches back and forth between them in order to be understood by two different sets of listeners. It internalizes, in the speech of one person, a dialogue between languages, between communities.

This 1606 text is the first example I have found of stage 5 (where *white* is used to describe, positively, European populations only). Its tentative formulation—"Englishman or white man"—testifies to the unfamiliarity of the idiom, by incorporating a more widely recognized definition or synonym within the utterance; variations on the word *English* occur 40 times in the book (twice on the title page). The author, an otherwise unknown merchant named Edmund Scott, had left England in April 1601 and did not return until May 1606; he remained in Bantam from February 1603 to October 1605, one of a handful of Englishmen alongside a much larger and better equipped group of Dutchmen. The English needed the Dutch, and interacted with them routinely, so Scott could have picked up his generic sense of whiteness from them. Indeed, on one occasion he attributes the phrase "a white man" to a Dutch speaker (perhaps speaking Dutch).[69]

These inaugural examples of generic whiteness originated in Indonesia, not Africa or America. Americans—including African Americans—have naturally been more interested in narratives about the epochal importance of the African slave trade or the discovery of America. But the earliest example in English of "Christians" being called "white men" (1553) occurred in the translation of an account of India. Vasco da Gama's successful voyage to India, in 1498, brought back much more lucrative cargo than had the unsuccessful third voyage of Columbus, that same year, which was aiming for the Indies but got no farther than the Caribbean. Likewise, Drake's return from the Indian Ocean in 1580 was much more lucrative than anything the English brought back from America before the tobacco boom of the 1620s. The economic success story of the first decade of the seventeenth century was not the settling of Jamestown in 1607 but the founding of the East India Company in 1600. By 1620 the East India Company, with two dockyards on the Thames, had built 76 ships and was one of London's largest businesses, allegedly capable of employing 2,500 sailors and 500 carpenters and other workmen.[70] As late as the mid-1660s, East India Company imports exceeded shipments of sugar and tobacco from the American colonies.[71] Within England itself, human beings imported from the tropics were first appraised as purchasable property in 1621; the owner of the "thirteen negroes or Indian people" was a member of the East India Company, who had acquired them on a voyage to Asia. Moreover, the joint-stock organization of the company meant that experience—and language—accumulated in one voyage was not dispersed but perpetuated within the company's relatively stable community of employees and investors.[72]

The tentative "Englishman or white man" of 1606 soon gave way, in texts issued or inspired by the East India Company, to the confident use of "white" alone. Of all the English books I have searched, up to the end of the seventeenth century, the single volume with the most examples of generic *white* is Robert Knox's autobiographical *An historical relation of the island Ceylon, in the East-Indies* (1681).[73] Knox used the adjective (stage 5) 35 times and the noun (stage 6) another 5. By contrast, the three huge volumes of Hakluyt's *Principal Navigations* (1598–1600) contain only 5 examples of stage 3, 5 of stage 4—and none of stages 5 or 6. Moreover, all Hakluyt's 10 examples are translations from other languages (European or Amerindian), and 6 were originally written by foreigners. By contrast, in 1606 an English author—for the first time—put the generic *white* into the mouth of an English speaker. That author, Edmund Scott, had just returned from the East Indies, where that speaker had spoken. This 1606 example not only inaugurates a new sense of the word *in* the English language (stage 5), but a newly active, newly internalized use of the word *by* the English—or, at least, by one or two of them.[74]

This inaugural utterance is also, of course, a lie. A "white man" is as capable as a black man of doing "such a bloody deed." White men did, and continue to do, many bloodier deeds.

Speaker Evaluation

The complications of classical and humanist theories of human color succumbed, in the end, to the simplicity of a repeated threshold experience, a social ritual that initiated a new social identity within a new set of social practices. An Englishman saw someone darker who called that Englishman white. After that christening the Englishman felt himself to *be* white and began to *act* white. The change in the word's meaning derives from a change in the dialogic context, and that change of dialogic context also explains the complete reversal of the word's evaluative register. As a description of English males, *white* suddenly goes from insult to compliment.

In itself, such a change is not uncommon; evaluative criteria are inherently unstable.[75] Whether a word carries a positive or negative charge depends, fundamentally, on who does the charging. In the elite textual legacy of southern Europe, the whiteness of Englishmen has been asserted in contexts that labeled them inferior. But when encountering non-Europeans, Englishmen were characterized as white in a context where they were technologically superior to the people calling them so—as demonstrated by the fact that the English had crossed the Atlantic, southward or westward, and in some cases the Pacific too.[76] As early as 1582, Englishmen could read, in an account of the conquest of Peru, an Inca prophecy that "when a white people, bearded, should come into that country," the original inhabitants should submit to them.[77] In 1609 they could read Hakluyt's translation of a prophecy (made "long ago . . . by their forefathers") that "a white people should subdue" the Amerindians living along the Rio Grande.[78] Both these prophecies were described by Spanish authors, but the ambiguous generosity of the word *white* made them equally appealing to English readers.

By 1621 the English were hearing prophecies of their own. Jobson recorded a similar belief, among Gambian peoples, that "they shall be subdued, and remain subject to a white people." Jobson also explained the prophecy: his African interlocutors "say . . . they see God loves us better than them, in giving us such good things, they see we have and are able to bring unto them, and likewise they do admire our knowledge, being able to make such vessels as can carry us through such great waters."[79] Likewise, according to the English the Algonquins in and around Roanoke in 1584 to 1586 were so amazed by English technology that "some people could not tell whether to think us gods or men."[80] In Wood's anecdote, the whiteness of English faces was coupled with the power of English guns in frightening the most fearsome of Amerindian peoples; in Bantam, the English declare their whiteness in positive contrast to a black murderer about to be executed. Whether or not non-Europeans meant *white* (or some equivalent color word in another language) as a compliment, they spoke it in a context where the English *felt* themselves to be superior, materially and intellectually—and morally.[81] *White* began to be internalized by the English once it could be equated with "superior."

That happened before the English were significantly involved in the slave trade, and it happened to Englishmen—like Jobson—who explicitly refused to own or trade slaves. But it could not happen until significant numbers of the English had personally experienced contact with darker peoples in territories outside Europe and the Mediterranean. And it could hardly be widely internalized by speakers back home in England until voyaging outside of Europe—and returning—had become routinized for large numbers of Englishmen. Those conditions were met only in the first two decades of the seventeenth century, with the rise first of the East India Company and then of the Virginia and Bermuda colonies. All those events affected inhabitants of the port city of London more quickly and more regularly than other Englishmen. But even in London the idiom spread slowly. By contrast with the three volumes published by Hakluyt at the end of the sixteenth century, the four volumes published by Purchas in 1625 contain 71 examples of the modern generic sense of the adjective "white." But 60 of those examples occur in texts translated from other European languages. The 11 written by Englishmen all came from just two voyagers (Richard Jobson and Andrew Battel), who both picked up the idiom from foreigners.

As historian Winthrop Jordan observed, "England's principal contact with Africans came in West Africa and the Congo where men were not merely dark but almost literally black"—or, as Jobson said, "perfectly black."[82] As a generic adjective, *black* preceded *white*—just as, in all these texts, from Ptolemy to Jobson, blackness grammatically preceded whiteness. The same asymmetry appears in the history of the noun. Jobson, who used the generic adjective *white* 18 times, never used *white* as a noun, but he did use the generic noun *black* 14 times.[83] The noun *black*—in the sense "a person with 'black' skin; an African negro . . . or member of another dark-skinned race" (*n.*6a)—is first recorded by the *Oxford English Dictionary* in the journal of a seagoing Englishman written in 1570.[84] Even earlier, the corresponding Spanish noun had been adopted into English: *negro* is first recorded in 1555 (in Eden's translation), soon to be followed by *niger* (1574), *nigro* (1582), and *neger* (1587). With nouns as with adjectives—not to mention human evolution—*white* enters after *black.*

The binary logic that made northern Europeans "white" was spelled out—in one of those rare moments of transparency for which any historian must be grateful—by Jean Bodin. "The contraries have opposite traits. So if the southerner is black, the northerner must be white."[85] If X, then Y. The south is the opposite of the north; if people from south of the Mediterranean basin are black, then logic requires that people north of the Mediterranean must be the opposite of black. It does not really matter whether the complexions of the English empirically satisfied any definition of the color category "white." If sub-Saharan Africans and tropical Asians are black, then the English—like other Europeans—*must be* white.

In Alexandria, in Senegambia, in America and the East Indies, darker peoples told the inhabitants of the islands northwest of Europe that they were white. The English sense of whiteness originated on a distant shore, far far from England.

Part II

Consolidation

Chapter 6

Popular Whiteness

On the title page of his autobiographical *Narrative* (1847), William Wells Brown identified himself as "An American Slave." Frederick Douglass had used the same formula on his title page two years before, and so would Henry Bibb two years later. In 1854 Brown published a collection of his travel writings, entitled *The American Fugitive in Europe,* where he again wrote of himself as "an American slave" and as "an American by birth."[1] Brown, like many blacks, had ambivalent feelings about the United States, but *Clotel* mocks the campaign of the American Colonization Society to return "emancipated slaves to Africa" (183) and recalls with evident pride that a "negro, by the name of Attucks, was the first that fell in Boston at the commencement of the revolutionary war" (161). Brown's own sense of identity depended on his complex connection to the word *American.* But for two centuries after its first use in 1578, the noun *American* had referred to the New World's indigenous peoples, what we today differentiate as "Native Americans," the members of what Canadians call "First Nations." Not until 1765 was *American* used in the sense that Brown, Douglass, and Bibb took for granted.[2] Brown and others of "his race" (61) agonized over their relationship to a community that had first been named less than a century before they wrote.

The speed with which that new community had established its identity derived in part from the newspapers that *Clotel* so frequently quotes. In 1830, when he was only 16, Brown had worked in the printing office of a newspaper publisher, and his first publication, in 1843, was a letter to an abolitionist paper; throughout his five years in England and while writing *Clotel,* he was also writing for the British and American press. The "imagined community" of a race or nation is, according to Benedict Anderson's influential and persuasive formulation, dependent on print capitalism to form a myth of shared identity between people who have never met each other. Anderson's most compelling examples of the influence of print capitalism are the newspaper and the modern novel.[3] Both are notoriously cheap, and by that means reach mass audiences, virtually simultaneously saturating a vernacular market. The impact of a text in contributing to myths of collective identity obviously depends on how many people read it within a relatively short space of time.

The Renaissance texts I have been examining so far were relatively esoteric and expensive documents, reflecting the intellectual preoccupations of a tiny elite. Of all the early modern non-English authors I have cited, the one most influential in England was Bodin.[4] "You cannot step into a scholar's study," a Cambridge scholar claimed, "but (ten to one) you shall likely find open either Bodin's *de Republica* or Leroy's *Exposition* . . ."[5] But, then as now, outside a scholar's study you would have been very unlikely to find Bodin open. Without knowing Latin you could not read his *Methodus,* or Ptolemy's *Tetrabiblos,* or Albertus Magnus's *Liber de natura locorum;* the only available English version of Aristotle's *Problems* was a selection that did not include the relevant passages; Bodin's *de Republica* was not translated until 1606. Such texts were available only to bilingual or multilingual readers, who—however powerful—constituted a small fraction of the population. As for the texts written or translated into English, they were almost all big books, and their size was not only intellectually but economically daunting. Book prices were regulated on the basis of the number of sheets of paper they contained. Really popular books contained no more than four to six sheets, and if a text hoped to reach a massive market it could not exceed a price of two pence (the cost, at the time, of about a pound and a half of ordinary household bread).[6] By contrast, even an unbound copy of Hakluyt's earlier, shorter *Principal Navigations* (1589), with 219 sheets and an engraved title page, probably cost 25 or 30 times that much—and, unlike cheap pamphlets, such big books had to be bound, further inflating the price.[7] *Hakluytus Posthumus* (1625) cost three pounds (180 times the price of a popular pamphlet).[8] Heavily illustrated books, like Holinshed's *Chronicles,* might cost double the price of an unillustrated book of the same (vast) length.

Easily the cheapest of all the early authorities on generic whiteness I have so far cited—from the 1553 description of Asia to the *Map of Commerce* published by an East India merchant 85 years later—was John Norden's *Vicissitudo Rerum* (1600). Consisting of only six sheets, it should have sold for three pence, not far from the "popular" price. The Latin title would have put off most English readers, and booksellers sometimes artificially inflated the price of poetry and plays. Nevertheless, Norden was undoubtedly the most affordable of the authorities I considered in the three preceding chapters—and Norden did *not* include Britain among the "white" nations of the far north. John Davies's *Nosce Teipsum,* which calls all Europeans white, would have been twice as expensive as Norden's *Vicissitudo Rerum.* With 11.5 sheets, *Nosce Teipsum* probably sold for six pence, three times the "popular" price; its Greek title deliberately discouraged readers familiar only with their mother tongue, and (unlike Norden) Davies did not offer a helpful translation as a subtitle. Even so, Davies outsold all the other titles, with four reprints between 1599 and 1617. However intellectually incoherent, his image of "the Moor black, and th'European white" probably reached more English readers than any of the other, more nuanced and respectable discussions I have cited. Nevertheless, only the wealthiest and best educated 5 percent of the population might even consider buying such a book, and all five editions over 18 years together amounted to no more than 10,000 copies (and probably closer to 2,500).

Such books do not tell us much about popular prejudices and assumptions, comparable to those presupposed by *Clotel* and the newspaper articles Brown quoted and wrote. The first American edition of Brown's book was published as a dime novel in a series of "Books for the Camp Fire," advertised as "Just the books to read to the soldiers" and "Equally adapted to home fires."[9] The early modern equivalent to *Clotel* is not an expensive scholarly tome but a London dramatic performance. The maximum print run for a book allowed by law (1,500 copies) was half the number of spectators that could be accommodated for a single performance at the Globe Theatre (3,000 people). Anyone could attend the annual Lord Mayor's pageant for free; entry to an open-air theater could be secured for a penny; neither spectacle demanded literacy. Urban pageants and commercial plays undoubtedly reached and reflected a much larger and more varied population than any of the big pretentious volumes that debated the problem of generic whiteness. And early modern drama has, fortunately, been comprehensively digitized. As a result, we can pinpoint with absolute confidence and precision the first popular use of the emerging trope.

"White People"

The earliest unmistakably generic, unmistakably positive use of *white* in an extant dramatic text occurs in a pageant performed in the streets of London on October 29, 1613—four months after the premiere of Shakespeare's last securely datable play, and more than a year after Purchas finished writing *Purchas his Pilgrimage,* where whiteness was still a contested and confusing category.[10] The most lavish and expensive show that had ever been performed to inaugurate a mayor of London, Thomas Middleton's *The Triumphs of Truth* was seen by many thousands of spectators, far more than could have crowded into a theater; the Grocers' Company paid for the printing of 500 copies of the quarto text, which were either given away or sold at a heavily discounted price.[11] Even at full price, with only four sheets the text would have cost just two pence.

That autumn four East India Company ships returned to London, carrying more than a million pounds of (very profitable) pepper.[12] The mayor Londoners celebrated on October 29 was Sir Thomas Myddleton, one of the founding members of the East India Company, named in its charter of 1600; a pamphlet entitled "Trade from England unto the East Indies" has been attributed to him; his cousin Sir Robert Myddleton had been on the first and second East India voyages (with Edmund Scott, author of the 1606 text that contained the first example of *white* in stage 5, its modern generic sense).[13] The Russian ambassador reported that "many people, men, women, and children—the whole City—watched this ceremony."[14] In the middle of the pageant, "a strange ship" appeared, carrying "a king of the Moors, his queen, and two attendants of their own color"; apparently astonished by "the many eyes of such a multitude," the king addressed the crowd, beginning:

> I see amazement set upon the faces
> Of these white people, wond'rings and strange gazes;
> Is it at me? Does my complexion draw
> So many Christian eyes that never saw
> A king so black before? (407–24)

A socially and morally undifferentiated crowd of English men and women is here characterized as "white people," their individual and collective white identity assumed and asserted in an address to them spoken by a black stranger: from the perspective of his alien blackness, they are all "white." Popular generic whiteness is first defined, literally, by a black gaze and a black speaker. Whiteness is created by a speech-act, fixed by the gaze and speech of a black-face performer. Middleton re-creates, for thousands of people who had never left England, the littoral experience of being seen to be white.

The black-faced speaker who calls them white is not a slave on a slave ship, or even a passenger on a European merchant ship manned by a European crew. He is a king, standing on a ship without any white crew or passengers, a ship that (seemingly miraculously) moves on its own power. Even more remarkably, this black king is the first unequivocally positive representation of a black speaker in the entire surviving corpus of English dramatic texts.[15] He is not lustful, not jealous, not a liar, not a murderer; he does not belong to the police line-up of violent black men arraigned in the preceding decades by George Peele, Thomas Dekker, and William Shakespeare. He is not even called ugly or foul, as other black-faced characters were almost inevitably labeled.[16] Nor is he mute spectacle (like the two Moors in Marlowe's *Tamburlaine* or the blackamoors in Shakespeare's *Love's Labour's Lost* or the black queens in Jonson's *Masque of Blackness* or the black servants in so many seventeenth-century English portraits); not mere orientalism, or mere ornamentalism (like the mute blacks paired with exotic animals in the pageants of Anthony Munday, John Webster, and Thomas Dekker); not a walking trope (like the mute black figures in Anthony Munday's 1616 pageant, "hurling gold and silver every way" into the crowd).[17] The blank blackness of such apparitions makes them objects, not subjects. By contrast, Middleton's black king is—as Eldred Jones noted decades ago—less "shallow" than the black figures in other pageants, "more closely woven" into the plot and argument of the pageant.[18] He is not a silent sign. He asserts the same (illusion of) sovereign subjectivity projected by any other protagonist in a dramatic text: he speaks. He speaks, in fact, 47 lines of verse.[19] Moreover, Middleton's black king is not alone. He stands beside his black queen, who also speaks. This is the first positive portrayal of a black marriage in English literature. Indeed, it is the first portrayal of black monogamy. Up until this point, black sexuality had been delineated solely within the frame of violent or ambivalent bicolor couplings, or of the sexual excess associated with polygamy.[20]

Middleton's positive depiction of the Black King might have been influenced by a literary and pictorial tradition that one of the Three Kings who came to adore the Christ child was black.[21] Common throughout Germany by 1470, the black Magus had been borrowed "by every other significant school of artists in Western Europe"—including the English—by 1510 (Illus. 5).[22] Like the Magi, Middleton's Black King, Queen, and entourage have come from a distant land to celebrate an inaugural moment; they have "arrived in blessèd time" (454) to see where Christians are "bred" (453); their appearance culminates in an act of "adoration" (441), not of the pagan sun, but of a Christian "temple" of "Truth," St. Paul's cathedral, to which they all "Do reverence" and "bow low" (464–65), as the Magi did before the Christ child.[23]

Middleton's Black King and Queen seem to be the first "good" black people in English literature. They are as admirable and sympathetic as the black protagonists of antebellum fiction. The long-suffering black hero of Harriet Beecher Stowe's abolitionist blockbuster was, in some sense, whiter than whites, having more thoroughly internalized the values of Christianity than his masters. But in the many nineteenth-century theatrical adaptations of *Uncle Tom's Cabin* ("Tom shows"), Uncle Tom became a farcically subservient toady and race traitor. He became, in fact, what William Wells Brown had already portrayed, in *Clotel,* through the figure of the chief house slave, Sam. Sam is the fictional prototype of what African American critic Trudier Harris identifies as "the emasculated black male": he is "a buffoon," effacing "all traits of his personality except those which were acceptable to his master." Sam "is emasculated because he cannot control his destiny to the extent that those in power above him can, and he can never claim property, a house, or the kind of job which should accrue to him

Illustration 5. Hieronymous Bosch's *Adoration of the Magi* (1509?), like many paintings from the fifteenth and sixteenth centuries, assumed that one of the three Wise Men was black. © Museo Nacional del Prado.

by virtue of his masculinity. . . . He must reign over the kitchen, not the parlor."[24] By contrast, Middleton's Black King is not emasculated; he reigns over a kingdom, not a kitchen. Like George Green and Clotel's daughter Mary, whose long-delayed union ends *Clotel,* Middleton's King and Queen are a moral and married black couple who have left their native land, at least temporarily, to observe and admire England.

Nevertheless, the very features required to make these "good blacks" good, for the original white spectators or white readers, also inevitably make them more problematic for modern black readers. George Green "was so white as easily to pass for a white man, and being somewhat ashamed of his African descent," in England "he never once mentioned the fact of having been a slave" (217); the former slave he marries has a complexion even "lighter" than her mother, Clotel (101); Mary is described as a "white slave-girl" and a "white nigger." This last cutting epithet is spoken by a black woman and fellow slave: "Dees white niggers always tink dey sef good as white folks" (156). The cook collaborates with the "unfeeling and fiendish designs" of her white mistress against her fellow slave. Brown explains that "The cook was black, and was not without that prejudice which is to be found among the Negroes, as well as among the whites of the Southern States" (156). But the cook undoubtedly speaks for many black readers, impatient with a black writer whose allegedly "black" protagonists are in fact perfectly white. In the 1864 American revision (*Clotelle: A Tale of the Southern States*), George is renamed Jerome, and recomplexioned: Jerome "was of pure African origin, was perfectly black." But even Jerome has "thin" lips and "nearly straight" hair.[25] Linguistically Jerome, like George before him, remains absolutely white, elevated by his language above characters like the cook Dinah and "Marser Sam" (164), who speak in dialect.

Brown's heroes—like Brown himself, like the Black King and Queen of Middleton's pageant—have mastered white English. Like Brown, Middleton's black paragons admire English political institutions: they celebrate "That honorable man," the new Lord Mayor. They have adopted English social customs and internalized English beliefs. They are Christians, and attribute their conversion to the beneficent effects of imperial capitalism:

> My queen and people all, at one time won
> By the religious conversatïon
> Of English merchants, factors, travelers,
> Whose Truth did with our spirits hold commèrce,
> As their affairs with us: following their path,
> We all were brought to the true Christian faith.(444–49)

The "white nigger"—the person with a black body who adopts cultural practices associated with white people—is a necessary fiction. Just as whiteness can be defined only by blackness, so it is only "white niggers" who can authoritatively affirm the moral and political superiority of white folks.

But if the "white nigger" is a necessary fiction, he is also a destabilizing one. To give a black man moral authority is to make him the moral equal of any white man—indeed, potentially his moral superior. Clotel, "indignant," shames the white husband who abandons her (120), becomes a corrupt politician, then drinks himself to death. George rebukes the white court that condemns him (212–13); Ellen commits suicide, rather than submit to the "degradation" planned for her by her white master (197); Jane dies "of a broken heart" after "her cruel master" murders the man she loves (199). The white parson's black slaves celebrate his death with the chorus, "Old master has gone to the slaveholder's rest; He has gone where they all ought to go" (154), and no reader has any doubt exactly where the white parson and his kind all ought to go. Likewise, Middleton's Black King, as Jack D'Amico argues, "subverts the simplistic division of races and cultures."[26] In the very moment that Middleton invokes the generic category of English whiteness, he absolutely denies its importance:

> I being a Moor, then, in opinion's lightness,
> As far from sanctity as my face from whiteness;
> But I forgive the judgings of th'unwise,
> Whose censures ever quicken in their eyes,
> Only begot of outward form and show.
> And I think meet to let such censurers know,
> However darkness dwells upon my face,
> Truth in my soul sets up the light of grace.(432–39)

The full significance of this speech can be understood only within the context of the entire pageant, which is organized as a recurring contest between light and darkness, Truth and Error. Error has already declared that she has many English acolytes:

> I can bring
> A thousand of our parish (besides queans)
> That ne'er knew what Truth meant, nor ever means.
> Some I could cull out here, e'en in this throng,
> If I would show my children, and how strong
> I were in faction.(304–09)

The "throng" to which Error here gestures is the same crowd that the Black King will address. It contains "some" of the children of Error, just as the city itself contains "a thousand" who belong to the "parish" of Error. Therefore, Middleton's pageant already has established that at least some of the "white people" addressed by the Black King belong to the "faction" of Error. The pageant explicitly insists that some "white people" are morally corrupt.[27] By contrast, Error has been forsaken by the blacks—whom he calls "my sweet-faced devils" and looks on with a combination of "scorn and anger to see such a devout humility take hold of that complexion" (472–75). The black couple and their entourage belong to the shock troops of Truth.

One may, of course, object to Middleton's privileging of "the ethnocentric doctrines of white Christianity."[28] For many of us, Christianity is not "Truth." But Christianity, it must be acknowledged, would become the chief source and weapon of the abolitionist movement. The Anglo-Saxon heroine of *Clotel,* Georgiana, defends the Bible against free-thinkers like "Rousseau, Voltaire, and Thomas Paine," arguing that it reviles slavery (108–10, 127–31); Brown ends his novel with one of its many biblical quotations. Nor is Christianity necessarily "white." The founding gesture of Christianity, as a separate religion rather than a mere sect of Judaism, had been the assertion that what matters is not the body but the spirit. Saint Paul's mission to the Gentiles replaced Jewish circumcision with a new incorporeal "circumcision of the heart" (Romans 2:29), available to anyone. The first recorded gentile convert to the new religion was a eunuch from Ethiopia (Acts 8:26–40).[29] Rembrandt made that black convert the central figure of one of his paintings.[30] Allegorically, both Jerome and Augustine had argued that all nations and individuals are "naturally black" because sinful and made white only by repentance. Within that tradition, Middleton's Black King—like the black Magus—demonstrates the equality of all peoples before God.[31]

For committed Christians like Middleton and the Puritan mayor he celebrated here (or William Wells Brown), what separates the sheep from the goats is not biology but religion. Middleton's 1622 pageant *The Triumphs of Honor and Virtue* contains another Black Queen, "representing India." *The Triumphs of Truth* does not specify whether its black sovereigns come from Africa or India. To Middleton, continents do not matter, complexions do not matter; what matters is the boundary that separates Christians from non-Christians. And that boundary is permeable. As the Black Queen of 1622 reminded her London audience:

> This black is but my native dye.
> But view me with an intellectual eye
> (As wise men shoot their beams forth), then you'll find
> A change in the complexion of the mind:
> I'm beauteous in my blackness. . . .
> All wealth consists in Christian holiness.(54–58, 79)

Like Sir Thomas Browne and Sir Walter Ralegh, Middleton here acknowledges the perspective that would make "blackness" "beauteous." In both pageants, Middleton insists on what, to ethnocentric Englishmen, must have seemed an outrageous paradox: black truth, black virtue, black Christianity.

Why? What purpose does that paradox serve? "The subject of the dream," Toni Morrison insists, "is the dreamer."[32] In fictions written by and for whites, blacks are deployed only for what they might tell whites about themselves. In 1613 Londoners were called "white people" by a white actor speaking words written by a white author, but projected into the mouth of a fictional black king.[33] Middleton describes the Black Queen of *Honor and Virtue* as "*lending* a voice to these following words" (italics added); the words are Middleton's own, transmitted through the voice of an English actor, doubly disguised as a woman and a black. Through this Black Queen or that Black King, Middleton addresses his own people. To maximize the dramatic effect of that address, he foregrounds and maximizes a series of paradoxes. In his pageants—as in the New Testament, or the poetry of John Donne, or *Clotel*—paradox is a rhetorical strategy for surprising the listener into a thought experiment. Black-faced mutes had become a common feature of civic pageants in the sixteenth century. But the traditional iconographic significance of blackness as evil or falsehood or monstrosity meant that mute signs alone could not convey to an audience the paradox of "black truth." Within the performance conventions that Middleton was adapting, the paradox could be communicated only by speech. The speeches of Envy, the Black King, and the Black Queen all work to overcome the traditional iconic associations of blackness, and thereby enforce Middleton's oxymoron.

Middleton's unconventional representation of black truth, of a black saint or black angel, takes place within, is generated by, and depends on a whole series of conventional binary oppositions: not only black/white and truth/falsehood, but also hereditary king/elected mayor, king/people, one/many, male/female, foreign/native, speaker/listener. But most of these binaries are merely instrumental. The rhetorical purpose of Middleton's paradox was to force listeners (including the new mayor) to think about, and acknowledge, their own sinfulness. Middleton achieved that purpose by insisting on the binary disjunctions between the speaker and the listeners, the king and the people, the one and the many, the foreigner and the natives. Because for the paradox to work at all the angelic truth-speaker must be black, then (to maximize the disparity between speaker and listener) the audience must be the opposite of black. That is, the audience *must be white.* As in Bodin's formulation, if X is black, then the opposite of X must be white. Therefore, the thousands listening to the Black King's speech must be white, but not necessarily white in a moral sense. In what other sense could they all be white? They could be white in terms of the contrast between their complexions and the Black King's. Whatever else they were, whatever else united them, epidermally they were all unblack. Middleton, accordingly, for the first time told the natives of London—whether or not they could read—that all their many different complexions could be included in the category *white.* He called them all, for the first time, "white people."

"White Kingdom"

The whiting of English identity that Middleton began in *The Triumphs of Truth* was extended and secured in another, even more spectacular Middleton text, where generic whiteness was again defined by black characters.[34] *A Game at Chess* was written in the spring of 1624, not long after the publication of Jobson's *The Golden Trade.* But Middleton emphasized whiteness much more self-consciously than Jobson. In *A Game at Chess* the word *white* is spoken 56 times, and various "white" compounds another 8 times: 64 occurrences altogether. The entirety of English drama up to the English Civil War and the closing of the theaters in 1642 contains nothing remotely comparable to this insistent iteration of *white.*[35] In any reading of Middleton's play—and three separate editions were published in 1625 alone—the word is even more ubiquitous and unparalleled than these statistics suggest, because it appears in stage directions and speech prefixes for half the play's characters (White Queen's Pawn, White Knight, White King, etc.).

These unspoken repetitions of the word correspond to, but underestimate, the visual repetitions of whiteness created, in performance, by the movements onto the stage of all these "white" characters. The actors were divided into the two competing sides on a chessboard, representing the Black House and the White House. The black costumes worn by members of the Black House would not have been intrinsically remarkable; black clothing was often worn in early modern England, and any soiled garment of another color could continue to be used by dyeing it black and thus concealing the damage. But as the theater historian Jean MacIntyre observes, white clothing "was not much used either in the theater or in practical life."[36] It was not much used precisely because, as a White Pawn in the play remarks, "white quickly soils, you know" (3.2.11–12). White clothes do not stay white. Even today, when we drive climate-controlled cars to climate-controlled offices, it can be hard to keep fashionably white summerwear white; so you can imagine how difficult it would have been in early modern London when food was cooked and buildings heated by smoky open fires, when Londoners walked dirty streets or rode dirty horses. The royal palaces of James I would not have met the hygenic standards demanded today of a hole-in-the-wall bar. In such environments whiteness was always temporary. As a result, "when the King's Men needed white costumes for Middleton's play, they probably had to have most of them made," specially tailored and usable for this play only. Costumes for the White King, White Queen, White Knight, White Duke, and White Bishop "seem likely to have translated clothes worn by the real persons into white satin, velvet, and cloth of tissue, fabrics of decorum for those of high rank."[37]

A Game at Chess translated to the popular stage expensive fabrics normally restricted to the court, and whiteness itself was one of those luxuries. White clothing was used occasionally, as a special effect among other special effects, in court masques like Ben Jonson's *Hymenai* (1613) and James Shirley's *The Triumph of Peace* (1634).[38] Such masques demonstrate the great variety of clothing and accessories that could be made spectacularly white for rituals of conspicuous consumption, but even in the luxurious circumstances of a royal masque whiteness was not a uniform, and it did not uniformly signify, and it was not uniformly contrasted with anything else.

A Game at Chess, for the first time in English literature, organized and unified whiteness. It was the first "designer play." Never before had the popular theaters staged a drama whose very meaning and structure depended on a prescribed design that controlled every aspect of the visual field. It is widely recognized that the early modern stage used almost no scenery, and that most of the spectacle was provided by costuming. Special costumes were sometimes created to highlight a particular character or a particular dramatic moment. But in *A Game at Chess* special and expensive costumes had to be created for all the White characters. Although the black clothing and accessories may not have been purpose-made, their distribution on stage was systematized in opposition to the White pieces. Moreover, the Black and White sides were distinguished, not only by their costuming, but by their makeup. The Black characters were black not only in their clothes, but in "their complexion" (3.1.263).[39] Most of the Black characters are Spanish. Middleton's known sources for the play asserted that the Spanish were of mixed blood, as much Moorish African as European.[40] Spaniards insisted on their "pure blood," but it was hard to deny the brownish complexions evident in many portraits from Golden Age Spain (Plate 18). In *A Game at Chess* the White King represented King James, a pale Scot with white hair and a white beard, in contrast to the Black King, representing the young black-haired Spanish king Felipe IV. Clothes, accessories, beards, makeup: everything contributed to the same coherent visual pattern.

The play's visual field is not only systematized but polarized. The actors speak various forms of the word *white* 64 times and of the word *black* 62 times. The total for *black* is more than double the number in any other play of the period.[41] (In *Othello* the word is used only 11 times.) Other colors of the visible spectrum never occur in the stage directions of *A Game at Chess,* and only a handful of times in the spoken text: a green fig, a golden-headed fish, a red hat—in each case, referring to a property that does not appear on stage. *A Game at Chess* imagined and embodied a world artificially stripped of color: a vision artfully, elegantly black and white.

This division of the world into competing armies of black and white seems (to us) a self-evident allegory; indeed, it seems (to us) so obvious as to be trite. Modern commentators explain the play's black/white binary—if they feel obliged to explain it at all—as a mere moral frame, or a consequence of the chess allegory. But the two sides in chess were not, at the time, or in other chess allegories, inevitably color-coded as white and black.[42] Nor were Protestant moral allegories inevitably so coded. Middleton's play is sometimes compared to Thomas Dekker's *The Whore of Babylon* (ca. 1606), another allegorical play that—like Middleton's *A Game at Chess*—recasts recent historical events in the

Illustraion 6. This broadside (1615) contrasts the black vestments of Christian penitence and simplicity with the revealing white fashions of a corrupt court. Courtesy of the Society of Antiquaries, London.

form of a struggle between Protestant virtue and Catholic vice. But Dekker's nationalistic and moral binaries do not inhabit visual binaries, or any kind of coherent visual design.[43] Indeed, in the social iconography of the day, Protestant piety was usually indicated not by expensive and wasteful white vestments, but by plain black clothes (Illus. 6). One need only think of the visual clichés associated with Puritans.

As Richard Dyer says, whiteness is so pervasive an image in our own culture that it has become for us a signifier whose signifying we hardly consciously register as such; "whiteness needs to be made strange."[44] In this case, criticism does not need to *make* it strange, but to *recover* its original strangeness. The massive symbolic deployment of whiteness in *A Game at Chess,* so unremarkable to us, was in 1624 a wholly unprecedented act of artistic creation.

What does that whiteness signify? The white chess pieces all belong to what Middleton calls "the White House." It is six times described as "the White Kingdom." All the identifiable White characters are British[45]; indeed, they all belonged to the English court, and all were often resident in London and familiar to London audiences.[46] When the Black Knight—the most important Black character—brags about his Machiavellian exploits against the White House, he describes events that actually had happened in England. England was still sometimes called Albion, in allusion to the white cliffs of Dover—the only thing visible from across the Channel, and the first thing encountered by Julius Caesar and other Roman invaders.[47] The first line of the play describes the setting as an "angle of the world" (Ind.1), and a later line reiterates "the most fortunate angle of the world" (3.1.108); these are traditional characterizations of England—or, as the play calls it, "Anglica," the land invaded and settled by the Angles and Saxons.[48] The White House is thus, absolutely unmistakably, "the English House" (2.1.199). It may or may not include Scotland and Wales, and therefore it may or may not represent Great Britain; but there can be no denying the sustained focus on England. The kingdom of the Whites is England. Whiteness is Englishness.

England's white community is set against the dark community of another kingdom, Spain. All the identifiable Black characters are Spanish.[49] The real Spanish ambassador in London in August 1624 vehemently protested that the Black characters were libels against his homeland. The kingdom of the Blacks is Spain. Blackness is Spanishness.

A Game at Chess is sometimes dismissed as an offensively jingoistic play; once we recognize the ethnic logic of its color coding, we also might dismiss it as offensively colorphobic. But Middleton's black villains—unlike Shakespeare's, Peele's, Dekker's, Heywood's, Marston's, Rowley's, or Webster's—are not Africans. They are Spaniards. That is, they are other Europeans. What Middleton attacks in *A Game at Chess* is the great European imperial power of his time, the Austro-Spanish Hapsburg empire, and its efforts to impose a "universal monarchy," the global dominance of a single ideology, enforced by an Atlantic superpower. A modern equivalent would be a Cuban, Vietnamese, Afghani, or Iraqi play in which the inhabitants of a small country outsmart sinister, powerful American invaders.

The victims of the Black House—cataloged by the Black Knight as a menu of "the large feast of our vast ambition"—include "the White Kingdom" (England), France, Germany, Venice, Italy, Savoy, Geneva, the Netherlands, Portugal, Holland, Switzerland, Poland, and "Indians and Moors" (5.3.93–102). The first thing to notice about this list is that England (or Great Britain) is the only "white" kingdom: whiteness is not extended to other Europeans, even Protestant northern Europeans like the Germans and Dutch. Generic whiteness originates, in popular English texts, not as a pan-European or even northern European category, but as a very local one, addressed to Londoners and applicable to no one outside Britain. The second thing to notice is that, in the conceit that describes each country as a type of food, the "Indians and Moors" are "blackbirds." (Birds—as "four-and-twenty blackbirds baked in a pie" reminds us—were at the time a regular part of the European diet.) Thus, Hapsburg ideology and power victimize both the "white" kingdom of England and the "black" kingdoms of the New World, Africa, and Asia. As in *The Triumphs of Truth,* the black King of Moors and the "white people" of England are on the same side. What unites them is the threat posed by the Counter-Reformation Hapsburg empire.

Nevertheless, the play is not really interested in Indians or Moors, Spain or Spanishness. The most important Spanish political figures—the Black King, Black Queen, and Black Duke—have very small parts, and speak only a handful of lines.[50] The chief Black characters are the Spanish ambassador to the Court of King James (Black Knight), a Jesuit and Jesuitess in England (Black Bishop's Pawn, Black Queen's Pawn), and a member of the Spanish diplomatic delegation in England (Black Knight's Pawn).[51] The first has been notoriously successful in duping King James (White King); the second and third join forces to convert/seduce an ideologically naïve English virgin (White Queen's Pawn); the fourth has castrated an English Protestant minister (White Bishop's Pawn). Thus, the most important Black characters are those operating within the White Kingdom of England. Blackness is interesting only insofar as it endangers whiteness.

Nevertheless, *A Game at Chess*—again, unlike *The Whore of Babylon*—does not celebrate or advocate retaliatory war with Spain, or the excitements of patriotic slaughter, or even the self-satisfied execution of would-be assassins. By play's end, the Black House already has been defeated (although, outside the theater, the Hapsburgs still dominated Europe and the rest of the world). What defeats the Black House in Middleton's play is not an army but a public exposure of imperial hypocrisy. The chief White character is a woman who risks her own reputation to denounce publicly the private vices of a respected public figure. What does the play celebrate? A refusal to respect imperial ideologues who are not respectable. The triumph of truth.

That triumph of truth is figured, by Middleton, as the victory of whitehood, the victory of an Englishness systematically equated with an undeniably positive collective whiteness. Whiteness is the focus of the play; Black characters matter only insofar as they live in the midst of White ones and directly threaten them. Within the play's unique visual design, it is whiteness—the rare, expensive, unprecedented spectacle of systematic whiteness—that the design's black/white contrast emphasizes. White triumphs.

Middleton's White Kingdom had an extraordinary cultural impact. In nine consecutive days in August 1624, *A Game at Chess* was seen by perhaps one-seventh of the total population of London, and many more who did not see it heard about it, or heard the "extraordinary applause" and "extraordinary concourse" of its audiences. Never before had any English play had so long a run of consecutive performances—and that run would certainly have continued if the play had not been suppressed (and the author thrown in jail) by order of King James himself. Each day the large Globe Theatre was packed to capacity: "There was such merriment, hubbub and applause that," even if the Spanish ambassador "had been many leagues away, it would not have been possible" for him not to have noticed. The play made the King's Men an unprecedented, scandalous amount of money. It stimulated more immediate commentary than any play, masque, or pageant of its age. It was the subject of letters sent to Brussels, Florence, Madrid, Paris, and Venice. It survives in many more manuscripts than any other play of the period; it was published in more illicit editions than any other play; it was the first individual play published with an engraved title page (actually, with two, in two different editions). For four decades after its nine performances, it was remembered as the most spectacular success in English theatrical history, the benchmark of exorbitant popularity.[52]

A Game at Chess helps explain the casual use of *white* as an ethnic marker in the two London plays of the 1630s that I cited at the end of chapter 2. Between Heywood's *The Fair Maid of the West, Part One* (ca. 1603) and *The Fair Maid of the West, Part Two* (1631), or between Jonson's *Masque of Blackness* (1605) and Brome's *The English Moor* (1637), what happened? Many things: the spectacular rise of the East India Company, the establishment of English colonies in North America and the Caribbean, the publication of Jobson's account of his trip to Africa and of the four volumes of *Hakluytus Posthumus*. All those events contributed to the evolution of English identity. But the main conduits of linguistic change and influence are personal networks, and Heywood and Brome have no known personal connection to any of these larger historical movements.[53] The personal connections point, instead, to Middleton. Middleton collaborated with Heywood, and Heywood later collaborated with Brome. The events during those decades most likely to have influenced the word choices of a London playwright and pageant writer like Heywood—or a London playwright like Brome—were Middleton's Lord Mayor's shows and Middleton's spectacularly successful play.[54] But if Middleton was the source that influenced Heywood and Brome (and other Londoners), who was the source that influenced Middleton?

England's First White Writer

Sociolinguist William Labov has shown that, in modern American cities, the leaders of linguistic change are usually rebellious individuals who straddle social boundaries, moving back and forth across thresholds that usually separate neighborhoods and economic classes; they belong, consequently, to an exceptional number of different social networks.[55] Middleton perfectly fits this profile: a rebellious poet who at one end of his career wrote a book banned and burned when he was only 19, and at the other end penned a play that provoked an international diplomatic incident and got him thrown in jail; a born gentleman who never owned any real estate and was often in debt; a student at Oxford University who never took a degree; a born Londoner who grew up a few blocks from St. Paul's Cathedral but eventually moved to the south bank suburbs, who commuted between his suburban home and his urban workplace, who is famous for city comedies filled with an extraordinary, detailed, and nuanced knowledge of the diverse neighborhoods and inhabitants of London. But Middleton also had a unique personal connection to the history of England's emerging generic identity.

The "chief factor" or "cape merchant" of the 1585 expedition to found a colony at Roanoke was a young bachelor named Thomas Harvey. Despite his important position as supplier of provisions and investor in potential export commodities, Harvey spent a miserable year in America, losing everything, and in July 1586 he returned from Roanoke "without a penny." To recoup his fortunes, he quickly courted and married a wealthy London widow, Anne Middleton, whose husband had died a few months before. As soon as the marriage was consummated, Harvey tried to get possession of the money Anne had set aside, in a carefully constructed trust, for her two young children. It took him 15 years of acrid legal battles, but English courts gave married women few legal rights independent of their husbands, and Harvey eventually won.[56] One of Anne's two children—age 5 when his father died, 6 when his mother married a colonial adventurer, 21 when his stepfather finally won—was Thomas Middleton.

At the very outset of England's effort to become an Atlantic colonial power, Middleton experienced the messy, sour backwash of imperialism, what intellectual historian Michel Foucault (more clinically) called "a return effect." Colonialism required a constant movement outward and back, and those who came back had been altered by their outing. They brought with them "a return of colonial practice," a "whole series of colonial models" that could be applied to "the mechanisms of power" back home, creating something like "an internal colonialism."[57] Foucault devoted only a paragraph to this subject, and never descended to specifics. Thomas Harvey was one of the specifics. In 1586 Harvey was among the few Englishmen who had encountered large numbers of profoundly alien, pretechnological brown and black people.[58] He spent much of his adult life in the multilingual polychromatic maritime contact zones where the English sense of whiteness was forged. (See chapter 5.) If Harvey resembled other English voyagers—including two who reported on Roanoke—those Atlantic encounters convinced him that he belonged to a "white" genre. That reflux of whiteness was surely the most significant of the many "techniques of power" that European colonists brought back to Europe.

Harvey might easily have been the muse who inspired Middleton's assumption or assertion that Londoners were "white people." After all, Middleton wrote *The Triumphs of Truth* for the Honorable Company of the Grocers, to which his stepfather had belonged. It was his first commission to write a mayoral pageant, and his family link to the company might even have helped him secure it; the Company of the Grocers was a small network of London households with its own rules, its own hierarchy, its own social rituals (like company dinners). Even if Middleton did not owe the commission to that personal connection, he could hardly have avoided thinking about his Grocer-stepfather when writing *The Triumphs of Truth.* And he was demonstrably thinking about his own childhood when writing *A Game at Chess.*[59]

Harvey might also have been the source of Middleton's ambivalence about the relationship between generic and moral whiteness. Harvey was no advertisement for whiteness. Any sense of his generic superiority abroad was combined with, and confounded by, his dubious ethical and economic status at home. Harvey's case was, in fact, pretty typical. The bankrupt, argumentative Harvey fits the profile of the class of impoverished European colonists that would later be called "redlegs" or "white trash." The relatively unsuccessful, unindustrious, unlucky majority of the imperial folk eventually would be consoled for their failures by the "vastly ego-warming and ego-expanding distinction between the white man and the black."[60] But that distinction was not much help to Harvey. He died years before the first African laborers were imported into Bermuda and Virginia, and decades before white identity had consolidated around the contrast with black slavery. To most Londoners in the 1580s and 1590s, it would not have been self-evident that "white" men like Harvey were superior to anyone. It certainly would not have been apparent to a fatherless six-year-old.

Complex cultural transformations do not have a single author or a single point of origin; new ideas slowly percolate, before they saturate a society. But at some point a catalytic agent must combine and articulate the emergent half-thoughts generated by the diversity of new experiences. For English whiteness, Middleton was that catalyst. By the end of his life, he apparently thought of himself as in some sense "white."[61] That cannot be said of any popular English writer before him.

Middleton invented the complex literary fiction of English whiteness. He did so because he was trying to create something original and powerful out of an inherited set of dramatic conventions and intellectual binaries. But he was not working in a hermetically sealed aesthetic space. In the years that he wrote *The Triumphs of Truth* and *A Game at Chess,* Middleton lived in the South Bank neighborhood of Newington; he would have walked into London along what is now Borough High Street, but was called in his lifetime Blackman Street.[62] As a university-educated humanist who could read Latin, Greek, Italian, French, and Spanish, Middleton could easily have been aware of the ongoing debates about climate and color. As a lifelong inhabitant of Europe's most populous city and busiest port, he was immersed in a "soundscape" remarkable for "the assemblage of different nations" in its markets and the "vast confusion of languages" that could be heard in its central cathedral, a community that contained enough foreigners to justify church services held in Dutch, French, and Italian.[63] Writing for portside theaters and celebrating the mayoralty of a man who had made his fortune in overseas trade, Middleton might well have talked to men like Barlow and Jobson and Battel, whose encounters with dark foreigners had left them with an impression of their own whiteness. He might have talked to those men; he certainly did talk and listen to Thomas Harvey. Unlike any of his predecessors or contemporaries in the London theater, Middleton had been exposed to a powerful postcolonial sense of whiteness when he was only six years old.

Toward the end of the seventeenth century, John Locke reported that even English children unselfconsciously thought of themselves as "white."[64] Middleton was among the first Englishmen who might have had something like that childhood experience. But Middleton's sense of whiteness would have come not from his biological parents, but from the ambivalent figure of his stepfather. Whiteness had not yet been naturalized. Unlike Locke (or me), Middleton was not born white. He *became* white.

As a fully embodied popular trope rather than an ethnographic description, the ideology of whiteness did not originate in the American colonies in the 1650s and did not develop as a direct consequence of English involvement in the Atlantic slave trade or the English colonization of Ireland.[65] It originated in

London, as a self-consciously symbolic fiction. Popular whiteness sprang from English mercantile encounters with darker peoples in Africa, India, America, and the East Indies, filtered through the ideological and commercial rivalries of the Counter-Reformation. In popular as well as elite usage, blackness preceded whiteness. Blackness had to be encountered and mythologized before generic whiteness could be imagined, because *white* was first publicly spoken and authorized by Middleton's black kings and black politicians.[66] For those black speakers to create the myth of whiteness, they had to have credible authority; they could not be, and were not, slaves. But color-coded slavery soon would transform the meanings Middleton had given whiteness.

Chapter 7

White Servitude

In the sequence of events that leads to her death, Clotel's whiteness fails her. She had disguised herself successfully as a white man, but her real legal status as a "black" slave is discovered after whites become more vigilant, searching for rebels led by a "full-blooded negro . . . who went by the name of 'Nat Turner'" (201). Brown thus ties the plot of his novel to the most famous of all American slave rebellions, which he describes in terms that fuse Turner's failed insurrection in Virginia with the successful black revolution in Haiti, led by Toussaint L'Ouverture. That revolution had overthrown white rule and established the first black republic in the western hemisphere. Brown imports into his story "a large, tall, full-blooded negro, with a stern and savage countenance," actually based on a Haitian revolutionary. "Brought from the coast of Africa," the escaped slave Picquilo weds "a negro woman," oiling her body in a traditional African "marriage ceremony." This is the only union between two fully black characters in the entire novel; it presents, like the Black King and Black Queen of *The Triumphs of Truth,* a positive image of black monogamy otherwise hard to find in English literature. But Brown's black couple do not mimic the civil deference of Middleton's. In revenge for his enslavement, Picquilo "imbrued his hands in the blood of all the whites he could meet." In a spiral of reciprocal violence, "carnage was added to carnage, and the blood of the whites flowed to avenge the blood of the blacks." One of the recaptured slaves, addressing a white court after it has condemned him to death, equates the black insurgents with the heroes of the Revolutionary War. "You say your fathers fought for freedom—so did we" (212). The man who says this—and whose words leave "nearly everyone present" in the courtroom "melted into tears"—is George, the novel's hero, who in the end will escape, become a prosperous free black, and marry Clotel's daughter.

Slave rebellions also can be found in the literature of the English Renaissance. The title character and hero of Philip Massinger's 1623 play *The Bondman* is a "slave" (1.1.41) named Marullo, living in the ancient city of Syracuse.

The Syracusans regard their slaves, "Valued at the best rate," as no better than "horses, or other beasts of carriage" (1.3.338–39). Too cowardly to stand up to their own social superiors, masters vent their frustrations on their slaves: "How brave we live! That have our slaves to beat" (2.2.23–24). One slave remarks, "I am bruised to jelly; better be a dog / Than slave to a fool or coward" (2.2.21–22). Marullo ("Mar-rule") persuades the other slaves that "Our lords are no Gods!" and that "Equal nature fashioned us / All in one mold," teaching them "to love . . . liberty"; "Is't not pity then Men of such eminent virtues should be slaves?" The inspired slaves leave the stage crying "Liberty, liberty!" (2.3.27–114). Hearing that "the slaves revolt" (3.1.31), the absent Syracusan army returns to the city. Standing on the walls of the town the slaves now control, their leader Marullo rebukes the Syracusans for having treated their slaves worse than horses, mules, and dogs: "man, to man more cruel, Appoints no end to the suff'rings of his slave" (4.2.77–78). When Marullo subsequently is captured, they "Stop his mouth" and "load him with irons" (4.4.66–67), and he is then

> dragged to prison
> With more than barbarous violence, spurned and spit on
> By the insulting officers, his hands
> Pinioned behind his back, loaden with fetters;
> Yet, with a saint-like patience, he still offers
> His face to their rude buffets.(5.1.45–50)

This sympathetic portrayal of Christ-like suffering is accompanied by the comment that, although "Marullo is a slave, he's still a man" (5.1.42). But his unrepentant master still responds to his self-defense by saying "Confute him with a whip" (5.3.150).

Massinger's sympathetic portrait of a slave and a slave rebellion might seem comparable to Brown's treatment of the subject in *Clotel.* However, Marullo turns out not to be a real slave at all. He is a "gentleman" named Pisander who has disguised himself for love and arranged for his own sale into the family of the woman he wants. His virtues—including his ability to lead others—are ruling class virtues; like others of his caste, Pisander/Marullo was born to rule. He never behaves violently or lasciviously. As a slave, he literally loves the person who owns him. By contrast, although the "mutinous slaves" are portrayed sympathetically in their servitude, once they become "lords of the town" they turn into "libidinous beasts," beginning "with violent rapes Upon the wives and daughters of their lords" (3.2.17–23). We see them, later, "drunk and quarrelling," deciding to "use" a woman as a "common good," because they will "have nothing private" (3.3.119–21). They duplicate the brutality of their former masters, dressing one "in an ape's habit, with a chain about his neck"

(3.3.0.1–2), using others as literal "footstools" (3.3.21), and beating them with a "tyranny" as brutal as what they once suffered (3.3.131). In the final battle for the town the masters need only "shake their whips" and the slaves, as if by a natural reflex of abjection, "throw away their weapons, and run off" (4.2.126–9). Their former leader is himself disgusted by "the baseness of These villains" (4.3.3–4). At play's end they enter with halters around their necks, on their way to the gallows; they confess they "have deserved" to be hanged (5.3.242–43); they dance for a pardon and swear to be as "obedient and humble" as their master's "spaniel, Though he kicked me for exercise" (5.3.258–61). Massinger's happy ending restores everyone—masters and slaves—to their proper original condition. The masters do not even promise to treat their slaves less brutally; the pardon itself constitutes an act of gratuitous magnanimity.

The Bondman is not as liberal as it looks. In itself that is predictable enough. Who needs a historian to see that a fugitive slave like William Wells Brown probably would represent a slave rebellion more radically than an Oxford-educated English gentleman whose father was legal counsel to the Earl of Pembroke? But the contrast between *Clotel* and *The Bondman* does more than highlight the elitist social assumptions of one forgotten seventeenth-century play. The contrast also reminds us that, taken out of context, phrases or speeches or even whole scenes in any early modern play can seem strikingly liberal and modern, even when the text as a whole supports a profoundly conservative view of society. Nobody nowadays has much motive for spin-doctoring the words of Philip Massinger; but a massive international educational-theatrical-media complex is dedicated to air-brushing the image of Massinger's canonical contemporary, William Shakespeare. Shakespeare's collected *Comedies, Histories, and Tragedies* were first published in the year in which Massinger's play premiered. In this chapter I will be analyzing four plays by Shakespeare—*The Tempest, The Comedy of Errors, The Taming of the Shrew, The First Part of the Contention*—and patterns of vocabulary throughout his canon. Shakespeare's representations of human servitude turn out to be as conservative as Massinger's. But Shakespeare's modern liberal apologists have done everything in their power to conceal that unpalatable fact about the world's most adored white writer. Those apologists, by making Shakespeare anachronistically modern, have warped our views of the entire period.

But traditional literary history has concealed more than Shakespeare's politics. Everyone recognizes that *Clotel* is a text relevant to the history of colorphobia in the Anglophone world. But *The Bondman* and *The Comedy of Errors* are equally relevant to that history. Why does no one acknowledge that fact? Nat Turner's significance to William Wells Brown is obvious, but why did Massinger represent a slave rebellion at all? Why was his play so popular in the 1660s?[1] And why has no one connected Massinger's slave rebellion to Brown's?

All these questions have the same answer: Massinger's slaves, and almost all of Shakespeare's, were Europeans.

European Slaves

The original audiences of *The Bondman* owned few if any slaves, and those they might have owned were black. But Massinger's play makes no ethnic distinction between slaves and masters. Marullo "plucks off his disguise" (5.3.154) to reveal his true identity as Pisander. What distinguishes slave from master must be sartorial, not epidermal. Consequently, social categories can be turned inside out as easily as a reversible jacket: "he that is a lord today May be a slave tomorrow" (3.3.138–39). "Today a mistress, tomorrow a slave" is a chapter title in *Clotel* (149); but that reversal is made possible in Brown's novel by the extraordinary and anomalous whiteness of his heroine. In *The Bondman,* all the slaves are as European as their masters, ethnically indistinguishable from the English actors and the English audience.

In 1623 slavery had not yet been stabilized by being color-coded. A few English colonists probably began enslaving blacks by 1616 in Bermuda and 1619 in Virginia, but at first the number of such slaves remained small.[2] Massinger did not automatically associate slavery with black bodies. Not only in English (from the ninth century) but in virtually every language in western Europe, the word *slave* originally meant "Slav," referring to the vulnerable eastern Europeans who provided many of the slaves sold for centuries by Muslim, Venetian, and German traders.[3] In early modern plays only a handful of slaves were black.[4] "An Ethiopian slave" who is also explicitly a "negro" appears in John Marston's *Sophonisba* (1605)[5]; but because that play is set in North Africa, the presence of an African slave does not entail any assumptions about the color of servitude.[6] In Shakespeare and Peele's *Titus Andronicus* (1592?), Aaron the Moor enters as a captive/slave, but none of the other captives on stage with him is similarly color-coded. In fact, in most plays slaves are explicitly European, not African. The people sold in John Fletcher's slave market scene, in *A Very Woman* (1615–25?), are as likely to be pale Europeans as dark Muslims. In Robert Daborne's *A Christian Turned Turk* (1610), a shipload of Frenchmen are captured by an English pirate; enslaved and shipped to Tunis, they are displayed for sale, while the captain selling them counts the gold he is being paid for "the sale" of his "own fellows" and "countrymen."[7] In Dekker and Massinger's *The Virgin Martyr* and in Markham and Sampson's *Herod and Antipater* (both first printed in 1622), a slave is specifically British.[8]

This portrayal of slavery as predominantly European, not African, accurately reflected English experience. In the sixteenth and early seventeenth century the enslavement most familiar in England was that of English sailors by Mediterranean pirates and slave traders.[9] W. E. B. DuBois was right to insist that in the sixteenth century black "Mohammedan" rulers in Egypt "were buying white slaves by the tens of thousands in Europe and Asia."[10] Indeed, until the 1640s "there were more English slaves in North Africa than there were African slaves under English control" in North America and the Caribbean.[11] Early English plays about Islam, from Robert Greene's *Selimus* (1592) to Lodowick Carlell's *Osmond the Great Turk* (1637), invariably surround powerful Moors with a retinue of slaves. The category of slave most often specified in play texts (at least 23 times) was a specifically Mediterranean type, the galley slave, as likely to be European as African and as likely to be rowing in Christian as Ottoman ships.[12]

When we read or perform early modern texts, we tend to color-code slavery anachronistically. During his trial Shylock asks, "What judgment shall I dread, doing no wrong? You have among you many a purchased slave Which, like your asses and your dogs and mules, You use in abject and in slavish parts, Because you bought them." In the 1987 Royal Shakespeare Company production of *The Merchant of Venice,* Shylock, at the words "purchased slave," seized a black attendant and held him forward, as a kind of living prop, throughout the remainder of the speech.[13] In 1998, in Stratford, Ontario, the Shakespeare Festival production of *Julius Caesar* cast a black actor as the freed slave Pindarus. The same year, at the other Stratford, the Royal Shakespeare Company production of *The Tempest,* directed by Adrian Noble, cast black actor Evroy Deer as Ferdinand; after he was captured by Prospero, Ferdinand entered "carrying logs" with his neck and ankles in chains, in an unmistakable visual allusion to black slavery.

As feminist critic Celia R. Daileader has argued, such allegedly "color-blind casting" grossly perpetuates modern racial (and gender) stereotypes.[14] The use of any reference to slavery as a cue to cast a black actor in a Renaissance play reproduces the characterization of blacks as disempowered accessories; it implies or assumes that there is something natural, transhistorical, aesthetically satisfying about the enslavement of black people. No wonder playwright August Wilson vehemently rejects the translation of modern black bodies into early modern white roles. For Wilson, "Colorblind casting is an aberrant idea that has never had any validity other than as a tool of the Cultural Imperialists. . . . The idea of colorblind casting is the same idea of assimilation that black Americans have been rejecting for the past 380 years."[15] The full round of black experience does not fit into the white boxes of canonical English literature. What's more, "colorblind casting" falsifies white history as much as it falsifies black history.

The Tempest

The most canonical English play that dramatizes a slave rebellion is undoubtedly *The Tempest* (1611). Caliban is described in the dramatis personae list as "a savage and deformed slave" and six times called *slave* in the first scene in which he appears (1.2.311, 316, 322, 347, 354, 377). A "savage" (1.2.158) and a "thing of darkness" (5.1.275) belonging to a "vile race" (1.2.361), he is said to be the child of an African woman and the (traditionally black) devil; the child of these two black parents is also presumably black. Caliban is called "monster" 40 times, and Africa more than any other continent was described by Europeans as the abode of monsters. Theatre historian Rosalyn Knutson has shown that the character might have been inspired by an African baptized in London in 1611.[16] Another theatre historian, Errol G. Hill, has documented that "Caliban was one of the first roles" in the Shakespeare canon "offered to black actors" in multiracial acting companies.[17] Beginning in America with Canada Lee's performances in Boston and New York in 1945, this tendency reached mainstream British theater in Jonathan Miller's famous "colonialist" production in London in 1970. Miller also cast Ariel with a black actor, playing the role of "houseboy" to Caliban's "uneducated field Negro."[18] In the same year, in Washington, D.C., both roles were played by black actors, with Ariel the lighter-skinned "Uncle Tom."[19] These theatrical interpretations cohabit with, and in many cases derive from, literary treatments—by Octave Mannoni, Frantz Fanon, Aimé Césaire, and others—that identify Caliban and/or Ariel with the slavery of the African diaspora.[20] But the first such representation of Caliban occurred not in twentieth-century postcolonial interpretations or adaptations, but in a colorphobic 1863 cartoon in the London magazine *Punch* (Illus. 7). Caliban embodies almost every prejudice, early modern and modern, about blacks, about slaves, and about black slaves: lazy, gullible, superstitious, drunk, ungrateful, treacherous, a monstrous would-be rapist, "a born devil, on whose nature nurture can never stick" (4.1.188–89). Because the only extant early text of *The Tempest* does not anywhere explicitly call Caliban "black," Bardolaters always can deny that Shakespeare penned English's literature's first colorphobic portrait of an African slave; but an African Caliban remains plausible, on- and offstage.

But the fact that *The Tempest* can so easily be performed and understood in modern generic terms is more important, historically, than whether Caliban was actually originally performed in blackface. If he was, then English colorphobia had been linked to the enslavement of Africans as early as 1611. Middleton's *The Triumphs of Truth* demonstrates that some Londoners lacked such prejudices; Middleton elsewhere deliberately contradicted Shakespeare, and his 1613 portrait of a black king might have been a conscious rejection of *The Tempest*'s colorphobic portrait of a black slave. But even if Caliban was not portrayed as a recognizably black African in 1611, Shakespeare's play demonstrates that all the later generic stereotypes already existed, already had been tied together in a tidy package. In 1611, though, that package of prejudices had not yet been clearly color-coded. It prejudged something other than pigment.

After all, Caliban is not the only character called Prospero's "slave." So is Ariel (1.2.270), and nothing in the text suggests that Ariel is black. Prospero enslaves Ferdinand too: Ferdinand calls himself a "slave" (3.1.66) and endures "bondage" (3.1.90) and "wooden slavery" (3.1.62), fetching wood, as Caliban earlier was ordered to do. Ferdinand is Alonso's son and clearly European, not African. In *The Tempest,* as in his other plays, Shakespeare did not limit slavery to people with dark complexions. However, he did portray the certainly African and probably dark slave much more negatively than his paler European counterparts. Caliban is the bad "abhorred slave" (1.2.354), contrasted with the good "industrious servant, Ariel" (4.1.33); both are contrasted with the temporarily enslaved Prince Ferdinand, whose brief bondage is a test, "nobly undergone," and whose love for his mistress makes his "labours pleasures" (3.1.3–7). In the end, Prince Ferdinand is released to marry a duke's daughter, and Prospero manumits his delicate Ariel. But Caliban remains a mere "thing," of which Prospero continues

SCENE FROM THE AMERICAN "TEMPEST."

CALIBAN (SAMBO). "*YOU* BEAT HIM 'NOUGH, MASSA! BERRY LITTLE TIME, I 'LL *BEAT HIM TOO.*"—SHAKSPEARE. (*Nigger Translation.*)

Illustration 7. A black "Sambo" offers a "Nigger translation" of one of Caliban's speeches in this pro-Confederacy political cartoon from *Punch* (January 24, 1863).

to claim ownership ("I acknowledge mine"); he is last seen obeying his master's orders (5.1.278–301). Modern productions that cast Ariel or Ferdinand as black simultaneously reinforce the association of blacks with slavery and obscure the colorphobic characterization of Caliban (giving the impression that Shakespeare was magisterially even-handed).

"What does the exclusive and aggressively eager focus on racism and colonialism in *The Tempest,*" white American literary critic Sharon O'Dair asks, "allow mostly white, upper-middle-class American literary critics to avoid both in the play and, more importantly, in their own lives?"[21] The critical focus on Caliban's colonized "racial" identity has distracted attention from two facts: most of the slaves in *The Tempest* are not black, and most of the rebellious working people in *The Tempest* are not black. One of Shakespeare's acknowledged sources for the play was an account of Englishmen shipwrecked in Bermuda in 1609–10; there, "five distinct conspiracies"—mostly by commoners and sailors, but including on different occasions a dissident minister and a rebellious gentleman—defied the authority of the colonial governor and other stranded gentlemen/masters.[22] In Shakespeare's play, three servants plot to "knock a nail into" Prospero's head, "or with a log Batter his skull, or paunch him with a stake, Or cut his weasand" with a knife (3.2.62, 90–92). Two of the three conspirators, the Neapolitan Trinculo and Stephano, are undoubtedly of European working-class stock. When white British literary critic Terence Hawkes claims that "the roots of the Prospero-Caliban relationship extend beyond that of Planter and Slave to find their true nourishment in the ancient home-grown European relationships of master and servant, landlord and tenant," he is wrong only in limiting the master-servant relationship to Prospero and Caliban.

The working-class European Trinculo and Stephano completely disappear from Hawkes's account of the planned "revolution" against Prospero.[23] Indeed, even to call it a revolution is to lend the event a romantic glamour that Shakespeare's text hardly warrants. As in Massinger's play, the underclass in Shakespeare's play initially is represented with some sympathy: "What cares these roarers for the name of king?" the Boatswain asks, and when the aristocrats insult him he sarcastically retorts, "Work you, then" (1.1.15–16, 41). But—unlike the Boatswain—Caliban, Trinculo, and Stephano are never shown doing a lick of labor. Some recent critics, trying to escape from the obsessive focus on Caliban and colonialism, have argued that the play is a "portrait of playhouse labor" or a representation of "coerced labor" or of the "labor" of "bound apprentice, paid servant and unpaid slave," but there is precious little labor performed by the three working-class rebels.[24] Like the mutinous English commoners on Bermuda, in the absence of proper authority Caliban, Trinculo, and Stephano immediately succumb to "sloth, riot, and vanity." The only "work" or "project" they even contemplate is the murder of Prospero (3.2.152, 4.1.175). The three lower-class comedians are initially united by a bottle, not a revolutionary agenda. As Felix Holt would say in George Eliot's novel of 1866, "while Caliban is Caliban, though you multiply him by a million, he'll worship every Trinculo that carries a bottle."[25] Alcohol—as abolitionist temperance activists like Frederick Douglass and William Wells Brown knew—was the enemy of resistance, not its ally. O'Dair romanticizes Caliban's desire to burn Prospero's books, claiming that "he wants the knowledge that enslaves human beings erased from the earth."[26] Caliban himself makes no such abolitionist affirmations. Historically, O'Dair may be right: literacy has flourished in, and perhaps helped to create, profoundly unequal societies. But Shakespeare's play does not endorse this anthropological critique of literacy. Instead, Caliban's projected book-burning, like the crowd's murder of Cinna the Poet in *Julius Caesar,* obscures the fact that book-burning was and is the favorite pastime of the state, not the proles.[27] In what Clotel calls "the Southern States of America," it was a crime to teach slaves to read; it was the defenders of slavery who burned abolitionist texts and murdered abolitionists. For Brown and Douglass and many others, literacy was the link to freedom.

Hawkes and O'Dair are not the only modern critics, or even the first, to romanticize Caliban. Before them, Leslie Fiedler had idealized the underclass conspirators by describing their goal as "not just the substitution of one master for another but the annihilation of all authority and all culture, a world eternally without slaves and clowns."[28] One wonders what play he was reading. In the very act of planning their takeover of the island, Caliban tells Stefano, "Thou shalt be lord of it, and I'll serve thee." Irritated by Trinculo, Caliban encourages Stefano to "bite him to death." After Stefano strikes Trinculo, Caliban says, "Beat him enough; after a little while I'll beat him too." Caliban wants his "valiant master" Stefano to "destroy" Trinculo as well as Prospero (3.2.34, 47, 58, 86–87, 149). There is no idealism here. Stefano plans to bed Miranda, just as Caliban had earlier tried to do; neither worries about her consent. Here as elsewhere, Shakespeare portrays underclass resistance as an act of indiscriminate, drunken destruction: book-burning, murder, rape, chaos.

As was often the case with slave rebellions, the plotted killing in *The Tempest* is thwarted by another slave, who reveals the conspiracy to the master (and is rewarded for his perfidy). The three "varlets" are first gratuitously humiliated: hearing Ariel's music, "like unbacked colts they pricked their ears . . . lifted up their noses As they smelt music," and are thereby led through briars and left dancing, up to their chins in a "foul lake" (4.1.170–84). Nat Turner, too, "fled to the swamps," Brown explains in *Clotel:* "The Dismal Swamps cover many thousands of acres of wild land, and a dense forest, with wild animals and insects," and in such places "runaway negroes usually seek a hiding-place," where "neither the thickness of the trees, nor the depth of the water could stop" a man like the rebellious African Picquilo (201–02). But Trinculo is no Picquilo. What for real runaway slaves was a desperate flight into the refuge afforded only by wilderness has become, in Shakespeare's play, ridiculous: a drunk aimlessly chasing music. The clown conspirators come on stage to enact their "bloody thoughts" in clothes torn and muddied: "I do smell all horse-piss," Trinculo informs us (4.1.199), and in live performances he actually may stink. Our proletariat heroes then are immediately distracted from their strategic political objective by the opportunity to do a little looting. Finally they are chased offstage by "a noise of hunters" and "divers spirits in shape of dogs and hounds, hunting them about."

Prospero's dogs were a proven mechanism for terrorizing slave populations (Illus. 8). Las Casas, the most famous critic of Spanish atrocities in the New World, had explained how the Spanish "taught their hounds, fierce dogs, to tear" the natives of the Caribbean islands "in pieces at the first view, and in the space that one might say a *Credo,* assailed and devoured an Indian as if it had been a swine. These dogs wrought great destructions and slaughters." Elsewhere he described the Spaniards "casting them to the dogs" or "giving them to the dogs."[29] *The Tempest* endorses what Las Casas condemned. More generally, Shakespeare's Machiavellian justification of Prospero's conquest contrasts with the emphasis on justice, found in earlier English descriptions of legitimate colonization.[30] By the 1640s Englishmen in Barbados were routinely using hunting hounds to track down runaway slaves.[31] William Wells Brown himself had been chased and discovered by dogs; in *Clotel,* he reprints newspaper advertisements for dogs to chase blacks. "These dogs will attack a negro at their master's bidding and cling to him as the bull-dog will cling to a beast" (96). Brown describes a "slave hunt" in Natchez, where two slaves had run away "into the swamps, with the hope that the dogs when put on their scent would be unable to follow them through the water." Blacks are the dogs' "favourite game," and as the "faithful animals" get closer "what was an irregular cry, now deepens into one ceaseless roar, as the relentless pack rolls on after its human prey." As one of the desperate blacks tries to climb a tree, "the catch-dog seizes him by the leg, and brings him to the ground" (96–99). Prospero and Ariel sic their hounds on three mud-spattered drunks, inciting each dog by name (Mountain, Silver, Fury, Tyrant). The goblin dogs chase the farcical fugitives offstage, their plot forgotten. But Shakespeare's audience is spared any discomfort that might be caused by seeing the physical consequences of such mauling. When we next see the "few odd lads," they are wearing "their stolen apparel" (5.1.258). Although "sore," they enter and exit on their own locomotion, festooned in filched fripperies, still drunk. And like the defeated slaves at the end of *The Bondman,* they are all forgiven. Happy endings all round, courtesy of a benevolent master class—instead of the exemplary massacres and showcase mutilation that followed real uprisings, or even real insubordination. In Bermuda, as Shakespeare knew, a man had been summarily executed for verbally insulting the shipwrecked governor.

Like Massinger's *The Bondman,* Shakespeare's *The Tempest* tells a story about rebellious European servants who are defeated, forgiven, and restored to a servitude they have come to appreciate and embrace. Sometimes Shakespeare, like Massinger, puts in his rebels' mouths sentiments that now sound revolutionary: "This island's mine" or "Freedom, high-day, freedom!" or "Thought is free" or "You taught me language, and my profit on't Is I know how to curse." But in both texts the rebels are, or become, violent clowns. In both, aristocratic masters restore the structure of class and comedy, disarming the threat posed to the social and aesthetic order by truculent underlings. To us, living in a pervasively color-coded society, it matters enormously whether Shakespeare intended Caliban to be performed in blackface. But it may not have mattered much to Shakespeare or his audiences. At the level of comedy and cruelty, Caliban does not differ

Illustration 8. This 1594 engraving shows the Spanish use of dogs to terrorize native populations. Courtesy of the Folger Shakespeare Library.

much from Trinculo or Stefano. One may be African, the others European, but all three are lumped together down in the bottom world where servants and sewage belong.

"Servants" and "Slaves"

Caliban and Ariel are both called "slave," but each is also called a "servant." By focusing on the word *slave* and on the color of Caliban's body, the "mostly white, upper-middle-class American literary critics" indicted by O'Dair can avoid talking about the words *servant* (as in "civil servant") and *service* (as in "service industry"), words that can refer to whites as easily as blacks or browns. But the fact that both words are applied to both characters in *The Tempest* makes it obvious that, for Shakespeare, the two words had not yet been separated by the color line.

What differentiates a character identified as a "slave" (like Shakespeare's Dromio in *The Comedy of Errors*) from one identified as a "servant" (like Shakespeare's Grumio in *The Taming of the Shrew*)? Theatrically, the roles are almost identical and likely to be played—then as now—by the same actors. Each specializes in the comic misconstruction of English; each gets physically abused, onstage, by his frustrated master, but the beatings are—as in *The Tempest*—comic; each speaks repeated asides, purveying the kind of confidential information available to servants who know all the intimate secrets of a household; each, like Ariel, remains faithful to the end. Because *The Taming of the Shrew* takes place in modern Christian Europe, Grumio is identified as a servant; because *The Comedy of Errors* takes place in the ancient pagan world, Dromio is identified as a slave. Most of the characters explicitly identified as slaves in early modern plays are, like Dromio, inhabitants of the ancient classical world, beginning with George Gascoigne's *Jocasta* (1566) and continuing through to Massinger's *The Bondman* and beyond. Ancient slavery was not color-coded, and certainly not Africanized; to signal that he was a slave, a Roman actor wore a red wig, implying if anything that he was eastern European.[32] To imagine those classical slaves as black would be to import our own assumptions not only onto the early modern world, but onto the classical world as well. For Plautus, slaves were an immediately recognizable social category, although one that did not overlap with twentieth-century racial assumptions; for Shakespeare, adapting Plautus in *The Comedy of Errors,* the two slaves named Dromio are indistinguishable from the English household servants of Elizabethan London.

Shakespeare does not recognize or represent a functional distinction between the two positions, but uses *slave* as if it were simply the pagan term for *servant.* Massinger and Fletcher's *A Very Woman* includes both "servants" and "slaves," but both perform similar functions onstage, and the "slaves" perform functions that in other plays are performed by servants. We see the slaves being purchased, but we do not see the servants signing contracts of employment, and unless they are differently clothed an audience cannot tell which is which. Although the categorical distinction between slaves and servants seems obvious and important to us, the words *servant* and *slave* overlapped in early modern theatrical practice and in early modern English. Both words are applied to both Grumio and Dromio, Ariel and Caliban. Indeed, the English *servant* derives from the Latin *servus* ("slave").

But the two words did differ in one crucial respect. *Slave* was widely used, from 1537 until at least the end of the eighteenth century, as a mere "term of contempt" (*OED n.*1.b). Of the noun's almost 900 occurrences in dramatic texts written between 1560 and 1642, most are loose insults, rather than strict descriptions of legal status. In *The Comedy of Errors,* when Antipholus of Ephesus addresses Dromio of Ephesus as "thou drunken slave" (4.1.96), he could be any English master berating any English servant; in *The Taming of the Shrew,* Petruccio includes Grumio among the servants he lambasts as "heedless jolt-heads and unmannered slaves" (4.1.152). Shakespeare uses the noun *slave* 173 times, but only 41 of those nouns could possibly be literal, and in many even of those 41 phrases insult dominates denotation ("Have you run from slaves that apes would beat?").

Usually such insults reflected the bigotries of the master class. The adjective most frequently coupled with *slave* was *base* (at least 79 times in plays of the period): slaves were by definition base (plebeian, illegitimate, immoral, servile), and anyone who could be stigmatized as "base" also could be labeled "slave." Less frequent but more specific compoundings of *slave* with *peasant* (11 times), *muddy* (6 times), and *mechanic* (5 times) targeted agricultural and industrial laborers. In Shakespeare slaves are base, peasant, mechanic, common, weak, oft-subdued, shrinking, straggling, one-trunk-inheriting, whoreson, ragged, wretched, vile, loathed, abhorred; unmannerly, unmannered, rude, rascally, rascal-bragging, false, deluding, lying, most perfidious, slander-coining, cogging, cozening, counterfeiting; drunken, tippling; poisonous, pernicious, murderous, transgressing, debauched, past-saving, damned, devilish, unhallowed, cursed, inhuman, cold-blooded, barbarian, black, thick-lipped, tawny, wall-eyed, hare-brained, mindless, heedless, trustless, worthless, soulless; sometimes silken-coated, neat, proud, and overweening, but always rogues, wretches, bastards, cowards, vassals, villains, traitors, liars, joltheads, fools, dogs, curs.[33]

By contrast, servants in Shakespeare are above all trusty (5 times) and true (3 times), but also honest, loyal, faithful, bound, household, industrious, gentle, high, noble, ancient, pleasant, most obedient, humble, poor, devoted, sworn, learned and well-beloved, affectionate, and good. Shakespeare never used any of these adjectives in connection with the word *slave.* In *As You Like It,* Orlando praises "good old" Adam as an exemplar of "The constant service of the antique world, When service sweat for duty, not for meed" (2.3.56–58). In fact, the servants of the antique world were usually slaves, who did not sweat for "meed" (reward) because they were not paid for their labor. But in Shakespeare, as in other English playwrights of his time, what determines whether someone was called *slave* or *servant* was not that person's legal status but the speaker's attitude toward and evaluation of that person. In *The Tragedy of King Lear,* the Duke of Cornwall's unnamed servant spontaneously interrupts the duke's torture of the Earl of Gloucester, respectfully addressing Cornwall as "my lord" and saying "I have served you ever since I was a child, But better service have I never done you Than now to bid you hold" (3.7.70–73); like "good old" Adam, this exemplary servant is a loyal retainer who has given a lifetime of service to a single master, and his "better service" consists in advising his master to restrain from illegal violence against another aristocrat. The duke is outraged that his own serf ("my villein") should dare contradict him, and his duchess Regan stabs the recalcitrant "peasant" in the back; Cornwall then orders the other servants to dispose of the dead body: "Throw this slave Upon the dunghill" (3.7.76, 78, 94–95). In both early texts of *King Lear,* speech prefixes and stage directions identify the man killed as a "servant," endorsing his own positive view of himself and his action. By contrast, the man is negatively described as a "slave" by someone the scene shows illegally blinding an old, helpless, sympathetic character. That Cornwall regards his servants as slaves reveals something about him, not about them.

Slave was the negative term for a social position that *servant* described positively. *Slave* was an insult; *servant* was a compliment. A slave was a servant you could not trust; a servant was a slave you could trust. A "slave . . . rebels" (*Timon of Athens* 4.3.393); by contrast, a "servant" will, under extraordinary provocation, without premeditation or conspiracy, on his own "stand up," spontaneously rising to his feet in protest (*Lear* 3.7.78). As Jerald Spotswood insists, the scene in *King Lear* "portrays not group rebellion, but individual action."[34] Even that individual action is not undertaken for his own sake or the sake of other servants. The heroic "servant" in *King Lear* stands up for another aristocrat, indeed dies in defense of an aristocrat (who is himself suffering for loyalty to his king). Although either *slave* or *servant* primarily evaluates the person to whom it refers, either also can evaluate the relationship attached to that person: tyrants enslave slaves, but servants voluntarily serve those who deserve service. By calling his servant a "slave," the Duke of Cornwall implicitly calls himself a "tyrant." To avoid such implications, what the languages of the ancient Bible called a "slave of God" got translated in English Bibles, from Wyclif to the 1880s, as "servant of God." The Christian English God is not a tyrant, and would not wish to be served by slaves. For exactly the same reason, in North American English the term *servant* would become the "usual designation for a slave" from 1643 to *Uncle Tom's Cabin.*[35] Euphemism did not improve the condition of the slave, but it did protect the conscience and reputation of the master from daily reminders of his own tyranny.

The slippage between *slave* and *servant* explains why Massinger and Shakespeare both wrote plays featuring a slave rebellion at a time when Englishmen owned few slaves. What *The Bondman* and *The Tempest* represent, what interested their audiences, was the rebellion of English *servants* against English masters. Because we have since come to associate *slave* with one human genre and one distinctive legal status, we are prone to misread such plays, where *slave* and *servant* are interchangeable terms, applied routinely to European domestic laborers. More profoundly, we are prone to misread the historical transition to color-coded slavery. The linguistic slippage from *servant* to *slave* expressed and encouraged a corresponding social ambiguity, which made possible the coming institutionalization of mass murder.

Murdering Clowns

No one gets murdered during *The Bondman* or *The Tempest.* Partly for that reason, perhaps, both plays were exceptionally popular in the years immediately after the Restoration.[36] As Shakespeare and Massinger bestowed gracious theatrical pardons on their comic rebels, so the Act of Oblivion legally blessed most of the rebels of the English Civil Wars. Massinger's and Shakespeare's satiric portrayals of underclass rebellion no doubt appealed to royalists in the early 1660s, who savored their own almost bloodless victory over the rebellious commoners who had deposed and executed Charles I. The 1660s and 1670s were also—as I will argue in subsequent chapters—the years when England decisively redefined itself as a white nation naturally entitled to enslave black people. But English masters had feared mass insurrection long before their nightmares came true in the 1640s. Shakespeare's and Massinger's uppity underlings were portrayed, in 1611 and 1623, no more satirically than the rebellious peasants in Sir Philip Sidney's Elizabethan romance, *The Countess of Pembroke's Arcadia,* written between 1577 and 1580, more than 60 years before "the great rebellion."

Sidney is less forgiving than Shakespeare or Massinger, and *Arcadia* is more useful than *The Bondman* or *The Tempest* in explaining the brutality of the seventeenth-century English slave system. Reading Sidney's vision of rebellious multitudes, we hear "the savage howlings the rascals made" before they are dignified with intelligible speech; the narrator then tells us that their "raging . . . tumult" began with a drunken conversation ("winy conference"), in which "public affairs were mingled with private grudge." This "scummy remnant" are, according to Sidney, "in the constitution of their minds little better than beasts," and when confronted by an armed opponent they "stand further off, crying and prating against him, but like bad curs rather barking than closing." When "the noble prince Musidorus" counterattacks, they immediately "(like so many swine when a hardy mastiff sets upon them)" disperse.

But neither the aristocratic author nor the aristocratic hero of *Arcadia* will let them go. One, "as he ran away, carrying his head as far before him as those manner of runnings are wont to do, with one blow [Musidorus] stroke [the other man's head] so clean off that, it falling betwixt the hands, and the body falling upon it, it made a show as though the fellow had had great haste to gather up his head again." Decapitation is funny, when the victim is a "clown." But one grotesque joke is not enough for Sidney and Musidorus. "Another, the speed he made to run for the best game bore him full butt against a tree, so that tumbling back with a bruised face and a dreadful expectation, Musidorus was straight upon him, and parting with his sword one of his legs from him, left him to make a roaring lamentation that his mortar-treading was marred for ever." The cartoon comedy of a fugitive running smack into a tree is compounded by the witty "parting" of a leg, as if the leg were simply departing; the pain and grief of the amputee are reduced to another bout of "roaring," as the ridiculously bruised face laments the loss of an occupation that Sidney and his elite readers would have considered contemptible. ("One might naturally regret *being* a mortar-treader," one can imagine Sir Philip saying, "but surely no reasonable creature could regret *ceasing* to be one.") Musidorus, meanwhile, is already "parting with his sword," simultaneously crippling one victim and moving on to his next.

Sidney's vicious romance was one of the most admired literary works of its time, but those who admired it were educated and relatively prosperous. Its title insisted on its aristocratic origin and intended audience, and it was available only in big expensive volumes, like the kinds of authoritative discourse discussed in chapter 4. Indeed, in a celebrated essay by the most admired Renaissance scholar of our time, Stephen Greenblatt compares *Arcadia* to the genre of public monuments, big expensive commemorations of military victories. Greenblatt notes that "a given genre . . . may have great difficulty accommodating a particular representational object," because genres themselves are always "social, contingent, and ideological." The problem of rebellious laborers was thus, for Sidney, primarily a problem of genre. How did one maintain decorum when describing an outbreak of indecorum? By categorizing early modern representations of rebellion in this way, Greenblatt situates them as competitors in a generic arena: confronted by this "great difficulty," how well did Sidney—or the artist Dürer, the poet Spenser, the playwright Shakespeare—overcome the technical obstacle? This early modern generic problem, in turn, is related to Greenblatt's own twentieth-century generic problem: how does a contemporary literary critic find ways to praise canonical Renaissance writers who celebrate such things as the state-sponsored murder of 100,000 German peasants in 1524–25? That is to say (although Greenblatt of course does not say this): how can modern white writers deplore the authorized violence of early modern European history while simultaneously whitewashing and reinstating the canonical masterpieces of white culture?

Greenblatt solves his own generic problem by concluding his essay with a celebration of one "sixteenth-century artist grappling with this problem" who provides "a solution that reconstitutes the social status of the hero and in so doing fundamentally alters the heroic genre." In other words, by reconfiguring the representation of violent repression as a problem of genre, Greenblatt the critic can celebrate an artist for providing "a solution" to an aesthetic problem. "The artist" who solves our problem is—no surprise—Shakespeare. Greenblatt thereby situates his own bravura critical performance within the genre of bardolatry, claiming that Shakespeare in one of his earliest plays provided a more satisfying solution to this fundamental problem than Dürer, Sidney, or Spenser were able to do in their own mature masterpieces. But Shakespeare did not simply write a good play; he did something of much more historical significance. Claiming that *The Second Part of King Henry the Sixth* "fundamentally alters the heroic genre," Greenblatt positions the play as a turning point in the history not only of drama, but of the interdisciplinary cultural genre of memorial celebration. Even more profoundly, Shakespeare's solution "reconstitutes the social status of the hero." As a result, in the play "status relations . . . are being transformed before our eyes into property relations," as "symbolic estate gives way to real estate" until "the aristocrat has been replaced by the man of property." In these memorable sentences, Greenblatt's repeated passive verbs do not identify the agent of these massive transformations and therefore do not distinguish between representing social change and causing it. In either case, Greenblatt rhetorically has associated Shakespeare with the social changes that shifted power from hereditary aristocrats to middle-class homeowners. Greenblatt's middle-class readers can be expected to approve. Hence, Shakespeare's negative depiction of rebellious laborers and positive depiction of those who kill them has been transformed: no longer the expression of an embarrassingly conservative politics, Shakespeare's play has become a profoundly innovative representation of profound social change.[37]

From the viewpoint of the masses being murdered, nothing had changed. In *The Second Part of King Henry the Sixth*—also called *The First Part of the Contention of the Two Famous Houses of York and Lancaster,* and in either title primarily concerned with the history not of England but of its ruling aristocracy—the man who kills the leader of the rebellion is not a peer of the realm, but he is, nevertheless, a landowning member of the gentry; the gentry constituted no more than 5 percent of the population, and not all of them owned land. (Middleton did not, although he was technically a born gentleman.) Moreover, Shakespeare made it clear that the killer's land is not simply owned but inherited: nobody is doing any social climbing here. Nor is there any shift from "status relations" to "property relations," because the killer has both. He has less of both than some other members of the ruling elite, but there is no sense that he possesses more of one than of the other. To find the sort of transformation Greenblatt claims to find in Shakespeare's play we have to travel, in fact, from the sixteenth to the nineteenth century. In 1841 a popular American play made Jack Cade, the leader of the rebels in Shakespeare's play, its titular, democratic hero.[38] In 1852—the year before the publication of *Clotel*—an American critic, comparing Shakespeare's treatment with the new American play, concluded that Shakespeare was "incapable of sympathizing with the cause and feelings of the mass of the lower classes." The contemporaries of William Wells Brown realized that "the derision and contumely which have been heaped [by Shakespeare] on Cade, would have been heaped on those who achieved the liberty of this country, had they been equally unsuccessful in their struggle."[39] Greenblatt's celebrated celebration of Shakespeare's play falsifies both social history and the history of literary genres. Its critical conservatism (in endorsing what has long been the orthodox canonization of Shakespeare) mirrors the political conservatism of the playwright (in endorsing the received view of dynastic history and political violence).

Just as the emotional reactions to slavery taken for granted by Fletcher in *A Very Woman* differ radically from the emotional reactions to similar stimuli taken for granted in Brown's *Clotel,* so Shakespeare's *Second Part of King Henry the Sixth* presupposes an affective community that differs radically from the affective community presupposed by Robert Taylor Conrad's *Jack Cade.* These two sets of differences are related, because attitudes toward slavery affect and reflect attitudes toward worker resistance. The scene in *Clotel* in which George compares rebellious slaves to the heroes of the American Revolution directly links the affective politics of Conrad's *Jack Cade* (another Anglo-Saxon rebel) to the issue of black slavery and black insurrection. To understand the evolution of the affective order that governs Victorian social life, we have to trace slow changes in responses to political resistance by common people. Genre does matter to such a history, but not in the way that Greenblatt assumes. Genre gives us a constant against which we can measure change. Artists are still competing with each other within an arena, and we can relish the virtuoso performance, but we also can see that the architecture of the arena itself has changed and therefore that the game has to be played differently. Part of the architecture of every arena of genre is the affective predisposition of the spectators it attracts.

If the competitors and the arena and the affective assumptions have all changed, what has remained constant? The spectators. Not literally, of course. Individuals die; generations die; hierarchies remain. *The Countess of Pembroke's Arcadia* belonged to a different genre from any of the works in the previous paragraph, not because it was prose or because it was fictional or because it was a romance but because it was aimed at and consumed by a different kind of spectator. Indeed, as its title declares and its known textual history confirms, it was written for a particular reader, the writer's sister, the Countess of Pembroke, and for a decade it circulated only in manuscripts passed among a small circle of elite readers connected to her and her brother. Even when it was abducted into print, it remained a luxury commodity; few could afford the price and time it took to buy and read so conspicuously frivolous a fiction. By contrast, *The Second Part of King Henry the Sixth*—like *Jack Cade* and *Clotel*—offered a much cheaper textual commodity to an undifferentiated mass of consumers, packaged with the promise of historical truth. Shakespeare's play differs from Sidney's romance not because Shakespeare's political sympathies differed from Sidney's, but because Sidney's arena was a quiet, expensively furnished room in a gentleman's country house, and Shakespeare—like William Wells Brown—was pitching his product in a big, noisy, urban, commoners' market. An Elizabethan playwright or a Victorian novelist could not know each of his potential customers as well as Sidney knew his sister; instead, he had to guess at and address the assumptions and affections of a burgeoning urban public. That is why the contrast between Shakespeare and Robert Taylor Conrad, or the contrast between Fletcher and Brown, indicates a real change in social perceptions, while the contrast between Shakespeare's play and Sidney's romance may reflect only a contrast of markets.

Theater as a genre uses visual, aural, and dialogic instruments that prose romances do not need or cannot duplicate. Consider the climax of Sidney's description of the encounter between the rebellious "clowns" and Prince Musidorus: "A third, finding his feet too slow as well as his hands too weak, suddenly turned back, beginning to open his lips for mercy, but before he had well entered a rudely compiled oration, Musidorus's blade was come between his jaws into his throat; and so the poor man rested there for ever with a very ill mouthful of an answer." The wit of this depends entirely on Sidney's absolute control of perspective. No Elizabethan playwright had such complete artistic control of his medium. An audience watching one man thrust a sword into another man's mouth will not necessarily see it the way Sidney makes us see it; a theater audience may not feel that any discernible wit in the swordplay erases its brutality. The "third" whatchamacallit—without proper names, Sidney's victims are simply a sequence from "the first" to "another" to "the third," seen successively from the perspective of an aristocrat and his sword—the third is a blazon of body parts: slow feet, weak hands, pleading lips, jaws, throat, mouth. In the theater he would be a real, whole person, not a rhetorical flourish. In the theater, moreover, he would be aurally as well as visually present; even an actor given no lines to speak will make noises. But Sidney's victim is never given the chance to speak; the "rudely compiled oration" he intended to deliver is metamorphosed into "a very ill mouthful," the grotesquely literal filling of his mouth with a sword, the only "answer" such "clowns" deserve.

If it had been left to men like Sidney, no one would ever have heard the oratory of men like Douglass and Brown. Not because they were "niggers," but because they were "clowns."[40] To understand the representation of rebellion and resistance, we have to attend not only to the history of classical literary genres (which is always a history of elite rules and elite performances) but to the history of individual words. Words, like genres, are "social, contingent, and ideological," but they do not all inevitably represent elite preferences. *Nigger* has been contested, appropriated, adopted, and adapted in a way that challenges its original function as a term of denigration—and the word *denigration* itself contains an educated Latinate prejudice against blackness.[41] Moreover, even when a word clearly represents elite preferences, there will almost always be one or more alternative words contesting that perspective. Just as Cornwall's description of a *servant* as a *slave* reveals his own tyrannous contempt, so Sidney's choice of the word *clown* betrays his. The people Sidney calls "clowns" could instead have been described, in his own time, as *farmers, peasants, servants, husbandmen, countrymen, yeomen,* or *freemen.* Even when we do not have literary works written by the people Sidney dismisses as clowns, we do, in those alternative words, have records of an alternative perception of their identity, records of resistant speech. Moreover, in another century the people Sidney calls "clowns" would have been called "poor whites." That difference, too, tells a story.

The word *clown,* from the beginning of its English use (in the 1560s), combined the senses "peasant" and "ignorant fool." Because schools were overwhelmingly concentrated in towns, country people were consistently less literate and less educated than their urban or aristocratic counterparts. For aristocrats and gentlemen reading *The Countess of Pembroke's Arcadia* on their country estates, clowns/peasants were dangerous because they were all around; for urban audiences watching *The Second Part of King Henry the Sixth,* clowns/peasants were dangerous because they were invading London and threatening its inhabitants; for whites running the sugar and tobacco plantations that developed in the English colonies in the seventeenth century, black slaves were doubly dangerous, because they were invaders who were all around. Boatloads of strangers who did not speak English disembarked so rapidly in the southernmost colonies that they soon outnumbered their white owners. Like Sidney's and Shakespeare's despised peasants, the overwhelming majority of black slaves in the Anglophone colonies would be agricultural laborers, deliberately and systematically deprived of any education. Blacks slaves thus were naturally subject to the same prejudices already deployed against impoverished English farmworkers. One could not take seriously the protests of people predefined as idiots.

The moment that they stepped off the boat, black slaves entered a social niche already defined by the derogatory word *clown.* They were ignorant country people, superstitious, speaking an unintelligible dialect, preoccupied with eating and drinking and fornicating, dumb as dirt. Their stupidity sometimes made them threatening, but more often it made them amusing. As early as the 1640s, black slaves in Barbados were being described as "jovial" folk, with "as merry a soul as any there is." Merry themselves, the blacks were also a source of merriment for their masters. Their "ignorance" made them ask funny questions, like the "neger" named "Sambo" who, seeing a compass for the first time, asked "whether it were alive." They were asked to perform physical tricks, engaging in "sport" for the "recreation" of white audiences.[42] Blacks rapidly became—and remain to this day—the occasionally dangerous clowns of the new white world.

Murdering Christians

The real rebels that worried men like Sir Philip Sidney and his father Sir Henry Sidney (Lord Deputy of Ireland) were not, in fact, uneducated. One of the rebels in Bermuda was a Puritan minister, a university-trained dissident who later caused trouble even on the *Mayflower.* Inspired by coherent alternative ideologies, such men persuaded laborers that they had a right, or even a duty, to rebel. Like the later abolitionist movement, the outbreaks of popular resistance in early modern England, Ireland, and northern Europe were informed and sustained by liberation theology, by a radical reading of Christianity itself. Most conservative apologists simply ignored the Christian credentials of the insurrectionary underclass. Massinger and Sidney situated their rebellions in the pagan classical world; Shakespeare made Caliban a worshipper of Setebos.

But sometimes even Christians could not ignore Christianity. Thomas Nashe was no more sympathetic to the rebellious Anabaptists of Munster than Sidney was to rebellious Arcadian (or Irish) peasants, but—unlike Sidney—Nashe could hardly pretend not to notice the rebels' ideological pretensions. It was their 70-year-old challenge to political and clerical authority that made the Anabaptists relevant to London readers in 1594, when Nashe wrote and published *The Unfortunate Traveller.* Between 1581 and 1602 London was disturbed by 35 recorded outbreaks of disorder, including one (in 1591) led by a self-declared prophet.[43]

Like Sidney's peasants, Nashe's Anabaptists are allegedly "ignorant" people, "without wit," who "howl" their "long babbling" prayers, "shouts and clamors." Like Sidney's peasants, they are made rhetorically ridiculous. Nashe describes them arming themselves for battle with "a round twilted tailor's cushion" for a shield, "a chamber pot" for a helmet, or "a couple of iron dripping pans" for body armor. Lacking aristocratic swords, they instead make weapons out of "dung-forks" (pitchforks for spreading manure). Like Sidney's peasants, the Anabaptists come to a bad end: their leader "died like a dog," and his followers "were all killed, and none escaped, no, not so much as one to tell the tale of the rainbow." But Nashe immediately follows this mocking report of annihilation with an exhortation that reveals the crucial distinction between this rebellion and that of Sidney's peasants: "Hear what it is to be Anabaptists, to be Puritans, to be villains."

Unlike Sidney's peasants, the Anabaptists cannot be called clowns, because they are not agricultural laborers. They are urban rebels; their occupations are "all base handicrafts." In this as in almost every other respect they resemble London's anti-episcopal radical Protestants, whose opponents called them Puritans. "Very devout asses they were," Nashe explains, the noun quickly deflating the adjective, "such as thought they knew as much of God's mind as richer men." That may seem to us a reasonable proposition, until Nashe gives his own interpretation of what it means. "Why, inspiration was their ordinary familiar, and buzzed in their ears like a bee in a box every hour, what news from heaven, hell, and the land of whipperginny." The very devout asses are inspired to rebel by a "familiar," a devil in the form of an attendant animal; the messages they receive from God become, once again, not words but the unmeaning noises made by animals, in this case the buzzing of a bee in the ear of an ass; they do not distinguish heaven and hell from the entirely imaginary land of whipperginny. "They would vaunt"—and the verb declares in advance that these claims are nothing but bragging—"They would vaunt there was not a pea's difference betwixt them and the Apostles: they were as poor as they, of as base trades as they"—true enough, so far, but for one crucial distinction—"and no more inspired than they, and with God there is no respect of persons." The difference between the Anabaptists and the Apostles is that the Apostles, although otherwise ordinary, were inspired by keeping company with Jesus. The egalitarian principle that "with God there is no respect of persons" is here transformed into a claim, attributed to the Anabaptists, that the presence or absence of Jesus is immaterial; to pay too much attention to Jesus would constitute "respect of persons." What appears to be an exceptionally devout community is transformed into a blasphemous "army of hypocrites."

The rebellious Anabaptists were not black and were not slaves. They were not even domestic or agricultural servants, but independent urban craftsmen. Nevertheless, in rebuking them Nashe cites the savior's words to his disciples: "*Verily, verily, the servant is not greater than his master.* Verily, verily, sinful men are not holier than holy Jesus, their maker. That holy Jesus again repeats this holy sentence, *Remember the words I said unto you, the servant is not holier nor greater than his master.* As if he should say, Remember them, imprint in your memory, your pride and singularity will make you forget them."[44] First, Nashe equates the craftsmen with servants; second, he rebukes them for failing to heed the truth of a statement backed not only by divine authority, but by the self-evident transparency of tautology. Servants are obviously not "greater" than their masters, because by definition masters have more power than servants. But power is then equated with efficacy: servants cannot claim to be better than their masters at doing anything, any more than an apprentice would know his craft better than the master craftsman who trains him. Competence is then equated with morality: servants cannot claim to be morally superior to their masters. Working people cannot rebuke their governors, because the weak cannot claim to be holier than the powerful, because for servants to be holier than their masters would be tantamount to ordinary people being holier than God. Which is impossible. By this chain of slippery signifiers, Nashe arrives at the conclusion that any criticism of a member of the master class by members of a lesser class constitutes evidence of the foolish and unholy "pride" and eccentricity ("singularity") of the subordinate/critic.

William Wells Brown described Nat Turner as "a preacher among the negroes, and distinguished for his eloquence" (201). Turner described himself as "a prophet" whose exceptional intelligence was "perfected by Divine inspiration." The white editor who published Turner's confession described him, instead, as "a complete fanatic."[45] Nashe did not call the Anabaptists fanatics, because in 1594 *fanatic* had not yet acquired its modern meaning (a person "prompted by excessive or mistaken enthusiasm, esp. in religious matters"). Only in the seventeenth century, and particularly after the explosive 1640s and 1650s, did the English begin to need a word to indicate and deplore *excessive commitment to Christianity.*[46] Irish rebellions always could be dismissed as the product of Catholic superstition, but it was harder to explain the rebellion of English Protestant workers against English Protestant rulers. The problem, in that case, could not be the religion itself, but something about the worker's relationship to the religion shared by master and servant. Christian devotion became excessive if it led common people to revolt against their rulers. Black slaves were not initially described as fanatics, because their English masters in Barbados and other plantation colonies did not allow them to become Christians. English property owners had learned, by then, that Christianity could be a dangerous weapon in the hands of a servant. But when black slaves did become Christians, conservative whites derided their subversive use of the English Bible by means of the same rhetoric Nashe had used about the Anabaptists and that royalists used about the "Great Rebellion" of the 1640s and 1650s. Nat Turner's editor believed that Turner had dared "to raise his manacled hands to heaven" because his mind had been warped by "endeavouring to grapple with things beyond its reach," becoming first "bewildered and confounded, and finally corrupted and led to the conception and perpetuation of the most atrocious and heart-rending deeds."[47] Like Nashe's "ignorant" urban artisans, black slaves naturally lacked the mental equipment needed to interpret the Bible properly.

Laborphobia

Nashe's satire was not aimed at exactly the same target as Sidney's, and Sidney's was not aimed at exactly the same target as Shakespeare's and Massinger's. But the target, in each case, was a rebellious group of manual laborers. That canonical prejudice against England's poorest and least powerful people can be found in other popular plays, other urban pamphlets, other elite fictions. Although there are differences between writers and differences between genres, the same foundational hostility shows up almost everywhere. It saturates the literature of the period. Beyond Elizabethan England, it belongs to a much more general social phenomenon, "a cultural fact" that the great sociologist Thorstein Veblen characterized as "the conventional aversion to labor."[48] In Genesis, labor is literally a curse, indeed part of the first curse; labor defines the human condition as fundamentally onerous. In early modern England, this aversion to labor and laborers—what I call "laborphobia"—was more pervasive and more virulent than colorphobia.

In the sixteenth and early seventeenth centuries, the educated elite had far more reason to fear clowns than blacks. As a group the servants and laborers, workers and workfolk, were most often identified as *the multitude,* or even—redundantly—*the many-headed multitude* (as in *Coriolanus* 2.3.17); their most significant characteristic was their sheer overwhelming numerical magnitude.[49] Africans were a few drops of ink in the ocean of sixteenth-century England; working people were the sea itself, potentially tempestuous, everywhere surrounding the tiny archipelagoes of educated and propertied privilege. Like the slaves of antebellum America, the workfolk of early modern England simultaneously sustained and threatened the prosperity of their masters. In both cases the threat produced the fear that produced a regime of brutal repression, and in both cases that state-sponsored terrorism was justified by characterizing the exploited population as a chaos of irremediably ignorant, immoral, misguided, violent animals. The negative stereotypes that would come to dominate colorphobic and racist descriptions of black slaves are already fully articulated in Sidney's, Nashe's, Shakespeare's, and Massinger's depictions of servants, peasants, and urban workmen. Shakespeare's references to *the multitude* spit contempt as consistently as the associations that he clusters around *slave:* the multitude is rude (twice), foul, buzzing, still-discordant, wavering, giddy, distracted, ragged, barbarous, many-headed, and (naturally, since anything born with more than one head is monstrous) a monster. In *Julius Caesar* as in *The Second Part of King Henry the Sixth,* a political uprising by "the multitude" of urban artisans is terrifying, arbitrary, misguided, and stupid, as simultaneously brutal and comic as Sidney's or Nashe's depictions of popular resistance.[50] Shakespeare advocates obedience as tirelessly as the slave owners in *Clotel.*[51]

Laborphobia expressed the fears and prejudices of those who *owned* the land against those who *worked on* the land. What distinguished English elites from "the inferior sort" was real estate. As in most predominately agricultural societies, in early modern England wealth, social position, and political power all depended on landownership. Hence, men who aspired to higher social status wanted, above all else, to acquire land—and particularly farmland, the kind of land that formed the large country estates of the aristocracy. A wealthy London craftsman, like the draper Quomodo in Middleton's *Michaelmas Term,* imagines land in terms that explicitly compare land-fantasy to sex-fantasy: "O, that sweet, neat, comely, proper, delicate parcel of land, like a fine gentlewoman i'th' waist, not so great as pretty, pretty; the trees in summer whistling, the silver waters by the banks harmoniously gliding" (2.3.91–94). When he finally acquires it ("The land's mine; that's sure enough"), he anticipates the immediate effect of this change in his social status: "Now shall I be divulged a landed man Throughout the livery: one points, another whispers, A third frets inwardly." Quomodo expects his transformation to be talked about, and in particular he expects, and wants, to be envied: "Especially his envy I shall have That would be fain, yet cannot be, a knave, Like an old lecher, girt in a furred gown, Whose mind stands stiff, but his performance down" (3.4.2–11). Again, the desire for land mimics sexual desire, which Middleton characterized as primarily a form of envy, the desire to have what others have. But in the end Quomodo's fantasy fails. Because all the land in England is already owned by someone else, an unlanded man like Quomodo can get land only by taking it away from someone else; to acquire land you must therefore become, as Quomodo says, "a knave." He tries to get land by defrauding a country gentleman, but by play's end the gentleman has successfully recovered his estate (and cuckolded Quomodo).

It would have been much easier for Quomodo to acquire land by leaving overcrowded, overowned England and migrating to a place with plenty of unclaimed real estate, waiting to be worked. In 1604, when *Michaelmas Term* was written, England had no successful overseas colonies. By Middleton's death, in 1627, the new Irish plantation in Ulster was thriving, and the English had begun colonizing Virginia, Bermuda, Plymouth, St. Kitts, and Barbados, had moved into what would eventually be recognized as the separate colony of New Hampshire, had secured their first foothold on the Indian subcontinent; in 1614 sporadically, and in 1619 systematically, the Virginia colony began granting land to individuals, establishing the incentive that would eventually attract most immigrants. By occupying uninhabited islands or violently evicting indigenous tenants, the English made available to men like Quomodo hundreds of thousands of acres of "new found land."

To get that land, unpropertied laboring people in England were willing to sign bonds or indentures that committed them to work for a certain number of years in exchange for their transatlantic passage and initial maintenance. These documents combined elements of two kinds of labor contract common in early modern England. Most servants in England were unmarried young men who contracted with a master to do agricultural work for an extended period, usually a year; an apprentice was an urban servant, bound to several (usually seven) years of service to a master in exchange for training in a recognized trade.[52] Most servants in the new colonies were agricultural laborers bound for terms as long as an apprentice; like agricultural servants and urban apprentices, they were overwhelmingly male and young.

Especially in the first decades, when mortality rates were appallingly high, many of the men who landed in North America as servants did not survive long enough to finish their contracts; they worked and died as bound laborers. Just as the early modern theater did not effectively differentiate the slave Dromio from the servant Grumio, or the servants from the slaves in *A Very Woman,* so in the English colonies in the early seventeenth century English masters treated English servants in ways often indistinguishable from the treatment of black slaves. Modern historians have extensively documented that equivalence.[53] Many colonists went involuntarily; thousands of criminals, vagrants, and political prisoners were legally deported, and thousands of others were kidnapped and shipped out by organized criminal gangs. Whether or not they went voluntarily, laborers were in such high demand that their contracts, good for years of work, were bartered and sold as lucrative commodities in a sellers' market. Virginia dispatched its first cargo of tobacco to London in 1617; by 1619 English tobacco planters there were "buying and selling" English "men and boys"; in 1623 an English woman complained that her servitude to her English master "differeth not from her slavery with the Indians"; in 1625 an observer reported that "servants were sold here up and down like horses"; in 1633 masters were gambling at cards with their servants as stakes—just as they gamble with slaves as stakes in an episode of *Clotel,* the subject of one of the novel's four illustrations (92–93).[54] In 1639 a foreign observer described the English servants in Bermuda living "poorly and practically in a state of slavery."[55] In Barbados as in Virginia, for the first decades servants were the most valued form of property.[56] Economic historian Hilary Beckles has collected appalling proof that "Pioneer Barbadian planters quite freely bought, sold, gambled away, mortgaged, taxed as property, and alienated in wills their indentured servants."[57] Not surprisingly, English servants rebelled against such treatment. In Barbados an armed insurrection of servants in 1634 "had conspired to kill their masters and make themselves free," and by 1647 another insurrectionary conspiracy was organized by servants "whose spirits were not able to endure such slavery."[58]

In 1667 an English observer who had been in Barbados the year before reported that "poor men" who had been imported to labor there—"and a very great part Irish"—were "derided by the Negroes and branded with the epithet of white slaves."[59] Shakespeare and Massinger had not called the European slaves in their plays "white," Sidney had not called his rebellious peasants "white," Nashe had not called the rebellious Anabaptists "white." Europeans we would now call "white" were slaves before 1666 and were subjected to the prejudices of laborphobia before 1666, but the phrase reportedly spoken in Barbados in 1666 is the earliest use of *white slaves* I have found in English. That reported speech repeats the pattern I described in chapter 5: inhabitants of the British isles were first called *white* by darker people. In Barbados the black population, initially small, by 1673 outnumbered whites by three to two[60]; between 1660 and 1680 the black population doubled.[61] Many of the blacks in England's Caribbean colonies already had encountered other Europeans. Sugar plantations in Brazil, originally Portuguese but conquered by the Dutch in the 1630s, were the model for Barbados, which switched to sugar manufacture in the 1640s, using thousands of black slaves.[62] As observers in the 1640s and 1650s reported, many of those imported blacks were culturally Portuguese.[63] But by 1667 "many thousands" of the black slaves in Barbados spoke English.[64] Thus, the situation of the English in the Caribbean colonies in the 1660s and 1670s resembled in crucial respects the situation of Jobson on the river Gambia in 1621: a group of Englishmen surrounded by blacks who lumped all Europeans into a single linguistic category. In these circumstances, the *speech community* had become profoundly dialogic, the product of pervasive interaction between black and white speakers of English, even though the *text community* remained completely monologic, the social product and social instrument of white writers and readers.

One of those white writers was the Quaker leader George Fox, the first Englishman to put the generic word *white* on a title page. Describing his missionary visit to Barbados in 1671, Fox refers to "the *white people,* so called by the *Blacks.*"[65] Before 1671 Fox had not used generic *white;* he learned it from the blacks of Barbados.

What can these early white records of black speech teach us? Fox explicitly confirms what the 1667 report implies: that the so-called "whites" of Barbados were given that verbal identity by black speakers. The gift was not lovingly given. *Branded* was a loaded metaphor. From the beginning of European conquest of the Caribbean, the Spanish had used hot irons to mark their Indian captives as slaves, "branding with the king's mark all that they might."[66] On Barbados in the seventeenth century, blacks were, on arrival, literally branded with the name or mark of their owners. Blacks could not retaliate by branding their European masters. Nonetheless, by calling poor European laborers "white slaves," they seared the minds of their British listeners, leaving a permanent and painful mark. The phrase confirms much other evidence of the harsh treatment of British laborers in the early British colonies. But in the mouths of those black slaves in Barbados in 1667, as in the novel by a black ex-slave published in London in 1853, *white slaves* was an aggressive oxymoron. It "derided" the assumption that *whites should not be slaves* (even though, in practice, in both cases, some were). Between London in the 1620s and Barbados in the 1660s, the casual acceptance of the enslavement of Europeans—now called "whites"—had disappeared. In Barbados at least, by 1667 one of the assumptions that *Clotel* would set out to challenge was already in place.

CHAPTER 8

WHITE SUPREMACY

"SOME AMERICAN WRITERS," *CLOTEL* TELLS US, "have tried to make the world believe that the condition of the labouring classes of England is as bad as the slaves of the United States" (150). As early as 1705, Virginians had insisted that their black slaves were better treated than English laborers.[1] But in the 1820s, defenders of southern plantation slavery began claiming that it was more humane than the "wage slavery" or "white slavery" of the northern factory system; the only difference between North and South, these southern slaveholders told northern abolitionists, was that "your slaves are white."[2] In a fateful alignment, a conservative pro-slavery argument echoed the language (if not the intent) of a radical pro-labor argument. "The socialists say wages is slavery," one Virginian wrote in 1854. "It is a gross libel on slavery . . . wages is worse than slavery."[3] At least part of this claim is true: socialists were indeed saying that wage labor constituted a form of slavery. In 1843 John A. Collins, an advocate of the redistribution of land who was also a lecturer for the American Anti-Slavery Society, had briefly upstaged Frederick Douglass when he "quickly turned the audience's attention from the 3,000,000 of his countrymen held in slavery to the 800,000,000 people worldwide whom he described as living with the evils deriving from property."[4]

But such comparisons were not limited to "American writers." The "peculiar institution" of color-coded chattel slavery focused attention on one region of one country; wage slavery, by contrast, was international. In 1824 William Cobbett had described conditions in an English factory as a "slavery" worse than anything that "negroes were ever subjected to." According to Cobbett, "The blacks, when carried to [slave plantations in] the West Indies, are put into a paradise compared with the situation of these poor white creatures in Lancashire, and other factories of the North."[5] In 1847 Friedrich Engels had described *The Condition of the Working Class in England* as "the slavery in which the bourgeoisie holds the proletariat chained."[6] In February 1848 the first edition of *The Manifesto of the Communist*

Party had been printed in London, describing "the modern working class" as "a class of labourers" who "must sell themselves piecemeal" as mere "commodities"; these "masses of labourers . . . are slaves of the bourgeois class, and of the bourgeois State" who are "hourly enslaved by the machine, by the overseer, and, above all, by the individual bourgeois manufacturer himself."[7] Karl Marx began his exile in London in the same year as Brown, 1849, and he might well have been one of the "young men with moustaches" whom Brown saw in the reading room of the British Museum: "each pursues in silence his own researches. The racing of pens over sheets of paper," Brown wrote, his pen racing over his own sheet of paper, "was all that disturbed the stillness of the occasion."

Whether or not Brown saw Marx, he apparently never met him. He did, however, meet Charles Dickens.[8] Dickens was an abolitionist, as he had made clear during his American tour of 1842, and in *Martin Chuzzlewit* he had travestied Americans like Thomas Jefferson—"(oh noble patriot, with many followers!)"—who "dreamed of freedom in a slave's embrace, and waking sold her offspring and his own in public markets."[9] More generally, Dickens had famously made reformist social satire (of child exploitation, parliamentary peculation, land speculation, legal obfuscation) the foundation of his fiction. As popular satirist, sentimentalist, and sensationalist, Dickens—more than any other novelist—inspired the form and ambition of both *Uncle Tom's Cabin* and *Clotel.* After both those novels, Dickens published the century's most famous fictional critique of English industrial capitalism. In *Hard Times* (1854), as in the works of Cobbett and Engels and Marx, the "down-trodden operatives of Coketown!" are called "the slaves of an iron-handed and a grinding despotism!" However, it is not the narrator Dickens who calls them slaves, but the character Slackbridge, union orator and labor agitator, a man with a "corrugated forehead" and "features crushed into an habitually sour expression." Dickens attributes the language of wage slavery, the equation of English industrial workers with black plantation chattels, to the manifestly manipulative mouthpiece of the United Aggregate Tribunal. The attribution discredits the equation. In distinguishing slavery from labor, Dickens also distinguished laborers from labor leaders, simultaneously encouraging sympathy for workers and suspicion of unions. "A plague on both your classes!" middle-class Dickens seems to say, balancing the despicable capitalist Gradgrind against the despicable agitator Slackbridge.

Brown could hardly adopt this Dickensian stance. Like Slackbridge, Brown was orator, agitator, fund-raiser, and organizer; he had dedicated his life to fighting a class of powerful property owners; when he stood on a stage and addressed a crowd of earnest faces, he spoke for oppressed laborers. Brown could not satirize the "oratorical arm" of Slackbridge, or lament the puzzling spectacle of a "crowd of earnest faces" engaged "in the act of submissively resigning itself to the dreariness of some complacent person" who addresses them, "above the mass in very little but the stage on which he stood."[10] Nor could he so easily dismiss the equation of laborers and slaves by attributing it, as Dickens did, to self-interested propagandists. Yes, the equation had been used by Southern slaveholders, but in England in 1840 the leading white abolitionist William Lloyd Garrison had been handed a leaflet asking "Have We No White Slaves?"[11] That "We" registered a communal—at least British, arguably global—protest. At the same time, that "White" set the plight of British workers against the plight of America's unnamed but implicit "Black Slaves." Because American chattel slavery was color-coded, prioritizing the abolition of chattel slavery inevitably also prioritized the liberation of blacks. That made sense to black abolitionists, but how could it be sold to their white audiences?

Early on in his first public address on British soil, Brown had acknowledged that "it was common in Europe"—not America, not the South, but in Europe, the land of freedom to which he and other fugitive slaves had fled—"to ask, 'Were not the slaves in America better off in their supply of food and clothing than the poorer classes in Europe?" Brown replied that he "had not seen a poor man, woman, or child since he landed upon the British soil who was worse off than the slaves in the United States." Just off the boat, fêted at the World Peace Congress in Paris, Brown had a limited acquaintance with Britain's working poor; when he claimed that he "would rather be a beggar in England than the best conditioned slave in America," he might be accused of pandering to English complacency. Because Britain had abolished slavery in its Caribbean colonies in 1833, the British middle classes could condemn American slavery much more comfortably than they could condemn the exploitation of their own poor. But Brown knew what it was like to be a poor working man in America.

> I have felt the chains upon my own limbs, and I have never seen a single moment since I escaped from slavery in Missouri that I would exchange for the best portions of slavery which I have left behind. And yet, since I made my escape from slavery, I have had to struggle for existence as hard as the poorest man in England, having come out from under the institution of slavery destitute of education or friends, in the coldest winter season, without a penny in my pocket or any friend to appeal to. And yet I had rather grope my way along, and try to get my living under the most disadvantageous circumstances than serve a single moment under the institution that I have left behind me.

Brown did not disparage the poorer classes or their leaders. Instead, he insisted on a real difference between the condition of slaves and the condition of other impoverished workers. That difference was not simply material. He did not "stop to inquire whether" American slaves "were or were not better off as far as food and clothing were concerned." Instead, he asked, "What was food and clothing to a man as long as he knew that he was a chattel slave—the property of another person?" Even if "the slaves in America did get enough to eat and wear—grant it all—what compensation was that for being robbed of every right as men?"[12]

In the dispute between crusaders for the abolition of slavery and crusaders for labor rights, the claims of class competed with the claims of race. That conflict is still with us, in theory and in practice. It depends on an equation of *white* with "superior class" that was already explicit in 1780, when the black Londoner Ignatius Sancho referred (sarcastically) to "the well-known dignity of my Lords the Whites." From the plebeian perspective of Sancho and his "sable brethren," all Whites were aristocrats, and expected to be treated with the appropriate deference.[13] But William Wells Brown tried to circumvent that equation. When he wrote of "the labouring classes" or spoke of "the poorer classes," he acknowledged the existence of class as an operative social category; when he spoke or wrote of his own "race" or of the "Anglo-Saxon race," he acknowledged the existence of race as an operative social category. But when dismissing the metaphorical equation of chattel slavery with wage labor—in this speech, or in *Clotel*—he did not speak of race at all and avoided describing American slaves as "Negroes" or "black" or "colored." To do so would have set the oppression of a black minority against the oppression of a white majority—a contest for sympathy that blacks could never win. In *Clotel,* Brown contrasted "the oppression of English operatives" (not of *white* factory workers, but of *English* ones) with that of "American slaves" (not *black* slaves, but *American* ones), a contrast of nations rather than colors. "The English labourer may be oppressed, he may be cheated, defrauded, swindled, and even starved," Brown admitted, "but it is not slavery under which he groans. He cannot be sold; *in point of law* he is equal to the prime minister" (150, italics added). Slavery was, for Brown, not a metaphor, but a specifically and explicitly *legal* category.

Brown made these observations in the course of describing Clotel's situation after she is sold to a new master in Vicksburg. She is "ordered to cut off her long hair," but this and other "degradation and harsh treatment" do not affect her so deeply as "the grief she underwent at being separated from her dear child," who had been "taken from her without scarcely a moment's warning" (150–51). Brown responded to the comparison between wage slavery and chattel slavery by emphasizing the humanity of American slaves, not their race. "What was the utmost amount of food and clothing to a man when he knew that he might be placed upon an auction-stand, sold to the highest bidder, and torn from his wife and children and everything that was dear to him?"[14] *A man*—not "a Negro."

But *Clotel* emphasized this shared humanity even more assertively. These reflections on "a society which is divided into two classes, masters and slaves" (150) are prompted by the situation of a slave who is, as we are constantly reminded, "white." The complexion of Clotel and of the novel's other "white" slaves is Brown's answer to the rift between abolitionists and socialists. By neutralizing the issue of color, he could emphasize differences in the scale of brutality, degradation, and suffering. Brown defined America as a society "divided into two classes," not "into two races."

English Slavery

Brown's story of "white slaves" was not meant to taunt or mock whites, but to convince them to unite with blacks against the institution of chattel slavery. Consequently, Brown's insistence on the whiteness of these slaves may seem radically different, in tone, from blacks' use of the phrase *white slaves* to "deride" European labourers in Barbados in 1666. But that negative interpretation of the phrase's use in 1666 comes not from the black speakers themselves, but from a visiting English witness. The black slaves in Barbados could have been urging their white coworkers to see that the actual daily slavery that united field hands on tropical sugar plantations mattered more than the color that allegedly divided them. Like Brown, blacks in Barbados in 1666 may have been trying to form alliances with the white "labouring classes"—and particularly the Irish. In 1655 the Governor and Council in Barbados had ordered the capture, and if necessary the destruction, of "several Irish servants and Negroes out in Rebellion."[15] In *The Tempest,* an enslaved African had joined with two European servants in a plot to murder the island's European master. Most early black slave rebellions in Barbados and other British colonies were joined, or led, by oppressed whites; individual white and black laborers collaborated to flee or kill their masters; white and black laborers ignored prohibitions on sexual relationships between them.[16] Moreover, some linguists argue that the distinguishing features of African American Vernacular English (AAVE) owe less to African languages than to the dialect spoken by the seventeenth-century English working classes.[17]

Nevertheless, from the perspective of at least one educated Englishman reporting in 1667 on what he had heard in 1666, *white slaves* was an insult. *Slave* was well established as an insult; yoking it to the adjective *white* intensified its impact, especially when spoken by someone black. That compounded sense of defamation derives from the perception of paradox, which in turn depends on the assumption that one of the meanings of *slave* was "black."

Historians continue to disagree about whether that was true from the very beginning of the English colonial enterprize. But a Maryland law of 1639 granted the full rights of Englishmen to "all Christian inhabitants (slaves excepted)."[18] It did not specify who the slaves were, but it did recognize their existence, and its discounting of their Christianity legalizes the religious hypocrisy that would be satirized by *Clotel,* which insists that Christ's "whole life was a living testimony against slavery and all that it inculcates" (130). In Virginia as early as 1641 a black had to "purchase" the freedom of his own infant child, and in 1648 it was possible for an English colonist to sell a "negro woman and all her increase (which for future time shall be born of her body)."[19] A series of acts passed by Chesapeake legislatures in the 1660s institutionalized such color-coded enslavement. In 1664 in Maryland (and six years later in Virginia), imported Negroes were declared slaves for life; that principle leads Clotel to decide, in the end, that only "death is freedom" (204). The Maryland statute reiterated "Negroes and other slaves"—the four occurrences of *other* in this repeated phrase grammatically equating "all Negroes" with "slaves."[20] In 1671 a Virginia statute dealt with the problems of appraising inherited or bequeathed "Negroes" in the same way as "sheep, horses, cattle"; the word *slaves* was not used, but the text of the legislation presumes that the word *Negroes* meant "slaves."[21] That is the linguistic, legal, and social equation that Brown's whole novel challenges.

By the end of the 1660s, and probably sooner, *Negro* and *slave* had become synonyms in at least three southern colonies: Maryland, Barbados, Virginia. The same equation may have been made even earlier, even farther south, on Providence Island, the Puritan colony in the southwestern Caribbean: historian Karen Kupperman believes that a 1638 reference to "cannibal Negroes" actually refers to a group of Pequots deported as slaves from New England, and that the Indians were called *Negroes* because they were slaves.[22] Since the 1570s Portuguese colonists in Brazil had been using the word *Negro* to describe Amerindian as well as African slaves.[23] Whether the English had adopted that definition by 1638 is less certain.[24] But early Providence Island shared with later Barbados and the Chesapeake a shift from white to black labor. Black slaves became the majority of the population on the two islands of the Providence colony in 1636 and 1638.[25] What fueled that shift to black labor was, in each of these colonies, capitalist calculation. Geographically, Providence Island was closer to existing slave trader routes, farther from England, and more vulnerable to Spanish attack than any of the other colonies; these factors simultaneously depressed immigration of English servants and made Africans affordable. As the Providence Island Company in London recorded in 1638, "Negroes" were "procured at cheap rates, more easily kept, and perpetually servants."[26] In Barbados servants outnumbered slaves into the 1650s, but between 1660 and 1670 the emigration of English servants to the island plummeted; as the incoming supply dropped 70 percent, prices for indentured servants more than doubled. By 1676 the Governor stated that a planter could "keep three blacks who work better and cheaper than one White man."[27] In Virginia, only as life expectancy rose did black slaves become a better buy than English servants; that economic turning point "was probably reached by 1660."[28]

According to historian Ira Berlin's acclaimed synthesis of recent research on American slavery, once *Negro* became synonmous with *slave,* "whiteness and blackness took on new meanings."[29] Although undeniably true, Berlin's phrase unfortunately treats *whiteness* and *blackness* as an inevitable symmetrical pair, and defies the alphabet by placing *white* before *black.* In fact, the change in the meaning of blackness demonstrably preceded—and arguably created—the change in the meaning of whiteness. *Negroes* first appeared in the statutes of an English colony in 1623, in Bermuda's "Act to restrain the insolencies of the Negroes"; the word *white* did not make its debut in Bermuda law until almost seven decades later—and I have not found it in any Bermuda document before 1679.[30] Likewise, in Virginia legislation there was a gap of more than half a century between the first use of *Negro* and the first use of *white.*[31] The English called themselves *English* before they called themselves *white,* and the evolution of the modern generic meaning of whiteness depends, in part, on the way *white man* eventually absorbed many of the existing meanings of *Englishman.*

English Liberty

Although an English servant might be "bought and sold like a damned slave," Englishmen were not born slaves, and they did not expect to die slaves. Like Ariel and Ferdinand in *The Tempest,* like Marullo/Pisander in *The Bondman* or Don John in *A Very Woman,* like all the other gentlemen and aristocrats disguised as slaves or servants in other early modern plays, an Englishman expected bondage to be an interlude, a temporary status, in no way altering his true nature, to which he would revert at the end of his play or the expiration of his contract. If some were "gentleman born," all were *free-born* (a compound recorded as early as 1340). Despite English laborphobia, by the early seventeenth century laborers and other servants had well-established legal rights, including most important the right to choose their masters at the expiration of a set term of employment, usually a year; that concept of "free labor" had been developing in England since the middle of the fourteenth century, when the rapid and severe depopulation caused by the Black Death gave the surviving laborers unparalleled negotiating power.[32] Because for centuries Englishmen had considered themselves free by birth, enslavement would constitute a violation of every Englishman's birthright.

Consequently, even educated English gentlemen could celebrate the violent rebellion of ordinary Englishmen against their *foreign* masters. After 14 years as a slave in Ottoman galleys, "John Fox, an Englishman"—as the title page proudly announced—"in the year of our Lord 1577" led a slave rebellion in Alexandria. Fox began by striking his keeper "so main a blow as therewithal his head clave asunder, so that he fell stark dead to the ground." The other slaves then ritualistically stabbed and dismembered the dead body, "cut off his head, and mangled him so that no man" would be able to recognize the corpse; next coming to the warders, they "dispatched these six quickly," and eventually succeeded in stealing a ship and escaping, against overwhelming odds. "Our God showed himself a God indeed" by delivering 266 Christians ("His Elect") from "so great a thraldom and bondage."[33] This "worthy enterprise" was registered for publication in London in 1579, included in Hakluyt's *Principal Navigations,* and retold by Anthony Munday in a separate edition of 1608.

All that happened before the English became significant slaveholders. The story of the "Miraculous Deliverance of William Okeley," by contrast, was published in 1675, and Okeley had been captured and enslaved in 1639 on his way to Providence Island—an English colony that had already by then enslaved the (non-English) majority of its inhabitants. The text never acknowledges that fact, instead dwelling indignantly on the conduct of buyers at the slave market in Algiers ("Their cruelty is great, but their covetousness exceeds their cruelty"). Okeley urged that "whoever has known Turkish slavery is obliged to become a more loyal subject, a more dutiful child, a more faithful servant." Rather than supplying a model for resistance by English servants, the rebellion of an English slave was intended to convince any English servant to "learn from our slavery to prize and improve his own liberty," lest God should "whip out of him that restive spirit of grumbling and disobedience."[34] These exhortations to grateful deference and warnings of the consequences of disobedience pop up in innumerable texts justifying to the powerless the power of the powerful, in all ages and all languages. But in the midst of these conventional prescriptions Okeley presupposes the normal "liberty" of Englishmen, including English servants. He urges them to "prize" it, but they could appreciate it only if they all already had it.

Neither John Fox nor William Okeley is called "A Fugitive Slave," the phrase used to identify William Wells Brown on the title page of *Clotel.* For Londoners in 1853, the noun *slave* described Brown's normal or natural or originary condition; the adjective *fugitive* modified but did not cancel that primary identity. By contrast, for early modern Londoners, John Foxe was not a slave but "an Englishman," and Okeley's title page promised his return "Safe to England." Englishmen were, by definition, not slaves. Hence, the reports that English servants in the English colonies were being treated "like slaves" were all complaints against what was perceived as unnatural exploitation. Hence, also, the "restive spirit" that fractured and transformed English government from the "Blessed

Revolution" of the 1620s to the "Glorious Revolution" of 1688 was consistently justified as a defense of existing or traditional English liberties against the "tyrannous" encroachments of an alien absolutism that threatened to make "slaves" of all Englishmen.

This political language of liberty, tyranny, and enslavement does not bear a direct or proportional relationship to English involvement in the African slave trade. It had always been a trope of European hostility to Islam, and was used by Protestants to attack the papacy decades before the first English trafficking in slaves; Dutch and English nationalists deployed it against Spain long before the English or Dutch had a single working plantation outside Europe. In England in particular liberty was linked to defense of the common law (as opposed to the Roman code), and tyranny was tied to the "Norman yoke" of foreign conquest.[35] None of this had anything to do with the purchase or sale of captured Africans. Although John Hawkins organized three notorious slave-trading voyages in the 1560s, they were atypical of English contact with Africa before 1640.[36] The third was an unmitigated disaster, and after 1569 English involvement in the African slave trade languished for more than half a century. Richard Jobson sailed up the Gambia River in 1620–21 as a representative of the Company of Adventurers of London trading to Guinea; that company, founded in 1618, thought it could make a profit in Africa from gold, not slaves. In the same text that invoked generic whiteness so often and so unselfconsciously, Jobson explained that, when an African showed him "certain young black women . . . which he told me were slaves, brought for me to buy, I made answer, We were a people, who did not deal in any such commodities, neither did we buy or sell one another, or any that had our own shapes."[37] In 1625 Virginia had only 23 blacks in a population of about 1,200 (less than 2 percent); in 1648 it still had only 300 blacks, in a sea of 15,000 English (exactly 2 percent).[38] In 1628 Barbados had a mere 50 slaves—including both Africans and Indians—out of a population of about 1,800 (less than 3 percent).[39] Before 1640 the English were probably responsible for only about 5,000 of the 676,000 Africans transported to European states or colonies: less than 1 percent of the total traffic.[40] England and its early colonies were "societies with slaves," not "slave societies," and the massive enslavement of Negroes by Anglos did not occur until the second half of the seventeenth century.

Consequently, "it would be difficult," historian David Eltis argues, "to attempt to link any of the political or religious upheavals of England in the 1640s and 1650s to a nascent slave system on one small island [Barbados] over 4,000 miles away, involving at most 30,000 people in 1650—less than half of whom were slaves." Slavery has been a feature of innumerable societies; the Anglo-Dutch "idea of full membership in society and, ultimately, freedom as independence from others deserves the title 'the peculiar institution' to a much greater degree than did slavery."[41]

That indigenous political tradition explains why two Englishmen, deported to indentured servitude in Barbados, could petition "the High Court of Parliament" in 1659, complaining about what they called "England's Slavery." On behalf of themselves and 70 other "freeborn people of this nation now in slavery in the Barbados," they complained of being treated as "goods and chattels," "bought and sold still from one planter to another, or attached as horses and beasts for the debts of their masters, being whipped at the whipping-posts . . . and sleeping in sties worse than hogs in England." This was, "to Englishmen," an "unparalleled condition," an exercise of "arbitrary power . . . made upon the free people of England," and "on behalf of themselves and all the free-born people of England" they asked Parliament to "curb the unlimited power" that had enslaved them.[42] In two days of parliamentary debate, it was said that the petition, printed and widely circulated, had "almost set the nation in a flame." The story had been "noised abroad, as if the Secretary of State could enslave, and had enslaved, the people of England, at his pleasure." Members spoke of it as "a matter that concerns the liberty of the free-born people of England," a violation of "the liberty and property of the people of England." One boasted, "We are the freest people in the world," and he pleaded "for the liberty of an Englishman"; another reminded the House of Commons that "our ancestors have ever been tender of the liberties of Englishmen." Such "arbitrary and tyrannical actings" violated the axiom "that no Englishman may be used contrary to the law."[43]

But neither the petitioners nor the speakers in Parliament ever used the phrase *white slavery* to describe this egregious example of English "men sold like bullocks and horses."[44] As late as 1659 the political classes of England—including men who had been "enslaved" in Barbados and others who were deeply invested in trade with Barbados—did not relate liberty to whiteness.

Jurisdiction

Freedom or slavery is a political condition, naturally linked to a political jurisdiction; even if it seemed scandalous for an Englishman to be subjected by other Englishmen to a condition tantamount to slavery, that very sense of scandal recognized the essentially jurisdictional relationship among English birth, English legal and political institutions, and English liberty. But no such intrinsic jurisdictional relationship connects liberty (a political condition) to pale complexions (an anatomical condition). To be insulted or appalled by the idea of "white slavery," in 1667 or in 1840, the English had to associate their peculiar political institutions with the color of their bodies. *White slavery* is a second-order oxymoron: *slavery* is incompatible with *whiteness* because *whiteness* has been equated with *Englishness,* and *Englishness* is incompatible with *slavery.* But if Englishness guarantees certain liberties, why did the English not simply continue to insist on their political Englishness, rather than adopting an identity constructed on their physical whiteness? After all, the fact that blacks called them white did not force the English to accept that designation. Whites do not normally call themselves *cracker, gringo, honky, pale-face, pig, spook, whitey,* or any of the other ethnic labels others have invented for us; why then was *white* adopted and internalized? Why, in particular, did *white* take on the political meanings of the word *English?*

As a purely jurisdictional identity, Englishness was vulnerable to jurisdictional ambiguity. Such ambiguities, rare in the sixteenth century, ballooned in the seventeenth. Between the accession of James I (in 1603) and the Act of Union (in 1707), England and Scotland were ruled by the same king but remained distinct kingdoms. In the century between those landmarks, England fully conquered and subjugated Ireland, but most of the king's Irish subjects were denied the rights of Englishmen. In 1655 the English took Jamaica from the Spanish. In 1664 the Dutch surrendered the colonies that the English would christen New York and Delaware. Conquered territories were subject to royal prerogative, not common law. "The laws of England do not extend to Virginia," one chief justice explained; "being a conquered country, their law is what the King pleases." Colonists in Maryland, Pennsylvania, and South Carolina were subject to the prerogative of proprietary lords to whom the king had given feudal powers. Within the imperial patchwork that developed from decades of separate ventures under individual charters, each colony had a different status, but all were effectively outside the normal application of English law. This ambiguous autonomy created the space in which slavery could be institutionalized, without ever being explicitly validated by English courts or parliaments.[45]

But Africans were not the only victims of the colonies' ad hoc legal status. Colonial autonomy created a private legal space in which the traditional rights of Englishmen were also uncomfortably vulnerable. The colonies all straddled a fundamental jurisdictional gap: putatively governed by England, on a day-to-day basis they were controlled by local elites. That jurisdictional gap was exposed and widened by the English Civil War, which for almost two decades left the authority of English law suspended ambiguously between rival claimants. Thousands of laborers perished in that gap. Rights guaranteed in England could be difficult to preserve or regain in the colonies—as indentured English servants discovered to their cost.

Further ambiguities were created by the mixing of European populations. New England averted this problem by systematically excluding non-English colonists.[46] Not coincidentally, the New England colonies were also the last to adopt *white,* in its modern sense, as a legal term. But all the colonies south of New England contained—and needed—representatives of other European nationalities (including Jews).[47] In New York and Delaware, much of the original polyglot community remained after the English conquest, as it did also in the land chartered as New Jersey. In 1654 a visitor to Barbados reported that the island was "inhabited with all sorts: with English, French, Dutch, Scots, Irish, Spaniards (they being Jews)."[48] Two decades later Sir Peter Colleton, President of the Council of Barbados, was more precise, counting "9,274 white men over 16 years of age, 3,600 boys, and 8,435 women and girls, of which one half may be English and the rest Scotch, Irish, French, Dutch, and Jews."[49] By 1673 only half the "whites" in Barbados were ("maybe") English. The legal status of most of these foreigners was disputable and disputed.[50]

But Jews, foreigners, and imported English laborers were nevertheless better off, legally, than imported African laborers. The English had first transported African slaves to Spanish colonies in the 1560s; the legal guarantees of English liberty did not apply in Africa or in Spanish America, which were both patently beyond the jurisdiction of English courts. No international law forbade slavery; most interpreters of "natural law" defended it; Portuguese and Spanish precedent legitimated it. English jurisdictional rules did not apply, and the rules of other jurisdictions supported enslavement of captives. Such reasoning, which justified the slave-trading of sixteenth-century English pirates, also supported the piracy of seventeenth-century English colonists: the ship that carried the first English settlers to Barbados captured, en route, an Iberian "prize," from which they took "ten Negroes," who were immediately classified as "slaves" on the island.[51] Since the Negroes had already been enslaved by other people from whom the English stole them, their enslavement by the English simply perpetuated their status at the time of English acquisition. Such reasoning even more comfortably justified the colonial purchase of African laborers from Dutch traders. In the colonies, the English were simply purchasing Dutch property. In recognizing Dutch property rights to their African cargoes, the English colonists accepted and cemented the mutual contractual obligations upon which international trade depended. In 1587 a Portuguese doctor in London learned that "the common laws" of England would not compel the Ethiopian he had purchased "to serve him during his life."[52] In 1614, when a Portuguese slave named Diogo set foot in England, "he immediately became free, because in that Reign nobody is a slave."[53] But in 1677 a London court ruled that Negroes were "usually bought and sold among merchants, as merchandise," and consequently an Englishman might reasonably regard them as "property."[54]

The "ten Negroes" enslaved in Barbados in 1627 were outnumbered by the "thirty-two Indians" who suffered the same fate the same year.[55] Unlike the Negroes, the Indians had not already been reduced, by someone else, to the status of property, but were free at the time of their first contact with the English settlers. Captain Henry Powell had brought them from Guiana, where he sailed to fetch supplies for the new colony; the Arawaks came voluntarily, and happily, in response to Powell's promises of fertile land in exchange for their labor. But once on the island, they were immediately classified as slaves.[56] When Powell returned to the island, in 1656 or 1657, he discovered that "some of them were yet living," but although he "left them here free people, . . . the former Government of this Island hath taken them perforce and made them slaves." Powell petitioned the government in England "to set these poor people free that had been kept thus long in bondage."[57] He made no such plea for the release of the Africans he had helped enslave. Powell felt personally responsible for the fate of the Indians, because his commitment to them had been broken. No such commitment had ever been made to the Africans.

Powell's Indians were enslaved because his promise to them was not written down. Moreover, Powell himself was exiled from the island for almost 30 years, as the consequence of a power struggle between rival groups of colonists; the Indians therefore lost the patron who had guaranteed them their liberty. Unlike English servants, captive Indians and Africans arrived in English colonies without paperwork specifying a term of service. In 1636—well before the "sugar revolution" and the massive importation of slaves—the Governor and Council of Barbados decreed "that Negroes and Indians, that came here to be sold, should serve for Life, unless a Contract was before made to the contrary."[58] It was not in the seller's or the buyer's economic interest to supply such a contract or specify such a term.[59] Other colonies did not spell out this logic as explicitly as Barbados did, but they all confronted the same legal and economic situation: no piece of paper bound the Indians' or Africans' master to end their bondage at a definite date. This absence of paperwork combined with the ambiguity or absence of jurisdiction to create (for Indian and African laborers) a legal vacuum where (for English laborers) there was an unequivocal legal deadline. As a result, an English colonial master would have had to go out of his way to impose on himself and enforce against himself a limit to the value of his African or Indian investment. Even if, at the time of purchase, a master intended to release his non-European laborer at a certain date, simple inertia was on the side of prolonging the slavery. The African or Indian laborer would continue to serve until his master chose to set him free. Many masters, in such circumstances, would choose never to do so.[60] Thus, widespread enslavement of imported laborers could become "the custom of a country" without any legal decision to enslave them. The very absence of written guidelines made their enslavement legally and psychologically possible.

The slave trade transported individuals born in Africa or the Americas to a jurisdiction that owed them no rights whatsoever. But the servant trade also transported individuals thousands of miles from their home jurisdictions. The analogous situational vulnerability of slaves and servants made it tempting for their masters/owners to treat them in analogous ways. In the seventeenth century, even English laborers who possessed and could read the appropriate paperwork often found it hard to secure in the New World the terms of employment and reward they had been guaranteed in Old England. African and Indian laborers had no such paperwork and—with no exceptions at first and few exceptions in the first decades of the seventeenth century—could not read English. How then could they invoke the paper rules that protected English laborers? English laborers could, and did, complain to their relatives back in England about their treatment in the colonies, appealing to those relatives to invoke English legal institutions on their behalf. Because African and Indian laborers in the English colonies could not appeal to such kinship networks, they were effectively "unkinned," and therefore stripped of any appeal beyond the immediate power of their masters.[61] De facto slavery is the default position for a displaced laborer transplanted from, and without recourse to, his native jurisdiction. Liberty generally, and the liberation of displaced laborers in particular, requires the creation and enforcement of special rules within a specified institutional jurisdiction.[62]

However, a pressing jurisdictional problem was introduced as soon as transported non-European slaves began to reproduce in their new environments. In *Calvin's Case* (1608), Sir Edward Coke had tied the rights and duties of English subjects to birth within any jurisdiction governed and protected by the king of England.[63] The key concepts here are "birth" and "jurisdiction." Coke's ruling was itself an attempt to solve (by invoking "birth") the problem of "jurisdiction" created by the accession in 1603 of James Stuart, who was King James VI of Scotland before he became King James I of England. James and his son Charles I ruled both kingdoms, but only by virtue of a physical coincidence: the king of Scotland and the king of England just happened to cohabit in the same human body. English Parliaments refused to ratify a legal union of England and Scotland, so they remained separate jurisdictions. Cromwell's military victories for the first time consolidated England, Ireland, Scotland, and all their territories into what was, effectively, a single political unit with a single head.[64] That single head was English. Nevertheless, by the early 1650s the problem of *English* whiteness—the subject of this book, so far—was becoming inseparable from the expanded problem of *British* whiteness. But "the rights of Englishmen" were only slowly extended to the Scots and Irish (many of whom did not speak English). Members of Parliament in 1659 were outraged specifically by the treatment of *Englishmen* as slaves. No such sympathy was extended to the much larger number of Scots and Irish opponents of Cromwell dispatched, involuntarily, to labor on plantations in Barbados. It is no accident that the men labeled "white slaves" in 1666 were Irish.[65]

The children of African slaves born in English colonies satisfied the conditions laid down by *Calvin's Case,* and therefore they should have become English subjects, automatically protected against enslavement. But Africans had even more trouble securing justice from English courts than the Scots and the Irish.[66] As early as 1643 it was widely known, even in London, that black children were enslaved at birth in the English-speaking world. The author of an anonymous commentary on Ephesians 6:5 noted, in passing, that "servants are either more slavish, or else more free and liberal: the first are such whose bodies are perpetually put under the power of the Master, *as Blackmores with us;* of which kind servants are made sometime forcibly, as in captivity: sometime voluntarily, as when one doth willingly make himself over; sometime naturally, *as the children of servants are born the slaves of their Masters*" (italics added).[67] The casual tone of this statement is as revealing as its content. By 1643 someone in London knew that, among "us" Englishmen, Africans were routinely enslaved for life and their children were born into perpetual slavery. After 1643 any English reader of this commentary (reprinted in 1645, 1647, and 1658) knew as much. By contrast, Coke's ruling in *Calvin's Case* was not separately printed until 1705.[68] Buried amid voluminous reports of miscellaneous cases, it was relatively unlikely to be read in the colonies, which throughout the seventeenth century suffered (or enjoyed) a shortage of lawyers.[69] Coke's interpretation of English law in respect to the children of resident aliens would have endangered the economic interest of slaveholders, who controlled the political and legal system in the colonies. Enforcement of Coke's ruling in colonial jurisdictions depended on people who would profit from not enforcing it.

In the seventeenth century, the English confronted two new problems created by the use of jurisdictional criteria for the division between slave and free. First, multiplying jurisdictions created gaps and ambiguities that made too many colonists subject to forms of servitude they regarded as a violation of their rights as free-born Englishmen. Second, the criteria of birth within English jurisdiction threatened to deprive too many Englishmen of what they regarded as their property rights in African and Amerindian livestock. The shift from Englishness to whiteness solved both problems. Whiteness abandoned the criteria of jurisdiction: in an increasingly mobile Atlantic world, exactly where a person was born mattered less and less. At the same time, whiteness preserved the criteria of birth: those born white were born free, and those born not-white were born not-free.

Linguistic Geography

That linguistic equation of the freedom line with the color line did not exist in 1659 when Parliament debated whether the suppliers of laborers to Barbados had illegally "enslaved, the people of England." But it did apparently exist in 1666, when blacks in Barbados applied the paradoxical phrase *white slaves* to European laborers. The difference between these two sets of speech-acts is not only chronological but geographical and hierarchical. The most powerful men in the London-Westminster conurbation in 1659 did not share the assumptions of the least powerful (ungendered) speakers in Barbados in 1666. Those distinctions are crucial to any understanding of the process by which the newly generic word *white* spread across the Anglophone world, accumulating new speakers and new senses as it went.

Forty years ago sociolinguist William Labov, discussing "the problem of explaining language change," distinguished between the "separate problems" of "the origin of linguistic variation" and "the spread and propagation of linguistic changes."[70] For intellectual historians, the moment of invention is the real turning point; for social historians, invention must be followed by diffusion ("the process by which an innovation is communicated through certain channels over time among the members of a social system").[71] By diffusion an innovation gradually accumulates critical social mass, culminating in the moment of saturation, when it has been distributed evenly throughout the society. Most innovations fail to reach saturation point; those that do usually take a surprisingly long time to do so. From the perspective of saturation, Jobson's routinely repeated use of the generic adjective *white* in the early 1620s matters much more than the presence of a couple of examples in Barlow's text from the late 1580s; likewise, the pervasive deployment of whiteness in the fantastically popular play *A Game at Chess* in 1624 matters much more than the single phrase *white people* in *The Triumphs of Truth* in 1613. Whenever he first heard it or used it, by 1621 or 1623 *white* had entered Jobson's active everyday vocabulary; by 1624 it had become part of Middleton's mental furniture. Even then we cannot say that those individuals are representative; indeed, we can demonstrate, statistically, that they were atypical.

A word's routine use in a certain sense by one person does not guarantee its routine use by a whole speech community; its routine use by one person necessarily precedes its use by others, who decide to reproduce it. This process of "lexical diffusion" is sometimes conceptualized as a wave, radiating outward from a single point of impact or creation, moving through geographical space over time. But that metaphor "implies too regular a movement to account for the reality" of language change.[72]

How quickly a new usage saturates a language community depends on the size, density, and structure of that community and on the mechanisms of linguistic transmission available to it. Language changes can spread rapidly in a compact, densely populated speech community, because of the number and rapidity of linguistic contacts between members of the community; by contrast, language changes spread slowly in a widely dispersed population, because of the relative infrequency of linguistic contacts between one set of speakers and another. In other words, language changes most rapidly in cities such as London.[73] Although the modern generic sense of *white* probably originated in various littoral contact zones, once sailors brought it back to the port city of London it began multiplying fairly rapidly. Stage 4 showed up first in a couple of phrases in Hakluyt's 1589 *Principal Voyages;* stage 5 appeared in 1606 in an account from the East Indies—then in a 1613 mayoral pageant written by a lifelong Londoner who seems never to have ventured farther than Oxford. After that inaugural "native" use of stage 5, the new sense of *white* continued to be reinforced by reports from the contact zones—most emphatically by Jobson's account of Gambia (1623) and by Purchas in the massive compilation called *Hakluytus Posthumus* (1625)—but it also showed up in other London texts by the Inns of Court poet Peyton (1620), the London cartographer Speed (1627), and the London playwrights Middleton (1624), Heywood (1631), and Brome (1637). None of these literary Londoners was translating from a foreign language; none had any personal experience of the contact zones. Beginning in 1613, generic *white* began to circulate, with increasing frequency, within London's concentrated speech community, as a local rather than merely an imported idiom.

Of course, the new idiom did not remain a peculiarity of London dialect, but became an active part of the language habits of English speakers worldwide. Originally imported to London from overseas, *white* must later have been exported to other English speech communities. To understand how that happened, we need to take account of changes in the number and distribution of speakers of English. Between 1520 and 1680 England's population doubled.[74] Moreover, beginning slowly in the 1560s but accelerating in the seventeenth century, it dispersed over a massively enlarged geographical area. Something like 100,000 people from England and Scotland moved to Ireland before 1641; perhaps 80,000 people left England for various overseas destinations during the single decade of the 1630s.[75] Outmigration peaked between 1630 and 1660, with estimates of 378,000 leaving England for American colonies, and of 495,000 for all destinations, in the seven decades after 1630.[76] Significant English-speaking communities developed as far away as India and the Spice Islands, on both sides of the North Atlantic, and in the western hemisphere from Newfoundland to Surinam.

Physical distance is the single most important obstacle to the diffusion of innovations.[77] Technology can offset the effects of such dispersion only to the degree that it rapidly and comprehensively disseminates linguistic data throughout the expanded population. All the London uses of *white* I have identified so far occur in printed texts; unlike speech or private letters, hundreds of copies were potentially transmittable anywhere that the English could transport themselves. But communication between England and its new colonies and trading posts, or between the scattered overseas communities, depended on shipborne haulage of persons, manuscripts, and printed matter—the latter so vanishing small, and so frivolous (by comparison with the supplies needed for survival and profit) that it is almost never mentioned. Within the colonies, settlement was primarily agricultural, population density low, literacy a luxury. The first printing press in the North American colonies did not begin operation until 1639, in Cambridge, Massachusetts; until 1689 its output was strictly controlled by the Massachusetts government, and chiefly ecclesiastical. In 1671 there were still no printing presses in Virginia, and when one appeared in 1683 it was promptly shut down by the government. None of the texts that I have considered so far, using *white* in a collective sense (stages 2 to 5), was reprinted in America. Throughout the seventeenth century, the colonies produced only a minuscule fraction of the volume of printed sheets generated in London.[78] Goods, people, texts, and ideas certainly circulated within the North Atlantic English speech community, but they did so much more slowly than they would in the dense and hurried swirl of seventeenth-century London, which within a few square miles packed a larger, more literate population than all the colonies combined. If London was the kind of community in which language changes spread most rapidly, thinly populated and widely dispersed agricultural communities like the early American colonies were the kind in which they spread most slowly.[79]

While poor communication between dispersed groups militated against the spread of London's new idiom to the colonies, other factors favored it. But those favorable factors were very unevenly distributed. Most of the new colonies created new contact zones that pale Englishmen cohabited with darker natives or imported slaves. Roanokes in 1584, Mohawks in western New England in the early 1630s, and Africans in Barbados in 1666 apparently told the European immigrants that they were "white" or "white-faced." Such contact was intense and regular—indeed, daily—on slave plantations with large numbers of imported Africans; it was much less frequent between Europeans and Amerindians. On St. Kitts, Nevis, and Barbados, Africans were a majority by the early 1670s, perhaps earlier.[80] Most of the colonists in the English Caribbean came from, or at the very least through, London; most of the merchants who invested in those islands were Londoners.[81] Moreover, the Leeward Islands were small, and they rapidly became overcrowded, creating interactive speech communities more similar to those in London than to the dispersed farming population of the Chesapeake. Movement within and between Atlantic colonies became increasingly common as the century wore on, but movement by sea was much easier and faster than overland transportation.[82] Finally, more commodities (and more valuable ones) were exported from the southern island colonies to England; at the same time, those island colonies needed more imported labor, and were closer to the supply of African slaves, and also—given the prevailing winds and currents—a shorter voyage away from the supply of British indentured servants.[83] For all these reasons, there was much more sea traffic to and from the southern islands, particularly Barbados. Barbados also boasted the largest English town anywhere in the Americas and had the best road system of any seventeenth-century English colony, permitting frequent interaction between rural plantations and urban ports.[84] As intense contact zones, densely populated English speech communities, and favored nodes in the Atlantic's most important transportation system, the populations of the Caribbean islands are those intrinsically most likely to have led the way in the colonial adoption of the new generic sense of *white.* They were also populations in which the social relationships between Englishmen and non-Europeans were most brutally hierarchical.

Morgan Godwyn complained that "These two words, *Negro* and *Slave,*" had by the 1670s in Barbados "by custom grown homogeneous and convertible; even as *Negro* and *Christian, Englishman* and *Heathen,* are by the like corrupt custom and partiality made *opposites.*" In contrast to these Negroes/slaves were "the *White Servants.*" That is, in Barbados, *servants* differed from *slaves* as *Negro* differed from *white* (which Godwyn explains was "the general name for *Europeans*").[85] Godwyn was an Anglican minister who had lived for a decade in Barbados (and in Virginia for several years before that), and his account of Barbadian vocabulary is supported by much anecdotal documentary evidence.[86] In 1675 *white* was being used casually in a gossipy letter written by an Irish householder in Barbados.[87] Between 1673 and 1688 *white* appeared repeatedly in texts written by three different governors of Barbados and in other official correspondence from the island.[88] Moreover, the first colonial example of *white* as a generic noun (stage 6) is recorded in the most densely populated parish of Barbados in 1669.[89] In 1670 the noun appeared in official letters written by three Barbadian planters who had moved to Jamaica, Antigua, and St. Lucia.[90] This pattern of distribution of early examples fits the thesis that linguistic change happens earliest in densely populated contact zones, like Barbados; in 1670 the movement of the idiom can be traced to the movement of individuals from Barbados to other nearby islands. Such migration also might be responsible for the first unambiguous use of the noun *whites* in legislation (in Montserrat in 1669). All this evidence suggests that the generic sense of *white* saturated the language in Barbados earlier than in any other English colony and that speakers in the English West Indies used the idiom before their counterparts in the continental colonies.

But this conclusion might rest on an unreliable selection of evidence. I cannot claim to have read every surviving seventeenth-century scrap of script from all England's Atlantic colonies. Even if I had done so, the survival of unique letters and manuscripts is much more haphazard than the survival of books; for instance, partly because of the climate, almost nothing remains from the early decades of the Leeward Island colonies. Barbados is a partial exception, but even for Barbados there is relatively little before 1650, especially by comparison with the textually prolific New Englanders or the bureaucratic papermills of the Virginia and East India companies. Is there any more reliable method for tracking when and where the concept of English generic whiteness reached saturation point among elites in the Anglophone Atlantic world?

Legal Language

In the absence of tape recorders or even newspapers, our best measure should be the emergence of the term *white* in legislation. Statutes are more likely than other texts to be copied and preserved, and although some early colonial statutes have perished, a great many survive. We possess seventeenth-century statutes for all the significant Anglophone colonies. Those statutes have been extensively discussed by scholars interested in the legal history of American slavery. I will not tell that story again. Instead, I want to track the related, but distinct, story of the legal history of the word and the concept *white.*

Laws are fictions with consequences, and like other fictional texts, statutes are written according to the generic conventions dominant in a particular time and place.[91] The English colonies fundamentally differed from the colonies of other European powers—Spain, Portugal, France—in relation to the legal problem of slavery. Continental law derived its procedures and authority from Roman law, an interrelated system of texts promulgated and rationalized by imperial decree; because Romans owned slaves, Roman law defined and regulated slavery, and the relevant provisions could be revived, amended, and applied to the Indian or African slaves of the new American colonies. By contrast, English jurisprudence was based on common law, an unsystematic collection of historical precedents drawn from parliamentary statutes and actual cases. Common law knew how to handle servants and contracts of employment. But because no body of accumulated English case law dealt with lifelong, inherited slavery, English colonists with slaves had—as Barbados legislators complained in 1661—"no track to guide us where to walk" in the legal jungle created by trafficking in human beings.[92]

Eventually those colonists would enact systematic slave codes, but initially they dealt with the problem piecemeal. They did not immediately recognize their need for new laws, because the English habit was to rely on judgments in individual cases. We might therefore expect *white* to emerge in colonial case law before it entered the statutory vocabulary. But most of what was said in courts was not written down, and in the surviving colonial case reports *white* either does not appear at all or postdates the word's appearance in statutes.[93] Because colonial judges in the middle decades of the seventeenth century had no historical precedents to guide their reasoning in cases involving slaves and their masters, colonial legislatures intervened to supply statute law to fill the vacuum. Individual legislative assemblies enacted specific (and usually short) statutes to deal with specific problems that had recently arisen. To solve those problems, they adapted precedents from English common and martial law, drawing on English statutes that regulated property, treason, apprenticeships, and vagabondage.[94] The resulting colonial legislation was, as historian Alan Watson observes, "more geared to local conditions than was the law in Spanish or Portuguese colonies."[95]

Colonial statutes also reflected local language use. They could not mimic the inherited language of Roman law (which did not recognize ethnic and color distinctions), or even the inherited language of the English common law (which did not recognize slavery).[96] Colonial statutes regulating slavery were, as English common law in general claimed to be, the expression of communal experiences, and because those experiences were new, they could be expressed only through a new or at least modified language. Unlike narratives or letters written by individuals, statutes embody a communally shared, authorized, and legitimated discourse, and for the new generic sense of *white* to appear in such a text, it must already be recognized as normal, at least among the European elites who drafted and enforced such laws. Moreover, such texts come out of speech acts comparable to the English parliamentary debate of 1659 (which did not use *white*). As such, they should enable us to trace the changing status of whiteness in comparable linguistic contexts in London and in all of its separate Atlantic colonies. At the same time, they should illuminate *the legalization of whiteness,* its transformation from an epidermal to a political category. The first appearance of generic *white* in a statute indicates that a sense of white identity has been both normalized and politicized in that particular speech community. In the Anglophone world as a whole, whiteness became a legal status in the half century between 1644 and 1691, when *white* entered the statute books of 13 separate English communities.

The first use of *white* in colonial legislation is usually attributed to the divided Rhode Island legislature of 1652. Although this was not in fact the first use, it does differ from all the others.

> Whereas, there is a common course practised among English men to buy negers, to that end they may have them for service or slaves forever; for the preventing of such practices among us, let it be ordered, that no black mankind or white being forced by covenant bond, or otherwise, to serve any man or his assigns longer than ten years. . . . And at the end or term of ten years to set them free, as the manner is with the English servants.[97]

Here as elsewhere, *white* literally and grammatically followed *black;* the word only arose at all when the legislature had to deal with the problem of black enslavement. Here as elsewhere, *slave* and *servant* easily overlapped ("for service or slaves"); the situation of black slaves was conceptualized in terms of indentured English servants; the intent of the legislation was to eliminate any distinction between the two categories. Here, too, *white* was subordinated and enfolded by an older, more familiar idiom ("English men . . . white . . . English servants").

But *white* in this 1652 text probably did not have the same meaning it took in all the other seventeenth-century legislation. What Winthrop Jordan called "this famous Rhode Island protest" has, I think, been misread, because interpreters have anachronistically imposed on it the division between "black mankind or white" that prevailed in subsequent centuries.[98] Since the grammar of the law requires "white" mankind to be treated in the same way as "the English servants," *white* is here not being equated with, but in some way distinguished from, *English.* The adjective *white* was still being applied, in the seventeenth century, to non-European peoples (stage 3); native North Americans were not, at first, color-coded differently from Europeans.[99] (The word *redskin* is first recorded in 1699.[100]) By contrast, at least nine early colonists reported that North American Indians were "fair" (1634) or "white" (1600, 1612, 1637, 1642, 1643, 1666).[101] The 1643 witness was Roger Williams, founder of the Rhode Island colony, famous for his respect for Indians; Williams believed that "Nature knows no difference between Europeans and Americans in blood, birth, bodies, etc."[102] There was no need for the Rhode Island legislature to proclaim the enslavement of Englishmen illegal; under English law, it already was. There was no history of enslaving other European nationals in New England. But the enslavement of Indians—men, women, and children, hence the totality of "mankind"—had become a general practice in the New England colonies after the Pequot War of 1636–37.[103] In 1644 the commissioners of the other New England colonies had decided on a policy of raiding Indian settlements and seizing their inhabitants "either to serve or to be shipped out and exchanged for Negroes."[104] In these circumstances—the kind of specific local conditions that stimulated the creation of colonial statutes—*white* was probably intended to protect Indians, the non-black people most vulnerable to enslavement.[105] Certainly we cannot presuppose that "black mankind or white" bifurcates the human universe along exactly the same dividing line that prevailed in the nineteenth and twentieth centuries.[106] At the very least, *white* is ambiguous here, as it is not in other seventeenth-century legal texts. The Rhode Island statute does not have the same clarity (about which people it specifies) or the same intent (toward slavery) as any of the century's other legislative uses of *white.*

Before I examine the texts that inaugurate the legalization of whiteness in other Anglophone speech communities, it is worth surveying the overall pattern (setting aside the ambiguous Rhode Island statute, which does not use *white* in the modern racial sense). The first known occurrence of *white* in colonial legislation occurred in Antigua in 1644 (the first year for which we possess any record of legislation there), followed by Barbados in 1652 (the first year for which we possess a full record of legislation there); followed thereafter in quick succession in Montserrat (1669), Nevis (1670), St. Kitts (1672), and Jamaica (1674), then by Maryland (1681), New Jersey (1683), New York (1684), Bermuda (1690 or 1691), South Carolina and Virginia (1691).[107] It did not arrive in Massachusetts statutes until 1712. The modern legal discriminatory usage apparently began in the Caribbean colonies: it had been used by all six West Indies legislatures before its inaugural appearance—in 1681—in any of the continental or Atlantic island colonies. Moreover, this chronological distribution is clearly related to another pattern in colonial legal history: Barbados slave laws directly influenced the slave codes of Jamaica, Antigua, and South Carolina.[108]

This movement from south to north may have been facilitated by emigration from the English Caribbean. Because they were so small, the island colonies quickly filled up; colonists in search of more and better land began leaving as early as 1647, and the mainland colonies from Carolina to New England were their favorite destinations.[109] The Carolina colony was founded by Barbados immigrants, who took *white* with them from the very beginning.[110] Like the plantation system and the wholesale enslavement of many thousands of Africans, the generic word *white* moved from the Caribbean islands to the mainland colonies of English North America. But in the Caribbean, generic *white* usually followed the shift to large-scale plantation slavery; on the mainland, it preceded that shift. The language and ideology of generic whiteness migrated to the mainland before, and independently of, the economic and social conditions that had prompted its general adoption in the Caribbean. After all, linguistic idioms could move as quickly as people moved; societies and institutions moved more slowly. But changes in institutions might be accelerated by widespread changes in the shared language, changes that had originated in the interpersonal circumstances of a different place. A mutated mentality that arose in one specific social ecology could be carried linguistically into different social ecologies. The linguistic carrier of that mutant mentality, the word *white,* is a perfect example of what has been called a meme (the social, cultural, and memorial equivalent of a biological gene).[111] In the interactions between the transplanted word/carrier/meme *white* and the different ecologies into which it was introduced, two kinds of transformation might occur: the environment might transform the meme, and/or the meme might transform the new environment. Consequently, although the *white* meme reached all English-speaking communities before the end of the seventeenth century, the initial uses to which it was put varied, depending on the specific social needs of each community.

Legalized Whiteness

That variety can be seen in the different inaugural uses of *white* in different colonies, beginning in 1644 when Antigua passed "An Act against Carnal Copulation between Christian and Heathen." As its title suggests, this first legalization of whiteness generally used the language of religious rather than epidermal difference ("if any Christian man or woman shall be lawfully convicted to have had carnal copulation with a heathen man or woman"). The law comprehensively considers the possible sexual combinations of Christian and heathen, sorting penalties by gender, marital status, and rank ("if it be a free woman and married"); it thus systematically combines religious and political distinctions ("if the man so defiling himself with any heathen be a servant"). The categories of master, free, servant, and slave were already in place. Color categories enter the statute only at the end, when it considers the problem caused by a case where the (Christian) man "named for the father" by "the heathen woman with child" denied his paternity. In that case, a month after the child's birth "four discrete men" would examine it and, under oath, declare "upon the best of their judgement whether they conceive the child to have been begotten by a white man, Indian, or negro." If the majority "judge the child to have been begot by a white man," he would be "liable to all the penalties of the statute against defiling himself with a heathen, as if he were thereof lawfully convicted by two sufficient witnesses."

In contrast to the Rhode Island statute of 1652, *white* here explicitly excludes "Indian." Also in contrast to the Rhode Island statute, and to almost all the early uses of *white* previously cited in this book, this Antiguan statute reverses alphabetical order to re-affirm a social order that places *white* before all other categories. Moreover, *white* enters the statute at a point where religious and political distinctions necessarily gave way to purely biological criteria. A one-month-old baby does not look Christian or heathen, free or servile. Paternity could be decided only by the physical features of the child, including explicitly the color of its body. But the arbitrators of paternity are not asked whether the baby looked like any particular male, white, Indian, or Negro. Instead, they are asked only to determine whether the child appears to have had a "white" father, because only in that case will the law have been violated. If the father does appear to have been white, then the court will accept the heathen woman's testimony as to *which* white male fathered her child. The important legal issue being addressed here is whether the testimony of a (Negro or Indian) "heathen" could convict a "white" (Christian). Normally, in cases of bastardy, "according to the statute of the kingdom of England," the testimony of a woman in labor was sufficient to establish paternity. But in Antigua, the woman's testimony had to be supplemented with the "judgement" of "four discrete men" as to the generic identity of the newborn's father. That is, the law presumes that, in normal circumstances, the testimony of a (Negro or Indian) "heathen" would not be sufficient evidence to convict "a white man" who denied his guilt. But if the arbitrators agree on the child's white paternity, "their judgement and the accusation of the woman shall be taken for a sufficient conviction of the party, as if the woman were a Christian and should father it upon him in her labor." Whiteness thus enters statute law to provide extra protection for white males, in a situation where there was already a legal presumption that white testimony normally outweighed Negro or Indian testimony.[112]

This 1644 law echoes the 1634 bigotry of Thomas Herbert who, tempted by libidinous foreign women, reminded his readers that "a perfect Christian values his salvation at a higher rate than by a devilish mixture with pagan beauties or sorceries to throw his dear soul into endless tortures and perdition."[113] The law demonstrates that official hostility to such unions began early, and cannot easily be attributed to economic factors. It punished freeborn Christian masters and mistresses, not just servants and slaves. English settlement of Antigua had begun in 1632, only 12 years before passage of this statute; although Barbados had switched to sugar production by 1644, Antigua certainly had not, and indeed continued to rely on tobacco until at least the 1680s.[114] Antigua had slaves, but it was seldom if ever the first port of call for slaving ships from Africa, which preferred to go directly to the larger markets in Barbados and Nevis. As the statute recognizes, many of the island's early slaves were Indians; Antigua belonged to the sphere of Carib inhabitation, migration, and resistance, and English clashes with the Caribs continued throughout the seventeenth century.[115] Bicolor sex did not require massive numbers of black slaves or a fully developed plantation economy. It required only the presence of a mixed population. The punishment of such liaissons simultaneously demonstrates two contradictory facts: (1) from the beginning, some whites were sexually attracted to some nonwhites, and (2) from the beginning, some whites were appalled by such couplings. Two centuries later the white community was still riven by that contradiction, which Brown would make the foundation for *Clotel*'s critique of color-coded slavery.

Two of the statutes that inaugurated the legalization of whiteness in other colonial jurisdictions also forbade bicolor unions, but both differed significantly from the Antigua original. Maryland in 1681 passed "An Act concerning Negroes and Slaves," in which "all negroes and other slaves already imported or hereafter to be imported" (and their children) were declared slaves for life; but the remainder of this discriminatory statute regulated the white master class. Any "freeborn English or whitewoman servant" who married a slave would be immediately released from her indenture and freed from service; her children would be born free; her master and mistress, punished by loss of their servant and by loss of the slave's offspring, would also be heavily fined, as would "any priest, minister, magistrate, or other person whatsoever" who should "join in marriage any negro or other slave to any English or other whitewoman servant freeborn as aforesaid." Like the phrase "Englishman or white man" in the 1606 inaugural use of stage 5 (discussed in chapter 5), the phrase "English or other whitewoman" is an example of code-switching, designed to secure the meaning of an unfamiliar idiom. The paired synonyms illustrate the use of *white* to resolve legal ambiguities created by the presence of several European nationalities within a single colonial jurisdiction. This law presupposed that such bicolor unions were encouraged by the "procurement or connivance" of the woman servant's white master or mistress, and then legitimated by white clergy or officials; to prevent marriages that it regarded as a "disgrace not only of the English but also of many other Christian nations," the Maryland legislature restricted the freedom of the most privileged members of Maryland society.[116]

A decade later the legislature in adjacent Virginia, equally horrified by "that abhominable mixture and spurious issue" created by "Negroes, mulattoes and Indians intermarrying with English, or other white women," solved the problem in a radically different way, enacting "that whatsoever English or other white man or woman, bond or free, shall intermarry with a negro, mulatto, or Indian man or woman, bond or free, he shall within three months be banished from this dominion forever."[117] Here as in the Maryland law, "English or other white" resolves any jurisdictional ambiguity than would be created by "English" alone. Unlike Maryland, Virginia punished the white (man or woman) who married a nonwhite. Unlike Antigua, which punished mere copulation, Maryland and Virginia first used *white* to punish marriages. These laws limiting the white right to marry nonwhites established the legal tradition still in place in 1853, which prevented the white Virginia gentleman Henry Green from marrying Clotel.

Unlike the inaugural Antigua statute, the first uses of *white* in Maryland and Virginia were not forced on lawmakers by the biological problem of determining paternity. Instead, in those later statutes, *white* was a recognizable idiom used to identify persons subject to the law in question. In all other colonial jurisdictions the inaugural statutes deploy *white* to clarify political identities (as in Virginia and Maryland) rather than biological identities (as in Antigua). This shift can already be seen in the first white statute after Antigua's. In 1652 Barbados decreed that

> whosoever, either Master of Family, or Captain, or Master of a Ship, or other that shall entertain any man, or woman, White or Black, above one night, if he doth not know him to be a Free-man, shall for every night after the first, forfeit one hundred pounds of Sugar, and if he know him to be a servant, or slave to another man, and do notwithstanding wilfully entertain him, he shall forfeit five hundred pounds of Sugar for every night.[118]

In this text, "White or Black" is the equivalent of "servant, or slave" later in the sentence. In context, the anti-alphabetical phrase *White or Black* does not separate but collapse the two categories, legally erasing differences between Euro-American servants and Afro-American slaves. Both servants and slaves belonged to someone else, and one's relations with them should therefore be governed by recognition of their status as someone else's property. Consequently, the law punishes members of the white colonial elite (masters and captains) for any refusal to recognize the more important distinction between "a Free-man" and a bondman. By treating a bondman (servant or slave) as a freeman, an elite European was infringing the property rights of some other elite European. This Barbados law, like the later Maryland statute, regulated conduct between elites: the solidarity of masters in their treatment of bound laborers mattered more, in this instance, than any difference between the laborers themselves. Such attitudes led, easily enough, to the 1666 description of European laborers as "white slaves." They also led St. Kitts in 1672 to define "the Carrying off this Island any Slave or Slaves by Stealth or any white person or persons, Servant or Servants to be Felony."[119] Again, this law lumped (black) slaves and "white" servants in the same category, as valuable property that—like cattle—was dangerously mobile and had to be secured against felonious stealth.

Similar assumptions are implicit in Montserrat's first white statute, despite the absence of the words *servant* and *slave*. Farmers preferred to plant cash crops like tobacco instead of edible ones like cassava, and as a result "there hath been of late a general Complaint over the whole Island of the want of Provision" (i.e., of the lack of food). Since the free market in greed was leaving people without anything to eat, the Montserrat assembly in 1669 was forced to decree that "All Masters of families living or residing on this Island shall plant or cause to be planted One Acre of Provision for every two working persons, Whites or

Blacks."[120] The telltale phrase here is "working persons," which excluded masters, mistresses, and their children, but included indentured servants, slaves, and hired laborers. Montserrat's "Whites or Blacks" thus performed the same function that "White or Black" had performed in Barbados: recognizing the distinction between white servants and blacks slaves in the very moment that, in practice, it was temporarily ignored.

On Nevis in 1670 the apparent binary again abolished difference. In an effort to attract and retain Church of England ministers, the Nevis assembly and the new governor ordered "that every Minister within this Island in their respective parishes shall have ten pounds of suger per poll for every person or persons, as well black as white, in their several parishes."[121] Despite appearances, this law did not tax blacks; instead, the legislation taxed white masters for each of their black slaves and white indentured servants. Throughout the tobacco and sugar colonies, wealth could be roughly indexed by the number of laborers a man owned, and the wording of this statute insisted that planters be taxed for those they owned temporarily as well as those they owned permanently.

All the preceding statutes, from Barbados in 1652 to St. Kitts in 1672, presuppose that temporarily indentured servants are white, in contrast to slaves who are *black*. But although they assume that distinction, the statutes do not themselves grant special privileges on the basis of color. The distinction between freeborn Englishmen and heathen slaves had, in each colony, been articulated—when articulated at all—using traditional political terms to distinguish traditional political categories. But early in 1674 *white* itself began to be used to define the political privileges of one group over another. Jamaica's inaugural legalization of whiteness prescribed special penalties for "any Slave either man or woman" who "shall offer any violence to any white Christian."[122] This 1674 statute revised Jamaica's 1664 slave code, which contained a similar provision but had worded it differently: "shall offer any violence to any Christian."[123] In turn, Jamaica's 1664 slave code—including the word "Christian" in this specific clause—copied, verbatim, the comprehensive Barbados slave code of 1661.[124] Here, in the most elementary and explicit transformation imaginable, *white* was simply added to an existing sentence. Between 1664 and 1674 the Jamaica legislature had recognized that slaves might (and perhaps should) be Christians; Jamaica was the first English colony conquered from the Spanish, and therefore contained blacks who had already been converted by the previous imperial power. The religious distinction was no longer sufficient to protect the privileges to which English colonists were accustomed. This law did not punish slaves for violence against their masters, but for violence against any member of the master class, a master class initially defined by religion but later defined by color-and-religion.

It was soon defined by color alone. Less than a decade later Jamaican authorities were routinely using *white* in legislation dedicated to the creation of special privileges for European colonists.[125] In 1682 the Jamaica assembly ordered "that all and every Master or mistress of Slaves, for the first five Working Slaves, shall be Obliged to keep one White Man Servant," with the number of obligatory white servants increasing in proportion to the number of black slaves. In the same legislative session, "An Act Encouraging the Importation of White Servants" provided subsidies for any ship that imported "fifty White Male Servants." Another act demanded that "all Owners of Neat Cattle shall keep one White Man at each respective Pen," and "two white Men" if the pen held more than 200 cattle.[126] These laws constructed a white welfare system, providing guaranteed employment for white workers and preferential treatment for suppliers of white labor.

Similar attitudes governed the inaugural legalization of whiteness in more northerly colonies. Jamaica could not rely on white labor alone, but New England could. Massachusetts, "being differently circumstanced from the plantations in the islands," in 1712 passed a statute "prohibiting the importation or bringing into this province any Indian servants or slaves," because the ready supply of slave labor constituted "a discouragement to the importation of white Christian servants."[127] Here again, as in Jamaica, the composite "white Christian" represents a transitional legal formula. The province had already, in 1705, imposed a duty of four pounds on each imported Black, and in 1718 the Council for New England resolved "that the Importation of White Servants be encouraged, and that the Importation of Black Servants be discouraged."[128] Between 1712 and 1718 "Christian" was dropped, and "white" could stand on its own. New England preserved white jobs simply by excluding from its territory, whenever possible, anyone who was not "white." By the eighteenth century, Indians had lost any legal title to the privileges of pallor.

Legalized white privilege had arrived in the middle Atlantic colonies decades before, probably because their populations were less homogeneously English than those of New England. What became New York and New Jersey originally had been Dutch colonies, so that the English from the outset settled alongside other European immigrants, who needed to be distinguished from non-Europeans. In 1683 New Jersey passed an act to protect any "white servant" from serving more than four years of indentured bondage, from involuntary transportation to another jurisdiction, and from maiming by his or her employer.[129] Implicitly, any of those things might be done legally (as actually they *were* done) to servants who were not "white." By contrast, neighboring New York in 1684 passed "a Bill against Fugitive Servants," dealing generally with "any apprentice Servant or Slave"; like earlier laws in the Leeward Islands, this legislation covered both servants and slaves. But one provision specified distinct penalties to be imposed on "whosoever shall counsel, persuade, entice, inveigle, or allure any white servant" to abscond from his or her obligation.[130] The similarity in these two statutes is more important than the difference: explicitly or implicitly, both colonies distinguished the treatment allowable for white servants from the treatment allowable for black slaves.

New Jersey sought to protect white servants while New York sought to protect white property owners from loss of their investment in such servants. Bermuda protected both categories. In 1690–91 it decreed that the testimony of "One White Person" was sufficient to convict any "Negroes . . . or other slaves" accused of a felony.[131] This law explicitly granted white testimony a different and superior legal status, leaving blacks and Indians with no legal protection against false accusation by even one white. It did not matter whether the white was a master or a fellow servant.

Two other aspects of white dominance were enforced by South Carolina's 1691 "Act for the better ordering of slaves." Like Jamaica before it, South Carolina decreed that "if any negro or Indian slave shall offer any violence, by striking or the like, to any white person, he shall for the first offence be severely whipped," and so on. Where Jamaica's version of this law had gone from "Christian" (1664) to the composite "white Christian" (1674), South Carolina's 1691 rewrite abandoned "Christian" altogether. The same law also forbade "any negro or Indian slave . . . to go out of their plantations . . . without a ticket, or one [or] more white men in their company."[132] Slave mobility had been legally restricted for decades in English colonies, but the provision for "white men" as escorts departed from previous procedure, which had been suspicious of collaboration between white servants and black slaves. The South Carolina legislature in 1691 assumed that it could count on any white man—including a white indentured servant—to police the movement of blacks and Indians. Moreover, like the Jamaican laws of 1682, this provision for white escorts guaranteed jobs for whites: even if they did no work, their presence was required to accompany the non-European slaves who actually worked. Blacks worked; whites watched. This statute legalized the status of whites as privileged observers, a privilege they continue to enjoy: whites are still preferentially given "white-collar" managerial jobs, supervising the more demanding but poorly paid manual work of blacks.

In these first unambiguous legislative uses in the English colonies, generic *white* served two functions. First, it institutionalized the equally privileged treatment of European immigrants and the unequal treatment of imported Africans and native Amerindians. It resolved the problem of jurisdictional ambiguity, creating a new "white" social identity by expanding the definition of the English colonial community to include other European colonists. That new communal Euro-American identity was founded on contrast with African or Amerindian slaves, whose customary exclusion from the circle of rights guaranteed to freeborn Englishman had by then been explicitly formalized already. *White* followed, was built on, the backs of blacks. By the 1680s *white* was also being used to guarantee additional legal privileges, vis-à-vis nonwhites, that had never been guaranteed to every freeborn Englishman. Once *white* had been introduced into legislation as a defining property of certain persons but not others, then whiteness became a form of property, conferring on those who possessed it certain legal, economic, and social advantages. In subsequent centuries, as legal historian Cheryl I. Harris has demonstrated, American law "recognized a property interest in whiteness."[133]

Second, the legalization of whiteness regulated Euro-American behavior toward Afro-Americans and Amerindians. This second function forced whites to collaborate in maintaining the first function. By outlawing alliances of various sorts between Europeans and non-Europeans, such laws insisted on the continuously visible separation of black from white. This enforced separation can be seen not only in the various attempts to regulate copulation and marriage, but in statutes like the one passed by Nevis in 1675, which forbade "the unchristianlike association of white people with Negroes; their drinking together in Common upon Sabbath days" or more generally "playing or conversing with Negroes."[134] Although the new category of *white* was invested with the freedoms previously guaranteed to the old category of *English,* whites were not free (as Englishmen had been) to endanger the distinction between white and black. To endanger that distinction—as *Clotel* systematically does—would endanger the entire institution of slavery.

The legalization of whiteness began in Antigua in 1644, and in 1697 Antigua also inaugurated a new and fateful statutory extension of the word *white.* The island's first comprehensive slave code referred to "all free people (not being whites)."[135] The clause in question was in attempt to deal with the social problem, within a color-coded slave society, of manumitted slaves. Once the legal system had installed the equation of slavery and color, then "free black"—like "white slave"—became a paradox, an oxymoron. Like other statutes in other colonies in the late seventeenth century, this clause of the Antigua slave code restricted the freedom of freed slaves. However, the 1697 statute set a legal and linguistic precedent by articulating that problem in negative terms. In 1655 the philosopher Thomas Hobbes had coined the compound "not-whites" (Latin *non-albi*). Hobbes used the word to illustrate a point in logic; he had not intended it demographically.[136] But when the Antigua legislature wrote "not being whites," it turned a logical into a legal and demographic category. At the same time, it conferred grammatical primacy on generic privilege. As Hobbes had observed, "positive names" (like *albi*) are logically "prior to negative names" (like *non-albi*).[137] By the end of the seventeenth century, the generic meaning of *white* was so self-evident in the British Caribbean that it could conveniently define all other population groups. The parenthetical phrase "not being whites" lumped together blacks, Indians—and the offspring (mulattos, mestizos, quadroons, octoroons) of sexual unions between whites and others.

The 1697 Antigua statute recognized the failure of the 1644 statute, which had attempted to prevent whites from copulating with "heathens." But copulation continued. So did the pregnancies resulting from copulation. As early as 1656, in a Virginia court, a "mulatto" was "held to be a slave."[138] By 1697 some of the enslaved "heathens" had become Christians, and some of the "mulattoes" had grown up and fornicated with whites; some tawny Christian children had one black and three white grandparents, some mulattoes had been freed by their white masters/lovers/fathers. Nevertheless, those category-confusing mixtures still could be stigmatized for "not-being-whites." Anyone who was not unequivocally white could be defined, by legal fiat, as nonwhite, and hence nonfree. The 1697 Antigua statute marked the beginning of what would become the notorious principle that "one drop" of nonwhite blood was sufficient to deprive a person of the privileges that legally belonged to whites only.[139]

The social acceptance of slavery depended on erecting and maintaining boundaries between those who could and those who could not be enslaved. *White* replaced a chaos of geographical, linguistic, religious, ethnic, political, and class identities with an initially simple, initially visible binary opposition. Between 1644 and 1697 English colonial law adopted and adapted the new generic term *white* to clarify the distinction between free and slave. That is why *Clotel* later unclarified whiteness: to muddy that distinction between free and slave, and thereby to enlist free people in the cause of slaves.

Capital Punishment

English Parliaments passed no comparable laws. But by the 1660s England was as deeply entangled in African slavery as any of its colonies. Until 1631 the English had not erected a single settlement in West Africa; the Portuguese dominated African trade until the Dutch successfully attacked their outposts there in 1637, and that destruction of the Portuguese monopoly was followed by divorce of the Spanish and Portuguese kingdoms in 1640, effectively opening the continent to free-for-all competition among European powers.[140] In Barbados, blacks were seldom mentioned in the 1630s, but the Portuguese-Spanish split in 1640 and the Spanish conquest of Providence Island in 1641 changed all that. Providence was the first English colony to use massive numbers of black slaves, and in 1641 Captain Philip Bell (who had been governor there) became de facto

Governor of Barbados.[141] Before Providence, Captain Bell had been governor of Bermuda; he there had married the daughter of the captain who shipped the first known cargo of slaves to Virginia in 1619, and shipped another cargo of slaves to Bermuda in 1620.[142] In 1641 a Guinea Company ship sold a cargo of slaves in Bell's Barbados—the first such shipment recorded—and from 1642 reports of slaves and slave ships rocket. Throughout the 1640s and 1650s English ships were heavily involved in the slave trade, particularly in supplying Barbados and other West Indies colonies that switched to sugar plantations. From February 1645 to January 1647, 19 English slaving ships were reported off the Gold Coast; between 1652 and 1657, there were reports of at least 75. In 1654 James Drax helped organize and finance a voyage of two ships from England to Africa to purchase slaves for the sugar plantations.[143] Drax had been one of the first settlers of Barbados, in 1627, and was one of the leaders of the conversion to sugar production; by 1654 he owned a 700-acre plantation, worked by 200 slaves; in 1660 he was named to the king's new Council for Foreign Plantations.[144] That year a new Company of Adventurers to Africa was formed; by 1662 it had contracted to supply all the slaves needed in the West Indies, and in 1663 its new charter for the first time identified slaves as one of its commodities. The Second Dutch War (1664–67) was precipitated by English attacks on Dutch slaving outposts in Africa.[145]

Until the 1650s few African slaves had lived anywhere in England.[146] By contrast, in the 1660s Pepys mentions the black house servant of Sir William Batten, the black servant of the goldsmith Sir Robert Viner, George Cock's blackamoor servant, and W. Batelier's two black servants; Pepys himself had a black maid working in his kitchen in 1669.[147] The Stuart royal family continued the enthusiasm for black servants they had brought to England in 1603. In the 1650s Prince Rupert had his portrait painted with a black page, and there are at least four Restoration paintings of mistresses of Charles II, similarly attended.[148] Before the Restoration, black figures in London civic pageants (like Middleton's *Triumphs of Truth*) had been played by English actors in blackface; by 1672 such pageants seem to have begun using real Africans.[149]

Like the English colonies, by the 1660s England itself—and especially London—had become a bicolor contact zone, where white masters owned black slaves. But because English Parliaments did not face the jurisdictional problems that puzzled English lawmakers in the colonies, they never needed to legalize whiteness.[150] In fact, English lawyers systematically avoided discussion of the flourishing English trade in human commodities.[151] That does not mean Londoners were free of colorphobia, or that they never acquired a sense of their own generic whiteness; it does mean that we cannot use the language of statutes as an index of white consciousness.

But if London lacked one genre of white text found in the colonies, it was overflowing with another genre, rare in the seventeenth-century colonies: literature. In particular, in the first century of English occupation, English colonists in North America and the Caribbean did not produce a single dramatic text. As we have already seen, from 1613 to 1637 London plays and pageants included some of the first examples of the generic use of the adjective *white.* In a 1613 pageant Middleton had put that adjective in the mouth of a Black King addressing the crowd. By 1672 the adjective had become an unselfconscious part of an English playwright's own vocabulary: a stage direction for that year's mayoral pageant describes the entrance of "two white Virgins."[152] Whiteness no longer required dialogue with a dark speaker; it had been internalized by Londoners themselves. Another, more significant index of such internalization is the transformation of *white* from generic adjective to generic noun. I discuss that change—which began in the early 1660s, in very unliterary texts—at greater length in chapter 10. But the timing and context of its emergence in London literature registers a shift in English identity parallel to the shift visible in colonial legislation between 1644 and 1697.

The generic noun *white* makes its first appearance in English literature in Edward Ravenscroft's adaptation of *Titus Andronicus,* written and performed in London in 1678. The evolution of London attitudes toward slavery and whiteness can be seen in the differences between the original Elizabethan play and its Restoration adaptation. *Titus Andronicus,* by the young Shakespeare and his more experienced contemporary George Peele, was probably completed in 1592.[153] Renaissance scholar Francesca Royster persuasively argues that the original *Titus* was written before the black-white binary had "been completely accomplished."[154] Ethnic and moral blackness is represented by Aaron, the "barbarous Moor" (2.3.78, 5.3.4), and his newborn son. Black father and black son are contrasted with two other males, Chiron and Demetrius; holding his black son in his arms, Aaron derides the other two males for their pallor:

> What, what, ye sanguine, shallow-hearted boys,
> Ye whitelimed walls, ye alehouse painted signs,
> Coal-black is better than another hue
> In that it scorns to bear another hue;
> For all the water in the ocean
> Can never turn the swan's black legs to white,
> Although she lave them hourly in the flood.(4.2.96–102)

Obviously, Aaron is not praising Chiron, Demetrius, or whiteness. Chiron and Demetrius are "barbarous Goths" (1.1.28), the sons of Tamora, the "Queen of Goths" (as she is called six times in the first scene); within the play the Goths are, as Royster notes, an ethnically distanced "Other." Moreover, the home of the Goths was located in Scandinavia, the far northern region conventionally associated with white bodies.[155] The extreme geographical and epidermal contrast between black Aaron and the whitelimed Goths thus resembles the contrast in another early Shakespeare play, *Love's Labours Lost,* between the men disguised as "Muscovites" (and so probably as pale as inhabitants of Moscow were thought to be) and the otherwise-unexplained and functionless "blackamoors with music" who accompany them (5.2.156).

The "whitelimed" complexion of Chiron and Demetrius thus does not represent an English norm or ideal, but a specifically northern, alien ethnicity. (See chapter 4.) The extreme pallor of the northern Goths is united sexually with the contrasting southern blackness of Aaron the Moor, who commits adultery with Tamora and encourages her sons to rape the Roman wife Lavinia. Goths commit adultery and rape; the rapists mutilate their victim; the adulteress encourages the rape and orders the murder of her own baby. The white ethnicity of the Goths is consistently as "barbarous" as the black ethnicity of the Moor. In the scene where Aaron defends his black son, two sets of males are contrasted with each other; *black* is spoken four times in this part scene (half its occurrences in the entire play), and explicitly contrasted with "another hue," the "whitelimed" complexion of Chiron and Demetrius. The adjective *whitelimed,* unlike the adjective *white,* suggests that epidermal pallor results from the exterior application of chemical pigments; as I pointed out in chapter 2, English actors used white makeup whenever they performed female characters. *Whitelimed* suggests that the complexions of the actors playing Demetrius and Chiron have been similarly artificially whitened, to signal their alien and Gothic ethnicity. They are performing in white-face, just as Aaron is performing in black-face.

Aaron's black son is, as Aaron insists, the "brother" of Chiron and Demetrius (4.2.87, 121, 125); all four men are physically linked to Tamora (Aaron by copulation, the others by birth). Black and white are not moral or natural opposites here, but twinned extremes, like Laura and her black servant (Plate 12). The conflict between the two black males and the two "whitelimed" males is only temporary; by the end of the scene they again "join in league" (4.2.135), collaborating to conceal a crime by committing more crimes. By contrast with these despicable and alien extremes, most of the characters in *Titus Andronicus*—and all of the sympathetic ones—are neither Goths nor Moors, neither white nor black, but Roman. London spectators almost certainly identified not with the villainous "whitelimed" Goths, but with the high civilization of Rome, the focus of the humanist curriculum everywhere in Elizabethan England. Shakespeare, in particular, almost certainly identified with Rome, given the other evidence for his allegiance to Roman Catholicism.[156] In *Titus Andronicus,* as in *Othello,* the authorial and spectatorial gaze was neither white nor black, but somewhere between, in the civilized middle. (See chapter 2.)

The assumptions that inform the Elizabethan play had changed radically by 1678, when Ravenscroft adapted it as *Titus Andronicus; or, The Rape of Lavinia.* The original had last been printed separately in 1611, and Ben Jonson derided it as old-fashioned in 1614; there are no records of any performances in the intervening decades. But Ravenscroft's adaptation quickly became a "stock play" in the Restoration repertoire, and remained so for half a century. In new lines Ravenscroft wrote for Aaron's first soliloquy, an unmistakably modern generic binary was for the first time interpolated into a Shakespearean text:

> Hence abject thoughts that I am black and foul,
> And all the Taunts of Whites that call me Fiend.[157]

It should by now not surprise any reader that this sentence, apparently the inaugural example of the generic noun *white* in English drama, is spoken by someone black. *Whites* here is not (as *whitelimed* was) a derogatory theatrical metaphor aimed at specific characters with an alien generic identity. Instead, the word's placement in a soliloquy presumes that an audience will immediately recognize it as a literal biological label for a population that includes all the other characters—and all the audience as well. Indeed, the lines that follow seem to describe the relationship between the black actor on the stage and the spectators in the pit:

> Lifted on high in Power, I'll hang above
> Like a black threat'ning Cloud o'er all their heads
> That dare look up to me with Envious Eyes.

Rather than balance two specific black males against two specific pale males, Ravenscroft generalized the conflict. Which "Whites" taunted Aaron, and why they did so, do not need to be explained, because the contempt of whites for blacks is taken for granted. Aaron is not holding his black child; instead, his singular blackness is set defiantly against the plural whiteness of everyone else in the theater.

The ethnic particularity of the original play has been erased. Chiron and Demetrius are still Goths, but in Ravenscroft's version of the scene with his black baby Aaron does not call them "whitelimed walls."

> What, what ye sanguine hollow-hearted Boys,
> Ye gaudy blossoms, checquered white and red,
> See, here is a gloss that will not sully
> Like your water-coloured complexions,

> Which Chance does fade and Sickness washes out.
> I say that black is better than another hue,
> In that it scorns to bear another hue.
> For all the water in the Ocean
> Can never turn the Swan's black legs to white,
> Although she lave them hourly in the flood.(5.1; pp. 39–40)

Since *white* had, by 1678, become a positive generic marker, Aaron could no longer use it as an obvious insult. Instead, he denigrates their complexions for being gaudy and changeable: gaudy like the "white and red" of a woman's mixed and painted complexion; changeable like thin watercolor tints that can be dirtied, faded, or washed out (and were not used as stage makeup, and did not become fashionable in the art world until the early nineteenth century).[158] The last three lines have not been changed, but their meaning has altered: *white* has become an English or European generic marker, as it was not in the Elizabethan play.[159] Once normative collective whiteness has been introduced into a semantic context, it can spontaneously transform the meaning of previously innocuous utterances. Thus, in Elizabethan texts women often are praised for white complexions; as I argued in chapter 2, that whiteness is not "racial" but gendered. But once generic whiteness has been widely attributed to men, the whiteness of an individual woman also can be understood generically. In both plays Aaron encourages Chiron and Demetrius to rape Lavinia; but in Ravenscroft's version he tells them, "Bath your Limbs in fair Lavinia's Snow," having just described "Snow / As white and Crisp as when at first it fell" (2.1, p. 18). The fact that this is spoken by Aaron, only minutes after the soliloquy in which he referred to "the Taunts of Whites," makes it very easy to interpret his euphemism in generic terms, as the rape of a "white" woman. In a play published in 1664, *white woman* had been used in its modern sense, so Ravenscroft and his audiences were almost certainly familiar with the idiom.[160]

Notably, the adaptation's references to whiteness—one certainly generic noun and two probably generic adjectives—are all spoken by Aaron. Ravenscroft expanded Aaron's role, not only writing new material for him but giving him speeches that originally had been written for other characters. Ravenscroft also highlighted Aaron's blackness, adding 38 new examples of *dark, black, swarthy, crow, raven,* and *Moor* to the original script.[161] This intensified emphasis on Aaron and his color cannot be separated from Ravenscroft's changes to the ethnicity of whiteness, because in the new generic economy *white* and *black* had become locked in a reciprocal relationship. The meaning of Aaron's blackness, like the meaning of whiteness, had been altered by the decades since the play's original composition. Even in the original play, the six appearances of the words *slave* and *slavish* all referred to the two black characters, but in context those all could just be examples of the figurative, abusive idiom (described in chapter 7). But Ravenscroft added two examples that must refer to literal slaves. Saturninus, seeking the murderers of Bassianus, orders, "Look round and see if any Slave be near" (3.1; p. 25). Earlier, Tamora explains how her husband,

> . . . with Wine and Luxury o'ercome,
> Is fallen asleep—in's pendant-couch he's Laid,
> That hangs in yonder Grotto rocked by Winds,
> Which raised by Art do give it gentle motion,
> And Troops of Slaves stand round with Fans perfumed
> Made of the feathers plucked from Indian Birds,
> And cool him into golden slumbers—
> This time I chose to come to thee, my Moor.(3.1, p.19)

There is nothing remarkable about a Roman emperor attended by slaves, but the "pendant-couch" is clearly a hammock, introduced to Europeans by New World natives; the first Englishmen to adopt them wholesale were colonists in Barbados—who were also notorious for their drunkenness and for employing "Troops of Slaves." The "Indian" birds could come from Asia, but they also could be West Indian. This description serves no dramatic purpose, except to situate Tamora's adulterous assignation with her black lover. The interpolated new context suggests wealthy white colonists, whose wives cuckold them with their own black slaves. Certainly in his other plays Ravenscroft refers often enough to the colonial world.[162]

But even if we ignore these overtones, Ravenscroft's introduction of real slaves changes the significance of the original lines that call Aaron or his black son a "slave." For audiences accustomed to routine black slavery, *slave* conjures up a specific set of social relationships. Once the English got used to the idea that black children were slaves from birth, calling a newborn black baby "the black Slave" (5.1; p. 40) means something different than it had meant in 1592 (4.2.119).[163] Likewise, although in both plays the Goths and Aaron enter the play as Roman captives, the appearance of a black man "in chains" (1.3, p. 8; 2.1, p. 11) had much fuller and more specific meaning for Londoners in 1678 than in 1592.[164] Moreover, if the captives enter in chains, the chains must be removed when Saturninus gives them—in a line not present in the original—"their liberty" (1.3; p. 8). The onstage manumission of Aaron, the obviously foolish freeing of a black man from his chains, unleashes a concatenation of violence that culminates in Aaron's rebinding: in the final sequence, he enters "bound" (5.1; p. 51) and then later is discovered bound and stretched "on a Rack" (p. 53), where he is tortured till he dies, bound at the end as he was at the beginning, alone against the world as he was in his first soliloquy, still the target of "the Taunts of Whites."

Nevertheless, in Ravenscroft's ending (as in the colonial legalization of whiteness), some whites also are punished. In both cases whites are condemned for failing to respect the color line. In the original play, Aaron's capture, confession, and offstage execution had been separated from the deaths of Saturninus and Tamora. In the adaptation, Aaron's torture and confession is intertwined with the deaths of Saturninus (who had freed him and furthered various of his schemes against other "Whites") and Tamora (who had fornicated with him). By giving Aaron two speeches originally written for Tamora, early in the action Ravenscroft deprived Tamora of her independence, making her from the outset Aaron's agent and partner. By transposing Aaron's torture and confession, Ravenscroft made Aaron's relationships with Saturninus (whom he cuckolded), Tamora (whom he impregnated), and her two sons (whose career as rapists he encouraged and facilitated) the focus of attention in the play's final moments. As Tamora and Saturninus lie dying, as the mutilated corpses of Chiron and Demetrius are displayed to the audience, the playwright shames and torments those four white characters by emphasizing how they collaborated and fraternized with a bad black slave. Tamora, just before her death, kills her own mulatto child (which had survived in the original play). Then Aaron—who in both versions had confessed only to save his beloved child—completely reverses himself and says, "I'll eat it." The original Senecan horror, in which an aristocratic parent unwittingly devoured its child and heir, is trumped by the specifically early modern European horror of the *cannibal* (a sixteenth-century word). Ravenscroft displays to his white audience a black man who consciously desires to devour human flesh, even the flesh of members of his own family, and who would certainly do so if white power did not restrain his brutal black impulses.[165]

"Ravenscroft not only presents a black character who has internalized whites' evaluation of the meaning of blackness," African American critic Joyce Green MacDonald argues, "but also confirms the correctness of the evaluation."[166] Aaron's soliloquy identified the "Whites" who taunt him with the audience, and given the presumption of a white audience, the play's final spectacle is not, as white critics have suggested, simply "sensationalist" and "royalist";[167] it is not simply "melodramatic."[168] It is sadistic. And the sadism is racially graded. Whites might be punished for fraternizing with blacks, but black violence against whites provokes a much more ferocious reprisal. Ravenscroft ends with "Aaron in Torment!" (5.1; p. 53): the climactic violence is the onstage color-phobic execution of Aaron, "at once . . . burnt and racked to death" (p. 56). When white critic Jonathan Bate claims that "the rack and flames symbolically consign [Aaron] to hell" and compares Ravenscroft's Aaron to Milton's Satan, symbolism and literary allusion are covering up an atrocity; when Bate celebrates "the spectacular style" in which Ravenscroft satisfied "the sophisticated audience of his age," he erases Aaron's color-coded identity.[169] Ravenscroft assumed—rightly—that white audiences would find it satisfying to watch a black man tortured, then tied down so that he cannot move while "his Funeral Fire" is kindled "around him."

Aaron is punished in the same way that recalcitrant blacks in English-speaking North America have been punished from the seventeenth century to the lynch mobs of the early twentieth century and the electric chairs still operating in some states as I write this book: bound, tortured, and burned alive in front of an approving white audience. *Clotel* quotes an 1842 Mississippi newspaper account:

> The body was taken and chained to a tree immediately on the banks of the Mississippi, on what is called Union Point. Faggots were then collected and piled around him. . . . The torches were lighted, and placed in the pile, which soon ignited. He watched unmoved the curling flame that grew, until it began to entwine itself around and feed upon his body; then he sent forth cries of agony painful to the ear, begging some one to blow his brains out; at the same time surging with almost superhuman strength, until the staple with which the chain was fastened to the tree (not being well secured) drew out, and he leaped from the burning pile. At that moment the sharp ringing of several rifles was heard; the body of the negro fell a corpse on the ground. He was picked up by some two or three, and again thrown into the fire, and consumed, not a vestige remaining to show that such a being ever existed. (98–99)

In 1675—three years before Ravenscroft's adaptation—six blacks in Barbados were burned alive for organizing a slave revolt, with the alleged objective of exterminating all the whites on the island (except the fairest white women). One of the six blacks refused to confess, and in response to the Taunts of Whites (who, "observing, cried out . . . *Sirrah, we shall see you fry bravely by and by*"), he "answered undauntedly, *If you Roast me today, you cannot Roast me tomorrow.*" These brutal judicial executions were celebrated in London as "Great News from Barbados."[170] In the summer of 1678—a few months before the premiere of Ravenscroft's adaptation—slaves in Jamaica revolted, and one of the captured rebellious blacks was similarly punished: "he was fastened upon his back to the ground—a fire was made first to his feet and burned up by degrees; I heard him speak several words when the fire consumed all his lower parts as far as his navel. The fire was upon his breast—he was burning near three hours—before he died."[171] Ravenscroft's play allowed white spectators in London to enjoy the same pleasure that white spectators in Barbados and Jamaica had experienced, watching stubborn black flesh fry.

The black slaves who led the 1675 revolt in Barbados called their European masters "Baccararoes."[172] In 1684 another English writer put "Baccheraro's" in the mouth of a black slave on an English plantation in the West Indies, and in a marginal note he explained the unfamiliar word to his London readers: "So the *Negroes* in their Language called the *Whites.*"[173] But the English never learned to call themselves "baccheraroes." The word is not in the *Oxford English Dictionary,* despite its use by at least three seventeenth-century English authors.[174] Indeed, until the middle of the twentieth century it continued to be used, in the shortened form *bakra,* by the descendants of African slaves living on islands off the coast of Georgia and South Carolina. It comes from the word $m_{1ba}1ka_{2ra}2$, shared by the Ibibio and Efik languages of what is now southern Nigeria. It means, literally, "he who surrounds or governs."[175] *Backra* is still used, in Jamaican and Caribbean English, as a synonym for "white man."[176] By 1675, for at least some African slaves on Caribbean islands, the defining characteristic of Europeans was no longer color. What distinguished Europeans was their shared power over Africans.

The English word for that new ruling class was *whites.*

Part III

Ramification

Chapter 9

White Right

The Reverend John Peck, owner of a plantation of 70 slaves near Natchez, "was educated for the ministry," *Clotel* informs us, "in the Methodist persuasion" (106). In his first speech in Brown's novel, Peck declares, "I believe that the sons of Ham should have the gospel, and I intend that my negroes shall." Accordingly, he employs a New York "missionary to the poor" who, as he says, "preaches to our 'people' on Sunday" (110). William Wells Brown modeled Peck on an actual Rochester minister, and the sermon preached by his "missionary" (111–14) is based on one of the *Sermons Addressed to Masters and Servants* by the Maryland minister Thomas Bacon (1700–68), originally published in 1743.[1] After his sermon, the preacher reads various questions and answers, including the question "Why may not the whites be slaves as well as the blacks?" and the answer "Because the Lord intended the negroes for slaves" (115).

Both "the sons of Ham" and "the Lord intended the negroes for slaves" depend on an interpretation of Genesis widely accepted in nineteenth-century America—so popular that Brown did not need to explain the allusion, so orthodox that Brown did not attempt to challenge its exegetical credentials. That interpretation seemingly gave biblical sanction for American slavery, and its "webs of meaning" unified what one historian has called the "mythic world" of antebellum southern culture.[2] Peck refutes Enlightenment political philosophy by an appeal to the authority of scripture: "The Bible is older than the Declaration of Independence, and there I take my stand." Peck's young white friend Carleton endorses this association of Christianity with slavery, but rejects both institutions: "I am no great admirer of either the Bible or slavery" (108). Some blacks put it more bluntly, rejecting Christianity as a cynical white ploy: "Dees white fokes is de very dibble . . . I think de people dat made de Bible was great fools . . . 'Cause dey made such a great big book and put nuttin' in it, but servants obey yer masters" (115).

Like other abolitionists, Brown realized that slavery could be overthrown only by breaking its link to Christianity. The first chapter of Frederick Douglass's *Narrative* addresses the argument "that God cursed Ham, and therefore American slavery is right" and that "the lineal descendants of Ham are alone to be scripturally enslaved"; the last chapter contrasts America's "*slaveholding religion*" with "the Christianity of Christ;" in-between, Douglass describes "the religion of the south" as "a mere covering for the most horrid crimes,—a justifier of the most appalling barbarity."[3] Likewise, *Clotel* devotes whole chapters to religious disputation ("The Religious Teacher," "The Young Christian," "The Liberator," "The Christian's Death") and religious satire ("The Parson Poet," "A Night in the Parson's Kitchen," "A Slave-hunting Parson," "Death of the Parson"). Nor is such hypocrisy limited to the South. "We once visited a church in New York," Brown writes, describing the escaped slave William's disillusioning encounter with northern colorphobia, "that had a place set apart for the sons of Ham." As the ambiguous pronoun *we* indicates, Brown slipped easily from William's fictional exasperation to his own: "It was a dark, dismal looking place in one corner of the gallery, grated in front like a hen-coop" (175). From first chapter to last, withering quotations and asides skewer the hypocrisy of slaveholding Christians.

Genesis does not say that Ham (sometimes translated "Cham") or his son Canaan, or Canaan's son Cush (sometimes translated "Chus"), was black or African. Recent scholarship has convincingly demonstrated that Peck's interpretation of the Curse of Ham arises very late in the history of biblical (and geographical) interpretation; its various elements coalesced in Islamic thought between the ninth and eleventh centuries, but in English the curse was not related to African color until the sixteenth century.[4] Like Douglass and Brown, modern historians have focused—naturally and properly enough—on the devastating implications of this myth for the treatment of Africans. I want to focus instead on its role in the evolving history of white manhood.

The implications of the curse for whites depend, in part, on identifying the descendants of Ham's brother Japhet. Noah's three sons were first assigned to separate geographical regions, and Japhet's line confined to Europe, by Alcuin (732–804),whose commentary on Genesis was followed, two centuries later, in Aelfric's introduction to his Anglo-Saxon translation of the Bible, and by the anonymous Middle English poem *Cursor Mundi* (ca. 1300).[5] But the association of Europe with Japhet was first widely disseminated in the great secular best-seller of the fourteenth century, Sir John Mandeville's *Travels.*[6] Mandeville, though, also included "the people of Israel" in Japhet's family, and in the seventeenth century commentators were still furiously debating the exact geographical destinations of Japhet's 14 children.[7] Nevertheless, by the 1690s, when asked "From which of the three Sons of Noah did the Europeans proceed?" a London newspaper answered, "There's little Question to be made, but that they came from Japhet."[8] The movement from Latin commentaries to London newspapers matters as much to the evolution of Christian consciousness as the actual content of these interpretations. But even a confident equation of Japhet's posterity with Europeans did not necessarily equate them with "white" people.

In the preceding chapters, I have traced the slow emergence of the new generic meaning of the word *white.* Generic whiteness cannot be found in Alcuin or Mandeville, Augustine or Luther.[9] I have not found *white* in any English biblical commentary before 1574—and even that example is translated, ironic, and ambiguous.[10] Once used almost exclusively of women, by the 1660s *white* had lost its original gender coding, and both the adjective and the noun were being routinely and positively applied to English men. But by then the word was no longer merely a neutral description of the relative paleness of English complexions. As a marker of collective identity, and therefore of self-identity, it had acquired an ad hoc collection of idealized associations. It remained as true in 1660 as in 1560 that every early modern cultural ideal is "also an ideal of manhood."[11] So the idealized associations that whiteness acquired during the seventeenth century were adapted from, and helped re-create, codes of male conduct. *By the 1660s it meant something for a man to be white.* In this and the two following chapters, I will try to unpick the knot of the word's new connotations. Some of those connotations are directly tied to interpretations of Noah's curse on his son Ham.

Damned Work

Logically, any putative biblical explanation of black bodies and slavery was also, inevitably, an explanation of nonblack bodies and liberty. Several early English texts that expound the biblical theory of blackness also use *white* in a generic sense. Moreover, unlike Ptolemy's explanation of the distribution of human colors, any biblical explanation had ethical, social, and theological implications for white Christians, and particularly for white males. Even Brown phrases the curse in male terms—the phrase he uses, twice, is "sons of Ham," as if the female descendants of Ham had not also been cursed, as if the curse of slavery were somehow specifically male. Ham is one of Noah's three sons; in cursing Ham's son to slavery, Noah simultaneously blesses Ham's brothers with the promise that their descendants shall be masters of those slaves. The curse and the blessing form a single system of male relationships. Any change in the interpretation of one element of that system (Ham) has implications for the others (Ham's father and brothers). Every relationship within that system is governed by the binary opposition between labor (a curse) and inherited property (a blessing).

The biblical theory's English debut took place in George Best's 1578 account of Frobischer's voyages to what is now northeast Canada; it first appeared in an all-male context that had no obvious relation to either Africans or slavery. So unexpected is this context that it seemed self-evident to black historian Winthrop D. Jordan that Best "veered off" from his proper subject "to the problem of the color of Negroes," and Jordan took this swerve as evidence of "the blackness within" at "a deep and almost inaccessible level of Elizabethan culture."[12] Jordan, that is, took Best's theory as evidence for an essentially psychoanalytic reading of the Elizabethan male unconscious.

But Jordan fundamentally misread the context. In the first place, the Frobischer voyage—like all Atlantic navigation, like all English economic and social life—was structured by the exploitation of denigrated labor in the pursuit of idealized property. Best himself, as an educated gentleman in a position of command, depended on the blessing of inherited property and status, which saved him from the cursed manual labor performed by the unnamed sailors on whom Frobischer's and Best's success and survival depended. As historian Paul Freedman has shown, in Christian exegesis the curse of Ham had been used most often as a justification of social inequality, including serfdom. From Petrarch to Chekhov, the biblical curse explained the exploitation of the bottom layer of European laborers. Long before Best, Ham had been invoked to justify the status of English serfs and peasants in *Cursor Mundi* (early fourteenth century), *Dives and Pauper* (early fifteenth century), and *The Book of St. Albans* (late fifteenth century).[13] In *Vox Clamantis,* a dream vision of the Peasant's Rebellion of 1381, John Gower—as hostile to uppity peasants as Sir Philip Sidney would be two centuries later—had described the rebellious laboring multitudes (*multitudine seruorum*) as the cursed progeny of Ham (*progenies Chaym maledictas*).[14]

A legal treatise compiled earlier in that century reported that "serfage, according to some, comes from the curse which Noah pronounced against Canaan, the son of his son Ham, and against his issue."[15] That fourteenth-century treatise was cited by Sir Edward Coke in his enormously influential summary and codification of the English common law in 1628, which stated "that bondage or servitude was first inflicted for dishonoring of parents: for Cham, the father of Canaan (of whom issued the Canaanites), seeing the nakedness of his father Noah, and showing it in derision to his brethren, was therefore punished, in his son Canaan, with bondage."[16] In the massive volume in which this sentence forms a negligible part, Coke was systematizing the entirely male judicial powers that regularly deprived some English men and women of their lives, or liberties, or properties; at the same time he was laying the intellectual and historical foundations for a legal and political defense of traditional

"Anglo-Saxon" common-law liberties against the absolutist state. Coke did not associate the curse with Africans, but with the legal history of English servitude.

The curse of Ham thus originated in laborphobia, not colorphobia, and the interpretive shift from English peasant to African slave needs to be understood as a change in the object of exploitation. That change coincided with England's complex transition, over the sixteenth and seventeenth centuries, into something approaching a capitalist economic system. Thus, any account of changing interpretations of the curse of Ham cannot help but become entangled in the so-called Origins Debate, which has raged among American historians since 1944.[17] In that year the Afro-Caribbean historian Eric Williams proposed that "slavery was not born of racism; rather, racism was the consequence of slavery."[18] This proposition was, in fact, only one of the four elements of what has come to be called "the Williams thesis."[19] It actually had been articulated by William Wells Brown 90 years before Williams: "The prejudice that exists in the Free States against coloured persons, on account of their color, is attributable solely to the influence of slavery" (*Clotel,* 171). The difference between Brown and Williams is indicated by the title of the 1944 book: *Capitalism and Slavery.* In the second half of the twentieth century, those who blamed slavery for racism attributed slavery to capitalism. "Capitalism," as Sharon O'Dair points out, "is routinely demonized in critical discourse"; that comfortable anti-capitalism serves the professional interests of "privileged intellectuals" whose own status depends on an antipopulist rejection of the market.[20]

Which came first, racism or capitalism? While I would not presume to resolve what historians cannot, it seems to me—from the predictable perspective of a literary critic—that much of the confusion generated by this debate stems from a failure to attend to the relationship between language and social experience. The answer to the historical question obviously depends on how one defines *racism* (a twentieth-century word) and *capitalism* (a nineteenth-century word). Within the postmodernist academy, the thesis that racism preceded slavery now is often condemned as the product of a naive *essentialism* (another twentieth-century word, first demonized by French existentialists, and installed in the American academic canon of vilification by Judith Butler in the 1990s). All these -ism words, and the analytical techniques associated with them, can be valuable; after all, *colorphobia*—which I prefer to *racism*—is not a seventeenth-century word either (although it is earlier than any of these others). The words used in the seventeenth century probably would have been *greed* (instead of *capitalism*) and *prejudice* or *opinion* (instead of *racism* or *essentialism*). Brown, in *Clotel,* wrote of the "prejudice . . . against colored persons, on account of their color." Middleton's Black King in *The Triumphs of Truth* had used *opinion* in much the same sense, to acknowledge that some Londoners assumed that a black body was incompatible with sanctity: "in opinion's lightness," a blackamoor was "as far from sanctity as [his] face from whiteness." Middleton does not attribute this opinion or prejudice to any particular social group, status, or class: "But I forgive the judgings of th'unwise, Whose censures ever quicken in their eyes, Only begot of outward form and show." *Unwise* is not the same as *uneducated;* as Middleton's plays show, no single social rank monopolizes unwisdom. Some people in London in 1613 *judged* others on the basis of the color of their faces; this prejudgment presupposed and expressed a *prejudice* against black bodies. But Middleton's testimony to this prejudice also demonstrates that not every Londoner shared it, because in describing it Middleton also challenges it.

Historians and literary critics have provided plenty of proof of English color-phobia. From their first encounters with African peoples, some of the English were prejudiced against humans with dark complexions.[21] That prejudice was not—and never has been—universal. But it was demonstrably common enough in the sixteenth and seventeenth centuries. Moreover, historian David Eltis has proven that "even the most cursory examination of relative costs" shows that, if pure profit were the determining factor, English or European slaves should have been preferred to African slaves. The capitalism of the plantation system was constrained by a European "value system" that discounted African rights.[22]

Nevertheless, those black slaves were purchased by a minority of relatively wealthy Englishmen. Almost all early modern books were written by that elite male minority. By dismissing such texts as elite male propaganda and such actions as elite male prejudice, we can imagine an ungendered utopian solidarity of worker resistance. Certainly, in the seventeenth century African-born and English-born labourers in the Anglophone world sometimes joined forces to frustrate, resist, escape, or kill their oppressors. Indeed, where English servants were forbidden to marry or mate with African slaves, even fornication could be (and has been) interpreted as evidence of color-blind intergender solidarity of labor against capital.[23] Theodore Allen, who has emphasized such cases, is the most formidable advocate of the argument that racism was a capitalist class solution to a "labor problem" and a "problem of social control," alienating white workers from black workers to disempower the laboring majority of inhabitants; but even Allen has to concede that a generalized hostility to blacks or Indians occasionally was expressed by English laborers in Virginia, as early as the 1660s.[24] I think it was expressed even earlier. In 1623—only four or five years after the first Africans were imported into Virginia—an English servant complained that his master had "sold" him "like a damned slave."[25] Why did he use the word *damned?* "Like a slave" would have made the point; *damned* is unnecessary but emphatic, condemning other oppressed laborers, rather than sympathizing with them. Since all actual slavery in the New World up to 1623 was

Amerindian or African, and since it was Africans who were routinely "sold" as slaves in the Atlantic world in the first decades of the seventeenth century, and since an Englishman probably would not refer to Englishmen enslaved by the Turks as "damned," it seems to me pretty likely that "damned slave" expressed a poor English laborer's prejudice against African slaves (who were damned because not Christian, and whose black color was associated with hell, and possibly with the curse of Ham). In Virginia, some English laborers felt from the beginning contempt for African laborers.

If this single phrase does not persuade you, you can find less ambiguous examples of prejudice against black people in the works of England's first famous working-class poet, John Taylor (1578–1653). Taylor made his living as a waterman, rowing passengers back and forth across the Thames: watermen have been called the early modern equivalent of cab drivers, but they were less respected than cab drivers, since they did not need to memorize the traffic grid of a huge metropolis, but simply to row back and forth from one side of the river to the other.[26] Taylor lumped into one despised category "Heathens, Jews, Turks, Negroes black as soot."[27] Since this line of verse includes both "heathens" and "Negroes," Taylor's prejudice against Africans was not simply religious bigotry; he had a more particular animus against the subcategory of heathens who were also black. He was fond of such negative catalogs throughout his career: "Turks or Jews or Moors"—"the Moors and barbarous Indians"—"Jews, Turks, Moors, and Infidels"—"Turks, Infidels, Moors, Pagans, Heathen, Jews"—"Jews or Moors." As its frequent coexistence with "Turks" indicates, *Moors* for Taylor meant "blackamoors" or "blacks," and it was never positive or even neutral. In 1614 Taylor referred to America, India, and "black Barbaria" as "black nations that adore" the Devil, and claimed that "Moors and Pagans are all like to" the Devil (who is "black").[28] In 1620 Taylor called "The Egyptians . . . cursed sons of Cham," and compared Newcastle coals to "black Indians" that come "in fleets, like fishes in the shoals."[29] Whether coals or fishes, the blacks do not look human; they seemed to him chiefly remarkable for their numbers, packed into the holds of ships like coal or dead fish. In the same year he described a chimneysweep in Prague who—in addition to his unmanly devotion to his spoiled wife—"like a slave all sooted, Looks like a courtier to infernal Pluto" [the god of the underworld, and therefore a synonym for Satan].[30] Taylor thus equated slavery with a "sooted" complexion, which in turn suggested allegiance to the devil. In 1638, in a particularly degrading reiteration of classical climate theory, he wrote that in "hot Afric and the Libyan coast" the sun's "flames doth seem the world to roast," and there "Negro Moors are dried and blackly dyed."[31] In Taylor's imagination, "Negro Moors" were black because they had been overcooked, like burned and dried-out meat. Or like the Newcastle coals, to which he had earlier compared them.

John Taylor, who belonged to one of the lowest niches of London laborers, at the beginning of the seventeenth century was as prejudiced against blacks as any eighteenth-century Virginia plantation owner could have wished. He did not see them as fellow proletarians, oppressed by the same evil capitalists who were oppressing him. We may dismiss Taylor as a mere dupe, aping the prejudices of his masters and internalizing the values of those who oppressed him, or we may claim him as evidence that a pecking order has always been as common among humans as among other social animals (including primates). But in either case Taylor demonstrates that color prejudice predated the plantation revolution. English ethnocentrism and colorphobia preceded the systematic targeted enslavement of Africans by English colonists, whether one locates the origin of such enslavement in 1617 (with the first blacks imported to Bermuda), the early 1640s (with the first sugar plantations in Barbados), or the late 1670s (after the suppression of Bacon's rebellion in Virginia).

The anti-African interpretation of the curse of Ham united two formidable English prejudices: laborphobia and colorphobia. The curse of painful agricultural labor (linked to expulsion from Eden) fused with the curse of black bodies (linked to Noah's flood and, through Ham's descendants, to the diaspora from the Tower of Babel). In the system of plantation slavery developed in the English Atlantic colonies, those cursed with dark complexions would also be cursed to labor in a slavery as permanent as their blackness. But although, once in place, that genocidal combination of laborphobia and colorphobia would prove enduringly stable, it took decades to develop into its final form.

Climate or Curse?

The English gentleman George Best was laborphobic and colorphobic enough, but in 1578 he was not justifying the English enslavement of Africans, or (as Jordan would have it) channeling the sexual neuroses of his age. His discussion of the curse of Ham immediately follows his discussion of the color of the Inuit people whom the English had encountered on their voyages to the Northwest—"which thing cannot proceed by reason of the clime." It immediately precedes his contrast between the "black and loathsome" complexions of the sub-Saharan descendants of Ham and the lighter complexions of inhabitants of "Spain, Sarigna and Sicilia" who, "by reason of the sphere," should have exactly the same color.[32] I have already cited (in chapter 4) Best's statements about the Inuit (and about "white" people in various tropical and equatorial regions) as evidence of his contribution to the collective sixteenth-century attack on classical theories of the relationship of color to climate ("the Sphere" or "the clime"). His invocation of the curse of Ham belongs to the same project; literally surrounded by that discourse, it forms part of a single coherent argumentative chain. If authoritative classical texts could not predict the distribution of human complexions, how could those troubling new facts be explained? Best found his answer in another authoritative ancient text: the Old Testament.

That idea was not original to Best. It can be traced to the great Islamic scholar Tabari (838–923), who in turn cited earlier Islamic and Hebrew sources.[33] Some Portuguese apparently were using the curse of Ham (or Cain) to justify enslavement of Africans as early as the mid-fifteenth century.[34] Martin Frobisher, the leader of the expeditions on which Best sailed, had spent at least nine months in Portuguese captivity. Best could have heard it from Frobischer, who could have heard it from his Portuguese captors, who could have picked it up from Islamic or Judaic traditions. Indisputably, a Dominican friar in Peru in 1575 claimed that the color of Africans, and their slavery, resulted from an inherited divine curse that went all the way back to the Book of Genesis.[35] Best did not have to cite an angel (or Frobischer), because the curse as the cause of blackness had been explicitly articulated, in print, a dozen years before he sailed west. In 1566 Jean Bodin had acknowledged its existence, in a reference to Ham's son Cush [or "Chus"]: *vix enim persuaderi possum, quod quidem vir doctus tradit, ab execratione Chusis homines atros fieri* (I can hardly be persuaded that men are made black from the curse of Chus, as a certain learned man reports).[36] Bodin did not identify the "certain learned man" who had proposed this theory, but the French orientalist Guillaume Postel had done so in several books, published between 1551 and 1561, which attempted to synthesize ancient and modern, Christian and Judaic and Islamic, cosmography. Postel did not often identify his sources, but he had been educated at Sainte-Barbe, "the center of geographical learning at Paris, as young men from Spain and Portugal brought news of the discoveries," and he had certainly read Islamic and Judaic texts (from which he could have learned of the alleged curse), as well as the new travel literature challenging the climate theory (from which he would have learned that many Amerindians had complexions like Europeans—which he explained by asserting that the Americas were originally populated by European colonists, allegedly sent across the Atlantic in Biblical times).[37] Another Frenchman, the Benedictine monk Gilbert Genebrard, published in 1580 another Latin book arguing "that Chus, the ancestor of the negroes, was made black by the curse on his father, Ham." As evidence for this conclusion, he noted that "not all peoples living in the tropics . . . were black; hence climate had nothing to do with human pigmentation."[38] In 1574 Genebrard had published an edition of the Latin text of the *Homilies on Genesis* by the early Christian theologian Origen; Origen, at the beginning of the third century, had traced the "origin" of the darkness and enslavement of Egyptians back to Noah's curse on Ham.[39] Neglected for a millennium, Origen's *Homilies* were published in five separate editions between 1503 and 1574.[40]

The Ham theory thus surfaces in four different northwestern European authors (three French, writing in Latin) published between 1551 and 1580. All four situate it within a critique of climate-based theories, based on recent geographical evidence. Three decades later, in a book published in Germany, another learned Latin writer, Augustine Torniellus, again invoked descent from Ham as an explanation for African blackness. Citing Ortelius and the Portuguese, he dismissed the "common opinion" that climate caused color: white men (*homines albos*) were born in the American tropics, dusky men in Abyssinia, and blacks (*nigerrimos*) in Malabar. "In the Arctic and Antarctic regions, the natives were black as night, and all the inhabitants of the Cape of Good Hope were Negroes. Then too, though the sun darkened the skins of European field laborers, it never turned them into Negroes."[41] In the continental learned tradition, as in Best's English argument, appeal to a biblical explanation followed directly from the failure of classical geographical theory to account for the observable phenomenon.

None of these Latin texts was translated into the vernacular in the sixteenth or seventeenth century. But in 1600 John Pory Englished *The Description of Africa,* written by Leo Africanus, based on travels chiefly in northern Africa in the early sixteenth century. To cover the intervening three-quarters of a century, Pory added his own long introduction. His "general description of all Africa" drew not only on Leo but on the many European voyages to areas of sub-Saharan Africa that Leo had never seen. Pory, like Best and everyone else familiar with the literature, recognized that classical theory could not account for the observed geographical distribution of color, which must instead be primarily "hereditary." Pory also, like Best, concluded that "the greatest part" of the population of the entire continent "are thought to be descended from Ham the cursed son of Noah: except some Arabians of the lineage of Sem, which afterward passed into Africa."[42] He located most of the Arabians "near the sea shore" (especially the Mediterranean) or "in the deserts" (the Sahara). Pory's passive construction does not tell us who "thought" Africans were descended from Ham, but most of his knowledge of sub-Saharan Africa came from Portuguese sources.

In 1615 another English adventurer (and future Virginia colonist), George Sandys, followed in the intellectual footsteps of Best and Pory. Describing his travels in Egypt in 1610, Sandys asserted that black parents there who sold their black children into slavery "are descended of Chus, the son of cursed Cham; as are all of that complexion. Not so by reason of their seed, nor heat of the climate: the one confuted by Aristotle, the other by experience: in that countries as hot produce of a different color, and colder by thirty degrees have done of the same. . . . Nor of the soil, as some have supposed; for neither (haply) will other *races* in that soil prove black, nor that *race* in other soils grow to better complexion: but rather from the curse of Noah upon Cham in the posterity of Chus" (italics added).[43] This passage was reprinted in 1625 among the excerpts from Sandys in *Hakluytus Posthumus;* the running title at the top of the page advertises "Cham's Curse continuing still. Black color, whence," and the same summary appears in the margin next to this paragraph.[44] Purchas himself, who excerpted the passage and presumably was responsible for highlighting it with these additions, declared, in his own introductory contribution to the collection, that "Africa fell to Cham's part."[45] Two years later Peter Heylyn—who had ignored the curse of Ham in 1621, in the first edition of his compendious *Microcosmos*—felt compelled to acknowledge it in the second edition. Like Bodin, he rejected it; like Best and all these intervening writers, he situated it in the context of the failure of classical geographical theories.[46]

By 1627 the curse theory was so widespread among intellectual elites that it had to be acknowledged, even by a writer who did not accept it; by 1646 it had become so common that an English writer included it in a compilation of "epidemic" beliefs. Sir Thomas Browne rejected the biblical theory, but he dedicated an entire chapter to it. By including it in his compilation of "vulgar and common errors," Browne's attack on the theory testified to its popularity.[47] George Frederickson reminds us that spontaneous violence against minorities occurred in the Middle Ages, long before such hostility was rationalized or justified by racial theories, and another historian concludes that "popular racism can arise with little or no validation from the writing of social theorists and other intellectuals."[48] Like innovations in pronunciation, vocabulary, and grammar, an emergent paradigm can saturate folk thought long before hypereducated elites accept it. Often enough, slang first appears in print when some conservative pedant complains about how common it has become. Browne's rebuttal, likewise, demonstrates the popularity of the theory he opposes.

Browne identified "the curse of God on Cham and his posterity" as one of only two "generally received" explanations "Of the Blackness of Negroes." The other, predictably, was the ancient climatological theory, with which he began, demonstrating at length that it had been refuted by "modern geography."[49] Only then did he turn to the biblical alternative. Before he did so, however, he had conceded three points central to the biblical case. First, the title of Browne's chapter phrased the problem in a new way: the problem is "the Blackness of Negroes," rather than the larger variety of human coloring (as it had been for ancient and medieval philosophers) or the anomalous appearance of "white" bodies where they should not have been found (as it was for Columbus and many sixteenth-century investigators).[50] Second, Browne's discussion presupposed that "Europeans" were "white."[51] Third, he concluded that, by whatever means "this complexion was first acquired, it is evidently maintained by generation," transmitted "from father unto son" by the "sperm of Negroes."[52] Notice that Browne does not say "parent unto child" or "blood of Negroes," but specifies male fathers, sons, and sperm. This emphasis on male lineage depends on the Aristotelian theory that mothers provided nothing more than raw matter (Latin *mater*), into which fathers infused spirit, form, and life. But the imagery of paternal inheritance also reiterates an essential element of the very theory that Browne set out to refute. This reproductive hypothesis would only be strengthened by the rise of modern biological science (which I discuss in the next chapter).

The climatic theory of Ptolemy and pseudo-Aristotle had satisfied European elites, as an explanation for the evident diversity of human populations, for at least a millennium and a half. When western European voyages undermined that theory, some other explanation had to be found. The Bible was the most authoritative single text in early modern Europe; both "the Book of God" and "god of books," it was "central to all spheres of intellectual life," not simply religion but astronomy, meteorology, magnetism, medicine, music, arithmetic, geometry, rhetoric, mechanical arts, moral philosophy, politics. The Bible had been equally central to medieval intellectuals, but the printing press unified, simplified, regularized, and popularized it. Probably more than a million copies were printed, in English alone, between the Reformation and 1640.[53] It would have been astonishing if European men had *not* searched the Bible for a new hypothesis to replace Ptolemy's. Nor is it surprising that this alternative theory gained adherents. Unlike the Ptolemaic theory, it could not be refuted. The Ptolemaic theory predicted a certain global distribution of color; when that prediction was repeatedly falsified by experience, defenders had to supplement it with more and more complicated subtheories. By contrast, the biblical theory depended on interpretation of an ambiguous curse, followed by identification of certain peoples as descendants of the cursed man. Both the interpretation and the identification could be disputed, but they could not be falsified.

Sir Thomas Browne complained that the curse theory "was sooner affirmed than proved, and carrieth with it sundry improbabilities." This is a logician's complaint. For most people, the proof was not textual and did not depend on the complex questions of biblical exegesis and genealogy surveyed by Browne. The proof, for most Europeans, was a social fact: the widespread enslavement of blacks by "whites," begun by the Portuguese two centuries before Browne published his book, transplanted to English colonies in the 1620s if not before, and increasingly visible even in London after 1660. If any people had been cursed to slavery, it had to be Africans.[54] Moreover, the more brutally they were treated, the more evident it became that they were cursed; the prophecy was therefore self-fulfilling (as the most influential prophecies usually are). It was also, to some extent, self-generating. Anyone who read the first book of the Bible could collate any of its curses with the ongoing enslavement of Africans. The Dominican friar who in 1575 assured the Inquisition that "the blacks are justly captives by reason of the sins of their forefathers, and that because of that sin God gave them that colour" claimed to have acquired his information from "an angel."[55] In other words—whether or not we believe in angels—his interpretation came to him as a flash of insight. The Inquisition did not approve of individuals who claimed direct access to divine revelation (thereby bypassing the appropriate official channels). But Protestants found it much more difficult to police claims to inspiration—especially in the colonies, which were to some extent used as dumping grounds for nonconformists. Even in allegedly orthodox outposts, the shortage of churchmen made it impossible to impose any particular authorized interpretation of the Bible: Anglican Virginia did not have its own bishop until the American Revolution. It allegedly belonged to the diocese of the Bishop of London, but in fact individual parish vestries were self-governing assemblies of laymen who employed and deposed ministers. As early as the 1660s, colonial laymen were punishing ministers who objected to their treatment of blacks or refuted their interpretation of the curse of Ham. Even in New England, where ministers were more plentiful and powerful, their arguments against the theory demonstrate its stubborn currency among parishioners.[56]

Browne's second objection to the theory was that "whereas men affirm this color was a Curse, I cannot make out the propriety of that name, it neither seeming so to them, nor reasonably unto us."[57] I applaud Browne's objectivity here, as presumably will most readers of this book; but the beauty standards of human beings are usually more self-centered, or at best ethnocentric. And whatever the intrinsic beauty of black bodies, physically brutalized slaves—of whatever color—are not likely to remain beautiful for long. Halle Berry's looks would not have survived the Middle Passage. (And Berry is, of course, like many Americans, of mixed ancestry.)

Modern anthropology and statistical studies of genetic drift decisively contradict the account of human origins presupposed by the "African" interpretation of the curse of Ham. But until the late twentieth century, no intellectual or material technology could identify the genetic and therefore genealogical relationships between scattered human populations, and no archaeological evidence could establish the chronology of ancient human migrations. Until the late eighteenth century, orthodox European historical thought was monopolized by biblical chronology, which placed Noah's flood less than 4,000 years before Columbus crossed the Atlantic.[58] Even now fundamentalists reject any evidence that might contradict (their interpretation of their translations of) the Bible; their faith in the authority of that single book outweighs all other evidence. It does so, in part, because popular interpretations of the Bible are easily comprehensible. Anyone can understand the curse of Ham as an explanation of color ("Noah cursed the descendants of Ham, and that is why black people are black, and why they are slaves"). As chapter 4 shows, every early modern version of climate theory was so complicated that it can baffle even dedicated scholars. Between 1566 and 1646 the curse theory was rejected by a few secular intellectuals; it was embraced by many clergymen and pragmatic laymen. The spread of the "Ham" theory of blackness can be explained without resorting to a loose psychoanalytic reading of the Elizabethan unconscious.[59]

Nevertheless, the biblical explanation does have psychological causes and consequences. One set of these can be seen in the work of Thomas Peyton (1595–1626), the son and heir of a landed esquire, educated at Cambridge University and at the London legal college called Lincoln's Inn. Peyton attributes black skin to the curse of Cain, not the curse of Ham; there is a long history to the confusion of the two, and in Christian commentary the curse of Cain antedates the curse of Ham as an explanation of black bodies.[60] In *The Glass of Time* (1620), Peyton explains that

> Cain's most fearful punishment and mark
> Was that his skin was all to *blackness* turned . . .

Peyton acknowledges that "Some have alleged . . . The sun himself to be the cause of it," citing various classical authorities for the belief that black complexions arise "in the hot and torrid burning Zone" because of "the heat extreme." But like other educated Europeans of his time, he realizes that this explanation is no longer plausible, because the geographical distribution of "white" people contradicts the climate theory.

> If this be true, how is it that there be
> In Africa, America, to see
> Under the line both people white and fair,
> As many men that now in Europe are,
> There born and bred by courteous *Nature's* laws—
> A pregnant *Sign* that cannot be the cause.

In contrast to Peyton's distaste for black skin, he associates *white* with *fair* (not only "light" but "beautiful"). Others attribute blackness to "the dryness of the soil" that makes some men look

> Much like the *black* and curséd Cain himself
> From top to toe, from head unto the foot,
> As if with grease they were besmeared, and soot.

But he replies that people in "the Libyan deserts" are "*white* (or *tawny* at the most)." He also recognizes that whites and blacks now inhabit the same places. He asks defenders of the geographical theories to explain

> How we and they are born within one place,
> And we are *white,* and they are *black* and base.

Although there is demonstrably human "variety" on the earth, "none more differ than the white from *black.*" The difference is easily summarized:

> The *Southern* man, a black deforméd elf;
> The *Northern* white, like unto God himself.[61]

Peyton, like other Elizabethan and Stuart writers, "proves" his biblical hypothesis by citing the new demographic evidence against the old geographical hypothesis.

But Peyton also demonstrates that the biblical hypothesis springs, in part or whole, from sheer ethnocentric repugnance. He takes it for granted that black skin is a "most fearful punishment" associated with *hell, grease, soot.* So viscerally revolting does Peyton find black skin that he seems unable to mention it without adding some other insulting term *(stained, smeared, base, deformed).* Most of these words demean black skin by associating it with degraded forms of "base" labor: the soot of chimneysweepers, the grease of cooks, the stained and smeared bodies and clothes of manual workers, the deformity of overworked and abused bodies. Peyton cannot imagine black skin (or laboring skin) as anything other than a curse, a loathsome "mark" placed on the body of sinners. Which curse—Ham's, or Cain's—hardly matters. This poem spits prejudices as poisonous, and as self-satisfied, as anything quoted in *Clotel.*

Peyton does not specifically justify the enslavement of Africans: the justification of slavery depends on the curse of Ham, and he has chosen instead the more primal curse of Cain. Because Cain was guilty of murder, his crime associates blackness with homicidal violence: a "black" face is a "murderous face." That association organizes most depictions of black men in early modern plays, from *Titus Andronicus* to *Othello,* and four centuries later it still dominates the representation of black men in white media. The violence of Cain is specifically fraternal; it is the violence of someone with whom you share a home. Peyton (an elder son and heir) condemns the "black" murderous envy of a dispossessed younger brother. Implicitly, Peyton identifies whiteness with Abel, the innocent victim. Explicitly, Peyton smugly equates his own "white" identity with "God himself." A very gratifying self-conception, no doubt, which does much to explain the subsequent popularity of whiteness. The perfectly virtuous white God has an obligation to punish what the black man has done, or would do, to innocent white victims. White identity is here constructed as, simultaneously, helpless victim and all-powerful avenger. The very helplessness of the victim justifies the unrestrained power of the avenger. The aristocratic logic that justified the brutal repression of peasants and urban laborers justifies Peyton's violent contempt for black bodies, and soon would justify white violence against black laborers.

Genesis rushed in to fill the vacuum left by Columbus's puncturing of the climate theory. But Peyton's was not the only possible interpretation of the biblical hypothesis. Indeed, it was a minority view, because it preferred Cain to Ham. The curse of Ham, by contrast, specifically justified slavery, and once color-coded it would justify the wholesale enslavement of Africans in the early modern Atlantic world. But the terms of that justification had consequences for white men more complicated than Peyton's.

Bible Reading

Any curse is a second-order explanation: to attribute blackness to a curse inevitably presupposed some anterior action to justify that curse. The exact nature of that anterior action could be (and has been) debated, but the biblical source restricted the possibilities. For our immediate purposes, we can ignore the complex history of the transmission, translation, and interpretation of the original Hebrew text, and read the story of Ham as it was read by most Elizabethan and Jacobean Englishmen, in the English of the Geneva Bible:

> Now the sons of Noah, going forth of the Ark, were Shem and Ham and Japheth. And Ham is the father of Canaan. These are the three sons of Noah, and of them was the whole earth overspread. Noah also began to be an husbandman and planted a vineyard. And he drunk of the wine and was drunken, and was uncovered in the midst of his tent. And when Ham the father of Canaan saw the nakedness of his father, he told his two brethren without. Then took Shem and Japheth a garment, and put it upon both their shoulders and went backward, and covered the nakedness of their father with their faces backward: so they saw not their father's nakedness. Then Noah awoke from his wine, and knew what his younger son had done unto him. And said, "Cursed be Canaan: a servant of servants shall he be unto his brethren." He said moreover, "Blessed be the Lord God of Shem, and let Canaan be his servant. God persuade Japheth, that he may dwell in the tents of Shem, and let Canaan be his servant." (Genesis 9:18–27)

The word *white* does not appear here. From such a text, the only thing absolutely clear is that the curse was provoked by some violation of the proper relationship between father and son. The marginal glosses in the Geneva Bible reinforce that emphasis: Ham displays "derision and contempt of his father," and Noah "pronounceth as a prophet the curse of God against all them that honor not their parents: for Ham and his posterity were accursed." The Hebraism "servant of servants" is glossed as "a most vile slave," and Ham's son Canaan (to whom it applies) is identified as progenitor of "the Canaanites that wicked nation, who were also cursed of God."[62] Noah's drunkenness is condemned, but nothing more is said about his nakedness. These glosses echo early Christian exegesis, but more directly they endorse the interpretation of this passage in the *Commentary on Genesis* published—also in Geneva—in 1554 by John Calvin. Calvin was the single most popular author in England up to 1640, and an English translation of his commentary was published in 1578.[63]

The "Authorized" King James version, published in 1611, differs in one (significant) detail: in the last verse, Geneva's "God persuade Japheth, that he may dwell in the tents of Shem" becomes "God shall enlarge Japheth, and he shall dwell in the tents of Shem." The Geneva note recognizes the alternative "enlarge," but prefers to interpret the verse as evidence "that the Gentiles, which came of Japheth and were separated from the Church, should be joined to the same by the persuasion of God's spirit and preaching of the Gospel." That is, the Geneva exiles—in the immediate throes of the Reformation's splitting of Christendom—saw a prophecy of reunification and return, based on the efficacy of persuasion, preaching, polemic. In 1611 a British king's translators saw a prophecy of imperial expansion.

The Authorized Version did not reprint the Geneva glosses, or any glosses at all, to explain or justify the curse. Best had provided a much more elaborate paratext. He began with the proposition that all the world's inhabitants must be descended from "Shem, Cham, or Japhet, as the only sons of Noah, who all three being white, and their wives also, by course of nature, should have begotten and brought forth white children." Whiteness here—as in all versions of the ethnic interpretation of the curse of Ham—is the originary human condition. The explicit statement that "Ham was a white man" before God's curse blackened him can be traced, in Arabic texts, as far back as the eighth century.[64] But this is its first appearance in English. Satan—"our great and continuall enemy"—intervenes: "he caused one of them to disobey his father's commandment, that after him *all his posterity* should be accursed" (italics added). The "fact"—which, in Elizabethan English, meant "a crime"—punished by the curse was "disobedience." Noah had strictly and immediately "commanded" his sons and wives that, "while they remained in the Ark, they should use continency, and abstain from carnal copulation with their wives," but these "good instructions and exhortations notwithstanding, his wicked son Cham disobeyed," and "used company with his wife" to beget the first child, who would disinherit the children of his brothers. This "wicked and detestable fact" provoked God to decree that "a son should be born whose name was Chus, who not only itself, but *all his posterity* after him should be so black and loathsome, that it might remain a spectacle of disobedience to all the world. And of this black and cursed Chus came all these black Moors which are in Africa" (italics added).

Best's repeated insistence on the cursing of "all his posterity" represents a crucial hermeneutic shift. In Genesis, only one of Ham's sons (Canaan) is cursed; in Best, the penalty is first expanded to all Ham's descendants and then specifically related to the black skin of all the descendants of a different son of Ham (Chus). A similar move had been made by Postel, who spoke of the "divine curse" (Diviniae vindictae) against Chus (which the Bible does not contain) as an explanation for blackness (which the Bible does not explain). Likewise, Best's moves were anticipated in the scholarly apparatus that surrounded the Geneva translation. Its marginal notes to chapter nine explain that "Ham *and his posterity* were accursed" (where the text itself cursed only his son Canaan) and that "the Canaanites that wicked nation . . . were *also* cursed of God" (implying that others were cursed too). The words I have italicized, expanding the scope of the curse, alter the Hebrew original in the first direction that Best will make explicit. Another marginal note, just below on the same column, anticipates Best's second change, glossing the reference to Cush (in the list of Ham's sons at 10:6) by explaining that "of Cush and Mizraim came the Ethiopians & Egyptians." Cush is the same son Best calls Chus; the Geneva note's syntax makes him progenitor of the Ethiopians. Likewise, an appendix on the meaning of Hebrew names asserts that "Cusan, Cusi" mean "black, or an Ethiopian."[65] These words refer to inhabitants of the land of Cush. Thus, a careful reader of the Geneva apparatus might infer that all Ham's descendants were cursed and that the descendants of Ham's cursed son Cush/Chus were black Africans.

These confusions about exactly who was cursed can be found throughout centuries of biblical exegesis by Jewish, Christian, and Islamic scholars. In one sense, it makes all the difference in the world who was cursed; in another, it makes no difference at all. Genesis, the shared foundation of three monotheistic religions, for millennia (a) legitimated enslavement (b) on the basis of a divine curse (c) of an entire population (d) including the descendants of those originally conquered and enslaved.[66] Genesis blessed the enslavement of others by God's "chosen people," a license more important and enduring than any changes in the specific identity of the chosen or the enslaved.

Nevertheless, whatever millennia of misery it caused, Genesis did not celebrate white skin, and the Geneva Bible's marginalia did not claim that the blackness was itself a curse, and it did not target any curse specifically against the descendants of Cush/Chus. The explanation of African difference by Best does both.

Best's interpretation is (like Peyton's) clearly motivated, in part, by an ethnocentric revulsion against African bodies ("so black and loathsome") and by a firstborn heir's rage at a younger man's attempt to usurp the inheritance that belongs to his elder brother. But Best's account also differs from Peyton's, and those differences will have large social and psychological consequences for whites.

Best changed the filial disrespect of Calvin and the Geneva glosses into an explicit act of filial disobedience, and he added to them an entirely extratextual act of sexual transgression. Again, Best was not inventing this sexual explanation for blackness, which can be found in various rabbinic, Christian, and Islamic sources.[67] Best's sexual emphasis recurs in two Jacobean clergymen.[68] But Jobson's 1623 description of Africa gave this religious explanation an ethnographic twist:

> undoubtedly these people originally sprung from the *race* of Canaan, the son of Ham, who dis-covered [=uncovered, revealed] his father Noah's secrets [=genitals], for which Noah awaking cursed Canaan (as our Holy Scripture testifieth); the curse, as by schoolmen hath been disputed, extended to his ensuing *race,* in laying hold upon the same place where the original cause began; whereof these people are witness, who are furnished with such members [=penises] as are, after a sort, burdensome unto them. . . . (italics added)

Jobson then explains that these abnormally large African penises are "burdensome" because they make intercourse with a pregnant wife dangerous. His argument about the disadvantages of a big dick may seem strange to us now, but it reflected European medical orthodoxy at the time.[69] Jobson bolsters the plausibility of his interpretation of the curse by citing another biblical text (Ezekiel 27:20), and thereby "right and amply explaining these people." He compares the African women to the two Old Testament sisters who, "being charged with fornication, . . . dote upon those people whose members were as the members of asses, and whose issue was like the issue of horses." (That is, African men had penises as huge as those of asses, and like horses they ejaculated streams of semen.) Jobson does not mention disobedience at all, focusing entirely on sexual transgression. For exposing his father's genitals, Ham was cursed to sire (black) descendants with penises so disproportionately large that they are cumbersome.[70] Samuel Purchas, in the marginalia he added to his reprint of Jobson, emphasized the "monstrosity" of the genitals of the black men he called "Priapian Stallions" (thereby compounding paganism and bestiality).[71] This image of the "Great Privy-membered Guineans" was repeated by other seventeenth-century English writers.[72] Whether or not linked to biblical curses, these anecdotal claims about macrophallic blacks eventually fed one of the most powerful themes of twentieth-century American racism.[73]

There are rabbinic and Christian sources that attribute aberrant sexuality to Ham, but historian Benjamin Braude "has yet to find any medieval Christian source explicitly connecting Ham, sex, and blackness."[74] It is possible that the addition of "black" to this compound originated in strong English reactions to the very different sexual customs of Africans (remarked on by all early modern European witnesses).[75] It may also have sprung from an association of the textual nakedness of Noah and the absolute or partial nakedness of most sub-Saharan Africans (also remarked on by all early modern European witnesses). But it is also possible that the association had nothing to do with African sexual endowments or habits at all. Ham was associated with sexual license long before he was associated with black bodies. Why?—because slaves and other manual workers were always accused of lechery. An eleventh-century physician in Baghdad, describing "white" Caucasian slaves, claimed that "chastity is unknown" among them.[76] In early modern jigs the fool or clown was equipped with exaggerated genitals, and in the competition for a woman's favor his superior physical performance always defeated his gentlemen rivals.[77] As chapter 7 argues, rebellious laborers were represented as figures of lust, rape, uncontrollable sexual excess. Once Africans inherited the curse of Ham, they also inherited "the lower bodily stratum" perennially associated with the lowest social stratum.[78]

Whatever its exact origins, the new compound Ham-Africa-sex, by equating blacks with unregulated sexuality, simultaneously equated nonblacks with sexual control. Calvin had praised the "magnanimity" of Shem and Japheth, in extenuating their father's fault, but he laid most stress on their "modesty," three times reiterated; for Calvin, the whole story confirmed that "there is something so unaccountably shameful in the nakedness of man, that scarcely any one dares to look upon himself, even when no witness is present."[79] Calvin did not align this (ridiculous, flesh-phobic) claim with any ethnic or geographical typology. But Jean Bodin did, arguing that northerners (Europeans) were naturally continent, in contrast to the inhabitants of hot climates (Africans) who were naturally lascivious. Neither Bodin nor his most important source for the idea of African sexual excess (Leo Africanus) identified Africans as the descendants of Ham.[80] But the subsequent development of an anti-African interpretation of the curse of Ham easily appropriated this alleged distinction between African and European sexual culture, and helped make sexual self-control a defining characteristic of English whiteness.[81]

However, Ham's crime was much more commonly described as violation of a specifically filial obligation. Patriarchal cultures equate disrespect for a father with disrespect for all other forms of social or political authority. It makes sense, within the logic of penalty, that a lack of proper respect for authority should be punished by enslavement: voluntary deficiency provokes compulsory overcompensation. Augustine had consistently allegorized Ham as the father of heresy, mocking what it should revere; the "father" here is God, and more generally the authority of the church.[82] But Augustine never associated Ham with blackness. Not until 1627 did an English interpretation of Noah's curse link it to disobedience *and* slavery *and* Africans: "this curse to be a servant was laid first upon a disobedient son, Cham, and we see to this day that the Moors, Cham's posterity, are sold like slaves yet."[83]

It would be hard to argue that the Scottish minister John Weemes, who wrote this sentence, was preoccupied with justifying British enslavement of Africans. The passage I have quoted is a minuscule fraction of a very big book. Like other ministers, Weemes was engaged in the project of regulating the behavior of British Christians by reference to an authoritative standard of legitimate conduct. Weemes was expounding the moral laws that British Christians should internalize, regulating their own behavior in ways that reinforced but also supplemented the civil law. Moreover, in words that Sir Edward Coke probably would have endorsed, Weemes identified liberty as the original human condition: "Servile subjection was contrary to the first state of man; therefore everyone ought to seek freedom, providing he may have it with lawful means." The logic of binaries means that justification of black bondage also justifies white freedom.

But there were also other, less comforting corollaries of Weemes's recognition that "Servile and unwilling subjection came in after the fall." First, "these who have commandment over their *affections* now, are morally Lords over these that cannot command their affections." These principles still were being reiterated by Reverend Peck, in *Clotel,* more than two centuries after Weemes. "I have searched in vain for any authority for man's natural rights," Peck says; "if he had any, they existed before the fall. . . . These were not 'inalienable rights,' however, for they forfeited both them and life with the first act of disobedience" (107). Ham's act of disobedience (against a father) was preceded by the greater disobedience of Adam and Eve (against God); not only the specific descendants of Ham, but all the descendants of Adam, were vulnerable to what Weemes calls "servile and unwilling subjection." As for any rights given to us by the Bible—including, presumably, the right given to the descendants of Shem and Japheth to rule over Ham's descendants—those depend on how successfully we "command" our own inclinations and impulses and emotions, on how successfully we internalize biblical ethical injunctions. "Our rights are there [in the Bible] established," Peck contends, "but it is always in connection with our duties. If we neglect the one we cannot make good the other" (108).

White control over others depends on white self-control. This reasoning reinforces the emphasis on white sexual modesty, but it extends that imperative regime of inhibition over the entire behavioral field. Of course, Christianity had always railed against the pleasures of the flesh. But the new interpretation of the curse of Ham directly tied abstinence to the legitimation of slavery. The white right (to rule, to be master of slaves) depends on white righteousness. That is why the nineteenth-century abolitionist movement was so often allied with the temperance movement. In 1836, only two years after his escape from slavery, Brown helped organize a temperance society in Buffalo, and in *Clotel* Horatio Green seeks relief from his political and personal failures "in that insidious enemy of man, the intoxicating cup" (149).

Second, if slavery is the consequence of sin, then "seeing all men are sinners now, why are not all men slaves?" Weemes answered that question by an appeal to the Calvinist doctrine of arbitrary election: "If God would deal in justice with us now, all should be slaves, but God hath mitigated this to some, to the end that commonwealths and families might stand." Weemes here echoes the question Calvin had asked: "Why among the many sons of Ham, God chooses one to be smitten?" And the answer is much the same: God "chooses whom he sees to be good, that he may show forth in them an example of his grace and kindness; others he appoints to a different end, that they may be proofs of his anger and severity." God is himself an absolute sovereign, whose "liberty . . . to extend his vengeance as far as he pleases" should not be questioned. But although Weemes shares Calvin's conviction of divine election, he explicitly extends it in a collective direction. For Luther and Calvin, as for Augustine before them, the reprobate belong to every nation.[84] Even in the Ark, "in the hallowed sanctuary of God, among so small a number, one fiend was preserved," which proves that everywhere "the wicked are mingled with the good."[85] But Weemes's God has, instead, "mitigated" his vengeance specifically for the sake of "commonwealths and families." Not individuals, but groups.

Chosen People

Weemes makes explicit the theological reasoning behind the colorphobic interpretation of the curse of Ham. It depends on the belief in an elect nation, a chosen people. Augustine had seen in Genesis a distinction between "the elect" or "the godly" (Shem and Japhet) and "the reprobate" or "the ungodly" (Ham).[86] The colorphobic reading of Ham played to a strain of apocalyptic thought, first influentially articulated by John Foxe's *Book of Martyrs,* that saw England as the new Israel, the godly flock destined to restore the kingdom of God on earth. As early as 1559, the axiom "God is English" appeared in print; in 1579, in the enormously popular and influential *Euphues his England,* John Lyly wrote that "the living God is only the English God."[87] The nationalist reading fed on providentialist interpretations of the Protestant defeat of the Catholic Spanish Armada in 1588 and the Protestant discovery of the Catholic Gunpowder Plot (a conspiracy to blow up the King and Parliament) in 1605. "And if [the Lord] be with us," preacher Thomas Cooper asked in 1615, citing such evidence, "who can be against us?" Cooper's rhetorical questions assumed that the answers were self-evident. "Hath not God wonderfully preserved this little island, this angle of the world? that in former ages was not known, or accounted to be any part of the world? Hath it not been the sanctuary of all the Christian world? Have they not joined themselves to us, because the Lord is with us? Are they not happily sheltered under our gracious government?" Cooper's collection of sermons was entitled *The Blessing of Japhet;* it was dedicated to the Lord Mayor of London and commissioners for the plantations in Ireland and Virginia. "Hath the Lord begun to enlarge us far and near to Virginia, and Ireland," he asked, and prayed that God would "bless all our holy designs far and near, for the establishing of peace, and setting up the kingdom of his Christ, both abroad and at home." Citing the 1611 translation's "God enlarge Japheth," Cooper then defined "the posterity of Japheth" as "the Gentiles, confined especially in this part of the world which we inhabit, called Europe; and extending to all those nations, in all parts of the world, that are not either properly Jews" (descendants of Shem), "or of that cursed *race* of Cham, scattered towards the south in Africa, etc." (italics added). The realm of Japheth was to be enlarged because "the true believer alone is the right owner of all God's blessings."[88]

The separate strands of colorphobia, Calvinist theology, and English nationalism had come together by 1634, when all three coalesced in Thomas Herbert's account of his travels around Africa to Asia. Herbert noted, in a matter-of-fact way, that "the Sun-burnt Ethiopians have a pedigree and curse" from Ham. He also recorded how the "coal black Moors" of Sierra Leone and Guinea expressed "their immeasurable admirations" for the color of Englishmen:

> An English ship not long ago, coasting out for discovery, here under the Equinoctial and elsewhere he anchored. The Negroes, repairing to our ship, earnestly desired one or two of our men to go ashore, leaving hostage in our ship for their safe return. Two Englishmen alloted by the Captain went with them, who were no sooner ashore, but thousands of the Ethiopians flocked about them, extremely admiring their color; so passing along, they were often presented with flowers, fruits, toddy, and like things.

Describing the "savage inhabitants" of the Cape of Good Hope, who were "of a swarthy dark color," Herbert contrasted sexual customs there with those in England. "If you give a woman a piece of bread, she will immediately pull by her flap and discover her *pudenda.* A courtesy commanded them, I suppose, by some Dutch ill-bred sailor—for taught it they are, they say, by Christians. And

English men, I know, have greater modesty." Herbert returned repeatedly to the lasciviousness of the natives of other countries, in stark (naked) contrast to the modesty of his own responses. He described how the women of Siam "go naked . . . unto their middles, where with a fine transparent taffeta they are covered, for though the loins are girded with a dainty lawn, yet by device 'tis so made to open that, as they go along, the least air gives all to all men's immodest views, denudating those parts which every modest eye most scorns, each thought most hates to see and think upon."[89] Obviously, he kept revisualizing this temptation, but by displaying it to others he demonstrated the magnitude of his own self-control. As Thomas Cooper had asked, describing the "burden of corruption" that afflicts even the blessed race of Japheth, "What peace then can there be, since the whoredoms of our nature are so rife, and corruptions so rebellious continually? Is there any way to procure our peace, but by maintaining continual war against our corruptions?"

For Cooper and Herbert and all the other descendants of Japhet, the price of peace is perpetual repression. Surrounded by sexual temptation, the godly Englishman must demonstrate, again and again, his vigilant self-control, his "holy discipline."[90] The price of power is willpower. Herbert expressed his gratitude for "God's infinite mercy towards ourselves, to whom He has vouchsafed not only a sufficient portion of wealth and worldly pleasure, but enriched us above all with that invaluable pearl, the Gospel, and benefit of his son's satisfaction for our sins."[91] Englishmen like Herbert could combine the conviction that black bodies were the result of God's curse with a sense of the blessings vouchsafed their own nation, admirable among other things for sexual self-restraint and the color of their bodies. Like that self-restraint, that elect nation was as explicitly male as the son of God.

Even for those who identified the elect nation not with England in particular but with the international community of godly Protestants, the people so elected were overwhelmingly northern European. Until the 1570s Spain and Portugal were two of England's major trading partners, and relations with the Iberian peninsula were generally friendly. In 1555 Richard Eden's preface to his translation of Martyr and Gómara had elevated King Ferdinand above the "famous princes in whom the Greeks and Romans have so greatly gloried" and defended recent kings of Spain against their critics.[92] But some of those critics were English Protestants, exiled during the reign of Queen Mary and her Spanish husband, Felipe II, and within a decade of their return the English attitude toward Spain began to shift. Eyewitness accounts of the Spanish Inquisition's treatment of Protestants were published in Latin in 1567, in English translation in 1568; in 1570 Foxe added an appendix on Spanish victims to his "Book of Martyrs." The long and brutal Spanish campaign to suppress the revolt of the

Netherlands (1565–1609), particularly the sack of Antwerp (1575) and the assassination of the Prince of Orange (1584), fed the Protestant image of Counter-Reformation Spain as the incarnation of imperial cruelty.[93] The damning *Brevissimas Relación* of Las Casas was translated into English in 1583, and it described the Spanish enslavement, slaughter, and rape of the Indians in horrified and horrifying detail.[94] After Spain absorbed Portugal in 1580, the two Iberian empires were united under one crown; from 1586 to 1603 Spain and England were at war.

The enemy empire was, for the English, not only morally but epidermally dark. Early modern English writers often commented on the dark complexion of Spaniards. In 1590 an anonymous propagandist described "the Spaniards" as "Africans, tanned, hot, parched."[95] In the same decade Shakespeare wrote of "tawny Spain," and Edmund Spenser declared that, having intermarried with "Moors and barbarians breaking over out of Africa," Spaniards had "no pure drop left" of European blood.[96] In Ben Jonson's *The Alchemist* (1611), to disguise himself as a Spaniard an Englishman need only "dye [his] beard, and umber o'er [his] face" (5.5.52). The sign of Spanishness was a black beard and a dark brown face. Dozens of other English examples could be cited from the seventeenth century.[97] The English sense of their own whiteness, epidermal and moral, developed alongside their sense of the darkness of a southern European enemy, the "Black House" that Middleton in 1624 would set against the English "White House" in *A Game at Chess.*

There is nothing intrinsic to Christianity about generic whiteness. The religion originated in the southeastern Mediterranean, and many of its early converts—including the Egyptian founders of monasticism and the enormously influential Augustine of Hippo—were North African. Not until about 700 did the Islamic conquest of the southern Mediterranean make Christianity a specifically European religion. Even then its political and theological and sacramental centers, in Byzantium and Rome, remained Mediterranean. Nevertheless, the Islamic conquests defined the clash of religions along a north–south border, and the fall of Byzantium in 1453 eliminated one of Christianity's Mediterranean bases (and its only remaining Asian stronghold). The fifteenth-century Portuguese voyages down and around Africa, followed by the Spanish exploration and colonization of Central and South America, revealed expansive populations of non-Christians south of Europe. The relative pallor of Iberians, by contrast with those darker southern peoples, coincided with a contrast of faiths, making it possible for the first time to associate different body tints with different religions. But those associations did not reach the English until the sixteenth century. By then the Reformation begun by a German monk in Wittenberg in 1517 had split Christianity itself between two competing centers of authority, one southern (Roman), one northern (German). After the Counter-Reformation defeated Protestantism in France, Austria, and the Spanish Netherlands, the sectarian dividing line was pushed farther north. Catholics controlled not only southern Europe, but all the southern continents. By the early seventeenth century, the self-defined "godly" were concentrated in England, Scotland, the Dutch Republic, Denmark, northern Germany, and Scandinavia. Some of those countries were certainly "white," according to the classical climatic scheme; England was the southernmost of the lot, and "northern" or "white" according to at least some of the traditional typologies. Moreover, in 1603 King James I united the crowns of England and Scotland, bringing an influx of Scots (and a Danish queen) into London and simultaneously extending the kingdom's communal identity northward, for the first time encompassing highlands and islands that were undoubtedly northern. Hence, Peyton's distinction between the "Southern . . . black deformed elf" and the "Northern white, like unto God himself" overlays a classical geographical scheme with colorphobia, laborphobia, and a Protestant map (see Illus. 9).[98]

Only at that point, in the third decade of the seventeenth century, did a (con)fusion of English whiteness and Christian righteousness become possible, plausible, or necessary. Peyton's poem seems to be the first concentrated expression of the whole toxic compound. John Taylor the waterman, who was colorphobic and nationalistic enough, never used *white* in a generic sense. Neither did the aristocratic traveler Thomas Herbert. Neither did the Reverend Thomas Cooper, who linked African blackness to the curse of Ham and English nationalism to the blessing of Japhet, but followed the Puritan commitment to drabness (Illus. 6). "The true Church of Jesus Christ . . . is black," she is "black and contemptible," and "is it not good that she should be thus black, to prevent spiritual pride? . . . Is not the Lord glorified in accepting such blackness?"[99] Thus, although we can find elements of modern colorphobic ideologies in Taylor, Herbert, and Cooper, none of them put all the pieces together. Purchas came close to embodying the emergent white/English/Protestant/imperialist generic identity—including the claim (translated from the Dutch) that "your God is white as we are."[100] All the ingredients are present in *Hakluytus Posthumus,* but they are scattered across four expensive volumes and several different voices.

Before those ingredients could be mixed in the poison chalice, *white* had to begin to be widely used in a generic sense. As the preceding chapters show, European whiteness did not enter the popular lexicon at all until 1613. Even then the mere invention or availability of generic *white* does not establish that the social identities later implied by it were already fully articulated and practised. Middleton, who did use *white* generically, did not attribute blackness to the curse of Ham and explicitly rejected the negrophobia evident in Taylor, Peyton,

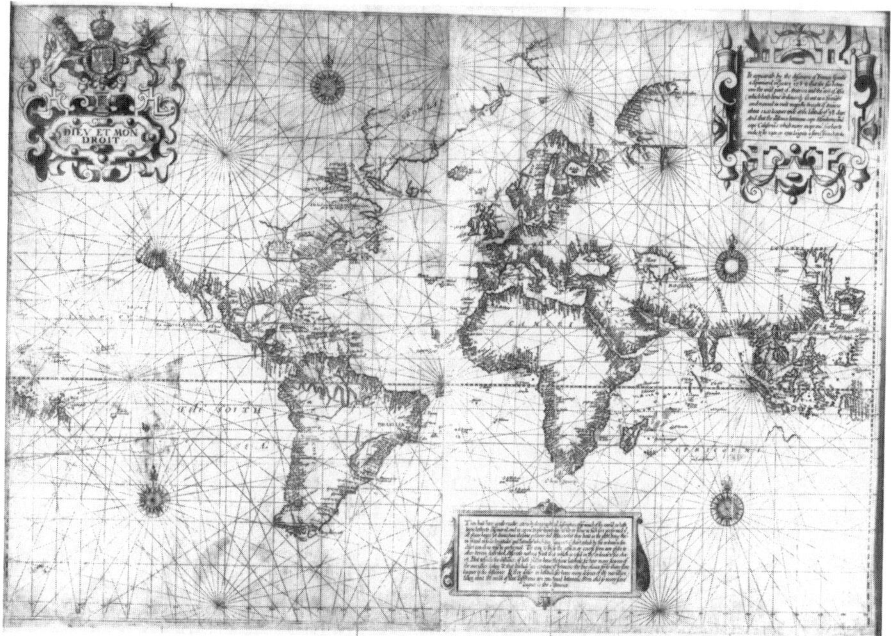

Illustration 9. Medieval world maps were centered on Jerusalem, but Edward Wright's map, included in Hakluyt's influential collection of *Principal Navigations* (1600), put Britain at the center of the world. By permission of The British Library.

and many other English authors. Until the collective senses of both *black* and *white* had become part of the unthinking vocabulary of thousands of speakers of English, modern color-coded identities could not be constructed, rationalized, enforced, or massively transmitted.

One of the meanings of the English adjective *white* always had been "morally or spiritually pure or stainless; spotless, unstained, innocent."[101] But that idiom always had been applied to individuals, and explicitly or implicitly to their invisible souls. In the apocryphal *Gospel of Philip* Jesus throws 72 different colors into a vat at a dyeworks and brings them all out white.[102] The 72 different colors presumably represent the diversity of human sins; only the Lord ("the dyer") can remove the stain of any sin. Whiteness in this parable is not a condition granted by birth to a particular ethnic group, but something miraculous. For the same reason, the prestige of white colorless glass derived from the fact that it was the most difficult to manufacture.[103] In the ancient and medieval world, whiteness was *achieved,* not received. Within Augustine's doctrine of original sin, or Luther's and Calvin's insistence on the centrality of grace, every human being was *naturally black,* unless and until they were whitened by the grace of God. Within that conceptual framework, inherited communal righteousness was inconceivable.

Rather than take the specifically moral or spiritual sense of whiteness as evidence for an intrinsic ethnocentric prejudice, we should regard the association of ethnic whiteness with moral superiority as an example of exaptation. Evolutionary biologists Stephen Jay Gould and Elizabeth Vrba coined the word *exaptation* to describe cases where a particular organ or ability, hitherto of little or no significance to an organism's survival, becomes important because of a change in the environment.[104] The organism did not consciously *adapt* to changed circumstances; instead, fortuitously, it already had a dormant quality that became an unexpected asset, or an ability previously used for one purpose that could now be used for another. For example, to enforce conformity with the Protestant Reformation, in 1538 Henry VIII ordered every English parish to record the date of every baptism, marriage, and burial, identifying by name the person receiving each sacrament; more than a century later, in 1662, those religious records provided the database for the new secular science of demographics, and they continue to be used ("exapted") in modern population studies, in a way Henry VIII never anticipated. Likewise, one or two odd details recorded during many centuries of rabbinic speculation about the details of Noah's curse suddenly, in the late sixteenth century, became useful and important to western European Christians and were plucked from their dormant marginality to become the foundations of a new orthodoxy.

Something similar—what linguist Salikoko Mufwene calls "linguistic exaptation"—happens to languages. Languages ceaselessly evolve in part because changes in the social environment lead speakers to seize on certain existing features of the language, hitherto dormant or used in another domain, and exploit their appropriateness to the new circumstances.[105] At the level of semantics, polysemous words are particularly prone to such appropriation, because the availability of different meanings for the same word leads speakers to make connections between the different meanings. Those connections—like "false etymologies" or "false cognates"—often are unauthorized by history or logic, but they are difficult to prevent, precisely because they involve a kind of code-switching.

Once *white* began to be used by English speakers in a positive ethnic sense, as a self-identifying badge of belonging to an esteemed community, that changed social and linguistic environment gave a new significance and importance to the ancient moral sense of *white.* Logically, speakers always should have distinguished the code for "*white* = ethnic category" from the code for "*white* = moral category," but code-substitution and imperfect replication are an inevitable part of ordinary language use. Folks make mistakes when they talk, and some mistakes are sure easier to make than others. The positive moral sense of *white* helped cancel the residual negative senses of the adjective as a description of male bodies. The very feature condemned by the classical tradition could now be embraced, thanks to its identification with an embattled but evangelical Protestant Christianity. In this new linguistic and social context, those who advocated "the golden mean" could be condemned as "lukewarm" Christians. So-called moderates were vilified for striving "to choke all forward holiness and zeal by commending the golden mean."[106] Golden Mediterranean bodies and ancient Mediterranean centrism began to be replaced by a Christian and epidermal polarity, in which one extreme (white) was good and the other extreme (black) was bad—and the once-ideal middle (mulatto) was a contaminated mongrel mix.

But there is also another, simpler, crasser explanation for the breakdown of the distinction between the two codes: self-interest. By reading the color of their bodies as a moral sign, Englishmen could cloak greed in the vestments of virtue.

Hypocrisy

Like the notion of European whiteness, African blackness was first linked to the curse of Ham and slavery in authoritative discourse, in difficult and expensive books aimed at an intellectual and economic elite.[107] The earliest popular expression of the African interpretation occurred in a sermon preached at Paul's Cross in 1607. Paul's Cross was an open-air pulpit next to St. Paul's Cathedral, which attracted the best preachers and large crowds. London preachers like Robert Wilkinson resembled London playwrights like Thomas Middleton: themselves highly educated, they addressed large and diverse audiences, including the illiterate, and they were therefore natural conduits by which elite theories trickled down into common knowledge.[108] By definition, ministers were more likely than any other group of people to be satisfied by biblical explanations of puzzling phenomena. The subject of Wilkinson's 1607 sermon was Lot's wife, whose transformation into a pillar of salt demonstrated God's tendency to deliver "strange punishment to the workers of iniquity"; among other examples of such punishment, Wilkinson mentioned that "thus the accursed seed of Cham, the Egyptians, Moors and Ethiopians had for a stamp of their father's sin the color of hell set upon their faces."[109] As the rest of the sermon indicates, Wilkinson apparently had read modern geographical works, but he spared only a sentence for this subject; he did not mention slavery or generic whiteness. Rather than identify Englishness with virtue, Wilkinson spent most of his time berating the audience, reading in the fate of Lot's wife a dozen warnings to London's sinful inhabitants. "You hypocrites," he thundered. "The more blesings ye have, and the more knowledge ye have, and the better that name is which ye abuse, the more heavy shall your judgement be. . . . For an ill Christian is the worst creature in the world."[110]

English hypocrisy was also the subject of a sermon preached by Thomas Adams at Paul's Cross in 1613, but that sermon specifically associated hypocrisy with whiteness. Entitled *The White Devil, or the Hypocrite Uncased,* the sermon explained that Judas was "a devil . . . black within and full of rancor, but white without, and skinned over with hypocrisy; therefore to use Luther's word, we will call him the white devil." Whiteness here is associated with skin, the "white skin of profession," the thin outer surface of what one professes or claims or pretends to be.[111] This sense of the shallowness of skin (epitomized by the derogatory expression "skin-deep") was new in 1613.[112] Adams was a popular preacher, and this sermon was printed five times between 1613 and 1617.[113] As Adams acknowledged, he owed the theological paradox of the "white devil" to Martin Luther, who had articulated it in his commentary on Galatians (the most popular of all his works in England).[114] Luther's paradox was inspired by 2 Corinthians 11:14 ("Satan himself is transformed into an angel of light"). Since a devil—as noted by Luther and subsequent theologians treating this theme—was normally black, a "white devil" was a devil in disguise, a person whose evil was covered by a righteous Christian facade. Luther's image was elaborated in 1583 in Pierre Viret's *The World Possessed with Devils.*[115] In Luther and Viret, the white devil was theological, not demographic. Whiteness in Luther's paradox represented a spiritual fault of which any human being was capable. The hypocrite is spiritually black, but pretends to be morally white: white is the color of hypocrisy. "All have the same corruption," Adams preached, because "who hath not sinned in hypocrisy?"[116] But the binary logic that enabled the paradox of "white devils" also enabled, and in some ways generated, the complementary paradox of what the Paul's Cross sermon emphatically called "*black Saints.*" Those who had sinned and repented were preferable to those who, by "artificial whitings," pretended to virtues they did not have: "a *black Saint* is better than a *white Devil.*"[117] Adams's sermon, preached at Paul's Cross in the spring of 1613, probably influenced Middleton's black Christian king in *The Triumphs of Truth,* staged there in the autumn of that year.[118]

But it would have been indecorous for Middleton's Black King to accuse the "white people" in his audience—including the new Lord Mayor, Middleton's patron—of hypocrisy. Accordingly, although *The Triumphs of Truth* contains the first popular expression of generic whiteness, and although it acknowledges the sinfulness of many Londoners, it does not associate their whiteness with hypocrisy or invoke the image of white devils. But elsewhere Middleton did use Luther's paradox. In fact, the first extant example in English drama occurs in Middleton.[119] In Middleton and Rowley's *The World Tossed at Tennis* (1620), Middleton created a character called "White Starch" (one of five Starches, each "habited" in her proper color). "Am not I the primitive starch?" she asks rhetor-

PLATE 1: This example of rock art from Sicily, 9000 years old, is typical of the reddish brown coloring of human figures in prehistoric European art. Museo Archeologico Regionale, Palermo.

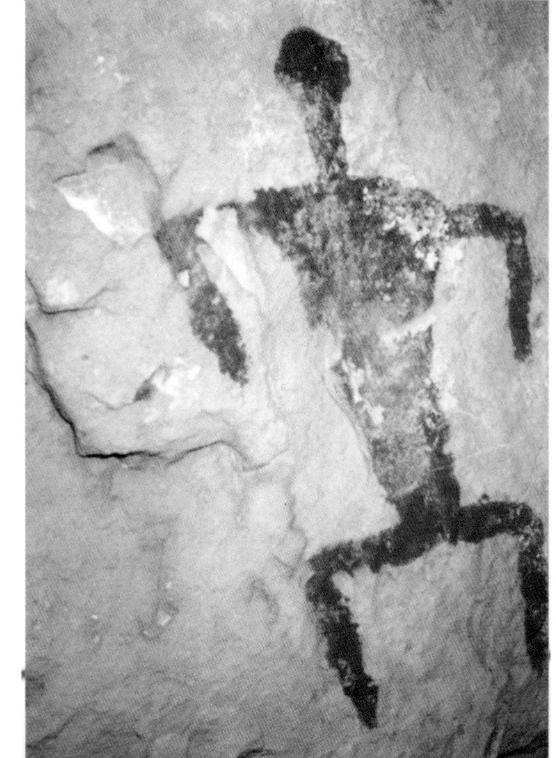

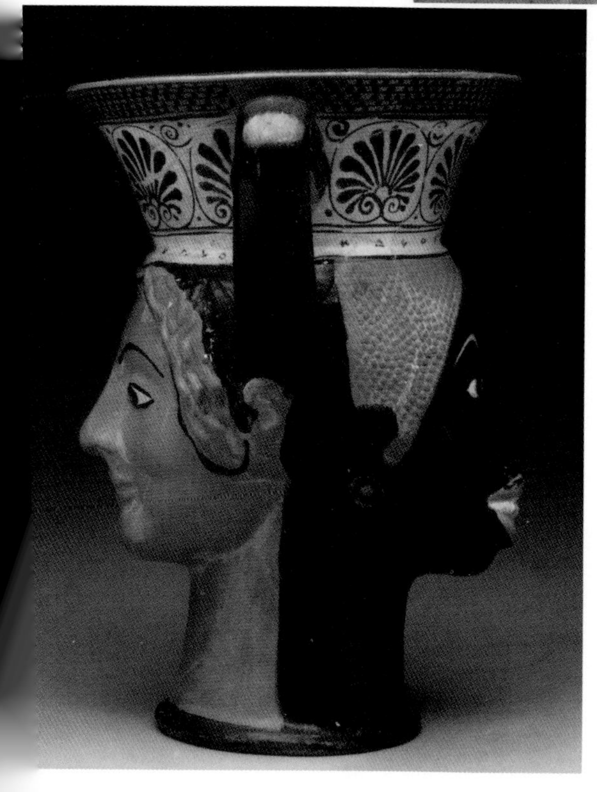

PLATE 2: This Janus-faced Athenian kantharos (c.510–480 B.C.) is one of several surviving specimens that contrast an Ethiopian woman (black) with a Greek woman (red). Photograph © 2003 Museum of Fine Arts, Boston.

above PLATE 3: The complexions of Christ and the twelve apostles in this third-century catacomb mural are as reddish brown as we would expect of Mediterranean outdoor laborers ("shepherds" and "fishers of men"). © Pontificia Commissione di Archeologia Sacra, Vatican.

left PLATE 4: This Christian family portrait, dating from the early fifth century, shows an aristocratic mother, son and daughter, their olive complexions highlighted by contrast with the son's white toga and daughter's white pearl necklace and earrings. ©Museo Civico, Brescia, Italy.

right PLATE 5: Paolo Veneziano's *Crucifixion* (*c.*1349) represents Christ, six angels, and eight human figures with brown complexions against gold backgrounds (Plate 4). National Gallery of Victoria, Melbourne, Australia

below PLATE 6: The dozens of faces in Sassetta's Siena altarpiece *The Burning of a Heretic* (1423–26) are all dark brown. National Gallery of Victoria, Melbourne, Australia

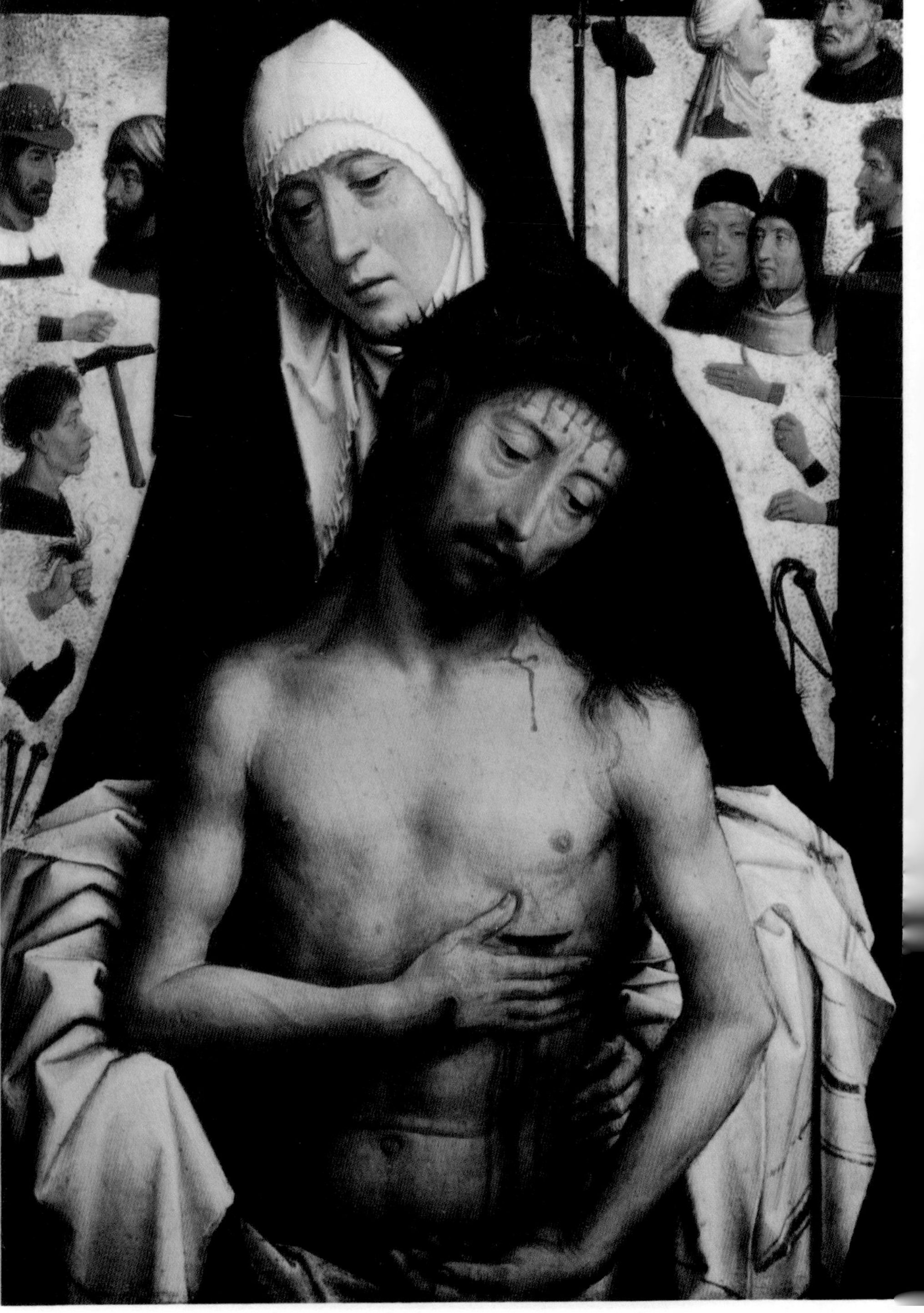

left PLATE 8: Piero della Francesca's *Baptism of Christ* (c. 1460) may be the first painting of a "white" Jesus, but even here his face and neck are tanned brown (in contrast to the three angels on the left). The tan demonstrates Christ's humanity, which suffers corporeal change. National Gallery, London

far left PLATE 7: The Flemish painter Hans Memling's *The Man of Sorrows in the Arms of the Virgin* (1475) depicts a brownish Christ, whose coffee tones contrast with the Virgin's milk-white robes; her face is lighter than his, but framed in white linens that bring out its reddish beige; the seven human males in the background are all much the same color as Christ. National Gallery of Victoria, Melbourne, Australia

right PLATE 9: The brown face and hands of St. Thomas Becket, in the stained glass portrait at Canterbury Cathedral (c. 1185), contrast strikingly with the white elements of his vestments. By kind permission of the Dean and Chapter, Canterbury.

above PLATE 11: Nicholas Hilliard's self-portrait (1577)—which did not have to please anyone but himself—shows a pale peach face set on a contrasting white lace ruff. Victoria & Albert Picture Library, London.

left PLATE 10: Hans Holbein the Younger's 1537 portrait of Henry VIII reveals the same reddish brown complexion evident in other likenesses. ©Museo Thyssen-Bornemisza, Madrid.

next page PLATE 12: Titian's *Laura dei Dianti* (c. 1523–5) initiated the portrait tradition of depicting an aristocratic European woman alongside an anonymous black male servant. Private Collection

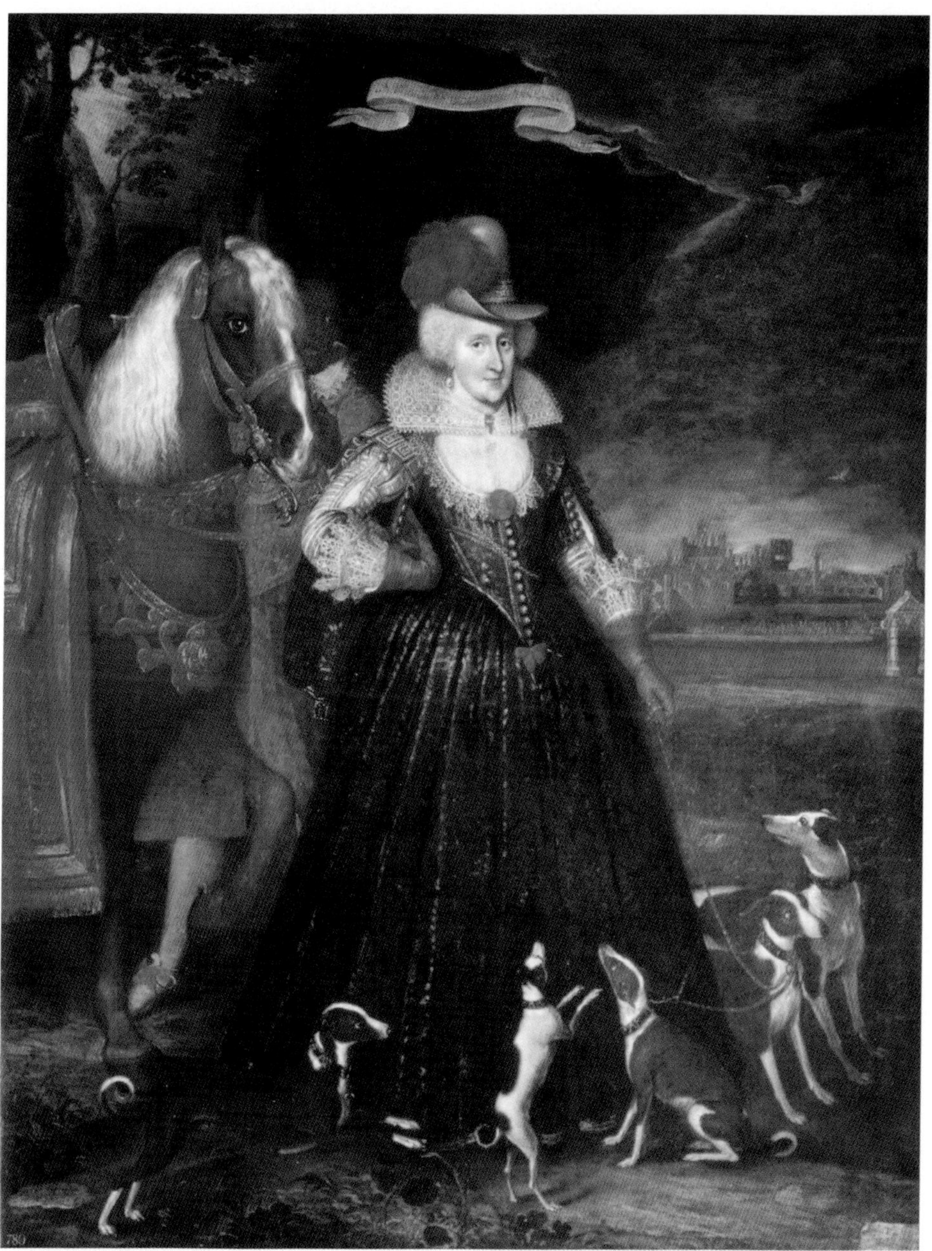

PLATE 13: This 1617 portrait of Queen Anne and her black male servant is the first British example of the genre inaugurated by Titian (Plate 12). The Royal Collection © 2003, Her Majesty Queen Elizabeth II.

left PLATE 14: Titian's self-portrait (c. 1555) shows a man as ruddy as Henry VIII (Plate 10), and quite unlike either Laura or her slave. Staatliche Gemäldegalerie, Berlin-Dahlem.

above PLATE 15: The brown flesh of the only certain color likeness of Shakespeare—the bust on his funeral monument (1616–23)—so offended colorphobic neoclassical taste that it was whitewashed in 1793. By permission of the Shakespeare Birthplace Trust Records Office.

above PLATE 17: Like many other angels in medieval churches, this fourteenth-century image of the Angel Gabriele is anything but white.

left PLATE 16: In *Charles I and Henrietta Maria departing for the Chase* (c. 1630), Daniel Mytens does not separate the British king from his white wife, but contrasts the united couple with their black stableboy. The Royal Collection © 2003, Her Majesty Queen Elizabeth II.

above PLATE 18: The figure in El Greco's so-called *Portrait of a Cardinal* (c. 1600–5) may not be a cardinal, but his dark complexion is typical of the men who visited the painter's Toledo studio. National Gallery of Victoria, Melbourne, Australia

right PLATE 19: This watercolor illustration of the carotid artery (1797?) seems to be the earliest surviving image of a dissected Negro body, though such anatomies were reported by Piso, Boyle, and Malpighi as early as the 1640s and 1660s. National Library of Medicine, Bethesda, Maryland.

Plate 4th

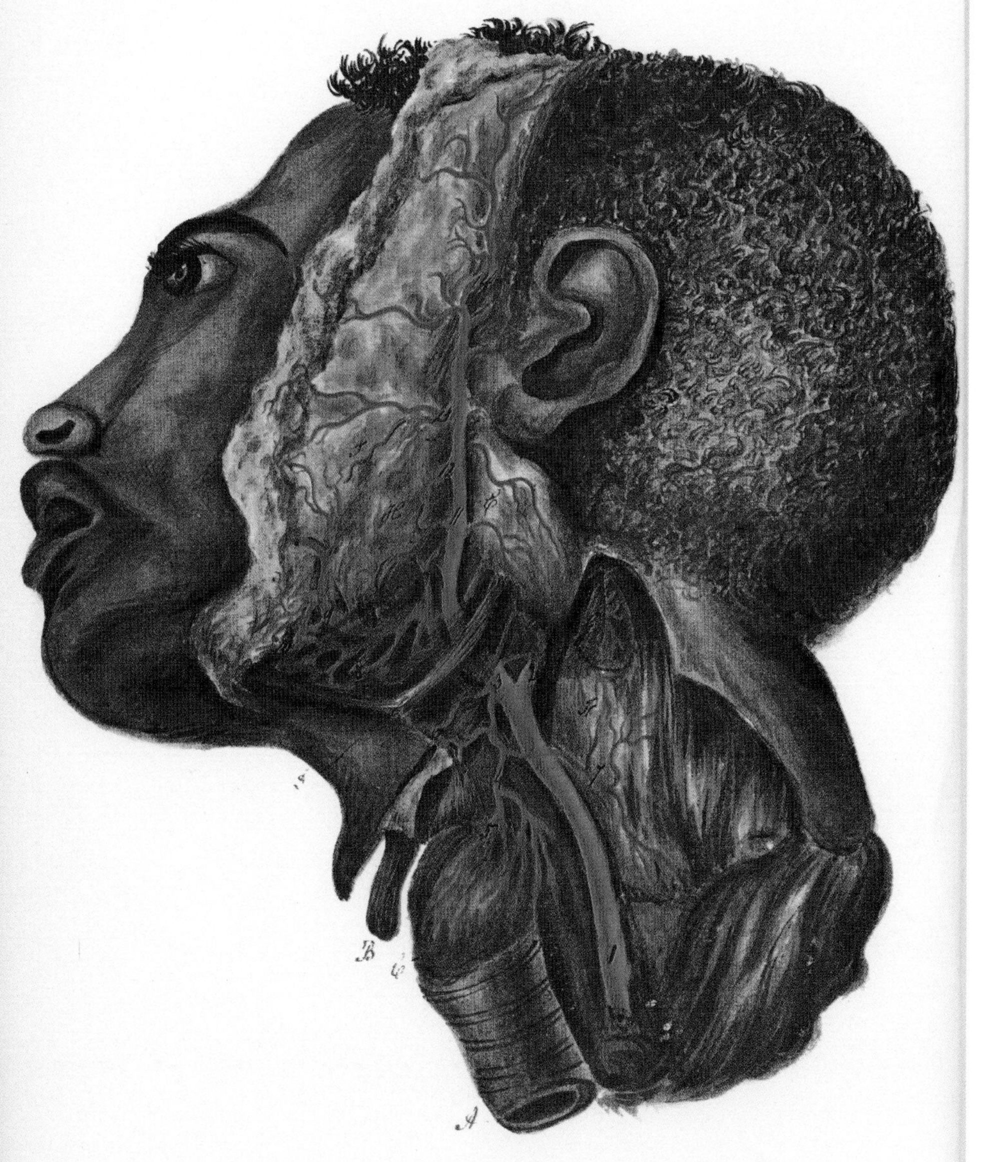

PLATE 20: "A Man is White": John Locke (c. 1685) is so pale that this color plate looks almost identical to a black and white reproduction of the same image. It is hard to discern any distinction between the white of the eye and the cheek. By courtesy of the National Portrait Gallery, London.

ically; "I'm Starch Protestant" (378–88). She is promptly accused of being "a white-faced hypocrite, Lady Sanctity . . . starched like innocence, But the devil's pranks not uglier" (391–94). Hypocritical whiteness is specifically associated with Protestant righteousness and attributed to a recognizably English character.[120] Whiteness, the color of hypocritical English Protestantism, is not the opposite of demonic blackness, but its natural ally and companion.[121]

In 1624, in *A Game at Chess,* the tropes of ethnic whiteness that Middleton had acquired from travel narratives combined with the trope of white hypocrisy that he had acquired from Luther and Adams. Like Peyton, Middleton believed that "we are white." But unlike Peyton, he did not imagine that white people were "like to God himself." In the play's central scene, the Fat Bishop—initially dressed in white robes, attended by a white servant, and honored by the White King with various English ecclesiastical titles—reveals that he is actually "one that's all black" (3.1.285). In the same scene, the White King's Pawn reveals that he is "black underneath" (3.1.261.1) and has been secretly working for the Black House all along. The Fat (White) Bishop and the White King's Pawn visually embody Luther's paradox, and they provoke more iterations of *hypocrite* and *hypocrisy* than occur in any other work by Middleton. Whiteness is a lie.

In *A Game at Chess* whiteness is vulnerable and unstable. "White quickly soils, you know" (3.2.11–12). Two of the play's characters spectacularly display the transformation of whiteness into blackness. At that point, the play's ethnic allegory completely breaks down. It is hard to believe that the characters who change sides also change complexions. Whiteness has slipped from a physiological to a moral and theological sign. But it would be equally accurate to say that, elsewhere in the play, whiteness had slipped from a moral and theological sign to a physiological one. The social power of the fiction of ethnic whiteness depends on precisely such slippages, such movements back and forth across the color line. *A Game at Chess,* the first popular text to elaborate a full-blown fiction of white Englishness, is also the first to display those white slips. It does not do so inadvertently, but deliberately and conspicuously. By making the whiteness of chess pieces an ethnic marker, Middleton created a play of polarities and ironies, a dialogue of contexts, between that emergent ethnic meaning and the older moral meanings, including Luther's image of hypocritical whiteness.

The first systematic representation of English whiteness was thus also the first sustained critique of English whiteness. Middleton's white kingdom features a weak duped white king, a greedy and ambitious white politician willing to betray his king, his faith, and his country for his own gain, a lecherous white duke vainly obsessed with his own good looks, a corpulent and carnal white bishop whose theology wavers between Protestant and Catholic positions, an ideologically naive white woman, a castrated white minister, and a white knight who achieves his greatest success by lying. As in *The Triumphs of Truth,* in *A Game at Chess* the whiteness of Englishmen is simultaneously ethnic and ironic. In its first popular manifestation, the fiction of generic whiteness was a trope of satire. The ethnic whiteness of England, the purity that establishes the right to receive the blessing of Japhet, is simultaneously an image of hypocrisy that must be chastised. *A Game at Chess* epitomizes the "chaste thinking" that critic Arthur Little Jr. sees as intrinsic to ethnic whiteness: self-castigation casts part of the self out of the self in order to purify and justify what remains. As a result, generic whiteness from the outset is the target of a relentless "hermeneutics of suspicion."[122]

But although *A Game at Chess* links ethnic whiteness to white righteousness and white hypocrisy, it does not invoke the curse of Ham. When the treachery of the White King's Pawn is revealed, the White King condemns his lack of loyalty to the royal favor that had raised him "from a condition next to popular labor" (3.1.265). In the next scene, a Black Pawn wishes he could capture "one of these white pawns now; I'd make him do all under-drudgery" (3.2.1–2). But then he is captured by a White Pawn, who declares that he will force the Black Pawn to "do all the dirty drudgery That slavery was e'er put to" (3.2.15–16). But then another Black Pawn enters and captures the White Pawn. There is no solidarity among pawns. There is also no sense that blacks have a monopoly on labor, drudgery, or slavery.

Early in 1625 *Hakluytus Posthumus* reprinted and endorsed George Sandys's attribution of African blackness and slavery to the curse of Ham. That same work also explicitly combined the ethnic sense of whiteness with Luther's white devil. It did so in a marginal note appended to its translation of a description of the Gold Coast of Guinea by the Dutch voyager Pieter de Marees. Marees had explained that the blacks there—in the words of a modern literal translation—"used to be very poor traders, because they trusted the Dutch so much that it amazed us, for they thought that whites" (that is, the Dutch) "were Gods who would not tell lies or deceive people; and they took goods upon their word, without checking the account. As a result, they were deceived."[123] Unlike the Dutch, the English had not yet turned the generic adjective into a noun, and Samuel Purchas translated the key sentence here as "they were of opinion, that white men were Gods." But Purchas added his own sardonic marginal note: "White Devils can hardly make black Saints."[124] Since Purchas was himself a minister, he probably had read Thomas Adams's sermon, with its conjunction of white devils and black saints. But by appending those images to a description of dishonest "white men" cheating blacks, he made *white* and *black* ethnographic, as Adams had not.

Although *Hakluytus Posthumus* contained both a color-coded curse of Ham and generic white hypocrisy, the two concepts occur separately in a vast and expensive compilation. But once the English invested massively in the slave trade, white hypocrisy became directly and explosively relevant to the white right to enslave blacks. In 1684 Thomas Tryon published in London a fictional dialogue between a black slave and his Christian master in an English colony in America. After listening to a long list of accusations, the master asks, "Do you *black Heathenish Negroes* then dare compare yourselves with us brave *white Christians?*" The slave replies that "we made not ourselves *Black,* nor do you make yourselves *White;* wherein then have you anything to brag of above us? . . . though *White* be an Emblem of *Innocence,* yet there are *whited Walls* filled within with Filth and Rottenness . . . have a care therefore that you be not found as *black within,* as we are externally."[125] Tryon's black speaker repeatedly accuses the "*Hypocrite Christians*" of ignoring the commandments of their own religion.[126] He does not mention the curse of Ham, but instead insists that "they are *White,* and we *Black,* because they are born in one Climate, and we in another." And "since *White* is as contrary to *Black,* as *Black* is to *White,* there is as much reason that *you* should be our *Slaves,* as we yours." The black slave denies that the English can claim any intrinsic moral superiority.

> By what right, or on what pretensions is it, O you nominal *Christians!* that you take upon you to make us your Slaves, to overlabor, half-starve, beat, abuse and kill us at your pleasure? Is it because we are not of your Religion and Belief? Hath God anywhere given a Commission to those that profess *Christianity,* that they may, when they list, fall upon any Persons whom they call *Heathens,* and dispossess them of their Lands, or lead them away Captive, and make Merchandize of them, and use them in all respects as Beasts, or rather much worse?[127]

Tryon ignored the curse of Ham, but four years earlier it had been discussed at length in another book published in London. Calling himself *The Negro's and Indian's Advocate,* Morgan Godwyn claimed that the colonists "bespeak [the Negroes] as descendants from Cain, and to carry his Mark," and also "make them the Posterity of that unhappy Son of Noah, who, they say, was, together with his whole Family and *Race,* cursed by his Father" (italics added). Godwyn was not describing arguments made in learned treatises printed in Virginia or Barbados; at the time there were no presses in either place. Instead, Godwyn recorded the speech acts of ordinary English men and women, expressing their opinions "privately (*and as it were in the dark*)," opinions he had "heard . . . more than a thousand times over." Godwyn wanted to refute the biblical explanation for black bodies as it was "usually discoursed" in the colonies: "Because they are *Black,* they are *Ham*'s Seed, and for this under the *Curse.*" He also reported (in order to challenge) popular opinions that had never been articulated by geographers or theologians, such as the "strange and before unheard-of conceit in Divinity, *viz. That Colors are a means of Grace,* and have a power in them to *recommend us to God.*"[128]

Like Sir Thomas Browne, Godwyn set out to cure epidemic errors, but Godwyn gave much more precise information about the popular circulation of these opinions, their status as a widely reiterated consensus among people who would not be considered particularly learned.[129] He noted that it was illogical to invoke both the curse of Cain and the curse of Ham, or to combine the curse claim with the claim that blacks were a different species; but incompatible propositions routinely cohabit in human minds (even in the minds of professional intellectuals), and few of Godwyn's informants busied their brains mastering the theory of theory-building. The complexities of geohumoralism did not concern them; indeed, those complexities hardly concerned Godwyn or Tryon either, who in their zeal to defend black slaves attributed their color to the equatorial sun, as if all obstacles to that ancient climate theory had up and vanished. Colonists in Barbados and Virginia were primarily interested in the use-value of theories. As Godwyn complained, slaveholders made a "*blessed use*" of their "*distortions of Scripture,*" since they "are hereby set at Liberty, and freed from those importunate Scruples" of "Conscience" that would otherwise afflict them.

The curse theory initially was used by white men for white men, in conversation with other white men; it justified the behavior of white male slaveholders to themselves and to other white males who—like Godwyn and Tryon—doubted the legitimacy of plantation practices. Those who disputed that theory and those practices were white men, arguing with their white brothers about the terms of their Father's will. While Godwyn devoted most of his pages to damning slaveholders, he also cited the criticisms leveled by "insolent" Quakers against Anglicans like himself: "*Who made you Ministers of the Gospel to the White People only, and not to the Tawneys and Blacks also?*"[130] Although Godwyn did not specify his source, he was quoting the Quaker leader George Fox, who had visited Barbados in 1671.[131] It was imperative for Anglican ministers—all, of course, male—to be able to defend themselves against such charges (by extending their pastoral care to blacks and Indians). By the 1670s, at the latest, Christians and Englishmen were divided over the enslavement of Africans, as they would continue to be through the nineteenth century. William Wells Brown took the names "Wells Brown" from the Ohio Quaker who had helped him escape from slavery.[132]

There was never any logically consistent defense of slavery, and never any homogeneity of colorphobic opinion, among whites or among Christians. Colorphobia and racism never required logical consistency or unanimity to institutionalize slavery. "Slavery," as Godwyn noted, "is but a lower degree of Poverty and Misery," and the black slaves were just "*poor People,* from whose labour their [the slaveholders'] Wealth and *Livelihoods* do wholly arise." Like laborphobic aristocratics, colorphobic plantation owners "put little difference between the Multitude and brute Beasts." Indeed, Godwyn at one point claimed that many of "these Miseries" of brutal overwork were not "the Fate only of the *Blacks,* but, in a proportionable measure, of the *English* and *White People* also." He was not speaking about all "White People," but specifically of what he had just called "the *White Servants.*"[133] Early plantation owners treated indentured white laborers as badly, in some respects, as they treated enslaved black laborers: hence that epithet "white slaves" applied to white laborers in Barbados in 1666.

Nevertheless, although for polemical purposes Godwyn on this one occasion compares black slavery to white servitude, his whole long angry treatise demonstrates that a fundamental difference in the treatment of blacks had already been put in place. That difference did not need to be universally accepted, or logically defensible, to dominate colonial life. But the anti-African interpretation of the curse of Ham did require, was conditional on a presumption of, white righteousness. Godwyn points out that the curse itself does not "therefore confer any *Right* or Authority over them upon any, nor *commission us* to be the Executioners of the Sentence." Even if the claim that the Africans are descendants of Ham were correct, the whites still would have to prove "that we are the *Brethren* whom they were to serve; and that the *Curse* did confer on us a full and perfect *Right of Dominion* [over] them." And how could white brothers prove their "*Right*" to rule, their "*Right of Dominion*"? Only by their righteousness. The whites "*that Sell them say, Blessed be the Lord, for I am rich.*" But Godwyn reminded his white readers of "the *Terms,* by which only they can pretend a Right to God's Temporal *Blessings.* '*He gave them the Lands of the Heathen,*' saith David, '*that they might observe his Statutes, and keep his Laws.*' So that *obedience to God's Laws* can only entitle Men to the *good things* that they here enjoy." And he packed his book with evidence that, compared to their black slaves, those who went by the "*Appellative* of *Christians*" were, in practice, "the *blackest* and rankest *Heathens.*"[134] The whites were, morally, blacker than the blacks.

Middleton, Godwyn, and Tryon demonstrate that, from the beginning, the sword of ethnic righteousness could cut both ways. Its identification of white male rights and white male righteousness would help create and sustain the system of color-coded slavery attacked in *Clotel.* But that justification also was haunted by the specter of white hypocrisy. Allegories are dangerous allies. Nevertheless, if they wanted to think of themselves as white, the English could not avoid allegory. They just needed allegories simpler than Genesis and *A Game at Chess.*

Fundamentalist Fables

John Bunyan was born in 1628, the year after Thomas Middleton died. Middleton's allegory of the White House had been the most spectacular theatrical hit of the seventeenth century. *The Pilgrim's Progress* would be the most spectacularly best-selling prose fiction of the seventeenth century. Whiteness had been central to Middleton's dream allegory. It was peripheral to Bunyan's. That does not mean that whiteness had become, between 1624 and 1678, less important. What Middleton had to imagine and create—the allegory of Protestant England as a white nation—Bunyan took for granted.

Bunyan dreamed that, near the end of their journey to the Celestial City, Christian and his companion Hope had come to a fork in the road. "And as they were thinking about the way, behold, a man black of flesh, but covered with a very light Robe, came to them, and asked them why they stood there." They explained; he offered to guide them; they followed him; he led them into a net, "in which they were both so entangled, that they knew not what to do; and with that, *the white robe fell off the black man's back*" (Bunyan's italics). They realized their error and lay crying a while in the net. But finally they saw "a shining One coming towards them, with a whip of small cord in his hand." He asked them how they got there; they explained that they had been "led out of their way by a black man, clothed in white." Then "he with the Whip" explained that the black man was "a Flatterer, a false Apostle, that hath transformed himself into an Angel of Light." Then he led them back to the right path, and "whipped" them for their carelessness.[135]

Bunyan does not say that Christian is "white of flesh." Nonetheless, by calling the false Apostle "black of flesh" and "a black man," Bunyan insists on the correspondence between moral and corporeal color. By three times calling attention to the stranger's blackness, Bunyan implies that it is remarkable, and thus implies that the pilgrims are *not* "black of flesh." In his marginal note, Bunyan cites 2 Corinthians 11:13–14: "For such are false apostles, deceitful workers, transforming themselves into the apostles of Christ. And no marvel: for Satan himself is transformed into an angel of light."[136] This is the same passage that had inspired Luther's image of the "white devil," an image Luther had articulated in one of Bunyan's favorite books.[137] But although Saint Paul's epistle contrasted angelic light with the (implicit) darkness of Satan, it did not do so ethnographically, or invoke the particularity of "a black man." Neither did Luther. Luther's image had continued to be used without epidermal significance at least as late as 1649.[138] Samuel Purchas had turned Luther's metaphor into an ethnographic trope, but his blacks and whites were Africans and Europeans. By contrast, Bunyan's epidermal allegory is lopsided. Whereas Satan is "transformed," in Bunyan the whiteness of the false Apostle is not even skin deep. It's just a white robe. Consequently, although Bunyan takes for granted the transparent moral significance of the color of a black man's body, he does not associate corporeal whiteness with hypocrisy. The false Apostle's white robe does not contaminate the presumptively white body of Bunyan's protagonist or Bunyan's readers. Bunyan's allegory is much less volatile, for white people, than St. Paul's, Luther's, or even Purchas's.

Bunyan returned to the contrast between black and white in a brief episode in the second part of *The Pilgrim's Progress,* published in 1684. Christian's wife, Christiana, and her companions "saw one Fool, and one Want-wit, washing of an Ethiopian with intention to make him white, but the more they washed him, the blacker he was. They then asked the shepherds what that should mean. So they told them, saying, Thus shall it be with the vile Person; all means used to get such an one a good Name, shall in Conclusion tend but to make him more abominable. Thus it was with the Pharisees, and so shall it be with all Hypocrites."[139] Bunyan does not cite a biblical source for this allegorical episode, but he probably had one in mind. "Can the Ethiopian change his skin, or the leopard his spots?" the prophet Jeremiah had asked, in the sixth century B.C.E., and he had replied to his own rhetorical questions with the sarcastic dictum "then may ye also do good, that are accustomed to do evil" (13:23). The marginal note in the Geneva Bible had glossed this passage as a reference to "the cloak of hypocrisy." But Bunyan has conflated the biblical image with a secular proverb about the futility of "washing an Ethiopian." Art historian Jean Michael Massing has traced the history of that image, verbal and visual, "from Greek proverb to soap advert." But the word *white* (or its equivalent in other languages) does not even appear in Jeremiah, or the earliest Greek and Latin versions of the proverb, or in most of its early modern uses. The central paradox, the epitome of futility, is expressed by "wash the Ethiope"—as if the blackness of the African's body were simply dirt (which could be washed off), as if a natural or biological fact could be altered by human effort. This paradox is not necessarily colorphobic. Indeed, it targets the stupidity of the washer, who imagines that the Ethiopian's body is dirty: hence, a visual image of someone washing an African was sometimes given the motto "Labor in Vain." When the proverb took the form "washing the Ethiop white," the word *white* was simply the opposite of *black,* a way of intensifying the paradox. Within traditional premodern geographical theories, white and black were polar extremes of human complexion, both in some ways defective. (See chapters 3 and 4.) None of the classical, medieval, or sixteenth-century examples uses *white* in a demonstrably generic sense or attaches it specifically to Europeans.[140]

The first English example of an unmistakably generic rendering of the proverb does not occur until 1637, in Richard Brome's play *The English Moor.* A lecherous Englishman, anticipating sexual contact with a black woman, swears "if I rub her not as white as another can, / Let me be hanged up with her for a new / Sign of the 'Labour in Vain.'"[141] Brome's play uses *white* as a generic adjective repeatedly and unambiguously. Undoubtedly this passage imagines washing an African body until it becomes as "white" as an English one. But the woman in question is really already English, having blacked up to disguise herself, and she does return to white-face (and virtue) by play's end. The same thing happens in Massinger's *Parliament of Love* (1624), where a black character has "this varnish from her face washed off," and in William Berkeley's *The Lost Lady* (1637), where a black woman's "blackness falls away," literally.[142] In all these plays what we witness is the mutability of blackness, not its permanence. Allegorically, that epidermal transformation fits the "ecumenical" interpretation of black body found in most of the early Christian theologians: it may be fruitless for a mere human being to try to turn black into white, but God's grace can convert even the most obdurate sinner.[143] That ecumenical interpretation fed the image of the converted Black King in Middleton's *Triumphs of Truth*.[144]

The visual image of blacks becoming Christian (in Middleton) or becoming white (in Massinger, Brome, and Berkeley) directly contradicts the logic of Bunyan's visual allegory. Although Brome in 1637 alluded to the proverb about washing the Ethiop, the visual and moral action of his play contradicted it. Theologically, the immutability of predestined damnation had been articulated by Calvin in his interpretation of Jeremiah 13:23. "Blackness is inherent in the skin of the Ethiopians," Calvin observed; "Were they then to wash themselves a hundred times daily, they could not put off their blackness." He then explained that the biblical image referred here to "the Jews," who "could not repent."[145] Calvin does not use the word *white* at all here, and his anti-Semitism is more conspicuous than any prejudice against the conversion of Africans.[146] In 1641 the young religious poet Thomas Beedome expressed the trope of impossibility by imagining Ethiopia "changed to a milk white Nation."[147] Beedome was apparently the first author in English to use the phrase "white nation," and he did so by denying the possibility that blacks could change their identity. But he did not allude to washing.

The first example of the proverb that deploys *white* in an immutable generic sense, comparable to Bunyan's, was not published until 1673. It debuted in an edition of Aesop's fables aimed at "the generality" of readers, who could not afford more expensive and learned translations.[148] In other words, the 1673 fables were aimed at the same class of readers that Bunyan reached.[149]

> He washed, and scrubbed and rubbed him every day,
> Supposing he was made of as white clay
> As other men, but found himself deceived:
> Blackness in Blackmoors cannot be retrieved.
> As well may you make day of what is night
> As wash a Blackmoor till that he be white.[150]

Even if we did not already know that, by the 1670s, *white* had acquired a generic meaning, the phrase "made of as white clay / As other men" would tell us that some Englishmen believed that their own bodies were white, and that white was normative.

Bunyan's allegory goes further. The traditional idea of "washing . . . white" foregrounds the notion of cleaning: cleaning restores something to its original, natural state. By contrast, Bunyan's "intention to make him white" suggests metamorphosis: "to make X into Y" forcibly transforms an original state into a new one. Bunyan then adds the idea that "the more they washed him, the blacker he was." Although Luther profoundly influenced *The Pilgrim's Progress,* Bunyan's allegory of hypocrisy here exactly reverses Luther's image of the white devil.[151] The hypocrite is not white; the hypocrite is someone who aspires to be white, and fails, becoming in the process even blacker. The hypocrite, in Bunyan, is not a white man, but a black trying to mimic a white.

Between the first part of *The Pilgrim's Progress* (with its "black man") and the second part (with its "Ethiopian"), Bunyan published *The Holy War* (1682), with its story of "one *Diabolus,* a mighty *Giant,*" who "was King of the *Blacks* or *Negroes.*" Not only is the Devil black; the Devil is the King of Negroes. Allegory has become ethnography. Bunyan began this tale of Christian jihad by echoing elements of innumerable narratives of European exploration.[152] "In my Travels, as I walked through many Regions and Countries, it was my chance to happen into that famous *Continent* of *Universe;* a very large and spacious Country it . . . lieth between the two Poles . . . a place well watered, and richly adorned with Hills and Valleys. . . . The People are not all of one complexion, nor yet of one Language, mode, or way of Religion; but differ as much as ('tis said) do the Planets themselves. Some are right, and some are wrong." *The Pilgrim's Progress* allegorized Christian theology as an individual's journey toward a divine city; one individual dominates the narrative, and his urban goal is reached only at journey's end. *The Holy War* instead allegorized Christian theology as the defense of a human city ("Mansoul"), transparently modeled on Bunyan's native Bedford; images of bustling collective life dominate the narrative. *The Holy War,* like *A Game at Chess,* turned local politics into color-coded allegory. But there had been no war in *A Game at Chess,* no Miltonic sweep of Christian history, no spacious universe—and the Black House had been as European as the White. *The Holy War* instead shows us innocent, victimized Mansoul/Bedford attacked by a giant Diabolus/Negro. Middleton's first representation of an allegorical Black King had been the good Christian of *The Triumphs of Truth.* There are no good blacks in Bunyan.

There are no good blacks because Bunyan subscribed to the colorphobic interpretation of Noah's curse. In his *Exposition on the Ten First Chapters of Genesis* (almost certainly written in the 1680s), he called Ham "the Father of the

Children of the Curse of God," and commented that his "mighty offspring" were "wicked Men, Idolaters, Persecutors, Sinners," notable for "Wickedness and Rebellion against the Way of God." Such men God was "resolved to number to the Sword, both in this World, and that to come." But for Bunyan these moral attributes had an epidermal corollary. He glossed "Cush" (the name of one of the cursed sons of Ham) as "Black." The damned descendants of Ham included "the Ethiopian, or Blackamoor."[153]

So far generic whiteness has been implicit in Bunyan: the unspoken opposite of "the black man" and the "King of the Blacks or Negroes," the unidentified color of Noah's blessed descendants, the explicit but unattainable goal of those washing the Ethiopian. If these texts had been written a century earlier, we could hardly deny that they demonstrated Bunyan's prejudices against blacks; nevertheless, in themselves they would not prove that Bunyan considered himself "white." But Bunyan was not writing in the 1580s. His contemporaries could casually refer to "the white skin of our Lord Jesus."[154] (Contrast Plates 3, 5, and 7.) And in the allegory "Of Moses and his wife" (1686), Bunyan's white race fully exposed itself.[155]

> This Moses was a fair and comely man;
> His wife a swarthy Ethiopian:
> Nor did his Milk-white Bosom change her Skin;
> She came out thence as black as she went in. . . .
> Therefore as Moses' wife came swarthy in,
> And went out from him without change of Skin:
> So he that doth the Law for Life adore,
> Shall yet by it be left a Black-a-moor.(1–4, 13–16)

Bunyan found this Ethiopian wife in Numbers 12:1 ("And Miriam and Aaron spoke against Moses because of the Ethiopian woman whom he had married; for he had married an Ethiopian woman").[156] The ancient Jewish historian Josephus confirms the Ethiopian wife, and provides more details.[157] But neither the Old Testament nor Josephus ever called Moses white, or commented on the color of his wife. Bunyan's seventeenth-century Moses has milk-white skin. Since Moses was thought to have been the author of the first five books of the Old Testament, by giving Moses white skin Bunyan projected seventeenth-century generic whiteness back onto the author of what were, at the time, the most ancient texts known to Europeans.

By contrast, the unnamed Ethiopian wife's skin is black and swarthy, and like the unnamed Ethiopian in *The Pilgrim's Progress* she cannot change her color, or escape from her predestined damnation. Bunyan's parable reverses the moral of the biblical text, where God had punished Miriam for her complaint by giving her leprosy, which turned her skin "white as snow" (Numbers 12:10).[158] He obscures this reversal by conflating the Ethiopian wife of Moses with Hagar, an "Egyptian" slave who became the concubine of Abraham (Genesis 16:1). Bunyan reiterates that the Ethiopian "came . . . in" to Moses, then "went out from" him and "came out thence." That corresponds to nothing in the ancient Jewish story of Moses. But Hagar the concubine went to Abraham and later was evicted from the household: she "came in" and "went out." For Bunyan, one black woman was sexually and morally interchangeable with another. Both, after all, were descendants of Ham. The middle of Bunyan's poem, which allegorizes the whiteness of Moses and the blackness of his wife, indicates the source of Bunyan's conflation of the two women.

> Now Moses was a type of Moses' Law,
> His Wife likewise of one that never saw
> Another way unto eternal Life;
> There's Myst'ry then in Moses and his Wife.
> The Law is very Holy, Just and good,
> And to it is espoused all Flesh and Blood:
> But this its Goodness it cannot bestow,
> On any that are wedded thereunto.(5–12)

These couplets versify a commonplace of Protestant theology. Obeying the Mosaic law in itself is not enough to guarantee salvation. In his Epistle to the Galatians—which became one of the central texts of Protestant divinity, and of Bunyan's own religious conversion—Saint Paul had offered "an allegory" of "the two covenants." Paul linked Hagar to "Mount Sinai" (from which Moses brought the tablets of stone with the divine commandments); that link between Hagar and Moses encouraged the slippage in Bunyan's poem, between Hagar and the Ethiopian wife.

For Paul, Luther, Calvin, and Bunyan, Hagar and Sinai are dual symbols of the covenant "of the flesh," which led to "bondage." Christians, by contrast, belonged to the covenant of "the Spirit." They are "not children of the bondwoman, but of the free" woman (Abraham's wife, Sarah). "What saith the Scripture?" Paul asks. "Cast out the bondwoman and her son; for the son of the bondwoman shall not be heir with the son of the freewoman" (Galatians 4:22–31).[159] But none of these texts—not Paul's epistle, not the passages in Genesis that tell the story of Hagar, not Luther's commentary, not Calvin's commentary—overlay the contrast between Grace and the Law with a contrast between white and black skin. That is Bunyan's special contribution to the allegory. Moses, with milk-white skin, represents the saving union of Grace and Law; the Ethiopian, by contrast, is "wedded to" the Law, and will therefore remain forever black and damned. Like the Ethiopian whom washing cannot make white, the Ethiopian wife will not be saved, no matter how scrupulously she mimics the outward rituals and commandments of Christianity. The planters of Barbados could hardly have asked for more.

Later in the same book, Bunyan returns to the subject of whiteness in a poem "Upon the Chalk-stone."[160]

> This Stone is white, yea, warm, and also soft,
> Easy to work upon, unless 'tis naught.
> It leaves a white Impression upon those
> Whom it doth touch, be they its Friends or Foes.
>
> The Child of God, is like to this Chalk-stone,
> White in his Life, easily wrought upon:
> Warm in Affections, apt to leave impress,
> On whom he deals with, of true Godliness.
>
> He is no sullying Coal, nor daubing Pitch,
> Nor one of whom men catch the Scab, or Itch;
> But such who in the Law of God doth walk,
> Tender of heart, in Life whiter than Chalk.

Nothing in this poem explicitly enforces an ethnographic interpretation. But since Bunyan had used "white" epidermally, only a few pages before, that meaning can hardly be excluded from his celebration of the whiteness of "The Child of God."

The child, after all, was literal, and English. So was the chalk, used then as now in teaching children to read. Both poems appear in *A Book for Boys and Girls; or, Country Rhymes for Children.* It belongs to a larger genre of Puritan books specifically aimed at children.[161] *The Pilgrim's Progress* quickly became one of the most popular and influential classics of children's literature, but it was not originally written for them.[162] *A Book for Boys and Girls,* by contrast, advertises its intention on the title page, and begins with an alphabet, advice on spelling, lists of names and numerals; most of the poems are short, some are set to familiar tunes. Bunyan did not model his poetic style on the complex verbal gymnastics of canonical intellectuals like Donne and Herbert, but on the anonymous verse of ballads, broadsides, and penny chapbooks.[163] The putative subjects of his little poems are such ordinary objects as eggs, candles, toys, glasses, mirrors (and chalk). But these are also "country rhymes," so their subjects include frogs, fish, bees, birds, trees, bushes, butterflies, spiders, ants, horses, hens, and snails. By his own admission, Bunyan's rhymes are "homely" and his language "mean." But that is the best method for "catching Girls and Boys." And others too: Bunyan also aimed his book at "Boys with Beards, and

Girls that be / Big as old Women." What pleased children also pleased the uneducated rural poor. Bunyan knew that "the wiser sort my Rhymes may slight"—but he didn't care, because he predicted that "The Foolish will delight / To read them."[164] They did. For centuries.

"Whether subtly or blatantly," a historian of children's literature has said, all such books were "propagandistic . . . tools for social, moral, religious, and political conditioning."[165] She might have added "colorphobic." With Bunyan we see the generic sense of whiteness—which began in difficult and expensive books written by and for a small intellectual elite, and then slowly moved into the language of a cosmopolitan port city—arriving in books written by the son of an illiterate tinker, born in a small cottage on the edge of a rural village. By the 1680s generic whiteness was being linguistically reproduced and circulated by a man who never trusted cities, courts, or intellectuals, and who spent many years of his adult life in prison. With Bunyan, finally, generic whiteness reached and conquered the last stronghold of linguistic conservatism: the teaching of children.[166]

Historians have tended to treat racism as an intellectual enterprise. If we are interested in the history of ideas about a "white race," then it is important to notice that Georg Horn (a.k.a. Georgius Hornius), a professor of history at the University of Leyden in the Netherlands, published in 1666 a book entitled *Arca Noae* (Noah's Ark). A committed Lutheran with strong links to England, Horn already had written a pioneering history of philosophy (which began with the sons of Noah), an important book on the ethnic origins of indigenous Amerindians, and a polemical treatise calculating the biblical age of the earth.[167] *Arca Noae* was reprinted four times—in Leyden, Rotterdam, Frankfurt, and Leipzig—between 1666 and 1675.[168] It claimed that the descendants of Noah were "of diverse colors": those who were "white" (*albus*) were the offspring of Japhet, those who were "black" (*nigros*) the offspring of Ham, those who were "yellow" (*flavos*) the offspring of Shem. Japhet's offspring initially obtained Europe, northern Asia, and America, "all the most ample spaces of the earth and multitudes of people, with majestic kingdoms and empires, culture, literature . . . and divine grace." Only to the family of the Japhites belonged dominion over "the whole orb of the earth, of all empires, kingdoms, peoples in Europe, Asia, America, and Africa."[169] In 1666, for the first time, a European intellectual color-coded all the descendants of the three sons of Noah and claimed imperial global dominion for "white" Europeans.

But have you ever heard of Georg Horn? Like its title, his long book was written in Latin, and has never been translated into English. John Bunyan, on the other hand, has been translated into more than 200 languages; by 1938 (the last time anyone attempted a comprehensive count), more than 1,300 editions of *The Pilgrim's Progress* had been printed.[170] *The Holy War* was quickly translated into Dutch and German and later into an untold number of other languages; it was printed in English at least 40 times before the end of the nineteenth century.[171] *A Book for Boys and Girls*—Bunyan's most popular book of verse, and one of the most popular children's books of the seventeenth century—was printed at least 12 times between 1686 and 1793.[172] All these books were adapted, abridged, parodied, and quoted widely. *The Pilgrim's Progress* and *The Holy War* are still in print (and available on audiocassette). And Bunyan himself is alive and well on the Internet, celebrated as one of the giants of "the Baptist tradition."

Bunyan does indeed epitomize the history of Protestant evangelical prejudice: an anti-Semitic, anti-Catholic, anti-Irish, misogynistic, and colorphobic hellfire-and-damnation preacher, most popular with the undereducated white rural poor. Although in his own time he was a persecuted dissenter, after his death—in the same year as the triumph of Protestantism in the Glorious Revolution of 1688—Bunyan became the moral darling of persecutors. Most of the many translations of his works were prepared by Christian missionaries, riding successive waves of European imperial conquest.[173] Few if any of the white soldiers and white missionaries of the eighteenth, nineteenth, and twentieth centuries had read Georg Horn's *Arca Noae,* but almost all of them had read Bunyan. Bunyan's people did not need to read many other books, because their sense of superiority was not complicated. Bunyan did not read Hebrew, Greek, or Latin, but that in no way impaired his confidence in interpreting the polylingual collection of ancient Mediterranean religious texts he called, simply, "the Bible." The Bible—Bunyan will tell you, Bunyan's people will tell you—is simple, as simple as chalk, as simple as the milk-white skin of Moses. For Bunyan's people, whiteness and righteousness are simple and sufficient. Bunyan's people became the "poor whites" of the antebellum rural South described by William Wells Brown. Bunyan's people elected George Wallace governor of Alabama in the 1960s. Bunyan's people put George W. Bush in the White House at the beginning of the twenty-first century. Bunyan's people are simple people: simple, white, and right.

CHAPTER 10

WHITE SCIENCE

CLOTEL IS STATISTICAL FICTION. IT DOES NOT SEEK the aesthetic unity of the number one. Such aesthetic unity had already been achieved by African Americans in the autobiographies of Frederick Douglass and William Wells Brown himself. These "slave narratives" tell one story about one person; they provide the easily understood whole satisfaction of one individual's quest for and achievement of freedom. Douglass went beyond that paradigm when he wrote the second version of his autobiography, but even then he told the story of "*My* Bondage and *My* Freedom," the binary of opposed nouns united by that persistent pronoun, that distinctive voice, that personal trajectory. But *Clotel,* despite the first word of its title, is not the story of one person. In fact, the title page immediately retracts that proper name: *Clotel; or, The President's Daughter* redefines its subject as a generic relationship between a [free and powerful] president and his [enslaved and powerless] daughter, between the democracy represented by an elected male president and the tyranny embodied in a female slave. The subtitle widens the focus even further: *A Narrative of Slave Life in The United States* does not promise us the life of one slave, but a comprehensive account of the living conditions of slaves throughout the republic.

Brown's fiction is fragmented, because slavery fragments any community. In the first chapter, the family has already been split by the legal separation of the white free father (Jefferson) from his enslaved concubine and their enslaved children. The temporary unity of mother and children is shattered when Clotel, her sister Althesa, and their mother, Currer, are sold to separate owners and dispersed across the continent. But Brown does not focus the rest of the novel on the experience of these three separated women, because to do so would have fraudulently reunited that family within the aesthetic experience of readers. Whiteness is not gigantic, globe-trotting, unitary, tragic, and mythic (as in *Moby Dick*), but petty, parochial, fractional, parodic, and ordinary.[1] Its full meaning cannot be contained within the experience of one family or one generation.

Currer, Clotel, and Althesa all die well before the end of the novel, and in the sites to which they have been scattered they are not socially central; no slave ever is. *A Narrative of Slave Life in The United States* attempts to represent a complex social whole, a clutter of voices and geographies, a terrible totality. A system.

Accordingly, the first sentence of the preface does not begin with a first-person pronoun or a proper name, but with a number ("More than two hundred years"). The first paragraph continues with six more: "From the introduction of slaves in 1620, down to the period of the separation of the Colonies from the British Crown, the number had increased to five hundred thousand; now there are nearly four million. In fifteen of the thirty-one States, Slavery is made lawful by the Constitution, which binds the several States into one confederacy" (46). What begins in the preface continues in the first chapter of the novel proper. Its first paragraph explains that "In all the cities and towns of the slave states, the real negro, or clear black, does not amount to more than one in four of the slave population" (81). Clotel herself is introduced with the advertisement that "Thirty-eight negroes will be offered for sale on Monday, November 10th, at twelve o'clock" (85). The chapter culminates in her sale, a riot of numbers: five hundred dollars, five hundred, seven hundred, eight hundred, nine hundred, nine fifty, ten, eleven, twelve hundred, thirteen, fourteen, fifteen, fifteen hundred dollars, a girl of sixteen, five hundred dollars, two hundred, one hundred, three hundred, four hundred (87–88).

We might attribute these numbers to the inevitable mechanics of a sale, but there had been no such emphasis in John Fletcher's much more extended scene of slaves being sold in *A Very Woman.* To the contrasts between *Clotel* and *A Very Woman* enumerated in my introduction must now be added a contrast in the literary treatment of quantities. Fletcher did not specify the number of people for sale ("diverse Slaves") or the time ("ring the bell") or the number of customers ("Citizens"). Thirty-one of the 274 words describing Clotel's sale are numbers (11 percent); in Fletcher's sale, by contrast, of 1,144 words, only 16 are numbers (1 percent).[2] Moreover, the numbers in Clotel's sale are structured in a way that emphasizes the mathematical logic of the action (rising to a climax and then recapitulating ironically); Fletcher distributes the arithmetic randomly.[3] Only about half Fletcher's numbers refer to price, and the prices form no coherent numerical or emotional sequence. The drama and meaning of Fletcher's scene is not shaped numerically. But numbers do create the corresponding moment in *Clotel:* the tension of the escalation, the clash between mathematical and moral values.

Fletcher's numbers never rise above 100; Brown's begin with 500. In the first paragraph of *Clotel*'s preface the numbers have already risen to 4 million, and by the second paragraph to 25 million. The conclusion quotes a "Statistical Acount of the Connection of the Religious Bodies in America with Slavery," published in 1851: "It is estimated that in the United States, members of the Methodist church own 219,363 slaves; members of the Baptist church own 226,000 slaves; members of the Episcopalian church own 88,000 slaves; members of the Presbyterian church own 77,000 slaves; members of all other churches own 50,000 slaves; in all, 660,563 slaves owned by members of the Christian church in this pious democratic republic!" (226). Here again, as in the auction scene, the numbers rise to a rhetorical climax. Against the claim to virtue in words like *church, Christian, pious,* and *democratic* Brown sets the claim to objectivity in numbers like "219,363." Numbers annihilate. Mathematics annihilates hypocritical verbiage. But numbers also reduce thronging longing beings to objects. Brown's massed digits batter at Methodists, Baptists, Episcopalians, Presbyterians. Unfortunately, the calculus that embarrasses the owners simultaneously depersonalizes the owned. The strings of numerals that strip the owners of their pretensions also strip the 665,563 individual slaves of any individuality. They are counted up and parceled out into labeled boxes of Protestant denominations. The numerals vary, but the noun remains: "slaves . . . slaves . . . slaves . . . slaves . . . slaves . . . slaves." They're all the same. Just so many interchangeable nouns.

Numbers numb. They anesthetize those counting and those counted. Brown's statistics echo, eerily, the account books of slave traders, calculating the number of slaves per ship, the percentage of fatalities per voyage, the margin of profit per life. Brown tries to turn the objectivity of numbers against the objectification of numbering. But although a bigger number should produce a bigger emotional response, our sympathy depends on our ability to imagine someone suffering, one someone at a time. As the digits pile up, the someones disappear, lost in the clutter of counting. The numbers become unimaginable, unmanageable. To stay sane, we have to find a way to manage the unimaginable, mathematically.

Management

Celebrating the restoration of the monarchy in 1660, young John Dryden greeted King Charles II with a poem proclaiming that "now time's whiter Series is begun."

> Oh Happy Age! Oh times like those alone
> By Fate reserved for Great Augustus' Throne!
> When the joint growth of Arms and Arts foreshew
> The World a Monarch, and that Monarch *You.*[4]

Within months of his return to power, Charles II centralized administration of the global colonial empire he had inherited. The need for new management structures had been apparent for at least a decade. In the 1640s London's overseas merchants had begun to exercise more political clout, and in 1651 the Navigation Act for the first time had legislated an overall policy for foreign trade.[5] During the same years major changes to army organization, tax collection, ship design, and naval policy had transformed the British state into a more efficient fiscal and military organization. Simultaneously, British colonies in New England, the Chesapeake, and the West Indies were achieving levels of political complexity and economic activity that seemed to demand more careful supervision and promise more lucrative tax revenue.[6] During the Interregnum sporadic efforts had been made to create a coherent colonial policy and a standing imperial bureaucracy; by 1656 influential English merchants had begun to lobby "to draw all the Islands, Colonies and Dominions of America under *one and the same management* here" in London (italics added).[7] By 1657 one element of their proposals was that "a more *certain* . . . and *uniform*" government of colonial affairs could be secured, in part, by "a *continual correspondence*" between the various colonies and London, thereby creating "*one* Commonwealth" (italics added).[8]

These proposals were renewed and expanded after the Restoration, and the commission for a Council for Foreign Plantations was formally approved on December 1, 1660. Its instructions repeated, verbatim, the foregoing details and many other specific proposals made by the merchants' chief lobbyist, Thomas Povey (a member of the Royal Society who became the Council's secretary and most active member).[9] The Council held its first business meeting on January 7, 1661, and immediately appointed a committee to begin drafting letters.[10]

The formation of the Council for Foreign Plantations initiates a shift in the evolution of whiteness. *White* had been used as a legislative adjective in the West Indies since at least 1644, but in 1659 it was not used by any of the speakers in the parliamentary debate about English servitude in Barbados. Two years later information from and to England's many disparate overseas enterprises began for the first time to flow through the hands of a group of less than 50 influential men and their appointed staff, meeting routinely (40 times in 1661). This London nucleus received and transmitted regular communications with important men in all the scattered colonial speech communities; both filter and sounding board, it was uniquely positioned to broadcast new idioms across the entire English language-scape. Moreover, the London group was not linguistically neutral. It consisted of men already familiar with the most important linguistic contact zones. Eight members of the Council (including Thomas Povey, Martin Noell, and John Colleton) were also members of the Council of Trade and the Royal African Company. Seven signed a petition of "Planters of Barbados inhabiting in and about London," read in the Council on March 1, 1661.[11] Committees did most of the real work, and the first committee consisted of six Barbados plantation owners (including Colleton, Noell, and Sir Anthony Ashley Cooper), two additional overseas merchants (including Povey), four sea captains, General Venables (who had captured Jamaica in 1655), the chemist Robert Boyle, and the poet Edmund Waller.[12]

Povey's manuscript of the "Minutes" taken at the meeting of "the Committee of the Council of Foreign Plantations" on January 10, 1661—only three days after the Council's first business meeting—contains the first use of the generic noun *white* I have found anywhere (Illus. 10).[13] The committee was discussing the problem of the new and precarious English colony in Jamaica. The

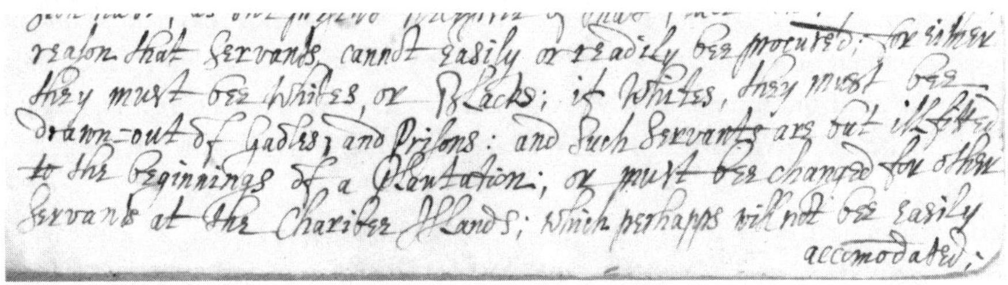

reason that Servants cannot easily or readily bee procured; for either they must bee Whites, or Blacks; if Whites, they must bee drawn-out of Gaoles, and Prisons: and such Servants are but ill-fitted to the Beginnings of a Plantation; or must bee changed for other Servants at the Charibee Ilands; which perhapps will not bee easily accomodated;

Illustration 10. First recorded use of the noun *whites* (January 10, 1661). By permission of the British Library.

first question was "What numbers [are] now there?" If the colony was to survive, it needed a massive infusion of "Servants (which are the Wealth of Planters, and the Seed of Plantations)." But "Blacks" were "such treacherous, and unsteady People" that a vulnerable and underpopulated colony could not afford to import many slaves, "although they be justly esteemed, as much the best and the most necessary" servants. The committee concluded that "servants cannot easily or readily be procured; for either they must be Whites, or Blacks; if Whites, they must be drawn out of Jails, and Prisons: and such servants are but ill-fitted to the beginnings of a Plantation."[14] *White* may have been used as a generic noun by speakers in the West Indies before its appearance in this London bureaucratic document; it might have been spoken in the committee meeting by one of the plantation owners who had learned it in Barbados. But I have not found the noun in surviving texts from the West Indies before 1669.

Before that colonial debut, the noun appears in at least two other memos. One comes (again) from the Committee to the Council of Foreign Plantations. Probably written in August 1664, "Certain Propositions for the better accommodating the Foreign Plantations With Servants" contained twenty numbered paragraphs.[15] For our purposes, the most important are the first four.

1. It being Universally agreed that People are the Foundation and Improvement of all Plantations and that people are increased principally by sending of Servants thither, It is necessary that a Settled course be taken for the Furnishing them with Servants.
2. Servants are either Blacks or Whites.
3. Blacks are such as are brought by way of Trade and are Sold at about 20 pounds a head, one with another, and are the principal and most Usefull appurtenances of a Plantation and are such as are perpetual Servants.
4. Whites are such as are diverse ways gathered up here in England (Very few from Ireland or Scotland) and being transported at the charge of about 6 pound a head are there entertained by such as they are consigned to from hence, or are exchanged for Commodities with such as have occasion for them, at different rates according to their Condition or Trade by which they are rendered more Useful and beneficial to their Masters. These after certain Years are free to plant for themselves or to take Wages for their service.

The distinction between *blacks* and *whites,* between "perpetual" black slavery and "free" white labor, is clearly understood. *Whites* includes people from the separate jurisdictions of England, Scotland, and Ireland.

The noun reappears in another bureaucratic memo among the papers of the Council, dated October 3, 1664. Specifically concerning Jamaica, this anonymous report to the king notes that "It is not good to overstock a young plantation with Servants: 30 Blacks and as many Whites, at first entering, is thought sufficient . . . and as the plantation increases, there must be constant supplies sent both of blacks and whites."[16] Again, *whites* and *blacks* are subcategories of servant; again, the memo is concerned with the economics of population management.

The economics of population management had been part of the Council's mandate from the beginning. Following the merchants' advice, Charles II had instructed the Council to "write letters" to each colonial governor, requiring an "exact account" of their charters or commissions, laws, institutions—and "what numbers of men" inhabited their territory. The first inquiry, intended to serve as "a precedent" for letters to the other colonies, went to Barbados on February 11, 1661.[17] "And seeing the principal subsistence and improvement of every Colony consists in the numbers of Planters and servants, upon the knowledge of which a more certain Judgement of your condition may be raised, We do further desire you to give us a conjectural Account of what numbers of men are upon the Island . . . how many Planters there now are as Freeholders, how many conditional servants, and how many Blacks."[18] In response to this letter, the president and council of Barbados, on May 10, directed the compilation of a "list in every Parish of all the white men and blacks therein and to distinguish how many freemen, and how many Servants."[19] By 1661 London knew that the welfare of a colony depended, more than anything else, on sheer numbers of inhabitants. This population logic, developed from decades of colonial experience, would soon be applied to England and other European states, leading to laws and policies designed to increase the national birth rate. The importance of what Michel Foucault would christen "bio-power" originated in colonial experience, in a mercantile calculation of subsistence economics, market size, and profit thresholds.[20]

Between 1665 and 1670 the Council disappeared, leaving Sir Anthony Ashley Cooper and his circle to take charge of active colonial initiatives; in the summer of 1670 Cooper engineered creation of a new council of "Commissioners of Foreign Plantations," with instructions from the king to inform themselves of "the number of parishes" in each colony, "the number of planters" and "the number of servants"—and "whether the said servants are Christian, or slaves that are brought from other parts."[21] In September 1670, pursuant to that brief, the new committee sent a list of questions to Sir William Berkeley, Governor of Virginia since 1641.[22] Among other things, they asked "What number of people have yearly died, within your plantation and government for these seven years last past, both whites and blacks?"[23] From London, the imperial bureaucracy in 1670 reduced all colonial inhabitants—not just "servants"—to two complementary categories, *whites* and *blacks.* If a "racialized society" is one that "keeps official records according to categories of race," then by 1670 at the very latest England was a racialized society.[24]

The official color-coded categories became increasingly entrenched. In September 1672 management of the colonies was again reorganized; instructions for the new Council of Trade and Foreign Plantations were drafted by Cooper (now the Earl of Shaftesbury) and his protégé John Locke, who would become the salaried Secretary of the new Council. Those guidelines again authorized population inquiries, but unlike their antecedents of 1660 and 1670, the new orders specified: "What number of Whites and Blacks do yearly come" and "What Number of People do yearly die within the said Colonies and Plantations, both Whites and Blacks."[25] Thus, in 1672 *whites* became an official demographic category within the explicit mandate of the imperial bureaucracy. Thereafter, ever more regular inquiries were sent to the colonies; surviving examples, all using the noun *white,* went to the Leeward Islands (1672), Bermuda (1676), and Connecticut (1679).[26] In the extant exchanges from the 1670s, the London questions used *whites* more often than the colonial replies.

Historians have understandably concentrated on the evolution of color-coded categories in the slave plantations of the colonies. But the generic noun *white* seems to have begun, and was certainly officially encouraged, in London.

The most sophisticated current model of linguistic diffusion—the "hierarchical model"—would lead us to expect that, like other new usages, the term *whites* should have originated in a large, heavily populated city that had long been a cultural center, and then moved to another densely concentrated but smaller group of English speakers under the influence of the first.[27] If the hierarchical model is right, then the generic noun should have begun in London and then should have jumped from London to Barbados. The surviving textual evidence seems to confirm that theory.

It is important to distinguish here between two changes to the meaning of the English word *white.* First, the English adjective acquired its modern, collective, positive ethnic sense. Second, that generic adjective became a generic noun. The second change may, like the first, have been stimulated by bilingual contact. The Spanish and Portuguese, predictably, were using the noun long before the English. Even the Dutch apparently preceded the English in this usage by more than half a century. Dutch voyagers to Africa were using *blancken* as a generic noun as early as 1602. In 1652 an official Dutch colonial document contrasted the Indians in New Netherland with "*blancken*" (whites); the Dutch had by then been a major player in the African slave trade for two decades, regularly supplying North American coastal colonies.[28] In New Netherland as in Dutch Brazil, the color-coding of Europeans as *blancken* derived from the littoral experience of a multicolor colony, in which Europeans dominated other complexions. By 1661 the English had conquered the Spanish colony of Jamaica, the king of England had a Portuguese wife, and the Dutch were England's major competitor in international trade. The English could have picked up the generic noun from any of those languages.

But the noun also could have happened without the invidious influence of foreign agitators. Adjectives turn into nouns all the time in English. Laziness—why use two words when one will do the job?—triumphs over prescribed grammar. In the right context, instead of saying *white people* you can spare yourself the exertion of two extra syllables—sometimes you get bored with a sentence before you reach the end of it—and just say (or write) *whites.*[29] By that common process Middleton's "white people" (1613) could become the Council of Foreign Plantation's "Whites" (1661).

It is one thing to say "The English are white," and quite another to say "The English are whites." Whether we call the difference grammatical or semantic, it turns an attribute into an object. Not all nouns do that. For example, although the following sentences are identical grammatically, "Those are Christians" and "Those are whites" are not equivalent semantically. *Christians* refers to a system of beliefs and to the conduct associated with those beliefs, with no hint of physical appearance; for the purposes of classification as *Christian,* the body does not matter. By contrast, *whites* refers to one aspect of physical appearance, with no hint of beliefs or actions; for the purposes of classification as *white,* only the body matters. ("Those are whites" need not refer to people at all. It could be describing a load of laundry.) In the noun *blacks* or the noun *whites,* body color—hitherto just one attribute among many—has been reified as the determinant condition of a group identity. That began to be done to "blacks" or "Negroes" in the second half of the sixteenth century. Insofar as nouns constitute identities, for users of the English language, African subjectivity was reduced to color more than a century before English subjectivity suffered a similar fate. But by January 1661 English colonists and African slaves were being treated as *grammatically equivalent,* by at least some London speakers of English.

In 1661 whites and blacks were not socially, politically, or economically identical (witness the very memo in which the generic noun *whites* debuted). Why make them grammatically equivalent? The effect of the noun *whites* is not to make whites equivalent to blacks. No, grammatical equivalence insists on semantic difference. For instance, in a song sung by one of the plantation slaves in *Clotel*—"The black folks makes the cotton / And the white folks gets the money" (145)—the exact repetition of sentence structure in the second line only emphasizes the economic distinction between the grammatically parallel "black" and "white" folks. Nevertheless, the new noun *whites* did, in the early 1660s, establish a new form of equivalence. The noun made every person with a "white" body equivalent to every other person with a "white" body. It erased individual difference—just as the noun *Negroes* had, long before, erased the individuality of people with "black" bodies. In a certain context, for certain purposes, whites had become interchangeable entities. The linguistic context was a social, political, and economic world where whites had become only one part of a larger whole. The world of British governance now included a significant number of entities who were not white. By January 1661, from the perspective of management, certainty, and uniformity, whites had become functionally interchangeable and quantifiable fractions of a heterogeneous British whole.

Populations

Members of the Council of Foreign Plantations were not the only Englishmen, in the early 1660s, interested in counting the inhabitants of each parish. John Graunt's *Natural and Political Observations . . . made upon the Bills of Mortality,* published in January 1662, inaugurated the statistical study of human populations; it was reprinted again that same year, and then again in 1665, with additions and revisions recommended by Graunt's old friend, Sir William Petty, "the outstanding economist of the seventeenth century."[30] Petty's own *Treatise of Taxes and Contributions,* also published in 1662, inaugurated what he would soon call "political arithmetic." Graunt's work was entirely based on parish statistics; Petty's begins with a calculation of the excessive number of separate parishes and the correspondingly excessive tax burden. In Graunt's and Petty's work, individuals were conceptualized as so many fractions of a political and economic whole that was described and evaluated mathematically. Graunt's demographic work and Petty's analysis of public revenues and expenses—often related to population, as indicated by Petty's reference to Graunt—together mathematicalized the state. What was revolutionary in 1662 seemed, by 1701, so basic that John Arbuthnot could claim that mathematics ("the great instrument of private commerce") was the basis of all "true political knowledgement."[31]

"Private commerce" certainly inspired Graunt's method. A prosperous London draper—and the son of a draper—Graunt studied the bills of mortality from London parishes as carefully as a tradesman might study financial accounts.[32] His book depended on what he called, in its dedication to the Royal Society, "the Mathematics of my Shop-Arithmetic." From the perspective of a London tradesman, Graunt argued that states were "not only powerful but Rich, according to the number of their people," and that the "little hint" afforded by reliable statistics provided a "model of the greatest work in the World, which is the making of England as considerable for Trade as Holland." He concluded that, by the knowledge of population, "Trade and Government may be made more certain and Regular." Indeed, "a clear knowledge of all these particulars"—especially in the hands of "the Sovereign and his chief Ministers"—is "necessary" to produce "good, certain, and easy Government, and even to balance Parties and Factions both in Church and State."[33] This argument so impressed Charles II that he recommended Graunt be admitted to the Royal Society, which published the second and subsequent editions of his book.

What Graunt called "the Science and Certainty that we aim at" could be achieved only by finding a method of inquiry immune to what Petty called "passion or interest, faction or party."[34] That agenda reacted against, but at the same time acknowledged, the preceding decades of ideological contention, civil war, and political uncertainty.[35] The midcentury chaos in the British islands also had divided many colonists in the western Atlantic (as members of the Council for Foreign Plantations were constantly reminded).[36] Graunt's solution to the problem of consensus in a dissentious society was to replace "idle, and useless Speculations" with something "downright Mechanical." Numbers seemed beyond political or theological dispute. Of course, the reliability of all counting depends on agreement about what to count, and part of Graunt's originality lay in his careful analysis of the limitations of data. Graunt argued that, even when the sources of demographic information were "ignorant and careless" people, their reports were nevertheless "sufficient" insofar as they involved distinctions that were "but matter of sense"—that is, as we would say, "merely matters of easily perceptible physical fact."[37] Even the stupidest or most contentious informants could distinguish dead from alive, male from female, black from white.

Graunt created the model for all future demographic studies, including Benjamin Franklin's 1751 *Observations Concerning the Increase of Mankind,* which anxiously noted how few "purely white People" inhabited the planet and proposed "excluding all Blacks and Tawnies" from America.[38] But although Graunt considered it "necessary to know how many People there be of each Sex, State, Age, Religion, Trade, Rank, or Degree," the London shopkeeper had not included color among his categories. Petty did. In 1671 he reported that Barbados contained "six Blacks and Slaves to one White and freeman," and later in the 1670s he noted that there were "500 Whites born" in Boston annually, that "eight hundred Whites" had been born in Plymouth (Massachusetts) in seven years, and that in the Rhode Island colony were born about 200 people a year, including both "Whites and Blacks."[39] In his *Political Arithmetic* (circulating in manuscript by 1676), Petty calculated "The value of the slaves brought out of Africa to serve in our American plantations" at "twenty thousand pounds." But Petty, like the Council of Foreign Plantations, was equally willing to reduce whites to economic counters: he calculated the value of "a newborn [white] child" in terms of "the price of negroes' children in the American plantations."[40]

Nevertheless, despite the grammatical symmetry of "Whites and Blacks," or the application of economic logic to both sets, Petty's attitude toward the two categories was anything but neutral. He drafted a hierarchical "Scale of Animals," which included the observation that "of man itself there seems to be several species," noting the extreme contrast "between the Guinea Negroes and the Middle Europeans." Petty's "Middle Europeans" here probably echo Bodin's division of the northern hemisphere into three zones: France, England, Germany, and the Netherlands constitute the norm, explicitly contrasted with the "very mean sort of men" found in "the northernmost parts of the habitable world" and implicitly contrasted with the Mediterranean Europeans (Spanish and Italian) who more closely resembled Africans. According to Petty, the Middle Europeans "do not only differ from the aforementioned Africans in color, which is as much as white differs from black, but also in their hair . . . in the shape of their noses, lips and cheekbones, as also in the very outline of their faces and the mould of their skulls. They differ also in their natural manners, and in the internal qualities of their minds."[41] Petty's account of the "several species" of man—not published until the twentieth century—was apparently written between 1676 and 1678. It therefore antedated the "new division of . . . the different species or races of men" (published in French in Amsterdam in 1684), which is often taken as the earliest example of "scientific racism."[42]

Petty's description of the gap between blacks and whites was mainly and particularly anatomical; unspecified cultural and psychological differences were secondary. This anatomical emphasis anticipated eighteenth-century racial theory, but it also reflected Petty's own biography. Having gone to sea as a cabin boy, he was cast ashore in France at the age of 14, and educated by Jesuits there in the 1630s, before studying medicine in the Netherlands in the 1640s; in the 1650s he became Professor of Anatomy at Oxford and a member of the Royal College of Physicians. In the same decade he played an important role in Cromwell's suppression of Irish resistance; he produced the first detailed survey and map of all Ireland, the cartographical foundation of subsequent English governance and land ownership.[43] His attitude toward the differences between human populations, evident by the 1670s, came out of a mix of Franco-Dutch education and English imperial experience in Ireland.

But Petty's colorphobic categories also belonged to a specifically English subculture. After all, although Petty may have influenced or encouraged the demographic and statistical preoccupations of the London imperial secretariat, those officials were using *white* as a generic noun years before it showed up in Petty's work, and his statistics about blacks and whites in Barbados, Boston, and Rhode Island must have come from them, directly or indirectly. The medium for the circulation of such information may well have been the Royal Society, which was always particularly attractive to civil servants.[44]

The Royal Society of London for Improving of Natural Knowledge received its first endorsement by Charles II in December 1660 (almost simultaneously with the commission for the Council for Foreign Plantations). Petty was one of its original members; so was his friend Robert Boyle, who was undoubtedly its most influential figure. Like Petty, Boyle had experienced firsthand the Protestant conquest of Ireland. (His father was the first Earl of Cork.) But unlike Petty, Boyle was an original member of the Council for Foreign Plantations, and in 1662 he was named governor of the Company for the Propagation of the Gospel in New England; in the 1670s he invested in the East India Company, the Hudson Bay Company, and the Turkey Company.[45] In August 1664 the Royal Society formed a Committee of Correspondence, to send systematic inquiries on various topics to knowledgeable Europeans around the world, including the English colonies.[46] Boyle was a member (as was Thomas Povey), and at that committee's first meeting that August he was to supply "Queries for Guinea"—that is, inquiries to be sent to, and about, the west coast of Africa.[47] In 1665 Boyle published in the society's *Philosophical Transactions* the protocols of inquiry ("Articles of Inquisition") for compiling a "Natural History" of countries, specifying that observers should supply (among other things) "a careful account given of the Inhabitants," including "in particular, their Stature, Shape, Color."

Boyle's "their" cannot be intended as a request for descriptions of the different statures, shapes, and colors of *each* of the individuals in a foreign country; "their . . . Color" presupposes that all the inhabitants of a particular country have a single collective observable body color. In its first year, Europe's first scientific journal thus asked—in the interests of "a Solid and Useful Philosophy" (first sentence) and "the welfare of Mankind" (last sentence)—for generalized physical descriptions of population groups.[48] Extending the inquiries that the Council for Foreign Plantations had already begun making, Boyle's protocols enlisted large numbers of white observers in the accurate recording of physical differences between Europeans and other peoples.

Boyle provided the model for specific inquiries developed by other members of the Royal Society for specific regions, including these questions about West Africa asked in 1666 in the *Philosophical Transactions*[49]:

7. Whether some People on the River Gambia, be only Tawny, as others very Black?
8. Whether the Negroes have such sharp sights, that they discover a ship at Sea much farther off, than the Europeans can?

Since Boyle had legitimated and indeed solicited questions about color, it is not surprising that the word *Negroes* entered the official vocabulary of the Royal Society by 1666, and that it did so in the specific context of physiological difference. Indeed, Negroes were implicit in Boyle's original directive.[50] In addition to color and other physiological features, Boyle had asked for information about "what diseases" the inhabitants of other countries "are subject to," and this quickly led to reports like this one, from the English colony in Jamaica: "the Spanish Negroes wash their heads with soap once a week to prevent being lousy; whilst the other Negroes lose a great deal of time in looking after their heads, which by reason of their curls breed Lice more than the English, insomuch, that he affirms to have seen great holes eaten by Lice in the heads of some of them that were lazy." Soon after, a Dr. Stubbs reported from Barbados that certain parasites "overrun the whole Body of some idle Negroes."[51] Parasitic infestations and laziness had become observable "facts" about blacks, part of the scientific record, by 1668. But the most important fact about blacks was anatomical.

Bodies

Early in 1664 Boyle published *Experiments and Considerations Touching Colors . . . The Beginning of an Experimental History of Colors;* Part II was a long and detailed consideration *Of the Nature of Whiteness and Blackness.* Praised by Robert

Hooke, Christopher Wren, and many others, Boyle's treatise was soon translated into Latin and reprinted in London, Amsterdam, Rotterdam, and Geneva.[52] In it Boyle denied that the blackness of Negroes could be due to "the Heat of the Sun."[53] Here and elsewhere, he rehearsed the earlier arguments against climatic explanations for color (discussed in chapters 3 and 4), including the presence of different complexions at the same latitudes.[54] But he also cited new sources.[55] Appropriately for a chemist, Boyle had an abiding interest in extreme temperatures, including their effects on skin. Neither his own experiments nor the observations of travelers supported the geohumoral theory.[56] Like Sir Thomas Browne (another member of the Royal Society), Boyle rejected the curse of Ham as an explanation. Like Browne, Boyle recognized that color was transmitted sexually; like Browne, he categorized "European Bodies" as "White."[57] Like Browne, Boyle added to his theological critique of the curse of Ham a specifically secular argument about the protocols of scientific inquiry. But where Browne ended, Boyle began, insisting from the outset on a search for "the Proper, Immediate, and Physical Cause of the Jetty Colour of Negroes."[58]

Much more emphatically and effectively than Browne, Boyle redirected the debate among European elites from climate and religion to the anatomical body. That body was understood differently than it had been in the ancient or medieval world, or even in the sixteenth century.[59] Galen, the greatest medical authority of the Roman empire, never dissected a human body, and that inhibition persisted in Christian Europe until the 1540s. The Royal Society, which included more doctors than any other profession, was licensed to perform medical dissections. Boyle himself had been enthusiastically practicing animal vivisection and human autopsy since the 1640s, and in the 1660s he often performed them for the Royal Society.[60] Dissection and vivisection had been crucial to Dr. William Harvey's discovery of the circulation of the blood, published in 1628, which Boyle regarded as one of the great achievements of the century.[61] Harvey's work became the basis of research by a group of Oxford physiologists (including Boyle), who from the late 1640s to the middle 1670s revolutionized understanding of human bodily functions.[62] Once understood and widely accepted, Harvey's discovery "cashiered" the classical theory of the four humors, or at the very least undermined and confined its relevance.[63]

In fact, the humoral model of the human body—which was fundamental to the classical explanation of complexion as a function of climate—had been under attack since the 1550s, when the works of the Swiss physician and chemist Paracelsus began to be widely published; Paracelsus was especially influential in northern Europe and among utopian and humanitarian English Puritans in the seventeenth century.[64] In 1651, a century after Paracelsus began its destruction, the whole edifice of Hippocratic and Galenic medicine could be mocked for its "threadbare and short-coated descriptions and discourses of Heat and Cold . . . with the Nature, Elements, temperaments, humours, powers."[65] Boyle himself, in *The Sceptical Chemist* (1661), demonstrated the absurdity of the Aristotelian four elements (upon which depended the four humors of Hippocratic and Galenic medicine).[66] In 1663 Boyle had specifically argued that "Physicians have ascribed too much to the Humors, under the notion of their being hot and dry, cold and moist, or endowed with such other Elementary Qualities" and that "the Juices of the Body" should instead be "more Chemically examined."[67] Boyle's book on colors does not even mention the alleged colors of the four alleged humors. Some other explanation of human diversity had to be found.

Having recorded and evaluated the accumulated testimony of many European observers, Boyle offered as his own modest contribution the conjecture that "the Seat" of human pigmentation "seems to be but the thin *Epidermes,* or outward Skin."[68] Here Boyle redefined the issue of color in the terms that we now take for granted. Whereas Columbus had said "these *people* . . . are white," Boyle wrote, more precisely, of "the Blackness of the *Skin*" (italics added). Whereas Browne's chapter title had announced a discussion "Of the Blackness of Negroes," Boyle's table of contents promised a chapter on "The eleventh Experiment, about the Blackness of the *Skin,* and Hair of Negroes, and Inhabitants of Hot Climates" (italics added).[69] Unlike Ptolemy and the whole geohumoral medical tradition, Boyle argued that color was only skin deep, and that, like other issues affecting pigmentation, it could be investigated by determining which specific organic structures produced colors.

Further investigation would, as Boyle suggested, require microscopes.[70] For early anatomists, skin was simply an obstacle, cut away to reveal the organs beneath it.[71] Consequently, the sixteenth and early seventeenth century perpetuated "the confusion and uncertainty of medieval authors" in relation to what we would now call dermatology.[72] England's first hospital specialist in skin diseases was not appointed until 1632.[73] But in 1645 Sir Kenelm Digby performed the first recorded experiment on skin allergies.[74] And by 1664 Boyle's protégé and experimental assistant had for the first time examined human skin under a microscope (Illus. 11). Robert Hooke placed a captured louse on his own skin and then observed parasite and epidermis under magnification, concluding that "there is no part of the skin but the blood is dispersed into, nay, even into the *cuticula.*" Hooke knew this because he had measured the length of the louse "nose": the blood it sucked up could not be "more than a three-hundredth part of an inch" below the surface.[75] What Hooke saw under the lens contradicted traditional humoral theories about the relationship between blood and skin.[76] Because skin contained no visible veins or arteries, the blood Harvey's louse found must have been dispersed by some organic structure that was simultaneously pervasive and invisible. Such a mechanism—a network of very small blood vessels, which we now call capillaries—had been seen and described in 1661 by the Italian anatomist Marcello Malpighi, who first examined lungs under the microscope. Malpighi's discovery confirmed Harvey's claim about circulation and destroyed the humors theory.[77] In 1665 the Italian turned his microscope on skin. But unlike Hooke, Malpighi did not confine himself to the surface; he looked through his lenses at the skin's dissected interior structure. He found there an organic mechanism that produced the "blackness of Ethiopians" and "the variety" of human pigmentation generally.[78] Malpighi was working independently of Boyle and Hooke. But the Royal Society soon learned of his work and elected him to their membership; by the early 1680s Boyle was praising Malpighi's description of skin structure.[79] In 1698 an English book, published by a Fellow of the Royal Society, included engravings that displayed the microscopic anatomy of skin (Illus. 12).[80]

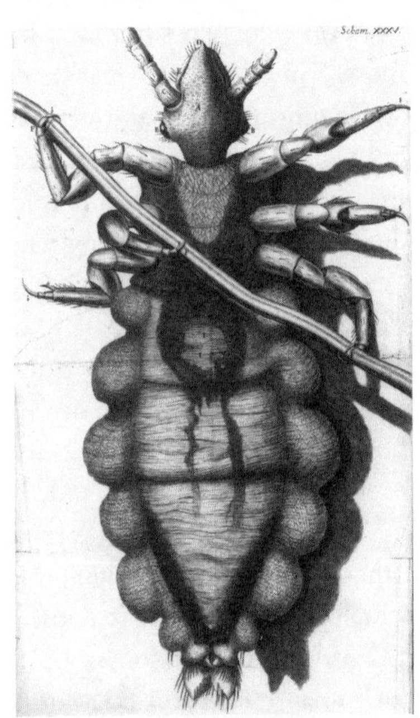

Illustration 11. Robert Hooke's engraving (1665) of a magnified louse on its back, clutching a strand of Hooke's hair. By permission of The British Library.

By that time Boyle was dead. But earlier and more clearly than anyone else, Boyle defined the research agenda that led to the discovery of the unknown chemicals that pigmented human skin and the unknown biochemical mechanism that transmitted skin color from parent to child. That scientific agenda would, by the late twentieth century, disprove the prejudices of colorphobia and racism. Even as early as 1744, the Royal Society published a description of anatomical experiments undertaken by Dr. John Mitchell of Virginia, demonstrating that—with the exception of certain "fibres" between the two layers of human skin—"all other parts" of the bodies of black people are "of the same Color" as the bodies "of white People."[81]

Boyle deserves some credit for the subsequent history of antiracist science. When he jettisoned the geohumoral explanation of human variety, he broke the classical link between human color and human nature.[82] Although the medical theory of four humors was not "racist" in a modern sense, it did assert that external color was symptomatic of interior constitution. It read the color of skin as a "sign," a reliable index of the characteristics of the body that skin enclosed.

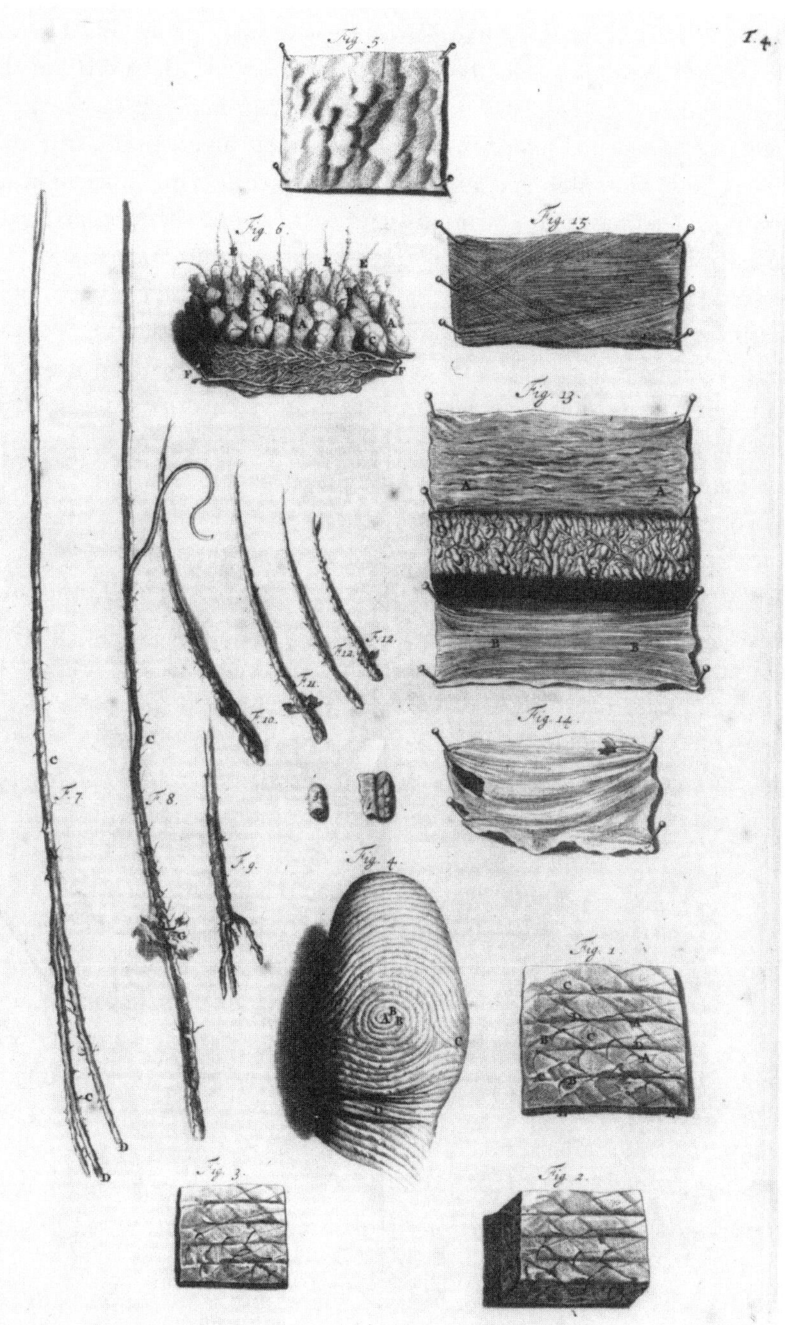

Illustration 12. The first microscopic images of human skin published in England—by William Cowper in 1698—show the outer layer (*cuticula*) of the back of the hand (Fig. 1) and bottom of the foot (Fig. 2), and the "Internal Structure" of the underlying "True Skin" (*cutis*), including "The Capillament of the little Aqueous Vessels . . . in which some have placed the Seat of that Tawny Tincture of the *Ægyptians,* and that Black one of the *Æthiopians*" (Fig. 6). By permission of the British Library.

Moreover, certain types and tinctures of body were inescapably linked to certain kinds of mind. A monstrous body—like the hunchbacked Richard III, in Shakespeare's popular play—signaled a monstrous soul. In humoral theory, physiology and psychology had shared the same complexion: an excess of white phlegm produced both white skin and a phlegmatic personality. Thus, ancient humoral tradition read skin as a sign of mind—and so, of course, does modern racism. In both theories of human variation, the color of your skin indicates what kind of person you are and what kind of behavior can be expected of you. Some recent scholars have celebrated the good old days of geohumoralism because the classical theory did not valorize white complexions, and because it insisted that a change of climate would change a man's nature (something slave traders and owners did not want to hear).[83] But geohumoralism, like racism, told Europeans that a man's nature was displayed in the color of his skin.

By contrast, Boyle's theory made color the consequence of a minute chemical process, confined to one layer of skin. Discussing the blackness of Negroes, he reported an elementary experiment in which the color of European skin could be "changed to an amber-like blackness" by the "simple and natural juice" of a certain American fruit.[84] Color was a local dermatological condition, without any necessary or intrinsic or essential relationship to other aspects of the corporeal or psychological self. The human body as a whole was, in Boyle's image, an "hydraulo-pneumatical engine."[85] In the new robotic philosophy of the French philosopher René Descartes, the mind ran a machine called the body; the subject-mind stood outside the object-body, like an overseer operating and supervising a complicated piece of equipment (or a slave).[86] That dualism has not survived the rise of neuroscience, but it did sunder skin color from character. Mind and body interpenetrate each other in manifold and complex ways, but color does not cross that line. A body with dark skin can do or think anything that a body with light skin can do or think. Boyle began the process of empirical investigation that has proven the irrelevance of color to intellectual achievement and psychological health. The scientific method, at its best, is color-blind.

But the scientific method is not always at its best. Just because he limited pigment variation to the outer layer of skin does not mean that Boyle himself considered "the differences between whites and blacks . . . quite slight."[87] Boyle explicitly called the blackness of Negroes "ugly" and associated it with "deformities."[88] Like William Petty, he attributed to the anatomical black body not only the "true Blackness" of Negro "Skin" but also "the Blobber-Lips and Flat-Noses of most Nations of Negroes." Describing an albino born in Brazil of Negro parents, Boyle reported that, despite his "very white skin," his nose was still "clearly of negro form."[89] The reactions of Englishmen to Africans had never been limited to their color: Othello was nicknamed "the thick-lips," and Samuel Purchas had described blacks in terms of their "great lips . . . wide mouths . . . woolly pates" and "flat-nosed" faces.[90] Hence, for Boyle, as for Locke and other seventeenth-century natural philosophers, color was just one part of an ensemble of physical differences between the inhabitants of England and the inhabitants of sub-Saharan Africa.[91]

Those physical differences produced distinct social and emotional responses. As evidence for his theory of epidermal pigment, Boyle cited the published testimony of a German physician, Willem Piso, who had "the opportunity in Brazil to Dissect many Negroes," and the private testimony of a physician who recently "had Dissected a Negro here in England."[92] There is nothing intrinsically ethnocentric about dissecting human corpses. The cut-open torsos displayed in the illustrations of Andreas Vesalius's revolutionary *De fabrica corporis humani* (1543) are all European, as are those in other anatomy textbooks of the sixteenth and seventeenth centuries. By contrast, in *Clotel* William Wells Brown quotes two nineteenth-century documents that describe an explicitly racial regime of anatomical inquiry. One is a newspaper advertisement:

> TO PLANTERS AND OTHERS.—*Wanted fifty negroes.* Any person having *sick negroes,* considered *incurable* by their respective physicians (their owners of course,) and wishing to dispose of them, Dr. Stillman will pay cash for negroes affected with scrofula or king's evil, confirmed hypochrondriacism, apoplexy, or diseases of the brain, kidneys, spleen, stomach and intestines, bladder and its appendages, diarrhea, dysentery, &c. *The highest cash price will be paid as above.* (132)

("Their owners of course" is Brown's sarcastic addition to the original advertisement.) Brown's second document is the prospectus of a small college, where the said Dr. Stillman gave lectures[93]: "Some advantages of a peculiar character are connected with this institution, which it may be proper to point out. No place in the United States offers as great opportunities for the acquisition of anatomical knowledge. Subjects being obtained from among the coloured population in sufficient numbers *for every purpose,* and proper dissections carried on *without offending any individuals in the community!*" (133). In 1853, in *Clotel,* doctors are white, and the corpses they dissect are black. Part of Brown's satire of the ignorant black servant Sam is a description of his aspiration to the paradoxical status of "Black Doctor"—without, of course, any proper medical training, and without any possibility of treating white patients (137). White knowledge gives whites the power to turn black bodies into the material that creates more white knowledge (Plate 19).

How did we get from Vesalius to Brown? Boyle's reference to the German doctor's enviable "opportunity . . . to dissect many Negroes" represents a turning point in the relationship between medicine and colorphobia.[94] Boyle did not theorize or justify the newly routine white dissection of black bodies. It did not seem to require explanation. Like other investigators of the natural world in the seventeenth century, Boyle was fascinated by oddities; he collected reports of such curiosities in 274 manuscript pages of what he called his "Outlandish Book."[95] But there was, apparently, nothing outlandish about European doctors cutting up countless African corpses. (Imagine, though, how whites would have reacted to reports that a black "witch doctor" had been cutting up countless white bodies!) From an African point of view, what Boyle mentioned so casually—and with evident admiration for the "excellent" and "commended" white doctor—would simply have been further evidence for the belief, widespread on the west coast of Africa in the era of the slave trade, that white men were cannibals.[96] The Africans were not exactly wrong. In Barbados in the 1670s, Morgan Godwyn heard rumors of "dissecting [Negroes] alive," and reported that such vivisection was "certainly affirmed by some of them, as no less allowable than to a Beast, of which they did not in the least doubt but it was justifiable."[97]

Boyle himself did not practice, or endorse, such atrocities. But he did remain blind to the white destruction of black bodies. Whether living black bodies in Barbados were ever cut up on a vivisectionist's table, they were certainly, routinely, and painfully sacrificed in the sugar mills that supported the island's economy. "If a mill-feeder be catched by the finger," a Barbados planter explained, "his whole body is drawn in, and he is squeezed to pieces." Likewise, "if a boyler gets any part into the scalding sugar, it sticks like glue, or birdlime, and 'tis hard to save either limb or life."[98] Another account of the sugar-making process in Barbados reported an accident that "burnt the poor Negro to death."[99] Boyle knew that 25,000 to 30,000 black "Slaves" in Barbadoes were "imployed almost totally about the planting of sugar canes and making of sugar," in an extremely lucrative industrial process imported directly from Brazil.[100] He also knew a great deal about those factories, thanks to "the accurate account . . . of the art of making sugar" that had been given by "the formerly commended Piso."[101] Piso's account includes what may be the earliest visual record of black slaves at work in New World plantations (see Illus. 13–15). Boyle apparently did not find anything odd about the color line that separated a small number of white (clothed) managers from a large number of black (almost naked) laborers. He was apparently not disturbed by the interlacing of anonymous black bodies with huge, dangerous modern machinery. He did not connect Piso's "opportunity . . . to dissect many Negro corpses" to the fact that black men—and women—had become cheap, interchangeable, replaceable parts of the ingenious new machines owned and operated by white men. Like other Protestant Englishmen, Boyle was prepared to condemn the Spanish mines in Peru, because of "the multitudes of unhappy men that are

Illustrations 13–15. One or two supervisors (with white skin and European clothes) direct the labor of many black, almost naked slaves working dangerous sugar-refining machinery on plantations in Dutch Brazil. By permission of the Houghton Library, Harvard University.

made miserable, and destroyed in working them"—but he never acknowledged that Englishmen were also destroying multitudes of unhappy men.[102] He never condemned the enslavement of blacks by his contemporaries. In fact, he repeatedly publicly praised individual white men who owned slaves. The suffering of "many Negroes" was an unimportant detail or unintended side effect.

The dissections in Brazil constituted, for Boyle, simply a piece of authenticating circumstantial detail in support of a scientific hypothesis. In the rhetoric of the new experimental science developed in England in the 1650s and 1660s, and epitomized by Boyle, "many" dissections were more valuable than one, and the testimony of a German physician working on a Dutch plantation in Brazil became more credible when supported by the independent testimony of a physician in England, repeating the same anatomical experiment. Vesalius had of course dissected many bodies, but in Restoration England "a multiplication of the witnessing experience" was for the first time explicitly theorized as a condition for establishing matters of fact.[103] Boyle compared his new experimental protocols to the common-law "practice of our courts of justice here in England," which required "the testimony of two witnesses" to convict anyone of murder. Thomas Sprat, the propagandist for the Royal Society, made the same analogy, but magnified the authority of the experimentalists by contrasting the "two, or three witnesses" of legal protocol with "the concurring Testimonies of *threescore or an hundred*" (Sprat's italics) who witnessed experiments performed at Gresham College.[104] Moreover, witnesses of these experiments, and readers of published descriptions of them, were encouraged to duplicate them on their own, thereby adding to the stock of testimony, as new cases added to the stock of common law. Boyle's theory that the proper, immediate, and physical causes of blackness should be sought in "the superficial parts of Bodies" would be independently verified, in 1674, by the "experimental knowledge" of another member of the Royal Society, Massachusetts colonist John Josselyn.[105] Multiplication equaled verification.

But the new anatomical theory of biologically distinct human genres originated in England, not the colonies. It developed in the same intellectual environment that stimulated the medical innovations of Dr. Thomas Sydenham (1624–89), the "English Hippocrates." Studying in Oxford in the 1650s, Sydenham had met Boyle, who inspired his interest in the experimental study of disease. In 1666 Sydenham dedicated his first book to Boyle, and reported that they sometimes visited the sick together; in London Sydenham and Boyle were next-door neighbors.[106] Sydenham worked chiefly among the poor, focusing not on the (wealthy) individual patient but on groups of patients suffering the same malady. In an effort to "reduce all the Species of Epidemics into Classes, according to the variety of their *Phenomena,*" Sydenham collected, organized, and published voluminous observations on the epidemics "that did rage from the Year 1661, to the Year 1676."[107] Sydenham's emphasis resembled John Graunt's analysis of the causes of London mortality over decades. But Graunt collected his evidence from parish registers, and Sydenham collected his from living and dying patients. In this agenda, treatment was a form of research, and victims—ideally, large numbers of victims—became evidence of the nature of a specific disease. Identifying and categorizing diseases required repeated "experiments" and a multitude of cases. Sydenham (in the words of medical historian Andrew Wear) made "the individual patient anonymous, hidden as one amongst the many from which knowledge would come," part of a process by which "medicine changed from being patient-centered to being disease-centered."[108] Sydenham's radical transformation of medical practice belonged to the same interest in analyzing whole populations evident in the work of Graunt, Petty, Boyle, the Royal Society, and the Council for Foreign Plantations.

Sydenham's patients were white. But by the 1660s enslaved black bodies and dead black bodies had become part of the personal experience of affluent and curious men living in London and Oxford. Black bodies had become part of the "Matter" from which English intellectuals would manufacture "a Masculine Philosophy" (that is, modern science, as opposed to the allegedly ineffectual, effeminate, subjective verbosity of traditional humanism).[109] Unlike Sir Thomas Browne in 1646, Boyle in 1664 was not limited to continental sources. "I knew a young Negro," Boyle reports, and later cites the testimony of "an Intelligent acquaintance of mine (who keeps in the Indies about 200 of them, as well Women as Men, to work in his Plantations)."[110] The blacks his friend kept were, of course, slaves, as Boyle knew perfectly well; but he does not say that. In 1662 civil servant Samuel Pepys was "pleased to hear" several captains discussing what was to him the new and interesting fact "that Negroes drownded look white and lose their blackness" (information acquired courtesy of the Middle Passage).[111] In 1665 an acquaintance showed Pepys "a black boy that he had that died of a consumption; and being dead, he caused him to be dried in a Oven, and lies there entire in a box." In 1667 Pepys read Boyle's book on color, finding in it "many fine things worthy observation."[112] In 1676 Sir Thomas Browne wrote to his son in London, urging him "to take notice of the *cuticula* and *cutis* of negroes, and to examine it well and to make a vesicatory"—that is, by applying an irritating ointment, deliberately create blisters—"and observe how the *cutis* looks when the *cuticula* is off."[113] By 1686 the Royal Society was exhibiting, in its London museum, both "the entire SKIN of a Moor" and "A Male Human Foetus" whose skin was "white and smooth."[114] As cultural critic Cristina Malcolmson observes, this juxtaposition assumed and asserted that "To be a male human is to be white; to be a Moor is to be notable because of one's skin."[115] It also associated whiteness with an originary human state. In 1664 Boyle assumed that Adam and Eve were "White Parents."[116] The fetus displayed by the Royal Society was as white as the Adam and Eve of Robert Boyle.

Science

Boyle was the first white scientist.[117] Because he was a European who believed that Europeans were "white"—and did not apply that word to any other population—he considered himself white in a recognizably modern generic sense.[118] He also helped to create the disciplinary protocols of observational and experimental investigation of the material world, the foundation of what we now call science. Boyle was the first European intellectual to construct his own identity on both those categories and to feel that there was no conflict between them.[119] In fact, the Honourable Robert Boyle was instrumental in the social evolution of both categories. The influential historian of science Steven Shapin has shown that "Boyle did not *take on* the identity of experimental philosopher, he was a major force in *making* that identity."[120] He personified the ego-ideal for the emergent profession of scientist. Boyle created that influential new form of vocational identity, according to Shapin, out of existing social materials (gentleman, Christian, philosopher), which he eventually defined and combined in an original way. But Boyle also belonged to the first generation of Englishmen to have widely, unselfconsciously, and positively characterized themselves as white. He was born in 1627: the year that Thomas Middleton died and the English settled Barbados (the first colony to begin with a combination of English freemen and black slaves). By the time Boyle died, in 1691, 13 English colonies had legislated whiteness, and *white* had become a generic noun routinely used as an official demographic category.

Shapin did not consider whiteness a part of Boyle's constructed public identity. For the elements of gentleman, Christian, and philosopher, Boyle (and Shapin) could mine an enormous inherited mountain of texts; for the new generic whiteness, there was no such legacy. In part, whiteness did not seem to need definition because it did not seem to need to be constructed. The whiteness of Boyle's body was a matter of fact. According to his contemporaries, the sickly Boyle was "pale," and one friend "frequently compared him to a crystal, or Venice glass."[121] The whiteness of the new science did not seem to need definition because *white,* in its new ethnographic sense, was initially a synonym for Christian, English, British, or European, words that already carried complex social traditions. In emergent colonial law, every white was becoming, in relation to blacks, a "Master" (abbreviated "Mr."), the honorific traditionally accorded gentlemen; but as the very wealthy son of an earl, Boyle did not need to be white to receive automatic deference. The Royal Society—funded in part by the profits of the East India Company—resembled one of London's "gentleman's clubs."[122] For Boyle's class, gender, and generation, whiteness might seem redundant. It just colonized and connected several existing genres of discourse.

Boyle began to give whiteness a discourse of its own. He devoted his life to the development of a powerful new genre, what we call science, what he and his contemporaries called experimental or mechanical philosophy. That new discourse was written in English (rather than Latin), but it could not be categorized as simply English, because the English were not the only participants. Boyle himself was Anglo-Irish; after Eton, rather than attending an English university, he spent five years with a tutor in Europe, mostly in Geneva, with important trips to Italy, and in 1648 he visited the Netherlands. The scientific revolution was begun by a Pole (Copernicus), a Belgian (Vesalius), a Dane (Brahe), an Italian (Galileo), a German (Kepler), and a Frenchman (Descartes). Technologically, gunpowder and the printing press had been invented by Germans, the telescope by a Dutchman; even the air pump, instrumental in the discovery of "Boyle's Law," was a German import. The noun Boyle used to describe the new professional identity he exemplified was the Italian word *virtuoso,* introduced into English in the 1650s. In science as in colonization, the English arrived belatedly.

What Boyle's generation added to their predecessors' achievements was the creation of a scientific community. That community was multinational, held together in part by a correspondence network (like the one created by the Council for Foreign Plantations).[123] A key figure in that network was Henry Oldenburgh, German-born multilingual secretary of the Royal Society of London, publisher of Boyle's *Experiments and Considerations concerning Colors* and of *Philosophical Transactions,* link between Malpighi and the Royal Society. For his account of the causes of blackness in Negroes, Boyle consulted not only books but living "Travellers," including "the best Navigators and Travellers to the West-Indies," the physician to a Russian ambassador, "a *Virtuoso* who lately Travelled through Livonia to Moscow," another man "that had for some years been an Eminent Physician in Russia," another "very Ingenious Physician" in England, and the "Possessor" of a white raven, as well as the "Intelligent acquaintance" who owned 200 slaves in the West Indies.[124] Like the free community in the English colonies, the scientific community was not just English but pan-European. Geographically, it was more than European, because it included from the outset European-born and European-educated men living in colonies outside of Europe. Among scientific virtuosi as among enfranchised colonists, the one word that applied to all members of the new community was *white.*

All the enfranchised members of the colonial and scientific communities could also be called *male* and *Christian.* But although manhood was crucial to these new seventeenth-century communities (and I will return to the subject of gender), almost half the global human population was male. Sex alone was not a sufficiently restrictive category for defining a new community. Christianity was also problematic. After all, scientific inquiry had begun before Christianity: Epicurus, like Aristotle, was a pagan. As for living authorities, on the subject of skin color Boyle consulted Protestant, Catholic, and Greek Orthodox sources. But more than a century of religious warfare had shown Europeans, and the mid-century civil wars had painfully proven to Englishmen, that sectarian difference divided communities more often than nominal Christianity united them. There was in 1664—and still is—no universally accepted definition of *Christian.* Boyle's England contained Roman Catholics and Anglicans, Presbyterians and Quakers and Baptists, but each of these groups contested whether the others were actually "Christian." The scientific community could remain a community only insofar as it banished theological discussion (as did the Royal Society). Moreover, although Boyle and Newton and many others devoted enormous energies to demonstrating the compatibility of Christianity and the new science, that compatibility has never been self-evident and has often been denied. From Copernicus to Darwin, from astronomy to cloning, Christianity has been the chief opponent of science. Even in calling himself "the Christian Virtuoso," Boyle's adjective acknowledged that his noun was not intrinsically Christian; the expression was, to some minds, as oxymoronic as "white slave." Whatever the religious beliefs and passions of its individual members, the shared and defining activity of the new scientific community was secular.[125]

White, rather than *Christian,* defined membership of the new scientific community for the same reasons it superseded *Christian* in colonial communities. Although some blacks and Indians had been converting to Christianity since the sixteenth century, that did not qualify them for membership in the new scientific community. The new science established its authority by drawing on existing social assumptions about which witnesses and technologies were intrinsically credible.[126] The Royal Society prided itself on accepting a few members, like John Graunt, who were tradesmen rather than gentlemen; like whiteness, science could (at least temporarily) suspend class boundaries. But it did so only within the white community. Natives of Africa, America, and Asia were not credible witnesses, and they did not possess reliable instruments. Boyle believed that "matters of fact"—including in particular medical remedies—could and should be acquired even from "Indians and other barbarous nations," but those people did not themselves become Fellows of the Royal Society.[127] Rather, their knowledge was to be appropriated and reported by qualified white observers, like Boyle's friend that "learned Gentleman" the Reverend Mr. John Clayton.[128] In 1687 Clayton sent a letter from Virginia—

later published by the Royal Society—describing how the Indians "by making many Trials and Experiments . . . find out the Virtues of Herbs." Most of Clayton's letter described the proven efficacy of various Amerindian medical practices. But Clayton began his letter by emphasizing the need to make a careful verbal distinction between "the *English* or *Whites*" who had been "born here [in Virginia]," and might therefore be "called *Natives,*" and "the *Aborigines*" or "*Indians.*" The Indians, Clayton reported, "know little of the Nature or Reason of things."[129] Their practices constituted science only when filtered through the observations of a white man, capable of reason, who could reliably report significant and verifiable matters of fact, filtering out Indian claims that depended on mere "Pretence" or "Accident."

Science began as a white monopoly, and long remained a club for whites only. Even when whiteness was not verbally specified, it was visually explicit (see illus. 16–19). The body of the invisible objective scientific observer appears only once in Robert Hooke's rhetorically illustrated *Micrographia:* in the single strand of hair clutched by a louse (illus. 10). That thin, long, transparent cylinder does not come from the "woolly pate" of an African.

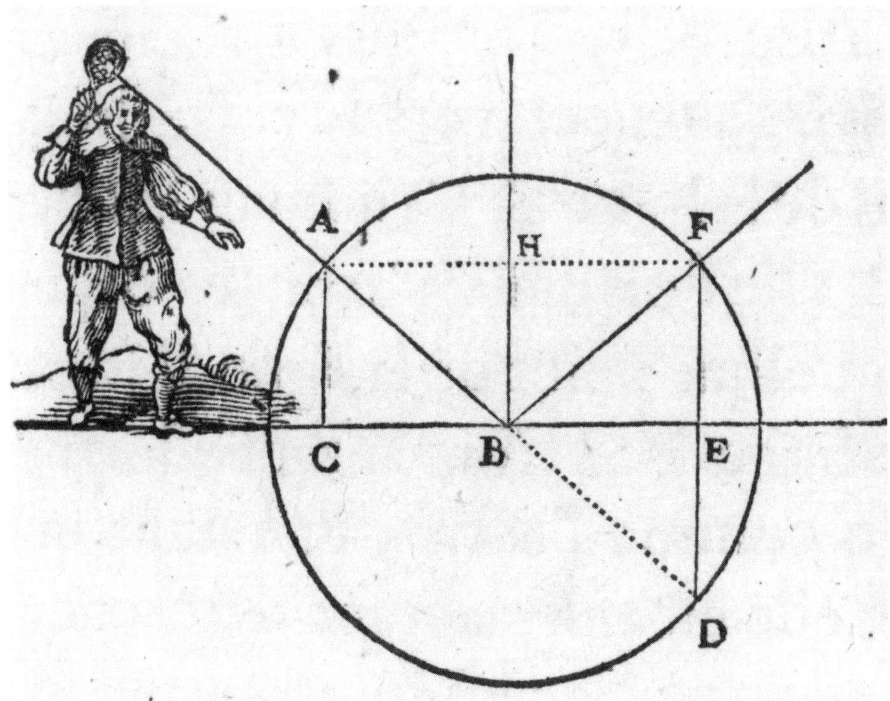

Illustration 16. The man conducting optical experiments in this engraving from Descartes's *Discours des Sciences* (1637) has white skin and wears European clothes. By permission of the British Library.

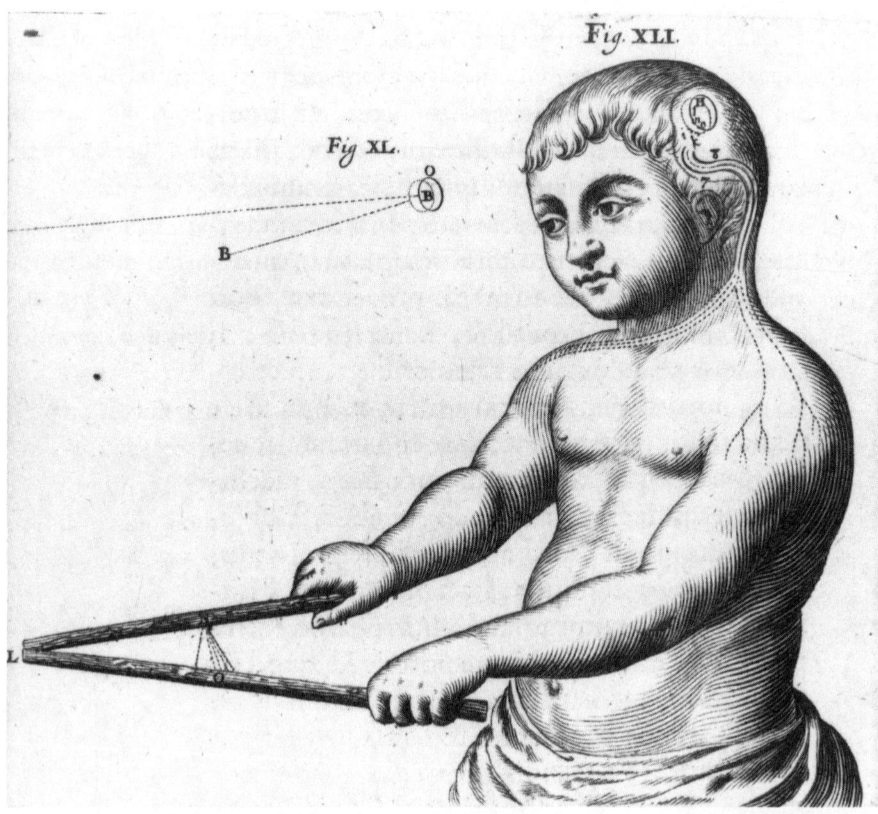

Illustration 17. The experimenter in this engraving from Descartes's *De Homine* (Paris, 1662) is a child with white skin and European hair and facial features (visually anticipating Locke's emphasis on the white child as an unprejudiced observer of phenomena). By permission of the British Library.

Most whites are not scientists, and people like Boyle were an even smaller proportion of the population in the seventeenth century than now. But the new science affected the identity of all whites. It established the validity of secular and empirical criteria—the criteria that slaveholders in Barbados used to defend themselves, when challenged by the religious and moral outrage of someone like Reverend Godwyn. Just as important, the new science provided a constant supply of visible evidence for the supremacy of white culture. Every new discovery, every new invention, increased the shared intellectual capital of whites as a whole. By 1758 that booming intellectual stock underwrote David Hume's conviction that "there never was a civilized nation of any other complexion than white, nor even any individual eminent either in action or speculation. No ingenious manufactures amongst them, no arts, no sciences."[130] It furnished the foundation on which Thomas Jefferson, in 1785, built his belief that blacks are

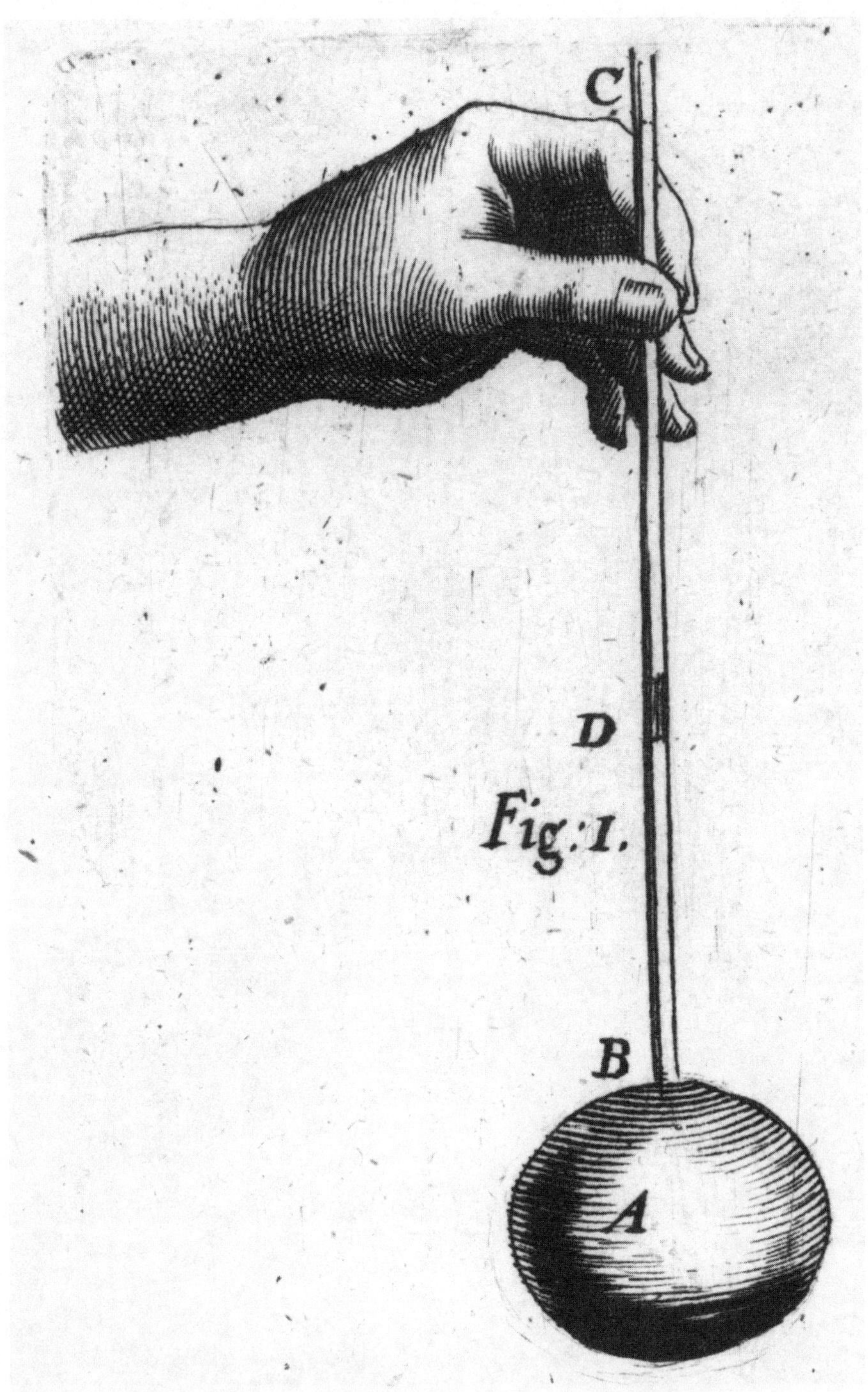

Illustration 18. The experimenter holding the laboratory vial in this engraving from Robert Boyle's *Experiments Touching Cold* (1665) is white: the palm (in shade) is darker than the back of the arm and thumb. By permission of the British Library.

Illustration 19. The French sculptor Roubiliac's white marble bust of Newton was widely copied, and seen by generations of Cambridge undergraduates. Wordsworth described it as "The marble index of a mind forever Voyaging through strange seas of thought, alone" (i.e., a mind autonomous, imperial, and marble white). Contrast the bust of Shakespeare in Plate 15. By permission of the Master and Fellows of Trinity College, Cambridge.

"in reason much inferior" to whites, and that "nature has been less bountiful to them in the endowments of the head."[131] *Clotel* was, in part, an answer to such attacks, a palpable "proof of the capability of the Negro intellect" (77). In 1662 Brown published another refutation, his book *The Black Man, His Antecedents, His Genius, and His Achievements.* Few whites read either book. But every white could see, everywhere, material evidence of white genius.

The accelerating accumulation of knowledges and technologies sparked by the white scientific revolution increased white pride and white power over native Americans, Africans, and Asians, but it also altered the balance of power between whites. The debate between "the ancients and the moderns"—did recent European achievements surpass those of the classical world?—was also, more subtly, a debate about the authority of Mediterranean culture. The centrist Mediterranean contempt for both southern (black) and northern (white) barbarians long seemed justified: for millennia, the civilizations of Egypt, the Middle East, Greece, Rome, and Islam dwarfed the accomplishments of peoples north of the Alps. Italians led the European Renaissance; Italians, Portuguese, and Spaniards spearheaded the global expansion of European power. England's "victory" against the Spanish Armada in 1588 had been entirely defensive, and it was followed by half a century of military embarrassments. But Cromwell's conquest of Scotland and Ireland (1649–52), victory in the First Dutch War (1652–54), and seizure of Jamaica from the Spanish (1655) demonstrated that England had become, for the first time, a major international power. Its most serious competitors—the Dutch and the French—were both northern European. By the mid-seventeenth century the scientific center of gravity had also moved north. If one separated Boyle's brand of experimental empiricism from Cartesian rationalism, the new scientific community was overwhelmingly Protestant, and dominated by the palest Europeans: British, Dutch, Danes, and Germans. Until the scientific revolution, western Europeans had belonged to what Rémi Brague calls an "eccentric culture," a secondary civilization always measuring itself against a superior, primary culture somewhere else (Jerusalem, Athens, Rome).[132] But science convinced northwestern Europeans of their own centrality, originality, and supremacy.

The pigmentation of the skin of the person(s) using an air pump to investigate air pressure should make no difference to the outcome of the experiments; it need not be recorded as a significant variable and need not affect interpretation of the results. But as a matter of fact the rhetoric of the Royal Society, its enormously influential protocols for scientific reporting, insisted that "knowledge about the world was to be provided by a definite occurrence happening to a particular person."[133] What then was important about that particular person? Not his voice. Boyle had an embarrassing stutter.[134] Newton was a notoriously boring lecturer. Fortunately for both, the white scientific revolution happened in a culture, an experimental setting, where seeing had begun to dominate hearing.[135] The visible book, the scientific illustration, or the mathematical table drowned out the colorless voice. That shift from sound to sight is evident in, and surely in part caused by, the millions of pages of text generated by the new technology of the printing press.[136] In the dialectic of the sixteenth-century French logician Ramus—whose influence can be seen in the analytical table of contents of Boyle's *Experiments and Considerations Touching Colors*—"the world is thought of as an assemblage of the sorts of things which vision apprehends: objects or surfaces."[137] The most spectacular early achievements of the new science depended on visual observation (of dissected human corpses, the movements of planets, sunspots, the moons of Jupiter) and on new technologies for magnifying vision (the telescope, the microscope) and reproducing it (the printing press, engraving). Consequently, the technicalities of optics preoccupied the seventeenth century's intellectual giants, from Galileo to Newton. *Experiments and Considerations Touching Colors* was the first significant English contribution to the science of light, and Boyle's vision of the visible immediately influenced Robert Hooke and Isaac Newton—and, hence, the future of optics.[138]

Whiteness interested Boyle in a way it had never interested anyone else. He advertised the novelty of his focus on it. "When I applied myself to consider how the cause of Whiteness might be explained by Intelligible and Mechanical Principles," he wrote, "I remembered not to have met with anything among the Ancient Corpuscularian Philosophers, touching the Quality we call Whiteness." Readers of this book—having suffered my accounts of Aristotle, Ptolemy, Pliny, Albertus Magnus, and others—may be surprised by Boyle's ignorance. But Boyle was limiting himself to "Corpuscularian" philosophy, which he distinguished from the aridity of the Aristotelian and medieval tradition. *Corpuscularian* was a brand-new word in English (not recorded before this example), based on the new word *corpuscle* (first recorded in 1660, in Boyle's *New Experiments Physico-Mechanical*). Boyle defined *corpuscle* as the smallest visible particle, itself a combination of the even smaller invisible particles described by the Greek word *atom.* Corpuscularians like Boyle accepted the ancient theory (championed by Democrites, Epicurus, and Lucretius) that the universe consisted of tiny particles of matter, variously arranged. This materialist conception had long been associated with atheism, and Boyle coined *corpuscularian* as a way of avoiding the negative associations of *epicurean;* he insisted that God created the corpuscles and the rules that governed their motion.[139]

Boyle was not the first of "the moderns" to revive "the Atomical Philosophy," or even the first to have "delivered something towards the Explication of Whiteness upon Mechanical Principles."[140] The earliest published atomist system had been written by the avid English experimental chemist Sir Kenelm Digby in

1644.[141] Among many other matters, Digby tried to explain "the generation of white and black."[142] Boyle knew and admired Digby: they were both cosmopolitan English aristocrats with an interest in literature, alchemy, and experiments.[143] Moreover, Digby anticipated several of Boyle's elucidations of whiteness.[144] Nevertheless, Boyle did not acknowledge Digby's influence on his discussion of whiteness (perhaps because Digby continued to defend the four elements and four humors of Aristotelian philosophy, perhaps because Digby declared himself a disciple of René Descartes).[145] Boyle preferred to associate himself with a different French philosopher, the explicitly Christian atomist Father Pierre Gassendi.[146] Before describing his own "Experiments and Observations," Boyle quoted six Latin sentences on the subject of whiteness delivered—but only "incidentally"—in an "ingenious" work that Gassendi, a "most learned" professor of mathematics, had published in 1642.[147]

Despite the fact that in the entirety of western philosophy he could find only six sentences on the subject worth quoting, Boyle began with whiteness. This priority determined not only the organization of his essay, but its title ("Of the Nature of Whiteness and Blackness"), and his consistent practice of reversing the alphabetical order of the two nouns, whenever he put them together in a phrase ("a Satisfactory account of Whiteness and Blackness").[148] Boyle used his conclusions about "Whiteness . . . to form a Notion of Blackness, those two Qualities being Contrary enough to Illustrate each other."[149] Given that opposition, he might just as easily have begun with blackness. In 1637 Descartes—whose conclusions anticipated and influenced Boyle—had begun with "black" (*noirs*) and then proceeded to "white" (*blancs*).[150] But for Digby in 1644 and for Boyle in 1664, whiteness was "the chiefest color."[151] It therefore made sense to begin with what Petty called, in 1667, "the primitive fundamental Colour, White."[152] Black was to be understood in and through its presumed binary opposition to an already-established white. Blacks were to be understood by defining their deviance from a white baseline.

Although I began my account of Boyle's book with his chapter on Negroes, in his text the categories white and black were not initially anatomical or demographic. When Boyle first referred to "a White Body," he was not describing the anatomical and organic frame of a European; he was using *body* as a synonym for *object.*[153] As Boyle proceeded to demonstrate, the "Quality we call Whiteness" originated in the chemistry of color and the physics of light; it could be mechanically investigated and intelligibly explained. Whiteness was a matter of fact. Within this domain of fact, late in a sequence of precise physical experiments precisely described, Boyle's eleventh experiment addressed "the Blackness of the Skin, and Hair of Negroes." Only in that chapter did Boyle use *white* in its new generic sense. In this ethnographic turn he again departed from

Descartes, whose *Optics* did not discuss skin color—and whose "Description of the Human Body and All Its Functions" discussed skin without once referring to differences of pigmentation.[154] Descartes had analyzed both colors and skins in mechanistic terms, but he did so in separate works, and did not relate the two. Boyle for the first time enfolded the metaphorical generic sense of corporeal whiteness into a larger, indisputably factual category. He wrote—in the same words, in the same essay—of the "White Bodies" of inanimate objects and chemical substances and of "White . . . European bodies."[155] Corporeal demographic whiteness was no longer confined to travel narratives, sermons, political documents, plays, collections of popular falsehoods. Boyle firmly and canonically situated it among "matters of fact."[156] The 461-page context of Boyle's 16-page discussion of skin color, and the even larger context of the life and authority of Boyle as "Father of Chemistry" and exemplar of the new science, matter as much as the particulars of Boyle's account of population pigmentation. "Racial science" began with Boyle, because Boyle first melded the new scientific investigation of color to earlier investigations of ethnic difference.

But Boyle did not simply extract facts from recalcitrant matter. White facts were attended by white theories, including a "Philosophy of Colors." Boyle's theory—what he called, with characteristic rhetorical modesty, his "Rude and General account of Whiteness"—was that "White Bodies reflect more Light than Others." White simply "Reflected a far greater Light, than any of the other Colours." The surfaces of a white body "reflect the beams it receives . . . without otherwise considerably Altering them; whereas in most other Colours, they are wont to be much Changed, by being also Refracted."[157] Boyle's account of whiteness (and its corollary blackness) interested his contemporaries more than any other part of his book.[158] It was the most "singularly successful" and "brilliantly conceived" element of his investigation of color—containing "what were to become the classic experiments repeated again and again in succeeding centuries, demonstrating that white objects reflect nearly all the incident light whereas black ones absorb nearly all the incident light."[159]

What then is "the Nature of Whiteness"? Because black objects absorb light, they also absorb heat; what reaches them from the exterior world changes their interior condition. Whiteness, by contrast, does not internalize light or heat, and therefore its interior remains independent of outside influences. Whiteness is stable, impermeable, unalterable. Nothing could be farther from John Fletcher's picture of Englishmen as apes and mimics, or Middleton's insistence that "white quickly soils." Boyle's whiteness mimics, instead, the ideal experimentalist, epitomized in the Royal Society's motto: *Nullius addictus iurare in verba magistri.* Boyle probably played a role in the choice of that motto; certainly, his financial and intellectual autonomy embodied the Royal Society's commitment to free inquiry, "dedicated to swear allegiance to the words of no master."[160] Like slaves, black bodies could be mastered by outside forces; like the new scientists, white bodies maintained their autonomy. Boyle's characterization of whiteness radically reversed the traditional geohumoral explanation, which attributed white complexions to the pervasive influence of a human being's physical environment. Mary Floyd-Wilson rightly emphasizes that "a disavowal of both environmental and somatic influences on the mind" made possible "the formation of the autonomous—and white—subject."[161] But there is no logical or inevitable connection between "autonomous" and "white." Boyle's study of light made that connection, and canonized it as a "scientific" fact.

Thanks to its perfect autonomy, whiteness does not hide or distort the light that falls on it; instead, whiteness faithfully reflects and retransmits the illumination it has received. Whiteness thus resembles Boyle's account of his own scientific method. In writing *Experiments and Considerations Touching Colors,* he did nothing more than "clearly and faithfully" report what had happened in a series of experiments. "I am," Boyle claimed, "so little Wedded to the Opinions I have proposed, that what I am to add shall be but the Beginning of a Collection of Experiments and Observations towards the history of Whiteness and Blackness, without at present interposing my Explication of them, that I may assist your Enquiries without Fore-stalling or Biasing your Judgment."[162] Personal "Opinions" might bias or forestall; "Experiments and Observations" instead "clearly and faithfully" reflect a pure reality, unmediated by any "interposing." Boyle here, as often elsewhere, insists on what one of his fans (Thomas Sprat) would call the "Innocence" of the Royal Society's experimental method, a method one of his friends (William Petty) characterized as "without passion or interest, faction or party, but . . . according to the eternal laws and measures of truth."[163]

Boyle did not invent the worship of objectivity. Historians in many disciplines have traced the complex development of that new ideal—so central to the scientific revolution of the seventeenth century and to the epistemology of modern science—to the cultural impact of the printing press, to the rise of merchant capitalism, to the adaptation of legal concepts of evidence, to the breakdown of medieval epistemes and the resulting theological wars of the sixteenth and seventeenth centuries.[164] As Boyle and the Royal Society acknowledged, Francis Bacon was an inspiring pioneer. But Boyle was far more important than Bacon in standardizing a methodology for making objectivity not only possible but routine. Boyle *practiced* objectivity. He made objectivity a lived experience, a recognizable and repeatable social identity. Boyle also, unlike Bacon, believed that he belonged to a people who could be objectively called white. In practice and in theory, Boyle for the first time linked whiteness to an ideal of perfect, unbiased reflection. Whiteness and experimental science innocently and objectively reflect, without distortion or mediation. In Boyle is born what two recent British critics, David Lloyd and Richard Dyer, identify as a key feature of white identity, a secular justification for white rule: the claim to an intrinsic and unique disinterestedness, a dispassionate neutrality.[165] Objectivity is painted white.

Language

In linking Boyle's theory of color to ethnocentric assumptions about whiteness, I might seem to be denying the validity of his contribution to optics by attributing it to colorphobia. I mean no such thing.[166] However, I do mean that Boyle's sustained interest in investigating whiteness probably arose, at least in part, from the increasing importance of whiteness to English generic identity. I do mean that Boyle's observations and conclusions were described in colorphobic terms, in a language that did express and perpetuate what Boyle himself called "bias," a bias that contributed to the emerging mythology of what it meant to be white. And I do mean that Boyle's bias weakened his analysis of blackness—as at least one of his friends complained.[167] Even the eccentric seventeenth-century feminist critic of the Royal Society, Margaret Cavendish, who contributed nothing to experimental optics, realized that "black requires as much Perception as white." In the world of objects surrounding us, both black and white are sensory experiences, which must be perceived and interpreted. In the human environment, "black is not black through the absence of Light, no more than white can be white by the presence of light; but blackness is one sort of color, whiteness another, redness another, and so of the rest."[168]

Consider the contrast between Boyle's claim that "Whiteness appeared to proceed from an Innumerable company of Lucid Reflections" and his claim that blackness "does as it were Dead the Light" (as in the modern expression "kill the lights").[169] Blackness is associated with the verb *dead* (to kill, deprive of vigor, deprive of sensation or consciousness, benumb, stupefy). Whiteness, by contrast, is associated with the adjective *lucid* (brilliant, transparent, calm) and the noun *reflection* (recollection, thought, blame reflected back on someone else for their actions). In the decades immediately following publication of Boyle's authoritative description of whiteness, *reflection* also came to mean "meditation, deep thought," a sense that may already be present in his *Occasional Reflections* (1665). In 1690 John Locke, in *An Essay Concerning Human Understanding,* defined *reflection* as "that notice which the Mind takes of its own Operations, and the manner of them."[170] By this chain of semantic associations, reflection is white, thinking is white, thinking about thought is white. But the same physical phenomena could have been described in very different terms. "Whiteness," one might say, "lacks the capacity for retention; but blackness absorbs all the lucid multiplicities that it encounters." Whiteness would then be associated with lack, and particularly with incontinence or failure of memory.

I might be accused here of the typical vices of a literary critic: "overreading" and therefore "misreading," confusing the intellectual issue by reading metaphorically what should be read literally. But what exactly *is* the literal meaning? Recent studies of early scientific culture have demonstrated the pervasive verbal maneuvering behind the claim to have renounced verbal maneuvering.[171] Boyle's own style owed more to seventeenth-century French romances than to Francis Bacon.[172] He did not renounce metaphor; in fact, he explicitly defended it.[173] *Whiteness* meant, for Boyle, both a visual property of material objects and a generic identity; *bodies* referred both to inanimate matter and to human corporeality; *reflection* was both a physical phenomenon and a human act. Boyle could not write—and his readers could not read—a sentence like "White Bodies reflect more Light than Others" without one set of meanings leaking into the other set. The more often such sentences were repeated and the more widely such concepts circulated, the more leakage was bound to occur.

"White Bodies reflect more Light than Others" functions so efficiently, as a verbal and cultural trope, because it does not seem metaphorical at all. It works its insidious magic without any flourish of the magician's cape to call attention to the trick that has just been played on us. By 1664 the sort of readers Boyle could expect were generally hostile to any conspicuous flourishing of verbal capes. In 1651 Thomas Hobbes had deplored "the use of metaphors, tropes, and other rhetorical figures, instead of words proper." Hobbes had been one of Petty's teachers; Petty admiringly—and hyperbolically and metaphorically—called him "clarissimus Hobbius" (Hobbes of superlative clarity).[174] As early as 1648 Petty was complaining about the (metaphorical) "rabble of words" that obstructed the advancement of learning; as late as 1687, three weeks before his death, he was still thinking about his "Dictionary of Sensible Words," which would "translate all words used in argument and important matters into words that are *signa rerum et motuum*."[175] "Signs of things and motions" produced phrases like "500 whites born" in Petty's description of Boston's population: the things were whites, the motion was birth. The innumerable genetic and social differences between individuals, the particularities of each pregnancy and parturition, disappeared into generic categories of matter and motion.

"Matter" and "Motion" were the constituent elements of the universe imagined by Thomas Hobbes, Robert Boyle, and Isaac Newton.[176] The messy abundance of experience, "the richness of being," was conquered by the new language of abstraction.[177] We can see this shift taking place, generationally, in the contrast between two Restoration descriptions of an apple tree, written by two of the most brilliant English minds of the seventeenth century.

> Of Man's First Disobedience, and the Fruit
> Of that Forbidden Tree, whose mortal taste
> Brought Death into the World . . .

So John Milton began *Paradise Lost,* published in 1667, when he was 59 years old.[178] For Milton, one tree stood for a world and a work of art, but his ancient biblical tree was—above all—fruited. Isaac Newton's tree was also fruited, but what mattered about the fruit was not taste or reproduction, but motion. In 1666, while 24-year-old Newton "was musing in a garden, it came into his thought that the power of gravity (which brought an apple from the tree to the ground) was not limited to a certain distance from the earth but that this power must extend much farther than was usually thought. 'Why not as high as the moon?' said he to himself, 'and if so that must influence her motion.'" This observation seeded Newton's revolutionary theory of motion and would eventually bear fruit in his *Principia Mathematica* (1687).[179] Milton's ancient tree had been numinous, sexual, sensual, historically specific, singular ("*that* Forbidden Tree"). Newton's new tree was tasteless, sexless, secular, transhistorical, generic ("*an* apple"). Milton's "fall" of man (an event at once psychological and theological) is replaced by Newton's falling apples.

In Milton's universe, there is only one apple. In Newton's, there are many; indeed, apples and moons are interchangeable. One apple plus one moon equals two falling objects. The same process of abstraction, reclassification, and addition produced Petty's description of Boston, a city characterized entirely in terms of number ("500"), matter ("whites"), and motion ("born"). Petty delivered the "Mathematical plainness" desired by Thomas Sprat's *History of the Royal Society of London.*[180] By contrast, there was and is nothing "plain" about calculus or Newtonian mechanics. But the complexity of Newton's arithmetical rhetoric did not diminish its authority. Newton succeeded Boyle as the idealized role model for generations of scientists. Unlike Boyle, Newton dressed whiteness in the purity of mathematics. But behind Newton's new tropes—geometrical diagrams and formulas of refraction—lay Boyle's abstracted metaphors of white superiority.

If Newton saw farther than other men, it is because he stood on the shoulders of Boyle.[181] Newton's revolutionary theory of light appears in his notebooks by the end of 1664—before he had performed any of the experiments or calculations that would eventually justify that hypothesis.[182] Undergraduate Newton had been reading Descartes, Gassendi, and Boyle, but only Boyle discussed whiteness at any length, provided experimental proof of the proposition that whiteness resulted from undistorted reflection, and made use of prisms in his investigation of whiteness; Newton's pages on the subject of color were full of quotations from Boyle's book, then hot off the press.

In his first letter to the Royal Society—where his new refracting telescope caused a sensation—Newton called attention to the fact that his invention "represents things distinct and *free from colors*" (italics added).[183] Color was something from which things were liberated. A few weeks later his first published paper appeared, the lead item in the *Philosophical Transactions* of February 19, 1672. By his own reckoning, emphasized by his own italics, his "most surprising and wonderful" discovery in that paper was of the "composition . . . of *Whiteness.*" On the basis of experiments with prisms, Newton claimed that white light was generated by "all the aforesaid primary Colors." Whiteness therefore was an "aggregate of Rays indued with all sorts of Colors."

Newton was certainly correct about the composite nature of white light.[184] But in describing his discovery, here and elsewhere, Newton transformed a tentative suggestion of Boyle's into an axiom that is demonstrably false.[185] "*Whiteness,*" announced Newton, "is the usual colour of *Light.*" The experiments Newton was describing all involved sunlight, as we are reminded by the sentence in which he first formulated his revolutionary theory: "I have often with Admiration beheld, that all the Colours of the Prism being made to converge, and thereby to be again mixed as they were in the light before it was Incident upon the Prism, reproduced light, entirely and perfectly white, and not at all sensibly differing from a *direct* Light of the Sun."[186] But sunlight is not "entirely and perfectly white." Any child can see as much. Although our galaxy contains many brilliant white stars, our sun belongs to the yellow range of the stellar spectrum. That is why Milton, Shakespeare, and many other early authors wrote of the *golden sun* or of *golden sunlight:* those phrases can be found at least 78 times in English literature before 1700.[187] Likewise, *golden light* shows up at least 69 times in English literature before 1800. In the same centuries, *white light* and *white sun* never appear. But the authority of Newton eventually triumphed over the evidence of mere eyesight. In 1735 the much-admired poet James Thomson compared Socrates, the Father of Philosophy, to "the sun, From whose white blaze emerged, each various sect Took various tints, but with diminished beam."[188] Beginning with Shelley's *Prometheus Unbound* (1820), English and American authors of the nineteenth century—including Disraeli, Melville, and Ruskin—wrote of *white light* 115 times; in the twentieth, the phrase was repeated more than 250 times in poetry and drama alone. Beginning (again) with Shelley, nineteenth-century authors declared the existence of Newton's *white sun* or *white sunlight* at least 35 times.[189]

By equating *white* with *light,* Newton profoundly altered the symbolic register of whiteness. The classical "golden mean" lost even more of its intellectual prestige, replaced by a glorification of radiant extremism. More pervasively, after Newton any reference to light, in the writings of the past or present, could be read—and, increasingly often, *was* read—in ethnographic terms. This change of meaning particularly affected religious and literary texts. The Hebrew and Greek testaments do not favor white skin, but they do celebrate light, and *Paradise Lost* comprehensively rewrites the Bible as a galactic struggle between "dark idolatries" and "celestial light." Because Milton had lost his eyesight, his "Hail, holy light!" was personal, moving, and not intrinsically colorphobic: Milton never used *white* in a demographic sense, did not associate Noah's curse with dark skin or Africans, and has been reasonably described as a "poet against empire," opposed to the imperial pretensions of the Stuart kings and Cromwell.[190] But Milton's "God is light" (A = B) plus Newton's "light is white" (B = C) produces "God is white" (A = C). Reading Milton by the light of Newton—as every educated Englishman of the eighteenth and nineteenth centuries did—generated a vernacular Christianity at once imperially sublime and insidiously color-coded.

It took decades for the implications of Newton's mistake to saturate European thought. When his paper was read to the Royal Society, it "met with a singular attention and an uncommon applause."[191] But it was also the first paper published by the Royal Society to provoke prolonged international debate.[192] That debate, however, did not rage over the false equation of light with whiteness. Instead, it was the generation of "*whiteness by mixtures*" that particularly disturbed his readers.[193] As Newton acknowledged, "this assertion above the rest appears *Paradoxical,* and is with most difficulty admitted."[194] Some of that resistance resulted from real weaknesses in Newton's theory.[195] But some of it was probably psychological. Whiteness had traditionally been, and would continue to be, an emblem of originary unpolluted innocence. Unsurprisingly, white readers balked when Newton—lacking Boyle's verbal subtlety—described whiteness as "a confused aggregate" of "Rays promiscuously blended."[196] With such phrases Newton seemed to be transforming whiteness into a symbol of confusion instead of order, undiscriminating accumulation instead of discrete selection, blending instead of purity.

The imperial and generic meanings of whiteness may not yet have reached the isolated rural-born Newton, but they could hardly be ignored by sophisticated metropolitan readers of his first paper, which was preceded and followed, in the pages of the *Philosophical Transactions,* by "A Description of the *EAST-INDIAN COASTS, MALABAR, COROMANDEL, CEYLON, etc.,*" an eyewitness Dutch white account of the "Indian Heathens," of recent events involving the "Dutch, English, Portugueses, Moors, etc.," and of the lucrative trade in indigo and other dyes.[197] Moreover, one of the current meanings of Newton's word *mixture* was "sexual intercourse."[198] Imperial readers in London, Paris, and the Netherlands knew very well, by 1672, that the sexual mixture of different colors did not produce whiteness. In the words of Anthony Van Leeuwenhoek—the man who discovered spermatazoa—in another paper published by the Royal Society, "from a *White* Man and *Negro* Woman a *Mestizo* is born."[199] The Spanish (and by now English) word *mestizo* is simply the past participle of the Spanish verb meaning "to mix."

Under attack, Newton more diplomatically formulated the principle as "*Whiteness* is produced by the Convention of all Colors."[200] But his new theory did not finally triumph until 1704, when he published a book-length treatise proving what he called "the Immutability of Color."[201] By then *Principia Mathematica* had earned him unassailable intellectual authority. Moreover, the *Optics* appeared in English rather than Latin. Infinitely more readable than his mathematically dense exposition of celestial mechanics, Newton's *Optics* was his first popular work, and it profoundly influenced eighteenth-century poetry, philosophy, science, and theology.[202] "God said, 'Let Newton be!'" Alexander Pope declared, famously rewriting Genesis, "and there was light."[203] His *Optics* has recently been described as not only "one of the most influential scientific books ever written," but as "one of the most influential books" of any kind—in part because its text "ranged from the humblest facts about light to the deepest truths about the universe, humanity, and God."[204]

Newton still began by asserting "the Whiteness of the Sun's Light."[205] But he described the composition of white light in more appealing terms than he had used in 1672. Thus, when a white paper "was *equally* or almost equally distant from *all* the Colours, so that it might be *equally* illuminated by them *all* it appeared white"; "being mixed with the rest of the Colors in a *due proportion,* it made the Paper look white" (italics added). The language of indiscriminate confusion has been replaced by equality, proportion, all-inclusiveness. Those qualities were apparent in one of Newton's most appealing and influential inventions, the color wheel; circles were classic images of perfection, and in Newton's circle of colors "the center" is "white of the first order," and all other tints are situated in relation to their "distance from Whiteness." Since white results from perfect balance, reflections "lose their Whiteness" as a result of the "*Excess*" of some specific pigment. In the classical theory of humors, whiteness itself resulted from an excess (of phlegm); in Newton's new theory of light, everything except whiteness results from excess. Although initially "the Light appears totally white and *circular,*" if any color is intercepted at the lens, "the whiteness will cease and *degenerate* into that Colour which ariseth from the composition of the other Colours which are not intercepted" (italics added). In contrast to this degeneration from a circular and balanced white ideal, "there will appear, to one that shall view [a froth of bubbles on the surface of a liquid] intently, *various Colors* everywhere in the Surfaces of the several Bubbles; but to one that shall go *so far off, that he cannot distinguish the Colors from one another,* the *whole* Froth will *grow* white with *a perfect Whiteness*" (italics added). Perfect whiteness corresponds to the achievement of an appropriate distance from the object of observation, which allows one to see the whole, without being distracted by the apparent variety of transient superficial surfaces. Like Boyle's impartially reflective whiteness, Newton's universal whiteness is dispassionately comprehensive: "the white of the first order" will "reflect all the Light" that falls on it.[206] Above the fray of competing colors, "perfect Whiteness"—or, in Newton's alternative phrase, the luminousness of "perfect Whites"—is a compound of equality, proportion, comprehensiveness, centrality, and distance. It is not a limited part of the spectrum, but the combination and summation of all.

When a modern film critic like Richard Dyer remembers being "taught the scientific difference between black and white" in elementary school, what he is remembering is Newton: "white, which looked just like empty space (or blank paper) was, apparently, all the colors there were put together. . . . white is no color because it is all colors." Dyer does not trace this paradox back to Newton, and does not even realize that it remains a textbook truth. But he does recognize that the "colorless multi-coloredness of whiteness secures white power" by making it hard for white people to "see" whiteness.[207] In Newton's whiteness originates the conceptual "snow-blindness" I described in my introduction, which so routinely prevents white people from realizing that their own point of view represents a particular point on the ethnic spectrum. "God said, 'Let Newton be!'" and we were white.

I might be accused, here, of importing colorphobic and ethnocentric meanings into a text innocent of such prejudices. But a few pages before his explanation of whiteness Newton had written that, at times, he "would be understood to speak not philosophically and properly, but grossly, and accordingly to such Conceptions as vulgar People in seeing all these Experiments would be apt to frame." And in the analysis of whiteness from which I have extracted all the preceding quotations, Newton notes that "the Experiment succeeded best" when a compound "became of a Color equal in Whiteness to that of Ashes, or of Wood newly cut, or of a Man's Skin."[208] Newton here went even further than Boyle in linking demographic whiteness to high science. Boyle had separately discussed differences in human skin color in the same book that described revolutionary experiments in the chemistry and physics of light; but Newton imports the image of the white man's skin into the very paragraphs that describe experiments justifying a revolutionary theory of light. Boyle had considered himself white, but had worried over the problem of different complexions. Newton, by contrast, not only assumes that he is white himself, but attributes that color to "a Man's Skin," as if all men had white skin. Just as white light incorporates all other colors, so a white-skinned man can stand for all others (and for all women too).[209] By contrast, Newton's brief and secondary description of blackness is as colorphobic as Boyle's: black bodies "reflect . . . very little light," and "Bodies look black" when light is "stifled in them" or "lost in them." By "mixing Whites and Blacks" we produce bodies that "differ from perfect Whites . . . in degree of Luminousness."[210] By the time this last sentence was published, *Whites* had been in use as a demographic noun for more than 40 years (and *Blacks* even longer). When Newton's scientific theory of whiteness carried the day, it did so in a language that was explicitly ethnocentric, in a London even more deeply embroiled in the slave trade than it had been when Boyle had published the first scientific theory of whiteness.

Boyle had focused on the color of objects ("bodies"); Newton focused instead on the spectrum of light itself. But in most respects Newton's work confirmed and complemented Boyle's. Neutral, autonomous, accurate reflection easily coexisted, as a white ideal, with distance, equality, dispassionate and centered comprehensiveness. Newton endorsed and reiterated Boyle's conclusions about the perfect reflectivity of white bodies: "such substances are known to reflect colors without changing them." Thus, if light is reflected off any colored object onto "a sheet of White Paper," the paper will reflect the same color as the object.[211] In another experiment, Newton compared the whiteness of paper to the white powder he had already described as that "of a Man's Skin," trying to determine "Which of the two Whites were the best," and concluding that "they were both good Whites."[212] The good, perfect whiteness of white paper (or of Englishmen) did not in any way diminish its ability accurately to reflect all other color(s).

Newton had learned this trick, of reflecting light off "White Paper in a dark Room," from Boyle:

> I did in the Darkened Room, formerly mentioned, hold not far from the Hole, at which the Light was admitted, a Sheet only of White Paper, from whence casting the Sun-Beams upon a White Wall, whereunto it was Obverted, it manifestly appeared both to Me, and to the Person I took for a Witness of the Experiment, that it Reflected a far greater Light, than any of the other Colours formerly mentioned, the Light so thrown upon the Wall notably Enlightning it, and by it a good part of the Room.[213]

For Boyle, white paper reflected light more intensely than other colors of paper; for Newton, white paper—"or any other white Body"—reflected any color cast on it. In either case, the experiment glorified the perfect reflectivity of whiteness. But the experiment performed this rhetorical function only because both Boyle and Newton called the paper "white." Initially a technical term for fresh stocks of paper that had not yet been inked by the printing press, *white paper* was synonymous with the earlier (and still current) phrase *blank paper.*[214] Although

English *blank* derives from the French word *blanc* (meaning "white"), it had accumulated a different set of connotations in English ("empty, fruitless, unsuccessful, speechless, prostrated, bare, rhymeless"), and those connotations might seem more appropriate to descriptions of matter empty of color or devoid of tint. Because *blank* never acquired the demographic meanings of *white,* it would more accurately represent unprejudiced neutrality. Blankness has no content, no theory, no allegiance to one perspective or another. By calling blank paper "white," Boyle and Newton internalized its association with an emergent generic identity. They proved that their own color reflected and contained all other colors, and therefore was no color at all. They described their own point of view as point of view-lessness. They claimed, in the name of one ethnic group, an objectivity beyond ethnicity. The new white consciousness asserted that ideal whiteness had no specific consciousness. Whiteness was instead *a*temporal, *dis*-embodied, *im*pervious, *in*dependent, *un*biased: a series of negatives. An accumulation of subtractions. A compelling new abstraction, created by extraction.

In the words of the first white philosopher: "Let us then suppose the Mind to be, as we say, white Paper, void of all Characters, without any Ideas" (II.i.2). In the Gospel according to John Locke, in the beginning there was an entirely white mind.

CHAPTER II

WHITE NATION

> We hold these truths to be self-evident: that all men are created equal, that they are endowed by their Creator with certain inalienable rights, and that among these are LIFE, LIBERTY, and the PURSUIT OF HAPPINESS.

WILLIAM WELLS BROWN QUOTED the Declaration of American Independence on the title page of *Clotel* and then ended its first chapter with the statement: "Thus closed a negro sale, at which two daughters of Thomas Jefferson, the writer of the Declaration of American Independence, and one of the presidents of the great republic, were disposed of to the highest bidder!" (89). Thomas Jefferson, gentleman scientist and slaveholder, the heir of Japhet and of Boyle, was also the father of Clotel and one of the founding fathers of the United States.

"Were it not for persons in high places owning slaves, and thereby giving the system a reputation," Brown's preface insists, "slavery would long since have been abolished." Slave autobiographies had focused on individual brutalities, because what every slave knew, firsthand, was the hand that had whipped or beaten him. But anecdotes did not get at the authority of "the system." Brown, after 19 years as a free black, had realized that "It does the cause of emancipation but little good to cry out in tones of execration against the traders, the kidnappers, the hireling overseers, and brutal drivers, so long as nothing is said to fasten the guilt on those who move in a higher circle" (46).

In exposing and mocking Jefferson's sexual and moral hypocrisy, Brown reenacts the role of Ham, who had dared to call attention to the shameful drunken nakedness of his father. Anyone who satirizes people in power reenacts the role of Ham and risks the corresponding punishment. The myth of Ham creates a self-perpetuating sense of white righteousness, because a slave who refuses to respect his master's claim to rightful mastery re-creates the very offence that justifies his enslavement. "What are servants to count their masters worthy of?" the northern missionary asks in his catechism of the southern slaves, and answers, "all honour." The slave, he tells them, has a Christian obligation not only to "obey" but "to love" his master (114). The master insists that he be respected and loved as a father. In fact, when their master dies, Sam and the other slaves do not mourn, but sing an impromptu song of celebration: "I laughed to myself when I heard That the old man's spirit had fled" (153–54). Like Sam, like Ham, Brown mocks and derides "respectable" men in positions of authority.

Brown's attack on white elites was a direct and in some ways inevitable result of the notion that blacks were the cursed descendants of Ham. Insofar as the biblical explanation for blackness and whiteness replaced a geographical explanation, issues of climate gave way to issues of authority: the proper respect due to authority, the inheritance of authority, disinheritance as a consequence of mocking or resisting authority, the inheritance of property or poverty, the inheritance of skin color. What mattered was no longer the nature of the soil, but who owned it. If the defining property of blackness was to *be* property, the defining property of whiteness was to *own* property. Among European elites, the authority of Ptolemy gave way to the authority of the first great philosopher of property, John Locke.

Therefore, it was not enough to attack slave-owning (property-owning) individuals, however eminent. The authority of the passage from the Declaration of Independence that Brown quoted on the title page of *Clotel*—and which he also had quoted on the title page of his *Original Panoramic Views,* three years earlier—did not depend on the integrity of Jefferson or any individual. It articulated a political philosophy that could be traced back—sometimes verbatim—to John Locke's defense of the Glorious Revolution of 1688. That philosophy subordinated the will of individuals (monarchy) to the will of multitudes (democracy). The fact that individuals like Jefferson faltered did not undermine, but underwrote, the moral authority of the people. Thus, to delegitimate the system that justified chattel slavery, Brown had to unravel the authority of the American multitude. One whole chapter of *Clotel* consists of a speech by Henry Morton on the proposition "Despotism does not depend upon the numbers of the rulers, or the number of the subjects" (176). Tyranny is tyranny, whether under one tyrant or three, under "Thirty . . . Four Hundred . . . Three Thousand." In fact, "The smaller the number of subjects in proportion to the tyrants, the more cruel the oppression" (177). Political theory is therefore mathematical theory. In America, because "the free white citizens" are all sovereign, the proportion of subjects to sovereigns is uniquely high and the tyranny therefore uniquely oppressive. "You and I," white Henry Morton tells his white listeners, "and the sixteen millions of rulers are free. The rulers of every despotism are free. . . . You, and I, and the sixteen millions are free, while we fasten iron chains, and rivet manacles on four millions of our fellow-men" (178).

Clotel thus resolved, mathematically, the seeming "paradox" of a "despotism" of "free citizens" (178): the much-celebrated democratic freedom of America is the freedom of every despot, multiplied by millions; the freedom of white Americans is the freedom to tyrannize over every nonwhite. Brown described mathematically what philosopher Charles Mills calls the Racial Contract: "the general purpose of the Contract is always the differential privileging of the whites as a group with respect to the nonwhites as a group, the exploitation of their bodies, land, and resources, and the denial of equal socioeconomic opportunities to them. All whites are *beneficiaries* of the Contract."[1] As beneficiaries, white Americans are indeed superlatively privileged and uniquely free. Brown does not use the phrase *racial contract,* but he does show a succession of contractual sales of blacks by whites, and he does, like Mills, characterize the American system as a formal agreement solemnly made by whites at the expense of blacks: "Twenty-five millions of whites have banded themselves in solemn conclave to keep four millions of blacks in their chains" (46). This sentence, from the preface, combines the language of social and legislative contract ("banded themselves in solemn conclave") with the magnitudes of modern mathematics ("twenty-five millions . . . four millions"). Contracts and numbers are bound together by the objectified nouns of racial classification ("whites . . . blacks").

The theory that American society was founded on a "racial contract"—explicit in Mills, implicit in Brown—deliberately revises the Enlightenment theory that a "social contract" is the foundation of civilization. The founding fathers of the United States, and particularly Thomas Jefferson, had justified their rebellion against British rule on the grounds that Britain had violated the terms of that social contract, thereby absolving the colonists of any obligation to allegiance. Jefferson and the other American revolutionaries did not invent that theory. It was first articulated by two English philosophers in the second half of the seventeenth century: Thomas Hobbes and John Locke. Hobbes had used it to deny the legitimacy of resistance to existing political authority; Locke used it to justify resistance. Locke was therefore more useful to the American revolutionaries of the eighteenth century and to the black abolitionists of the nineteenth.

But the social contract and the racial contract both depend on another, anterior contract. Even if "all men are created equal," it is not at all self-evident what the word *men* means. A linguistic contract, an agreement about language, precedes all others. Political authority therefore depends on the meaning of words. Language was, according to Locke, "the great instrument and common tie of society."[2] Hobbes agreed: "seeing then that *truth* consisteth in the right ordering of names in our affirmations, a man that seeketh precise *truth,* had need to remember what every name he uses stands in for."[3] In the decades between Hobbes's *Leviathan* (1651) and Locke's *Two Treatises of Government* (1689), the word *white* became, for the first time in English, an objectified generic noun, almost inevitably linked to the objectified generic noun *black*—and routinely applied in specifically statistical and political forms of reasoning. "A man that seeketh precise truth" about the political philosophers of the late seventeenth century has to ask: What is the relationship between the generic noun *whites* and the generic noun *men?*

White Sisters

Published in the year of the Glorious Revolution, Aphra Behn's *Oroonoko: or, The Royal Slave* has been celebrated as the first English novel, the first American novel, the first abolitionist novel, the first novel by a woman. All those labels also have been contested. But it seems undeniable that *Oroonoko* was the first original literary work in English saturated with the modern generic sense of whiteness. (In the following extracts I reproduce the unsystematic use of italics in the first edition.)

> [The natives of Surinam] understand no vice, or cunning, but what they are taught by the *White Men.*
>
> Whoever had heard [Oroonoko] speak, would have been convinced of their errors, that all fine wit is confined to the *White* Men.
>
> I have seen an hundred *White* Men sighing after [Imoinda].
>
> And I have observed, 'tis a very great error in those, who laugh when one says, *A* Negro *can change colour;* for I have seen 'em as frequently blush and look pale, and that as visibly as ever I saw in the most beautiful *White.*
>
> *Oroonoko* . . . was more civilized, according to the *European* Mode, than any other had been, and took more delight in the *White* Nations; and above all, Men of Parts and Wit.
>
> *Trefy* . . . proceeded to tell him . . . he had done nothing but Sigh for [Imoinda] ever since she came; and that all the white Beauties he had seen never charmed him so absolutely as this fine Creature had done.
>
> . . . some Persons . . . feared a Mutiny (which is very Fatal sometimes in those Colonies, that abound so with Slaves, that they exceed the Whites in vast Numbers).
>
> However, [Oroonoko] assured me, that whatsoever Resolutions he should take, he would Act nothing upon the White-People.
>
> [We] resolved to surprise 'em [the *Indians*], by making 'em see something they never had seen (that is, White People).

> . . . one *Sunday,* when all the Whites were overtaken in Drink (as there were abundance of several Trades, and *Slaves* for Four Years, that Inhabited among the *Negro* Houses, and *Sunday* was their Day of Debauch . . .
>
> [Oroonoko] told him, there was no Faith in the White Men, or the Gods they Adored, who instructed 'em in Principles so false that honest Men could not live amongst 'em . . .
>
> [Oroonoko demanded] that it should be ratified by their Hands in Writing, because he had perceived that was the common way of contract between Man and Man amongst the Whites . . .
>
> [Oroonoko] replied that] he would declare, in the other World, that he was the only Man, of all the Whites, that ever he heard speak Truth.[4]

Othello (discussed in chapter 2) contained nothing comparable to even one of these 13 literal instances of generic *white.* Ravenscroft's adaptation of *Titus Andronicus* (discussed in chapter 8), written only 10 years before, contained a single example of the generic noun; the noun occurs five times in *Oroonoko.* And although whiteness was even more pervasive in *A Game at Chess,* Middleton's play (discussed in chapter 6) had sensationally mixed allegorical, sartorial, and epidermal senses; by permitting the Fat Bishop and White King's Pawn to change sides, Middleton privileged allegory as the dominant element in the compound. Unlike the virtuoso originality of Middleton's deployment of mass whiteness, or of Boyle's sustained repeated experimental analysis of optical whiteness (discussed in chapter 10), Behn's use of *white* was casual. Behn did not treat *white* as a metaphor, or a conspicuously paradoxical compound full of possibilities for semantic play, or a physical phenomenon that needed to be explained. She regarded it as a self-evident sign for a self-evident category. ("We hold these truths to be self-evident.") Like Jobson's account of his journey to the river Gambia (discussed in chapter 5), Behn's account of events in Surinam routinizes an internalized, seemingly literal sense of generic whiteness; indeed, the title page insisted that her account was, like Jobson's, "A True History," drawing on her own experience in the English colony in the early 1660s.

Whatever else Behn's text does, it canonizes whiteness as a pervasive, normal, "natural" generic sign. The *Oxford English Dictionary*'s last recorded example of the use of *white* to describe an individual, in the old pre-generic sense (stage 1), was written earlier in the 1680s (in an adaptation of a French text).[5] After *Orooonoko,* it disappears completely. Behn may be ambivalent about slavery, but she has no difficulty with the notion of generic white identity.

Behn also routinely uses the word *race* in a recognizably modern way. Describing her African protagonist Oroonoko, Behn says "he was adorned with a native Beauty so transcending all those of his gloomy Race" (a category described in the preceding paragraph as "Blacks"); encouraging the other black slaves to rebel, Oroonoko asks, "Shall we render Obedience to such a degenerate Race?" (a category described in the preceding paragraph as "Whites").[6] White Behn and her black hero both distinguish the white "Race" of English colonists from the black "Race" of enslaved Africans. The *Oxford English Dictionary* does not record the modern pseudoanthropological definition of *race*—"one of the great divisions of mankind, having certain physical peculiarities in common"—until 1774 (*n.*[2] 2.d). But *race* was being used in its modern anthropological sense in French—a language that Behn read and translated—by 1684 at the latest.[7]

That modern sense of *race* easily arose from the decline of the climate theory of skin color. Boyle's scientific study of color had concluded that black skin was transmitted biologically from parent to child. If that was true, then all blacks were related to one another, in a lineage that had at some point branched off from the lineage of whites. The earlier meanings of *race* referred to human or animal descendants of a single parent or couple.[8] The linguistic movement from "human race" (recorded as early as 1580) to Behn's identification of a "race" of blacks and another of whites implies also a fundamental shift of emphasis: "the human race" (Sidney) or "the whole race of mankind" (Shakespeare) emphasized that all human genres derive from Adam and Eve, whereas Behn's "gloomy Race" and "degenerate Race" emphasize derivation from different intermediaries. Politically, Behn insisted on the overriding importance of lineage. As many critics have observed, her sympathy for *Oroonoko* is difficult to disentangle from her sympathy for the dethroned Catholic king, James II.[9] The whole logic of her narrative insists that an individual like Oroonoko—a prince, the son of a king—should be treated differently from ordinary blacks, who do not have royal blood running in their veins.

Behn's sympathies extended to "the Brave, the Beautiful, and the Constant Imoinda," as the final words of the text describe Oroonoko's African wife.[10] The first heroic, tragic black woman in English literature, Imoinda laid the emotional and literary foundation for Clotel.[11] In *The Triumphs of Truth* Middleton had portrayed an equally admirable (and royal) black couple, but Behn's black husband and wife live in a world much closer to Clotel's: enslaved, transported involuntarily, betrayed rather than saved by Christians, tragic not comic. Moreover, that tragedy was brutally gendered. *Oroonoko* forces readers to inhabit an explicitly female point of view; the text's comments on "white men"—through Behn's own narrative voice, and Oroonoko's ventriloquized voice—are consistently scathing. Like Ravenscroft's adaptation of *Titus Andronicus* 10 years earlier, *Oroonoko* ends with the death of a defiant black man, judicially tortured and burned to death by white authorities. But Behn produces and presumes an emotional response radically different from Ravenscroft's: "Thus Died this Great Man." In *Titus,* only men are alive onstage at the end to witness the execution, but Behn creates a gendered division of sympathies. The atrocity is explicitly blamed on white men: Byam, his council of "Villains" ("not worthy the Name of Men"), and Banister ("a wild Irish Man").

By contrast, Behn and a group of women admire and comfort Oroonoko, and even at the end "My mother and Sister were by him all the while, but not suffered to save him; so rude and wild were the Rabble, and so inhumane were the Justices, who stood by to see the Execution."[12] Behn thus set in place a gendered division of attitudes toward slavery that would persist—in fact or in polemic—through the nineteenth century. Men governed; women emoted. Men enforced slave rule; women sympathized with slaves. That dichotomy remains in *Clotel,* where the curse of Ham is articulated and defended by two white men (both of them ministers), and the chief opponent of their version of Christianity is a saintly white laywoman, Georgiana.

Georgiana wants to abolish slavery, and after the death of her father she frees all her slaves. Behn, by contrast, protested the dastardly abduction of Oroonoko and condemned the enslavement of a prince, but she was not an abolitionist. For Behn, "Royal Slave" was an intolerable oxymoron (like "white slave" in Barbados in 1666), but the enslavement of Africans was not intrinsically objectionable. Notoriously, after his black followers abandon him, Oroonoko turns on them, "ashamed of what he had done, in endeavoring to make those Free, who were by Nature Slaves, poor wretched Rogues, fit to be used as Christians' Tools; Dogs, treacherous and cowardly, fit for such Masters" (109). Behn's named, extraordinary African prince thus endorses the white enslavement of ordinary, anonymous, nameless, interchangeable, and disposable blacks. Behn's attitude here resembles that of Tryon (whom she knew and admired). Both Tryon and Godwyn wanted to improve the working conditions of black laborers, but neither condemned slavery in principle. Tryon's fictional Negro ("Sambo") denied that he even wanted freedom. "Those that are wise amongst us, matter not their Freedom so much," and, if only they were a little better treated, they would "*Bless* you," and "we and our Posterity shall *willingly serve you,* and not count it any *Slavery,* but our unspeakable Happiness."[13]

Rejecting the curse of Ham as a justification for enslaving blacks, Godwyn passionately advocated "the Instructing and Baptizing of the Negroes and Indians in our Plantations" and "their Admission into the Church." Robert Boyle endorsed Godwyn's proposals. But Godwyn explicitly denied that baptism would entail "their release from servitude." As the example of other European colonies demonstrated, "*Bondage* is not *inconsistent* with *Christianity.*" Indeed, converting the heathens would make them better slaves: "That in regard *Religion* would be apt to *create a Conscience* in their Slaves, it might be convenient, *in order to make them the truer Servants.*" Christianity is a mighty convenient religion: "For *Insurrections* and *Revolts,* nothing can be imagined a greater *Security* against them, than a sincere inward persuasion of the truth of *Christianity.*"[14] The colonial authorities in Jamaica had come to the same conclusion when they revised their slave code in 1674, urging slave owners to "instruct their Slaves (Especially the younger Sort) in the Christian religion," because, "being thus baptized and made Christians they serve their masters with more fidelity and Respect."[15] Godwyn accepted the legitimacy of the "*Law*" in Barbados, Virginia, and Maryland that specifically and "carefully *barred all such Pleas*" for manumission on the basis of conversion; he supported the legitimacy of such colonial legislation even if or when it conflicted with the "*Laws . . .* of *England* itself."[16] The same colonial legislature in Jamaica that urged slave owners to instruct their slaves in religion decreed, in the same paragraph, that "all negroes Lawfully bought or born slaves shall here continue to be so . . . their Christianity or any Law, Custom, or Usage in England or elsewhere to the contrary notwithstanding." Oroonoko, endorsing the enslavement of the Africans he has learned to despise, ends his curse with the suggestion that they "be whipped into the knowledge of the *Christian Gods,*" which will make them "the vilest of all creeping things; to learn to Worship such Deities as had not Power to make 'em Just, Brave, or Honest." This curse is really directed at the hypocrisy of colonists who claim to worship Christ but behave barbarously; but Oroonoko was right to think that conversion would not change the status of blacks as whipped, vile, creeping things, worshipping gods powerless to improve their condition.

In 1613 Middleton had presented to an audience of "white people" an imaginary Black King converted to Christianity "By the religious conversation Of English merchants, factors, travellers." By the 1670s and 1680s English colonists had systematically resisted, for more than a generation, any effort to Christianize their black slaves. Tryon's 1684 speaking Negro is as imaginary as Middleton's had been in 1613, but Tryon's is a slave, not a king; Middleton's black speaker thanked the English for the gift of Christian truth, but Tryon's complains that the English colonists "endeavor to keep us *Heathens,* that we may continue their *Slaves.*"[17] In 1624 Middleton's *A Game at Chess* had satirized elements of political, religious, and sexual hypocrisy in the "White House," but the enslavement of Africans was not an item in his bill of indictment. By the 1670s and 1680s the English treatment of blacks had become the focus of sustained polemical attacks on white hypocrisy: when Oroonoko concludes that "there was no Faith in the White Men, or the Gods they Adored; who instructed 'em in Principles so false, that honest Men could not live amongst 'em; though no People professed so much, none performed so little," most readers must have read his condemnation of Christianity as a critique not of the religion itself, but of the un-Christian behavior of men like Byam. Nevertheless, by the 1680s the white enslavement of black people was so entrenched, so naturalized, that even critics like Behn, Godwyn, and Tryon could not imagine its abolition.

In effect, these white reformists accepted the Africanist interpretation of the legacy of Ham (that black people should be perpetually enslaved to white people), but did not like calling it a curse. "After all," we can imagine them saying, "working for a white person *like me* isn't a curse." If black slaves could be given the benefits of Christianity, if black slaves were just treated a bit better, if exceptional black slaves like Oroonoko were exempted from manual labor and adopted by white patrons, if white hypocrites were exposed and punished, if this, if that—then black slavery would stop gratuitously offending enlightened white sensibilities. It would stop being a curse and could continue as a rational, traditional, justifiable, just division of labor: "a kinder, gentler" slavery. The struggle between the brutal Barbados planters and Godwyn the self-appointed "Negro's and Indian's Advocate," or between the "Tyrant" Byam and sympathetic Mrs. Behn, amounts to no more than the difference between "White Rule!" and "whites rule, okay?"

The diatribes of the reformers, which began in the 1680s and continue into our own time, do not threaten or question the legitimacy of white dominance. They simply want to replace one set of white masters with another, better set. The new set advertises that it would be better because it understands blacks, and on certain issues sympathizes with them, as the first set does not; the new masters would therefore be able to manage the black labor force more effectively, without provoking so much black resistance, active (rebellion) or passive (laziness). The fact that these whites can sympathize so deeply—even with blacks—demonstrates the extraordinary white capacity for impartial liberal fairness. As sympathy separates tyrants from constitutional monarchs, as sincerity separates Christians from hypocrites, so sincere white sympathy legitimates white rule. Japhet, after all, had earned his father's blessing by sympathizing with the old man's nakedness and drunkenness.

I do not question the sincerity and sympathy of Godwyn, Tryon, or Behn. Their books broke through the silence surrounding white violence against people with darker skin. But over the long term the white claim to disinterestedness served the interests of whites. In the 1680s—when the English system of black slavery had been in place for more than a generation, and whiteness had become a self-evident generic category—the white siblings began squabbling over which of them should inherit the black siblings.

Black Brothers

The fissure in the white community, which opened in the 1680s, widened in the eighteenth century, in part because the bloodlines of Japhet and Ham were by then more and more often intertwined. Liaisons between English men and African women began only a few years after the English acquired slaves. In Virginia in 1630 Hugh Davis was "soundly whipped . . . for abusing himself to the dishonor of God and shame of Christians, by defiling his body in lying with a negro," and in 1640 a gentleman named Robert Sweet was sentenced "to do penance in church . . . for getting a negro woman with child." In Maryland in 1651 a man sued for damages someone who had libeled him by claiming "that he had a black bastard in Virginia." (Whether or not the charge was true, to be made it must have seemed plausible.[18]) We know about these early examples only because they were punished, but most such encounters left no legal record. In 1662 a Virginia law declared that the children of Negro women by an English father would be slave or free, depending on the status of the mother. (This is the principle, eventually adopted throughout the slave states, that would enslave at birth Frederick Douglass, William Wells Brown, and Clotel.) In English law the status of the child depended on the father, and Virginia's radical reversal of traditional practice served only one purpose: it protected white males from having to free the children they sired on their own slaves. Passage of the Virginia law proves that, by 1662, such practices must have been general enough to be recognized and protected by the legislature (dominated by large plantation owners).[19]

The sexual use of black slaves by their white male masters was even more pervasive in England's Caribbean colonies than in the Chesapeake.[20] The Antigua statute of 1644, punishing fornication between Christians and heathens, made special provisions—beyond English law—to protect any "white man" accused of impregnating a heathen woman. (See chapter 8.) In Barbados, a French visitor reported as early as 1654 that "the greatest of all the vices which prevail in this country is lewdness."[21] Much of that lewdness must have involved slave women, because there were relatively few free ones. Morgan Godwyn acknowledged that some of "our People" in Barbados had "Intermarried with" Negroes and that other "*Debauchees* . . . frequently do make use of them for their *unnatural* Pleasures and Lusts."[22] Behn claimed to "have seen an hundred *White* Men sighing after" Imoinda in Surinam in the early 1660s, "and making a thousand Vows at her Feet, all vain, and unsuccessful." In the real world of black slavery, white men were not often so successfully refused, but Behn's account of white male desire is entirely credible. The Frenchman who in 1684 had proposed that blacks and whites belonged to "different species or races" also reported that "I have also seen some very handsome [women] among the blacks of Africa. . . . I have seen at

Moka many quite naked for sale, and I may say that I have never seen anything more beautiful; but they were very expensive, for they wanted to sell them three times dearer than the others."[23] They were more expensive for the same reason that Clotel fetched so high a price: they were valuable sexual commodities.

The white male appetite for black female flesh had profound consequences for the legitimation of black slavery. If only the descendants of Ham were condemned to slavery, then the descendants of Shem and Japhet should not be enslaved. The sons of white fathers—Frederick Douglass, for instance, and William Wells Brown—should inherit the kingdom; they should not be inherited, like cattle. If the descendants of Ham were black, then the enslavement of whites violated God's blessing on Ham's white brothers. "White slaves" like Clotel, Clotel's daughter, Clotel's sister, and that sister's daughters were not only an anomaly; they were an execration. To permit such crimes would be to mock God's blessing and thereby risk bringing God's curse down on the entire white race. "Can the liberties of a nation be thought secure when we have removed their only firm basis, a conviction in the minds of the people that these liberties are of the gift of God? That they are not to be violated but with his wrath?" These worried questions would be asked, in 1785, by white slaveholder Thomas Jefferson. "Indeed I tremble for my country when I reflect that God is just: that his justice cannot sleep forever: that . . . The Almighty has no attribute which can side with us in such a contest."[24]

But such reflections did not convince Jefferson to free the slaves he had fathered, even at his death. He knew what he should do, but he could never bring himself to do it, at any particular moment. This "inability to act on a considered judgement" is one of the problems that also disturbed John Locke. In his *Essay Concerning Human Understanding* Locke tried—and failed—to explain it.[25] But Locke did perceive that the problem is partly optical. "Objects near our view," he observed, "are apt to be thought greater than those of a larger size, that are more remote: and so it is with pleasures and pains, the present is apt to carry it, and those at a distance have the disadvantage in the comparison."[26] In the pursuit of "happiness," the small immediate pleasure looked bigger, for Jefferson, than the huge but distant disaster. The pain of black people is "more remote" than the pleasure of white people. Whites, we might say, have trouble *seeing* blacks.

Why? Locke did not answer that question. He did not even ask it. But he did realize that, to understand the inaction of "good" men (like Jefferson, or himself), he needed to attempt to understand the nature of human understanding. Boyle had focused on the outer world of perceivable objects. Locke focused instead on the inner world of the perceiver of objects. But that perceiver was, for Locke, born white.

White Minds

Locke was hardly the first philosopher to argue that people are born without innate ideas. But Aristotle and others had described the newborn mind as an empty wax tablet, or one from which all previous impressions had been scraped or erased. Seventeenth-century English writers were still using the Latin phrase *tabula rasa* to express that Aristotelian concept.[27] The practical English equivalent of the classical wax tablet was the slate, especially popular in teaching, where repeated writing and erasing made something like a modern blackboard useful.[28] A "blank slate" or "clean slate" could, like the tabula rasa, easily serve as a metaphor for the impressionable empty mind. But slate is blue, brown, or gray; wax is bright yellow.[29] Modern blank paper, by contrast, is white.[30] Locke repeatedly used the image of "white paper" for the child's "as yet unprejudiced Understanding."[31] Although elements of that comparison can be found in three authors we have already encountered in this book—Richard Eden, Thomas Hobbes, and Robert Boyle—the metaphor "white paper = child's mind" was, apparently, original to Locke.[32]

So was Locke's approval of the child's blankness. Locke associated the word *white* with the word *power;* the "white paper" of the child's mind is not a defect but an impowering asset.[33] According to Locke, the child was not simply ignorant (an obviously undesirable condition); its mind had not yet been violated by propositions. Unlike Aristotelians or Catholic theologians or Cartesians, the child did not start with a theory and then deduce particulars. Instead, like the ideal scientist, like Robert Boyle, Locke's empirical infant observed, recorded, experimented, formed a preliminary hypothesis, but then observed and experimented again, if necessary repeatedly revising that hypothesis on the basis of new sensory data. In his *Essay Concerning Human Understanding,* Locke wrote what the authors of the great French Enlightenment *Encyclopédie* called "the experimental physics of the soul."[34] Children were exemplars of the method of induction. Like the neutral scientific observer, the child's blank mind was *unprejudiced* (a new and always positive word, first recorded in the middle of the seventeenth century, and much used by members of the Royal Society, including Boyle).[35] Just as the child is "unprejudiced," so Locke himself is "unbiased."[36] Through his analysis of a child's trial-and-error acquisition of concepts, Locke laid the intellectual foundation of the empiricism whose empire has outlasted Britain's. That foundation is a sheet of white paper, the image of an unprejudiced pretheoretical mind.

That mind is white. Its whiteness is far from innocent. Locke has been called, plausibly, "the most influential philosopher of modern times."[37] But he was also the first philosopher to use *white* in a colorphobic generic sense. It first occurs, in the *Essay,* in the context of Locke's discussion of words that indicate a relationship between one object and another. Locke uses as an example a man named Caius (or Cajus):

> when I consider him, as a Man, I have nothing in my Mind, but the complex *Idea* of the Species, Man. So likewise, when I say Caius is a white Man, I have nothing but the bare consideration of Man, who hath that white Colour.(II.xxv.i)[38]

It might be objected that Locke here was describing an individual and was not using the adjective in a generic sense. But by 1690 the generic meaning of "a white man" was well established, and Locke's early readers must have interpreted the adjective in that way. If they did so, they would have projected ethnic whiteness back onto the classical world. "Caius" (or "Cajus") is a Latin name; later in the same paragraph that person is married to someone named "Sempronia" (another Latin name). Locke was not, apparently, referring to any particular historical figure.[39] But he was assuming that ancient Romans were white. Moreover, the absence of an indefinite article at the end of the passage—supplied by many modern interpreters, but not present in any of the editions published during Locke's lifetime—seems to make a generic statement about the species *Man.* Locke is not talking about "a man who hath that white Colour," but about "Man, who hath that white Colour."[40]

Defenders of Locke might nevertheless insist that, whatever his readers may have assumed, Locke himself was innocently describing the pale complexion of a particular individual, without any assumptions about ethnic categories. But later in the *Essay* Locke used *white* in an unequivocally generic sense.

> a Child having framed the *Idea* of a *Man,* it is probable, that his *Idea* is just like that Picture, which the Painter makes of the visible Appearances joined together; and such a complexion of *Ideas* together in his Understanding, makes up the single complex *Idea* which he calls *Man,* whereof White or Flesh-colour in England being one, the Child can demonstrate to you, that *a Negro is not a Man,* because White colour was one of the constant simple *Ideas* of the complex *Idea* he calls *Man* . . . (IV.vii.16)

Like any good empiricist, the child bases his view "upon Collection and Observation," the collection of experiences, the observation of events.[41] Locke did not explicitly reject the child's conclusion, which some adult readers would have endorsed (as Locke knew); however, some modern apologists think that Locke implicitly dissociated himself from the child's colorphobia.[42] Locke's private opinion of the child may matter less than the public fact that Locke here, for the first time in western philosophy, takes for granted the collective whiteness of his own ethnic group.[43] Whether or not Locke thinks that a Negro is a Man, he clearly thinks that English men are White. He also—like his friend

Newton—treats *Flesh-colour* as a synonym for *White* (as if yellow, pink, red, brown, and black were not possible colors of human flesh).

This colorphobic passage was included in Locke's very first draft of the *Essay,* written in July 1671.[44] It persisted, substantially unchanged, through all revisions and editions until his death.[45] Having introduced *white* as an ethnic term when he began work on his masterpiece, Locke also used it in a passage he added to the 1700 edition. Describing an "old *Parrot*" in Brazil, the passage recounts how, "when it came first into the Room where the Prince was, with a great many *Dutch-men* about him, it said presently, *What a company of white Men are here!*" (II.xxvii.8). In the three passages so far considered, generic whiteness has been attributed to ancient Romans, Englishmen, and Dutchmen; for Locke all Europeans were, and always had been, "white." Across three decades, this European ethnic whiteness constituted part of his thinking about human nature and the nature of human knowledge.

White Species

It might be objected that, in this last example, Locke was quoting someone else, and that the phrase *white men* should be attributed to the parrot, or to Sir William Temple (Locke's source for the anecdote), rather than Locke himself.[46] But Locke chose to include the anecdote, Locke identified the source as "an Author of great note," and Locke cited it as evidence supporting his own conclusions about the boundaries of the human species. "If this *Parrot,* and all of its kind, had always talked as . . . this one did," Locke asked, would parrots "not have passed for a race of *rational Animals?*" Locke thought the parrot's identification of the Dutch as "white men" was a rational act. Locke nevertheless doubted "whether for all that, they would have been allowed to be Men and not *Parrots.*" The ability to reason, then, is not sufficient to determine whether an animal qualifies as a member of Locke's "race." Why not? Because "'tis not the *Idea* of a thinking or rational Being alone, that makes the *Idea* of a *Man* in most People's Sense; but of a Body so and so shaped joined to it." In determining the category *Man,* differences in the body may outweigh the shared possession of a reasoning mind.

Perhaps Locke was describing "most People's Sense," not his own. But he did not question the legitimacy of their reasoning here. Moreover, Locke denied that there was "any natural connection . . . between certain particular articulate Sounds and certain *Ideas.*" Words acquire their meanings "by a voluntary Imposition, whereby such a Word is made arbitrarily the Mark of such an *Idea*" (III.ii.1). That arbitrariness of linguistic signs—whether we use, for instance, *white* or *blanco,* when referring to the color of snow—is compounded when we come to use "general" or "abstract" nouns, like *man* or *human.* Locke argued that all general terms depend on human decisions about classification and that all such decisions are categorically arbitrary: "the sorts of Things, and consequently the sorting of Things, is the Workmanship of the Understanding, since it is the Understanding that abstracts and makes those general *Ideas*" (III.iii.12). In any system of classification someone has to decide which similarities count and which do not.[47]

In Locke's own classifications, color is one of the things that did count, as can be seen in the first paragraph of his chapter on the relationship between abstract and concrete terms (III.viii.1). Locke here was not quoting anyone or describing the reasoning of a child.

> For how near of kin soever they may seem to be, and how certain soever it is, that Man is an Animal, or rational, or white, yet everyone, at first hearing, perceives the falsehood of these Propositions: *Humanity is Animality,* or *Rationality,* or *Whiteness. . . . a Man is White,* signifies, that the thing that has the Essence of Man, has also in it the Essence of Whiteness, which is nothing but a power to produce the *Idea* of Whiteness in one, whose eyes can discover ordinary Objects: or *a Man is rational,* signifies, that the same thing, that hath the Essence of Man, hath also in it the Essence of Rationality, *i.e.,* a power of Reasoning.

The proposition *Humanity is Whiteness* was obviously false for Locke, not because it asserted a link between whiteness and the proper definition of mankind, but simply because the sentence illogically joined one abstract noun to another. The same idea, expressed in another way—*a Man is White*—was perfectly acceptable, because it correctly linked abstract ("Man") to concrete ("White"). The difference between the incorrect *Whiteness* and the correct *White* is simply, as Locke explained in the next paragraph, that the first is "a Substantive" [i.e., a noun], and "the other an Adjective." But Locke's grammatical distinction does not alter the intellectual substance of his definition. *A Man is White* is not a proposition about one particular man; it is not the same as saying "John Locke is white." *A Man is White* is parallel, for Locke, to *a Man is rational;* both are categorical statements, defining the word *Man.*[48] Locke's *a Man is White* is the logical equivalent of the traditional definition, *Man is a rational animal.*[49] But Locke has revised that definition. In this paragraph Locke, for the first time in western philosophy, presumed that *Man is a rational white animal.*

Of course, Locke did not write the sentence I have just written. I have put that sentence together from elements that Locke provided, and that proposition is certainly implicit in Locke's paragraph. But it would be possible to put Locke's elements together in a slightly different sentence, which perhaps would more accurately reflect his characteristically qualified mode of assertion: *It is as certain that man is white as it is certain that man is rational or that man is an animal.* For Locke, none of these propositions was any more certain than the others, because no proposition about the "Essence" of a general category like *Man* could ever be certain.[50] In a previous chapter, Locke had already made that clear. "There are Creatures," he reports, "that with Language, and Reason, and a shape in other Things agreeing with ours, have hairy Tails" (III.vi.22). Locke owned an enormous collection of travel narratives, and he was here presumably referring to reports of African primates.[51] "If it be asked, whether these be all *Men,* or no, all of human *Species*"—and notice that *Species* here could be singular or plural—Locke would reply that it depended on "the definition of the Word *Man.*" The definition of a word determined what he called "nominal Essence" (the essence of an arbitrary category we have constructed for our own convenience). Such a question could be answered, but the answer would be a purely linguistic assertion, a statement of fact about the conventional use of a particular word. On the other hand, "if the Enquiry be made concerning the supposed real Essence; and whether the internal Constitution and Frame of these several Creatures be specifically different, it is wholly impossible for us to answer." (By *specifically* here Locke meant "relevant to the definition of a species.")

This may seem simply an expression of Locke's skepticism, an innocent pessimism about the limits of human knowledge that can also be found in his teachers, Boyle and Sydenham.[52] In fact, the African American critic Henry Louis Gates Jr. has described "Locke's sweeping skepticism" about categories as an "antiessentialism" that provides us with "a conceptual grammar of antiracism."[53] My own argument in this book, that the racial category "white" was socially constructed, could be seen as a variant of Locke's. But different skeptics aim the weapons of doubt at different targets—and produce different patterns of collateral damage. One victim of Locke's skepticism in the *Essay Concerning Human Understanding* becomes obvious once we collate these doubts about the meaning of "species" with a sentence from *Two Treatises of Government,* where Locke claims that there is "nothing more evident, than that *Creatures of the same species* and rank promiscuously born to all the same advantages of Nature, and the use of the same faculties, *should also be equal* one amongst the other" (italics added).[54] Political equality, for Locke, depended on definition of the word *species.*

That word had not yet been restricted to its modern biological meaning; it also could mean "categories" more generally. But the biological meaning was available, and it is not hard to see why Locke's skepticism about species had a profound effect on eighteenth-century biology.[55] In the paragraph from his *Essay* quoted above (III.vi.22), Locke was using *species* in relation to human beings and other living "Creatures," and in the next paragraph Locke's example of such uncertainties took an explicitly biological turn. "Nor let anyone say, that the power of propagation in animals by the mixture of Male and Female, and

Plants by Seeds, keeps the supposed real *Species* distinct and entire" (III.vi.23). To this biological criterion Locke makes a specifically human objection: "if History lie not, Women have conceived by Drills." At first glance, this claim may seem obviously misogynist, but not necessarily racist. Reports of promiscuous simian sexuality have a long history in European, Islamic, and Asian culture.[56] In A.D. 49 a maidservant in Rome allegedly gave birth to a monkey; in the third century a Roman scholar reported that Egyptian apes had raped women and that reddish apes in India committed adultery with men's wives.[57] Classical "History" thus associated human-simian intercourse or offspring with Rome, India, and Egypt; early modern writers made similar claims about Borneo and Peru. The anomaly was not limited to a particular region or ethnic group.

But Locke's word *drills* changed the significance of such anecdotes. A drill is a black-faced West African primate, and the first examples of the word in English (in 1644 and 1654) specify "Guinea drill."[58] The word *Guinea* did not refer to the modern African state, but to the whole of central West Africa, between the Sahara and Angola. This chapter is the only one in the entire monumental *Essay Concerning Human Understanding* that refers to Guinea (twice).[59] The word *drill* occurs four times in this same chapter.[60] When Locke in 1671 had sketched his first draft of this argument about species, he had explicitly associated the drill with Negroes.[61] Throughout this chapter—and probably nowhere else in the *Essay*—Locke was actively thinking of West Africa and its native inhabitants. By using the specific word *drill* rather than the more general *monkey* or *ape* or *baboon* or *orangutang* (which were all available, and used by other writers in similar contexts), Locke made a geographically and ethnically specific assertion that "Women *in coastal tropical West Africa* have given birth to children sired by large apes."

Englishmen had not made the acquaintance of the primates they called *drills* (probably adapting a word from a local African language) until the early 1640s, when British ships began routinely buying slaves in Guinea.[62] But as early as the 1590s, and continuing into the first decades of the seventeenth century, Portuguese witnesses had reported the sexual interest of West African primates in the indigenous women.[63] In London John Bulwer saw, in 1652, what he called a drill, which appears to have been a chimpanzee (illus. 20).[64] Citing Dutch and Portuguese sources, Bulwer endorsed their view that such "rational Brutes" resulted "from the wicked copulation of man and beast," a conclusion supported by the fact that they "very much resemble them in the Face, especially in the Nose, which is very flat and camois, with expanded nostrils." The pronouns *they* and *them* in this last quotation are grammatically ambiguous, but the context makes it clear that Bulwer was comparing the flat noses of West African primates to what Boyle called the "Flat-Noses of most Nations of *Negroes.*" But Bulwer wavered between two theories: that the drill resulted from human copulation with an unnamed animal, or that copulation of humans with drills produced the native inhabitants of the tropical forests. "If you beheld their ugly visages," he says at another point, citing a European observer, "you would think that they had no other Sires than the Apes and Baboons of the neighboring Woods."[65]

Locke's reference to women impregnated by drills belongs to a larger discourse of "simian orientalism" that simultaneously disparaged primates, women, and Africans.[66] Many Muslims and some Christians had been associating Negroes with apes since the Middle Ages.[67] In 1634 Thomas Herbert, describing the "swarthy dark" inhabitants of the Cape of Good Hope, had concluded that "comparing their imitations, speech and visages, I doubt many of them have no better Predecessors than Monkeys: which I have seen there of great stature."[68] An English visitor to Barbados in 1655 described the "Injuns and miserable Negors born to perpetual slavery, they and their seed" as "slaves apes" (without punctuation).[69] In 1668 a play performed in a London theater featured a "Negro wench" dancing with a baboon, while the characters discuss whether such creatures were "begot upon Drills."[70] In the 1670s, according to Morgan Godwyn, many of the white colonists in Barbados believed "*Negroes* to be but *Brutes,*" and they justified that claim by referring to "the too frequent unnatural conjunctions . . . of some Africans" with "the Ape and Drill." Godwyn admitted that Jean Baptiste Tavernier had reported human-drill intercourse in Africa

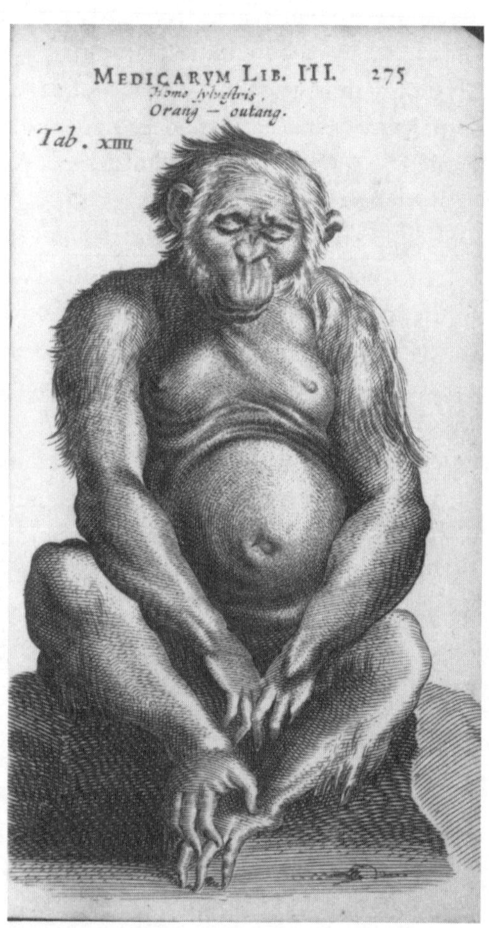

Illustration 20. The first reasonably accurate European image (published in Amsterdam in 1641) of a chimpanzee, here called *Homo Sylvestris,* "man of the woods." By permission of the Houghton Library, Harvard University.

and that some people "even in England have been heard to defend" the theory that Africans were not "of the like *species* with" whites.[71] In 1679 a Jamaican colonist and medical doctor, Thomas Trapham—who believed Africans were "the cursed posterity of the naked Cham"—warned against European "mixture with these animal people," whom he associated with "Baboons and Drills."[72] Locke owned copies of Godwyn, Tavernier, and Trapham, so he was certainly aware of the radical racist conclusion that was being drawn from the statement that "Women have conceived by Drills."

Godwyn dismissed that claim as a "monstrous opinion." Locke did not. Indeed, Locke cited it in the course of systematically undermining the traditional definition of the species/category "Man." And elsewhere, in the *Essay*'s only explicit reference to Africans in their native land, Locke characterized the "Thoughts and Notions" of the indigenous inhabitants of the Cape of Good Hope as "brutish" (I.iv.12).[73] Locke's skepticism about traditional categories, combined with colorphobic insults and his willingness to entertain unorthodox ideas about Negro-primate coupling, had particular and poisonous relevance to the status of Africans as members of the human species. Within a decade of the publication of Locke's *Essay*—and while Locke was still revising it for each new reprint—a fellow member of the Royal Society was describing "Neger Africans" as "a Race of Drills," noting that they "have their Foreheads, Nose and Faces extremely flat; great Heads; large, and full Eyes; blubber Lips" and "woolly hair."[74] Locke's reference to drills was anything but innocent or inadvertent.

In addition to Tavernier and Godwyn, Locke also owned Isaac La Peyrère's scandalous *Prae-Adamitae,* printed in 1655 in Amsterdam.[75] La Peyrère argued that God had created other, lesser races of men before Adam. This opinion was profoundly heretical, because it reduced the Bible to a history of the Jewish people only.[76] The comprehensiveness of biblical history had been challenged almost as soon as it became evident that Columbus had discovered not a shortcut to Asia, but the "new heavens, new earth" of a hitherto unsuspected continent. That happened in 1498, the same year that Columbus discovered whiteness and Vasco Da Gama discovered a sea route to India. As early as 1520, the unorthodox German chemist and physician Paracelsus was asserting that the natives of the New World were descended from "a different Adam."[77] In 1590 the unorthodox Italian philosopher Giordano Bruno expanded the list of peoples outside the genealogy of Adam to include yellow Indians, black Ethiopians, pygmies, giants, and other mythological beings.[78] In 1592 the English mathematician and colonist Thomas Harriot was associated with the same heresy.[79] By 1616, according to the French atheist Lucilio Vanini, "Other atheists, more mild, have thought that none but the Ethiopians are produced from a race of monkeys, because the same degree of heat is found in both."[80] But all these claims—made in four European countries, across almost a century—surfaced as unsubstantiated offhand remarks. La Peyrère, by contrast, expounded and defended the heresy in 294 printed pages, packed with evidence from respected modern authorities, including his own detailed anthropological study of the Eskimos (another book Locke owned). La Peyrère's thesis, although "certainly not racist in any modern sense," quickly lent itself to arguments for white supremacy.

Burned and banned on the continent, *Prae-Adamitae* was immediately translated into English.[81] Whether they read it in Latin or English, or only heard of it secondhand, planters in Barbados were, by the 1670s, "extremely fond" of "Pre-Adamitism." The theory that "there must be a numerous *race* of Men, not derivable from Adam" (italics added) was actually "preferred above the Curse" of Ham, as a justification for their enslavement of blacks.[82] Similar arguments were circulating among Portuguese and French colonists in the late seventeenth century.[83] But the heresy also evidently appealed to readers who voyaged no farther than the Thames. A pamphlet published in London in 1695 denied that "both *Blacks* and *Whites*" could have descended from Adam. The author (an Oxford M.A. with the initials "L. P.") combined arguments we have already seen articulated by Boyle and other authorities: "neither the Sun, nor any Curse from Cham could imprint upon" blacks "their Colour," which "appears to be as Ingenite and as Original as that in *Whites.*" The old climatic explanation has been discredited, because many peoples "living under the same Climates and Heats, are never Black . . . neither will any *White* ever become a *Black* in Guinea, Congo, or Angola, though born there; neither will any *Negroes* produce *Whites* in Virginia, or New England." Nevertheless, despite the reiterated parallelism of black and white, the author—like Browne and Boyle—redefined the mystery of human diversity as an explicitly black enigma ("The Origin of *Negroes* lies very obscure"). Like Boyle and Petty, he linked pigment to other anatomical differences ("*Blacks* with a woolly Substance on their Bodies instead of Hair. . . . The Textures of their Skins, and Blood, differ from those of *Whites*"). Like Locke, the philosopher L. P. articulated the problem in terms of species ("their Colour and Wool are innate, or seminal from their first Beginning, and seems to be a specific Character").[84] A Fellow of the Royal Society reported that this defense of polygenesis "was applauded generally by Men of loose Principles: such as make their small stock of Philosophy subservient only to Scepticism and Infidelity."[85] England's most famous living skeptic, in the 1690s, was John Locke.

Bruno and Vanini had been burned at the stake, La Peyrère arrested and forced to recant; Locke was celebrated throughout Europe and America. Even if he had supported La Peyrère's thesis, he would almost certainly have concealed the fact: no one before Voltaire dared publicly endorse it. Instead, Locke side-stepped the explosive issue of biblical authority by confining himself to recent "History."[86] Locke thus hints at the nontheological form of polygenesis that Hume would later make explicit.[87] Locke covered his ass by strategic use of the word *if:* "if History lie not, Women have conceived by Drills; and what real *Species,* by that measure, such a Production will be in Nature, will be a new Question." He did not say what that question was, but instead continued, "and we have Reason to think this not impossible." To what does the word *this* refer? As evidence for the plausibility of that ambiguous *this,* Locke cited the fact that "Mules . . . from the mixture of an Ass and a Mare . . . are so frequent in the World" (III.vi.23). So *this* may refer either to the copulation of chimpanzees with black women or to the birth of a distinct species from such unions.

A few paragraphs later Locke summed up his argument about human difference with a rhetorical question: "Wherein then, would I gladly know, consists the precise and *unmovable Boundaries of* that *Species?* 'Tis plain, if we examine, there is *no* such thing *made by Nature,* and established by Her amongst Men" (IV.vi.27). The issue, of course, was not Her, but Him: not what "Nature" had made, but what the Bible said about God's creation of mankind. But Locke reiterated that "these Boundaries of *Species,* are as Men, and not as Nature makes them" (III.vi.30).[88] Locke avoided heresy by ignoring God. Indeed, as an illustration of the arbitrariness of generic terms, Locke imagined Adam, after his expulsion from the Garden of Eden, inventing "two new Words, *Kinneah* and *Niouph*" (III.vi.44)—which are in fact Hebrew words that occur in the Old Testament. The words of the Bible were, like all other words, mere human inventions. In 1734 the Inquisition put Locke's *Essay* on the Index of prohibited heretical works.[89]

But by 1734 the Catholic Inquisition was less powerful than the European scientific community and its "Republic of Letters."[90] Locke was friends with the traveler and corpuscularian philosopher François Bernier, whom he met in Paris in 1677, and he owned a complete set of the 1684 *Journal des Sçavans,* including the issue that had published Bernier's "New Division of the Earth, by the Different Species or Races of Man who inhabit it."[91] That sub-Saharan Africans belonged to "a different species" was evident, according to that article, from "1. Their thick lips and squab noses," and "2. The blackness which is peculiar to them, and which is not caused by the sun." The cause of their blackness "must be sought for in the peculiar texture of their bodies, or in the seed, or in the blood."[92] These statements should sound familiar. The evidence of a distinct species repeats Boyle's characterization of blacks. The hypothesis about causes of blackness adds to Boyle's own explanation ("seed," semen) another possibility, "the peculiar texture of their bodies," which uses the word *texture* in the corpuscularian sense invented and popularized by Boyle.[93] The third possibility, "blood," might have been referring to an article published in the *Philosophical Transactions* in 1675, which reported that "The Blood of *Negros* is almost as black as their skin." The informant—a white doctor in Barbados—had "often seen drawn forth the Blood of at least twenty" Negroes, and their dark blood convinced him that "the Blackness of *Negroes* is likely to be inherent in them, and not caused by the scorching of the Sun."[94] Boyle did not publicly comment on this claim, published by his close friend Henry Oldenburgh, but Boyle dominated the content of the Royal Society's journal in its early years, and one of his first contributions to it had been an account of curiously "white blood" observed in an Oxford maid.[95] Locke owned all the volumes of the *Philosophical Transactions,* and "the author whose works Locke obviously collected and treasured, whose entry in the catalogues [of his library] is the most extensive and painstaking, is Robert Boyle."[96]

Locke was Boyle's disciple.[97] Following Boyle, he insisted on (1) the distinction between the microscopic real substance of matter and the secondary features accessible to human perception, and (2) the limits of human understanding; together, these two concepts justified (3) Locke's skepticism about our ability to identify the real boundaries of species.[98] Contrasting Locke's pragmatic treatment of essence with the universalism of (Catholic) Christianity and Cartesian rationalism, H. M. Bracken argued that "the empiricist model of man . . . made racism easier to justify."[99] This does not mean that all empiricists are racists, but it does mean that empirical procedures more readily lent themselves to intellectually codified colorphobia.

The difference between rationalist and empiricist approaches can be seen in G. W. Leibniz's detailed contemporary commentary on Locke's *Essay.* Leibniz consistently cut and ignored the examples of generic *white,* and he usually turned Locke's West African *drill* into a geographically unspecific baboon or orangutang.[100] He recognized that Locke's argument about species boils down to whether we are "able to distinguish members of the race of Adam from the descendants of some king or patriarch of a community of African monkeys," but he denied that there was much real difficulty identifying who was human and who was not: "the exercise of reason . . . is the essential point, and it cannot be settled by appearances."[101] Locke, by contrast, argued that neither the possession of a human "shape" nor the possession of "reason" was sufficient to identify an animal as human, concluding that "none of the Definitions of the word *Man,* which we yet have, nor Descriptions of that sort of Animal, are so perfect and exact, as to satisfy a considerate inquisitive Person; much less to obtain a general Consent, and to be that which Men would everywhere stick by, in the Decision of Cases, and determining of Life and Death, Baptism or no Baptism" (III.vi.27).[102] As Locke knew, Englishmen deeply disagreed over whether to baptize black slaves; he also knew that, in colonial law, "the Decision of Cases" determining "Life and Death" differed, depending on the complexion of the witnesses, the perpetrator, and the victim. An "Englishman bred in Jamaica" (III.vi.13)—where black slaves had long outnumbered whites—could kill a black man much more casually than he could kill a white one, and would suffer fewer (if any) consequences for doing so. Locke's skepticism about the criteria for membership in the human race had practical consequences.

Edward Stillingfleet, Bishop of Worcester, had been the first Englishman to attack La Peyrère's theories of polygenesis, and he also immediately attacked Locke's skepticism about the category *Man.* Intellectually, Leibniz and Locke undeniably outclass Stillingfleet, but the bishop's "common sense" did tease out the everyday implications of Locke's argument.

> a Laplander is as really a Man whatever you call him, if he hath the Essence of a Man. And it is strange to me to find any Man dispute such evident things. . . . Peter, James and John are all true and real Men; not by attributing a general Name to them; but because the true and real Essence of a Man is in every one of them. . . . Your Weweena, Cuchepy and Cousheda I have nothing to say to, they may be Drills for anything I know; but Peter, James and John are Men of our own Country, and we know them to be several Individuals of the Race of Mankind: And what is it makes them Men, but that the true and real Essence of a Man is in every one of them?[103]

Few Europeans would question the humanity of "Men of our own Country." Instead, as Stillingfleet's exotic names—"Weweena, Cuchepy and Cousheda"—demonstrate, Locke's skepticism was more likely to raise doubts about the human status of natives of other continents. When Locke defended himself, Stillingfleet again seized on Locke's skepticism about species. "Mankind are not so stupid," he insisted (optimistically), "as not to know a Man from a Horse or a Drill."

> If it be asked you, "whether Men and Drills be of the same Kind or not?" Could you give no other Answer, but that 'the Specific Name *Man* stands for one sort, and the Specific Name *Drill* for the other, and therefore they are not of the same Kind'?—Are those Names arbitrary, or are they founded on real and distinct Properties? If they be arbitrary, they have no other Difference, but what a Dictionary gives them. If they are founded on real and distinct Properties, then there must be a real Difference of Kinds founded in Nature.[104]

Locke in reply reiterated the arbitrariness of language: "these two names, *Man* and *Drill,* are perfectly Arbitrary, whether founded on real distinct Properties or no—so perfectly Arbitrary, that if Men had pleased, *Drill* might have stood for what *Man* now does, and Vice versa." This point can hardly be denied, and in itself has no implications about species. But Locke goes further: "these two

Names stand for two abstract Ideas, which are (to those who know what they mean by these two Names) the distinct Essences of two distinct Kinds; and as particular Existences, or things Existing are found by Men (who know what they mean by these Names) to agree to either of those Ideas, which these Names stand for; these Names respectively are applied to those particular things, and the things said to be of that Kind."[105] Behind Locke's characteristically complicated, lifeless prose lurks an assertion we could paraphrase as "men apply these words to objects that match their arbitrary ideas about the difference between the category *drill* and the category *man*." As Stillingfleet suspected, Locke was denying any "real Difference of Kinds founded in Nature" between men and drills.

Locke made this final denial in 1699. That same year Edward Tyson published a pioneering essay in comparative anatomy. Tyson believed that "Nature's Gradation in the Formation of Animal Bodies" was "so gradual, that there appears a very great similitude . . . between the lowest Rank of Men, and the highest kind of Animals"—and he made clear who was "lowest" when he conceded to some primates as much right to be considered human as "Certain Barbarians in Africa." Tyson's descending scale of humanity echoes William Petty's and anticipates eighteenth-century taxonomies. But Tyson enumerated 34 ways in which the body of a human being differs from the body of what he called an "Orang-utang" (perhaps what we would call a bonobo chimpanzee). To illustrate the differences he supplied fourteen anatomical engravings.[106] Tyson's conclusions have been confirmed by centuries of subsequent observation. "Locke's reasoning" on the indistinguishability of species is—as even his modern defenders have to acknowledge—"both extreme and false."[107]

Locke dangles in front of us a hypothesis he does not bother to verify; Tyson slams a body on the table and cuts it up in front of us. The contrast between Tyson and Locke belongs to a larger, emerging divide: the ancient discipline of "natural philosophy" was splitting into the competing modern communities of naturalists (Boyle, Tyson) and philosophers (Hobbes, Locke). As Catherine Wilson shows in her study of the impact of the microscope on early modern philosophy, "There is a reactionary aspect to empiricist epistemologies" like Locke's. Locke doubted the value of anatomy ("even if we dissect to the interior, we see only the outside of things, and only make a new surface to observe") and of optical magnification (someone with microscopic vision could not convey his experience to "the rest of Men . . . or have any Communication about Colours"). Locke here parted company with Boyle, who had applauded Malpighi's microscopic anatomical discoveries. Locke instead argued that "we are so far from being capable" of "a perfect *Science* of natural Bodies" that "I conclude it lost labour to seek after it."[108] Locke limited his attention to the immediately apprehensible world, the world any child could see.

What a child could see was that some people are darker than others. For Locke, that was enough. For Boyle, Malpighi and Tyson, it was not enough; they wanted to know *why* some people are darker. However colorphobic Boyle's own analysis of human variety might have been, his Christianity committed him to the unity of mankind, and his research agenda directed attention to the microscopic interiors where the causes of human color would eventually be tracked down and trivialized. Locke's skepticism, by contrast, prevented him from looking beyond what was right in front of him.

The Linguistic Contract

Although Locke found it difficult to define *Man,* there was no such problem defining *whiteness.* "He that knows once, that Whiteness is the Name of that Colour he has observed in Snow, or Milk, will not be apt to misapply that Word" (III.iv.15). Nevertheless, by 1690 Englishmen had grown accustomed to misapplying the word: Locke was not the color of snow or milk, but considered himself white. At the start of the chapter that puzzles over the meaning of the word *Man,* Locke had again invoked his image of white paper, explicitly comparing *himself* to "this white thing I write on" (III.vi.4).[109] Everyone, presumably, could agree that paper was white—and that Locke was white (Plate 20). Like other Englishmen who could afford to do so, Locke wore the powdered wigs that became popular in England in the early 1660s; by 1669 the great "white wig" had appeared on fashionable heads in London, where it would dominate important male faces for more than a century.[110] (It can still be seen in British courtrooms.) Like the white makeup that for centuries helped women approximate the ideal of feminine pallor, the elaborate white wig, quintessential accessory of Enlightenment Man, insured that the first visual impression made by an English gentleman was whiter than any face.

For Locke, each word was an idea.[111] The word *Man* represented a complex idea; the word *white,* a simple one. Such "*simple Ideas . . . are generally less doubtful and uncertain,*" and therefore "Men, for the most part, easily and perfectly agree in their signification: And there is little room for mistake and wrangling about their meaning" (III.iv.15). The linguistic problem boils down to a social problem: how to secure agreement with others about the meaning of words. Meaning, like government, results from a social contract; indeed, since a contract presumes the existence of a language in which agreement can be specified, the linguistic contract precedes all other contracts.

Because it is the most primitive of all contracts—usually made "in all Languages" by "ignorant and illiterate People"—agreement to a linguistic contract is most easily secured when it involves simple sensations. That is why, according to Locke, "*the ranking of things under general Names*" has always depended on "*their obvious appearances*" (III.vi.25). Inevitably, therefore, most of the words that define general categories refer primarily to "Shape" and "Color" (III.vi.29). And with words as with governments, children usually accept the contract they have inherited from previous generations: "if they would use these Words, as Names of Species already established and agreed on, they were obliged to conform the *Ideas,* in their Minds, signified by these Names, to the *Ideas,* that they stood for in other Men's Minds" (III.vi.45). With meaning as with government, the original contract was made long ago; but "all Men ever since" have the same "liberty" as their precursors. We are as capable as Adam of "affixing any new name to any *Idea.*" Nevertheless, "in Places, where Men in Society have already established a Language amongst them"—places like Britain—"the signification of Words are very warily and sparingly to be altered" (III.vi.51). Politics depends on language, and the political theory Locke articulated in his *Two Treatises of Government* presupposes the painstaking and enormously influential linguistic theory articulated in Book III of the *Essay Concerning Human Understanding.*[112] Indeed, since communal life requires a definition of membership in the community, Locke's political theory—the foundation of modern liberal democracies like the United States—depends, above all, on chapter six of Book Three, where Locke worries over the substance of the word *man.*

Locke's linguistic contract explains the social appeal of simple nouns like *blacks* and *whites.* Those words refer to an immediately apprehensible feature of animal populations. Moreover, by turning adjectives into nouns, they entirely elide the problematic term *man.* Using *black* instead of *black man* eliminates tiresome debates about whether Africans belong to the category "man"; using *whites* and *blacks* eliminates any shared term, and therefore any debate about what the two categories have in common. The social world—where meaning is made, where linguistic contracts originate—primarily values "convenience of Language and quick dispatch" (III.vi.32). The "*true end of Speech*" is "the easiest and shortest way of communicating our Notions," ideally in a "short monosyllable" (III.vi.33). Hence the appeal of *blacks* and *whites* to government committees, like the Council for Foreign Plantations (on which Boyle served) or its reincarnations in the 1670s and 1690s (on which Locke served). The relationship between the linguistic contract and the social contract is seen, and lived, when a subcommittee drafts letters of inquiry, using words that must be approved by a majority of the subcommittee and then revised and approved by a majority of the whole committee. From just such communal deliberations, from just such a sociolinguistic contract, emerged, apparently, the noun *whites.* We do not know which individual suggested that word in January 1661, because it occurs in the summary of a collective act.

Hence also the difference between Locke's attitude toward the indigenous peoples of America and those of sub-Saharan Africa. Modern scholars who have accused Locke of racism have generally conflated his attitude to the two continents.[113] But the great variety of human complexions recognized in the sixteenth century had by 1661 been reduced to the two categories ("blacks" and "whites") recognized by a bureaucratic memo. In 1646 Sir Thomas Browne had written of black, white, and "Tawny" complexions; three decades later he declared that "A greater division of mankind is made by the skin than by any other part of the body, that is into white and black, or negroes."[114] Within that binary, Amerindians were white—especially the Amerindians that the English knew best (those in North America from Carolina to Newfoundland). In his 1684 division of humanity, Bernier, who regarded blacks as a separate race, did not make that claim about "the Americans" (i.e., Amerindians): "I do not find the difference sufficiently great to make of them a peculiar species different from ours."[115]

Like Jefferson later, Locke showed much more sympathy for native Americans than for Africans.[116] He referred to "an intelligent *American*" (II.xiii.20) and to "some *Americans,* I have spoken with, who were . . . of quick and rational parts enough" (II.xvi.6). He expressed admiration for some native American practices and—like his patron the first Earl of Shaftesbury—in his practical management of colonial affairs Locke consistently opposed the enslavement, murder, or mistreatment of Amerindians by English colonists.[117] He explicitly argued, in his first *Letter Concerning Toleration,* that Christian colonists should never deprive Indians—even those who refused to convert to Christianity—of their political rights as equal members of the community.[118] English colonists could take "waste land" that the Indians were not farming in a European way; but Locke thought there was plenty of land for both natives and colonists.[119] This was a tragic misperception, but the same argument about "waste land" had been used to justify the expropriation, enclosure, and privatization of English "commons land" throughout the sixteenth and seventeenth centuries.[120] There is nothing specifically colorphobic about Locke's statements or actions toward native Americans. For Locke, Amerindians had the same inalienable moral and political rights as other white folks.

But blacks did not. Locke never called a Negro "intelligent" or "rational." He advocated a free college education for "as many Indian Children . . . as may be," but never mentioned such education for blacks, though in the same manuscript he repeatedly refers to them in other contexts.[121] He never expressed admiration for Africans, individually or collectively. "The Child certainly knows, that the *Nurse* that feeds it, is neither the *Cat* it plays with, nor the *Blackmoor* it is afraid of" (I.ii.25). This is the only explicit reference to transplanted Africans in the published text of the *Essay;* in this snapshot of a child's "unprejudiced" perception, the child is undoubtedly white, and of the three objects of his attention only the black is a negative figure. In earlier drafts, Locke had conjectured that "a child, unused to that sight, and having had some such descriptions of the devil, would call a Negro a devil," but that explanation has been removed from the published text[122]; the child's fear of blacks is now apparently self-explanatory, a spontaneous reaction, as natural as a nurse feeding a child or a child playing with a pet. Appearing in an English child's household in the 1680s, the black is presumably a servant, and probably a slave, but Locke did not specify a social or legal status, considering it either self-evident or unimportant. Unlike the nurse, the black has no function, no gender, and no social or personal identity beyond the black skin that frightens an innocent child.

Locke never protested the enslavement of blacks, privately or publicly. In 1669 he wrote out, in manuscript, "The Fundamental Constitutions of Carolina," including the provision that "Every freeman of Carolina, shall have absolute power and authority over his negro slaves, of what opinion or religion soever."[123] He never disassociated himself from that provision, reiterating toward the end of his life that slaves need not be freed just because they have converted to Christianity.[124] In 1674 he invested 400 pounds in the Royal Africa Company, and the next year invested another 200 pounds.[125] In a 1675 manuscript entitled "Trade," Locke recorded that "The Chief end of trade is Riches and Power, which beget each other. Riches consists in plenty of Moveables" (personal property, which would include slaves). "Power consists in numbers of men, and ability to maintain them" (the reasoning behind the London imperial bureaucracy's demographic inquiries). Trade contributes to both power and riches, and one thing that helps promote trade is "Cheap labour" (slaves being, as numerous memos noted, the cheapest labor pool).[126] In 1679, copying into his personal notebook useful information extracted from travel narratives, Locke listed the chief commodities exported from various countries—including (repeatedly) slaves.[127] Locke was instrumental in creation of the Board of Trade in 1696, and for the next four years he was, for 1,000 pounds a year, "its chief director and controller."[128] In 1697 Locke and three others signed a memo objecting to the establishment of an English colony in Panama, on the grounds that it would harm the colony in Jamaica by interfering with the existing advantageous "Commerce with the Spaniards for Negroes and European Commodities."[129] Locke was instrumental in drafting the Board's "Instructions" to Governor Nicholson of Virginia in 1698, which demanded radical reforms in the government of the colony, involving the legislative council, the judiciary, land grants, codification of laws, taxation, even surveying.[130] But neither those instructions nor Locke's own voluminous papers on the Virginia case question the legitimacy of black slavery. Like Behn and Tryon, the Board of Trade wanted—if politically possible, if the legislative consent of his Majesty's white subjects could be secured—to restrain the "Inhumane Severities" of some masters, and to convert slaves to Christianity.[131] But the Board apparently did not consider inhumane a law cutting off both ears of blacks convicted of hog-stealing.[132] And Nicholson was explicitly instructed "to give all due Encouragement . . . in particular to the Royal African Company."[133] The reason may have been, in part, demographic. Locke's own notes worried that Virginia was seriously underpopulated (as Jamaica had been in 1661), and he recommended solving the problem by stocking the colony with immigrants who were not British-born. Every new foreigner living in "the English Plantations" gave the king "a new subject."[134]

Defenders of Locke sometimes claim that we cannot be sure of his authorship of documents in his own handwriting (like "The Fundamental Constitutions of Carolina") or his agreement with all details of documents he signed (like the instructions to Governor Nicholson). Such documents represent the outcome of a process of collective deliberation, and Locke may not have initiated or endorsed every detail. Bureaucracies disperse responsibility. But Locke's own theory—of government and of language—rules out such a defense. Locke participated in the process; he did not withdraw his consent; by not withdrawing, he accepted and endorsed the social and linguistic contract represented by texts that legitimated the contractual sale of African bodies. He gave the slave trade a hand, literally. Locke would not have accepted the standard apology of defendants at the Nuremberg trials ("I was just obeying my superiors"). By deferring to superiors, by going along with the majority, one signed the contract.

It was always possible to refuse to sign. In the Glorious Revolution of 1688, the Protestant political nation had refused to accept the actions of a Catholic monarch and had deposed James II; Locke's *Two Treatises* provided the philosophical justification for that resistance. Also in 1688, the monthly Quaker meeting in Germantown, Pennsylvania, adopted a resolution condemning the slave trade: "though they are black, we cannot conceive there is more liberty to have them slaves, as it is to have other white ones. There is a saying, that we should do to all men like as we will be done ourselves; making no difference of what generation, descent, or colour they are."[135] In 1693 a printed Quaker proclamation protested the enslavement of blacks by "white men," insisting that "*Negroes, Blacks,* and *Tawnies* are a real part of Mankind."[136] During his political exile in Holland in the 1680s, where he wrote the *Two Treatises* and the final version of the *Essay,* Locke was on intimate terms with two abolitionists (Jean Le Clerc and the Quaker Benjamin Furly), but he never endorsed their views, publicly or privately. Even earlier, in 1673, the nonconformist Protestant minister Richard Baxter had condemned the slave trade: "To go as Pirates and catch up poor Negroes or people of another Land . . . and to make them slaves, and sell them, is one of the worst kinds of Thievery in the world." Locke, at about that time, was investing in the Royal Africa Company. Baxter commended "Princes who make Laws that Infidel slaves shall be free men, when they are duly Christened." Locke throughout his life denied that conversion and baptism freed a slave from his bondage. "If men buy Negroes or other slaves," knowing they had been illegally abducted, Baxter insisted that "undoubtedly they are presently bound to deliver them" [i.e., the owners are immediately required to free the slaves they have purchased].[137] Locke never suggested that his friend Sir Peter Colleton, or anyone else, had an obligation to free his black slaves.[138] Visiting the British Museum for the first time, William Wells Brown saw "a portrait of Baxter, which gives one a pretty good idea of the great nonconformist."[139] Locke was not such a great nonconformist.

Nobody's perfect, and a dead man can't defend himself. But Locke's culpability needs to be acknowledged, and his contradictory behavior needs to be analyzed, because both are generic. Locke conspicuously and influentially inaugurated a psychological and social complex typical of subsequent "white" nations. John Locke—skeptical philosopher of modern empiricism, passionate advocate of modern liberalism, godfather of the American Revolution, champion of (limited) religious toleration, libertarian hero—acquiesced in, profited from, institutionalized the enslavement of blacks.

When this contradiction is acknowledged at all, it usually is treated as an embarrassing personal weakness. That maneuver condemns the man, to acquit the ideology. It takes for granted a distinction between public and private life that Locke himself canonized. Theories of monarchy depended on a divine right to rule passed from father to child; political life mirrored family life. To undermine the legitimacy of inherited power, Locke divorced political from personal life. Government originated, said Locke, not in the divinely sanctioned power of fathers over their children, but in a contract, made by equal and independent adults. In place of rule by the father, Locke installed rule by the siblings. But the siblings of Locke's theory are all male. From Locke's fratriarchy, mothers and daughters disappear. But of course without mothers there would be no sons to grow up into adults and sign contracts, and without daughters there would be no women for those sons to impregnate and thereby produce another generation of contract-signing sons. Locke's frat-pack social contract presupposed what feminist philosopher Carole Pateman calls a "sexual contract," which it never acknowledges. Locke's theory of government makes sense only by consistently repressing one of its constituent elements.[140]

But more than the sexual labor of women is being repressed. Historically, the first slaves were women.[141] But slave labor was not limited to the sexual use of female slaves. African American philosopher Charles Mills describes the social contract as "a contract between those categorized as white *over* the nonwhites, who are thus the objects rather than the subjects of the agreement." This racial contract "includes an epistemological contract, an epistemology of ignorance. . . . Evasion and self-deception thus become the epistemic norm."[142] Most historians acknowledge that the English political system worked in this lopsided way in Locke's time. But most (white) philosophers and political theorists dismiss this collective history in the same way that they dismiss Locke's personal history: they describe it as a failure of practice, not a failure of theory. The theory of a social contract, they would say, is not intrinsically racist, or intrinsically self-deceiving. I agree. The social contract was first theorized, in English, by Hobbes, not Locke. Born in an isolated English village, way back in 1588, Hobbes did not call himself, or anyone else, "white." Nor did he articulate an epistemology of self-deception. Rather, Hobbes is notorious for speaking unpleasant truths no one wanted to hear, repeat, or applaud in public.

The racial and epistemological contract that Mills indicts was first articulated by Locke. *Leviathan* had defended absolute rule by a powerful individual. Locke's shift from individual to collective rule (constitutional monarchy, based on parliamentary democracy) intrinsically shifted legitimacy to mathematically dominant population groups: numerical majorities within Parliament itself, numerical majorities in the election of members of the House of Commons, numerical definitions of the property qualifications to vote. Locke owned copies of Graunt's demographic study of London and Petty's *Political Arithmetic,* and his social contract institutionalized rule by numbers. That shift in the locus of power, from the divine right of an individual monarch to the natural or secular rights of mathematical populations, can obviously coexist with a division of populations along color lines. Moreover, although the theory of a social contract between siblings represses female labor, it explicitly presupposes shared parentage. For Locke, government naturally originated in an agreement made within a biologically related population group. To the degree that Boyle's theory of the propagation of skin color by "seminal impressions" displaced the old theory of climatic color, skin color became a visible index of biological kinship. Locke's siblings were presumably of the same color.

Nevertheless, eventually that initial sibling group had to form a compact with siblings from other families, and nothing in Locke's theory requires that those other families be biologically related to the first. Locke's own society may have been colorphobic, but that does not prove that a democratic social contract always already entails a racial contract. In fact, rather than presupposing inequality, Locke's theory explicitly presupposes equality: government naturally and legitimately arises from an agreement between interchangeably equal siblings or interchangeably equal groups of siblings.

But Locke's theory of equality depends on the inequalities that it represses. Siblings are never identical, and therefore never physically or socially equal. Even in the case of twins, one must be born before the other; the birth canal can accommodate only one head at a time. Likewise, families are not equal: some parents have more children, or healthier children, than others. Once groups of siblings from different families meet, such inequalities *between* families compound the inequalities *within* families. Moreover, power in the second generation is distributed even more unequally than in the first. Locke's theory of property as the just reward for labor was subsidized by property he never labored to earn: he inherited a family estate (as did Boyle and Newton). It is a small step from inherited privileges to hereditary slavery. For instance, Locke argued that, if "his *Father [is] a Freeman,* the *Son is a Freeman* too."[143] According to this logic, if the father is a slave, so is the son. Locke acknowledged equality only among "Creatures of the same species *and rank*" (italics added). Consequently, "there is," as philosopher Jennifer Welchman argues, "no inconsistency between Locke's political philosophy and the institution of chattel slavery."[144]

However, inherited property or hereditary slavery need not entail the specific "white epistemology" described by Charles Mills. What may explain it is the fact that Locke seldom even visited the real estate that supplied his income; he paid someone else to manage his properties and collect rent from his tenants. Capital regularly flowed his way from the invisible labor of distant strangers. Surplus capital could be invested in the Royal Africa Company or the Royal Bank. As a shareholder in such joint-stock enterprises, Locke profited from the distant unseen labors of people he never met; in the seventeenth century Europeans could invest in companies that reaped thousands of pounds from the labors of thousands of persons thousands of miles away. Money happened. Locke, the first white philosopher, was also the first philosopher who internalized the mentality of investor capitalism. That new economic system radically distanced exploiter from exploited. White men like Locke, or his patron Anthony Ashley Cooper, could congratulate themselves on their astute investment in profitable enterprises without ever confronting the daily exercise of brute white power that made profit possible. "I that wish you the enjoyment of perfect happiness," Locke wrote to a friend in 1670, "desire and advise that you should feel nothing at all of others' misfortune."[145] He followed his own advice.

A series of classic experiments by the psychologist Stanley Milgram demonstrated an inverse ratio between our willingness to hurt other people and our proximity to the victims of our cruelty: inhumanity is a function of social distance.[146] The sociologist Zygmunt Bauman, trying to explain the anti-Semitic

Holocaust of the twentieth century, has argued that "racism is inevitably associated with the strategy of estrangement."[147] But that strategy originated long before Adolf Hitler was born. Early modern European trade—including the slave trade—depended on crossing oceanic distances.[148] It also depended on venture capital contributed by investors like Locke, who never left home, never dirtied their hands. The emotional consequences of such a business structure can be seen in David Hancock's recent study of a group of eighteenth-century British merchants. Managing at least 35 overseas plantations from their London base, juggling multiple activities simultaneously, coordinating businesses on four continents, Hancock's "Citizens of the World" epitomize what he calls "the practical Enlightenment." The records of their slave-trading operations are "cool and businesslike," and their few extant comments on the subject "do not even recognize the need to justify slavery, the slave trade, or their role in it." Any attempt to understand their "coldness, indifference and inhumanity" is frustrated by their consistent "silence."[149] Exactly the same problem confronts interpreters of Locke.

The business operations of Hancock's eighteenth-century merchants were deeply entangled in the political structures of imperial England. From its beginnings, transatlantic trade depended on the military and financial resources of the territorial nation-state.[150] In the 1650s the managerial needs of overseas merchants had created the demand for better political management of England's overseas empire. Capitalism could survive only with the help of a burgeoning government bureaucracy—exactly the sort of managerial structure that, according to Bauman, made possible the routines of organized and sustained racist genocide. Bureaucracies institutionalized "the substitution of technical for moral responsibility." To achieve "practical and moral distance from the final product," functionaries like Locke had to dehumanize the objects of their bureaucratic operations—which meant that human beings needed to be described "in purely technical, ethically neutral terms." Such dehumanization starts at the point when human beings "are reduced to a set of quantitative measures."[151] By the time Locke became secretary of the Council, it had already started keeping records of the number of "whites" and "blacks" in each colony. Individuals disappear in mathematical formulas of interchangeability.

Something similar happens in all Locke's writing. His style anesthetizes even the most determined reader. Locke inaugurates and exemplifies the axiom that *white men are boring.* Again, the boredom cannot be attributed to a mere individual personality defect. *Locke achieved boringness.* He created and canonized the industrial prose that dominates the "disciplines" of modern intellectual life. "The power of abstracting," Locke tells us, is what distinguishes "betwixt Man and Brutes" (II.ix.10). The more abstract we can become, the more human we will be. Locke's relentlessly abstracted, soporific style deadens the moral imagination.

The effect depends in part on Locke's endless digressions, repetitions, and subdivisions, which I cannot illustrate with excerpts. But consider the following slow train of abstract nouns, weak passive verbs, ambiguous referents, and subordinate clauses:

> For what greater connection in Nature, has the *Idea* of a Man, than the *Idea* of a Sheep with Killing, that this is made a particular Species of Action, signified by the word *Murder,* and the other not? (III.v.6)

Get it? Typically, Locke repeats the point later:

> the pulling the Trigger of the Gun, with which the Murder is committed, and is all the Action, that, perhaps, is visible has no natural connection with those other *Ideas,* that make up the complex one, named *Murder.* (III.ix.7)

In other words: dismembering Oroonoko, or assassinating Martin Luther King Jr., is just like killing livestock on a farm. Locke was not an animal rights activist. He is not outraged by people who eat lamb. Instead, he is undermining—intellectually, methodically—the legitimacy of our outrage at people who kill people. As the contemporary French philosopher Pierre Manent complains, Locke's argument about the interchangeability of generic sheep and generic people ignores the fact that "man has an idea of death and a word by which to name it. . . . A man knows he is killing a man who knows he is being killed."[152] But such particulars evaporate in the floating abstractions of Locke's prose. Indeed, the plausibility of his argument at one point depends on our forgetting what he has said at another point. Locke never intended his distinction "betwixt Men and Brutes" to be shoved into the same paragraph as his denial of a distinction between killing men and killing sheep, 289 mind-numbing pages later.

In Locke's description of murder, only the pulling of the trigger is "visible": we do not see the spinning bullet crash through the lungs of a beautiful 27-year-old, knocked backward by the impact, spraying blood on the face of his curly haired daughter. We do not hear her scream, then, or later, when she wakes from the nightmares that reenact her father's exploding chest. Locke focuses on what he can see. But the whole idea of "focus" presupposes an attention to particular details, at the expense of a larger eye-scape. The visible, voluntary, carefully defined contract between Locke and other white male investors in the Royal Africa Company rested on an obscure, complicated network of unwritten coercive subcontracts between various white intermediaries and their nonwhite victims. But Locke does not talk about the spider web of subcontractors and the wriggling life they trap. Hobbes, who was never so effectively insulated, had been more forthright than Locke about the inequalities of wealth and power. Hobbes recognized that people routinely acquiesce in unfair contracts, just because they cannot resist the power of a stronger opponent—one, for instance, with his finger on a visible trigger.

White liberal Locke systematically repressed his own indebtedness to Hobbes, not simply because he was dishonest, not simply because Hobbes was scandalously unpopular, but—and only this reason mattered in the long run—because the psychological and political appeal of Locke's theory depends on its utopian promise of even-handed justice. We admire Locke, as we admire Jefferson, because they imagined an ideal community and labored to make that ideal real. But racism comes into its own, according to Bauman, "only in the context of a design of the perfect society and an intention to implement the design through planned and consistent effort." Locke's and Jefferson's vision of a society founded on and regulated by a social contract between equals depended, like Hitler's vision of the Reich, on the legitimacy of "social engineering."[153] Locke began his political career developing, with Shaftesbury, a plan for a new society. Although it is as dull as everything else Locke wrote, the "Fundamental Constitution" of the not-yet-founded Carolina colony belongs to a literary genre founded by Sir Thomas More's *Utopia* (1516).[154] More claimed to describe a real place, discovered on a recent voyage to the New World; that world offered Europeans an empty space where they could project their frustrated desires for a better society. But More's vision also belonged—in both language and content—to the humanist project of recovering a classical ideal.[155] Slavery was normal in ancient Greece and Rome, and when humanism successfully installed classical texts in the classrooms of Europe, it also routinely associated slavery with an idealized political culture.[156] More's inaugural Utopia, like Locke's and Shaftesbury's, institutionalized slave labor. By Locke's lifetime, the texts of classical Greece and Rome had replaced the Bible as the most influential scripts of political self-definition.[157] Locke's and Jefferson's chief models for a glorious imperial republic were slave-holding societies. When Locke made his generic Roman "Caius" white, he projected his own generic whiteness back onto that authoritative ideal.

Locke's social contract resembles, in more ways than one, the deal offered by a used-car salesman. His very notion of a mutually beneficial contract between equals implies (or creates) an uneven-handed asymmetry between those who sign the contract and those who do not. In the world outside Locke's text, a contract gives a job, or property, or power, to one person rather than another. A contract excludes, even as it includes. It excludes not only those who refuse to sign, but those who are defined as incompetent to sign (children, for instance, or chimpanzees—or women, servants, slaves, Catholics, men who do not own land, blacks). Every social contract therefore presupposes a preexisting social contract about who should be entitled to negotiate contracts and—back beyond that—a preexisting sociolinguistic contract about the meaning of the words of the contract; the theory dizzyingly recedes into an endless cycle of pre-pre-pre^n . . . contracts. But Locke excludes from his theory the exclusions required by his theory.

Unlike Hobbes, Locke represses the repression that a social contract presupposes. Why? Not because Locke just happened to be a more evasive individual than Hobbes; that kind of personal psychological explanation would not account for the enduring influence of his political theory. The state imagined by Locke institutionalized evasiveness. It could have succeeded in doing so only if a significant fraction of the political nation desired and internalized evasiveness. Locke shifted the locus of legitimate rule from an individual (the monarch) to a group (Parliament). To secure consensus within a group, one must convince that group that the proposed contract represents the best interests of everyone, rather than the narrow interests of one individual or one faction. Brute power, as Hobbes knew, could be secured by mute physical means. But consensus can be achieved only through language—and most often by a rhetoric of all-inclusiveness.

As a theory of political legitimacy, Locke's social contract replaces the arbitrary individual point of view (of a monarch) with what claims to be a comprehensive view (of the whole group). This political ideal is parallel to the new, and explicitly white, ideal of unbiased objectivity. But that white/political ideal depends on repressing the fact that every observer is situated in space and time. Point of view can be repressed, but it cannot be abolished. A group, too, can have a point of view. Indeed, to define themselves as members of a group, individuals must internalize the point of view that defines the group—as anyone who has ever been ostracized knows. Even Locke's child, the paradigm of "unprejudiced" consciousness, occupies an inescapably particular point of view (one who lives in a family wealthy enough to have a nurse; one unfamiliar with and frightened by people with black skin). But white political legitimacy depends on repressing the fact that whiteness and democracy have a point of view.

White paper does not look; it reflects; it is looked at. Nevertheless, to be perceived or defined as *white,* the paper must first be observed—and lighted—from a particular perspective. Locke defined *whiteness* as an absolute term (like *Man*), rather than a relational one (like *husband,* or *whiter*). But *white* has meaning only in relation to other color terms (especially *black*), and *man* has meaning only in relation to other animal terms (like *woman,* or *drill*). To define oneself as "white," one must stand outside one's own skin and compare that skin to other skins. To be white, one must objectify oneself. Locke begins his analysis of the problem of defining *Man* by comparing "the Constitution of *Man*" to "the famous Clock at *Strasbourg*" (III.vi.3).[158] The first white philosopher looks at himself as if he were a tourist, gazing at a piece of machinery. Whiteness—which names itself for the color of its own body—is an out-of-body experience. It depends on estrangement not only of others, but of oneself. White subjectivity represses its own subjectivity.

White consciousness is systematically and intrinsically repressed. Locke's personal failings—his notorious unwillingness to acknowledge his intellectual debts to other people, his obsessive secrecy, his preference for anonymous publication even when anonymity was unnecessary or transparent, his investment in the slave trade—are not accidents, not quirks of an irrelevant individuality. They are expressions of the new generic identity represented by blank white paper. That new self, defined by selflessness, is inextricably imparadoxed. Boyle, Locke, Newton: by any normal standard the fathers of the English Enwhitenment were all neurotic, secretive, sexually repressed, paranoid, obsessive, self-contradictory. They all defended and attended the Church of England, without really believing in the Christianity it preached. The Restoration was based on a policy of studied oblivion: the majority agreed not to remember the majority's political infidelity. Boyle developed an elaborate system of self-regulation to make sure that he never wasted a single moment of his time; heaven he defined as "a perfect immunity from that slavery of sleep;" notoriously antisocial, he loathed the "frivolous and useless Conversation" of "senseless Visits"; he explicitly rejected Aristotle's golden mean, arguing that, when it came to saving time, avarice was "either Commendable or Impossible."[159] (Extremism in the pursuit of whiteness is no vice.) Newton suffered a massive nervous breakdown in 1693, long before they were fashionable among the whiter classes.

Unlike Newton and Bunyan, Locke suffered no nervous breakdowns. Unlike Boyle, he was not a lifelong hypochondriac, and did not torment himself with endless self-accusations or harass his confessors with an apparently unshakeable fear that he was damned.[160] Boyle and Newton both served on government committees, but of them all Locke was the perfect civil servant: efficient, methodical, systematic, rational, without any distracting eccentricities. Life, in Locke, is like a regularly scheduled meeting of a government subcommittee. A group of well-educated, well-behaved, well-dressed white men sit around a table, talking carefully about distant events. Someone takes notes. No one raises his voice or makes a fuss; everyone is admirably detached. Experts on various facets of the situation are consulted. The labor of the subcommittee is divided among its members, so that no one need shoulder too much responsibility. Its report is written in a deliberately impersonal style, reflecting an intellectual and stylistic consensus. "Segmented, routinized, and depersonalized, the job of the bureaucrat or specialist," according to historian Christopher R. Browning, "could be performed without confronting the reality of mass murder."[161] Browning was describing the "ordinary men" who administered the Nazi Holocaust in Poland, but his depiction just as easily sticks to Locke.

Goethe's last words were "More light!"[162] Locke—secretive to the end—had no last words. At three o'clock in the afternoon on October 28, 1704, John Locke lifted his hands to his face, and with his own white fingers (as if he were closing the eyes of a corpse) he lowered his own eyelids and died. The final solution of the first white philosopher was to refuse to see.

EPILOGUE

WHITE NOISE

I'm so glad dat I'm a niggar,
An don't you wish you was too

—"The Original Jim Crow" (1832)

I hear your name ain't really white
Man.

—Langston Hughes[1]

I'M WHAT'S CALLED WHITE, I TOLD YOU AT THE START, and now you know why. By 1704, when Newton published his *Optics* and Locke closed his eyes, the British had bought—lock, stock, and gun barrel—the metaphor that told them they were white, and that their generic whiteness was a sign of their superiority over all other peoples. In 1705, a man named Mathew Taylor was born in Wales; he later migrated to Maryland, where his son Henry Taylor was baptized in 1738. Henry Taylor was my great-great-great-great-great-grandfather. I belong to the ninth generation of a family of so-called white Americans.[2] My son Josh—the tenth generation, the hip hop generation—introduced me to *The Eminem Show,* the top-selling album of 2002, written and rapped by a man who grossed about $300 million that year and featured in 153 different stories in the New York Times.[3] Its first song is called "White America."

A lot has happened to whiteness in the three centuries between Newton's *Optics* and *The Eminem Show.* Nevertheless, some things have hardly changed at all. The continuities and changes both show up in the vernacular spoken by Marshall Mathers III (aka Eminem, aka Slim Shady). Although people will argue about almost anything connected to him, nobody doubts that Mathers/Eminem is "W-H-I-T-E," physically, phenotypically, generically. "I'm white," he says himself, "a corny lookin white boy" with a "big white ass."[4] The exact relationship between his work and his whiteness is sharply disputed, but the meaning of his lyrics and his life cannot be separated from his putative biological whiteness, which everyone treats as a fact rather than a metaphor. That allegedly factual whiteness is defined by its relationship to blackness. Musically, "White America"'s blasting guitar beat owes a lot to 1970s rock and 1980s punk rock, but the song describes itself as "hip hop," a genre that originated in a 1970s South Bronx fusion of black American and immigrant Jamaican party styles.[5] The word *hip* has an African origin, deriving from the Wolof word *hep.*[6] In addition to calling his music "hip hop," Eminem often calls himself "white trash," a much earlier compound that first surfaced in the 1830s; the first two recorded examples are both attributed to black speakers.[7] Eminem acknowledges that there are "cocky Caucasians who think I'm some wigger;" indeed, he has been described—by approving white critics and disapproving White Nationalists—as "the über-wigger."[8] The word *wigger,* a contraction of "white nigger," probably originated in the early 1970s in urban African American speech; it resembles other ironic black compounds—like *witch* ("white bitch") and *whitianity* ("white Christianity")—that whittle down *white* to a prefix.[9] This pattern should look familiar. I have argued that black slaves in Barbados apparently coined the compound *white slave* (chapter 7), and more fundamentally that non-European peoples taught the English the modern racial sense of the word *white* (chapter 5). In the twenty-first century, Anglos still get their sense of "white" identity from people darker than themselves.

But other things have changed. Both words of the title phrase "White America" (repeated 18 times in the song) have meanings that John Locke and Isaac Newton would not have recognized.[10] No seventeenth-century Englishman would have regarded Marshall Mathers, covered with black tattoos, as an ideal or even representative "white" man. Until 1765 the noun *American* referred to the Western Hemisphere's indigenous peoples (chapter 6). The political entity called "the United States of America" was created by a document signed in 1787, and the abbreviated singular term *America* only began to be routinely used as a name for the new nation sometime in the nineteenth century. Until the Civil War, "the United States" was considered a plural noun, and in some languages the country's name is still plural (*gli Stati Uniti, les États Unis*) and its citizens are identified as members of a plural community (Italian *gli Statiunitensi,* French *les Etatsuniens,* which we would have to translate as something like "United-statesians"). People in Canada and Latin America also consider themselves "American" in the broader geographical sense, and most of those I have met resent the way U.S. citizens appropriate the word *America* for themselves alone.

This monopolizing of the word *America* by a particular population belongs to a larger shift in linguistic power. Although *The Eminem Show* debuted at No. 1 in the music charts on both sides of the Atlantic, although it won the 2002

MTV Europe award for best album (and many other British and international awards), it originated in the United States.[11] During the centuries when Anglos decided that they were white, London dominated English language use (chapters 1 and 2). But the most important changes in the language—new words, meanings, pronunciations, grammars—now spread outward from major cities in the United States. (Eminem grew up in Kansas City and Detroit; the entertainment industry is concentrated in New York and Los Angeles; politicians and bureaucrats in Washington, D.C., determine what can be broadcast.) Even in Europe, Eminem's generation prefers to learn American, rather than British, English. U.S. English is not "better" than U.K. English, any more than sixteenth-century London English was superior to sixteenth-century Yorkshire English: U.S. dominance now, like London dominance then, reflects the unequal geographical distribution of linguistic power. Everyone speaks, but people in one place have more power than speakers in other places to determine which words get legitimated and reproduced. Linguistic power flows along the curves of economic and political topography. In the sixteenth century the most affluent and influential speakers of European languages in the Western Hemisphere were Spanish and Portuguese (chapter 3); in the seventeenth century they were Caribbean (chapter 8). But in the eighteenth and nineteenth centuries continental North Americans took over the pole position, and in the twentieth the United States surpassed Britain as the militarily, politically, economically, and linguistically dominant English-language population. That's why Marshall Mathers, rehearsing in London for an appearance on British television, could say "Shut your fuckin' face, Uncle Europe."[12] While tracks from *The Eminem Show* were saturating British airwaves, the Prime Minister was ignoring his own electorate and playing the role of faithful servant to his American master. In 2002 Britain became, for the first time, America's niggah. If American fundamentalism gets its way, the whole world will soon be America's niggah.

These radical changes to the meaning of the geopolitical noun *America* work in tandem with equally profound changes to the significance of the generic adjective *white.* The two words, the two concepts, are now impossible to disentangle. Inside and outside the United States, American power epitomizes what it means to be white. Eminem's English reached almost instantaneously a planetary marketplace, not only because American technology and American marketing techniques have created a global information network, not only because the U. S. government began in the summer of 2002 broadcasting Eminem's songs "in the Middle East as part of its propaganda campaign to enhance America's image to young radio listeners in the Arab world."[13] Why else? Because power stimulates mimicry: modern American power, embodied in a superstar like Eminem, creates an international desire to be American, to be modern, to be white.[14] As geographer Alastair Bonnett argues, white identity cannot be separated from modernity.[15] That link was forged in the 1490s with the triple European discovery of a "new world," a sea route around Africa to India, and an inexplicable whiteness (chapter 3).

But although it was the discovery of "white people" in the New World that precipitated the collapse of ancient explanations for skin color, the "White America" invoked by Eminem does not include any of the New World's original inhabitants. The seventeenth-century belief that the indigenous peoples of North America were white (chapters 2 and 8), including Locke's conviction that they should be better treated than Africans (chapter 11), has disappeared. Most of the actual Native Americans have disappeared too, victims of a sustained policy of ethnic cleansing by extermination and displacement; American apartheid has isolated most of the surviving remnant on depressed and depressing "tribal homelands." Although my family tree includes a fair number of acknowledged Amerindians—my maternal grandmother grew up on a reservation—they have left almost no trace on the family's self-definition, and in American popular culture living Amerindians remain virtually invisible.

The disappearance of Amerindians belongs to a larger erasure of non-European whites.[16] Although the anomalous presence of various white peoples in tropical regions had first challenged and eventually disproved the ancient climatic explanation of skin color, once biological lineage had replaced environmental influence those originally startling exceptions lost their intellectual importance. The research agenda switched from geography to anatomy. Abolitionists championed the old climate theory, ignoring the exceptions in the interest of emphasizing the common humanity of enslaver and enslaved. Racists ignored the exceptions in the interest of equating white racial superiority with European dominance. Having redefined themselves as "white" (rather than ruddy or red), Brits on both sides of the Atlantic could, in the eighteenth century, redefine Amerindians as "redskins" or "the red man." The originally "white" peoples of Asia were recategorized as "yellow." Although Western civilization undoubtedly originated in Egypt and the Middle East, even Arabs—called "white Moors" in the Renaissance—are now being stigmatized as an alien nonwhite race. Eminem's father's family came from Wales, his mother's family from Scandinavia.[17] His "White America" refers to a non-Amerindian, non-Asian, non-Arab, non-Latino population.[18] Only one white genre remains visible: Euro-American whites, conspicuously contrasted with African American blacks.

The Eminem Show is a minstrel show. Like all popular American musical entertainment, Eminem's performances and persona can be traced to the fertile originality of nineteenth-century black-face theatre. Like *Clotel,* those shows mixed elements of European, white American, and African American culture, combining songs and social satire.[19] Like *Clotel,* they were more likely to quote Shakespeare than any other British author.[20] In a few cases, they adapted an entire Shakespeare play. One of the first American Shakespeare travesties was *Ye Comedy of Errors* (ca. 1858), "written expressly for Charley White," which begins with the blackface Dummy of Ephesus referring to the audience as "dese knowing white folks."[21] Generic whiteness is not present in Shakespeare's own texts, but colorphobia is, and you have to work hard to ignore the racial profiling in nineteenth-century adaptations of his work.[22] The traffic between Shakespeare and minstrelsy worked both ways. In 1838 the London musical burlesque *Macbeth Modernized* included the American blackface tune "Jim Crow."

The blacked-face white-wigged title character of the 1834 London hit *Othello Travestie* anticipated that, when "lubbly" Desdemona bore him children, "De piccaninnies be most white." Ten years later that prophecy was satirically realized in Philadelphia, in a new adaptation called *Otello,* written by T. D. Rice, who also played the title role. For two decades the most popular actor in both the United States and Britain, Rice was a working-class, urban-born performer who had begun his theatrical career playing servant roles, including Pindarus in *Julius Caesar,* Peter in *Romeo and Juliet,* and Grumio in *The Taming of the Shrew*—roles that epitomize the lack of distinction, in Shakespeare's laborphobic art, between "servant" and "slave" (chapter 7). Rice could have blacked up for those Shakespearian roles. Certainly, white Rice made his blackface character Jim Crow what W. T. Lhamon, Jr. calls "an inaugural icon of international popular culture." Unlike Shakespeare's *Othello,* Rice's *Otello* is full of generic whiteness. Brabantio demands "a white man's justice" and objects to the marriage of "a white man's daughter and a black man's son;" the chorus is appalled by the prospect that "a black shall wed a white;" Iago declares "I'm . . . white;" Othello concludes that the moral of his story is that "If his wife had but been black, Instead of white, all had been right." But Rice's black characters are born survivors. Otello does not kill himself, "Missus Otello" survives, and the happy bicolor couple dance off the stage to happy-ever-after land, carrying with them their child, who is "colored . . . half and half." In *Otello,* an aggressively vulgar, blacked-up white actor rewrote Shakespeare's tragedy to celebrate the birth of mulatto America.[23]

That chaotic mixing of literary genres in nineteenth-century Anglophone culture belonged to the much larger mixing of population genres in an increasingly interdependent circumatlantic world.[24] If Desdemona had lived to bear Othello's children, they would have been—like Clotel, William Wells Brown, and Frederick Douglass, among millions of others—a compound of the traits of parents whose progenitors came from different continents. The geotemporal population groups of Africa and England, long separated by the Sahara and the Atlantic Ocean, have been massively intermingling, biologically and culturally, for more than five centuries. As usual in both art and biology, the intersection of two genres produces a new, third genre, different from either of its progenitors. Shakespeare wrote *Othello* for a group of male English actors, including one who blacked up to play Othello and another who whited up to play Desdemona (chapter 2). Since 1660 actresses have played Desdemona, and in the nineteenth century Othello began to be played, occasionally, by black men, including the famous African American actor Ira Aldridge.[25] Less famous than Aldridge, but more typical, was Joseph Jenkins, an African-born former slave who impersonated Othello in front of a packed London audience that included William Wells Brown. Jenkins (a.k.a. "Selim, an African Prince") played Othello "with a fine, full, and musical voice." He received "thunders of applause" from the patrons of the Eagle Saloon, where his performance took place.[26]

Jenkins, an African playing Shakespeare in a London saloon, was what we now call a "cross-over" artist. So was William Wells Brown. So was "Jim Crow" Rice. So is Eminem. Eminem is white, but he addresses "White America" in the same way that "Jim Crow" had addressed "O white folks, white folks," in the same way that Middleton's Black King had addressed the "white people" of London (chapter 6). In all three cases, the popular art form addresses a much larger (and socially more diverse) audience than academic monographs on the subject; in all three cases, the vocative defines that audience as white, but simultaneously defines the speaker as not-white.

The actors who played Middleton's Black King and Jim Crow were not "really" black, and neither is Eminem. Defined by those around him as both (biologically) white and (culturally) not-white, Eminem defines White America as "the Divided States of Embarrassment." Like Brown's "the Southern States of America," Eminem's phrase satirically rewrites the nation's name for itself. Brown's phrase had insisted on the geopolitical divide that would soon materialize as civil war; Eminem yokes the political to the psychological meaning of *states.* Throughout my adult life, from the police assault on a peaceful Civil Rights march in Birmingham to Dubya's invasion of Iraq, White America has often embarrassed me. Embarrassments are self-divided states, combining identification with alienation. I am an American but I don't want to be associated with *those* Americans; don't those Americans realize they are embarrassing themselves and the rest of us?

Eminem's self-division is evident in his names. Either in its original incarnation ("M&M") or in the later and more familiar form "Eminem," his stage name puns on a brand name (written *M&M's,* pronounced "em 'n' ems"); but it also plays on the initials of the name on his birth certificate, Marshall Mathers. In adopting the brand name of a famous American candy, he mocks (as his lyrics often do) the corporate culture that markets his music, a global entertainment complex that turns artists into sickly-sweet commodities for mass consumption. His own corporate logo Eminem runs dangerously close to infringing the trademark of a very powerful corporation, threatening to ruin the entirely positive public-relations image of M&M's® by associating them with a scandalously unsweet commodity called Eminem. He protects himself from lawsuits by spelling out and singularizing the permanent plural of the registered trademark initials.[27] (The candy corporation depends on mass production and mass consumption, so it does not encourage anyone to think of eating *just one* m&m.) Finally, the image of a human being as one popular American trademarked sweet (M&M) reverses the image of a human being as another popular American trademarked sweet (oreo). In racial slang, an "oreo" is someone "black on the outside, white on the inside," an African American who has internalized Anglo standards of behavior. (I once encountered a black man wearing a satirical t-shirt that identified "OREO" as "America's favorite cookie.") By contrast, whatever its glossy surface, an M&M is always chocolate—and therefore black—on the inside. As a white man internalizing black standards, Eminem turns the racial oreo inside out.

Eminem articulates the divided states of anyone forced to juggle two incompatible generic identities ("Since age 12, I've felt like I'm someone else").[28] This book has traced the emergence of a new population genre that called itself "white" and distinguished itself from other, allegedly inferior population genres it called black, brown, tawny, colored, red, or yellow. But the lines that divided these new color-based genres were, from the beginning, crossed by other population genres based on class, caste, gender, sexual preference, language, nationality, religion. These conflicts began as early as the 1650s, when the Irish in Barbados were treated as badly as blacks (chapter 8). Such fissures within whiteness have been a favorite topic of recent American historians looking at the nineteenth and twentieth centuries, asking *Are Italians White?* and *How the Irish Became White* and "How Did Jews Become White Folks?," calculating *The Wages of Whiteness* for the American working class.[29]

We can generalize from such examples, and many others, to conclude that, historically, an extraordinary proportion of "white" Americans have, like T. D. Rice and Eminem, been afflicted with a conflict between two generic identities. At the end of the nineteenth century W. E. B. Dubois identified just such a conflict between generic identities as the source of the "double consciousness" of American blacks; at the end of the twentieth, Paul Gilroy expanded that analysis to argue for an association between "modernity and double consciousness" that was not limited to African Americans, but to the culture of the entire "Black Atlantic." I cited Dubois and Gilroy, in the Introduction, to explain the significance of London in the double consciousness of William Wells Brown. But that double consciousness is also present in Rice and Eminem, and in all the generically conflicted varieties of American whiteness analyzed by recent historians. The pervasiveness of this phenomenon suggests four hypotheses.

1. Every individual identity incorporates more than one generic identity.

2. Whenever any of those generic identities conflict, the individual may experience double consciousness.
3. The emergence, between the fifteenth and the eighteenth centuries, of new generic identities based on skin color massively increased the number of potential conflicts between generic identities, and correspondingly increased the number of individuals experiencing the "modernity" of double consciousness.
4. The instabilities of personal identity produced by double consciousness, when multiplied by millions, increased both personal and social mobility, which in turn intensified the conflict between received generic identities, creating a spiraling feed-back loop of individual and social instability.

These conjectures may look like just another white appropriation of black labor, in this case intellectual labor. Eminem adopts and adapts black hip hop so that it can express white alienation; I am adopting, adapting, and "universalizing" the black concept of double consciousness for the purposes of explaining white history. In doing so I hope not to erase or undervalue the particularity of black experience. Here as elsewhere, the dynamic is "white after black" (chapter 5). Black America articulated and expressed generic double consciousness long before white America, which typically responded to its own experience of double consciousness not by inventing new aesthetic genres of its own, but by adopting and adapting genres created by blacks or (to a lesser degree) other non-white and not-yet-white immigrants. The direction of this influence, from black to white, has given African-American genres their undertow charisma for more than a century. But racial double consciousness was never canonical in twentieth-century white culture. At the beginning of the twenty-first century, Eminem has mainstreamed white double consciousness.

Eminem's fictive doppleganger, "Slim Shady," is only one sign of this doubling. More fundamentally, his adopted identity as a "wigger" (an oxymoronic "white nigger") sprang from the generic conflict inherent in his status as both white and lower working class (oxymoronic "white trash"). Marshall Mathers grew up, and still lives, in Detroit (described in another oxymoron as "America's first Third World city"). His hip hop angrily documents a ramshackle wasteland of poverty, ignorance, alienation, and violence, a falling-down drug-driven crime-ridden environment stereotypically associated with blacks, not whites. "I shoveled shit all my life," he explains, and now's he's "dumping it on / White America!" He shoveled shit because, in the economically and psychologically depressed cities described in the annually issued, annually ignored reports of the National Urban League, you're either unemployed or you're doing some kind of ill-paid dirty manual labor—in his case, five on-off years of minimum wage dishwashing, cleaning up the waste left behind by other people.

How did Marshall Mathers escape from what he calls "Shitville"? His whiteness did not rescue him ("nobody gave a fuck that I was white"). Instead, he was helped out by somebody rich and powerful who was *not* white, the black rap artist and producer Dr. Dre. In the multi-award-winning video of the most popular track from *The Eminem Show* ("Without Me"), Eminem plays junior sidekick Robin to Dr. Dre's Batman. "Every fan black that I got was probably his," Mathers raps, "in exchange for every white fan that he's got." But although Dre has certainly profited personally from Eminem's success, the overall cultural exchange may not be as equitable as this "rapper of the Caucasian persuasion" wants to believe. Eminem is a white man appropriating a black musical genre. He has been condemned as a "culture stealer," the mere "hood ornament" for a white corporate hostile take-over, even "the rap Hitler." Indisputably, he is a marketing manager's cross-over dream, and "his endorsement by the mainstream media has everything to do with the spectacle of whiteness."[30] White entertainers have been living off the spoils of "white ventriloquism of black art forms" for at least two centuries. Comparing himself to Elvis Presley, Eminem recognizes that he is not the first white singer "To do Black Music so selfishly And use it to get myself wealthy."[31]

Eminem differs from his white predecessors only because he knows, and publicly declares, how much he owes to the color of his skin. He does not confine that acknowledgement to interviews or the small print of production credits; he constantly foregrounds it in the songs themselves, making it impossible for his fans to ignore. "Look at my sales / Lets do the math, / If I was black / I would've sold half." He knows his fans connected with him because he "looked like them," because his eyes are "baby blue, baby." He knows his fans are not only buying his lyrics; they are buying his whiteness, too. He knows the media criticism of his music is color-coded. After all, "hip hop was never a problem in Harlem only in Boston." Whites expect blacks to be obsessed by sex, drugs, hatred, violence; but "it bothered the fathers of daughters starting to blossom" to see the same attitudes expressed by a white musician and bought by thousands of white teenagers. "Erica loves my shit," he knows, and that's what disturbs Erica's America. At the 2000 MTV Awards ceremony, Eminem clones in close-cropped shock blond hair and white t-shirts had marched behind him into Radio City Musical Hall: "it's like a fucking army," he raps in 2002, "marching in back of me."

But Eminem is not leading a white supremacist militia. Although he may be blonder than Britney Spears, that is only because he has been "standing in this mirror bleachin my hair, with some peroxide." (Something we actually see him doing in the video of "Stan.") Britney's breasts may be synthetic, too, but thousands of people and millions of dollars labor to make her look absolutely natural. Eminem's hair is as bleached as the emblematically original "white paper" of Locke's philosophy (chapter 11), but unlike Locke Eminem calls attention to the toxic chemicals needed to construct a white identity. White America is for Eminem "the democracy of hypocrisy." A fake labeled "fake" is not faking authenticity, but mocking it. No one who's paying attention would mistake Eminem for the aggressively Aryan counterfeit rapper, Vanilla Ice.

Nevertheless, for some critics what separates Eminem from lip-synching Milli-Vanilli is only the difference between a failed prototype and the successfully marketed final product. Both belong to a suspect cultural hybrid that Norman Mailer infamously christened the "white negro".[32] Certainly, Eminem exemplifies an increasingly globalized youth culture that mixes and plays with generic identities of all kinds. Equally certainly, the hybridized and commodified identities sold to young consumers do not necessarily undermine racism. To the extent that they depend on equating blackness with rebellion, transgression, sexuality, or primitive authenticity, they simply reinforce racial stereotypes. A white suburban teenager, listening to Tupac Shakur tell him "both black and white, is smoking crack tonight," may be doing nothing more than the latest and safest version of slumming. The murder of black rappers like Tupac and the Notorious B.I.G. enhances the thrill of the spectacle without ever endangering white consumers or white prejudices about black men.

However, the fact that some people are impervious to redefinition does not mean that all cultural hybrids fail, either aesthetically or politically. For at least some spectators, they create new genres of identity. "There's always going to be assholes," Marshall Mathers told an interviewer in 1998, "but if there's one music that could break down racist barriers, it's hip-hop." He should know. In 1984 Marshall Mathers, then 11, had decided to become a rapper after hearing Ice T's "Reckless." At one time Tupac was his favorite rapper; at another, he "wanted to be LL Cool J"; at another, he mimicked NWA in front of his mirror, "wanting to be Dr. Dre, to be Ice Cube."[33] Like every other wigger, Eminem had black heroes who gave him a living model of the kind of man he aspired to be. Both blacks and whites often compare hip hop to sports, especially basketball, because both are nakedly competitive, "Darwinian" arenas where black men have conspicuously bested their white rivals; hoop dreams and hip hop battles are "two contemporary definers of black male genius."[34] That black genius has helped shape the emergent identities of innumerable adolescents, black and white. What black rappers did for Marshall Mathers was done, for my son Josh, by black athletes, in particular Scottie Pippin and Michael Jordan. In both cases the ideal was performative, not physical; it was about style.

Every identity is aesthetic, a style and rhythm of being. What Michael Jordan's style means for Josh—and millions of other young men—is exemplified by his behavior in the critical fifth game of the 1997 NBA championship series. (In case you don't know: the Chicago Bulls had won both home games, then lost two away games in a row; the day of the fifth game, played in Utah, Jordan had severe flu, a high temperature, and dehydration; he played anyway.) I watched that tense game with Josh and still remember Jordan's performance—and not just because it changed my son's life.

GAME THEORY

Home game
blocked shot
fast break
slam dunk

away game
double-teamed
fever-struck
throwing up

    but still
    you will

that aerial
    corporeal
        ballet

It's easier to win at home
but heroes win away

Unlike Shakespeare's Othello (chapter 2) or Behn's Oroonoko (chapter 11), Jordan did not have to kill a woman to attract white attention; he is not a monster, tortured and burned alive, like Ravencroft's Aaron (chapter 8), but a man almost universally celebrated and admired. A sense of generic identity can survive only if it is internalized as an ideal by each new generation, and white generic identity as Locke knew it will not survive once "white" adolescents begin constructing their sense of self in the image of "black" heroes like Jordan or Tupac. Instead, the presence of such an abundance of such visible black icons makes inevitable what Cornel West called, in 1993, "the Afro-Americanization of white youth."[35] The color of America's future is not white.[36]

Jordan's performance in that fifth game inspired my son to climb out of the disabling depression that had afflicted him for almost his entire junior year in high school. For Josh, Michael Jordan is not an objectified black body. Instead, Jordan's heroism demonstrates that the mind can command the body, that will can overcome weakness, that concentration can outwit circumstance. Above all, Jordan exemplifies the determination not to let your team down. At the end of the sixth game, everyone wanted him to make the game-winning final shot, but Utah expected that and double-teamed him, so Jordan passed to his (white) teammate Steve Kerr, whose two-pointer won the championship.

Whether or not white men can jump, white men play basketball alongside black ones. Neither basketball, nor hip hop—nor the study of race—"belongs" to people who are "black." No aesthetic genre belongs to a single population genre. William Wells Brown wrote *Clotel* to prove that a man with dark skin and frizzy hair could write novels. He also proved that such a man could write plays, histories, and travel books. It is as racist to claim that "white people are boring" as to claim that "black people are insolent." John Locke's prose is certainly boring, but who would generalize about the style of Charles Dickens or Virginia Woolf on the evidence of *An Essay Concerning Human Understanding?* "White" people are all individuals. "Black" people are all individuals. There is no one, "white" or "black," quite like William Wells Brown, or John Locke, or Eminem. There are no generic human beings.

But there are genres. When Nobel laureate Seamus Heaney called Eminem "the saviour of new poetry," the Irish poet situated the American artist in the genre poetry rather than the genre shock-schlock pornopop.[37] Scholars have plausibly compared Eminem to the Roman satirist Juvenal.[38] Certainly, part of his appeal, for my sons Josh and Michael, is aesthetic in the strictest formal sense; they notice that he rimes *hinges* with *oranges* and then *syringes,* and contrast his precise originality with the repetitive predictability of most pop lyrics.[39] Eminem fans notice such verbal niceties because, like other rappers, he privileges words over music—and because, unlike many poetically gifted African American rappers, he very clearly articulates and enunciates a recognizably white dialect of English. Hip hop has been called "noise," and Eminem's Anglo adaptation has been dubbed "white noise."[40] But in contrast to the white boy genres of hard rock, grunge, and heavy metal, the most admired rappers are not particularly cacophonous: rap never revels in mere decibel riot.

Unlike other characterizations of whiteness, the expression "white noise" did not originate in the African American vernacular but in the whitest of authorized discourses, science. *White noise,* according to the *OED,* refers to a sound "having approximately equal intensities at all the frequencies of its range." The expression derives, specifically and precisely, by analogy with the spectral composition of white light.[41] It derives, that is, from Newton's colorphobic theory of whiteness (chapter 10). But whereas white light has always been idealized, the very first description of the aural combination of "all frequencies added together at once . . . producing a noise which is to sound what white light is to light" concluded that "white noise is annoying." Other scientists, comparing it to the noise made by "innumerable mice eating Rice Crispies," describe such sounds as so "random and heterogeneous that their pretenses to conveying information are negligible."[42] This absence of information content relieves the listener of any obligation to pay attention; you can buy recordings of white noise that promise to relax you or help you sleep. If we equate white people with white noise (rather than white light), they come across as annoying, boring, and meaningless. That is just how whites get stereotyped in the subversive counter-discourses of hip hop culture.

Hip hop began as party music. It makes people dance. It never put anyone to sleep. Unlike actual white noise, Eminem's songs do not simultaneously combine all signals, but depend instead on careful control of jarring juxtapositions. When he ironically calls himself "the motherfuckin spokesman now for White America!" he attaches a stereotypically "black" vulgarity to "White" America, and appends the undeleted mother-of-all-expletives to an official functionary ("spokesman") who specializes in flat spin-doctoring euphemism. He self-consciously fucks with language, including the "fucked-up" language of generic identity—especially the word *white* ("What the fuck does that mean?")[43] In his biggest hit, the ranting of a misogynistic, drugged-out, insecure, suicidal, homicidal, young white American male character is sung by Eminem; between these stanzas (verbally indistinguishable from the raging abuse that made Eminem/Slim Shady famous, and made this man his "biggest fan"), the female voice of the British artist Dido melodically sings a haunting lyric chorus ("It's not so bad"); the dead fan is finally answered by the "real" Eminem, rapping the last stanza ("I'm glad I inspire you but Stan / why are you so mad?").[44] The mixing of signals here produces a precise, powerful, six-and-a-half-minute meditation on the problem of artistic responsibility (which ends with a moment of recognition and the word "Damn").

I don't want to whitewash Eminem. He has told an interviewer that "hip-hop is all about manhood," and his brand of cock-rock has been so profitable in part because it embodies and articulates an image of post-feminist, backlash machismo that condemns single mothers struggling to survive on welfare while reveling in pornographic cartoon fantasies of date-rape and wife-murder.[45] From the beginning, the self-proclaimed whiteness of European men has had to dissociate itself from the allegedly effete pallor of women and homosexuals (chapters 2 and 3). Typically, Eminem singles out by name only two representatives of the "White America" he detests: Lynn Cheney and Tipper Gore. Who would guess, from these two female names, that White America is, and always has been, run by men? In the same song, Eminem defends himself against charges of misogyny by mocking the (white) media for "acting like I'm the first rapper to smack a bitch, or say faggot." Like Middleton long before him (chapters 6 and 9), Eminem here and elsewhere gleefully skewers whiteness as the color of hypocrisy. Despite the obligatory official pronouncements about liberty and justice for all, White America has always discriminated (often viciously) against women and homosexuals. Nevertheless, Eminem's criticism of the white media dissociates himself from white hypocrisy; unlike other whites, *he* is not a hypocrite. Unlike Middleton, Eminem uses this race-rhetoric of hypocrisy to redefine his own gender-bigotry as honesty. Moreover, his self-defense against charges of woman-bashing and gay-baiting depends on a characterization of (black) rappers as misogynistic and homophobic.

Eminem is not exactly wrong. At least some (and arguably a lot) of the appeal of many black rappers is their embodiment of a hypermasculine aesthetic that treats every woman as a bitch/'ho and every less testeronic male as a fag.[46] White observers like me are not supposed to mention such prejudices. Wiggerism—including much recent work in White Studies—sometimes uncritically romanticizes blackness, making every black morally superior to every white.[47] The fact that blacks have been, and are still being, oppressed does not make them perfect, or render them incapable of oppressing others. Condoleeza Rice is black, too.

The problem with Eminem defending himself by citing black precedents for his prejudices is the way that it positions him in racial space. His wigger identity lets him have his chocolate cake and eat the vanilla frosting too: he can be white when it suits him, and not-white when that suits him. "I don't do black music," he claims, "I don't do white music."[48] Out of context, as a statement without a speaker, who can criticize that admirable rejection of color categories? But the reiterated first person pronoun insists that this statement *does* have a speaker, a speaker identified in a song earlier on the same album as "the great white American hope."[49] Only whites have the privilege of temporarily renouncing their generic identity and declaring themselves non-raced. In that respect, Eminem's whiteness does not essentially differ from the white ideal articulated by Boyle and Newton (chapter 10). Whiteness confers on Eminem a capacious objectivity that incorporates all possible colors, all possible identities and points of view. "I am whatever you say I am."[50]

You may recognize, in Eminem's obsessive role-playing, a figure you encountered at the beginning of this book. In John Fletcher's representation of a slave market in *A Very Woman,* the English slave is a performing "ape" who can assume any identity on demand. Fletcher's English slave was not "white" and his shifting identity was a satirical joke, embodying on stage a long-standing prejudice against actors and against the English tendency to mimic continental fashions. But in the centuries between Fletcher and Emimen, just as pale skin went from evidence of inferiority to a globally-recognized sign of superiority, so Anglo role-playing, once cited as evidence of a weak and unstable identity without any personal integrity, has now become the sign and privilege of the strongest of all possible identities. It is no accident that the most admired of all white authors is an English playwright, whose works are allegedly "universal."[51] It is also no accident that, although Tupac actually read Shakespeare, it's Eminem who gets compared to the Great White Bard.[52] "White America" was performed by a gifted mimic who on his videos played Elvis (on the toilet), Osama Bin Laden (break-dancing), and Vice President Cheney (being electrocuted). Even before "White America" was released, its author had finished filming his starring role in *8 Mile,* the hip hop biopic that, when it premiered later in 2002, had the second-biggest opening weekend box office in history for an R-rated film.[53]

White America is, for much of the world, Hollywood. Movies work by projecting light onto a giant white screen—like Boyle and Newton aiming light onto white paper (chapter 10), or Locke imagining the mind as a sheet of white paper (chapter 11). The American movie business—as canonical pioneering films like *Birth of a Nation* and *The Jazz Singer* remind us—has its roots in "the first and most popular form of nineteenth-century mass culture, blackface minstrelsy."[54] Unlike Al Jolson and Bing Crosby, Marshall Mathers never actually performs in blackface, but the white star of *8 Mile* does mimic the performance of black entertainers, and does prove in the final scene that he can be, as it were, blacker than blacks. *8 Mile,* "a victory fantasy for whitey," belongs to "the long tradition of special elastic whiteys that began circa Tarzan," an elasticity that makes it possible for a heroic white man to understand non-whites better than they understand themselves.[55] "An orgy of black hands slapping a white back," *8 Mile* tells the familiar Hollywood tale of a white frontier hero, a misfit, loner and underdog who, by means of nothing but determination and hard work, wins against all odds and then walks away into "romantic white solitude."[56] Sylvester Stallone rides again.[57]

Marshall Mathers is not a racist; indeed, he has explicitly and consistently attacked anyone who wants to turn "facial tissue" into a "racial issue." In his most politically explicit song and video, released only a week before the November 2004 presidential election, Eminem criticized the war in Iraq, mocked President Bush and his "daddy," and imagined an interracial political coalition, "a sea of people, some white and some black, Don't mattter what color."[58] But he can no more escape his generic identity as a white man—or the privileges that go with it—than I can.

I have, until this point, deliberately avoided the genre of white confession that dominates so many contributions to critical race studies (and that dominates Eminem's lyrics). Personal anecdotes inevitably personalize the problem, implying that it can be solved by a conversion experience or a good therapist. But, duh, it's not that simple. Every institution in America was originally designed for the benefit of whites, and institutions change much more slowly than individuals. Eminem calls himself a "political" rapper, and a recent critic has heralded him as "America's most politically radical pop star."[59] But "White America" does not criticize the political and economic decisions that have devastated America's (primarily black and Latino) urban population, given America the world's largest (primarily black and Latino) prison population, and led to the greatest income gap in American history between the (primarily white) rich and the (primarily black and Latino) poor. "White America" does not criticize the privatization of prisons, which when combined with mandatory sentencing guidelines and widespread racial profiling have produced a (primarily black and Latino) captive, non-unionized, life-time slave-labor pool hired out to major corporations. These disasters have all happened in the lifetime of Marshall Mathers and other members of what Bakari Kitwana calls "the hip hop generation," born between 1965 and 1984.[60] Confronted with such crises, an African American rapper can recognize that "It ain't all about a black and white thing," but he also knows that "discriminatin different races, Tax payers pay for more jail for black latin faces." When Nas addresses American politicians, he raps about infrastructure and hunger: "Mr. Mayor imagine if this was your backyard, Mr. Governor imagine if it was your kids that starved."[61] By contrast, what does "America's most politically radical pop star" criticize? What Marshall Mathers most dislikes about White America is the unsuccessful attempt of some white women (his mom, Tipper Gore) to regulate his own freedom of misogynist self-expression. Eminem's complaint resonates with innumerable white adolescent Erics and Ericas whose parents object to their goddamn fucking vocabulary. Yes, America's puritanical policing of expletives is irritating and dumb. But shit, we've got bigger problems.

White confessional literature can not solve problems too big to fit in a confessional. The confessions may be emotionally satisfying, for white authors and white readers, but they don't change a thing. Indeed, they probably inhibit change, because—like Ecstasy, the white drug of choice for Eminem and his generation—they provide an unearned emotional climax. You can feel good without having any reason to feel good, and without caring whether anyone else does. Eminem's first hit—the alienation anthem "I don't give a fuck"—begins with "I" and ends with "fuck," and in-between those two poles of adolescent experience doesn't give anybody anything.

Mathers can't see beyond "me, me, me" because, as he says himself, "I don't really read too much." He failed ninth grade three times, and then dropped out of school entirely. A limited education did not prevent John Bunyan from turning his own life into verbal art (chapter 9), and it hasn't prevented Marshall Mathers from mastering the art of accusatory confession. "But anything that happened in the past between black and white," he say, defensively, "I can't really speak on it because I wasn't there."[62] I wasn't there either, but I do know something about what happened in the past, and as a result I know something about the relationship between that collective past and my personal present. Confessions, by definition, deal with my present or my very recent past. But the distorting effect of a white generic identity here and now can only be made fully visible by contrast with the larger history and geography of whiteness.

White confessional literature often reinforces the metaphor of a generic white identity. The value of that identity may have abruptly and radically changed from positive to negative, but it is still generic. Eminem's "I can't stand white people!" is as colorphobic as a Ku Klux Klansman's "I can't stand black people!" would be.[63] I did not write this book—and I would not want anyone to read it—in a paroxysm of self-loathing, or to expiate the sin of having been born "white." My years of work on it were driven by intellectual curiosity, by the excitement of one discovery that lighted the way to another (a kind of intellectual chain-smoking), by the desire to unpack a metaphor of pervasive aesthetic and political importance, by a determination to follow the trail of whiteness, wherever it led me. I am not responsible for the colorphobia of Bunyan, Boyle, Newton, or Locke, any more than I can take credit for Bunyan's *Pilgrim's Progress,* Boyle's *The Skeptical Chemist,* Newton's *Principia Mathematica,* or Locke's *Letter Concerning Toleration.* To take blame for their prejudices, to take credit for their achievements, would be to accept that I am linked to them, in some non-trivial way, by the pallor of a thin layer of constantly dying cells. To take pride or accept guilt would be to assume that something called "the white race" really exists. It doesn't. All that I have in common with Bunyan, Boyle, Newton, or Locke is the English language. And the English language is something I also have in common with William Wells Brown, Frederick Douglass, and Toni Morrison.

Nevertheless, I am writing this and you are reading this in the present, and neither of us should pretend that we can escape from racial space. The metaphor of generic whiteness, the idea of "being white," is undoubtedly, as James Baldwin insisted, a lie.[64] But it's a lie we have to live with. I may not *be* white, but I am still *called* white, and what people call me has affected how people have treated me, my whole life. It still does. It's as though, at birth, I had a remote control garage door opener implanted in my skin, which for fifty years has been opening doors for me, without my even knowing it was happening, without my realizing that those doors would have stayed slammed shut for millions of equally hard-working people who had not been given my magically enhanced skin. My being called white is, as William Upski Wimsatt says about himself, "the reason I am getting paid to write about hip hop," despite my physical and social distance from the people who have created it, many of them "in jail, dead, or strugglin, scramblin 'n' gamblin. This is neither something to fight, nor to gloat about, nor to sit back and be thankful over. It is merely a moral debt."[65]

Eminem exemplifies one way to deal with that moral debt, constructively. "America," rock critic Anthony Bozza claims, "has adopted Eminem like a troubled foster child whose problems could no longer be ignored."[66] But before America did, the black rap artist and producer Dr. Dre had "adopted" him. (The word *adopted* shows up repeatedly in descriptions of their relationship; it is found, for instance, in the bios on many Eminem websites.[67]) But before he met Dr. Dre, Marshall Mathers had already "adopted" hip hop and various "black" behaviors associated with them. Indeed, as the black music critic and hip hop historian Nelson George points out, white entrepreneurs were involved in hip hop from its very beginnings, and those "white stepmothers and fathers adopted the baby as their own and many have shown more loyalty to the child than more celebrated black parental figures."[68] Eminem has now become one of those stepfathers himself, not only producing individual tracks for Jay-Z and Nas but adopting Dr. Dre's role of patron, producer, enabler and father-figure for Fifty Cent and other black rappers. In a duet Fifty Cent calls him "my favorite white boy."[69] As a white rapper who routinely collaborates with black rappers, when Eminem says "We don't play that black and white shit" he speaks for, and helps create, a generic "we" that rejects color as the basis for group identity.[70] Born white, Eminem has adopted, and been adopted by, a family that includes but is not limited to whites.

These transracial relationships are controversial for some of the same reasons as actual transracial adoptions. Because of the racial profiling endemic in the criminal justice and social welfare system, a disproportionate number of children in foster care are black, and for decades the National Association of Black Social Workers has seen adoption of black children by white families as a threat to "preservation of the African American family." White adoption of black children (or black genres) can be patronizing or exploitive; the culture of the white majority can erase or absorb minority difference. Eminem has been accused of all that.

My reaction to such accusations is entangled in my own whiteness and, more specifically, in my experience of transracial adoption. In 1990 I adopted two non-white siblings. I first tried to adopt two brothers in foster care in Bridgeport, Connecticut, but I could not do so because they were black and I am white. Applying racial criteria to adoptions has since been banned by the Multiethnic Placement Act (1994, revised 1996)—a law which, like many of those I described in chapter 8, was designed to protect white privileges against black resistance. But in 1990 racial profiling of adoptions was still legal. Having for the first time in my life been denied something because of the color of my skin, I simply circumvented the problem by going to a private (Christian) charity, where a white social worker was happy to introduce me to another set of non-white siblings, aged 6 and 9.

The point of this anecdote is not that I was victimized by "reverse discrimination." I was not. Two months after being rejected by Bridgeport, I got what I wanted from Lowell. Almost certainly, if I had been black and had wanted to adopt white children, I would have encountered more obstacles, more difficult to overcome. The idea that whites have become the chief victims rather than the chief perpetrators of racial prejudice simply will not survive any serious examination of the statistical evidence.[71]

The point is not that, by adopting non-white children, I proved that I am really a good person, despite being white. My original motives had nothing to do with racial guilt or racial obligation. I already had two children; I did not want to contribute to global overpopulation by reproducing anymore, especially when there are millions of kids in care; unlike most adoptive parents, I wanted older kids, preferably in elementary school; I told the social workers that race was irrelevant, and they offered me two non-white children, and I liked them, and I brought them home, and I fell in love with them.[72]

The point is not that the National Association of Black Social Workers was wrong. Jessica and Michael did suffer from the transition to a white family. The adoption moved them from the racially mixed, predominantly non-white environment of Lowell, Massachusetts to the all-white suburb of Acton, thirty miles away. We joked that the adoption had doubled Acton's non-white population, but my two new children had to pay the price, every day, of being conspicuously different from every other kid in their school and their neighborhood. Undoubtedly, they would have suffered less disorientation if they had been adopted by a suitable African American and/or Puerto Rican family.

The point of the anecdote is that adoption changes both parties, the adopter as well as the adoptee. Both have to adapt to what they have adopted. My "white" son Josh and my "non-white" son Michael grew up together, and each has profoundly influenced the other. Hip hop generally, and Eminem particularly, is one of the many things they share. Although it was Josh who introduced me to "White America," it was Michael who first insisted that I listen to Tupac's "Dear Mama," and then later to Eminem's adoption and adaptation of black rap. It was the experience, as a parent, of seeing the difference between America's treatment of my white sons and America's treatment of my non-white son that made it impossible for me not to see the privileges my skin gets me. "What in the world gives me the right?" Eminem asks, and I now know that, for him as for me, a low melanin count is part of the answer.[73]

Which is to say: transracial adoption may or may not be good for non-white children, but it's good for white parents and white families. Which is to say: the suffering of non-whites contributes to the enlightenment of whites. Is this any different, or any better, than the situation of Robert Boyle (chapter 10), laying the foundations of modern science on a white man's opportunity to dissect many black corpses? I don't know. I do know that I am now asking such questions, which I never asked before I adopted Michael, and Michael adopted me.

In my favorite track from *The Eminem Show,* the über-wigger apologizes to his mother: "I'm sorry momma, I never meant to hurt you." But he is digging a grave as he sings this, and its rapt lyricism clashes with the rapper's spat catalog of his mother's (and father's) unforgivable sins against their own child. "Tonight," he explains, "I'm cleaning out my closet." My eyes, too, are baby blue, baby, and I love what some people would call white literature. But in this book I have tried to see my Anglo inheritance through the eyes of the black students who grew up in my "bad" (meaning "poor and racially mixed") Topeka neighborhood and attended the same underfunded public schools. I have tried to see it through the deep brown eyes of my son Michael, who is as "black" as I am "white." To do so, I have adopted, adapted, and appropriated genres of historical criticism pioneered and developed primarily by black scholars. William Wells Brown has been my Dr. Dre. I have been sampling him throughout this book, mixing him into the base-line of Anglo history.

"America, you know I love you," Eminem says at the end of "White America"—strategically dropping the adjective, declaring his allegiance not to the whites-only fraction of the nation but to a larger and more complicated whole. Like Eminem I love my country as much as I hate it. I respect my parents and teachers, I admire many canonical Anglo writers. But I now know that they filled my head with white noise; I now know that the static of white identity prevented me, for most of my life, from hearing many of the messages that the real world was trying to send me. "99% of my life," Eminem figures, "I was lied to," and he wasn't the only one.[74] That I am white, that I share a special genetic and cultural legacy with an identifiable white race who brought us the Bible and planned the Parthenon and raised the Roman empire, that I am better than other people because I am American and male and straight and white, that science is white, that objectivity is white, that Christianity is white—that's twisted shit. Whiteness is just some broken-down toxic junk that's been piling up way too long. It's time we all started cleaning out that closet.

Acknowledgments

THIS BOOK RESULTS FROM MY OWN DIALOGUES with many individuals, living and dead, and it will I hope contribute to dialogues with many other individuals, now and to come. My own effort to desegregate my reading and thinking would not have been possible without the personal courage of a handful of scholars—Kim Hall, Margo Hendricks, Arthur Little Jr., Joyce Green MacDonald, and Francesca Royster—who have reread the literature of the English Renaissance from a contemporary African American perspective. Where my black contemporaries have led, this old white guy tentatively follows.

The Coalition for Diversity and Inclusiveness, to which this book is dedicated, first made me aware of the impact of institutional racism. But institutions can also help dismantle racism, and this book would have been impossible without the help of institutions created and sustained over many years by many people. The Hudson Strode Program in Renaissance Studies, created through the generosity of Hudson and Therese Strode, funded my many trips to research libraries, and the cost of the illustrations for this book. It would have been impossible to write this book without the resources and the librarians of the British Library, the Public Record Office, the Bodleian Library, the Folger Shakespeare Library, the Huntington Library, the Houghton and Widener libraries at Harvard University, the libraries of the University of Alabama at Birmingham and the University of Connecticut, the public library in Lecce (Italy), and the Department of Archives in Barbados. But the librarians to which I owe most are those here at the University of Alabama. The John Simon Guggenheim Foundation funded a year of research which I had intended to devote to something else, but which this project devoured; without them I could not have visited the European catacombs, churches, museums and galleries that showed me the visual history of whiteness. I have formally recorded my debt to the institutions from which I have garnered the book's illustrations, but in each of those places—as in each of the aforementioned libraries—I am indebted to the efficiency and kindness of a particular individual (and sometimes more than one) who actually responded to my queries.

Other individuals are closer to home. I am indebted first to Philip Beidler (my partner in organizing the symposium where this project begun as an infant essay, before growing into a 300 pound gorilla). Barbara Fuchs, Mary Floyd-Wilson, and Francesca Royster (speakers at that symposium) made helpful comments on earlier drafts. Robert Young and Tony Bolden first called my attention to the relevance of *Clotel;* Arthur Little, Sharon O'Dair and Harold Weber all read drafts of parts of this book. Three linguists—Janina Brutt-Griffler, Catherine Davis, and Lucy Pickering—gave me indispensable guidance when I realized that I needed to investigate the scholarship on language change. Utz McKnight, newly arrived in the Political Science department, at short notice read the penultimate draft of the whole book, saved me from many mistakes of fact and tone, and loaned me half a dozen books I should have read earlier; I thank him for delaying publication for another month. Ted Miller, from the same department, who took time off from his own work on Hobbes to read chapters 9 and 11, was also a source of enlightening (and very different) criticism. My research assistants Heather Duerre (first and foremost), Emma Harper, Nathan Parker, Tobie Meinel, Ed Geisweidt, and Ron Tumelson (in the long final haul) over the years dealt patiently with my endless requests for books and articles, and for technical help finding and searching databases. Brandie Siegfried gave me the opportunity to try two slivers from the book on audiences at Brigham Young University, and called my attention to the two books I would otherwise never have discovered.

My sons Josh and Michael introduced me to the music of Eminem.

I am grateful to Karen Quinn—a lawyer who belongs to that mysterious category, the "intelligent general reader"—for reading some chapters of a draft of this book, and objecting to my tendency to assume that everyone is interested in the petty disputes between professors of English.

I owe more to Celia R. Daileader than can be indicated by my various citations of her published and forthcoming work. Issues of race and sexuality were almost entirely absent from my c.v. before 1995, when she and I simultaneously arrived at the University of Alabama. She has continually inspired my thinking about both subjects. My work, and my life, would be unimaginably poorer without her.

Notes

Unless otherwise noted, books cited were published in London. Publishers are not identified for books printed before 1900. The following abbreviations are used:

Add.MS	Additional Manuscript (class of documents in British Library)
Clotel	William Wells Brown, *Clotel; or, The President's Daughter: A Narrative of Slave Life in the United States,* ed. Robert S. Levine (Boston: Bedford/St. Martin's, 2000)
C.O.	Colonial Office (class of documents in PRO)
"Collective Degradation"	"Collective Degradation: Slavery and the Construction of Race," papers given at a conference at Yale University, November 7–8, 2003, http://www.yale.edu/glc/events/race/schedule.htm
CSPC	*Calendar of State Papers Colonial*
Davis, *Progress*	David Brion Davis, *Slavery and Human Progress* (New York: Oxford UP, 1984)
Dyer, *White*	Richard Dyer, *White* (Routledge, 1997)
Eltis, *African Slavery*	David Eltis, *The Rise of African Slavery in the Americas* (Cambridge: Cambridge UP, 2000)
Essay	John Locke, *An Essay Concerning Human Understanding,* ed. Peter H. Nidditch (Oxford: Clarendon, 1979)
Floyd-Wilson, *English Ethnicity*	Mary Floyd-Wilson, *English Ethnicity and Race in Early Modern Drama* (Cambridge: Cambridge UP, 2003)
Godwyn, *Advocate*	Morgan Godwyn, *The Negro's & Indians Advocate: Suing for Their Admission to the Church* (1680)
JBMHS	*Journal of the Barbados Museum and Historical Society*
Jordan, *White Over Black*	Winthrop D. Jordan, *White Over Black: American Attitudes toward the Negro, 1550–1812* (Chapel Hill: published for the Institute of Early American History and Culture at Williamsburg, VA, by the University of North Carolina Press, 1968)
Labov, *Principles*	William Labov, *Principles of Linguistic Change,* vol. 2: *Social Factors* (Oxford: Blackwell, 1994)
Morgan, *American Slavery*	Edmund S. Morgan, *American Slavery, American Freedom: the Ordeal of Colonial Virginia* (New York: Norton, 1975)
Mufwene, *Ecology*	Salikoko S. Mufwene, *The Ecology of Language Evolution* (Cambridge: Cambridge UP, 2001)
OED	*Oxford English Dictionary*
PMLA	*Publications of the Modern Language Association*
PRO	Public Record Office
SEL	*Studies in English Literature*
STC	*Short Title Catalog of Books Printed in England . . . 1475–1640,* rev. ed. (Bibliographical Society, 1976)
UP	University Press

Vaughan, *Roots*	Alden T. Vaughan, *Roots of American Racism: essays on the colonial experience* (New York: Oxford UP, 1995)
Wheeler, *Complexion*	Roxann Wheeler, *The Complexion of Race: Categories of Difference in Eighteenth-Century British Culture* (Philadelphia: University of Pennsylvania Press, 2000)

Chapter 1

1. John Ford, "Elegy for John Fletcher" (1625) in *English Renaissance Literary Criticism,* ed. Brian Vickers (Oxford: Clarendon, 1999), 543.
2. Ashley Montagu, *Touching: The Human Significance of the Skin* (New York: Columbia UP, 1971), 1–6.
3. C. S. Henshilwood et al., "Emergence of Modern Human Behavior: Middle Stone Age Engravings from South Africa," *Science* 295 (2002): 1278–80.
4. Thévoz, *The Painted Body* (New York: Skira/Rizzoli, 1984). See also Robert Brain, *The Decorated Body* (Hutchinson, 1979), and Victoria Ebin, *The Body Decorated* (Thames and Hudson, 1979). I discuss some of the implications of human bodies as surfaces to be marked in *Castration: An Abbreviated History of Western Manhood* (New York: Routledge, 2000), 159–66.
5. *The World Encompassed by Sir Francis Drake,* ed. W. S. Vaux (Hakluyt Society, 1854), 126. See also 53, 197, 223, 234.
6. William Allen Pusey, *The History of Dermatology* (Baillière, Tindall & Cox, 1933), 11–23; P. W. M. Copeman, "The creation of global dermatology," *Journal of the Royal Society of Medicine* 88 (1995): 78–84.
7. The American Anthropological Association's "Statement on Race," *American Anthropologist* 100 (1998): 712–13, and the American Association of Physical Anthropology's "Statement on Biological Aspects of Race," *American Journal of Physical Anthropology* 101 (1996): 569–70, both agree that race is socially constructed.
8. Nina G. Jablonski and George Chaplin, "The Evolution of Human Skin Coloration," *Journal of Human Evolution* 39 (2000): 57–106. Their bibliography of modern scientific studies of skin reflectivity contains 153 items.
9. Luigi Luca Cavalli-Sforza and Francesco Cavalli-Sforza, *The Great Human Diasporas: The History of Diversity and Evolution,* tr. Sarah Thorne (Cambridge, MA: Perseus, 1995), 229; see also more generally 74–105, 227–44.
10. For a fuller discussion see Gary Taylor, *Time, Space, Race: A Short Geography and History of Atlantic Racism* (New York: Palgrave, forthcoming).
11. The literature on genre is vast. A good place to begin is still Alastair Fowler's *Kinds of Literature: An Introduction to the Theory of Genres and Modes* (Cambridge, MA: Harvard UP, 1982).
12. H. Rap Brown, *Die, Nigger, Die!* (New York: Dial Press, 1969), 2.
13. Ferdinand de Saussure, *Course in General Linguistics* (1916), tr. Wade Baskin (New York: Philosophical Library, 1959), 67.
14. For prejudices against eunuchs and their pale skin, see Taylor, *Castration,* 140–44. My own investigation of the history of whiteness originated as a side effect of my research for that book and in particular from my discovery of the classical prejudice against white skin.
15. Brown, *The American Fugitive in Europe: Sketches of Places and People Abroad* (Boston, 1854), 312; Brown also uses "Negrophobia" (314).
16. *The Colored American* (New York City), September 28, 1838 ("'COLOR-PHOBIA' UNKNOWN IN ENGLAND AND FRANCE") and April 4, 1840 ("what a fit of 'color-

phobia' the squire had"). In *OED,* the first citation of *colorphobia* is dated 1863, but it comes in the text of a speech actually delivered on January 28, 1852: see Wendell Phillips, *Speeches, Lectures, and Letters* (1863), rpt. (New York: Negro UP, 1968), 35, 49. This first citation comes from a speech to the Massachusetts Anti-Slavery Society by a white Boston abolitionist; *OED*'s second and last comes from the Boston *Journal* for October 23, 1886 ("COLORPHOBIA IN CHICAGO"). Not surprisingly, *OED* made little use of texts written by African Americans. Outside of newspapers, the first occurrence I have been able to find is in the slave narrative of the black abolitionist lecturer and preacher Andrew Jackson, *Narrative and Writings of Andrew Jackson, of Kentucky; Containing an Account of His Birth, and Twenty-Six Years of His Life While a Slave . . . Narrated by Himself; Written by a Friend* (Syracuse, NY: Daily and Weekly Star Office, 1847), 26 ("they were violently attacked with colorphobia"). I have accessed this text from the electronic archive "Documenting the America South" at the University of North Carolina at Chapel Hill. For other African American examples, in addition to those I have quoted in the text, see: *The North Star* (Rochester, NY), August 10, 1849 ("COLORPHOBIA ON STEAMBOATS"), August 31, 1849 ("OFFICIAL COLORPHOBIA"), November 30, 1849 ("COLORPHOBIA ON THE RAILROAD AND ON THE RIVER" and a second article on "COLORPHOBIA IN THE CHURCH"); *Provincial Freeman* (Toronto, Ontario), September 2, 1854 ("prejudice towards colored people . . . colourphobia"); William C. Nell, *Colored Patriots of the American Revolution* (Boston, 1855), 113 ("American colorphobia"); *Cleveland Gazette,* March 8, 1884 ("COLORPHOBIA IN THE MEMPHIS SCHOOLS") and May 7, 1887 ("The extreme extent of colorphobia"), both accessible from the Ohio Historical Society's electronic archive "The African-American Experience in Ohio 1850–1920"; Joseph Butsch, "Catholics and the Negro," *Journal of Negro History* 2 (1917): 408 ("an address denouncing 'Colorphobia' as a 'malignantly unchristian disease'"), accessible on the UNC website; George S. Schuyler, "The Negro-Art Hokum," *The Nation,* June 16, 1926 ("the colorphobia of the mob"). See also *OED* citations for the related idioms *colour dread* (1889) and *colour prejudice* (1905+). An even earlier idiom was *negrophobia,* which *OED* records from 1819 to 1945, but almost all the examples come from white sources; *colorphobia* probably originated as a deliberate alternative to *negrophobia,* preferred because it applied also to mixed-race persons.

17. Douglass, "Colorphobia in New York!" *The North Star* (Rochester, NY), May 25, 1849.
18. Douglass, presumably quoting from memory, wrote: "It is impossible 'that nature so could err.' 'Charms, conjuration—mighty magic,' must have bewildered and misled them" (385). The words he places in quotation marks telescope several lines of *Othello* 1.3.62–101: Branbanzio's "For nature so preposterously to err, Being not deficient, blind, or lame of sense, Sans withcraft could not" (62–64) and "It is a judgement maimed and most imperfect That will confess perfection so could err Against all rules of nature" (99–101), and Othello's sarcastic summary of Brabanzio's charges, "what charms, What conjuration and what mighty magic—For such proceeding I am charged withal" (91–93). Douglass is describing New Yorkers' incredulity at the sight of two English "ladies, elegantly attired, educated, and of the most approved manners, faultless in appearance and position, actually walking, and leaning upon the arm of a person, with a skin not colored like their own! Oh! monstrous!" (384); Brabanzio is describing the behavior of his (white) daughter, "A maiden never bold, Of spirit so still and quiet that her motion Blushed at herself—and she in spite of nature, Of years, of country, credit, everything, To fall in love with what she feared to look on!" (1.3.94–98). Douglass may also have been thinking of *Othello* when he "quoted" the response of New Yorkers as "Oh monstrous"; that exclamatory collocation occurs three times in the play (3.3.377, 3.3.427, 5.2.190), more than in any other Shakespeare text. Citations from Shakespeare are keyed to *The Complete Works,* gen. ed. Stanley Wells and Gary Taylor (Oxford: Clarendon, 1986). In dating early

modern plays I will cite the known or estimated date of first performance, rather than first publication (when they differ).

19. See *OED phobia* (from 1786), *hydrophobia* (from 1547).
20. In addition to the passage from *Othello*—where "what she should fear to look on" is the "black" face and body of Othello—see "dread and black complexion" (*Hamlet* 2.2.455, where *dread* means "dreadful, causing dread"), "black and fearful" (*All's Well* 3.1.5, where *fearful* means "frightful, frightening"), "Your kingdom's terror and black nemesis" (*1 Henry VI* 4.7.78, where hendiadys equates "black" with "terror"), "Acts of black night, abominable deeds" (*Titus Andronicus* 5.1.64, where the acts are simultaneously "black" and abominable), "Black is the badge of hell" (*Love's Labour's Lost* 4.3.252), etc.
21. Pieter de Marees, *Description and Historical Account of the Gold Kingdom of Guinea (1602),* tr. Albert van Dantzig and Adam Jones (Oxford: British Academy, 1987), 44.
22. Chase, *Washington Bee,* February 27, 1915. See also Willard B. Gatewood, *Aristocrats of Color: The Black Elite, 1880–1920* (Bloomington: Indiana UP, 1990), 260.
23. Brown, *Clotel,* 135.
24. Lawrence Dennis, *The Coming American Fascism* (New York: Harper, 1936), 109.
25. "The Skin Aristocracy in America: An Address delivered in Coventry, England, on 2 February 1847," *The Frederick Douglass Papers,* ed. John W. Blassingame et al. *Volume 2: 1847–1854* (New Haven, CT: Yale UP, 1982), 1–8.
26. Gary Taylor, *Cultural Selection* (New York: Basic Books, 1996), 178.
27. See the recent study of the Pirahã by Dr. Peter Gordon, reported in *Science,* August 20, 2004; Jacques Derrida, "Racism's Last Word," tr. Peggy Kamuf, in *"Race," Writing, and Difference,* ed. Henry Louis Gates (Chicago: University of Chicago Press, 1986), 331.
28. See Gary Taylor, "Cry Havoc," *Guardian Review,* April 5, 2003, 16–17.
29. Orlando Patterson, *Slavery and Social Death: A Comparative Study* (Cambridge, MA: Harvard UP, 1982).
30. Raymond Williams, *Keywords: A Vocabulary of Culture and Society* (Oxford: Oxford UP, 1976). Williams does not include the word *white.*
31. Noel Ignatiev and John Garvey, *Race Traitor* (Routledge, 1996), 10.
32. Dyer, *White,* 42.
33. Lakoff and Turner, *Metaphors We Live By* (Chicago: University of Chicago Press, 1980), 7, 145. Lakoff and Turner do not discuss race as a metaphor.
34. On social space as a key index of racist practice, see Taylor, *Time, Space, Race.*
35. Bourdieu, "The Economics of Linguistic Exchanges," *Social Science Information* 16 (1977), 645–68; recycled as "Price Formation and the Anticipation of Profit," in *Language and Symbolic Power,* ed. John B. Thompson (Cambridge, MA: Harvard UP, 1991), 66–89.
36. Lemke, *Textual Politics: Discourse and Social Dynamics* (Taylor and Francis, 1995), 20.
37. For a sophisticated sociolinguistic examination of individual voice, see Barbara Johnstone, *The Linguistic Individual: Self-Expression in Language and Linguistics* (Oxford: Oxford UP, 1996).
38. In Edward Sapir's classic formulation, "Two individuals of the same generation and locality, speaking precisely the same dialect and moving in the same social circles, are never absolutely at one in their speech habits. A minute investigation of the speech of each individual would reveal countless differences of detail": *Language: An Introduction to the Study of Speech* (New York: Harcourt, 1921), 147. Subsequent "minute investigations"—including computer-based investigations of authorship—have amply confirmed his claim.
39. Vimala Herman, *Dramatic Discourse: Dialogue as Interaction in Plays* (Routledge, 1995).
40. Milroy, "Internal vs. External Motivations for Linguistic Change," *Multilingua* 16 (1997): 311.

41. See Edgar W. Schneider, "Chaos Theory as a Model for Dialect Variability and Change?" in *Issues and Methods in Dialectology,* ed. Alan R. Thomas (Bangor: University of Wales Bangor, 1997), 22–36, and Ronald R. Butters, "Chance as Cause of Language Variation and Change," *Journal of English Linguistics* 29 (2001), 201–13.
42. I take these examples from Charles Barber, *Early Modern English,* rev. ed (Edinburgh: Edinburgh UP, 1997), 240–41.
43. On title pages as advertisements, see Marjorie Plant, *The English Book Trade* (George Allen & Unwin, 1965), 248, and Tiffany Stern, "'On Each Wall and Corner-Post': Playbills, Title-Pages and Advertisements," *English Literary Renaissance* (forthcoming in 2005).
44. The Chadwyck-Healey database, Literature Online, is comprehensive for early modern drama, less so for poetry and literary prose. See MacD. P. Jackson, "Editing, Attribution Studies, and 'Literature Online': A New Resource for Research in Renaissance Drama," *Research Opportunities in Renaissance Drama* 37 (1998): 1–15.
45. For instance, in one of the most admired books on the rise of slavery in America, Edmund S. Morgan reports that Francis Drake's crew believed that attacks on them were "a result of the Indians' assumption that all *white men* were Spaniards or Portuguese" (italics added). But "white men" never appears in any of the texts describing those attacks. See Morgan, *American Slavery,* 14. Morgan also mistakenly locates all these incidents on "the east coast of South America" (13).
46. For example, see *Calendar of State Papers, Colonial Series* (hereafter *CSPC*), Volume 5: *America and West Indies, 1661–1668,* ed. W. Noel Sainsbury (Her Majesty's Stationary Office, 1880), 223 (item 784), dated August 10, 1664: "Article 1. That the King be prodigal in giving away the first million of acres, allowing 30 acres per head to men, women, and children, white or black, agreed." This is allegedly a summary of "Colonial Papers, Vol. XVIII, No. 93." But in fact that document—item 93, on folio 206a of what is now cataloged by the PRO as C.O. 1/18—reads "The First Article Agreed Vnto." *White* does not appear anywhere in the document. The quoted sentence occurs in a report of the Committee of the Privy Council for the affairs of Jamaica, in response to nine articles proposed by Governor Sir Thomas Modyford. Modyford's proposals occur in a letter to Secretary Sir Henry Bennet (Lord Arlington), written from Barbados on May 10, 1664, calendared as follows: "Advises (1) that his Majesty be prodigal in granting the first million of acres, allowing 30 acres per head to white or black" (*CSPC* 5:207–8). In fact, Modyford had advised "that his Ma^{ty} be Prodigall in giuing away the first Million of Acres allowing 30^{ty} acres p[er] head to men women & Children White or blacke" (C.O. 1/18, item 66, fol. 148b). That is, Modyford used *white* as an adjective, not a noun. The grammatical distinction is, as I argue in chapter 10, historically significant. Although Sainsbury's summaries can be defended, as a summary, in both cases, they are misleading to anyone interested in tracing the history of racial concepts—especially because the early 1660s seem to have been a crucial period for evolution of the racialized noun.
47. Jordan, *White Over Black,* ix.
48. Arthur L. Little Jr., *Shakespeare Jungle Fever: National-Imperial Re-Visions of Race, Rape, and Sacrifice* (Stanford, CA: Stanford UP, 2000), 87.
49. For examples of this critical genre see Norman Knox, *The Word "Irony" and Its Context, 1500–1755* (Durham, NC: Duke UP, 1961), and S. I. Tucker, *Enthusiasm: A Study in Semantic Change* (Cambridge: Cambridge UP, 1972). Knox specifically and immediately relates his inquiry to "New Critics" (vii), and its pedigree can be seen in the individual chapters of William Empson's *The Structure of Complex Words* (Chatto and Windus, 1951) and C. S. Lewis's *Studies in Words,* 2nd ed. (Oxford: Oxford UP, 1967).
50. Gretchin Gerzina, *Black London: Life before Emancipation* (New Brunswick, NJ: Rutgers UP, 1995), 5.

51. Vron Ware and Les Back, *Out of Whiteness: Color, Politics, and Culture* (Chicago: University of Chicago Press, 2002), 3.
52. See Terttu Nevalainen and Helena Raumolin-Brunberg, "The Changing Role of London on the Linguistic Map of Tudor and Stuart England," in *The History of English in a Social Context: A Contribution to Historical Sociolinguistics,* ed. Dieter Kastovsky and Arthur Mettinger (Berlin: Mouton de Gruyter, 2000), 279–337.
53. See Theodore K. Rabb, *Enterprise & Empire: Merchant and Gentry Investment in the Expansion of England, 1575–1630* (Cambridge, MA: Harvard UP, 1967), and Robert Brenner, *Merchants and Revolution: Commercial Change, Political Conflict, and London Overseas Traders, 1550–1655* (Cambridge: Cambridge UP, 1993), 577–613; Eltis, *African Slavery,* 136, 215.
54. Hugh Quarshie, *Second Thoughts about Othello,* International Shakespeare Association Occasional Paper, 7 (Chipping Campden: International Shakespeare Association, 1999), 3. The lecture was given in Stratford-upon-Avon and in Tuscaloosa, Alabama, in 1998.
55. For this logic see the examples collected and edited by David Roediger in *Black on White: Black Writers on What It Means to Be White* (New York: Schocken, 1998).
56. The word *octoroon* does not appear in *Clotel;* according to the *OED* its first occurrence was in the title of Dion Boucicault's play *The Octoroon* (first performed 1859, printed in 1861).
57. Article 1, section 2, clause 3 ("adding to the whole Number of free Persons . . . excluding Indians not taxed, three fifths of all other Persons"). Noticeably, this euphemistic clause avoids the words *white* or *black,* as well as the word *slaves.*
58. Even this fixed point is less fixed than it appears, since Brown revised and republished the novel in three different forms in America in the 1860s. But because I am chiefly interested in the movement from the English Renaissance to the American Renaissance of the 1850s, I have focused, unless otherwise noted, on Brown's first version (the only one published in London).
59. *Unchained Voices: An Anthology of Black Authors in the English-speaking World of the Eighteenth Century,* ed. Vincent Carretta (Lexington: University Press of Kentucky, 1996). As Carretta notes, Briton Hammon, whose autobiographical *Narrative* was published in Boston in 1760, "seems to have been a free man" (24). Jupiter Hammon published in New York the first known poem by an American slave (1760), but Wheatley's was the first book of such poems. For Mary Prince, see *The Civitas Anthology of African American Slave Narratives,* ed. William L. Andrews and Henry Louis Gates Jr. (Washington, DC: Civitas/Counterpoint, 1999), 22–77.
60. William L. Andrews, "Introduction," *African American Slave Narratives,* 3.
61. DuBois, *The Souls of Black Folk* (1903), ed. Donald B. Gibson and Monica M. Elbert (Penguin, 1989), 5; Wright, *The Outsider* (New York: Harper & Row, 1965), 129. DuBois originally articulated the concept of "double consciousness" in his 1897 essay "The Strivings of the Negro People," incorporated in the 1903 collection. For DuBois, the "two souls" were "an American, a Negro," but shortly thereafter (7) he quoted *Macbeth* 3.4.102–03, and later (183) quoted *Hamlet* 3.1.70–74. He regularly quoted nineteenth-century British poets: Arthur Symons (3), Byron (36), Fitzgerald (74), Elizabeth Barrett Browning (133, 186), Tennyson (153), and Swinburne (169). Clearly, for DuBois "an American" was someone steeped in English literary culture.
62. Gilroy, *The Black Atlantic: Modernity and Double Consciousness* (Cambridge, MA: Harvard UP, 1993), 1.
63. Brown, *American Fugitive,* 35, 303, 306, 313–14.
64. Brown uses Shakespeare for epigraphs to two chapters (124, 140). His casual invocation "of the milk of human kindness" (103) echoes *Macbeth* 1.5.16, and he describes the moment of his rechristening as a free man (63) with a quotation from *A Midsummer Night's*

Dream 5.1.17. (Levine does not notice these echoes.) For references to "the immortal Shakespeare" by Douglass, see *The Frederick Douglass Papers,* 2: 6, 75, 163, 255, 303, 307–08, 309, 310, 367, 384, 411, 457, 464, 466.

65. Brown, *American Fugitive,* chapter 19 (epigraph, quoting *Women Beware Women*).
66. August Wilson, "Writing Race in America," unpublished lecture at the University of Alabama, September 25, 2001.
67. For the term, see William L. Andrews, "The 1850s: The First Afro-American Literary Renaissance," *Literary Romanticism in America,* ed. Andrews (Baton Rouge: Louisiana State UP, 1981), 38–60. For a pioneering effort to link Shakespeare criticism to contemporary black American women writers, see Peter Erickson's *Rewriting Shakespeare, Rewriting Ourselves* (Berkeley: University of California Press, 1991).
68. Gilroy, *Against Race: Imagining Political Culture Beyond the Color Line* (Cambridge, MA: Harvard UP, 2000), 7–8.
69. *OED white a.*11.e.
70. R. L. Trask, in *A Dictionary of Grammatical Terms in Linguistics* (1993), defines *marked form* as "A form or construction differing from another with which it stands in a paradigmatic relationship (the *unmarked form*) by the presence of additional morphological material" (167).
71. Matthew Frye Jacobson, *Whiteness of a Different Color: European Immigrants and the Alchemy of Race* (Cambridge, MA: Harvard UP, 1998), 15–31.
72. The medical condition of albinism had been identified in the second half of the eighteenth century; the word *albino,* first recorded in English in 1777, derives from the Portuguese term for a "white negro," apparently coined by the seventeenth-century Jesuit Balthazar Tellez. The early discussion of albinism, especially in America, focused entirely on examples among people of African descent. See *OED albino,* and Charles Martin, *The White African American Body: A Cultural and Literary Exploration* (New Brunswick, NJ: Rutgers UP, 2002).
73. I cite the text of *A Very Woman* from *The Plays and Poems of Philip Massinger,* ed. Philip Edwards and Colin Gibson, 5 vols. (Oxford: Clarendon Press, 1976), IV, 207–89. As revised by Massinger, the play was first performed in 1634; for the attribution of this particular scene to Fletcher, and the consequent dating of its composition before Fletcher's death (in 1625), see the introduction, IV, 201. On the assumption that the original play was a Fletcher collaboration with Massinger, it is unlikely to have been written before 1613.
74. On the history of comparing people to pigs, see Peter Stallybrass and Allon White, *The Politics and Poetics of Transgression* (Methuen, 1986), 44–59. Unfortunately, they do not discuss pig color or the racial metaphor.
75. Thomas Phillips, "A Journal of a Voyage from England to Africa, and so forward to Barbados, in the Years 1693 and 1694," in *A Collection of Voyages and Travels,* ed. Awnsham and John Churchill, 6 vols. (1732), 6:231.
76. Thomas Wright compares the imitative English to "Stage-players" in *The Passions of the Minde in Generall* (1604), 136–37. See also George Wither's *Abuses, Stript, and Whipt* (1613), Book II, Satyre I: "The *Sunne* lights not a *Nation* / That more addicteth *apish imitation* / Then do we *English*" (157).
77. For this stereotype about the English, see Floyd-Wilson, *English Ethnicity,* 132–61; and Sara Warneke, "A Taste for Newfangledness: The Destructive Potential of Novelty in Early Modern England," *The Sixteenth Century Journal* 26 (1995): 881–96.
78. Besides the dismissive "Pig-complexion'd," the only verbal reference to color is the statement, about a "Red-bearded" slave, that "My Sorrel slaves are of a lower price, Because the colours faint" (3.1.27–29). Given attitudes toward northern Europeans analyzed in chapter 4, the pig complexion might have been, for Fletcher and his audience, Scandinavian.

79. In Act Three, scene four of *Love's Cure, or The Martial Maid*—first printed in Francis Beaumont and John Fletcher's *Comedies and Tragedies* (1647), but written much earlier and probably adapted by Massinger—a woman calls a man "White Sir," but in context this address to an individual male (who is being mocked) clearly belongs to what I describe, in chapter 2, as "stage 1."
80. Brown, *Clotel,* 69, 61. *Race* occurs repeatedly in *Clotel:* 66, 81, 89, 101, 135, etc.
81. Gary Taylor, "Feeling Bodies," in *Shakespeare in the Twentieth Century: Proceedings of the Sixth World Shakespeare Congress,* ed. Jonathan Bate et al. (Newark: University of Delaware Press, 1998), 258–79.
82. Sacks, *The Widening Gate: Bristol and the Atlantic Economy, 1450–1700* (Berkeley: University of California Press, 1991), 14, 363.
83. I have analyzed the relationship between cultural memory and literary canons at greater length in *Cultural Selection.*
84. For Dryden and Keats, see *Massinger,* ed. Edwards and Gibson, 5:252.
85. For Fletcher's early popularity, see Gary Taylor, "Shakespeare Plays on Renaissance Stages," *The Cambridge Companion to Shakespeare on Stage,* ed. Stanley Wells and Sarah Stanton (Cambridge: Cambridge UP, 2002), 1–27; for the slow growth of Shakespeare's dominance, see Gary Taylor, *Reinventing Shakespeare: A Cultural History from the Restoration to the Present* (New York: Grove Weidenfeld, 1989).
86. For instance, *The Making and Unmaking of Whiteness,* ed. B. B. Rasmussen et al. (Durham, NC: Duke UP, 2001), does not discuss the original "making" of whiteness. A complete list of such omissions would be a bibliography of White Studies.
87. For instance, in an otherwise sophisticated and invaluable book Richard Dyer traces the notion of racial degeneration "back at least to Johan Boemus, who in 1521 [*sic*] proposed that all humans were descended from Ham, Shem and Japeth, the sons of Noah, but those who descended from Ham degenerated into blackness, whereas the civilized, *who remained white,* were descended from Shem and Japeth" (*White,* 22; italics added). Dyer cites as his source George Fredrickson's *White Supremacy* (New York: Oxford UP, 1981), whose paraphrase of Boemus does not include the word *white* (10), and who himself cites as his source Margaret T. Hodgen's *Early Anthropology in the Sixteenth and Seventeenth Centuries* (Philadelphia: University of Pennsylvania Press, 1964), 234–35. Hodgen gives a good overview of Boemus and his influence (231–43), but the word *white* never appears in her many quotations from Boemus's *Omnium gentium mores, leges, et ritus ex multis clarissimis rerum scriptoribus* (Augsburg, 1520). Richard Watreman's 1555 English translation—entitled *The Fardle of Facions*—does not contain the word *white* in the relevant passage (sig. B3-B4v); nor does Ed. Aston's 1611 translation, *The Manners, Lawes, and Customes of All Nations,* B1v-B2v.
88. Theodore W. Allen, *The Invention of the White Race,* Volume 1, *Racial Oppression and Social Control* (Verso, 1994), and Volume 2, *The Origin of Racial Oppression in Anglo-America* (1997). The single sentence, in a paragraph on "the West Indies," is: "This was a scheme for class collaboration of Europeans that required a new term of social distinction, namely 'white,' that would include not only laborer and capitalist but also bond-labor as well as free labor" (2:228). The note to this sentence cites two books, published in London in 1675 and 1680, both referring to Barbados (2:351)—despite the fact that Allen was using them to explain events in Virginia. I discuss both books, and the larger history of the legislation of racial whiteness, in chapter 8.

Chapter 2

1. Child, "The Quadroons," in *Clotel,* 283. Levine prints the whole of Child's story.
2. Child, "Quadroons," 276, 281. Levine does not mention this change, perhaps because he is ambivalent about it. He does, however, supply an otherwise excellent analysis of

Brown's use of Child's story and contextualizes it as part of the larger issue of bricolage (6–8, 18–21, 231–37, 274). R. J. Ellis also notes some important differences between Child's text and Brown's reproduction of it: see "Body Politics and the Body Politic in William Wells Brown's *Clotel* and Harriet Wilson's *Our Nig*," in *Soft Canons: American Women Writers and Masculine Tradition,* ed. Karen L. Kilcup (Iowa City: University of Iowa Press, 1999), 119–20.

3. This incident is not based on Child's story, but on the actions of a real slave named Ellen Craft. Craft—as Brown reported in the first published account of her escape—was "so near white, that she [could] pass without suspicion for a white woman." See Brown, "Singular Escape," *The Liberator,* January 12, 1849, in *Clotel,* 273. Like Brown, Ellen Craft was in England at the time of *Clotel*'s publication, and Brown's account of his travels—*The American Fugitive in Europe*—includes a chapter on her. Ellen Craft's story was later told, by her husband, William Craft, in *Running a Thousand Miles to Freedom; or, The Escape of William and Ellen Craft from Slavery* (1860). The significance of Craft for Brown's rewriting of "The Quadroons" was noticed by Jean Fagan Yellin, *The Intricate Knot: Black Figures in American Literature, 1776–1863* (New York: New York UP, 1972), 172.
4. A point made by Roxann Wheeler, *Complexion,* 39–40.
5. Eldred D. Jones, *Othello's Countrymen: The African in English Renaissance Drama* (Oxford UP, 1965); G. K. Hunter, "Othello and Color Prejudice," *Proceedings of the British Academy* 53 (1967), rpt. in *Dramatic Identities and Cultural Tradition: Studies in Shakespeare and His Contemporaries* (New York: Barnes and Noble, 1978), 31–59; Jordan, *White Over Black,* 3–43. Since the 1960s there has been an explosion of such studies.
6. See, for instance, Kim Hall, "Sexual Politics and Cultural Identity in *The Masque of Blackness,*" in *The Performance of Power: Theatrical Discourse and Politics,* ed. Sue Ellen Case and Janelle Reinelt (Iowa City: University of Iowa Press, 1991), 3–18; Mary Floyd-Wilson, "Temperature, Temperance, and Racial Difference in Ben Jonson's *The Masque of Blackness,*" *English Literary Renaissance* 28 (1998): 183–209. The word *white* appears once in a stage direction describing the costume of the allegorical figure of the Moon: "Her garments White, and Silver" (187–88). The claim that King James can "blanch an Ethiope"—apparently impossible—refers to Scots law (Floyd-Wilson, 189–92). In any case, *blanch* is never used as a racial epithet, and as a verb is usually negative: see *Macbeth* 3.4.114–15 ("And keep the natural ruby of your cheek When mine is blanched with fear").
7. *Acts of the Privy Council,* ed. John Roche Dasent (Mackie, 1902), n.s. xxvi, 16 (July 11, 1596), 20–21 (July 18, 1596); *Tudor Royal Proclamations, 1588–1603,* ed. J. L. Hughes and H. F. Larkin (New Haven, CT: Yale UP, 1969), 221.
8. Similar asymmetries can be found in early modern French legal documents. In 1619 the charter for the Compagnie de Rouen, formed to buy Africans and sell them to the Antilles, stated that "The treatment of Negroes is not to differ from that of French indentured servants except that they will serve perpetually"—thus contrasting *Negroes* with *French.* See William B. Cohen, *The French Encounter with Africans: White Response to Blacks, 1530–1880* (Bloomington: Indiana UP, 1980), 37.
9. H. Henry Lefroy, ed., *Memorials of the Discovery and Early Settlement of the Bermudas or Somers Islands, 1515–1685,* 2 vols. (1877), rpt. (Toronto: University of Toronto for the Bermuda National Trust, 1981), 1:308–09.
10. For mainland racial legislation see June Purcell Guild, *Black Laws of Virginia: A Summary of the Legislative Acts of Virginia Concerning Negroes from Earliest Times to the Present* (Richmond, VA: Whittet & Shepperson, 1936), 40 (1660, Act XXII), "in case an English servant shall run away in company with any Negroes"; 22 (1662, Act XII), "an Englishman upon a Negro woman . . . if any Christian shall commit fornication with a Negro"; 128 (1668, Act VII), "Negro women . . . the English." For Providence Island and Barbados, see Jordan, *White Over Black,* 64.

11. Jordan, *White Over Black,* 95–97.
12. Benedict Anderson, *Imagined Communities: Reflections on the Origin and Spread of Nationalism,* rev. ed. (Verso, 1991). The two chapters added to this revised edition (163–206) are particularly useful in describing the retrospective construction of the historical continuity of "nation"; Anderson does not relate this logic to race, but many of the same arguments apply.
13. Gilroy, *Against Race,* 68.
14. Tacitus, *De Vita et Moribus Iulii Agricolae* (ca. 98), chapter 11 (*colorati; rutilae . . . comae*); *The Life of Agricola,* tr. Henry Savile (1591), 243 (sig. X2).
15. *Description of Wales,* tr. Sir Richard Colt Hoare, in *The Historical Works of Giraldus Cambrensis,* ed. Thomas Wright (1881), 500.
16. *Baedae Opera Historica,* ed. J. E. King, 2 vols (Heinemann, 1930), 1:16 (*Haec in praesenti . . . quinque gentium linguis . . . Anglorum vicelicet, Brettonum, Scottorum, Pictorum et Latinorum*).
17. R. A. Lodge, *French: from Dialect to Standard* (Routledge, 1993), 8.
18. *The Ancient Historie, of the destruction of Troy . . . Translated out of French into English, by W.C. Newly corrected, and the English much emended, by William Fiston* (1596), "THE PRINTERS to the curteous Reader," sig. a4. (My thanks to Ron Tumelson for calling my attention to this text.)
19. Peter Trudgill and Richard Watts, "Introduction: In the Year 2525," in *Alternative Histories of English,* ed. Watts and Trudgill (Routledge, 2002), 2 ("the English of King Alfred was a standard form that was in no way the forerunner of what we choose to call Standard English today").
20. Jonathan Hope, "Shakespeare's 'Natiue English,'" in *A Companion to Shakespeare,* ed. David Scott Kastan (Oxford: Blackwell, 1999), 248.
21. The chronological catalog in John Bale's *Illustrium Majoris Britanniae Scriptorum* (1548) is expanded in *Scriptorum Illustrium Majoris Britanniae . . . Catalogus* (1557–59).
22. Milroy, "The Legitimate Language: Giving a History to English," in *Alternative Histories of English,* ed. Watts and Trudgill, 7–26.
23. Stephano Guazzo, *The Civile Conversation,* tr. George Pettie and Bartholomew Young (1581), ed. Edward Sullivan, 2 vols. (New York: AMS, 1967), 1:140. I have modernized "Countrie" as "county" (one of its recognized meanings in the period), since in context it clearly means something smaller than a "nation" but bigger than a "city."
24. Ronald Hutton, *The Rise and Fall of Merry England: The Ritual Year 1400–1700* (Oxford: Oxford UP, 1994), 34–37, 85, 99, 105–06, 175–76.
25. On London population growth, see Keith Wrightson, *English Society 1580–1680* (New Brunswick, NJ: Rutgers UP, 1982), 128; Steve Rappaport, *Worlds Within Worlds: Structures of Life in Sixteenth-Century London* (Cambridge: Cambridge UP, 1989), 64, 76.
26. George Puttenham, *The Arte of English Poesie* (1589), sig. R3.
27. Helgerson, *Forms of Nationhood: The Elizabethan Writing of England* (Chicago: University of Chicago Press, 1992), 1, 303.
28. On the construction of English identity in contrast to Jews, see James Shapiro, *Shakespeare and the Jews* (New York: Columbia UP, 1996); in contrast to the Irish, see (among others) Brenden Bradshaw, Andrew Hadfield, and Willy Maley, eds., *Representing Ireland: Literature and the Origins of Conflict* (Cambridge: Cambridge UP, 1993).
29. In 1582 the manuscript diary of an Oxford scholar described a group of English seamen, anchored off the coast of Sierra Leone, as "Anglo-Saxons": see *An Elizabethan in 1582: The Diary of Richard Madox, Fellow of All Souls,* ed. Elizabeth Story Donno (Hakluyt Society, 1976), 184 (September 12, 1582).
30. Hugh A. MacDougall, *Racial Myth in English History: Trojans, Teutons, and Anglo-Saxons* (Hanover, NH: University Press of New England, 1982), 31–50.

31. The earliest example I have found in Literature Online occurs in James Thomson's patriotic poem *Liberty* (1735–36), where it is historical and literal.
32. *OED Anglo-Saxon,* III.b. James Fenimore Cooper used it in this sense 22 times between 1838 and 1849. On nineteenth-century developments, see Reginald Horsman, *Race and Manifest Destiny: The Origins of American Racial Anglo-Saxonism* (Cambridge, MA: Harvard UP, 1981).
33. Shakespeare, *Sonnets,* 130.
34. Randall Cotgrave, *A Dictionary of the French and English Tongues* (1611), defining "baillet" (sig. H4), the same word as the modern English "bay" (of the color of a horse), defined by modern French-English dictionaries as "sorrel." Cotgrave defines "vin baillet" as "red claret" and "bache baillette" as "A pide cow, red and white."
35. Dyer, *White,* 48 (color plates 2 and 3). The paragraph that follows this claim cites only two examples: Joshua Reynolds's *Portrait of a Lady* (ca. 1767–69) and James Whistler's *Symphony in White No. 3* (1865–67). In addition, the book's full-color frontispiece displays William Bouguereau's lubricious *Naissance de Venus* (1879). The first photographic portraits were not taken until 1845.
36. Michael Hatt, "Thoughts and Things: Sculpture and the Victorian Nude," in *Exposed: The Victorian Nude,* ed. Alison Smith (Tate, 2001), 37–38.
37. For an overview see Jean Clottes, *World Rock Art,* tr. Guy Bennett (Los Angeles: Getty, 2002). For paleolithic Europe in particular, see Jean-Marie Chauvet, Eliette Brunel Deschamps, and Christian Hillaire, *Dawn of Art: The Chauvet Cave: The Oldest Known Paintings in the World* (New York: Harry Abrams, 1996), 48, 110; Christopher Chippindale and Paul S. C. Taçon, eds., *The Archaeology of Rock-Art* (Cambridge: Cambridge UP, 1998), 114, 293, 297; Jean Clottes, "Paint Analyses from Several Magdalenian Caves in the Ariège Region of France," *Journal of Archeological Science* 20 (1993), 229; Jean Clottes and J. Courtin, eds., *La Grotte Chauvet. L'Art des origines* (Paris: Seuil, 2001).
38. There is a vast scholarly literature on ancient pottery—so extensive that such vases have been called "that great curse of archaeology" and an "archaelogical black hole": see Brian A. Sparkes, *The Red and the Black: Studies in Greek Pottery* (Routledge, 1996), 1. For accessible overviews with many color illustrations, see John Boardman, *Athenian Black Figure Vases: A Handbook* (Thames and Hudson, 1978), and *Greek Art,* rev. ed. (Thames and Hudson, 1985), 79–101.
39. John Gage, *Color and Culture: Practice and Meaning from Antiquity to Abstraction* (Thames and Hudson, 1993), 29–30.
40. See the imposing Etruscan statue currently in Palermo (Museo archeologico da Chiusi, ex. Collezione Casuccini, no. 143 Statua cinerario detta Plutone, 550–530 B.C.E., rosso e nero).
41. Boardman, *Greek Art,* illus. 232, 238, 239; Francesco Paolo Maulucci Vivolo, *Pompei e La Villa dei Misteri* (Narni: Plurigraf, 2001); Antonio Varone, *Eroticism in Pompeii* (Los Angeles: Getty, 2001)
42. For more examples see Wolfgang Fritz Volbach and Max Hirmer, tr. Christopher Ligota, *Early Christian Art* (New York: Abrams, n.d.).
43. The foregoing examples are all taken from H. W. Janson and Anthony F. Janson, *History of Art,* 6th ed. (New York: Abrams, 2001): 184–91, 262–72, 345, 358.
44. Dyer, *White,* 66–67.
45. See Ean Begg, *The Cult of the Black Virgin,* rev. ed. (Penguin, 1996), and Lucia Chiavola Birnbaum, *Black Madonnas: Feminism, Religion, and Politics in Italy* (Boston: Northeastern UP, 1993). Art historians describe these madonnas as Byzantine; Begg and Birnbaum see them as evidence of the subversive survival of pagan goddesses—but whatever their origins, they represent Christianity's most worshipped woman as nonwhite.
46. Peter Humfrey and Mauro Lucco, *Dosso Dossi* (New York: Metropolitan Museum of Art, 1998), 103–05.

47. For comprehensive reproductions see Pierluigi de Vecchi, *Michelangelo: The Vatican Frescoes* (New York: Abbeville Press, 1996). For close-ups of Michelangelo's very dark-skinned God separating light from darkness and creating the sun and moon, see Carlo Pietrangeli et al, *The Sistine Chapel: A Glorious Restoration* (New York: Abrams, 1994), 177, 181.
48. Marco Bussagli, "Centralità del nudo: Dal Quattrocento al Manierismo," in *Il Nudo: Eros, Natura, Artificio,* ed. Gloria Fossi (Florence: Giunti, 1999), 79.
49. See for example Boardman, *Greek Art,* illus. 68, 77, 109, 209.
50. Davis, *Progress,* 56.
51. On the geographical determinants of the racialization of Atlantic slavery, see Taylor, *Time, Space, Race.*
52. Excerpts from Cadamosto and the whole of Usodimare are translated and annotated in David P. Gamble and P. E. H. Hair's edition of Richard Jobson's *The Discovery of River Gambra (1623)* (Hakluyt Society, 1999), 244–58. "Blacks" occurs repeatedly; for "white men" see 246, 251 (Cadamosto), 258 (Usodimare). Cadamosto's extended Italian account circulated in manuscript in the fifteenth century and was printed in 1507 (Vicenza) and in 1550 in Ramusio's influential collection of voyages (Venice): for *homini bianchi,* see Tulia Gasparrini Leporace, ed., *Le Navigazioni Atlantiche del Veneziano Alvise da Mosto* (Roma: Istituto Poligrafico dello Stato, 1966), 81, 97, 113. Although Cadamosto's *Paesi novamente retrovati* (1507) was soon translated into Latin (1508), German (1508), and French (1515), it did not appear in English until 1745; the only annotated translation of the entire text is G. R. Crone's *The Voyages of Cadamosto and Other Documents on Western Africa in the Second Half of the Fifteenth Century* (Hakluyt, 1938), 1–84. Usodimare's short Latin letter was not published until 1802 and not translated into English until 1999. Thus, neither of these texts can have influenced English usage in the sixteenth and seventeenth centuries.
53. Castiglione supplies the earliest example of the use of *bianco* with the meaning "appartenente alla razza bianca" in the closest thing in Italian to the *OED:* Salvatore Battaglia, *Grande Dizionario della Lingua Italiana,* red. Giorgio Bárberi Squarotti et al., 21 vols. (Turin: Unione Tipografico-Editrice Torinese, 1961–2002), vol. 2 (1962), 208–09 (agg. 13, sm. 15). Although *Il libro del Cortegiano* was not published until 1528, Castiglione had been writing it—and circulating it in manuscript—for 20 years: see Amedeo Quondam, *"Questo povero Cortegiano," Castiglione, il Libro, la Storia* (Rome: Bulzoni, 2000). I have not attempted to determine whether the passage cited in *Grande Dizionario* occurs in any of the earlier manuscript drafts, but from the perspective of canonized Italian usage, the publication date is more important. Other early literary examples of the generic sense quoted in *Grande Dizionario* come from Tommasso Garzoni (writing between 1566 and 1589) and Francesco Carletti (writing between 1606 and 1636). It does not note the passages in Cadamosto.
54. Baldesar Castiglione, *Il libro del Cortegiano* (Venice, 1528), facsimile (Rome: Bulzoni, 1986): "non dico gia di quella manera totalmente contraria, come se ad un nano si dicesse gigante, & ad un negro bianco, overo ad un bruttissimo bellissimo" (115). See *The Courtyer,* tr. Sir Thomas Hoby (1561): "I speake not of the maner that is cleane contrarye, as if one shoulde call a dwarf a giaunt: and a blackeman, white: or one most ilfavoured, beawtifull" (sig. X1^{v}). Hoby's translation was reprinted in 1577, 1588, and 1603. The generic meaning of this passage is not absolutely indisputable, because *bianco* here might be describing the complexion of an individual (rather than a group), and because whiteness is not attributed to Europeans: it lacks any geographical or biological specificity. The phrase "*un negro*" (rather than *nero*) is clearly generic, but *bianco* is just its opposite (as *bellissimo* is the opposite of *un bruttissimo*), and need not imply that an entire ethnic group is white. Finally, it is not clear that *bianco* is being used as a positive self-representation. The parallel word *gigante* is not necessarily positive; like a dwarf, a giant is a freak-

ish or monstrous extreme, and—as I explain in chapter 4—white skin was long regarded as one of the undesirable poles of the continuum of human complexions. Nevertheless, the use of *bianco* for a man is unusual, outside of a racial context, and Cadamosto had used the generic idiom 70 years before, so Italian lexicographers may be correct in interpreting Castiglione's image racially. But the translation is even more ambiguous, because its original English readers would have lacked the racialized linguistic context available at the time for Italians.

55. For recent objections by British art historians to the "normalizing" of the Italian Renaissance, see Alice T. Friedman, "Did England Have a Renaissance? Classical and Anticlassical Themes in Elizabethan Culture," in *Cultural Differentiation and Cultural Identity in the Visual Arts,* ed. Susan J. Barnes and Walter S. Mellon (Washington, DC: National Gallery of Art, 1989), 95–111, and Lucy Gent, ed., *Albion's Classicism: The Visual Arts in Britain, 1550–1660* (New Haven, CT: Yale UP, 1995).
56. For these examples see David M. Wilson, *Anglo-Saxon Art from the Seventh Century to the Norman Conquest* (Thames and Hudson, 1984), 37, 98, 126, 162–63. The image of Christ carved in ivory (207) might seem to sanctify white skin, until we realize that green vines and brown cows were represented in the same medium in the same period (192–94). For another dark-brown figure from the Cuthbert tomb see James Campbell, ed., *The Anglo-Saxons* (Oxford: Phaidon, 1982), 178, which also reproduces a ruddy Christ and martyrs from the ninth-century Aethelstan Psalter (179) and a brown-faced divinity from the ninth-century Royal Bible (133).
57. See *OED ruddy,* 1.a., citing Gower's *Confessio Amantis* (1390), III.339, and 1.b ("of persons: having a fresh red complexion"); *rud,* n.1; *red,* a.1.d: "of the cheeks (or complexion) and lips (of a natural healthy colour); hence of persons." Many additional examples of the positive use of these words could be cited. See for instance Shakespeare and Fletcher's *Two Noble Kinsmen* (1613) 4.2.96–97, where we are told that a warrior's "complexion/ Is, as a ripe grape, ruddy."
58. *OED carnation*^{2} *n.* 1.a (flesh), 1.b ("pink"), 3 (cherry), *adj.* a,b. It is specifically distinguished from white in quotations from Cooper (1565–78) and Topsell (1607).
59. *Nicholas Hilliard's Art of Limning,* ed. Arthur F. Kinney and Linda Bradley Salamon (Boston: Northeastern UP, 1983), 31–35, 77–79.
60. Musée National du Moyen Age, catalogue no. 11499. White complexions only become normative in the museum's collective of tapestries representing French aristocrats in the late fifteenth and early sixteenth centuries; there is also a clear chronological development in its collection of stained glass portraiture, early dark complexions giving way to late whiter complexions.
61. Thus, one portrait of an unusually pale sitter, such as *Young Man Against a Background of Flames,* might give the impression that the English were already, by the late 1590s, thinking of themselves as a white race; but Hilliard's other portraits contradict that assumption.
62. DuBois, "The Souls of White Folks," in *Writings* (New York: Library of America, 1986), 924.
63. Charron, *Of Wisdom,* tr. Samson Lennard (1608), Bk. I, chap. 5 (C1^v-C2). The first French edition of *De La Sagesse* was published in Bordeaux in 1601. On its antecedents and influence, see Tullio Gregory, "Pierre Charron's 'Scandalous Book,'" in Michael Hunter and David Wootton, *Atheism from the Reformation to the Enlightenment* (Oxford: Clarendon, 1992), 87–110. Charron here reiterates conventional wisdom: see for instance, Levine Lemnius, *The Touchstone of Complexions,* tr. Thomas Newton (1576), which describes "a Complexion, perfectly and exactly temperate" as "a perfect hew of whyte and redde" (sig. E3-E4^v, 33–36).
64. In *The Optick Glasse of Humors* (1607), Walkington called the sanguine humor (dominated by red blood) "this happy temperature, and choise complection" (f. 56^v, sig. H8^v), "a monarch or prince to be constituted over all temperatures . . . the ornament of the

body, the pride of humors, the paragon of complexions" (f. 57, sig. I1), "the princeliest and best of all" humors, "most deckt with beautie . . . this best complection" (58, I2), "the paragon of all" (66[v], k2[v]).

65. Taylor, *Castration,* 140–44.
66. Aristotle, *Problems,* 10.33, 38.4, in *The Complete Works of Aristotle: The Revised Oxford Translation,* ed. Jonathan Barnes, 2 vols. (Princeton, NJ: Princeton UP, 1984), 1385, 1526.
67. Vivian Nutton, "Medicine in Medieval Western Europe, 1000–1500," in Lawrence Conrad et al., *The Western Medical Tradition, 800 BC to AD 1800* (Cambridge: Cambridge UP, 1995), 188–89. For England in particular, see P. W. M. Copeman and W. S. C. Copeman, "Dermatology in Tudor and Early Stuart England," *British Journal of Dermatology* 82 (1970): 186 ("By the Tudor period, there can be little doubt that in England, leprosy was no longer widespread as in former times or as it was still in Europe and Scandinavia").
68. John Webster, *The Duchess of Malfi* (1614), ed. John Russell Brown, *Revels Plays* (Methuen, 1964), 3.3.63–64.
69. *Middle English Dictionary, Part W.5,* gen. ed. Robert E. Lewis (Ann Arbor: University of Michigan Press, 2000), *whit* 6.b (citations from 1150 to 1426). This dictionary gives much fuller and more up-to-date coverage of Middle English than the *OED.*
70. For early modern changes in this humoral conception of whiteness, especially in relation to canonical English literature, see Floyd-Wilson, *English Ethnicity.*
71. For the association of phlegm with whiteness, see Sir Thomas Elyot's often-reprinted *The Castell of Helthe* (1539), A2[v] ("fleumatike . . . Colour whyte"), A8 ("Naturall fleume is a humour cold & moist, whyte"), B3 ("Of inequalitie of humoures, whereof doo procede . . . Whyte, colde of fleume"). Elyot was being entirely orthodox, as can be seen by comparing him with almost any early modern text that discusses the humors: for examples, see Claude Dariot's *A breefe and most easie introduction to the Astrologicall Judgement of the Starres,* tr. F. Wither (1583), E1 ("White . . . White"), or William Vaughan's *Naturall and Artificial Directions for Health* (1600), 128 ("The Flegmaticke humour is of colour white"). Likewise, in his best-selling *Cavelarice, or The English Horseman* (1607), Gervase Markham attributes "horses colours" to the predominance of particular humors, and explains that "Milk-whites" result "from Flegme" (Book 7, chapter 1).
72. For summaries of traits associated with phlegm and the phlegmatic person, citing many early modern texts, see John W. Draper, *The Humors & Shakespeare's Characters* (Durham, NC: Duke UP, 1945), 29–43, and Ruth Leila Anderson, *Elizabethan Psychology and Shakespeare's Plays* (New York: Haskell, 1964), 34. Walkington, for example, after describing the "passive and destructive qualitie" of this "clammy humor," associates it with people who are "pale coloured; slow pac'd; drowsie headed, of a weake constitution . . . dull of conceit, of no quick apprehension, fainthearted" (*Optick Glasse,* ff. 61, 63[v], 64). Floyd-Wilson notes that "phlegm carries few, if any, positive qualities in humoral discourse"—so much so that, by the middle of the eighteenth century, European naturalists like Linnaeus considered Africans "phlegmatic, bearing all of that humor's attendant negative conotations—except whiteness" (*English Ethnicity,* 13, 86).
73. *OED white,* a.3. The obsolete sense survives only in the early surname "White," which originally belonged to an individual with skin so unusually pale that it could be used to differentiate him from his neighbors.
74. See for example Mary Janell Metzger, "Jessica, *The Merchant of Venice* and Early Modern English Identity," *PMLA* 113 (1998): 52–63, and Barbara Bowen, "Aemilia Lanyer and the Invention of White Womanhood," in *Maids and Mistresses, Cousins and Queens: Women's Alliances in Early Modern England,* ed. Susan Frye and Karen Robertson (New York: Oxford UP, 1999), 274–304. In each case an entire racial identity is constructed from a single conventional instance of *white,* used to describe the complexion of part of a woman's body.

75. Dyer, *White,* 57–59.
76. In Shakespeare's *King Lear* (1605), the son of the Earl of Gloucester disguises himself by taking off his clothes. Tolstoy found this premise ridiculous, because disguise usually operates by addition or transformation, not subtraction: see *Tolstoy on Shakespeare,* tr. V. Tschertkoff and I. F. M. (New York: Funk & Wagnalls, 1906), 26, 30, 49. Edgar becomes unrecognizable not by changing his clothes or adding a false beard, but his disguise does result from addition and transformation. Having decided to take "the basest and most poorest shape That ever penury . . . Brought near to beast," he decides to produce this effect by adding dark make-up: "My face I'll grime with filth" (Sc.7.173–75).
77. Likewise, in Fletcher, Field, and Massinger's *The Knight of Malta* (1616–18), Zanthia has a "black shape"—"hell fire cannot parch her blacker than she is"—and so is metaphorically (and insultingly) described as a "chimney-sweeper" (5.2).
78. *The Telltale,* ed. R. A. Foakes and J. C. Gibson (Oxford: Malone Society, 1960), lines 1053, 1059, 1176. The play was written after 1605. In *As You Like It* Celia disguises her aristocatic femininity in a similar way: "I'll put myself in poor and mean attire, And with a kind of umber smirch my face" (1.3.110–11).
79. *The Captives by Thomas Heywood* (1624), ed. Arthur Brown (Oxford: Malone Society, 1953), 2.2; Dekker, *The Spanish Gypsy* (1623), 2.1.
80. Collocations of *muddy* and *slave* occur in the anonymous *Captain Thomas Stukeley,* the Cambridge play *Club Law,* Chettle and Munday's *Death of Robert Earl of Huntington,* Jasper Fisher's *Fuimus Troes,* and Brome's *City Wit.*
81. Margreta de Grazia, "The Scandal of Shakespeare's Sonnets," *Shakespeare Survey* 41 (1993), 45; Kim F. Hall, "'These bastard signs of fair': Literary Whiteness in Shakespeare's Sonnets," in *Post-Colonial Shakespeares,* ed. Ania Loomba and Martin Orkin (Routledge, 1998), 71–73, 81–82. Hall claims that "class intersects with race in the troping of fairness" (71), but the class identity is unmistakably central and the racial identity much less certain—and, if present, described in terms of *fair,* not *white.* Although *fair* could certainly be used in colorphobic contexts, that it was not synonymous with *white* is demonstrated by Lady Mary Wroth's *The Countess of Montgomery's Urania* (1621), *Part One,* ed. Josephine A. Roberts (Binghamton: Center for Medieval and Renaissance Studies, 1995), 545: "all women were pleasing to him, after a tall woman, a little one was most pleasing, after faire, browne, white, blacke, all came to his staidnesse welcomly" (sig. 3M3). In this passage *fair* is used to indicate a complexion, but distinguished from *white* (as well as *brown* and *black*); moreover, since all these complexion words are grammatically parallel to *tall* and *little,* none of them seems to anticipate modern racial categories.
82. See for example Jean E. Howard, "An English Lass Amid the Moors: Gender, Race, Sexuality, and National Identity in Heywood's *The Fair Maid of the West,"* in *Writing, "Race," Difference,* 101–17. Howard repeatedly calls Bess "white" in a racial sense (113, 114, 117), but in that sense the word is not used of any character in *The Fair Maid of the West, Part One*—the subject of her article, which does not discuss *Part Two* (102).
83. On women and phlegm, see Gail Kern Paster, "The Unbearable Coldness of Female Being: Women's Imperfection and the Humoral Economy," *English Literary Renaissance* 28 (1998): 416–40.
84. Gage, *Color and Culture,* 29.
85. S. F. Grieco, "The Body, Appearance and Sexuality," in *A History of Women in the West: Renaissance and Enlightenment Paradoxes,* ed. Natalie Zemon Davis and Arlette Farge (Cambridge, MA: Harvard UP, 1993), 62.
86. Shakespeare and Fletcher, *The Two Noble Kinsmen* 4.2.42 ("this brown manly face"). This praise of brown male faces also occurs in three other plays by Fletcher: *The Humorous Lieutenant* 2.3 ("a handsome brown complexion"), *The Prophetess* 3.2 ("Was not the Captain A fellow of a fiery, yet brave nature, A middle stature, and of brown complexion?"),

and *The Sea Voyage,* 4.1 ("The graine of thy complexion is quite altered. Once 'twas a comely browne"). But it was not unique to Fletcher: see Middleton, *A Chaste Maid in Cheapside* 1.1.19 ("pretty brown gentleman") and *Hengist, King of Kent* 4.2.84 ("brown men are honestest"). The alleged honesty of brown men presumably reflects a preference for men who were soldiers (and therefore tanned, because they earned their power through outdoor warfare) rather than courtiers (and therefore politicians, who earned their power through indoor cunning).

87. Vicki Bruce and Andy Young, *In the Eye of the Beholder: The Science of Face Perception* (Oxford: Oxford UP, 1998), 106.
88. Nancy Etcoff, *Survival of the Prettiest: The Science of Beauty* (New York: Doubleday, 1999), 104. For extensive evidence for this generalization see: P. J. Byard, "Quantitative Genetics of Human Skin Color," *Yearbook of Physical Anthropology* 24 (1981): 123–37 (esp. 132, 135–36); A. H. Robins, *Biological Perspectives on Human Pigmentation* (Cambridge: Cambridge UP, 1991), 37–47, 112–13; Japlonski and Chaplin, "Evolution of Human Skin Coloration," 63, 69, 78.
89. For early modern English examples of this idealization of female seclusion, see Linda Woodbridge, *Literature and the Natue of Womankind, 1540–1620* (Urbana: University of Illinois Press, 1986), 172. The many dramatic examples of the loose sexual morals of women who do venture out into public (172–76) presume the same logic.
90. Peter Heylyn notes that "the extraordinary and continuall vicinity of the Sun, is not (as some imagine) the efficient cause of blacknesse: though it may much further such a color: as wee see in our country lasses, whose faces are alwaies exposed to wind and weather": *Microcosmos* (1627), 771.
91. See Peter Erickson, "Representation of Blacks and Blackness in the Renaissance," *Criticism* 35 (1993), 517: "The cult of Elizabeth is a cult of whiteness. . . . The royal iconography of whiteness is established through the mutual reinforcement of official portraiture and the orchestrated live displays of her own person."
92. *The Works of Thomas Campion,* ed. Walter R. Davis (New York: Norton, 1970), 22–23.
93. A "brown wench" appears in Shakespeare and Fletcher's *Two Noble Kinsmen,* Davenant's *The Platonick Lovers,* Nabbes's *Tottenham Court,* and the anonymous *Nobody and Somebody,* as well as *All Is True.*
94. If the author(s) had wanted to identify this woman as a "Negro" or a "Moor," they would probably have used those words, as Shakespeare does in *The Merchant of Venice* (3.5.37).
95. Kim F. Hall, "'I rather would wish to be a black-moor': Beauty, Race, and Rank in Lady Mary Wroth's *Urania,*" in *Women, "Race," and Writing in the Early Modern Period,* ed. Margo Hendricks and Patricia Parker (Routledge, 1994), 178–94; Hall, *Things of Darkness: Economies of Race and Gender in Early Modern England* (Ithaca, NY: Cornell UP, 1995). Jordan claimed that "for Elizabethan Englishmen," whiteness "was, particularly when complemented by red, the color of perfect human beauty, especially *female* beauty" (*White Over Black,* 8). But Jordan's qualifier understates the importance of "red" in Elizabethan praise of "white"; as his own examples show, "white and red" are praised in a way "white" alone is not, at least until the seventeenth century.
96. On female whiteness and cosmetics, see especially Dympna Callaghan, "'Othello was a white man': Properties of Race on Shakespeare's Stage," in *Alternative Shakespeares: Volume 2,* ed. Terence Hawkes (Routledge, 1996), esp. 198–202. Like others, Callaghan assumes that whiteness already existed as an English racial category.
97. Dyer, *White,* 48.
98. Erasmus, in his massive and influential collection of classical adages (1500), cited the Latin phrase *Ebur atramento candefacere,* and explained that "To whiten ivory with ink is to apply external refinement and decoration to something naturally beautiful, so as to obscure rather than enhance its native charm." The idiom depended on a comparison of

skin to ivory, and therefore might seem to establish the ancient pedigree of racial whiteness. But Erasmus quoted the phrase from the *Mostellaria* of Plautus, where it was spoken by a bawd "to the naturally pretty girl who is asking for white pigment to smear on her cheeks . . . White-lead used to be used to produce a white complexion, and similarly rouge to redden the cheeks." See *The Collected Works of Erasmus,* Vol. 31, *Adages Ii1 to Iv100,* tr. Margaret Mann Phillips (Toronto: University of Toronto Press, 1982), 292 (adage I.iii.70), citing *Mostellaria* 259. This adage was included in the original (1500) edition, though later (1523) somewhat modified. White was not privileged over red, in this description of cosmetic practice; moreover, ivory skin was a specifically female ideal. See *OED ivory* 4 ("the color of ivory; ivory-white, *esp.* whiteness of the human skin"); the first three examples cited, from Spenser in 1590 to Pope in 1725, explicitly refer to women.

99. Lloyd A. Thompson, *Romans and Blacks* (Routledge, 1989), 105–06; Taylor, *Castration,* 148–52.
100. Shuger, "Irishmen, Aristocrats, and Other White Barbarians," *Renaissance Quarterly* 50 (1997): 520.
101. See *Macbeth* 2.3.112 (King Duncan's "silver skin"), *Cymbeline* 4.2.263 ("golden lads"), *Two Noble Kinsmen* 4.2.42 ("brown manly face," in a scene probably written by Fletcher), and *Troilus and Cressida* 1.2.89–94 ("Troilus for a brown favour . . . She praised his complexion above Paris'"). Cressida contests this praise of Troilus and succeeds in utterly confusing Pandarus; but she does this throughout the scene, in relation to every possible compliment. Pandarus is reporting Helen's praise of Troilus, and Helen clearly praised his "brown" complexion; her preference for it, over the complexion of Paris, would fit the normal preference for soldiers (like Troilus) over courtiers (like Paris). Cressida, despite her game with Pandarus, is actually in love with Troilus, who must have a complexion—whether "brown" or "brown and not brown"—in some way darker than that of Cressida or Paris, and certainly not "white."
102. Corpse: *Venus and Adonis* 364, 1170. Cowardice: *2 Henry IV* 1.1.68, *Lover's Complaint* 201 ("bloodless white"), 308 ("to turn white and swoon at tragic shows").
103. *Love's Labour's Lost* 1.2.102; *Venus and Adonis* 643.
104. See Hall's discussion of the "fair" young man of Shakespeare's sonnets, linking his pale complexion to the ambiguities of his sexual orientation, noted by many other critics ("Literary Whiteness," 73–76).
105. William Riley Parker, *Milton: A Biography,* 2nd ed., rev. Gordon Campbell, 2 vols. (Oxford: Clarendon, 1996), 1:43, 2:723, 739.
106. *OED white boy,* 1, citing Fuller's *Holy War* (1639), 1.13.20. See also the related idiom *white son* (*white a.*11.e), with examples from 1541. These are negative from the start: see *OED*'s anti-Catholic quotation from Coverdale's *Confutation* (1547), "when I see you follow your unholy mother, I call you her white son."
107. See for instance Levinus Lemnnius, *De Habitu et Constitutione* (Antwerp, 1561), translated by Thomas Newton as *The Touchstone of Complexions* (1576): "they bee but meere meycockes, and persons very effeminate, shrinking at the least mishap that hapneth, and with the smallest griefe and feare that can be, their hearts faile them, and they as white as a Kerchiefe" (20).
108. *Timon,* ed. J. C. Bulman and J. M. Nosworthy (Oxford: Malone Society, 1980), I.iii, 190–203. "White boy" is being used figuratively, not racially, because he has just remarked on his "purple coulored face." The only earlier use of the phrase cited by *OED* is difficult to interpret, but certainly not positive, given the speaker's consistent denigration of the person to whom it applies: see *The Two Angry Women of Abington 1599,* ed. W. W. Greg (Oxford: Malone Society, 1912), line 1531.
109. Thomas Adams, *The White Devil* (1613), 39 (F4). I discuss this work at greater length in chapter 9.

110. *OED white, a.*4. The generic sense of *blanc* is not cited in Frédéric Godefroy's *Dictionaire de L'Ancienne Langue Française . . . du ix⁰ au xv⁰ siècle,* vol. 1 (Paris: Librarie des Sciences et des Arts, 1937), or in Edmond Huguet's *Dictionaire de la Langue Française du seizième siècle* (Paris: Champion, 1925), or in Randall Cotgrave's *A Dictionarie of the French and English Tongues* (1611), sig. k4. The earliest examples I have found in searches of digitized French texts are from F. Garasse le Pere, *Doctrine Curieuse Beaux Espr.* (Paris, 1623), 23 ("les mores ne peindront jamais leurs dieux blancs, les europeans ne les peindront jamais mores," and J. L. Goez de Balzac, *Le Prince* (Paris, 1631), 67 ("hommes blancs").
111. I have checked *white* (in various spellings) in all these named authors in available print concordances or machine-readable texts; for "poets"—that is, authors of texts we would define as "literary"—who died before 1600 I rely on the database in Literature Online.
112. Newman, "'And wash the Ethiop white': Femininity and the Monstrous in *Othello,*" in *Shakespeare Reproduced: The Text in History and Ideology,* ed. Jean E. Howard and Marion F. O'Connor (New York: Methuen, 1987), 143–62.
113. The main title of Newman's essay ("And wash the Ethiop white") is placed in quotation marks, which implies that the phrase occurs in *Othello.* In fact, it is quoted from John Webster's later play, *The White Devil* (1612). For the history of the proverb (never quoted by Shakespeare), see chapter 9, below.
114. For the latest example, see Peter Erickson, "Images of White Identity in *Othello,*" in *Othello: New Critical Essays,* ed. Philip C. Kolin (New York: Routledge, 2002), 133–46.
115. The play's main source, acknowledged by all scholars, is Giambattista Cinzio Giraldi's *Gli Ecatommiti* (Ferrara, 1565), third decade, seventh novella. No English translation was published until the eighteenth century. For a convenient and reliable English translation of the source story, noting the Italian where relevant, see E. A. J. Honigmann, ed., *Othello,* Arden Shakespeare (Nelson, 1997), 368–87.
116. *White* also occurs once in *Othello* (2.1.136) as a noun; for a discussion of the complicated textual variants, concluding that Shakespeare could not have intended the modern racial sense, see Gary Taylor, "*Othello:* Titian, Shakespeare, and the Invention of the White Race," in *Rewriting, Remaking, Refashioning: Italian Culture in Early Modern English Drama,* ed. Michele Marapodi (forthcoming).
117. For a reading of the image that relates it to modern racial stereotypes—and that assumes that nonblack characters are *white*—see for instance Joyce Green MacDonald, "Black Ram, White Ewe: Shakespeare, Race, and Women," in *A Feminist Companion to Shakespeare,* ed. Dympna Callaghan (Oxford: Blackwell, 2000), 188–207.
118. Paul H. D. Kaplan, "Titian's *Laura Dianti* and the Origins of the Motif of the Black Page in Portraiture," *Antiquità Viva* 21, no. 1 (1982): 11–18, no. 4 (1982): 10–18.
119. On the historical Laura and her context, see Lynne Lawner, *Lives of the Courtesans: Portraits of the Renaissance* (New York: Rizzoli, 1987), 118, 121, and Rona Goffen, *Titian's Women* (New Haven, CT: Yale UP, 1997), 62–3.
120. On the rarity of black slaves in Venetian markets at this time, see Charles Verlinden, *L'Esclavage dans l'Europe médiévale,* 2 vols. (Bruges: De Tempel, 1957–77), 2:374, 588ff; on Isabella D'Este's particular desire for a slave "as black as possible," and the development of a northern Italian tradition of painting black Africans between 1495 and 1525, see Jean Devisse and Michel Mollat, *The Image of the Black in Western Art,* Vol. 2, Part 2, *Africans in the Christian Ordinance of the World (Fourteenth to the Sixteenth Century)*, tr. William Granger Ryan (New York: Morrow, 1979), 187–94.
121. For the importance of sixteenth-century ducal Ferrara to Renaissance English literature, see Gary Taylor, "Shakespeare's Mediterranean *Measure for Measure,*" in *Shakespeare and the Mediterranean,* ed. Thomas Clayton et al. (Newark: University of Delaware Press, 2004), 243–69. For patronage of the arts by Alfonso I and Ercole II, see *Dosso's Fate: Painting and Court Culture in Renaissance Italy,* ed. Luisa Ciammitti, Steven F. Ostrow,

and Salvatore Settis (Los Angeles: Getty Research Institute, 1998), and Andrea Bayer, "Dosso's Public: The Este Court at Ferrara," in Humfrey and Lucco, *Dosso Dossi,* 27–54.

122. On the white woman with black servant portrait genre in England and its racial meanings, see Hall, *Things of Darkness,* 211–53 (which obscures the chronology), and my discussion in "Titian, Shakespeare."
123. hooks, "Reflections on Race and Sex," in *Yearning: Race, Gender, and Cultural Politics* (Boston: South End Press, 1990), 57–64.
124. On Plate 15 see S. Schoenbaum, *William Shakespeare: Records and Images* (Scolar, 1981), 160. The "dark face" of the so-called Chandos portrait of Shakespeare, now in the National Portrait Gallery and attributed to John Taylor, has been described as "swarthy" (175); but whether it is actually Shakespeare, or someone else, remains a matter of conjecture—whereas no one can doubt the identity of the person represented by the Stratford monument.
125. John Harrington used the phrase "white divels" to describe Italian "women of good worth and of great modestie" who "have such a tempting power" that a man should be forgiven for succumbing to their seductions: see "The Life of Ariosto Briefly and Compendiously Gathered Out of Sundrie Italian Writers by John Harington" in Ludovico Ariosto, *Orlando Furioso,* tr. Harington (1591), sig. Nn3. Most critics agree that the title of John Webster's play *The White Devil* (1612) refers to its protagonist, the sexually active and amoral Vittoria. In both cases the "white devils" are—like Desdemona—Italian women, whose whiteness is clearly linked to their gender. In *Othello* Desdemona is called "the fair devil" (3.3.481) and Othello "the blacker devil" (5.2.140); in the same sentence Desdemona is called an "angel" (5.2.140), but that idealization also places her at one extreme of a continuum on which the normal European male occupies the center.
126. For the chief classical and patristic sources and their pervasive educational and cultural authority in sixteenth- and early-seventeenth-century England, see Joshua Scodel, *Excess and the Mean in Early Modern English Literature* (Princeton, NJ: Princeton UP, 2002), 2–8.
127. For these proverbs and examples see R. W. Dent, *Proverbial Language in English Drama Exclusive of Shakespeare 1495–1616* (Berkeley: University of California Press, 1984), M792, M793, W117.
128. Shakespeare and Thomas Middleton, *Timon of Athens* (1605?), 4.3.302–03 (a Shakespeare passage).
129. Horace, *Odes,* II.x.5; Jonson, *Volpone,* 3.4.47.
130. See Taylor, "Titian, Shakespeare."
131. The subtitle to Walkington's *Optick Glasse of Humors* is *The touchstone of a golden temperature, or the Philosophers stone to make a golden temper* (using *temper* in the obsolete sense now conveyed by *temperament*); his conclusion returns to the subject of "this excellent and golden temperature . . . this golden temperature" (f. 78).
132. One of the Seven Wonders of the ancient world was the statue of Zeus at Olympia, executed by Phidias in ivory and gold; for a surviving example of ancient Greek portraiture in gold, see Boardman, *Greek Art,* illus. 221 (third century B.C.E.). For two examples among many in surviving medieval and Renaissance art see the cover of the Judith Gospels (late eleventh century), reproduced in Campbell, ed., *Anglo-Saxons,* 219, and the sixteenth-century gold portrait of Isabella d'Este, reproduced in Lisa Jardine, *Worldly Goods: A New History of the Renaissance* (Doubleday, 1996), 326 (plate 16). Jardine emphasizes the importance of precious materials in representing idealized figures (21–23). Gage also discusses the enthusiastic medieval and Renaissance use of real gold (*Color and Culture,* 119, 129, etc.) and the relation of painting to alchemy (139–50).
133. Spenser wrote of "the face of golden mean," and Shakespeare of a "golden face" (Sonnet 33.3), "golden head" (*Lucrece* 777), "golden muse" (*Edward III* 2.1.65), "golden Phoe-

bus" (*Antony and Cleopatra* 5.2.311), "golden Apollo" (*Winter's Tale* 4.4.30), the "golden blood" of King Duncan (*Macbeth* 2.3.112), "golden cherubins" and "golden lads and girls" (*Cymbeline* 2.4.88, 4.2.263).

134. See *Two Gentlemen of Verona* 5.2.12 ("black men"), *Titus Andronicus* 4.2.66 ("black . . . issue").

135. The first use of *white* in reference to the play occurs in Thomas Rymer's *A Short View of Tragedy* (1693), in *The Critical Works of Thomas Rymer,* ed. Curt A. Zimansky (New Haven, CT: Yale UP, 1956), 133. I discuss all the early allusions to the play in "The Invention of White Literary Criticism," in *Race, Gender, and Genre in Early Modern England,* ed. Celia R. Daileader and François Laroque (New York: Palgrave, forthcoming).

136. *The Hawkins' Voyages during the reigns of Henry VIII, Queen Elizabeth, and James I,* ed. Clements R. Markham (Hakluyt Society, 1878), 5–81.

137. Vaux, ed., *The World Encompassed by Sir Francis Drake.* Vaux prints all 10 surviving contemporary accounts.

138. When Ralegh wanted to refer to Europeans, as distinct from Amerindians, he consistently used the word *Christian.* That is also the word and category he attributed to the Indians themselves, who allegedly believed, before Ralegh's arrival, that "no nation of Christians durst" resist the Spaniards: *The Discoverie of the Large, Rich and Bewtiful Empyre of Guiana* (1596), N4, H2^{v}.

139. See *The Original Writings & Correspondence of the Two Richard Hakluyts,* ed. E. G. R. Taylor, 2 vols (Hakluyt Society, 1935). For examples of the word in works written or translated by other authors, included in collections edited by the younger Hakluyt, see chapters 4 and 5. But the word was not part of his own active vocabulary. He uses "Christians" where later writers would use "whites" (2:405, 421, 468, etc).

140. Richard Verstegan, *A Restitution of Decayed Intelligence: In antiquities. Concerning the most noble and renowmed English nation* ("printed at Antwerp . . 1605. And to be sold at London in Paules-Churchyard, by John Norton and John Bill"). *Restitution* was printed five times between 1605 and 1670. On Verstegan and the evolution of racism, see Samuel Kliger, *The Goths in England: A Study in Seventeenth and Eighteenth Century Thought* (Cambridge, MA: Harvard UP, 1952), 114, and Ivan Hannaford, *Race: The History of an Idea in the West* (Washington, DC: Woodrow Wilson Center Press, 1996), 180–84.

141. P. E. H. Hair, *Sierra Leone and the English in 1607: Extracts from the Unpublished Journals of the Keeling Voyage to the East Indies,* Occasional Paper No. 4 (Freetown: Institute of African Studies, University of Sierra Leone, 1981), 16 (British Library, India Office MS L/MAR/A/iv, by an unidentified Englishman, entry for August 8), 37 (British Library Cotton MS Titus B VIII, journal of Anthony Marlowe, entry for August 30), 31 (Marlowe, September 4).

142. François Pidou de Saint Olon, *Estat present de l'empire de Maroc* (Paris, 1694), tr. Peter Anthony Motteux, *The Present State of the Empire of Morocco* (1695): [The Moors of Tetuan] "are White-men, pretty well Civiliz'd" (12).

143. Antoine Charant, *A letter, in answer to divers curious questions concerning* . . . (1671), an anonymous translation of *Lettre escritte en response de diverses questions curieuses sur les parties de l'Affrique* (Paris, 1670): "After him raigned his Brother Muley Elwaly, who was a White, his Mother a Spanish Moor" (10). *OED* may have misunderstood this passage, which might indicate that Elwaly was "a White Moor," as his mother was "a Spanish" one. This is hardly an unambiguous example of a new meaning. In any case, it clearly refers to non-Europeans, and originates in French (not English) usage.

144. *OED white a.*4, citing the 1604 translation of Acosta. See the discussion of Acosta in chapter 4.

145. The dictionary cites the London minister Christopher Ness, whose *Compleat and Compendious Church-History* (1680) describes a plot by Satan to "corrupt the *White Line,* (the Posterity of *Seth,*) and to make them as Black as those of the *black Line,* the Cursed brood of

Cain" (27). Excerpted from its context, this sentence looks like a clear example of a racial use of the adjective *white.* However, in context the sentence turns out not to be racial at all. Ness's detailed discussion of the curse of Cain explicitly denies that the "brand" was a physical or epidermal mark, describing it instead as "*an Hornet in his* Conscience," which resulted in "(probably) a *Trembling*" of his "whole *Body*" (22–23). God's curse did not make Cain physically black. Moreover, the paragraph that immediately follows the sentence quoted by the *OED* specifies that "the fair *Faces* of the *Daughters of Men*" were "*Cain's* Brood," who seduced "*the sons of God, the off-spring of* Seth" (28). That is to say, the offspring of Cain had "fair" faces, not black ones; in copulating with Cain's daughters, the sons of Seth were guilty of "thinking a fair Face enough, though covering never so foul a Soul" (28). The material both before and after the passage quoted by *OED* makes it clear that "black" and "white" are, for Ness, moral evaluations (referring to souls), not racial epithets (referring to skin). Satan intends to "corrupt" men, not to increase their melanin count.

146. The dictionary took its examples of forms and meanings from innumerable slips of paper, "pouring in at the rate of 1000 a day": see K. M. Elisabeth Murray, *Caught in the Web of Words: James A. H. Murray and the Oxford English Dictionary* (New Haven, CT: Yale UP, 1977), 171–88. Since each slip contained an illustrative individual sentence, the compilers of lexicographical entries—often never having read the original source—did not have access to the relevant contexts, and therefore the only "con-text" helping them to define the word, beyond the quoted sentence, was their own worldview. Since each slip was handled by five readers in Oxford before being included as an example of a particular meaning (Murray, 186), mistakes like the misinterpretation of *white* in the 1680 example reflected a worldview widely shared by English and American readers at the time. (For the dedication to Queen Victoria, see Murray, 289.)
147. R. A. Waldron, *Sense and Sense Development,* rev. ed (Andre Deutsch, 1979), 114.
148. Susie I. Tucker, *Enthusiasm: A Study in Semantic Change* (Cambridge: Cambridge UP, 1972), 4 ("here is the obvious difficulty, since what was once technical is now general, and, which is worse, is often a compliment instead of a disapproving label or signal").
149. Waldron, *Sense Development,* 154–55. Waldren cites (222) Brent Berlin and Paul Kay, *Basic Color Terms: Their Universality and Evolution* (Berkeley: University of California Press, 1969, rpt. 1991); Brent and Kay used data from almost 100 languages (152–6).
150. *OED white adj.*1.a, 2.a, 2.b. For a more recent and sophisticated analysis of the word's earliest meanings, see Seija Kerttula, *English colour terms: etymology, chronology, and relative basicness,* Mémoires de la Société Néophilologique de Helsinki, vol. 60 (Helsinki: Société Néophilologique, 2002). Kerttula concludes that Old English *hwit* was originally a term for luminosity (brightness) rather than for hue (what we would call whiteness).
151. Thomas Heywood, *The Fair Maid of the West,* ed. Robert K. Turner, Regents Renaissance Drama (Lincoln: University of Nebraska Press, 1968), *Part Two,* 2.6.66 ("white"); 2.6.76, 104, etc. ("black").
152. Brome, *The English Moore; or The Mock-Marriage* (1659), 61, 65–66 (4.4). In the same scene England is described as "the fairest Nation Man yet ever saw" (66), and in the context "fairest" clearly means "with the lightest complexion." Although the play was not printed until 1659, it was first performed in 1637.
153. Bishop Joseph Hall, "Upon the sight of a Blackamoor" (no. 38), *Occasional Meditations* (1630), 94: "That which is beauty to one is deformity to another; we should be looked upon in this man's country with no less wonder and strange coyness than he is here; our whiteness would pass there for an unpleasing indigestion of forme. . . . It is not for us to regard the skin, but the soul." This phrasing implies that, in southern England by 1630, "our whiteness" was the opposite of "unpleasing"—indeed, so automatically pleasing that his readers need to be reminded of the relativity of such aesthetic judgements.
154. "Mercurius Britannicus" [=Joseph Hall], *Mundus Alter et Idem* (1605?), allegedly first published in "Frankfurt," but printed by the London stationer Humphrey Lownes for the

London bookseller John Porter, 1605 or early 1606. The bibliographical history of this work is complicated: I quote from the Folger Library copy, p. 147 (sig. K2), and translate the Latin myself (because no existing translation is literal).

155. John Healey, tr., *The Discovery of a New World; or, A Description of the South Indies, Hetherto Vnknowne* (1609), p. 162 (M1^{v}). Healey's is a very "free" translation/adaptation, throughout. John Millar Wands's allegedly more literal translation, in *Another World and Yet the Same: Bishop Joseph Hall's "Mundus Alter et Idem"* (New Haven, CT: Yale UP, 1981)—"He enjoys Ethiopians in place of thrush, and Englishmen, in truth, in place of quail" (85)—also supplies a noun in the place of Hall's pronoun, but the disagreement between Healey and Wands demonstrates the ambiguity of the original.
156. Philip Vincent (b. 1600), *A True Relation of the late battell fought in New England, between the English, and the Salvages* (1637), 16. Vincent had earlier visited Guiana and Germany.
157. Lewes Roberts (1596–1640), *The Merchants Mappe of Commerce* (1638), 87.
158. John R. Elliot Jr., "*Mr Moore's Revels:* A Lost Oxford Masque," *Renaissance Quarterly* 37 (1984): 411–20. Elliot published the manuscript text of the masque for the first time. The relevant lines (81–86), addressed to the audience, are:

    The joyfull moore hath chang'd his native hew
    And pensive sable being made ffayre by you
    H'as left his mourning weeds chusing to bee
    Invested with your glorious livery;
    Since hees your candidate after this night
    Since y'have smild of's blackenesse heele be white

    Although *white* here is an adjective referring explicitly to a single individual ("he," the "joyful Moor"), that color has just been described as "your" (the audience's) "livery"; *livery* literally refers to clothing, but was elsewhere used of skin, and "native hue" or skin color is the subject here. Moreover, as Kim F. Hall demonstrates, the entire masque is preoccupied with what we would now call racial identity: see "'Troubling Doubles': Apes, Africans, and Blackface in *Mr. Moore's Revels,*" in *Race, Ethnicity, and Power in the Renaissance,* ed. Joyce Green MacDonald (Madison, NJ: Fairleigh Dickinson UP, 1997): 120–44. Although the passage requires a rather more complicated exposition than Heywood's "white men," in context *white* here undoubtedly refers to the collective skin color of an English (and primarily male) audience.
159. Thomas Morton, *New English Canaan* (Amsterdam, 1637), 32. Morton claims that Indians were, at birth, "of complexion white as our nation"—thus describing the English as a "white . . . nation" in the same breath that whiteness was also attributed to the native inhabitants (Stage 3).
160. Speed, *A Prospect of the Most Famous Parts of the World. Together with that large Theatre of Great Brittaines Empire* (1627), 6. The *Prospect* was subsequently reprinted, separately, in 1631, 1646, 1662, 1665, 1668, and 1676.
161. Franciscus Junius, *The Painting of the Ancients, in three Bookes . . . Written first in Latine . . . And now by Him Englished, with some Additions and Alterations* (1638), 270: "*Philostratus* cometh neerer, and openeth the nature and power of Lineall picture somewhat further; Lineaments consisting in light and shadow without any colour, sayth he [*De vità Apollonii,* lib. II, cap. 10], deserve the name of Picture: . . . although these lines, being put together after a most simple manner, doe not represent any mixture of bloud, nor expresse the flower of bright haire, and of a newly up-growing beard, yet doe they resemble the similitude of a tanie or a white man: yea if wee doe designe any one of the Indians in white lines, he shall for all that seeme to be blacke: seeing his flat nose, his standing haire, his plumpe cheekes, and a certaine kinde of dulnesse about his eyes maketh all black and sheweth him

to be an Indian to every one that doth view him not foolishly." Junius was the Earl of Arundel's librarian and resident philologist; his Latin *De pictura veterum* was published the previous year. He is here citing (and translating) a passage from the *Life of Apollonius of Tyana* by Flavius Philostratus (217 C.E.), ed. F. C. Conybeare, 2 vols. (Heinemann, 1912), where the key phrase of the original Greek was τῷ τε ξανθῷ ἀ νθρώπῳ ἔοικε καὶ τῷ λευκῷ (1:178, Book II, chapter xxii), more literally translatable as "of both tawny men and of white." In other words, the Greek clearly refers to collective attributes, making it clear that "a white man" has the modern generic sense. However, the Greek does not juxtapose the noun for *man* with the adjective for *white,* but instead connects the noun with the adjective equivalent to *tawny.* The Greek text therefore conforms to the typical Mediterranean pattern, which regards brown or tawny skin as normal, and then proceeds to discuss the extremes of white and black. The 1638 English translation instead regards "a white man" as normative. We see here the beginning of a process by which modern color categories are retrospectively and anachronistically given an ancient pedigree.

162. See Franciscus Junius, *The Literature of Classical Art,* ed. Keith Aldrich, Philipp Fehl, and Raina Fehl, 2 vols. (Berkeley: University of California Press, 1991), 1:xxvi-xlix, for the biography of Junius (born in 1591).
163. On Mytens (1590–1648) see Graham Parry, *The Golden Age Restor'd: The Culture of the Stuart Court, 1603–42* (Manchester: Manchester UP, 1981), 114–16, 224–25; Peter Erickson, "Representations of Race in Renaissance Art," *Upstart Crow* 28 (1998): 2–9; and Arthur Wheelock, "The Queen, the Dwarf and the Court: van Dyck and the Ideals of English Monarchy," in *Van Dyck 1599–1999: Conjectures and Refutations* (Turnhout: Brepols, 2001), 151–66. Arundel, who patronized Junius, also patronized Mytens, having brought him to England in 1618.

Chapter 3

1. Brown, *American Fugitive in Europe,* 222, 223, 226, 227.
2. For the role of the Atlantic in early modern racism, see Taylor, *Time, Space, Race.*
3. See Penelope Eckert, "The Whole Woman: Sex and Gender Differences in Variation," *Language Variation and Change,* 1 (1989): 245–67; William Labov, "The Intersection of Sex and Social Class in the Course of Linguistic Change," *Language Variation and Change* 2 (1990): 205–54; James Milroy and Lesley Milroy, "Mechanisms of Change in Urban Dialects: The Role of Class, Social Network and Gender," *International Journal of Applied Linguistics* 3 (1993): 57–77; Jack K. Chambers, *Sociolinguistic Theory* (Oxford: Blackwell, 1995), 102–45; Gerald J. Docherty et al., "Descriptive Adequacy in Phonology: A Variationist Perspective," *Journal of Linguistics* 33 (1997): 275–310; Janet Holmes, "Setting New Standards: Sound Changes and Gender in New Zealand English," *English World-Wide* 18 (1997): 107–42; Lesley Milroy, "Women as Innovators and Norm-creators: The Sociolinguistics of Dialect Leveling in a Northern English City," in *Engendering Communication: Proceedings from the Fifth Berkeley Women and Language Conference,* ed. Suzanne Wertheim et al. (Berkeley: BWLG, 1999), 361–76.
4. For this and other examples of female innovation in early modern English see Terttu Nevalainen, "Gender Differences in the Evolution of Standard English: Evidence from the *Corpus of Early English Correspondence,*" *Journal of English Linguistics* 28 (2000): 38–59, and Helena Raumoulin-Brunberg and Arja Nurmi, "Dummies on the Move: Prop-*One* and Affirmative *Do* in the 17th Century," in *To Explain the Present: Studies in the Changing English Language in Honour of Matti Rissanen,* ed. Terttu Nevalainen and Leena Kahlas-Taarka (Helsinki: Société Néophilologique, 1997), 395–417.
5. I quote and discuss Barlow and Lane—whose narratives are printed in Hakluyt's *Principall Navigations* (1589)—in chapter 5. Their texts refer to events in 1584 and 1585, and

if they were written at that time the gap between male and female first occurrences would be even greater.

6. Margaret Cavendish, Duchess of Newcastle, *Observations upon Experimental Philosophy* (1666): Cavendish there rejects the theory of whiteness formulated in Robert Boyle's *History of Colors* (1664), because if it were correct "a black Moor would have larger Pores then a man of a white complexion" (52). On the same page she refers to "a fair white Lady." This whole section ("18. Of the blackness of a Charcoal, and of Light") attempts to refute Boyle (whose work I discuss at length in chapter 10). But unlike Boyle, Cavendish attributes whiteness only to individuals, one of whom is female and upper class; "a man of a white complexion" is not necessarily "a white man" in the modern sense. No such ambiguities bedevil Behn's usage (discussed in chapter 11). In identifying the first female uses of modern racial *white* I have relied on the texts in Brown University's Women Writers database (in addition to my usual databases and my own reading).
7. Labov, *Principles,* 306–07.
8. Taylor, *Time, Space, Race.*
9. Douglass, *Life,* in *African American Slave Narratives,* 160. See also, at the beginning of the same episode, the forecast "You have seen how a man was made a slave; you shall see how a slave was made a man" (156), and the later conclusion "a contented slave . . . ceases to be a man" (177).
10. David Gwyn, "Richard Eden Cosmographer and Alchemist," *Sixteenth Century Journal* 15 (1984): 13–34.
11. *A treatyse of the newe India, with other new founde landes and Ilandes, aswell eastwarde as westwarde, as they are knowen and found in these oure dayes, after the description of Sebastian Munster in his boke of Vniversall Cosmographie . . . Translated out of Latin into Englishe. By Rycharde Eden* (1553), sig. D8[v]. Munster's *Cosmographia: beschreibung aller lander* (Basel, 1544) had been expanded and translated into Latin in 1550; Eden was here translating (as his first page announces) "*Libr. v. De terris Asiae Maioris.*"
12. Ludovico Varthema, *Itinerario dallo Egypto alla India* (Rome, 1510), ed. Enrico Musacchio (Bologna: Fusconi, 1991), VI:viii (*homini bianchi*). There were 40 editions in the sixteenth century, including Eden's own 1576 translation, "The Navigation and vyages of Lewes Vertomannus," posthumously published in *The History of Travayle in the West and East Indies,* ed. Richard Willes (1577): "This kyng useth not to geve his wyfe to the priestes to be defloured, as doth the kyng of *Calecut,* but committeth this facte to whyte men, as to the Christians or Mahumetans, for he wyll not suffer the Idolaters to do this. The inhabitantes lykewyse have not to do carnally with theyre wyves, before some whyte man, of what so ever nation, have fyrst the breakyng of them" (fol. 399a). This paragraph constitutes the whole of chapter eight, entitled "Of the maner which the kyng of Tarnassarie useth, when he permitteth his wyfe to be defloured of white men."
13. The word *Portugal(s)* appears 36 times in Eden's translation, always referring to events after 1498; this passage is sandwiched between two references to "the Portugals, whiche in this our daies sayle into the Eastpartes" and "how the Portugales subdued Malaccha."
14. Eden, ed., *The Decades of the Newe Worlde* (1555), fol. 239[v]: Eden uses the obsolete form "Portugales" (which I have modernized to "Portuguese"). I have not traced his source ("Of this Ilande with the other landes and Ilandes lyinge betwene Portugale and the same, a certeyne pylotte of Portugale hath wrytten a goodly vyage to Conte Rimondo"). Throughout I cite Eden from the 1555 original, but the text is also accessible in the reasonably accurate (racist) reprint in *The First Three English books on America,* ed. Edward Arber (1895), 270.
15. For another early example, explicitly attributed to a Portuguese speaker, see *An Elizabethan in 1582: The Diary of Richard Madox, Fellow of All Souls,* ed. Elizabeth Story Donno (Hakluyt Society, 1976): "the oldest of [the Portuguese living in the area] whose

name is Lewis and who has lived here twenty years . . . reported to us that these Æthiopian people are loyal and compassionate and they ardently love white men if they suffer no injury from them" (September 12, 1582). Since the Portuguese were more reticent than the Spaniards about putting information into print, much of the Portuguese influence on other Europeans was probably, as here, individual and spoken, and therefore usually invisible to modern historians.

16. "White moors" is first recorded by *OED* (*Moor n.*[2]1) in Andrew Boorde's *The Fyrst Boke of the Introduction of Knowledge* (1542), ed. F. J. Furnivall, Early English Text Society, extra series, no. 10 (1870), 212 (chapter xxxvi: in Barbary "ther be whyte mores and black moors"). Floyd-Wilson (*English Ethnicity,* 191) identified an even earlier example in John Major's *A History of Greater Britain* (1521), tr. and ed. Archibald Constable (Edinburgh, 1892), 90. For the same distinction, see *Decades,* fo. 242[v]: "chose rather to make warre ageinst the Moores of Granada, then to bye and sell with the blacke Moores of Guinea" (in Eden's translation of Gómara). Bartholemy notes that, in John Pory's English translation of Leo Africanus, "Moor" is a mistranslation of the original "Affricani," and that Pory also changed the original Italian "bianchi" to "tawnie" or "brown or tawnie" (*Black Face,* 12–16). For at least one Englishman, by 1600 "white" did not seem a word appropriate to Moors or Africans. By 1642 "white moors" was being used to describe Italians (*OED white a.*11e); the transference across the Mediterranean clearly indicates that the Italians are generically "white" (if atheistic and immoral).

17. See Gernot Rotter, *Die Stellung des Negers in der islamisch-arabischen Gesellschaft bis zum XVI. Jahrhundert* (Dissertation at Bonn University, 1966); Davis, *Progress,* 40–45; William McKee Evans, "From the Land of Canaan to the Land of Guinea: The Strange Odyssey of the 'Sons of Ham,'" *American Historical Review* 85 (1980): 15–43 (esp. 25–33). For "white man" and "whites" in particular, John Hunwick gives Islamic examples from the eighth and ninth centuries in "Arab Views of Black Africans and Slavery" ("Collective Degradation"). An accessible medieval source is Ibn Battuta's *Travels in Asia and Africa, 1325–1354,* tr. and selected by H. A. R. Gibb (Routledge, 1929), 317–37. (I do not read Arabic and am therefore dependent on translations for Islamic texts.) For Islamic influence on the anti-African interpretation of the curse of Ham, see chapter 9. Hakluyt's *Principal Voyages,* volume 2 (1599) contains "A description of the yeerely voyage or pilgrimage of the Mahumitans, Turkes and Moores vnto Mecca in Arabia" which includes the statement that "The attendants vpon these sepulchres are fifty eunuches white and tawny, neither is it granted to any of them to enter within the tombe, sauing to three white eunuches the oldest and best of credit" (211). Hakluyt's source seems to have been a Venetian Relazione (British Library, Royal MS 14.A.xv, ff. 41–87): see *The Hakluyt Handbook,* ed. D. B. Quinn, 2 vols. (Hakluyt Society, 1974), 2:419. But the category of "white eunuchs" (as opposed to black or tawny ones) originated in Islamic culture: see the article on k͟hāsī ("castrated man, eunuch") by Ch. Pellat in *The Encyclopedia of Islam: New Edition,* vol. IV (1978), 1087–93.

18. One of those zones was Sicily, and by the thirteenth century "Sicilian officials qualified the general designation for 'Moor' or 'Saracen' with the Latin terms for 'white,' 'sallow' and 'black'": see Davis, *Progress,* 55. These are Islamic distinctions applied to Muslims by Europeans and therefore do not constitute evidence that Europeans generally—or even Sicilians in particular, or their Norman then Catalan masters—were yet thinking of themselves as "white." But they do show the beginning of a process that would lead to a change of European identity.

19. James H. Sweet, "The Iberian Roots of American Racist Thought," *William and Mary Quarterly* 3:54 (1997): 143–66. Although the English texts I am discussing originated in Spain, Spanish contacts with sub-Saharan Africa postdated those of Portugal. On Portugal and early racism, see C. R. Boxer, *Race Relations in the Portuguese Colonial Empire*

1415–1825 (Oxford: Clarendon, 1963). But Portugal's influence on English colorphobia is more difficult to trace, because it depended on personal contacts rather than printed books. (See the discussion of Frobischer in chapter 4 and of Portuguese linguistic influence in African contact zones in chapter 5.)

20. George M. Fredrickson, in *Racism: A Short History* (Princeton, NJ: Princeton UP, 2002), sees the first signs of a "racial order" in "fourteenth- and early-fifteenth-century Iberia" (28–40), as does Barbara Fuchs, "A Mirror Across the Water: Mimetic Racism, Hybridity, and Cultural Survival," in *Writing Race across the Atlantic: Medieval to Modern,* ed. Philip R. Beidler and Gary Taylor (New York: Palgrave, 2005).
21. John Algeo, "Spanish loanwords in English by 1900," *Spanish Loanwords in the English Language: A Tendency towards Hegemony Reversal,* ed. Félix Rodríguez González (New York: Mouton de Gruyer, 1996), 18–22.
22. For this larger process see Anthony Pagden, *Spanish Imperialism and the Political Imagination* (New Haven, CT: Yale UP, 1990), and *Lords of All the World: Ideologies of Empire in Spain, Britain and France* (New Haven, CT: Yale UP, 1995); Barbara Fuchs, *Mimesis and Empire: The New World, Islam, and European Identities* (Cambridge: Cambridge UP, 2001); Taylor, *Time, Space, Race.*
23. Martyr, *De rebus oceanis et Orbe Novo Decades tres* (Alcalá, 1516). The First Decade, which includes the relevant passages, had been published in 1511, as part of *P. Martyris Angi mediolanensis opera. legatio Babylonica, Oceani Decas, Poemata, Epigrammatae;* pirated Italian editions of material from the First Decade had appeared in 1504 and 1507. For a bibliography of the early editions see F. A. MacNutt, tr., *De Orbe Novo,* 2 vols. (New York: Putnam, 1912), I, 49. I quote the 1516 edition because the 1555 English translation derives from it.
24. Richard Eden, ed., *The Decades of the Newe Worlde* (1555), First Decade, Book 6, fol. 29^{v}.
25. Martyr, *Decades* (1516), sig. c1^{v}: "aethiopes enim nigri.crispi.latini.non aunt capillati. hi vero albi capillis oblongis:protentis:flavis." Eden may have found Martyr's idiom confusing, because his English does not make it clear that "of yellow color" refers to the islanders' hair, not their skin: he might appear to be saying that their skin is both white and yellow.
26. Of the many modern accounts of the depopulation of the New World following European contact, see William H. McNeill, *Plagues and Peoples* (Garden City, NY: Anchor/Doubleday, 1976), Alfred W. Crosby's *Ecological Imperialism: The Biological Expansion of Europe, 900–1900* (Cambridge: Cambridge UP, 1986), and Matthew Restall, *Seven Myths of the Spanish Conquest* (New York: Oxford UP, 2003), 128, 140–42.
27. For a defense and illustration of the value of photo quotation and an argument that modernized editions radically misrepresent the linguistic thinking of early modern culture, see almost any essay by Randall McLeod (sometimes printed under pseudonyms like "Random Cloud"). Unfortunately, McLeod's scattered work has not been collected in a single volume, but for representative essays see: "Spellbound," in *Play-Texts in Old Spelling,* ed. G. B. Shand and Raymond C. Shady (New York: AMS, 1984), 81–96; "Information on Information," *TEXT* 5 (1991): 241–81; "Where Angels Fear to Read," in *Ma(r)king the Text: The Presentation of Meaning on the Literary Page* (Aldershot: Ashgate, 2000), 144–92.
28. For a recent analysis of the differences, see N. F. Blake, *A Grammar of Shakespeare's Language* (New York: Palgrave, 2002).
29. *False amici* is the Italian term for what in English are called "false cognates."
30. See *OED heaven n.*1.
31. As Mary B. Campbell notes in her splendid reading of Columbus in *The Witness and the Other World: Exotic European Travel Writing, 400–1600* (Ithaca, NY: Cornell UP, 1988), "It is only since the conquest of geographical science over legend that we have come to perceive a category distinction between such places as Ophir and Haiti" (178).
32. Martyr, *Decades,* Decade I, book 2, ed. Arber, 72. Martyr had more than one informant, as he indicates in this very chapter, distinguishing between what "the Admirall himself told me" and what "they all affirm."

33. *Select Documents Illustrating the Four Voyages of Columbus,* ed. Cecil Jane, 2 vols. (Hakluyt Society, 1933), 2:14–15. The original is lost; this edition, like others, derives from a transcript by Las Casas.
34. *Select Documents,* 2:20–21.
35. *Select Documents,* 2:23 (my translation). Jane translates "The color of these people is whiter than that of any other race that has been seen in the Indies" (2:22), but "race" is the translator's interpolation (not surprising in 1933); in *Select Letters of Christopher Columbus,* ed. R. H. Major (Hakluyt Society, 1870), the same Spanish text is translated "These people are of a whiter skin than any I have seen in the Indies" (128), but "skin" is the translator's interpolation. Both translators render "esta gente" as "these people," but the Spanish is singular, not plural; Columbus is not referring to multiple individuals, but generalizing about a people, a population.
36. Martyr, *Decades,* ed. Eden, fol. 31; ed. Arber, 89.
37. *The Diario of Christopher Columbus's First Voyage to America 1492–1493,* transcribed and tr. by Oliver Dunn and James E. Kelley Jr. (Norman: University of Oklahoma Press, 1989), 66–67. The *Diario* survives only in the abstracts and extracts from the original made in the 1530s by Fray Bartolomé de las Casas. But las Casas goes out of his way to specify that he was here reproducing the original exactly: "What follows are the very words of the Admiral in his book about his first voyage to, and discovery of, these Indies"; immediately after this claim, the next sentence begins "I" (*yo*)—meaning Columbus—where previously las Casas had used third-person singular forms ("the Admiral," "he") when referring to Columbus (64–65).
38. *Select Documents,* 2:28.
39. Martyr, *Decades,* f. 32.
40. *Select Documents,* 2:30–34.
41. Martyr, *Decades,* f. 32.
42. E. G. R. Taylor, "Columbus and the World-Map," *Select Documents,* 2:lxxxiii.
43. Ferdinand Columbus, *The Life of the Admiral Christopher Columbus by His Son Ferdinand,* ed. and tr. Benjamin Keen (New Brunswick, NJ: Rutgers UP, 1959).
44. Kirkpatrick Sale, *The Conquest of Paradise: Christopher Columbus and the Columbian Legacy* (New York: Knopf, 1990), 175.
45. Taylor—otherwise so scathing about the claims Columbus made on the third voyage—confirms his observation of magnetic declination: "After passing mid-Atlantic the declination was west of north, a phenomenon which had never been observed before Columbus's first voyage, and which well deserved emphasis" ("Columbus and the World-Map," *Select Documents,* 2:lxxxiii).
46. *The Times Atlas of the World: Tenth Comprehensive Edition* (New York: Times Books, 1999), 26.
47. *Select Documents,* 2:32, 30.
48. Martyr, *Decades,* f.29.
49. *Times Atlas of the World,* 32. More technical analysis can be found in works such as *Oceanography from Space* (Washington, DC: National Aeronautics and Space Administration, 1986), or Sandipa Singh and Kathryn A. Kelly, *Monthly Maps of Sea Surface Height in the North Atlantic and Zonal Indices for the Gulf Stream Using TOPEX/Poeseidon Altimeter Data* (Woods Hole, MA.: Woods Hole Oceanographic Institution, 1997).
50. For the "demographic disaster" in Trinidad that was the result of initial contact, see Linda A. Newson, *Aboriginal and Spanish Colonial Trinidad: A Study in Culture Contact* (New York: Academic Press, 1976), 30 (a report of 1612 that "of the 40,000 Indians that there were in Trinidad and the neighboring mainland only 4000 remained"), 76–103. On human and other extinctions in the Caribbean after 1492, see Richard L. Cunningham, "The Biological Impacts of 1492," in *The Indigenous People of the Caribbean,* ed. Samuel M. Wilson (Gainesville: University Press of Florida, 1997), 29–35. Cunningham notes

that the disappearance of the Taino Indians from the Bahamas—within two decades—was "probably the New World's first vertebrate extinction caused by contact with the Old World" (31).

51. Jablonski and Chaplin, in "The Evolution of Human Skin Coloration," confirm the ultraviolet radiation hypothesis, but underestimate the differences in skin color between Africans and South American/Caribbean peoples, precisely because there are almost no reliable samples from the western hemisphere representing skin color uncontaminated by the intervening five centuries of transatlantic contact. They pay no attention to the mass extinctions in America or to the interbreeding of Amerindians and Africans. On the latter, see for instance *Indigenous People,* ed. Wilson, 204–05.

52. Among the many recent studies of prehistoric human migration, see Clive Gamble, *Timewalkers: The Prehistory of Global Colonization* (Stroud: Alan Sutton, 1993), 201–38; Luigi Luca Cavalli-Sforza and Francesco Cavalli-Sforza, *The Great Human Diasporas: The History of Diversity and Evolution,* tr. Sarah Thorne (Cambridge, MA: Perseus, 1995); Jared Diamond, *Guns, Germs, and Steel: The Fates of Human Societies* (New York: Norton, 1997); Stephen Oppenheimer, *Out of Eden: The Peopling of the World* (Constable, 2003). The details of human evolution, migration, and genetic drift continue to be debated, of course, but the basic picture is not in doubt.

53. In 2003 "modern human" fossils apparently between 154,000 and 160,000 years old were found in Ethiopia: see Ann Gibbons, "Oldest Members of *Homo sapiens* Discovered in Africa," *Nature* 300 (13 June 2003): 1641. This agrees with Oppehheimer's figure—based on mitochondrial DNA—of the origin of modern humans in Africa "over 150,000 years ago."

54. Samuel Wilson, "Introduction to the Study of the Indigenous People of the Caribbean," in *Indigenous People,* ed. Wilson, 7; Adrian de Santo Tomas (1630s), reported in Juan Requejo Salcedo, *Relación histórica y geográfica de la Provincia de Panamá (año 1640),* in *Colección de libros y documentos referente á la historia de América,* vol. 8, ed. Manuel Serrano y Sanz (Madrid: V. Suárez, 1908), 130 (my translation); Lionel Wafer, *A New Voyage and Description of the Isthmus of America* (1699), ed. L. E. Elliott Joyce (Hakluyt Society, 1934), 80–82.

55. Richard Oglesby Marsh, *White Indians of Darien* (New York: Putnam, 1934), 198, 202. For other twentieth-century discussions, see Reginald G. Harris, "The San Blas Indians," *American Journal of Physical Anthropology* 9 (1926), 17–63; D. B. Stout, "Further Notes on Albinism among the San Blas Cuna, Panama," *American Journal of Physical Anthropology,* n.s. 4 (1946): 483–90, and Michael T. Taussig, *Mimesis and Alterity: A Particular History of the Senses* (New York: Routledge, 1993), 139–75. Harris, a eugenicist, accompanied the second Smithsonian expedition (1925); confirming Marsh's belief that the trait was genetically recessive and that "they are clearly Indians, not hybrids," Harris concluded that "The White Indians obviously express a form of albinism which has been termed imperfect or partial albinism by Geoffroy Saint Hilaire, Pearson and others. These terms signify that either the skin, hair, or eyes, any two or all three may fail to express the full albinotic condition, but that one or more are, partially at least, relatively free from pigment" (42–57). Since "partial albinos" may exhibit none of the three symptoms of albinism, and since "relatively free" permits the complete range of subjective judgements, Marsh was justified in retorting that "all of the whites races" could be described as "partial albinos" (214). "All the scientists" were agreed that "the white Indians were *not* ordinary albinos" (217), since they had "yellow hair, blue or hazel eyes, and were normally healthy, both mentally and physically" (214). Moreover, the incidence of such pale complexions among the San Blas Cuna "greatly exceed[ed] the usual expectation of albinism among human groups" (Stout, 485), and would have been even greater were it not for the "aboriginal practice of albino infanticide" (486, 489). For the emergent scientific category

of albinism, see Jordan, *White Over Black,* 249–52, 521–25. In *White Identities: Historical and International Perspectives* (Prentice Hall, 2000), Alistair Bonnett gives another twentieth-century example: a 1997 tourist's guide to Peru recommends an excursion to a remote community it calls "the village of the whites," which contains an "incongruous" native population that "could easily have just stepped off the five o'clock flight from Stockholm" (27). Bonnett does not mention that this surviving population of white Amerindians in Peru confirms the claim by sixteenth-century observers that they were "white" indigenous people there.

56. Given their yellow hair, it is unlikely that the fair-skinned people that Columbus saw in 1498 were descendants of Chinese navigators: see the claims made by Gavin Menzies in *1421: The Year the Chinese Discovered America* (New York: Bantam, 2003).
57. Campbell, *Witness and the Other World,* 225; Greenblatt, *Marvelous Possessions,* 14, 20.
58. Pigafetta, "A briefe declaration of the vyage or navigation made abowte the worlde," *Decades,* fol. 231a. The source for this information about China was "a Moore that was in the Ilande of *Timor*" (further evidence of "white" ethnic distinctions originating in Islamic cultures).
59. Munster, *Newe India,* tr. Eden, sig. f2^{v}.
60. For Munster's heavy dependence on Boemus see Margaret T. Hodgen, "Sebastian Muenster (1489–1552): A Sixteenth Century Ethnographer," *Osiris* 2 (1954): 504–29. See Book II, chapter 8 of *Omnium gentium mores,* tr. Watreman: "This people ware an offspring of ye Scithians" (*Fardle of factions,* sig. M4), and "Thei are all of colour shining white" (sig. M4^{v}). Likewise Aston's 1611 translation: "The people be of the Scythians race. . . . they be naturally white and pale of complexion" (*Manners,* 104).
61. *A briefe collection and compendious extract of the strau[n]ge and memorable things, gathered oute of the cosmographye of Sebastian Munster* (1572), 95.
62. See "Reportes from the province of China," tr. Richard Willes, in *History of Travayle* (1577), fol. 294a (sig. 2K1). Willes was translating Pereira's *Novi avisi delle Indie di Portogallo . . . Quarte parte* (Venice, 1565), 63–87, which I have not seen. Because Pereira also reported that "the rivers are frosen in the Winter for colde, and many of them so vehemently, that carts may passe ouer them," the whiteness of the Tartar inhabitants was not a challenge to the classical climatic theory.
63. "Certaine notes gathered by Richard Iohnson . . . ," in *Principall Voyages,* ed. Hakluyt (1589), 388; *Principal Voyages,* I (1598), 336.
64. Robert Coverte, *A True and Almost Incredible report of an Englishman . . . with a Discovery of a Great Emperour called the Great Mogoll, a Prince not till now knowne to our English Nation* (1612), 39. Earlier Coverte described the offshore capture, in southeastern Africa, of three boats full of "Moors" and of eight men the English thought were Portuguese, because they were "pale and white, much differing from the colour of the *Moores.*" However, these "white Roagues" turned out to be tattooed like the Moors, and in every other respect indistinguishable from them (16–17). Clearly, pale skin did not successfully differentiate Europeans from other populations, or good men from bad, and the episode leaves their ethnic identity undetermined.
65. Shakespeare, *History of King Lear,* 1.109. On Scythians more generally, see F. G. Butler, "The Barbarous Scythian in *King Lear,*" *English Studies in Africa* 29 (1985): 73–79, and Floyd-Wilson, *English Ethnicity,* 23–52, 89–110.
66. Arabic geography was much more knowledgeable than its classical or Christian counterpart, but it did not include the Americas and was still limited by an east-west axis not far north or south of the Mediterranean basin: see André Miguel, *La géographie humaine du monde musulman jusqu'au milieu du 11^{0} siècle,* vol. 2 (Paris: Mouton, 1975), 3–11, 58, 90–126.
67. Campbell, *Witness,* 173.

68. Claudius Ptolemeius, *Tetrabiblos*, ed. and tr. F. E. Robbins (Cambridge, MA: Harvard UP, 1940), Bk. II, chap. 2.
69. *The Complete Works of Aristotle: The Revised Oxford Translation*, ed. Jonathan Barnes, vol. 2 (Princeton, NJ: Princeton UP, 1984), 1415 (14.14), 1527 (38.8).
70. On the contrast among ancient Egyptian, Hebrew, and Greek terms for alien populations, see Benjamin Braude, "Black Skin/White Skin in Ancient Greece and the Near East," in *Micrologus: Nature, Sciences and Medieval Societies* (in press). I am grateful to Professor Braude for showing me this article in advance of its publication. Although Braude's reading of the linguistic evidence in ancient languages makes clear the Greek origin of color prejudice, his polar contrast between black and "white" skin is based on a misreading of Greek janiform vases. This mistake originates in Braude's source for the Greek vases, Frank M. Snowden Jr.'s essay "Iconographical Evidence on the Black Populations in Greco-Roman Antiquity," in *The Image of the Black in Western Art*, vol. 1, *From the Pharoahs to the Fall of the Roman Empire*, ed. Jean Vercoutier et al. (Cambridge, MA: Harvard UP, 1991), 133–245. Although Snowden says that "early Greek artists were struck by the obvious differences between the physical characteristics of whites and Negroes and dramatized the contrast by placing them in juxtaposition" (146), the vases actually contrast black figures with red ones. This contrast can be clearly seen in the color plates (no. 174, p. 154; no. 193, p. 163). The appearance of a black/white polarity is created by the polarity of black-and-white photographs, not by the Greek vases themselves. See plate 2.
71. *The Historie of the World. Commonly called, The Natural Historie of C. Plinius Secundus*, tr. Philemon Holland, 2 vols (1601), 1:36–37 (sig. d6^{v}-E1): "the Æthiopians by reason of the Sunnes vicinitie, are scorched and tanned with the heat thereof, like to them that be adust and burnt. . . . Also, that in the contrarie clime of the world to it, in the frozen and icie regions, the people have white skins, haire growing long downward, & yellow. . . . But in the middest of the earth, there is an holesome mixture from both sides: the whole tract is fertile and fruitfull for all things, the habits of mens bodies of a mean and indifferent constitution. In the colour also there sheweth a great temperature."
72. For the evolution and transmission of this tradition see Clarence J. Glacken, *Traces on the Rhodian Shore: Nature and Culture in Western Thought from Ancient Times to the End of the Eighteenth Century* (Berkeley: University of California Press, 1967); he discusses *De natura locorum* on 268–70.
73. The first English translation of Vesalius—by Richard Eden—was not published until 1559; thus, Eden's first readers were still living in the pre-Vesalian world of Columbus and Martyr.
74. *OED complexion n.*1, 2 (both referring to the humoral theory and to the whole constitution, with examples ranging from 1340 to 1761), 3 ("disposition, temperament"). The English word's Latin source also has this medical meaning ("physical constitution"), derived from the root etymology "combination, connection." The first clear example of the modern meaning—"the natural colour, texture, and appearance of the skin"—dates from 1580 (*n.* 4).
75. See Campbell's account (*Witness*, 216) of Stamler (1508) and Lilius (1512), and Hodgen's account (*Early Anthropology*, 134–35) of Boemus (1520).
76. Oviedo, "The Hystorie of the weste Indies," tr. Eden, in *Decades*, fol. 206^{v}, sig. 3F2^{v}. Actually, Oviedo had written *blanquissimos*, literally "whitest." See chapter 9 of Oviedo's *De la natural hystoria de las Indias* (Toledo, 1526), fol. xix, sig. C3: "los ombres que en una parte son negros/en otras províncías son blãquissimos/& los unos & los otros son hõbres." It is possible that Eden worked from some later text or translation—or that, dealing with an idiom unfamiliar to him and his readers, he simply ignored the unnecessary complication of the superlative. In terms of the argument I will develop in chapter 4, it seems

to me likely that Oviedo's superlative was designed to situate Spaniards in the ideal middle of the complexion spectrum, between the "black" of Africa and the "hyperwhite" of northern Europe.

77. Eden, *Decades,* f. 310^{v}–311 (Arber 338).
78. Once again, Eden has accurately translated the key terms: *blanco* ("white"), *negro* ("black"), *contrarios colores* ("colors utterly contrary"): compare Gómara, *La istoria de las Indias y conquista de Mexico* (1552), fol. 117 (sig. F3), from the chapter "Del color de los Indios." See also the original Spanish of the crucial statement, later in the paragraph: "De suerte que assi como en Europa son comunmente blancos, y en Africa negros, assi tambien son leonados en neustras indias" (fol. 117^{v}, sig. F3^{v}).
79. As linguist R. A. Waldron notes, "Influence on meaning is sometimes discernible even when there is no similarity of form between the English and the foreign word"; he calls these "sense-loans," as distinct from "loanwords" (*Sense and Sense Development,* 126).

Chapter 4

1. Brown, *American Fugitive,* 110, 119–20, 164, 226.
2. Josephine Brown, *Biography of an American Bondman, by His Daughter* (Boston, 1856), in *Clotel,* 302–06.
3. Bourdieu, *Language and Symbolic Power,* tr. Gino Raymond and Matthew Adamson, ed. John B. Thompson (Cambridge, MA: Polity Press, 1991).
4. For a more extended discussion of the spatial foundations of colorphobia, see Taylor, *Time, Space, Race.*
5. See Floyd-Wilson, *English Ethnicity,* 2.
6. The Loeb edition of the *Problems,* tr. W. S. Hett (Cambridge, MA: Harvard UP, 1936), reads "fair" instead of "white" (p. 323). This translates the same word Ptolemy uses (νευκοί).
7. *A Greek-English Lexicon,* comp. Henry G. Liddell and Robert Scott, rev. ed. (Oxford: Clarendon Press, 1968), 1042.
8. For a general history of the influence of modern racial theories on classical scholarship, see Martin Bernal, *Black Athena: The Afroasiatic Roots of Classical Civilisation,* Vol. I, *The Fabrication of Ancient Greece 1785–1985* (Free Association Books, 1987). One can accept the force of Bernal's analysis of the roots of modern scholarship without accepting all Bernal's own (controversial) claims about ancient Greek culture.
9. Pliny, *Naturalis historia,* 2:80 ("et adversa plaga mundi candida atque glaciali cute esse gentes flavis promissis crinibus"); Vitruvius, 6.1.3 ("candidis coloribus").
10. Pliny, *Natural History,* tr. H. Rackham, 10 vols. (Heinemann, 1938), 1:321: "For it is beyond question that the Ethiopians are burnt by the heat . . . and that in the opposite region of the world the races have white frosty skins, with yellow hair that hangs straight." Vitruvius, *On Architecture,* ed. Frank Granger, 2 vols. (Heinemann, 1931), 2:12–13: "the races of the north . . . are characterized by tall stature, fair complexion, straight red hair, blue eyes."
11. *Oxford Latin Dictionary,* ed. P. G. W. Clare, rev. ed. (Oxford: Clarendon, 1996), 264–65.
12. Thompson, *Romans and Blacks,* 10–11 (*albus*), 65 ("*candidi Galli . . . Candidi Germani . . . candidi Saxones*"); *Oxford Latin Dictionary,* 93–94.
13. Heinrich Zollinger, "Biological Aspects of Color Naming," in *Beauty and the Brain: Biological Aspects of Aesthetics,* ed. Ingo Rentschler, Barbara Herzberger, and David Epstein (Basel: Birkhauser, 1988), 155–56.
14. Robert S. Miola, "'An alien people clutching their gods'?: Shakespeare's Ancient Religions," *Shakespeare Survey 34* (2001): 31–45.
15. Ptolemy, *Tetrabiblos,* 124–25.

16. For this principle of moderation in Greek civilization, see for instance Michel Foucault, *The History of Sexuality,* Vol. 2, *The Use of Pleasure,* tr. Robert Hurley (New York: Vintage, 1985), 44, 86.
17. Floyd-Wilson, *English Ethnicity,* 2.
18. Thompson notes that the "blue eyes, blond hair (in the male sex, at any rate), and pale whiteness regarded as typical of the central and northern Europeans" were, by ancient Roman writers, "perceived with some disfavor" (*Romans and Blacks,* 35).
19. David Goldenberg, "Early Jewish and Christian Views of Blacks" ("Collective Degradation"); Shaye J. D. Cohen, *The Beginnings of Jewishness* (Berkeley: University of California Press, 1999), 29–30; I. F. Fikhman, "The Physical Appearance of Egyptian Jews according to the Greek Papyri," *Scripta Classica Israelica* 18 (1999), 134.
20. Bernard Lewis, *Islam from the Prophet Muhammad to the Capture of Constantinople* (Oxford: Oxford UP, 1987), 2:209.
21. See Bernard Lewis, *Race and Color in Islam* (New York: Harper, 1970): Arabs generally consider themselves white or light red, by contrast with northern people who are "dead white, pale blue, and various shades of red" (9). Like other peoples, Arabs regard their own skin color as normative and therefore tend to denigrate the pallor of northerners. Ibn Botlan, an Arabic-speaking physician living in Baghdad in the eleventh century, in his *Introduction to the Art of Making Good Purchases of Slaves,* wrote that "The Armenian is the worst of the white, as the Negro is of the black": see Adam Mez, *The Renaissance of Islam,* tr. S. H. Bakhsh (Patna, India, 1967), 162.
22. On the date of composition of *De Natura Locorum* see Jean Paul Tilman, *An Appraisal of the Geographical Works of Albertus Magnus and His Contributions to Geographical Thought,* Michigan Geographical Publication 4 (Ann Arbor: University of Michigan Department of Geography, 1971): 176. Tilman's treatise incorporates her translation (the first in English), which I use for all quotations from the work; as she notes, there is no modern critical edition of the Latin original, although it survives in an authorial copy currently in Vienna.
23. Heinz Meyer, *Die Enzyklopädie des Bartholomäus Anglicus: Untersuchungen zur Überlieferungs- und Rezeptionsgeschichte von 'De Proprietatibus Rerum,'* Münstersche Mittelalter-Schriften 77 (Munich: Fink, 2000), 41–137 (255 extant Latin manuscripts). *De Natura Locorum* survives in 43 manuscripts, and Tilman notes the existence of editions printed in Vienna in 1514 and Strasburg in 1515 (22).
24. *De Natura Locorum,* tr. Tilman, 101–03 (II, 3).
25. *De Natura Locorum,* tr. Tilman, 101–03 (II, 3), 108 (II, 4).
26. *De Natura Locorum,* 138, 141 (III, 7).
27. *On the Properties of Things: John Trevisa's translation of Bartholomæus Anglicus De Proprietatibus Rerum,* ed. M. C. Seymour et al., 3 vols (Oxford: Clarendon, 1975–88), 3:1–11. Steven Batman's 1582 edition is treated, by some modern scholars, as if it were an original Elizabethan work.
28. *On the Properties of Things,* 1:134, 136 (IV.2), 156–57 (IV.9), 2:753 (XV.100), 823–24 (XV.173).
29. *The Problemes of Aristotle, with other Philosophers and Physitions,* tr. Anonymous (1597): "*Question. Why do some women love white men, and some blacke?" Answer.* There are two answers: some women have a weake sight, and such delight in blacke, bicause the white doth hurt the sight more than blacke. The second reason is, bicause like doth delight in the like: but bicause some women are of a hot nature, such are delighted with blacke, bicause blacknes doth follow heate. And some of them are of a cold nature, and those are delighted with white, bicause cold is the mother of whitenes" (sig. F5^{v}). Notice that "white men" here is not necessarily an ethnographic category, but simply means "particular men with very pale complexions" (stage 1), who may be distributed randomly; they

are not associated with Europe or any other locale. This paragraph does not appear in modern editions of Aristotle's *Problems.* It can be found in the collection of academic medical disputations *Omnes homines,* ed. E. R. Lind, *Problemata Varia Anatomica: MS 1165 The University of Bologna,* Humanistic Studies 38 (Lawrence: University of Kansas Press, 1968); see M. Schleissner, "Sexuality and Reproduction in the late medieval *Problemata Aristotelis,*" in *Licht der Natur. Medizin in Fachliteratur und Dichtung. Festschrift für Gundolf Keil zum 60. Geburtstag,* ed. Josef Domes et al. (Göppingen: Kümmerk, 1994), 383–98.

30. As late as the 730s, Bede could describe Britain as "placed right in manner under the North Pole" (*prope sub ipso septentrionali vertice mundi iacet*): see *Baedae Opera historica,* 1:14–15.
31. For an interesting example of the perplexity created by the mismatch between ancient Mediterranean perspectives and late medieval northern ones, see *De Proprietatibus Rerum* 15.66: "Gallia . . . hath þat name of oolde tyme of whittenes of men. For *Gallia* is grew and is to menynge 'melke.' þerefore Sibille calleth hem *Galles,* þat is 'white', and seith þanne in on ȝere mylky nekkes shal be iuynede. For by þe dyuersite of heuene, face and colour of men and hertes and witte and quantite of bodyes ben dyuers . . . but now Frenshe men woneþ in þis prouynce and of hem þe londe hath þe name and hat Francia" (2:763). This passage acknowledges the ancient Roman reaction to "the whiteness of men" north of the Alps, but it situates that whiteness among the Gauls in an "old time," clearly distinct from the "now" of Frenchmen, who are not described as white, either in this entry or in that for "Francia" (15:57), to which it provides a cross-reference ("Loke tofore *in litera f de . . . Francia*").
32. *De Proprietatibus Rerum,* XV, 104 (2:785).
33. *De Proprietatibus Rerum,* XV, 17 (2:733–34).
34. Venerable Bede, *The History of the Church of Englande,* tr. Thomas Stapleton (Antwerp, 1565), Book II, chapter 1, p. 48 (M4[v]).
35. Matthew 28:2–3 ("the angel of the Lord . . . his raiment white as snow"), Mark 16:5 ("clothed in a long white garment"), Luke 20:12 ("two angels in white"), all three passages referring to the angel(s) at the sepulcher; Acts 1:10 ("in white apparel"); Revelation 15:6 ("the seven angels . . . clothed in pure and white linen"). Here and elsewhere I cite the King James translation, unless otherwise noted. *White* is not used of angels in the Old Testament, whose God ("the Ancient of days") is not white himself, but simply wears a "garment . . . white as snow" (Daniel 7:9).
36. *Baedae Opera Historica,* 2.1 (1:200).
37. For Bede's association in the sixteenth and seventeenth centuries with Catholic and Jesuit theological positions, see Colin Kidd, *British Identities before Nationalism: Ethnicity and Nationhood in the Atlantic World 1600–1800* (Cambridge: Cambridge UP, 1999), 110–11.
38. Foxe, *Actes and Monuments* (1563), instead reproduces the letter of commission from Gregory to Augustinus (16, sig. D2[v]), as part of his polemical account of "The first originall of the ii. metropolitane churches of Canterbury and York."
39. Holinshed, "History of England," in *Chronicles* (1577), 146 (K1[v]).
40. William Camden, *Remains Concerning Britain* (1605), ed. R. D. Dunn (Toronto: University of Toronto Press, 1984), 16.
41. Camden, *Britain,* tr. Holland (1610), 136. Camden also quotes (131) "a Poet of the middle time," who "sung not untunably in this manner:—*Saxonia protulit Anglos,/ Hoc patet in lingua, niveoque, colore.*—/That Englishmen from Saxons draw descent,/ Their colour white and tongue make evident." The marginal note opposite "white" changes it to "Faire."
42. Verstegan, *Restitution,* 140 (S2[v]).

43. Harrison, *Description,* in Holinshed, *Chronicles,* Vol. I, fol. 38v–39; chap. 14 in the 1577 edition, chap. 20 in 1587.
44. Elyot's *Castel of Helth* (1539) had listed climate and particularly temperature among the "outwarde causes" of "colour": hence "cold or heate" accounted for the fact that "as englysshe menne be whyte, Moriens be blacke" (B3). Elyot's book continued to be reprinted until 1610, but it is misleading to describe it as "a popular household text" (Floyd-Wilson, *English Ethnicity,* 195). Few English households could afford a book of more than 24 sheets. But Floyd-Wilson is right to emphasize that, within the humoral theory Elyot was rehearsing, whiteness was not valorized, but taken as symptomatic of a physiological and therefore psychological imbalance (stage 2).
45. Harrison had been anticipated to some degree by Ranulph Higden, whose fourteenth-century *Polychronicon* (printed in 1482 and often thereafter) contrasted "men in Europe" with "men of Affrike," claiming that "men beenge in the northe partes" are "more grete in body, more myghty in strenghte, moore bolde in herte, more feire in beaute" and also "more whyte." See *Polychronicon,* tr. John Trevisa, vol. I (1865), 51–53. As Floyd-Wilson notes, Higden chauvinistically locates "the British within the broader category" of Europeans; but he retains the classical emphasis on physical strength and courage, not civil or intellectual achievement. Moreover, like his classical sources, he does not identify all European men as white, but simply as "more white" than Africans.
46. *Travails in Guinea: Robert Baker's 'Brefe Dyscourse' (?1568),* ed. P. E. H. Hair (Liverpool: Liverpool UP, 1990), lines 265–540. On the basis of a Stationers' Register entry, Hair believes this text was separately published in a lost edition of 1568, but many books were entered without being printed, and he acknowledges that any such edition may have contained more material than Hakluyt printed in 1589 (19).
47. Huarte, *The Examination of Mens Wits,* tr. Richard Carew (1594), 116 (sig. I2v). Carew's translation was reprinted in 1596 and 1604. For Huarte in relation to climate theory, see Waldemar Zacharasiewicz, *Die Klimatheorie in der Englischen Literatur und Literaturkritik* (Stuttgart: Wilhelm Braumüller, 1977), 57–76. This particular passage was cited by Floyd-Wilson (*English Ethnicity,* 119).
48. Floyd-Wilson, *English Ethnicity,* 5 (and throughout).
49. Floyd-Wilson denies that "Renaissance writers' skepticism toward climatic explanations of blackness can be attributed to the rise of Baconian empiricism" (*English Ethnicity,* 5), arguing instead that "the racial stereotypes that facilitated the Atlantic slave trade were incompatible with geohumoral tenets" (6). Paradoxically, she claims, the collapse of geohumoralism was antiscientific and anti-empirical: "England's nascent expansionist ideology helped to disrupt the accepted paradigms of scientific knowledge" (6); for example, "as the Atlantic slave trade gained momentum, Europeans began to deny Africa its place in classical history, and they accomplished this in part by establishing a fixed boundary between North and West Africa" (6). The "fixed boundary" is the Sahara, and it was not established by Europeans. European intellectuals separated Egypt from West Africa when they discovered (after circumventing the Sahara) that the early modern societies of West Africa had almost nothing in common with ancient Egypt. Floyd-Wilson is right to deny "the rise of Baconian empiricism" as an explanation: Bacon, the theorist of empiricism and empire, offered a geohumoral explanation of African physical difference (79). With Bacon, a challenge to geohumoralism could easily be linked to imperial ambitions, but in fact no such link materializes, and she does not establish any such biographical link in other cases, simply asserting that writers were "motivated" by "nascent" colonizing desires that she assumes saturated the entire society throughout the sixteenth and early seventeenth century. The challenge to geohumoralism began before Bacon. This chronological point is important, because by invoking Bacon Floyd-Wilson can plausibly put England at the center of these intellectual developments. But neither the slave trade nor the cri-

tique of geohumoralism began in England. Floyd-Wilson claims that a 1554 voyage to Guinea represents "one of the earliest records of England's involvement in the Atlantic slave trade" (7); it is in fact the first, involving only a handful of Africans, and the English report of the voyage rehearses (rather than challenges) geohumoral explanations of difference. In interpreting an English text of 1578, Floyd-Wilson claims that "blackness was reinvented as a sign of inferiority to justify a growing slave economy" (10), claiming that the sixteenth century was "the first century of England's involvement in the Atlantic slave trade" (11). But England played almost no part in that trade before the 1630s. Europeans began shipping enslaved non-Europeans in 1402 from the Canary Islands and in 1441 from the West African coast; in 1492 Columbus immediately compared the Caribbean Islanders to the Canary islanders, captured some, and shipped them involuntarily back to Europe; in 1495 he sent almost 600 enslaved Caribbeans to Spain. The discovery of whiteness, and the challenge to geohumoralism, did not begin until 1498. Between 1402 and 1498 none of the Europeans involved in the Atlantic slave trade seems to have felt that it was incompatible with geohumoralism. (See Taylor, *Time, Space, Race.*) Ironically, Floyd-Wilson's critique of English racism is itself Anglocentric.

50. Lesley B. Cormack, *Charting an Empire: Geography at the English Universities, 1580–1620* (Chicago: University of Chicago Press 1997), 140.
51. *History of Travayle in the West and East Indies, and other countries lying either way* (1577), ed. Richard Willes, 4–4[v].
52. Best, *A True Discourse of the late voyages of discoverie, for the finding of a passage to Cathaya, by the Northwest, under the conduct of Martin Frobisher General* (1578), 61 (sig. N3), 29–30 (sig. F3[r-v]). The contemporary portraits of the Inuit captives brought back to England confirm Best's characterization of their skin: see *Meta Incognita: A Discourse of Discovery: Martin Frobisher's Arctic Expeditions, 1576–1578,* ed. Thomas Symons, 2 vols. (Hull, Quebec: Canadian Museum of Civilization, 1999), plates 10–13.
53. Best, *True Discourse,* 28 (sig. f2[v]).
54. In fact, Best implicitly characterizes as white everyone who is not African: "*Sem, Cham,* or *Japhet,* as the onely sonnes of *Noe,* who all three being white, and their wives also, by course of nature, should have begottten and brought forth white children" (*True Discourse,* 30, sig. f3[v]). This passage is reprinted in Hakluyt (1600), 3:52 (sig. E2[v]); it belongs to Best's ascription of African blackness to the curse of Cham. (For which, see chapter 9.) Since everyone else comes from white parents, all other peoples should be white. This of course contradicts Best's own experience with the nonwhite Inuit, as he acknowledges in his professed inability to account for the skin color of the inhabitants of "Meta Incognita."
55. See the essays by James McDermott and Richard I. Ruggles in *Meta Incognita,* 1:55–114, 179–256.
56. James McDermott, "Michael Lok, Mercer and Merchant Adventurer," in *Meta Incognita,* 1:119–46, and *Martin Frobischer: Elizabethan Privateer* (New Haven, CT: Yale UP, 2001), 103–19.
57. *Congo,* tr. Hartwell, 18 (C3[v]), marginal note. The head title of Book I, chapter 3 is "*Whether the children which are begotten by Portugalles, being of a white skinne, and borne in those Countries by the women of Congo, bee blacke or white, or Tawney like a wild olive, whom the Portugals call* Mulati."
58. *Congo,* tr. Hartwell, 19 (C3[v]-C4). In this passage and in the headnote Hartwell accurately translates the key color terms (*bianchi, neri*) of the Italian original, Pigafetta's *Relatione del Reame di Congo et delle Circonvicine contrade* (Rome, 1591), 8–9 (A4[v]-B1). In this respect Hartwell's translation is more accurate than that published in 1881 as *A Report of the Kingdom of Congo,* tr. Margarite Hutchinson (New York: Negro UP, 1969), which renders *bianchi* as "fair" (16–17).
59. *Congo,* tr. Hartwell, sig. *3[v].

60. Ortelius, *His epitome of the Theatre of the Worlde* (undated), sig. A3^{v}, opposite map of Africa (map 4). As evidence "against the general opinion: which seemes of reason to yelde that the whitenesse or blacknesse of the people proceedeth from the nearenesse of the Sonne," Ortelius notes that "near to the cape of good hope the people are very blacke, and yet neere the straight of Magillan theyre are most white: yet are they both almost of equale distance from th'equinoctiale to the southwarde. Therefore we esteeme the sonne doeth not make the people blacke: for both in Spaine and Italie where their are white, theyr are also whithin 30. & 40. degrees of theequinoctiall northwarde, as those of the cape of good hope are southwarde. But let us leave this questione unto them which searche the secrets of nature." This edition translates the abridgment printed in Antwerp in 1595; it is presumably no earlier than 1596, and no later than the *STC's* "1601?"
61. Ortelius, *Theatrum Orbis Terrarum* (Antwerp, 1570). The text to map 4 gives a fuller version of the objections summarized in the *Epitome,* noting for instance that the inhabitants of the straight of Magellan are "candidissimi." Antwerp was part of the Spanish Netherlands, so in an important sense this is another "Spanish" source.
62. Linschoten, *Discours of Voyages into ye Easte & West Indies,* tr. William Phillip (1598), 211.
63. Hakluyt, ed., *Principal Navigations,* 3 vols (1598–1600), 3:48. In Hakluyt's reprint, Best's 1578 description of various equatorial peoples as "white" became "tauney and white": see Alden T. Vaughan and Virginia Mason Vaughan, "Before *Othello:* Elizabethan Representations of Sub-Saharan Africans," *William and Mary Quarterly* 3:54 (1997): 26.
64. Benjamin Braude, "The Sons of Noah and the Construction of Ethnic and Geographical Identities in the Medieval and Early Modern Periods," *William and Mary Quarterly* 54 (1997): 135.
65. John Pory, "A particular description of all the knowne borders, coastes and inlands of Africa, which John Leo hath left undescribed: collected out of sundry ancient and late writers," in Leo Africanus, *The History and Description of Africa,* tr. Pory (1600), ed. Robert Brown, 3 vols. (Hakluyt Society, 1896), 1:68: "which very thing may be a sufficient argument, that the sunne is not the sole or chiefe cause of their blacknes; for in divers other countries where the heate thereof is farre more scorching and intolerable, there are tawnie, browne, yellowish, ash-coloured, and white people; so that the cause thereof seemeth rather to be of an hereditarie qualitie transfused from the parents, then the intemperature of an hot climate, though it also may be some furtherance thereunto." Without elaborating the argument in this way, Pory's introductory material elsewhere refers to "white" people in Africa: "the Africans or Moores, properly so called; which last are of two kinds, namely white or tawnie Moores, and Negroes or blacke Moores" (1:20), "of a colour inclining to white . . . The women are white" (1:55), "of colour whitish" (1:57). He also reiterates the point about people of different color on either side of the river Senegal: "the people on this side are of a dead ash-colour, leane, and of a small stature; but on the farther side they are exceeding blacke, of tall and manly stature, and very well proportioned" (1:18).
66. "*But hereunto if the* authors *reasons here alleaged do not sufficiently answere, I do refer them, that will not yeeld therein, to the excellent treatise of* Josephus a-Costa, *printed this last year . . . in which* Theological *and* Philosophicall *worke, he doth at large both by good reasons and also by his own experience prove this his position to be true. And therefore I protest unto you, it was one of the chiefe* Motives, *which moved me to translate this* Report, *to the end it might be more publikely knowen*" (*Congo,* tr. Hartwell, sig. *3).
67. Anthony Grafton et al., *New Worlds, Ancient Texts: The Power of Tradition and the Shock of Discovery* (Cambridge, MA: Harvard, 1992), 207; Anthony Pagden, *The Fall of Natural Man: The American Indian and the Origins of Comparative Ethnology* (Cambridge: Cambridge UP, 1982), 149, 153. Pagden's chapter on Acosta (146–200) is the most thorough and sophisticated account in English.

68. In discussing attacks on ancient climate theory in the sixteenth century Floyd-Wilson distinguishes between "the old knowledge and the newer ideological impulses" (*English Ethnicity,* 47). But the old climate theories could also be attributed to "ideological impulses" (of Mediterranean prejudice), and they were based on very limited "knowledge" of planetary geography and of human corporeal and cultural variety. We might just as easily say that early modern theorists were attempting to process an enormous amount of new data, and that their "newer *knowledge"* simply could not be reconciled with the "old *ideological impulses."*
69. José De Acosta's *Naturall and Morall Historie of the East and West Indies,* tr. Grimestone, book II, chapter ix (sig. H3^{v}), chapter xi (sig. H5^{v}); it accurately translates *Historia Natural y Moral de las Indias* (Seville, 1590), sig. G7^{v}-G8 (negra . . . negra . . . blanca). This passage of Grimestone's translation is *OED*'s first citation of the sense "applied to those of ethnic types (usually European or of European extraction) characterized by light complexion" (*OED white, a.*4). Eden's translation of Gómara antedates this passage by almost 50 years; Trevisa, by more than two centuries. *OED* does not distinguish between neutral uses of *white* as a collective demographic adjective (as in Trevisa and Acosta, which I would identify as stage 2 and stage 3) and the specifically ethnocentric European sense (which I would identify as stages 4 and 5). If *OED* includes Acosta, it should also include Trevisa and Eden. But it seems to me that these are quite distinct uses of the word, which *OED* confuses (misdating them both).
70. Interestingly, Acosta located white-skinned peoples on the north coast of South America, close to the "white" Trinidadians found by Columbus.
71. Linschoten, *Voyages into ÿ Easte & West Indies,* 14 (Book I, chapter 6), 28 (chap. 16), 29 (chap. 17).
72. In 1582 Richard Hakluyt published a collection in which Indians in what is now Virginia were described as "more white than those we found before," while "some" of the New England Narragansetts "encline more to whitnes"; in a book translated into English in 1587 Antonio de Espejo noted that in what is now New Mexico "the women are whiter skinned than the Mexican women"; in 1594 Thomas Blundeville reiterated—against the evidence of Columbus, Hakluyt, Acosta, and others—that the Indians in the tropics were "brown bay like a Chestnut, and the higher they dwell to either of the Poles Arctique or Antarctique, the whiter most commonly they be" (all cited by Vaughan, *Roots,* 8–9). These accounts all report shades of whiteness in the original inhabitants of North America, mirroring the diverse shades of whiteness Gómara had noted among Europeans. However, other accounts attributed darker skins to those native populations; notably, in none of these passages are the natives absolutely white, but only relatively "whiter" than others.
73. Mornay, *A Woorke Concerning the Trewnesse of the Christian Religion,* tr. Sidney and Golding (1587), chap. 2, p. 21 (sig. B3).
74. Mornay, *De la verité de la religion Chrestienne* (Antwerp, 1581), 30 (sig. B7^{v}).
75. Mornay, *Christian Religion,* 22 (sig. B3^{v}).
76. George T. Buckley, "The Indebtedness of *Nosce Teipsum* to Mornay's *Truenesse of the Christian Religion,*" *Modern Philology* 25 (1927): 67–78; James L. Saunderson, *Sir John Davies* (Boston: Twayne, 1975), 120–23.
77. Davies, *Nosce Teipsum* (1599), in *The Poems of Sir John Davies,* ed. Robert Krueger (Oxford: Clarendon, 1975), lines 925–32. Krueger's commentary notes, but does not analyze, the parallel with the translation of Mornay (343); he does not cite the French text.
78. Hans Pawlisch has shown that Sir John Davies' "juridical stance on Gaelic property right laid the basis for an imperial formula that was fundamental in the creation of the British empire": see *Sir John Davies and the Conquest of Ireland: A Study in Legal Imperialism* (Cambridge: Cambridge UP, 1985), 14.
79. "The Colonies," lines 575–76, in *The Divine Weeks and Works of Guillaume de Saluste Sieur du Bartas, translated by Josuah Sylvester,* ed. Susan Snyder, 2 vols. (Oxford:

Clarendon, 1979), 1:458. Sylvester was apparently translating "The Colonies" in 1603 (2:836); it was first published in 1605 in *Bartas his Devine Weekes and Workes* (1:34).

80. "Les Colonies," lines 551–52, in *The Works of Guillaume De Salluste Sieur Du Bartas,* ed. U. T. Holmes Jr. et al., 3 vols (Chapel Hill: University of North Carolina Press, 1940), 3:164.

81. Snyder, 2:835, identifies the source as Bodin's *Methodus ad Facilem Historiarum Cognitionem* (Paris, 1566), translated by Beatrice Reynolds as *Method for the Easy Comprehension of History* (New York: Columbia UP, 1945). Throughout my discussion of Bodin I have checked the translation against the Latin original, but I cite the Latin only when there is a significant difference. On the relation between Du Bartus and Bodin see also Frank Lestringant, "Du Bartas entre Du Plessis-Mornay et Jean Bodin: a propos des <<Colonies>>," *Du Bartas 1590–1990,* ed. James Dauphiné (Mont-de-Marsan: Editions InterUniversitaires, 1992):306–07. Lestringant points out that the passage in chapter V of *Methode* (1566) is virtually identical to that in Book Five, chapter 1, of *Six Livres de la Republique* (Paris, 1576). On Bodin and the evolution of racism, see Hannaford, *Race,* 155–58.

82. Bodin, *The Six Bookes of a Commonweale,* tr. Richard Knolles (1606), sig. 3C2 (Book V, chap. 1), translating *Republique:* "l'un a le poil blond, & la peau blanche, l'autre a le poil, & la peau noire" (sig. Z1, p. 541). The English translator changes Bodin's "blanche" to "faire"—clear enough evidence that "white" still seemed, in 1606, an odd or inaccurate characterization of Englishmen to themselves. For the English translation's dependence on the French text alone in this chapter—rather than using both the French and the revised Latin texts, as in the preceding four books—see Kenneth D. McRae's facsimile edition (Cambridge, MA: Harvard UP, 1962), 48–49.

83. Camden, *Britannia,* tr. Holland, 115 ("Scandia, called in times past Scythia").

84. See for instance the table of latitudes—without modern symbols for degrees and minutes—in Peter Heylyn's *Microcosmos or a little description of the great world* (Oxford, 1621), 281 (London "51 30," Paris "48," "Louvaine" "51," in contrast to Moscow "61," Stockholm "60 30")

85. In his notes to *Six Bookes,* McRae calls attention to material added in the revised Latin version (Paris, 1586), but absent from the French version (Paris, 1576), and therefore absent from the English translation of Book Five. Bodin's visit to England took place between publication of the French and Latin versions; he recognized that the greater mildness of its climate resulted from the fact that it is an island (McRae, A140). Jovius, in his *Descriptiones* (1578), had observed that England "exceeds many regions of France and Italy for mildness of temperature and as it were benignity of climate" (13), and William Camden claimed, in 1586, that Britain had the world's most temperate climate, neither too hot nor too cold (*Britannia,* tr. Holland, 2)—an effect we can now attribute to the Gulf Stream. If a cold climate produces white skin, then it would logically follow that the French should be "whiter" than the English (an implication Bodin does not acknowledge).

86. Bodin, *Six Bookes,* sig. 3A4; *Method,* 88; *Six Bookes,* sig. 3B6, 3C2, 3A4^{v}; *Method,* 97 (*Methodus,* sig. p1); *Method,* 89.

87. Best's (unpaginated) map, included in *True Discourses* (1578), is reproduced in *Meta Incognita,* I, 213.

88. Norton's plagiarism was first noticed by Katherine Koller in "Two Elizabethan Expressions of the Idea of Mutability," *Studies in Philology* 35 (1938): 228–37, and developed in *John Norden's Vicissitudo Rerum: A Critical Edition,* ed. Harry Gordon Rusche (Ph.D. dissertation, University of Rochester, 1962).

89. Louis Leroy, *De La Vicissitude ou Variété des Choses en L'Univers* (Paris, 1575), fol. 6^{v}, sig. b2^{v}; Leroy, *Of the Interchangeable Course, or Variety of Things in the Whole World,* tr. Robert Ashley (1594), sig. C1^{v}; John Norden, *Vicissitudo Rerum, an Elegiacall Poeme of the interchangeable Courses and Varietie of Things in this World* (1600), stanzas 113–14 (sig. E2).

90. Leroy, *Vicissitude,* fol. 9, sig. C1; Ashley, *Variety,* sig. C4; Norden, *Vicissitudo,* stanzas 129–30 (sig. E4). Norden, driven by the need to fill out his stanza and rhyme, adds that "some" people in the equatorial region are "*tawnie,* some are *dunne,*" thus reflecting the greater geographical knowledge of a professional mapmaker.
91. Camden, *Remains,* 5.
92. Charron, *Of Wisdom,* Book I, chapter 42 (p. 164, sig. M2[v]), translating *De La Sagesse,* Book I, chapter 38 (p. 214, sig. O3[v]): "Septentrionaux sont . . . Au corps . . . blancs & blonds," "Meridionaux sont . . . noirs."
93. Walkington, *Optick Glasse,* ff. 13, 15, 16. He also, when speaking of the inhabitants of "the septentrionall climate," explains that "many authors doe report of them, and wee see by experience in travaile" (f. 15); clearly, he is not speaking of his own countrymen, but of peoples they have read about in books, or heard about from travelers.
94. Morton, *New English Canaan* (Amsterdam, 1637), 11, 15–16 (chapter 1): "this goulden meane, to be scituated about the middle of those two extreames, and for directions you may proove it thus: Counting the space betweene the Line [equator] and either of the Poles, in true proportion, you shall finde it to be 90. Degrees: then must we finde the meane, to be neare unto the Center of 90, and that is about 45. Degrees . . ." New England "doth participate of heate and cold indifferently, but is oppressed with neither: and therefore may be truly sayd to be within the compasse of that golden meane, most apt and fit for habitation and generation . . . and is therefore most fitt for the generation and habitation of our English nation, of all other," because, although New England is a little farther south, it does not "exceede [old England] in heate or cold, by reason of the cituation of it" (15–16). A marginal note emphasizes "*New England is placed in the golden meane*" (15).
95. "Under the tropics they are unusually black; under the pole, for the opposite reason, they are tawny in color. After that, down to the sixtieth parallel, they become ruddy; thence to the forty-fifth they are white; after that to the thirtieth they become yellow" (*Method,* 89). This scheme—which contradicts other statements by Bodin himself, relegating whiteness to more northerly regions—puts England and most of France in the "white" category. Although Floyd-Wilson quotes this passage (*English Ethnicity,* 39), she does not acknowledge that it contradicts her claim that Bodin put "the French" in "the temperate zone," while locating Britain and whiteness "in the north" (36). Bodin's self-contradictory texts cannot be made to yield a single coherent theory of whiteness.
96. Bodin, *Method,* 97, 96; *Six Bookes,* 3B5. As Floyd-Wilson notes in her doctoral dissertation (but not her book), it is *within* this temperate zone, "from the thirtieth parallel to the sixtieth," that the English "are generally referred to as Northern" ("Temperature, Temperance, and Racial Difference," 185, n. 4).
97. Verstegan, *Restitution,* sig. †4.
98. "Airs, Waters, Places," para. 24, in *The Medical Works of Hippocrates,* tr. J. Chadwick and W. N. Mann (Oxford: Blackwell, 1950), reprinted in *Hippocratic Writings,* ed. G. E. R. Lloyd (Harmondsworth: Penguin, 1983), 168.
99. Glacken, *Rhodian Shore,* 82–88.
100. *De natura locorum,* tr. Tilman, 106 (II, 4); Glacken notes the resemblance (*Rhodian Shore,* 269), although not specifically in relation to the issue of skin color; he also more generally notes the influence of Hippocrates on medieval writers (256). On the originality of Albertus Magnus in this respect, see Tilman, 162.
101. Bodin, *Method,* 85.
102. See for instance Bodin, *Six Bookes,* 568, sig. 3C2[v]: "we see in climates that be alike and of the same elevation foure notable differences of people in color, without speaking for other qualities, for that the West Indians are generallie of a duskish color like unto a roasted quinze, unless it be a handfull of men that are black, whom the tempest carried from the coast of Affrike: and in Sivill of Spaine the men are white [*blancs*], at Cape

Bonne Esperance black [*noirs*], at the river of Plate of a chestnut color, all being in like latitude, and like climates, as we reade in the histories of the Indies which the Spaniards have left in writing" (*Republique,* 542, sig. Z1^{v}).

103. Bodin, *Six Books,* 567; *Republique,* sig. 3C2.
104. Bodin, *Six Books,* 572–73; *Republique,* sig. 3B5^{v}–3B6 ("les uns sont presque blancs, les austres du tout noirs").
105. Bodin, *Method,* 140; *Methodus,* 160–61 (sig. x4^{v}-y1).
106. Bodin, *Six Books,* 3B6; *Republique,* 539 (sig. y6). Bodin here refers to the work of Leo Africanus, originally written in Italian (1526), first published in Venice (1550), later translated into French (Antwerp, 1556) and Latin (Antwerp, 1556). See Africanus, *Description of Africa,* tr. Pory, 2:548 ("Their faces are white, and that perhaps for the coldnes of the mountain").
107. Glacken, *Rhodian Shore,* 434, 446.
108. On the consequences for Elizabethan literature of its belatedness, see especially Joel Fineman, *Shakespeare's Perjured Eye: The Invention of Poetic Subjectivity in the Sonnets* (Berkeley: University of California Press, 1986), and Alistair Fox, *The English Renaissance: Identity and Representation in Elizabethan England* (Oxford: Blackwell, 1997). Belatedness also underlies Helgerson's characterization of the Elizabethans as a people who "had to know themselves as the barbarous or inferior other, know themselves from the viewpoint of the more refined or more successful cultures of Greece, Rome, and contemporary Europe" (*Forms of Nationhood,* 243).
109. Selden, "Illustrations" to "The First Song" in Drayton's *Poly-Olbion* (1612), p. 17. He cites Ortellius.
110. *Purchas his Pilgrimage* (1613), Book vii, chapter x (p.587); *Hakluytus Posthumus, or Purchas his Pilgrimes,* ed. Samuel Purchas (1625), VII.iv.5 (980). For the second passage (which substantially repeats the first) there is also a marginal note ("Some white children borne among them"). The reports from Battel in both these sources are collected in *The Strange Adventures of Andrew Battell of Leigh, in Angola and the adjoining regions,* ed. E. G. Ravenstein (Hakluyt Society, 1901), 81, 48. Ravenstein's editorial paragraph headings, in both cases, anachronistically identify these white children as "albinos," but neither that word nor that concept was available to Battel or Purchas.
111. *Purchas his Pilgrimage* (1613), 545–46 (sig. 3b1–3b1^{v}). Braude calls attention to the textual variants in this passage, in its subsequent reprintings ("Sons of Noah," 135–37); "black" is the reading of the second edition, where the first edition has the nonsensical "other."
112. Burton, *The Anatomy of Melancholy,* vol. 2, ed. Nicolas K. Kiessling, Thomas C. Faulkner, and Rhonda L. Blair (Oxford: Clarendon, 1990), 41–42. This edition indicates, in its collations, the many variants between the different printings of Burton's expanding masterpiece.
113. On Burton's sources for these passages see *Anatomy of Melancholy,* vol. 5, *Commentary,* comp. J. B. Bamborough (Oxford: Clarendon, 2000), 123–26.
114. Floyd-Wilson characterizes this passage of Burton's *Anatomy* as "a jumbled survey of geohumoral tenets" and warns that "we should not assume that he is challenging older knowledge with empirical evidence" (*English Ethnicity,* 76). She does not distinguish between the different chronological layers of his text (attributing them all to "1621"), because she cites the 1977 reprint of the 1932 Everyman edition (ed. Holbrook Jackson), which prints a conflated text.

Chapter 5

1. J. Noel Heermance, *William Wells Brown and Clotelle: A Portrait of the Artist in the First Negro Novel* (n.p.: Archon Books, 1969), 49–50.
2. Brown, *American Fugitive,* 91.

3. See Thomas Jefferson's doubts about whether Phillis Wheatley and Ignatius Sancho actually wrote the works "published under [her, his] name," in *Notes on the State of Virginia,* ed. William Peden (Chapel Hill, NC: University of North Carolina Press, 1995), 140–41.
4. See for instance Nan Johnson, *Nineteenth-Century Rhetoric in North America* (Carbondale: Illinois UP, 1991), and Kenneth Cmiel, *Democratic Eloquence: The Fight over Popular Speech in Nineteenth-Century America* (New York: William Morrow, 1990).
5. Brown, *American Fugitive,* 217, 222, 209–16.
6. hooks, *Talking Back: Thinking Feminist, Talking Black* (Boston: South End Press, 1989), 12.
7. "Introduction," *Lift Every Voice: African American Oratory, 1787–1900,* ed. Philip S. Foner and Robert James Branham (Tuscaloosa: University of Alabama Press, 1998), 1–2.
8. Molefi Kete Asante, *The Afrocentric Idea* (Philadelphia: Temple UP, 1987), 17.
9. The book published in London in 1853 as *Clotel* includes, in addition to the novel, four illustrations and a third-person biography of Brown; the novel itself mixes literary English with slave dialect and interleaves fiction with a variety of documentary texts, including newspaper ads, statistics, quotations from the Bible, poems and speeches, and historical documents. The many clashing styles of Brown's novel are a large part of its appeal. For the heteroglossia of novels like Brown's, see M. M. Bakhtin, *The Dialogic Imagination: Four Essays,* ed. Michael Holquist, tr. Caryl Emerson and Michael Holquist (Austin: University of Texas Press, 1981), 259–422. I am not convinced by Ellis's claim that *Clotel* "never ventures far from confirming the accepted abolitionist 'facts,'" and is consequently a specimen of "authoritative (monologic) political abolitionism" ("Body Politics," 115). I find it disconcerting for a comfortable modern professor to dismiss the "facts" of American slavery by enclosing them in ironic quotation marks; abolitionism in 1853 was not "authoritative," but an opposition movement, and Brown himself a fugitive, in political exile; the abolitionist movement was not monologic, as recent historians of black abolitionists have demonstrated. Although abolitionist writing may have ceased to be subversive for modern readers (who can complacently condemn nineteenth-century slaveholders, without in any way having their own lives disturbed), it is a grotesque injustice to take for granted the emancipation that Wells and so many others dedicated their lives to securing.
10. *Lift Every Voice,* 213–17 (originally published in *The Liberator,* November 2, 1849).
11. For evidence that "red man" originated as a southeastern Amerindian idiom, see Nancy Shoemaker, "How Indians Got to Be Red," *American Historical Review* 102 (1997): 625–44.
12. *Discovery of River Gambra,* ed. Gamble and Hair, 246; *Navigazioni Atlantiche,* ed. Leporace, 77.
13. See Gary Taylor, "Hamlet in Africa 1607," in *Travel Knowledge: European "Discoveries" in the Early Modern Period,* ed. Ivo Kamps and Jyotsna G. Singh (New York: Palgrave, 2000), 223–48.
14. Manuel Álvares, *Ethiopia Minor and a Geographical Account of the Province of Sierra Leone* (MS, c.1615), trans. P. E. H. Hair (Liverpool: privately published, 1990), f. 56^v (chapter two, p. 8). Hair's "interim translation" has no through pagination; I therefore cite the foliation numbers from the Portuguese manuscript, combined with the page numbers of the translated chapter cited. (I have not seen the original manuscript.) See also Taylor, "Hamlet in Africa 1607," 247.
15. Brutt-Griffler, *World English: A Study of Its Development* (Buffalo: Multilingual Matters, 2002), 126–73.
16. Barber, *Early Modern English,* 222–26.
17. Ira Berlin, "From Creole to African: Atlantic Creoles and the Origins of African-American Society in Mainland North America," *William and Mary Quarterly* 53 (1996): 262.

18. Álvares, *Ethiopia Minor,* f. 78v (chapter 10, p. 8).
19. Jobson, *The Golden Trade: or, A discovery of the River Gambra, and the Golden Trade of the Aethiopians* (1623), sig. D1v, D2, E2v, K2v-K3, L1v, M3v-M4, N1, N3v, O1, O3v, P1, P3, Q4, X1. Since some of the marginal notes contain additional information not present in the text, I have assumed that Jobson was author of all the marginal notes.
20. *Hakluytus Posthumus; or, Purchas his Pilgrims,* ed. Samuel Purchas (1625), Book VII, cap. i ("a true Relation of master Richard Iobsons voyage . . . Extracted out of his large Iournall"), 921–24. The extracts describe two of the incidents where *Golden Trade* had used "white": "our thunder (so they called our Guns)" (923), "neither had they ever seen any white people before" (923). In the first of these, *Hakluytus Posthumus* prints "our" where *Golden Trade* had "the white man's"; this is reversed in the incident where *Hakluytus Posthumus* reports "ten white and four black" (923), but *Golden Trade* had a marginal note "We were 10 of our owne company, that went up in a shallop, and 4 Black that I hired to carry up a Canoe" (C2v). Purchas notoriously edited his texts, but was taking extracts directly from the journal Jobson kept on the voyage; *Golden Trade* is Jobson's own retrospective description of the country, based on his journals but significantly reorganizing and rewriting them. What is surely most significant is that either Jobson or Purchas or both regarded "the white man's" and "our" as synonymous.
21. British Library, Royal MS L8 A LVIII, 275, f. 2 (printed in *Discovery of River Gambra,* ed. Gamble and Hair, 199). Gamble and Hair suggest that Jobson may not have considered the Portuguese living in Africa (often of mixed Afro-Portuguese ancestry) "white" (143).
22. Jobson talks about the interpreter's "pretty English" on two separate occasions (M2, P2v). For evidence of another African native who spoke English in 1614 (in what is now Liberia), see Gamble and Hair, "Introduction," *Discovery of River Gambra,* 13.
23. *Hakluytus Posthumus,* 922, 924 ("More I might have known had not the emulations of my company hindered, who would not suffer the blacke boy to let me know what he spake"). See also Jobson, *Golden Trade,* N3 ("some other conference past betwixt us at this time, howbeit by reason of a disaster that fell in the way betwixt mee and my chiefe interpreter, I was hindred from understanding divers particulars, wherein Buckor Sano, seemed very desirous to give me full satisfaction").
24. See for example H3v ("I think, there is hardly any Englishman can say, he ever saw the Blacke-man kisse a woman"), M2 ("Thus we being ten Englishmen, and these foure Blackes, went . . .").
25. Ca' da Mosto, too, had normally differentiated Africans from "Christians" and had sometimes distinguished between the Portuguese and Venetians like himself; his three uses of "white men" (*homini bianchi*) had all been descriptions of African reactions to his appearance: "these remained for a while gazing upon a thing which neither they nor their fathers had ever seen before, that is ships and white men" (Crone, tr., *Cadamosto,* 58; Leporace, ed., *Navigazioni Atlantiche,* 81); "He was overcome with astonishment at the sight of us white men" (Crone, 67; Leporace, 97); "and gazed upon us in great astonishment, to see white men" (Crone, 76; Leporace, 113).
26. Marees, *Gold Kingdom,* tr. Dantzig and Jones: "before the Blanken or whites arrived here with their goods to trade, the Blacks of these Lands had little to use as clothes; so when the first people from Portugal arrived, they brought with them many goods for which there was a need; and then the Dutch . . ." (51). See Allison Blakely, *Blacks in the Dutch World: The Evolution of Racial Imagery in a Modern Society* (Bloomington: Indiana UP, 1993), 33: "Blanke became the most popular term for describing whites, as opposed to (the more Germanic) Witte."
27. "The voyage of Richard Rainolds and Thomas Dassel to the riuers of Senega and Gambra adioyning vpon Guinea, 1591," in *Principal Navigations,* ed. Hakluyt, II (1599), 2:190.

28. Nicholas Downton, "The firing and sinking of the stout and warrelike Carack called Las Cinque Llaguas," in *Principal Navigations,* ed. Hakluyt, II (1599), 2:200.
29. "The relation of the nauigation and discouery which Captaine Fernando Alarchon . . . ," *Principal Voyages,* ed. Hakluyt, III (1600): "Hee answered mee no, sauing that hee had sometime hearde of [= from] olde men, that very farre from that Countrey there were other white men, and with heardes like vs" (429), with a marginal note "Newes of bearded and white men." Later, another native "said likewise to the rest of the people . . . Now you see how long ago our ancesters told vs, that there were bearded & white people in the world, and we laughed them to scorne" (431), with a marginal note "Their ancesters told them that there were bearded and white men in the world." Hakluyt's is the first English translation of "Relatione Della Navigatione & scoperta die fece il Capitano Fernando Alarcone," in Ramusio's *Navigationi et Viaggi,* III (1556), ff. 363–70ᵛ.
30. *Principal Navigations,* ed. Hakluyt, II, 2:228—reprinting John Florio's translation, *A shorte and briefe narration of the two Nauigations and Discoueries to the Northweast partes called Newe Fraunce* (1580), 71; for a critical edition of the 1545 French original, see *Jacques Cartier Relations,* ed. Michel Bideaux (Montreal: University of Montreal Press, 1986).
31. Waldron, *Sense and Sense Development,* 126–27.
32. For the dominance of Portuguese as an intermediary language between English and Africans, see *Discovery of River Gambra,* ed. Gamble and Hair, 9–11, 34–35, 69–72.
33. *OED European n.*1 gives Massinger's *The City Madam* (1632) as its first example; *Nosce Teipsum* antedates that by more than three decades. It also antedates *OED*'s first example of the adjective (1603).
34. *African* dates from the ninth century and *Indian* from Trevisa's translation of *De Proprietatibus Rerum* in the late fourteenth century; both derive from classical languages. By contrast, Greeks and Romans knew nothing of the western hemisphere, which was named "America" in honor of the Italian Amerigo Vespucci; *American* is first used in English by George Best in 1578. For all these words see *OED.*
35. On the sense of collectivity created by Atlantic encounters, see Taylor, *Time, Space, Race.*
36. See for example Ligon, *A True & Exact History of the Island of Barbadoes,* 29 ("either by the Christian servants, or negroe slaves").
37. Ligon, *Barbadoes,* 50.
38. For the 1652 example, see the discussion of colonial legislation in chapter 8. It is of course entirely possible that some earlier use of *white* will be found in seventeenth-century records of Barbados. For the period 1627 to 1661 I have checked all the printed sources (including printed transcripts of manuscripts) listed in Jerome S. Handler, *A Guide to Source Materials for the Study of Barbados History, 1627–1834* (Carbondale, IL: Southern Illinois Press, 1973), and in Jerome S. Handler and Samuel J. Hough, "Addenda to *A Guide to Source Materials for the Study of Barbados History, 1627–1834,*" published in six parts in *JBMHS*: vol. 36 (1980–82): 172–77, 279–85, 385–97; vol. 37 (1983): 82–92, 296–307; vol. 38 (1987): 107–16. I have also checked all relevant manuscripts listed by these bibliographies in the British Library and those listed in Michael J. Chandler's *A Guide to Records in Barbados* (Oxford: Basil Blackwell, 1965).
39. For Virginia, see Morgan, *American Slavery,* 136; for London, see Wrightson, 128.
40. Mufwene, *Ecology,* 15–18.
41. See William Labov, "Objectivity and Commitment in Lingusitic Science: The Case of the Black English Trial in Ann Arbor," *Language in Society* 11 (1982): 165–201.
42. For the social status of early modern seamen, see Peter Linebaugh and Marcus Rediker, *The Many-Headed Hydra: Sailors, Slaves, Commoners, and the Hidden History of the Revolutionary Atlantic* (Boston: Beacon, 2000), and Taylor, *Time, Space, Race.*

43. For the African term *toubabes* (first recorded in 1637), see P. E. H. Hair, "An Ethnolinguistic Inventory of the Upper Guinea Coast before 1700," *African Language Review* 6 (1967): 37 (Wolof), 44–45 (Mandingo). Hair included Jobson among his sources, but did not record Jobson's translation of *tobabo condo* (published in 1623, based on conversations in early 1621) or of the Arabic/Wolof term *alcaid,* "tribal chief" (Hair, 34). However, Gamble and Hair annotate Jobson's *tobabo condo* with "*Mandika tubaboo* 'white man'; *kunda* 'village/town'" (*Discovery of River Gambra,* 128).
44. The Portuguese were undoubtedly contrasting "the blacks" with "white men" in their trade along the coast of west Africa as early as 1526: see P. E. H. Hair, "Sources on Early Sierra Leone (12): The Livro of the 'Santiago' 1526," *Africana Research Bulletin* 8 (1978): 37, 38 ("the blacks"), 41 ("white men"). This linguistic habit almost certainly dates from the fifteenth century. In 1444 the Portuguese chronicler Zurara contrasted African slaves who were "as black as Ethiops" with others who were "white enough" and others still who were "less white than mulattoes": see Gomes Eannes de Zurara, *Chronicle of the Discovery of Guinea,* tr. C. R. Beazley and Edgar Prestage, 2 vols. (Hakluyt Society, 1896–99), 1:82. Diogo Gomes, who sailed to the river Gambia in the 1450s and in the 1480s related his experiences there to a German visitor, also—if we trust the German's transcript into Latin—contrasted "blacks" with "whites": see *Discovery of River Gambra,* ed. Gamble and Hair, 260, 268. As already noted, Ca' da Mosto's use of "white men" in the account of his 1455 voyage probably represents the usage of black interpreters who spoke Portuguese.
45. See A. C. de C. M. Saunders, *A Social History of Black Slaves and Freedmen in Portugal 1441–1555* (Cambridge: Cambridge UP, 1982), and A. J. R. Russell-Wood, "Before Columbus: Portugal's African Prelude to the Middle Passage and Contribution to Discourse on Race and Slavery," in *Race, Discourse, and the Origin of the Americas: A New World View,* ed. Vera Lawrence Wyatt and Rex Nettleford (Washington, DC: Smithsonian Institution Press, 1995), 134–68.
46. Jobson, *Golden Trade,* D4^{v}, E3^{v}.
47. Jobson, *Golden Trade,* X1^{v} ("the familiar conversation, faire acceptance, and mutuall amitie, we finde the natives to embrace us withal"). Jobson's account is full of reported speech and reported conversation.
48. "Arthur Barlowe's Discourse of the First Voyages," in *The Roanoke Voyages, 1584–1590* ed. David Beers Quinn (Hakluyt Society, 1955), 102, 111–12. The use of "white" in this passage was noted—but not quoted, analyzed, or recognized as the first occurrence of a new racial idiom—by Vaughan, who observed that the idiom is "unusual in early English chronicles" (*Roots,* 15).
49. On the historical shift in citation practices, see Margreta de Grazia, "Sanctioning Voice: Quotation Marks, the Abolition of Torture, and the Fifth Amendment," in *The Construction of Authorship: Textual Appropriation in Law and Literature,* ed. Martha Woodmansee and Peter Jaszi (Durham, NC: Duke UP, 1994), 281–302.
50. "Ralph Lane's Discourse on the First Colony" (1585–86), also published by Hakluyt: *Roanoke Voyages,* 259–61.
51. Spanish voyages explored the coasts north of Florida in 1561, 1566, 1570, 1571, 1572, and 1573.
52. On Simon Fernandez, see David B. Quinn, "A Portuguese Pilot in the English Service," in *England and the Discovery of America, 1481–1620* (New York: Knopf, 1974), 242–63, and Donno, *An Elizabethan in 1582,* 147–8, 192.
53. *Roanoke Voyages,* 25, 79, 81, 189.
54. Malkiel, "Changes in the European Languages under a New Set of Sociolinguistic Circumstances," in *First Images of America: The Impact of the New World on the Old,* ed. Fredi Chiappelli, 2 vols (Berkeley: University of California Press, 1976), 2:583.
55. On the multinational and polylingual crews of fifteenth- and sixteenth-century Atlantic ships, see Roger C. Smith, *Vanguard of Empire: Ships of Exploration in the Age of Columbus*

(Oxford: Oxford UP, 1993), 135. In the seventeenth and eighteenth centuries, "English ships continued to be worked by African, Briton, Quashee, Irish, and American (not to mention Dutch, Portuguese, and Lascar) sailors" (Linebaugh and Rediker, *Many-Headed Hydra,* 151). On "the interchange of seamen between the different maritime countries" see also John Ehrman, *The Navy in the War of William III, 1689–1697* (Cambridge: Cambridge UP, 1953), 115, and *The Economic Writings of Sir William Petty,* ed. C. H. Hull (1899), 1:281: "Whereas the Employment of other Men is confined to their own Country, that of Seaman is free to the whole world" (from *Political Arithmetic,* 1690).

56. *The Standard Edition of the Complete Psychological Works of Sigmund Freud,* tr. James Strachey et al., 24 vols. (1955–74), 11:199, 21:114. For a revision of this along evolutionary lines, see Taylor, *Castration,* 160, 226.
57. See Bruce and Young, who report various modern experimental studies that all races are equally recognizable, but that members of one race find it more difficult to identify individuals of another; in particular, one study of 693 black and 752 white participants "found that the decrement in recognition of other-race faces compared with own-race was highly similar for both the black and the white participants" (*In the Eye of the Beholder,* 111).
58. For the logic of responses to Europeans (and by Europeans) in terms of surface features and collective similarities, see Taylor, *Time, Space, Race.*
59. For a summary of the evidence for the correlation between the number of basic color terms in a language and the level of technology in the host society, see Berlin and Kay, *Basic Color Terms,* 104.
60. "The relation of John de Verrazzano a Florentine" (1524), in *Principal Navigations,* ed. Hakluyt, II (1599): "we saw great store of people which came to the Sea side; and seeing us approch, they fled a way, and sometimes would stand still and looke backe, beholding vs with great admiration: but afterwards being animated and assured with signes that we made them, some of them came hard to the Sea side, seeming to rejoyce very much at the sight of vs, and marveiling greatly at our apparel, shape and Whitenesse. . . . they began to behold him with great admiration, marueiling at the whitenesse of his flesh" (2:295–96). Hakluyt's 1599 text reprints his translation in *Divers Voyages touching the Discoverie of America* (1582), ed. John Winter Jones (Hakluyt Society, 1850), 56, 57, which derives from Ramusio's *Navigationi et Viaggi,* III (1556), fol. 420–422ᵛ. For the Italian original, see Lawrence C. Wroth, *The Voyages of Giovanni da Verrazzano 1524–1528* (New Haven, CT: Yale UP, 1970), 123 (*biancheza*), 125 (*la bianceza de le sue carne*).
61. "These negroes"—poor people from the surrounding countryside, as distinct from those along the banks and mouth of the river Senegal—"crowded to see me as though I were a marvel. It seemed to be a new experience to them to see Christians, whom they had not previously seen. They marvelled no less at my clothing than at my white skin [*la mia biancheza*] . . . some touched my hands and limbs, and rubbed me with their spittle to discover whether my whiteness [*la mia biancheza*] was dye or flesh. Finding that it was flesh [*carne biancha*] they were astounded" (Crone, *Cadamosto,* 49; Leporace, *Navigazioni Atlantiche,* 68). Unlike his translator Crone, Ca' da Mosto refers to "white flesh," not "white skin."
62. In John Underhill's *Newes From America* (1638), a Pequot explains that "we distinguish not betweene the Dutch and the English, but tooke them to be one Nation" (12).
63. *World Encompassed,* ed. Vaux, 36, 61, 69, 99, 238–39, 37, 256, 96. For an equally ambiguous South American case, see Robert Harcourt, *A Relation of a Voyage to Guiana* (1613), 43: "A Nation of Indians, which never had seen white men, or Christians before, and could not be drawne to any familiar commerce, or conversation, no not so much as with our Indians, because they were strangers to them, and of another Nation." Notice the use of code-switching ("white men, or Christians"), and the Englishmen's dependence on their Indian guides and translators (who spoke Spanish, and who must be responsible for the conclusion that the other "Nation of Indians" had never seen Europeans before).

It is impossible to determine whether "white men" was somehow expressed by the new tribe, or expressed in Spanish by the guides, or interpolated by the English reporter.

64. Greenblatt, *Marvelous Possessions,* 7. Greenblatt's skepticism about whether European texts can tell us anything reliable about non-European peoples is excessively pessimistic. It seems certain, for instance, on the basis of accounts by several independent eyewitnesses, that on at least two occasions native peoples did attack and kill members of Drake's expedition. Given the fact that the European eyewitness accounts radically differ in their moral evaluation of Drake and his crew, and that the attacks clearly posed a problem for English apologists, it is hard to believe that they were simply invented. About the circumstances and motives of the attacks we can, of course, be much less confident, since the English might have reasons to misrepresent those and in any case had no opportunity to discuss with the natives, retrospectively, the motives for the attacks.
65. William Wood, *New England's Prospect* (1634), ed. Alden T. Vaughan (Amherst: University of Massachusetts Press, 1977), 92, 106. I cite Vaughan's edition, rather than the 1634 first edition, because Vaughan has collated variants in the 1634, 1635, and 1639 editions. None of the passages I quote is variant.
66. Wood, *New England's Prospect,* 76. Mortality rates in Virginia were appallingly high in the early decades, supporting Wood's account of their unhealthy appearance; moreover, a standard English medical treatment for disease was bleeding the patient, which would have had the effect of making victims even paler.
67. As noted in chapter 1, according to Roger Williams the eastern New England tribes identified Europeans as a group with the word *wautaconanog,* meaning "coatmen" or "men who wear clothes" (*Key into the Language of America,* 52). The 1643 testimony of Williams thus supports the 1634 testimony of Wood that the eastern New England tribes did not call Europeans "white"—just as Vincent's 1637 text (quoted in chapter 2) confirms the association of "white" with the Mohawks.
68. Edmund Scott, *An Exact Discourse of the Subtilties, Fashions, Religion and Ceremonies of the East Indians* (1606), C2^v, D4^v. This text is also discussed in Michael Neill's "'Mulattos,' 'Blacks,' and 'Indian Moors': *Othello* and Early Modern Constructions of Human Difference," *Shakespeare Quarterly* 49 (1998): 367. But the inferences Neill draws from it about the interpretation of *Othello* (completed before Scott's return) presume that the experiences of Englishmen in the very unfamiliar context of Indonesia would have been immediately apprehensible by Shakespeare and his audience—even before those Englishmen returned to tell some literate Londoners something about it.
69. Scott, *Exact Discourse,* D2^v. The Fleming had been mortally wounded by one of the English, and the English were trying to determine whether their "mullato" servant was the murderer. One of the English asked him if his assailant was "a white man, or a blacke," and the Fleming answered "a white man," but then acknowledged "it was darke, hee knew not well." The crucial issue, which would distinguish the suspected member of the English group from all the others, was skin color, and given the poor light the victim could not distinguish facial features; hence the contrast between "white" and "black" here represents, in very particular circumstances, the crudest of physical distinctions, and its generic significance—or the language of the exchange, reported at second hand—is not entirely clear. For Scott see *The Voyage of Sir Henry Middleton to the Moluccas 1604–1606,* ed. William Foster (Hakluyt Society, 1943), xix-xx, xxx; since the same publisher registered an earlier account of the voyage on May 20, 1606, shortly after the voyagers returned (xxxv), Scott's book can hardly have been published before July, and perhaps much later in the year.
70. K. N. Chaudhuri, *The English East India Company: The Study of an Early Joint-Stock Company* (F. Cass, 1965), 21, 90.
71. Eltis, *African Slavery,* 43.
72. Peter Fryer, *Staying Power: The history of black people in Britain* (Pluto, 1984), 8, 462. For additional East India Company examples of generic *white,* not discussed in the text, see Sir

John Skinner's *A true relation of the uniust, cruell, and barbarous proceedings against the English at Amboyna in the East-Indies* (1624), 30 ("The Priest, when he came to the place of execution, spake these words in the Mallaian Tongue: All yee, great and small, rich and poor, black and white, look to it: we have committed no fault"), and A. S., *A Terrible Seafight . . . betweene nine East India ships of the Hollanders and three great gallions, which happened about Goas Bare in the East Indies* (1640), C2 ("we got prisoners above 100 men, about 50 white, and 50 Negroes").

73. Based on a digital search of Literature Online and of Early English Books Online: Textual Coding Project, as of November 2003, as well as databases mentioned elsewhere, and my own old-fashioning reading.
74. *A true and large discourse of the voyage . . . set forth the 28 of April 1601* (1603) and *The last East-Indian voyage* (1606) do not use racial *white;* nor—as I noted in chapter 2—do the several texts of Keeling's 1607 voyage.
75. Waldron, *Sense Development,* 157.
76. On the importance of European ships ("proximity engines") in establishing the asymmetrical dynamic of European superiority at first contact, see Taylor, *Time, Space, Race.*
77. Agustin de Zurate, *The discoverie and conquest of the provinces of Peru,* tr. anonymous (1582), 34.
78. *Virginia richly valued . . . Written by a Portugall gentleman of Elvas . . . and translated out of Portugese by Richard Hakluyt* (1609), N1^{v}.
79. Jobson, *Golden Trade,* L1.
80. Thomas Heriot, *A Briefe and True Report of the New Found Land of Virginia* (1588), E4-F1^{v}.
81. As Jordan noted, many early English accounts of Africa "reported explicitly that the Negro's preference in colors was inverse to the European's" (*White Over Black,* 10).
82. Jordan, *White Over Black,* 6; Jobson, *Golden Trade,* F3.
83. Jobson, *Golden Trade,* D1^{v} (twice), F2^{v}, F3, G1, G1^{v}, M2, P2^{v}, Q1, Q3^{v}, S2^{v}, T3^{v} (twice). Jobson used *black* as a racial adjective more than 50 times.
84. *OED black n.*6 (dated 1625, from the date of its publication in *Hakluytus Posthumus,* but it comes from a journal of 1570). This early date is supported by a seaman on the Hawkins voyage of 1568, who used the idiom in testimony to the Inquisition in 1573 ("when we were off the Guinea coast picking up blacks . . ."): see P. E. H. Hair, "Protestants as Pirates, Slavers, and Proto-missionaries: Sierra Leone 1568 and 1582," *Journal of Ecclesiastical History* 21 (1970): 211–12. The sailors' idiom apparently did not become common in London until much later, but it occurs in "A project in the Days of Queen Elizabeth for the Settling her Subjects in Guinea; shewing of what conveniency it would be, Writ in the year 1597," printed in Churchill, *Collection of Voyages,* 5:428–30. Jobson in 1621 used it constantly, four years before *Hakluytus Posthumus.*
85. Bodin, *Method,* 124, translating "est autem contrariorum contraria disciplina. igitur si Australis ater est, Septentrionalis candidus" (*Methodus,* sig. t2, p. 159).

Chapter 6

1. Brown, *Travels,* 140, 226.
2. *OED American n.*1 ("An American Indian"), 2 ("An American of European descent"). This second definition literally applies to Brown and Douglass, whose fathers were white; *OED* seems not to recognize the existence of Americans who are wholly of African descent.
3. Anderson, *Imagined Communities,* 25–36, 61–64.
4. See Leonard F. Dean, "Bodin's *Methodus* in England before 1625," *Studies in Philology* 39 (1942): 160–66.
5. *Letter Book of Gabriel Harvey, A.D. 1573–1580,* ed. E. J. L. Scott (Camden Society, 1884), XXXIII, 79.

6. On book sizes, prices, and popularity see Tessa Watt, *Cheap Print and Popular Piety, 1550–1640* (Cambridge: Cambridge UP, 1991), esp. 260–64; on bread prices see B. R. Mitchell, *British Historical Statistics* (Cambridge: Cambridge UP, 1988), 769–70.
7. Eden's *Decades* was so expensive to produce that the cost had to be shared between a consortium of printers—who were worried that they could not recoup their investment (Gwyn, "Eden," 30). Gwyn is wrong to assume that shared printing indicates a large print run.
8. In a letter of June 25, 1625, Joseph Meade announced the publication of "a great Pilgrimage of Purchas of some 4 big volumes about 3[l] price" (British Library MS Harleian 389, f. 466). The prices of many of the books discussed in the preceding chapters are included in Francis R. Johnson, "Notes on English Retail Book-prices, 1550–1640," *The Library*, V, 2 (1950): 83–112, and David McKitterick, "'Ovid with a Littleton': The Cost of English Books in the Early Seventeenth Century," *Transactions of the Cambridge Bibliographical Society* 11 (1997): 184–234.
9. J. Noel Heermance, *William Wells Brown and Clotelle* (Shoe String Press, 1969), 192. The revised American edition was published in 1864.
10. Purchas must have completed *Purchas his Pilgrimage* before August 7, 1612, when it was licensed for publication; by that date it had been read and approved by the censor. See Edward Arber, ed., *A Transcript of the Registers of the Worshipful Company of Stationers, 1554–1640,* 5 vols. (1857–94), 3:223b. Shakespeare and Fletcher's *All is True; or, Henry VIII* was a new play, performed only a few previous times, when the Globe burned down on June 29, 1613; Shakespeare and Fletcher's *Two Noble Kinsmen* must be later than February 20, 1613, and is probably later than the burning of the Globe. See Taylor, "Canon and Chronology," *Textual Companion,* 133–34. It is often assumed or asserted that *Kinsmen* was the first play performed at the opening of the rebuilt Globe in June 1614, but the King's Men continued to play at the Blackfriars theater while rebuilding their outdoor arena, and the title page of the first edition of *Kinsmen* specified only the Blackfriars. The prologue's reference to "our losses" thus probably refers to the Globe fire, but would have been equally topical at performances at the Blackfriars in autumn 1613. *Triumphs of Truth* might therefore easily postdate even *Kinsman* and thus postdate the entire Shakespeare canon.
11. Jean Robertson and D. J. Gordon, ed., *A Calendar of Dramatic Records in the Books of the Livery Companies of London,* Malone Society Collections III (Oxford: Malone Society, 1954), 87. The actual number of copies printed by Okes is left blank in this manuscript, but Okes was paid the same sum for printing 500 copies of Middleton's Lord Mayor's pageant for another Grocer in 1617 (92).
12. Chaudhuri, *East India Company,* 156.
13. See "Sir Thomas Myddleton" (1550–1631) in *The Dictionary of National Biography,* and A. H. Dodd, "Mr. Myddleton the Merchant of Tower Street," in *Elizabethan Government and Society,* ed. S. T. Bindoff et al. (Athlone Press, 1961), 249–81.
14. "Report of the Russian Ambassador Aleksei Ziuzin," lines 143–44. This is reprinted, as an appendix to *The Triumphs of Truth,* in *The Collected Works of Thomas Middleton,* gen. ed. Gary Taylor (Oxford UP, forthcoming), to which I have keyed all my quotations from Middleton. David Bergeron's introduction to *Triumphs of Truth* is an excellent overview of the mayoral pageant tradition.
15. I stress "unequivocally positive," because there are always critics who will defend anything written by Shakespeare, and who will accordingly find sympathetic qualities in, for instance, Morocco in *The Merchant of Venice*—despite Portia's evident contempt for his "complexion," and despite the period's almost universal disapproval of miscegenation (at least if it involved a dark man and a fair woman), and despite his dramatic role as foil for Bassanio. For the overwhelmingly negative portrayal of blacks in Tudor texts, see Vaughan and Vaughan, "Before *Othello.*" They cite as an exception (36–38) "Blacke *Porus* the *Aethiopian* king" in George Chapman's *The Blind Beggar of Alexandria* (performed 1596,

printed 1598), claiming that Porus is "praised by the victor" for having fought bravely, and that, when someone calls him a devil, the woman who has chosen to marry him declares "the blackest is the fayrest." But in fact the victor never praises Porus for his valor: instead, Cleanthes calls him one of "these base miscreantes" (Sc.ix.151) and condemns "The vile presumption of [their] hated lives" (Sc.x.6). Porus is not called a devil before the woman's speech, but after it; Chapman thus leaves the comparison unrefuted, and indeed appends to it the expectation that Porus will "have hornes," like the devil, because he will be cuckolded (x.158–62). These exchanges "do much to disparage further the already humbled Porus" (Barthelemy, *Black Face,* 149). In a sense Porus is already cuckolded, because he is about to marry a woman who is not, as he thinks, a widow, but the abandoned pregnant mistress of Cleanthes. As Elliot H. Tokson observes, in *The Popular Image of the Black Man in English Drama, 1550–1688* (Boston, MA: G. K. Hall, 1982): "his instantaneous obsession with the swollen-bellied white woman" demonstrates that he is a suitably lecherous partner for the "white strumpet" (96). This is the play's final cruel practical joke, played on a character whom Chapman goes out of his way to identify as a pagan, swearing "by all my Gods whom I adore" (x.11). For Chapman's play see *The Plays of George Chapman: The Comedies,* gen. ed. Allan Holaday (Urbana: University of Illinois Press, 1970).

16. Even Celante, the otherwise virtuous "black" daughter (619, 621) in Peele's *The Old Wives Tale* (1595), is described by her own father as "so hard favoured, so foule and ill faced" and a "deformitie" (233–36), and routinely identified in stage directions as "the fowle wench" (614.1, etc.); in one of the play's many practical jokes, she marries a blind man, who is unaware of her ugliness. See *The Life and Works of George Peele,* gen. ed. Charles T. Prouty, vol. 3 (New Haven, CT: Yale UP, 1970).
17. For these mute black figures in civic pageants, see Rebecca Ann Bach, *Colonial Transformations: The Cultural Production of the New Atlantic World, 1580–1640* (New York: Palgrave, 2000), 160–61. Bach also quotes Middleton's *Triumphs of Truth* and *Triumphs of Honour and Virtue;* but she does not notice the originality of either, or their differences from preceding English portrayals of black figures. This failure is symptomatic of New Historicist and Foucauldian scholarship, dedicated as it is to the assertion of a synchronic epistemic totality, without individual agency and difference, without gradual systemic change.
18. Jones, *Othello's Countrymen,* 35.
19. He is perhaps not the first black character to speak in an English pageant. There is a speech by a figure "apparelled like a Moore" and possibly black, in George Peele's pageant for Wolstan Dixi (1585). But this figure simply serves as a presenter and is not characterized at all: see *The Life and Minor Works of George Peele,* ed. David H. Horne (New Haven, CT: Yale UP, 1952), 209–10.
20. Every survey of the representation of blacks in early modern drama remarks on the negative treatment of black sexuality: see for instance Tokson, *Popular Image of the Black Man,* 82–105. Jordan had shown that this stereotype was not confined to plays (*White Over Black,* 32–40).
21. Associations of one of the Magi with Ethiopia have been inferred as early as the fifth century, but the identification did not become explicit until the early thirteenth century, in Germany, when a Latin prayer called one of the Magi (Balthasar) "Rex . . . niger." See Paul H. D. Kaplan, *The Rise of the Black Magus in Western Art* (Ann Arbor, MI: UMI Research Press, 1985), 19–30. In the thirteenth century St. Maurice also became black in German iconography, and the visual image of a black saint—common in German art until at least the sixteenth century—belongs to the same intellectual agenda that produced a black Magus. See Jean Devisse, *The Image of the Black in Western Art,* Vol. II, Part 1, *From the Demonic Threat to the Incarnation of Sainthood,* tr. William Granger Ryan (New York: Morrow, 1979), 164–205. In 1324 Mansa Musa, King of Mali, made a spectacular pilgrimage to Mecca, laden with gold and slaves, and within a few decades the

image of such a rich black African pilgrim-king bearing gifts had reached western Europe (Davis, *Progress,* 46, 50). In John of Hildesheim's *Historia Trium Regum* (1364–75) there is "no doubt" that one Magus was a "black Ethiopian," and one Magus comes from "this land of Ethiopia" in the fantastically popular *Travels* of the fictitious Sir John Mandeville, probably written in the 1360s. At about the same time, the Black Magus/King became increasingly important in German iconography.

22. Kaplan, *Rise of the Black Magus,* 71, 112; *The Image of the Black in Western Art,* II.2:161–86. Baltasar was not married. The most familiar Black Queen, for early modern Christians, was almost certainly the Queen of Sheba, whose blackness in the Song of Songs was sometimes acknowledged to be literal: see Sujata Iyengar, "Thirteen Ways of Looking at a Black Woman," in "Mythologies of Color" (Ph.D. dissertation, Stanford University, 1998).
23. Albert Boime has argued—in *The Art of Exclusion: Representing Blacks in the Nineteenth Century* (Washington, DC: Smithsonian Institution Press, 1990)—that "instead of missionaries and slavers invading the black man's land and plundering its wealth and subjugating its people by force, a noble and 'wise' black ruler comes of his own volition to the white man's land and lays down his wealth and his power at the feet of the Christ child" (9). This cynical gloss might well be appropriate to depictions of a black Magus in the nineteenth century, but it is harder to sustain in the thirteenth or fourteenth, when Africa was not yet being plundered by Christian "missionaries and slavers." In any case, the Black King of 1613 does not bring any gifts and does not surrender his own political authority. Balthasar was normally subordinated pictorially to the other Magi: see Roger Bastide, "Color, Racism, and Christianity," *Daedalus* 96 (1967): 312–27. But Middleton replaced the mute and subordinated image of the black Magus with a foregrounded and individuated speaking subject, surrounded by other black subjects.
24. Trudier Harris, *Exorcising Blackness: Historical and Literary Lynching and Burning Rituals* (Bloomington: Indiana UP, 1984), 31–33.
25. Brown, *Clotelle* (1864), 57–58. In the revision Brown also presents Dinah more sympathetically, explaining that "Dinah was the mother of thirteen children, all of whom had been taken from her when young; and this, no doubt, did much to harden her feelings, and make her hate all white persons;" she also dissociates herself from the cruelty of her mistress, in an added speech spoken after "the mistress was out of the kitchen" (41).
26. D'Amico, *The Moor in English Renaissance Drama* (Tampa: University of South Florida Press, 1991), 59.
27. Bach claims that "Christian truth saves (whitens)" the Black King and Queen here, and likewise says that the black Queen in *Honor and Virtue* possesses a "spiritual whiteness that redeems her visible blackness" (*Colonial Transformations,* 159). But *white* is not used in this doubled ethnic and ethnical sense in either pageant; indeed, in *Truth* Middleton insists on the disparity between the two senses. Bach's description better fits William Strachey's dedicatory sonnet in the front matter to *For the Colony in Virginea Britannia Lawes Divine, Morall and Martiall* (1612), which she quotes; Strachey praises "the Lords of the Councell of Virginea" in London because their efforts at colonization make God's "truth in blackest nations shine," and "where white Christians turne in maners Mores" the Lords "wash Mores white with sacred Christian bloud" (final recto of unsignatured first gathering). Middleton might have been influenced by Strachey's contrast between errant white Christians and virtuous black nations, but he did not reproduce Strachey's ethical use of *white.*
28. Tokson, *Popular Image,* 109.
29. For a more extended analysis of the significance of this shift in the body politics of Mediterranean religions, see Taylor, *Castration,* 67–73, 162–4, 185–208.
30. For a discussion of the racial politics of the Rembrandt image, see Peter Erickson, "Images of White Identity," 134–37.

31. Jerome, Epistle xxii; Augustine, *Enarrationes in Psalmos,* col. 938; quoted by Hunter, "Othello and Colour Prejudice," 48–49. In the same tradition, Joseph Hall concluded that "it is not for us to regard the skin, but the soul" (*Occasional Meditations,* 93–94). Hall's distinction—published 87 years after the anatomy textbook of Vesalius—may be using *skin* as a synonym for *body,* or it may reflect a slowly emerging distinction between skin and temperament. Hall is the only contemporary preacher actually cited by Middleton (in the preface to *Two Gates of Salvation,* written in 1609).
32. Morrison, *Playing in the Dark: Whiteness and the Literary Imagination* (Cambridge, MA: Harvard UP, 1992), 17.
33. Callaghan claims that "Between 1585 and 1692, numerous civic pageants . . . specify the inclusion of 'negroe boys' or 'beautiful Raven-black negroes' (not just English people in blackface)" ("Othello was a white man," 193). But the source she cites to support this claim (Barthelemy, *Black Face,* 50, 47) cites such evidence—and the two phrases Callaghan quotes—only in pageants of 1672 to 1692. There is no evidence of actual Africans performing in London civic pageants before the Restoration (and England's official entry into the slave trade).
34. Scholars have noted some links between *A Game at Chess* and *The Triumphs of Truth;* both, for instance, contain the allegorical character of "Error." See Margot Heinemann, "Middleton's *A Game at Chess:* Parliamentary Puritans and Opposition Drama," *English Literary Renaissance* 5 (1975): 235.
35. The play that comes closest is Brome's *The English Moor* (1637), where *white* and its compounds is spoken 20 times—less than a third of the total in *A Game at Chess.* Likewise, in no dramatic text before 1624 does *whiteness* occur more than twice; in *A Game at Chess* it is spoken four times, the highest total in the entire period.
36. Jean MacIntyre, *Costumes and Scripts in the Elizabethan Theaters* (Edmonton: University of Alberta Press, 1992), 316.
37. MacIntyre, *Costumes and Scripts,* 317. The need to create an entirely new wardrobe for the play probably explains one of the puzzles about *A Game at Chess* that has much exercised modern commentators: why the 55-day delay between the licensing of the play on June 12 and the first performance on August 5? The answer: the King's Men would not have wanted to invest large sums of money in creating so many new and expensive costumes until after the play had successfully passed through the censor's office. Costumes were always the most expensive capital outlay for a new play, and in this case especially so.
38. Ben Jonson's wedding masque *Hymenai* (1613) had called for "five pages, attired in white" to accompany a bride, "her garments white" (38–50). In the costuming of various allegorical characters Jonson also calls for white undervestments, a white girdle, a white band, a white diadem, white cloth of silver, and white socks. But those specified white properties are mixed, in individual costumes, with many other colors: gold, purple, saffron, yellow, blue, several-colored silks, carnation, silver, sky color, flame color, tawny, azure. See Jonson *Complete Masques,* ed. Stephen Orgel (New Haven, CT: Yale UP, 1969), 75–106. Jonson's palette was surpassed, for the "richness of the habits" (and their expense), by James Shirley's masque *The Triumph of Peace* (1634), which called for a white fall, white hats and feathers, a white diadem, white robe, white wings and buskins, scallops of white, white undersleeves and bases, white stockings and white shoes; but again, these specific white accessories were mixed, in the same costumes, with a riot of other colors (black, crimson, scarlet, silver, gold, yellow, olive, green, carnation, several-colored, dark blue). See *A Book of Masques,* ed. T. J. B. Spencer and Stanley Wells (Cambridge: Cambridge UP, 1967), 275–314. In terms of the total occurrences of "white," Jonson's *Hymenai* and Shirley's *Triumph of Peace,* each with 24, both exceed Brome's *The English Moor;* but almost all the occurrences in Jonson's and Shirley's masques come from stage directions rather than the spoken text. They therefore represent a seen but not a spoken signifier.

39. For evidence that the darkness of the Black characters was epidermal, see Taylor, *Castration,* 133–35.
40. See Thomas Scott's *The Second Part of Vox Populi* (1624): Spaniards, speaking of the English, explain that "they living in the North, and we in the South . . . those of the North (howsoever goodlier in person, better faced, and more beautifull then our selves by reason of the coldnesse of the climate" (12, sig. B3v). This refers, clearly enough, to the classical climatic theory. The English are more beautiful and "better faced" because, being northerners, they have lighter skins than the Spanish. Another Spaniard ventures the explanation that "it may be they hate us for the same cause, that *France, Germany, Italie,* and the rest of the Countries of *Europe,* for that many of us are discended of the Moorish race" (13, sig. B4). Note the generic use of *race.*
41. The next highest total occurs in Thomas Goffe's *The Raging Turke* (30); for other high totals, see Dekker's *If It be not good, the devil is in it* (28) and *Lust's Dominion* (28), and Webster's *White Devil* (26).
42. Paul Yachnin notes that in earlier chess allegories, "no special significance is attached to color and in many, in Colonna and Rabelais for example, the colors of the chessmen are other than black and white": see "*A Game at Chess* and Chess Allegory," *SEL* 22 (1982): 325. As for the game itself, "chessmen may be of any hue," and the color distinction between the two sides may be white and red, or green and red, or silver and gold: see David Hooper and Kenneth Whyld, *The Oxford Companion to Chess,* 2nd ed. (Oxford: Oxford UP, 1992), 86. For early modern examples of different color contrasts in actual sets or games, see H. J. R. Murphy, *A History of Chess* (Oxford: Clarendon Press, 1913), 781, 823, 829.
43. "Truth" first appears in black, then shifts into "light" colors, carrying "silver" properties (Pro. 27–37) and in the final scene inhabits an actual onstage property described as a "green mount" (5.6.84). Evil and Catholicism are embodied in the Whore of Babylon, who wears purple robes (3.1.170, 4.4.4, 39) and scarlet veils (4.4.40), and rides on a "scarlet-colored" or "rose-colored" beast (3.1.171, 4.4.25). She carries a "golden cup" (4.4.44); she is usually accompanied by cardinals in their distinctive red vestments; "her face is full of . . . red pimples" (4.1.72). Against this female embodiment of evil the play sets a female embodiment of virtue, Titania (Queen Elizabeth). She is called, by her suitors, "fair" and "fairest," and as always in such Petrarchan contexts the words suggest a light complexion; but she is never called white, nor are her English followers, and there is no indication that she confines herself to white clothes, any more than Queen Elizabeth did.
44. Dyer, *White,* 10.
45. Contemporary observers and modern scholars agree that the White King represents King James; the White Knight is the Prince of Wales, the future King Charles I; the White Duke is the Duke of Buckingham; the White King's Pawn shares features of the Earl of Middlesex and the Earl of Bristol.
46. King James is a Scot, who styles himself King of Great Britain; but the other identifiable characters all belong to his English court, not to the separate government of Scotland. Even King James had, by 1624, been living in England for 21 years (the entire lifetime of most of the London population). The Fat Bishop, who begins on the White side, is Marcantonio De Dominis, a refugee and convert living in England and holding various English ecclesiastical positions (named in the text).
47. See for example *Batman uppon Bartolome* (1582), f. 218v, sig. 2P2v; Camden, *Britain,* tr. Holland, 24.
48. "Anglica" occurs twice in *A Game at Chess* (1.1.300, 2.1.198). For Britain as a "corner" of the world, see the classical citations in *De Proprietatibus Rerum,* XV, 14 (2:734), and the repetition in one of Middleton's sources, Thomas Scott's *The second part of Vox Populi* (1624), 26 ("that angle of the world, England").

49. The character who speaks more lines than any other, the Black Knight, is the former Spanish ambassador. The Black King is King Philip IV of Spain; the Black Duke is the Spanish favorite, Conde-Duke Olivares. The only named character in the play, Loyola, is also a Spaniard. The visit to the Black House by the White Knight and White Duke represents the trip to Spain by Prince Charles and Buckingham; they are welcomed to the Black House, in the play, by the Black Bishop's Pawn, speaking words quoted from an official Latin oration welcoming Charles and Buckingham to Madrid.
50. The Pope, whom the English called the Bishop of Rome, is once mentioned as an offstage second Black Bishop; he never appears. Neither does the Spanish Infanta, the all-important object of the Spanish Match, so detested by English Protestants and nationalists. The chief Catholic figures in the Thirty Years War—the Holy Roman Emperor Ferdinand II, Duke Maximilian of Bavaria, General Ambrogio Spinola—do not appear either and are never even mentioned, although they were the focus of intense English anxiety and hostility at the time. To appreciate how remarkable these absences are, we need only compare *A Game at Chess,* once again, with Dekker's *The Whore of Babylon.* In Dekker's allegory, the Pope, the Holy Roman Emperor, the King of Spain, and the (Catholic) King of France are all important characters in the enemy camp. In Middleton's allegory, the most powerful individuals of Counter-Reformation Europe are invisible or unimportant.
51. My definition of which characters are most important is based on a tabulation of the number of lines they speak, in descending order from Black Knight to Black Knight's Pawn.
52. For the sources of these statements about Middleton's last play, see Sara Jayne Steen, *Ambrosia in an Earthern Vessel: Three Centuries of Audience and Reader Response to the Works of Thomas Middleton* (New York: AMS Press, 1992). Several additional responses to *A Game at Chess* have been discovered and published since Steen; see my texts and commentaries on the play in *The Collected Works.*
53. See for instance Lesley Milroy and James Milroy, "Social Network and Social Class: Toward an Integrated Sociolinguistic Model," *Language in Society* 21 (1992): 1–21.
54. Heywood and Brome both belonged to the small community of practicing London playwrights in the 1620s; both almost certainly would have seen the most successful play of their lifetimes. Heywood collaborated with Middleton: see Gary Taylor, "Middleton and Rowley—and Heywood: *The Old Law* and New Technologies of Attribution," *Papers of the Bibliographical Society of America* 96 (2002): 165–217. Brome's *The English Moor* was demonstrably influenced (as Brome often was) by Middleton; see Sara Jayne Steen, ed., *The English Moore; or The Mock-Marriage* (Columbia: University of Missouri Press, 1983), 7–9. Heywood and Brome collaborated on *The Late Lancashire Witches* (1634).
55. Labov, *Principles,* 325–411.
56. For these and other biographical details, see Mark Eccles, "'Thomas Middleton A Poett,'" *Studies in Philology* 54 (1957): 516–36.
57. Foucault's 1976 lectures at the Collège de France, quoted and translated in Ann Laura Stoler, *Race and the Education of Desire: Foucault's "History of Sexuality" and the Colonial Order of Things* (Durham, NC: Duke UP, 1995), 75.
58. Before collecting the fed-up Roanoke colonists in 1586, Sir Francis Drake had raided Spanish colonies in the Caribbean and Florida, liberating hundreds of black slaves; unless he threw them overboard as he headed up the Atlantic seaboard—unlikely, given their commercial and propaganda value—the blacks were still with him when he reached Roanoke and may have crossed the Atlantic with Harvey and the others. We do not really know what happened to them: at worst sold back into slavery, at best dumped among strange Amerindians or strange Englishmen. See Morgan, *American Slavery,* 42.
59. See the reference to the Spanish Armada in "eighty-eight" (3.1.187–88) and to the alleged plot by "Doctor Lopez" to poison Queen Elizabeth (4.2.116–18).

60. W. J. Cash, *The Mind of the South* (1941), excerpted in *Critical White Studies,* 339–47.
61. In his poem "To King James," written to secure his release from prison after *A Game at Chess* was suppressed, Middleton described himself as a "man"—both a chess piece and a male human being—who had been placed "in the bag" by the Black House, despite the fact that the "White House" won the game. Since pieces taken by the black side must be white, Middleton clearly implies that he belongs among the "white" "men."
62. John Aubrey, *The Natural History and Antiquities of Surrey,* 5 vols. (1719), 5:130: "NEWINGTON is the last Parish within the Bills of Mortality on this Road, and lyes at the South end of *Blackman-street.*" See also David J. Johnson's *Southwark and the City* (Oxford UP, 1969), 114: "Blackman Street (as Borough High Street south of St. George's Church was known until 1889)." In the subsidy roll (PRO E/179/186/406) of 8 March 1621/22 (which records Middleton's residence in Newington and payment of the assessed tax), "Blackmanstrete" is included in the parish of Newington.
63. On these variant "soundscapes" of London, see Bruce R. Smith, *The Acoustic World of Early Modern England: Attending to the O-Factor* (Chicago: University of Chicago Press, 1999), 54–55, 61 (citing Hentzner, Platter, Dekker, and Earle).
64. See the detailed discussion of Locke, whiteness, and children in chapter 11.
65. For the Ireland hypothesis, see Allen, *Invention of the White Race;* for the argument about whether racism preceded or resulted from slavery, see chapter 9. Dyer claims that both Jordan and Bernal "locate the emergence of the term [*white*] in the American colonies" (*White Over Black,* 66). Jordan had noted "a shift during the seventeenth century in the terminology which Englishmen in the colonies applied to themselves. From the initially most common term *Christian,* at mid-century there was a marked drift toward *English* and *free.* After about 1680, taking the colonies as a whole, a new term appeared—*white*" (95). Jordan was discussing legal language in the colonies, not making a more general claim that *white* was a "new term" in 1680; or, if he was making such a claim, he was mistaken. Despite Jordan's own emphasis on 1680, Jordan is the only evidence cited by Bernal for his claim that "a more clear-cut racism grew up after 1650 and . . . was greatly intensified by the increased colonization of North America" (*Black Athena,* 1:201).
66. In *A Game at Chess,* "white" is first spoken by Error (who defines himself, in the same line, as belonging to the Black House), and then by the Black Bishop's Pawn; throughout the play, it is spoken much more often by Black than by White characters.

Chapter 7

1. For Massinger's biography, see "General Introduction," *Plays and Poems,* ed. Edwards and Gibson, 1:xv-xvi; for the early stage history of *The Bondman,* 1:307–8.
2. For the early history of slavery in Bermuda, see Virginia Bernhard, *Slaves and Slaveholders in Bermuda 1616–1782* (Columbia: University of Missouri Press, 1999), 18–93. Like many historians of colonial Virginia, Bernhard contends that "there is no evidence to indicate that" the first imported blacks "were slaves" (36). But Governor Tucker's instructions in 1616 listed "negroes to dive for pearles" among other commodities that would certainly have been bought: "Cattle, Sugar Canes . . . and what other plants are there to be had" (Lefroy, *Memorials,* 1:115–16). Bernhard identifies this diver as a skilled workman, not a slave, but enslaved Amerindians and Africans had been exploited as divers in the Caribbean from the beginning of the sixteenth century: see Taylor, *Time, Space, Race.* Bernhard notes that the ship which in May 1616—a month after Shakespeare's death—"brought with her also one Indian and a Negroe" came from the Lesser Antilles (19); "good store of neggars . . . brought from the West Indies" were delivered by another ship in 1617 (*Rich Papers,* 25). Blacks shipped from the West Indies would almost certainly have been slaves. In 1618 one English colonist expected to "procure . . . a neger" for "one

hundred pounds" (*Rich Papers,* 17, 59); at about the same time, another English colonist listed "James the negger" at the very end of his list of laborers, without a surname (81–82); 11 years later, at least one of those blacks still "belonged" to the company (Bernhard 36). In 1622 the governor described blacks as "a most necessary commodity" (Bernhard 22) and as "slaves" (29). Bernhard admits that by the 1630s blacks and Indians were subjected to lifetime servitude (49). Although some colonists may have treated black servants more humanely than others, at least some of them were almost certainly enslaved from the beginning.

3. Charles Verlinden, *L'Esclavage dans l'Europe médiévale,* vol. 2, *Italie, colonies italiennes du Levant, Levant latin, Empire byzantin* (Ghent, 1971), 2:999–1010.
4. In Marston's *Sophonisba* (1605) and in Webster's *The White Devil* (1612), a treacherous black woman is a servant, but not clearly a slave. In Marlowe's *The Jew of Malta* (1589), the slave Ithamoor is apparently Muslim, but he was born "in Thrace; brought up in Arabia" (2.3.130–31); European by birth, he might well be "white" and would at most be "tawny." The printed text does not indicate his color. See Marlowe, *The Jew of Malta,* ed. N. W. Bawcutt, Revels Plays (Manchester, NH: Manchester UP, 1978), 2.3.130–31.
5. "Vangue. *An Ethiopian slave*" is included in the authorial list of "Interlocutores"(sig. A2^{v}); "Dear Ethiopian Negro" (1.1.60), "gentle Negro" (1.1.70), "gentle Negro" (3.1.147), "The Negro's dead" (3.1.158); he is twice called "slave" in his final moments, by his master (3.1.184, 192). I cite here the line numbers from *The Selected Plays of John Marston,* ed. MacDonald P. Jackson and Michael Neill (Cambridge: Cambridge UP, 1986).
6. Less predictably, George Chapman apparently calls for black slaves in Virginia in *The Memorable Masque* (1613): see *Comedies* (566), which specifies "two Moores, attir'd like *Indian* slaves" (52) to attend each of the "Virginian Princes" (31) and "every Man his Moore, attending his horse" (62–3). "Moor" here presumably means "blackamoor" or "Negro." But the Moors here are enslaved to the Indians, not the English. Chapman's "Indian slaves" presumably result from confusion or conflation of Asian with American "Indians."
7. Daborne, *Christian Turned Turk,* 6.303–05, in *Three Turk Plays from Early Modern England,* ed. Daniel J. Vitkus (New York: Columbia UP, 2000).
8. *The Virgin Martyr,* 4.1.126–60, in *The Dramatic Works of Thomas Dekker,* ed. Fredson Bowers, 4 vols. (Cambridge: Cambridge UP, 1953–61); Gervase Markham and William Sampson, *The True Tragedy of Herod and Antipater,* ed. Gordon Nicholas Ross (New York: Garland, 1979), 1.5.88–89. In *Virgin Martyr,* the British slave refuses to rape a Christian, saying—in one of the period's many expressions of colorphobia—that he is now "But halfe a slave," but such an action would make him "A damned whole one, a blacke ugly slave"; sentenced to be punished for his refusal, he tells his master, "Thou art more slave then I."
9. Godfrey Fisher, *Barbary Legend: War, Trade and Piracy in North Africa 1415–1830* (Oxford: Clarendon, 1957); Stephen Clissold, *Barbary Slaves* (London: Elek, 1977). See also Philip Beidler's "Mustapha Rub-a-Dub Keli Khan and Other Famous Early American Literary Mahometans" in *Writing Race across the Atlantic,* ed. Beidler and Taylor.
10. DuBois, *The World and Africa* (New York: Viking, 1947), 52. See also Wayne B. Chandler, "The Moor: Light of Europe's Dark Age," *Journal of African Civilizations* 7 (1985): 144–75.
11. Eltis, *African Slavery,* 57.
12. On the ecumenical nature of Mediterranean slavery, see Fernand Braudel, *The Mediterranean and the Mediterranean World in the Age of Philip II,* tr. Sîan Reynolds, 2 vols. (Collins, 1972), 2:866–69.
13. *The Merchant of Venice,* ed. Jay Halio (Oxford: Oxford UP, 1993), 192.
14. Daileader, "Black Male Casting in the Royal Shakespeare Company: Beyond Othellophilia," in *Shakespeare and Race,* ed. Stanley Wells and Catherine Alexander (Cambridge: Cambridge UP, 2000), 177–202.

15. Wilson, *The Ground on Which I Stand* (New York: Theatre Communications Group, 2001), 29, 31.
16. Knutson, "A Caliban in St. Mildred Poultry," in *Shakespeare and Cultural Traditions: Proceedings of the Fifth World Shakespeare Congress,* ed. Roger Pringle et al. (Newark: University of Delaware Press, 1994), 110–26.
17. Hill, *Shakespeare in Sable: A History of Black Shakespearean Actors* (Amherst: University of Massachusetts Press, 1984), 107–10; Hill, "Caliban and Ariel: A Study in Black and White in American Productions of *The Tempest* from 1945–1981," *Theatre History Studies* 4 (1984): 1–10.
18. Alden T. Vaughan and Virginia Mason Vaughan, *Shakespeare's Caliban: A Cultural History* (Cambridge: Cambridge UP, 1991), 191–92.
19. Hill, *Shakespeare in Sable,* 157–58.
20. Mannoni, *Prospero and Caliban: The Psychology of Colonization* (Paris, 1950), 2nd ed., tr. Pamel Powesland (New York: Praeger, 1964); Frantz Fanon, *Black Skins, White Masks* (Paris, 1952), tr. Charles Lam Markmann (New York: Grove, 1967), 83–108; Césaire, *Une tempête; d'apres "La tempête" de Shakespeare. Adaptation pour un théâtre nègre* (Paris: Editions du Seuil, 1969).
21. O'Dair, *Class, Critics, and Shakespeare: Bottom Lines on the Culture Wars* (Ann Arbor: University of Michigan Press, 2000), 34.
22. Linebaugh and Rediker, *The Many-Headed Hydra* (Boston: Beacon, 2000), 26. Shakespeare's source was a manuscript of William Strachey's *A True Reportory of the Wreck and Redemption of Sir Thomas Gates, Knight, upon and from the Islands of the Bermudas,* written in 1610 but not printed until 1625.
23. Hawkes, *That Shakespeherian Rag: Essays on a Critical Process* (Methuen, 1986), 3. For the same emphasis on the one relationship, see also 2 ("Prospero as Planter, with the aboriginal Caliban as . . . Slave"), 6 ("Caliban's . . . relationship with Prospero"), 10 ("the ghost of Caliban confronted the spirit of Prospero"), 12 ("the creator of Prospero and Caliban"), 20 ("Prospero's relation to Caliban"), 22 ("the Prospero-Caliban relationship"), 23 ("encounter between Prospero and Caliban").
24. See Douglas Bruster, "Local *Tempest:* Shakespeare and the Work of the Early Modern Playhouse," *Journal of Medieval and Renaissance Studies* 25 (1995): 33–53; Daniel Vitkus, "'Meaner Ministers': Mastery, Bondage, and Theatrical Labor in *The Tempest,*" in *The Blackwell Companion to Shakespeare's Works,* ed. Jean E. Howard and Richard Dutton (Oxford: Blackwell, 2003), 408–26; Andrew Gurr, "Industrious Ariel and Idle Caliban," in *Travel and Drama in Shakespeare's Time,* ed. Jean-Pierre Macquerlot and Michele Willems (Cambridge: Cambridge UP, 1996). For the comparison with the Bermuda rebels, see Jerald W. Spotswood, "Labor and the Reworking of Hierarchy in Shakespeare's Plays" (Ph.D. dissertation, University of Alabama, 1996), 93.
25. Eliot, *Felix Holt, The Radical* (1866), ed. Peter Coveney (Harmondsworth: Penguin, 1972), 368–69.
26. O'Dair, *Class, Critics, and Shakespeare,* 36.
27. See Gary Taylor, "Bardicide," in *Shakespeare and Cultural Traditions,* 333–49.
28. Fiedler, *The Stranger in Shakespeare* (New York: Stein and Day, 1973), 238.
29. Las Casas, *The Spanish Colonie, or Brief Chronicle of the Actes and Gestes of the Spaniards in the West Indies,* tr. M. M. S. (1583), A4, B3^{v}, C1^{v}.
30. Andrew Fitzmaurice, *Humanism and America: An Intellectual History of English Colonisation 1500–1625* (Cambridge: Cambridge UP, 2003), 168–77.
31. Ligon, *Barbados,* 98. Speaking of "runaway Negres," Ligon notes that "there is nothing in that Countrey so useful as Liam Hounds, to find out these Thieves" (*Barbadoes,* 98), and later repeats that "only one kind" of hound "are useful here, and those are Liam Hounds, to guide us to the run away Negres" (105).

32. M. L. Gordon, "The Nationality of Slaves under the Early Roman Empire," in *Slavery in Classical Antiquity: Views and Controversies,* ed. M. I. Finley (Cambridge: Heffer, 1960), 174.
33. The only non-negative attributes attached to *slave* in the Shakespeare canon are "heedful" (*Errors* 2.2.2), "sad" (Sonnet 57.11), and "warm" (*1 Henry IV* 4.2.18)—and the last is ironic, since it is the only positive claim that Sir John can make about the men he has drafted to serve as "food for powder."
34. Spotswood, "Maintaining Hierarchy in *The Tragedie of King Lear,*" *SEL* 98 (1998): 265–80. Spotswood argues persuasively that Shakespeare's play "did not deconsecrate privilege, status, or hierarchy," or valorize the resistance of real commoners.
35. *OED servant n.*3.b. See also Robert McColley, "Slavery in Virginia, 1619–1660: A Reexamination," in *New Perspectives on Race and Slavery in America: Essays in Honor of Kenneth M. Stampp,* ed. Robert H. Abzug and Stephen Maizlich (Lexington: University of Kentucky Press, 1986), 12–14.
36. Massinger, *Plays and Poems,* ed. Edwards and Gibson, 1:307–08.
37. Greenblatt, "Murdering Peasants," in *Learning to Curse: Essays in Early Modern Culture* (New York: Routledge, 1990), 99–130.
38. Robert Taylor Conrad, *Jack Cade: The Captain of the Commons* (1868), first produced in Philadelphia (1835), revised and revived in New York and Philadelphia in 1841 and thereafter in America and London.
39. See Taylor, *Reinventing Shakespeare,* 201–02.
40. Sidney, *The Countess of Pembroke's Arcadia (The Old Arcadia),* ed. Jean Robertson (Oxford: Clarendon, 1973), 126–27, 306–08.
41. Randall Kennedy, *Nigger: The Strange Career of a Troublesome Word* (New York: Pantheon, 2002).
42. Ligon, *Barbados,* 47–49, 52–53.
43. Brian Manning, *Village Revolts: Social Protest and Popular Disturbances in England, 1509–1640* (Oxford: Clarendon, 1988), 187.
44. *The Unfortunate Traveller,* in *The Works of Thomas Nashe,* ed. R. B. McKerrow, 5 vols., rpt. (Oxford: Blackwell, 1966), 2:232–41.
45. *The Confessions of Nat Turner,* in *The Civitas Anthology of African American Slave Narratives,* 89–90, 99.
46. *OED*'s first example of the adjective with a specifically religious association dates from 1626 (*a.*1.a); but as applied to persons (as opposed to actions or words) that meaning first appears in 1647, in Clarendon's conservative *History of the Great Rebellion* (*a.*2), and the noun in that sense premiered, in 1644, in another royalist publication (*n.*2.a).
47. *Confessions of Nat Turner,* 100, 87.
48. Veblen, "The Instinct of Workmanship and the Irksomeness of Labor," *American Journal of Sociology* 4 (1898): 201.
49. Christopher Hill, "The Many-Headed Monster in Late Tudor and Early Stuart Political Thinking," in *From the Renaissance to the Reformation,* ed. Charles H. Carter (New York: Random House, 1965), 296–324, and Williams, *Keywords,* "Masses" (also "Class," "Labour," and "Work").
50. I have discussed the treatment of the plebeians in *Julius Caesar* at length in "Bardicide."
51. I have discussed Shakespeare's advocacy of obedience at length in "Forms of Opposition: Shakespeare and Middleton," *English Literary Renaissance* 24 (1994): 283–314.
52. For agricultural servants, see Ann Kussmaul, *Servants in Husbandry in Early Modern England* (Cambridge: Cambridge UP, 1981); for urban labor, see Steve Rappaport, *Worlds within Worlds: Structures of Life in Sixteenth-Century London* (Cambridge: Cambridge UP, 1989).
53. For influential overviews, see Abbot Smith, *Colonists in Bondage: White Servitude and Convict Labor in America, 1607–1776* (Chapel Hill: University of North Carolina Press, 1947); P. W. Coldham, ed., *English Convicts in Colonial America,* 2 vols. (New Orleans,

LA: Polyanthos, 1974–76); David Galenson, *White Servitude in Colonial America: An Economic Analysis* (Cambridge: Cambridge UP, 1981); Hilary McD. Beckles, *White Servitude and Black Slavery in Barbados, 1627–1715* (Knoxville: University of Tennessee Press, 1989); Allen, *Invention of the White Race,* 2:47–147.

54. Morgan, *American Slavery,* 90, 117, 128–29.
55. Alison Games, *Migration and the Origins of the English Atlantic World* (Cambridge, MA: Harvard UP, 1999), 90.
56. Morgan, *American Slavery,* 175; Beckles, *White Servitude,* 38.
57. Beckles, *White Servitude,* 71.
58. "Father White's Briefe Relation," in Clayton Colman Hall, ed., *Narratives of Early Maryland* (New York: Scribner's, 1910), 34; Ligon, *Barbadoes,* 45. For the 1634 rebellion White specified that "The ringleaders were 2 brothers named Westons, Westerne men" (i.e., from western England). In the report White sent to his Jesuit superiors in Rome, the word *servants* in his English text is the Latin *Famuli* (which could be "servants" or "slaves"): see *Voyage to Maryland (1633): Relatio Itineris in Marilandiam: Original Latin Narrative of Andrew White, S.J.,* tr. and ed. Barbara Lawatsch-Boomgaarden with Josef IJsewijn (Wauconda, IL: Bolchazy-Carducci, 1995), 59.
59. [Anonymous], "Some Observations on the Island of Barbadoes, 1667," C.O. 1/31, no. 170. For a transcript of the entire document, see Jerome S. Handler and Lon Shelby, "A Seventeenth Century Commentary on Labor and Military Problems in Barbados," *JBMHS* 34:3 (1973): 117–21 (quotation on 118).
60. Vincent T. Harlow, *A History of Barbados 1625–1685* (Oxford: Clarendon, 1926), 338. In 1655 whites had still outnumbered blacks; rough estimates in 1668 and 1669 gave blacks a two-to-one advantage.
61. For the doubling of the black population, see Beckles, *White Servitude,* 168.
62. For the importance of Dutch sugar plantations in Brazil to the transformation of the Barbados economy in the 1640s, see Robert Boyle's account, cited below on p. 456, note 100.
63. "Father Antoine Biet's Visit to Barbados in 1654," *JBMHS* 32 (1967): 67; Ligon, *Barbadoes,* 52.
64. "Some Observations on the Island of Barbadoes" (1667), 120 ("there are many thousands of slaves that speak English, either born there or brought young into the country").
65. Fox, *Gospel Family-Order,* 16–17.
66. Las Casas, *The Spanish Colonie,* E4.

Chapter 8

1. Robert Beverley, *The History and Present State of Virginia* (1705), ed. Louis B. Wright (Chapel Hill: University of North Carolina Press, 1947), 272; Hugh Jones, *The Present State of Virginia* (1724), ed. Richard L. Morton (Chapel Hill: University of North Carolina Press, 1956), 130.
2. Numerous examples are cited in Allen, *Invention of the White Race,* 1:163–64. *OED*'s first example of "wage-slave[ry]" (*wage n.*4.a) dates from 1886, but White cites examples from American pro-slavery advocates as early as 1820. See also Wilfred Carsel, "The Slaveholders' Indictment of Northern Wage Slavery," *Journal of Southern History* 6 (1940): 510–16.
3. George Fitzhugh, *Sociology for the South* (Richmond, VA: 1854), excerpted in *Clotel,* 403.
4. William S. McFeely, *Frederick Douglass* (New York: Norton, 1991), 105.
5. Cobbett, *Political Register* 52 (November 20, 1824), in *"Hard Times": Human Documents of the Industrial Revolution,* ed. E. Royston Pike (New York: Praeger, 1966), 60–61.
6. Engels, *The Condition of the Working Class in England* (1846), in *The Voice of Toil: Nineteenth-Century British Writings about Work,* ed. David J. Bradshaw and Suzanne Ozment (Athens: Ohio UP, 2000), 479.

7. Karl Marx, *The Communist Manifesto* (1848), ed. Frederic L. Bender (New York: Norton, 1988), 61–62. A partial English translation, by Helen Macfarlane, had appeared in 1850 (54).
8. Brown, *American Fugitive in Europe,* 116, 313.
9. Dickens, *The Life and Adventures of . . . Martin Chuzzlewit* (1844), chap. XXI.
10. Dickens, *Hard Times* (1854), Book II, chap. iv.
11. David Roediger, "Race, Labor, and Gender in the Languages of Antebellum Social Protest," in *Terms of Labor,* 173.
12. Brown, "Speech . . . 5 September 1849," in *The Black Abolitionist Papers,* Vol. I, *The British Isles, 1830–1865,* ed. C. Peter Ripley et al. (Chapel Hill: University of North Carolina Press, 1985), 170.
13. Sancho, *Letters,* 1:145–6 ("Jan. 5, 1780").
14. Brown, "Speech," *Black Abolitionist Papers,* 1:170.
15. See the Lucas transcripts of the "Minutes of the Council" (Department of Archives, Barbados), November 6, 1655 (pp. 161–62).
16. See Allen, *Invention of the White Race,* 2:148–62.
17. See for instance Shana Poplack, Gerard Van Herk, and Dawn Harvie, "'Deformed in the dialects': An Alternative History of Non-Standard English," in *Alternative Histories,* 87–110.
18. *Archives of Maryland,* 72 vols. (Baltimore: Maryland Historical Society, 1883–1972), 1:41.
19. Helen T. Catterall, ed., *Judicial Cases Concerning Slavery,* vol. 1 (Washington, DC, 1926), 77; Morgan, *American Slavery,* 154.
20. *Archives of Maryland,* 1:533–34: "*An Act Concerning Negroes & other Slaves* . . . That all Negroes or other slaves already within the Province And all Negroes and other slaves to be hereafter imported into the Province shall serve Durante Vita And all Children born of any Negro or other slave . . ." For the similar Virginia statute of 1670, see *The Statutes at Large; Being a Collection of All the Laws of Virginia,* ed. William W. Hening, 13 vols. (Richmond, VA, 1809–23), 2:283.
21. Hening, *Statutes at Large,* 2:288
22. Kupperman, *Providence Island,* 178.
23. James H. Sweet, "Spanish and Portuguese Influences on Racial Slavery in British North America, 1492–1619" ("Collective Degradation"), 8.
24. A. P. Newton had interpreted it as a reference to Africans: see *The Colonising Activities of the English Puritans* (New Haven, CT: Yale UP, 1914), 261.
25. Alison Games, "'The Sanctuarye of our Rebell Negroes': The Atlantic Context of Local Resistance on Providence Island," *Slavery and Abolition* 19 (1998): 1–21.
26. C.O. 124/1, fol. 124 (July 3, 1638).
27. Sir Jonathan Atkins to Lords of Trade and Plantations, August 15, 1676 (C.O. 1/37, No. 48); for prices and immigration, see Beckles, *White Servitude,* 123–25.
28. Morgan, *American Slavery,* 296–99.
29. Berlin, *Many Thousands Gone,* 114. Berlin is misleading about the chronology of this change: "Victory over the small holders, servants, and slaves who composed Nathaniel Bacon's motley army in 1676 enabled planters to consolidate their control over Chesapeake society. In quick order, they elaborated a slave code that singled out people of African descent as slaves and made their status hereditary" (109). But the legislative definition of discriminatory African slavery had been established by a series of Virginia statutes in the 1660s: what Berlin calls "the Africanization of slavery" (107, 111) was institutionalized in the 1660s (at the latest), before Bacon's rebellion.
30. For the legislation, see Lefroy, ed., *Memorials,* 1:308–09 (1623), and *Acts of Assembly, Made and Enacted in the Bermuda or Summer-Islands, From 1690, to 1713–14* (1719),

"An Act for Trying Negroes and Slaves" (12–13). For *white* more generally, there are no examples in *The Rich Papers: Letters from Bermuda, 1615–1646,* ed. Vernon A. Ives (Toronto: University of Toronto Press, 1984). The first use in Bermuda reproduced in Lefroy's *Memorials* occurs in a document signed July 15, 1679, replying to inquiries from London: "About four Merchants English, noe Strangers, about foure hundred Planters, about eight thousand Men, Women, Children, and Slaves, about a thousand White people able to bear armes" (2:432). This answer uses "White" even though the question from London did not (2:431). Later in the same document, the noun *whites* is used in both London question and Bermuda answer: "Q: What number of Whites, Blacks or Mulattos have been born or christened, for these seaven years last past . . . Ans: About one hundred and twenty of Whites, Blacks, and Mulattos are born in a year" (2:432).

31. Guild, *Black Laws of Virginia,* 36 (1639, ACT X), 24 (1691, Act XVI, "white women").
32. Robert J. Sternfeld, *The Invention of Free Labor: The Employment Relation in English and American Law and Culture, 1350–1870* (Chapel Hill: University of North Carolina Press, 1991).
33. "The Worthy Enterprise of John Fox," in *Piracy, Slavery, and Redemption: Barbary Captivity Narratives from Early Modern England,* ed. Daniel J. Vitkus (New York: Columbia UP, 2001), 63–66.
34. "Ebenezer; or, A Small Monument of Great Mercy, Appearing in the Miraculous Deliverance of William Okeley" (1675), in *Piracy, Slavery, and Redemption,* 147, 150–52, 139–40.
35. Christopher Hill, "The Norman Yoke," in *Puritanism and Revolution* (Secker and Warburg, 1958), 50–122.
36. P. E. H. Hair and Robin Law, "The English in Western Africa to 1700," in *The Oxford History of the British Empire,* vol. I: *The Origins of Empire: British Overseas Enterprise to the Close of the Seventeenth Century,* ed. Nicholas Canny (Oxford: Oxford UP, 1998), 241–63.
37. Jobson, *Golden Trade,* 88–89 (sig. M4v-N1).
38. *A Perfect Description of Virginia* (1648), 1 ("there are in *Virginia* about fifteene thousand *English,* and of *Negroes* brought thither, three hundred good servants").
39. Henry Winthrop to John Winthrop, January 1628, in *Winthrop Papers,* ed. A. B. Forbes et al., 5 vols. (Boston: Massachusetts Historical Society, 1929–47), 1:357.
40. Eltis, *African Slavery,* Table I–1, 9–10.
41. Eltis, *African Slavery,* 278, 22.
42. Marcellus Rivers and Oxenbridge Foyle, *England's Slavery or Barbados Merchandise, Represented in a Petition to the High Court of Parliament* (1659).
43. For the full parliamentary debate, see *Diary of Thomas Burton,* ed. John T. Rutt, 4 vols. (1828), rev. ed., Ivan Roots et al. (Johnson Reprint Corp., 1974), 4:254–73 (March 25, 1659), 300–09 (March 30, 1659). Quotations from 261, 301, 262, 263, 270, 271, 306.
44. Burton, *Diary,* 4:304. For another example of a historian using *white* when it is not in the sources, see Hilary McD. Beckles, "English Parliamentary Debate on 'White Slavery' in Barbados, 1659," *JBMHS* 36 (1982): 344–52. Beckles claims that "Some contemporaries called it 'white slavery'" (346)—but he does not provide a single citation of the phrase from the period. It does not appear anywhere in the reported parliamentary speeches. In Barbados itself, a complaint against "a slavish imposition beyond what Englishmen ever yet suffered," which would allegedly leave the inhabitants "meerely slaves to that company that shall have the sayd license as our *Negroes* are to us, they making theirs the whole advantage of our labours and industries here," consistently used the word *Englishmen* instead of *white:* see *A Declaration Set forth by the Lord Lieutenant Generall the Gentlemen of the Councell & assembly* (1651), 3.
45. See Jonathan A. Bush, "Free to Enslave: The Foundations of Colonial American Slave Law," *Yale Journal of Law and the Humanities* 5 (1993): 417–70, quoting (456) Chief Justice Holt's opinion in *Smith v. Brown and Cooper* (1702?).

46. In the seventeenth century, Massachusetts and New Hampshire limited "freeman" status to Englishmen; Connecticut and Rhode Island required special methods of approval for any "foriner, Dutch, French, or of any other nation" seeking to be admitted as a freeman. See Peter Kivisto, *Americans All: Race and Ethnic Relations in Historical, Structural, and Comparative Perspectives* (Belmont, CA: Wadsworth, 1995), 113–14, 138.
47. On January 9, 1654, the Barbados Coucil ruled that "Jews and Hebrews inhabiting in & about this Island . . . during their stay shall enjoy the privileges of Laws & statutes of the Commonwealth of England & of this Island, relating to foreigners & strangers" ("Minutes," 87). Like other Europeans, Jews belonged to international trade and kinship networks important to the Barbados economy.
48. "Extracts from Henry Whistler's Journal of the West India Expedition" (British Library Sloane MS 3926), Appendix E in *The Narrative of General Venables,* ed. C. H. Firth (1900), 146.
49. *CSPC,* vol. 7, *America and West Indies, 1669–1674,* ed. J. Noel Sainsbury (1889), no. 1101 (May 28, 1673), 495.
50. A small fraction of these foreigners had been naturalized as English subjects before their arrival; others were specifically naturalized by colonial governments. But in the seventeenth century the status of foreigners was bedeviled by jurisdictional ambiguities between England and the colonies and between one colony and another; moreover, established practices often had no legal basis whatever. See James H. Kettner, *The Development of American Citizenship, 1608–1870* (Chapel Hill: University of North Carolina Press, 1978), 65–105.
51. N. D. Davis, "Papers Relating to the Early History of Barbados and St. Kitts," *Timehhri: Journal of the Royal Agricultural Society of British Guiana* 6 (1892): 327–49 (transcribing depositions made in 1647, contained in Trinity College, Dublin, MS G.4, 15), 329 ("tenn negroes taken in a prize").
52. PRO Req. 2/164/117. The case was first described by Knutson, "Caliban in St. Mildred Poultry," 116. It continues to be overlooked by legal historians of slavery.
53. Sweet, "Spanish and Portuguese Influence," 11–12 (citing ANTT, Inquisição de Lisboa, Processos, No. 5964). As Sweet notes, this eyewitness testimony in Lisbon confirms the accuracy of William Harrison's claim, in 1577, that "if anie come hither from other realms, so soone as they set foot on land they become so free of condition as their masters" (cited by Jordan, *White Over Black,* 49).
54. 2 Lev. 201, 83 Eng. Rep. 518 (King's Bench 1677). In the same year, the Privy Council ruled that slaves were to be deemed commodities within the Navigation Acts, which meant they had to be carried by English ships: see *CSPC, America and West Indies, 1677–80,* 118, 120.
55. Bodleian Library, Rawlinson MS c.94, fol. 28. More generally, see Jerome S. Handler, "The Amerindian Slave Population of Barbados in the Seventeenth and Early Eighteenth Centuries," *JBMHS* 33 (1969): 111–136.
56. In a letter dated August 22, 1627, colonist Henry Winthrop described Barbados as "without any inhabytanse of any other people of other natyones saue Inglishe men saue a matter of 50 slaves of Indyenes and blacks," and in another dated October 15, 1627, he wrote that "here is but 3 score of christyanes and fortye slaues of negeres and Indyenes": see *Winthrop Papers,* I:357, 361. In both letters, he treats the Indians as slaves, indistinguishable from the enslaved Africans; in neither does he use *white* to identify himself and the other English colonists. *White* does not appear in any of the letters from or about Barbados in this collection (through December 1649), or in *Volume VI: 1650–1654,* ed. Malcolm Freiberg (1992).
57. Rawlinson MS c.94, fol. 29, 32, 33, 33^{v}.
58. William Duke, *Memoirs of the First Settlement of the Island of Barbados and Other the Caribbee Islands* (1743), 20.

59. Richard S. Dunn, *Sugar and Slaves: The Rise of the Planter Class in the English West Indies, 1624–1713* (Chapel Hill: University of North Carolina Press, 1972), 228.
60. On the European control of time, including the time that Africans and Indians would serve their masters, see Taylor, *Time, Space, Race.*
61. Claude Meillassoux, *The Anthropology of Slavery: The Womb of Iron and Gold,* tr. Alide Dasnois (Athlone, 1991), 23–26, 78–84, 99.
62. On freedom as a condition defined by "belonging" (rather than "individuality"), see Orlando Patterson, *Freedom in the Making of Western Culture* (New York: Basic Books, 1991), 20–44.
63. On the legal importance of *Calvin's Case* in colonial America, see Kettner, *Development of American Citizenship,* 6–16, and Rogers M. Smith, *Civic Ideals: Conflicting Visions of Citizenship in U.S. History* (New Haven, CT: Yale UP, 1997), 40–69.
64. David Armitage, *The Ideological Origins of the British Empire* (Cambridge: Cambridge UP, 2000), 120.
65. On prejudicial treatment of the Irish in Barbados, see Hilary McD. Beckles, "A 'riotous and unruly lot': Irish Indentured Servants and Freemen in the English West Indies, 1644–1713," *William and Mary Quarterly* 47 (1990): 503–22. On the more general English prejudice against the Irish throughout the seventeenth century—and its importance as a precedent for other English prejudices—there is a growing historical literature: the first volume of Allen's *Invention of the White Race* is entirely devoted to anti-Irish prejudice.
66. In the 1650s the Governor's Council in Barbados also acted as the Court of Chancery, hearing appeals based on equity rather than common law. On August 1, 1654, the Council upheld the complaint of an indentured servant against his master, reducing the term of his service (Lucas transcript, p. 44); on March 4, 1656, it freed "from any longer service" two Irishmen who protested "that they were Prisoners of War, taken at Sea, & contrary to law or custom sent as Slaves to this Island" (196). By contrast, on January 2, 1655, it denied the validity of Henry Powell's deposition in defense of the enslaved Indians and ordered a new trial under common law jurisdiction (84), and on January 13 it gave Colonel Ellis "liberty to sue the Indians at Judge Colleton's Court" (85). On March 20, having heard "part" of a petition from "Anthony Izard, a Negro . . . for his Freedom," it ordered "that the said Negro be referred to the Common Law for Trial" (99). The Council thus recognized the equity rights of indentured servants and Irishmen, but not of Indians and Negroes. Since common law privileged property rights, and local courts directly reflected local prejudices, the Council's procedural evasion deprived nonwhite plaintiffs of any hope of a sympathetic ruling.
67. *An Entire Commentary upon the Whole Epistle of the Apostle Paul to the Ephesians . . . Preached by Mr Paul Bayne* (1643), 695. Paul Baynes (d. 1617) had written *A commentarie upon the first chapter of the epistle to the Ephesians* (1618), which was posthumously published; but if Bayne had completed his commentary before his death, it would certainly have been published in 1618. There is, to my knowledge, no evidence identifying the author of the commentary to the other chapters of Ephesians. Given the Puritan credentials of Bayne, the anonymous author may have been familiar with the enslavement of Africans on Providence Island in the 1630s.
68. *The reports of Sir Edward Coke, knt. late lord chief justice of England . . .* (1658), 583–613.
69. On the shortage of colonial lawyers and the consequent dependence on "custom" and "local traditions," see Warren M. Billings, "The Transfer of English Law to Virginia 1606–50," in *The Westward Enterprise: English Activities in Ireland, the Atlantic, and America 1408–1650,* ed. K. R. Andrews, N. P. Canny, and P. E. H. Hair (Detroit: Wayne State UP, 1979), 220–21, 232, 236. Billings relates *Calvin's Case* to the jurisdiction of English laws in Virginia, but does not address its importance for slavery (243).
70. Labov, *Sociolinguistic Patterns* (Philadelphia: University of Pennsylvania Press, 1973), 1. The first chapter of Labov's foundational book was originally published in 1963.

71. Everett M. Rogers, *Diffusion of Innovations,* 4th ed. (New York: Free Press, 1995), 10.
72. David Crystal, *The Cambridge Encyclopedia of Language* (Cambridge: Cambridge UP, 1987), 332.
73. This so-called gravity model of linguistic change and diffusion was first articulated in Peter Trudgill's "Linguistic Change and Diffusion: Description and Explanation in Sociolinguistic Dialect Geography," *Language and Society* 3 (1974): 215–46, and in his book *The Social Differentiation of English in Norwich* (Cambridge: Cambridge UP, 1974), 9–10, 99–112, 129, 167–68.
74. E. A. Wrigley and R. S. Schofield, *Population History of England, 1541–1871* (Cambridge, MA: Harvard UP, 1981), 208–09.
75. Nicholas Canny, *Kingdom and Colony: Ireland in the Atlantic World, 1560–1800* (Baltimore: Johns Hopkins UP, 1988), 96; Games, *Migration,* 4.
76. Henry A. Gemery, "Emigration from the British Isles to the New World, 1630–1700: Inferences from Colonial Populations," *Research in Economic History* 5 (1980): 179–231; Wrigley and Schofield, *Population History of England,* 219–21.
77. On the diminution of interaction as a function of distance, see K. E. Haynes and A. S. Fotherinham, *Gravity and Spatial Interaction Models* (Newberry Park, CA: Sage, 1984). A century's work in linguistic geography has shown the crucial role of distance in the spread of innovations: see Lee Pederson, Susan McDaniel, and Carol Adams, *Linguistic Atlas of the Gulf States, Vol. 4, Regional Matrix* (Athens: University of Georgia Press, 1990) and *Vol. 5, Regional Pattern* (1991).
78. For the circulation and production of texts in the seventeenth century, see *A History of the Book in America,* Vol. 1, *The Colonial Book in the Atlantic World,* ed. Hugh Anmory and David D. Hall (Cambridge: Cambridge UP, 2000), 1–151.
79. For the urban/rural dense/dissipated distinction, see "Dialect Diffusion" in Walt Wolfram and Natalie Schilling-Estes, *American English: Dialects and Variation* (Oxford: Blackwell, 1998), 142–48.
80. *CSCP* 7:393–94 ("Answers to the inquiries of the Council for Foreign Plantations"). On St. Christopher's (no. 896.II), there were 496 English men able to bear arms, 349 French, and 41 Dutch, for a total of 886 able European men; the three nationalities had 352, 552, and 48 blacks respectively, for a total of 952. On the English territory, whites still significantly outnumbered blacks, but the black majority among the French and Dutch no doubt made all the Europeans on the tiny island nervous. On Nevis, wholly occupied by the English, there were 1,411 men able to bear arms, but 1,739 blacks (no. 896.VI). By 1678 blacks outnumbered not simply the white men on Nevis, but all whites: see the summary of the 1678 census in Dunn, *Sugar and Slaves,* 127.
81. Eltis, *African Slavery,* 216, 235, 255.
82. Gaw, *Migration,* 190–216.
83. On the importance of the wind-current system to the history of European generic identity, see Taylor, *Time, Space, Race.*
84. On Bridgetown as the seventeenth-century equivalent of Philadelphia and Boston in the eighteenth century, see Eltis, *African Slavery,* 219; on roads, see Jack P. Greene, "Changing Identity in the British Caribbean: Barbados as a Case Study," in *Colonial Identity in the Atlantic World, 1500–1800,* ed. Nicholas Canny and Anthony Pagden (Princeton, NJ: Princeton UP, 1987), 230.
85. Godwyn, *Advocate,* 36, 83. Godwyn also uses *white* in a generic sense elsewhere: "nothing doubted (tho *Black*) to be of the same *species,* with the *Whiter*" (24); "*English,* or of the *Whiter* sort" (39), "*White People*" (77); "to remember how unjust it would seem to one of us, that our *different White* should deprive us of the least Advantage" (160).
86. On Godwyn's career, see Vaughan, *Roots,* 55–81.
87. Dunn, *Sugar and Slaves,* 108: "Untill a neger wench I have be brought to knowledge, I cannot . . . be without a white maid" (John Blake, letter of November 1, 1675).

88. In addition to the statement by Governor Atkins in 1676 (quoted above), *white* appears in the following official documents: Governor Dutton to Lords of Trade and Plantations, June 10, 1683, and December 19, 1683, CO 29/3, fol. 214; Minutes of Council, February 16, 1686, *CSPC 1685–88,* 155; Governor Edwin Stede to Lords of Trade and Plantations, August 1687, *CSPC 1685–88,* 17; Sir Thomas Montgomery to the Lords of Trade and Plantations, August 3, 1688, *CSPC 1685–88,* 577; quoted in Beckles, *White Servitude,* 39, 38, 112, 104, 92.
89. "Records of the Vestry of St. Michaels," *JBMHS* 15 (1948): "8th of Mch. 1668" (old style, e.g., 1669): "the whole profitt for duties of all that shall be putt into the said Cage, both Whites and Blacks" (202).
90. *CSPC,* 7:107 (no. 277), September 28, 1670; 7:116 (no. 298), October 20, 1670; 7:205 (no. 508), 1670.
91. For the conclusion that "all of law's texts . . . are works of fiction," see Paul W. Kahn, *The Cultural Study of Law: Reconstructing Legal Scholarship* (Chicago: University of Chicago Press, 1999), 139. This needs to be distinguished from Lon L. Fuller's argument that *Legal Fictions* (Stanford, CA: Stanford UP, 1967) represent only "the pathology of the law," a verbal patch applied to conceal a difficulty, "propounded with a complete or partial consciousness of its falsity" (viii, 9). There is no reason to suppose that Englishmen in the seventeenth-century colonies regarded "white" as a false description.
92. "An Act for the better ordering and governing of Negroes," C.O. 30/2 (September 27, 1661), preamble.
93. For colonial case reports I have checked *Judicial Cases concerning American Slavery and the Negro,* ed. Helen T. Catterall, 5 vols. (Washington, DC: Carnegie Institute, 1926–1937). In Maryland as late at September 1681 a lawsuit contrasts "two English men" with "a negro" and "five Indians" (4:27), but a Maryland case in January 1685 refers to "One Roger Makeele, one called Mr. Smith, one other white man, and One negro" (4:27). This 1685 report is the first example I have found in continental colonial case law, but it is four years later than Maryland's first use of *white* in legislation. Catterall's collection does not include reports from any of the island colonies, and I am not aware of any comparable compendium that would make it possible to locate the first use of *white* in English Caribbean case law (though I have checked the manuscript of the Barbados Council/Chancery Minutes from February 1654 through July 1656).
94. Bradley J. Nicholson, "Legal Borrowing and the Origins of Slave Law in the British Colonies," *American Journal of Legal History* 38 (1994): 38–54.
95. Watson, *Slave Law in the Americas* (Athens: University of Georgia Press, 1989), 64.
96. The earliest use of *white* in English law apparently occurred in the landmark case of *Somerset v. Stewart* (1772), where, in arguments before the court, a supporter of slavery claimed that it was "necessary the masters should bring them [their black slaves] over [to England from the colonies]; for they [the masters] cannot trust the whites, either with the stores or the navigating the vessel" (*Judicial Cases,* ed. Catterall, 1:16).
97. John R. Bartlett, ed., *Records of the Colony of Rhode Island and Providence Plantations, in New England,* 10 vols. (Providence, RI, 1856–65), 1:243.
98. Jordan, *White Over Black,* 70.
99. Vaughan, *Roots,* 3–33.
100. Shoemaker, "How Indians Got to Be Red," 625–44.
101. John Francis de la Roche (1542) and Marco di Nita (1539), translated and printed in Hakluyt, *Principal Voyages* (1598–1600), 3:242, 370, 373; John Smith, *A Map of Virginia. With a Description of the Countrey . . .* (Oxford, 1612), 19; William Strachey, *The Historie of Travell into Virginia Britania (1612),* ed. Louis B. Wright and Virginia Freund (Hakluyt Socitey, 1953), 70; William Wood, *New Englands Prospect* (1634), 54–55; Thomas Morton, *New English Canaan* (Amsterdam, 1637), 32; Thomas Lechford, *Plain Dealing:*

or, Newes from New-England (1642), 50; Roger Williams, *Key into the Language of America* (1643), 52; Daniel Coxe to Robert Boyle, February 5, 1666 (*Correspondence of Robert Boyle,* 3:57). Strachey's manuscript and Coxe's letter were not published until much later, but the other seven accounts circulated in hundreds of printed copies (and reprints). Vaughan refers to, but does not quote, Wood, Morton, and Williams (*Roots* 10, 28). Coxe simply asserted that "in America . . . the natives are white"; Nita reported "a white man" and a people "somewhat white"; Roche insisted that "they are very white," indeed "as white" "as the French are," but explained that "they paynt themselues for feare of heat and sunne burning." The other six noted that the Indians were "fair" (Wood) or "indifferent white" (Strachey) or "white" (Smith, Morton, Lechford, Williams) at birth; Smith observed that they were "of a colour browne when they are of any age" without accounting for the change of color, but the other four all explained that the Indians deliberately darkened their skin by "their annoyntings" (Williams), thus situating their somewhat darker skin in the realm of nurture, not nature. It belonged with the other kinds of skin painting discussed in chapter 1.

102. *The Complete Writings of Roger Williams,* 7 vols. (New York: Russell & Russell, 1963), 1:141. Among many discussions of Williams and Native Americans, see for instance John Garrett, *Roger Williams: Witness Beyond Christendom, 1603–1683* (Macmillan, 1970), 119–44.
103. Almon Wheeler Lauber, *Indian Slavery in Colonial Times within the Present Limits of the United States* (New York: Columbia UP, 1913), 108–09, 123–27. For a New England example, see the January 1648 "Bill of Sale from John Winthrop Governour of the massachusetts in New England" which "sould . . . one Indian man called Hope" to "John Mainford of the iland of Barbados merchant" (*Winthrop Papers,* 5:196–97).
104. Nathaniel B. Shurtleff and David Pulsifer, eds., *Records of the Colony of New Plymouth in New England,* 12 vols. (Boston, 1855–61), 9:70–71.
105. In Newport, Rhode Island, in 1676 the Quaker missionary William Edmundson—the first Christian Englishman to declare slavery a sin—told his audience that "many of you count it unlawful to make slaves of the Indians: and if so, then why the Negroes?" See Thomas E. Drake, *Quakers and Slavery in America* (New Haven, CT: Yale UP, 1950), 12. This reproduces the parallelism in the 1652 statute.
106. Vaughan, *Roots,* 172: "In 1652, Rhode Island's legislature epitomized the prevailing English bifurcation of humanity when it referred to 'blacke mankind or white.'"
107. All the mainland colonies and Bermuda are noted in Jordan, *White Over Black,* 96. Jordan did not take account of the Caribbean legislation because, unlike the laws of the mainland colonies and Bermuda, "The main body of surviving island statutes for this early period is still in manuscript in the Public Record Office" (Dunn, *Sugar and Slaves,* 238). To identify first occurrences for Antigua, Barbados, St. Kitts, Nevis, and Jamaica I had to read through those manuscripts, and given the difficulty of some of the handwriting (and the scattering of material from the same colony in different manuscripts), it is possible that I have missed an earlier occurrence; without a critical edition of the Caribbean legislation comparable to those available for the mainland colonies, absolute certainty is impossible.
108. David Barry Gaspar, "With a Rod of Iron: Barbados Slave Laws as a Model for Jamaica, South Carolina, and Antigua, 1661–1697," in *Crossing Boundaries: Comparative History of Black People in Diaspora,* ed. Darlene Clark Hine and Jacqueline McLeod (Bloomington: Indiana UP, 1999), 343–66. (This article routinely uses "white" when its sources do not, but that does not affect Gaspar's compelling evidence of legal influence.)
109. All the available property on Barbados was already engrossed by 1647; "something like 10,000 Barbadians moved to other parts of English America during the course of the century." St. Kitts, likewise, was overpopulated by 1655, when it began exporting large numbers of whites; small planters were leaving Nevis by the later 1660s. In the detailed 1679

list, Boston had the second highest total among destinations (exceeded only by London); mainland colonies from Carolina to New England were the chosen new home of 230 emigrants, as against only 154 for other Caribbean destinations (Dunn, *Sugar and Slaves,* 111–12). There was, of course, much more land available on the mainland than in the Caribbean—and also less danger of attack by French and Dutch warships.

110. See Anthony Long, William Hilton, and Peter Fabian, *A Relation of a Discovery Lately made on the Coast of Florida (from Lat. 31, to 33 Deg. 45 Min. Nort-Lat.* (1664), 30: "the severall and respective Persons above-intended, shall within five years next ensuing, have one Person white or black, young or old transported at their Charge as aforesaid." This is an account of the first expeditionary party from Barbados, reconnoitering possible settlement sites in what became South Carolina.

111. For a general theory of the mechanisms of memory that help generate collective cultural identities, see Gary Taylor, *Cultural Selection* (New York: Basic Books, 1995). I do not there use the sociobiologists' term *meme* (a replicating unit of imitation), which was invented by Richard Dawkins in *The Selfish Gene* (Oxford: Oxford UP, 1976), and developed at length in Susan Blackmore's *The Meme Machine* (Oxford: Oxford UP, 1999). In its generic meanings, the word *white* surely qualifies as a "selfish meme": highly effective in encouraging its own replication and in transforming its environment—and highly noxious.

112. C.O. 154/1 ("Leeward Islands 1644–73"), folio 55–6 (stamped numeration). The Antigua statute has received little scholarly attention. Winthrop Jordan's account of "early reactions to sexual union between the races" overlooked it (*White Over Black,* 78–79). Richard Dunn's three-sentence summary (*Sugar and Slaves,* 228)—apparently the first modern discussion—did not mention its remarkable early legalization of whiteness. There are brief references in Fernando Henriques, *Children of Caliban: Miscegenation* (Secker and Warburg, 1974), 93–94, and Mindie Lazarus-Black, *Legitimate Acts and Illegal Encounters: Law and Society in Barbuda and Antigua* (Washington, DC: Smithsonian Institution Press, 1994).

113. Herbert, *A Relation of Some Yeares Travaile, Begunne Anno 1626. Into Afrique and the greater Asia . . .* (1634), 198. A "revised and enlarged" edition was published in 1638 and reprinted in 1664, 1665, and 1677.

114. Barbados had begun to use sugar "as unit of measure and medium of payment" by about 1645 (Eltis, *African Slavery,* 196); by contrast, tobacco "was still a major crop in Antigua in the late 1680s" (205).

115. For early Antigua, see Dunn, *Sugar and Slaves,* 17–18, 30–34, 118–26; Carl and Roberta Bridenbaugh, *No Peace Beyond the Line: The English in the Caribbean 1624–1690* (New York: Oxford UP, 1972), 13, 20–21, 32–3, 53, 172.

116. "An Act concerning Negroes & Slaves" (1681), *Archives of Maryland,* 7:203–05.

117. Act XVI (1691), in *Statutes at Large,* ed. Hening, 3:86–87.

118. *Acts and Statutes of the Island of Barbados. Made and Enacted since the Reducement of the same, unto the Authority of the Common-wealth of England. And Set forth the Seventh day of September, in the year of our Lord God, 1652. By the Honourable Governour of the said Island, the Worshipfull the Council, and Gentlemen of the Assembly,* 20–21 (sig. C2^v-C3). This undated London pamphlet includes statutes passed between January 17, 1651, and July 19, 1654; this one is specifically dated "7 of October, 1652 *Signed, Daniel Searle.*" This statute is not included in Richard Hall's *Acts, Passed in the Island of Barbados. From 1643, to 1762, inclusive* (1764).

119. C.O. 154/2 ("Leeward Islands 1668–82"), 4. I quote the title of the statute; *white* is not used in the body of the text, which instead at the corresponding point has "any Christian Servant or Servants." The law is indexed in *CSPC,* 7:362 (no. 832).

120. "An Act for planting of Provisions" (1669), in *Acts of Assembly . . . Montserrat 1668–1740* (1740), 17–18 (no. 16).

121. C.O. 154/1, fol. 117 (new). This is number "13" of a group of 15 Nevis acts; they are undated, but identify "Sir Charles Wheeler" as governor, a position he held for less than a year after his arrival in 1670.
122. "An act For the Better Ordering and Governing of negro Slaves," C.O.139/1, fol. 121a.
123. "An Act for the bett[r] ord[r]ing & Gouerning of Negro Slaues," C.O.139/1, fol. 66b. Another significant change between 1664 and 1674 is in the provision that "euery Owner of a Family in this Island shall cause all his Slaues houses to bee searched dilligently & effectually once eu[r]y fow[r]teene Dayes" (122b); this is the same in the 1664 statute, except that the "Slaues" of 1674 were "Negro Slaues" in 1664 (fol. 67b). Presumably, by 1674 "Slaues" so clearly implied "Negro" that the adjective could be omitted.
124. C.O. 30/2, clause 2.
125. The Jamaica Assembly had passed in May 1672 "An Act to provide that everyone for 10 working negroes be obliged to have one Christian servant, and so proportionably" (C.O. 139/1, fol. 138), and later in that same session had also passed an act (number 28) "For the encouragement of the importation of Christian servants into this island." Other examples of the so-called deficiency laws were passed in Barbados (1661), Antigua (1677), and St. Kitts (1679), but they also referred to the servants as "Christian": see C.O. 30/2, p. 78 (Barbados), C.O.154/2, pp. 326 (Antigua), 23–24 (St. Kitts).
126. *The Laws of Jamaica, Passed by the Assembly, And Confirmed by His Majesty in Council* (1683), 6, 78, 80, 65. These Jamaican statutes were approved at Whitehall in February 1683 (sig. A1) and were valid for the space of seven years "to commence from the First of October last preceding the Date hereof" (sig. 06, signed "John Nicholas").
127. *Acts and Resolves, public and private, of the Province of Massachusetts Bay,* 1:698. Jordan did not record this first (?) use of *white* in Massachusetts, presumably because he limited himself to seventeenth-century examples.
128. *Acts and Resolves,* 1:578; *Council for New England, Records,* 10:260.
129. Aaron Leaming and Jacob Spicer, eds., *The Grants, Concessions and Original Constitutions of the Province of New Jersey,* 2nd ed. (Somerville, NJ, 1881), 236–37: "That no white servant, whether male or female, if seventeen years of age, when bound or bought, shall serve above four years from the time of their arrival here, and then be free . . . and no white servant shall be sold or transported against hir or their consent to any place out of this Province. . . . If a man or woman, maim, or smite the eye of his or their man or maid servant, being a white servant, so that it perish, or smite out the tooth of his or their man or maid servant, such servant shall go free" (section XXV of "A Bill for the General Laws of the Province of New Jersey").
130. *The Colonial Laws of New York,* 5 vols. (Albany, 1894), I:148 (October 23, 1684): "Bee itt further ennacted by the authority aforesaid that whosoever shall Councell, perswade, entice, inveagle, or allure any white Servant whether Male or female either by promises of freedome Matrimony or by any other ways or means what soever to omitt or Neglect the Service worke and Imployment of his or her Master or Mistresse and be therof Convicted shall be adjudged to make full satisfaction to the said Master and mistresse."
131. In *Acts of Assembly, Made and Enacted in the Bermuda or Summer-Islands, From 1690, to 1713–14* (1719), among statutes passed in 1690 and 1691 is included "An Act for Trying Negroes and Slaves," which defines the correct legal procedures for cases in which "any Negroes, Molattoes, Indians, Mustees, Quarterroons, or other Slaves whatsoever, shall at any time or times hereafter be accused to have committed any Murther, Burglary, Felony, or other Capital Crime . . . in cases of this nature and kind, Be it Enacted, That the Oath of One White Person of Discretion shall be sufficient Proof to Convict any such Offender; and in case no such White Person can Swear to the Fact positively against him or them, yet with good Circumstances relating to the Fact, given upon Oath by one or more White Person or Persons, and the Testimony of one Black

agreeing therewith, shall be sufficient Proof to Convict such Offender or Offenders" (12–13).

132. *The Statutes at Large of South Carolina,* ed. Thomas Cooper and David J. McCord, 10 vols. (Columbia, SC, 1836–41), 7:343 (February 7, 1691). The same statute orders that "if any negro or Indian slave shall offer any violence, by striking or the like, to any white person, he shall for the first offence be severely whipped," etc. (essentially repeating the provision of the Jamaica statute, cited above, which in turn had essentially repeated a Barbados statute). South Carolina's relatively late use of legislative *white* is a function of the colony's late foundation. It began passing statutes only in 1682, and none survive until 1685: we know titles of 22 earlier laws for which we have no text. Most of the other colonial legislatures had already used *white* before South Carolina passed any of its extant laws.

133. Cheryl I. Harris, "Whiteness as Property," *Harvard Law Review* 106 (1993): 1709–91. Harris documents the property status of whiteness in (eighteenth-century) colonial and (nineteenth-century) American case law.

134. C.O. 154/2, 107–08: "White men not to keep Company with Negroes . . . Whereas many mischiefs arise by the vnchristianlike association of white people wth Negroes: their drinking together in Common vpon Sabbaoth dayes, when they should be at better Exercises, being mute to y[e] dishonnour of God, and the Scandall of Christianity: Therefore be it Enacted . . . y[t] all such white people as shall be found soe spending their times on the Lords or other dayes in drinking, playing, or conversing wth Negroes, shall for such Crimes be presentable, to y[e] Justicies of the peace in each respective diuision that they may receiue such Corporall punishment, he or they shall think meet to inflict" (Nevis, May 26, 1675).

135. "An Act for the Better Government of Slaves," C.O. 8/3, fol. 25–28 (December 16, 1697). For discussion of this code and the slightly revised code of 1702, see David Barry Gaspar, *Bondmen and Rebels: A Study of Master-Slave Relations in Antigua* (Baltimore, MD: Johns Hopkins UP, 1985), 135–36, 164–67.

136. Hobbes, *Computatio Sive Logica/Logic,* tr. Aloysius Martinich, ed. Isabel C. Hungerland and George R. Vick (New York: Abaris, 1981), 202–03 (chapter 2, section 7). *Logica* was originally published as Part First of *De Corpore* (1655); an anonymous English translation, *Elements of Philosophy: The First Section, concerning Body,* appeared in 1656. Hobbes contrasts whites with blacks, blues, and transparents (*nigri, caerulei, diaphani*), thus demonstrating that he is thinking of colors, not population groups. Martinich translates the plural Latin "*non-albi*" as the singular English "nonwhite," but this is part of the translator's systematic change of plurals to singulars. *OED*'s first example of the noun or adjective *non-white* dates from 1921.

137. Hobbes would have regarded "not being whites" as the equivalent of *non-albi:* he wrote of "some equivalent of [*non-albi*] in which the vocal sound 'white' [*albi*] is repeated (such as 'unlike white' [*albo dissimile*])" (*Logica,* tr. Martinich, 202–03).

138. *Judicial Cases,* ed. Catterall, 1:78.

139. The "one-drop" rule was first articulated in 1857: see Thomas D. Morris, *Southern Slavery and the Law, 1619–1860* (Chapel Hill: University of North Carolina Press, 1996), 26–27. But A. Leon Higginbotham Jr.—in *Shades of Freedom: Racial Politics and Presumptions of the American Legal Process* (New York: Oxford UP, 1996)—notes that "The 1662, 1705, and 1723 [Virginia] statutes codified into law, long before the scientific theories had been dreamed up, the idea that black blood was a corrupting agent and that the purity of white blood needed to be protected from its corrosive effects" (36); discussing the 1705 Virginia statute that defined as mulatto "the child of an Indian, or the child, grandchild, or great grandchild of a Negro," he points out that, since the statute was passed only about 85 years after the first blacks had arrived in Virginia, "there would barely have been time for four generations of offspring necessary to 'dilute the taint' of

black blood to the point that it did not count under law. Thus, few if any white/black mixtures would have qualified as white, though it is likely there were some white/Indian mixtures who did" (39). The problem of defining white and nonwhite began to preoccupy legislatures in both Antigua and Virginia at about the same time.

140. K. G. Davis, *The Royal African Company* (Longman, 1957), 1–14, 39.
141. On Bell's move from Providence to Barbados, see Duke, *Memoirs,* 21–22, and P. F. Campbell, "Aspects of Barbados Land Tenure 1627–1663," *JBMHS* 37 (1984): 141. Bell left Providence in 1637 and arrived in Barbados in 1640 or 1641. He was officially only the "deputy governor" between 1641 and 1645, but since the alleged "governor" was absent, Bell was in charge from 1641 to 1649; moreover, he adopted a policy of "neutrality" in relation to the dispute between king and Parliament in England, which (as Campbell notes) "amounted to virtual independence." To my knowledge, no one has called attention to Bell's possible role in the massive expansion of slave imports in Barbados after 1640. According to Robert H. Schomburgk, in *The History of Barbados* (1848), "during the war between the Dutch and Portuguese for the possession of Maranham, the Dutch governor sent fifty Portuguese of St. Luiz in 1643 to Barbados to be sold as slaves. The governor (Philip Bell) ordered them to be brought on shore, as if intending to bargain for them, and then set them at liberty, after indignantly reproving the agent, who had insulted him by offering white men and Christians for sale" (144). Schomburgk cites no source for his account, which may not have contained the idiom "white men," but the incident itself indicates that Bell by 1643 extended the rights of Englishmen to all Europeans, including Catholics.
142. Alan Burns, *History of the British West Indies* (George Allen & Unwin, 1954), 203.
143. Larry D. Gragg, "'To Procure Negroes': The English Slave Trade to Barbados, 1627–60," *Slavery and Abolition* 16 (1995): 65–84.
144. Dunn, *Planters and Slaves,* 58, 69.
145. Davis, *Royal African Company,* 12–13, 41–43.
146. Peter Fryer, *Staying Power: the History of Black People in Britain* (Pluto Press, 1984), 14.
147. *The Diary of Samuel Pepys,* 2:36 (February 14, 1661), 6:215 (September 7, 1665), 6:244 (September 27, 1665), 9:464 (March 2, 1669), 510 (April 5, 1669).
148. For the portraits see Hall, *Things of Darkness,* 211–53. See Patrick Moorah, *Prince Rupert of the Rhine* (Constable, 1976), for Rupert's acquisition of an African boy in 1652 (264) and subsequently of other blackamore servants (287), all of whom had by 1658 been disposed of or died (298).
149. As noted by Bartlemy, *Black Face,* 50, 47.
150. The brief reports of court cases involving the status of enslaved Africans (beginning in 1677) do not use the word *white:* see *Oroonoko,* ed. Catherine Gallagher and Simon Stern (New York: Bedford St. Martin's, 2000), 414–17.
151. On the extent—and peculiarity—of that legal silence, see Bush, "Free to Enslave," 428–56.
152. Thomas Jordan, *London Triumphant* (1672), 6 ("two *Negroes* . . . two white Virgins").
153. On the date of *Titus,* see Gary Taylor, "The Canon and Chronology of Shakespeare's Plays," in Stanley Wells, Gary Taylor, et al., *William Shakespeare: A Textual Companion* (Oxford: Clarendon Press, 1987), 113–15. For further evidence that the play was a collaboration between Shakespeare and Peele, see Marina Tarlinskaja, *Shakespeare's Verse: Iambic Pentameter and the Poet's Idiosyncracies* (New York: P. Lang, 1987), 124; Brian Boyd, "Common Words in *Titus Andronicus:* The Presence of Peele," *Notes and Queries* 247 (1995): 300–07; Gary Taylor, "Shakespeare and Others: The Authorship of *1 Henry VI,*" *Medieval and Renaissance Drama in England* 7 (1995): 179–82; MacD. P. Jackson, "Stage Directions and Speech Headings in Act I of *Titus Andronicus* Q (1594): Shakespeare or Peele?" *Studies in Bibliography* 49 (1996): 134–48; Ward E. Y. Elliott and Robert

J. Valenza, "And Then There Were None: Winnowing the Shakespeare Claimants" (Claremont, CA: Claremont McKenna College, 1996); Brian Vickers, *Shakespeare, Co-Author: A Historical Study of Five Collaborative Plays* (Oxford: Oxford UP, 2002), 148–243. In the forthcoming revised edition of the *Complete Works,* gen. ed. Wells and Taylor (Oxford: Oxford UP, 2005), *Titus* will be explicitly identified as collaborative.

154. Royster, "White-limed Walls: Whiteness and Gothic Extremism in Shakespeare's *Titus Andronicus," Shakespeare Quarterly* 51 (2000): 432–55 (esp. 440, n. 22). She identifies the Goths as "hyperwhite," but this formula is based on the assumption that the other characters would have been regarded as "white." It seems more accurate, historically, to say that the play's tripartite racial division separates the normative Roman characters from the "black" Aaron and the "white" Goths.

155. The association of Goths with Scandinavia was traditional: see for instance *De Proprietatibus Rerum* XV, 71, 152 (2:765–66, 813), and George Abbot, *A Briefe Description of the Whole Worlde* (1599), sig. A5v; numerous additional sources are cited in Kliger, *Goths,* 13ff.

156. For Shakespeare's Catholicism, see Gary Taylor, "The Fortunes of Oldcastle," *Shakespeare Survey* 38 (1985): 85–100; "Forms of Opposition: Shakespeare and Middleton," *English Literary Renaissance* 24 (1994): 283–314; "Divine [ ]sences," *Shakespeare Survey* 54 (2001), 13–30.

157. Edward Ravenscroft, *Titus Andronicus, or the Rape of Lavinia* (1687), 2.1 (p. 15). The adaptation had been performed in 1678.

158. Michael Clarke, *The Tempting Prospect: A Social History of English Watercolours* (British Museum, 1981), 14.

159. As noted in chapter 9, by 1673 the old trope of "washing an Ethiope" had been reinterpreted racially in a popular London text; that makes it more likely that the swan's inability to wash her black legs white also would be interpreted racially in 1678.

160. Thomas Killigrew, *Bellamira her Dream; or, the Love of Shadows,* in *Comedies and Tragedies* (1664), 563–64 (*Part Two,* Act Four, scene four).

161. "Dark is the case" (p. 10), "this black Vayle . . . my swarthy Cheeks" (11), "your Swarthy Cymerion" (20), "her Raven-colour'd Love . . . Like a frighted Crow" (21), "my dear black Angel, Did ever Raven sing so like a Lark" (31), "this Black and loathsome Child," "that Fiend" (38), "this black Imp," "a thing So foul and black" (39), "the Moor, The Moor, that dismall Fiend of darkness" 51), "his dark soul," "so muffled in black clouds" (52), "A Child of darkness . . . this black brat, This Babe of darkness" (53). *Moor* appears 13 times in the dialogue of the original, but 35 times in the dialogue of the adaptation.

162. "Poets are Planters, Stage is their Plantation . . . they are for Trade and Propagation": Ravenscroft, *Dame Dobson* (1684), "Epilogue" (p. 71). The "Plantation" he had in mind was probably Barbados, on the evidence of the immediately preceding couplet ("If Alderman did Spirit men away, Why may not Poets then Kidnap a Play?"). Ravenscroft alluded to such methods of supplying involuntary colonists again in *The English Lawyer* (1678), I.i ("Trepan'd to some foreign Plantation"). See also *The Canterbury Guests* (1695), I.vi: "The Son of an English Renegade: He was born a Ship-board, and never was ashore beyond a Sea Port Town—except up in the Countries amongst Indians and Spaniards" (where the "Indians" must belong to Spanish New World dominions), and "He brings with him sixty thousand Crowns, and doubtless will have good Employment—for from Captains of ships, and Governors of Plantations, the King has heard much of his Valour" (where the "Governors of Plantations" presumably refers to English colonies, in the sea-vicinity of the Spaniards and Indians just mentioned—which would therefore have to be in the Caribbean). In *The London Cuckolds* (1682), a character laments that "a whilrwind blows my Mistress into Asia and I am tost into America."

163. For Ravenscroft's familiarity with the principle, see *The Careless Lovers: A Comedy* (1673), Act Two: "he had sold me to the Master of the Ship, who was a Dutchman; he sold me, and this poor Child that was in my Belly, to Slavery and Bondage."

164. For the association of chains and slavery, see Ravenscroft, *Careless Lovers,* 2.1 ("comes like a Slave loaden with Feters, dull and out of humour").
165. On the western obsession with cannibalism in its encounters with nonwestern peoples, see Peter Hulme, *Colonial Encounters: Europe and the Native Caribbean, 1492–1797* (Methuen, 1986), 13–87. On early modern cannibalism and theater, see Gary Taylor, "Gender, Hunger, Horror: The History and Significance of *The Bloody Banquet,*" *Journal of Early Modern Cultural Studies* 1 (2001): 1–45. Both Shakespeare's and Ravenscroft's depictions of the eater differ radically from Montaigne's and Middleton's psychologically complicated representation.
166. MacDonald, "'The Force of Imagination': The Subject of Blackness in Shakespeare, Jonson, and Ravenscroft," *Renaissance Papers 1991* (1992): 68.
167. Michael Dobson, *The Making of the National Poet: Shakespeare, Adaptation and Authorship, 1660–1769* (Oxford: Clarendon Press, 1992), 62, 75.
168. Shakespeare, *Titus Andronicus,* ed. Eugene Waith (Oxford: Clarendon, 1984), 46.
169. Shakespeare, *Titus Andronicus,* ed. Jonathan Bate, Arden Shakespeare (Routledge, 1995), 54.
170. *Great Newes from the Barbadoes . . . with The number of those that were burned alive, Beheaded, and otherwise Executed for their Horrid Crimes* (1676), 12. "Some affirm, they intended to spare the lives of the Fairest and Handsomest Women (their Maistresses and their Daughters) to be converted to their use. But some others affirm the contrary; and are induced to believe they intended to Murther all the White People there, as well Men as Women" (10).
171. Dunn, *Sugar and Slaves,* 258, 260. Reports of the Jamaica revolt were sent in various letters to England in June and July 1678.
172. "[A]nother *Cormantee Negro* working with him told him boldly and plainly, *He would have no hand in killing the* Baccararoes *or White Folks* . . . He answered and told her freely, *That it was a general Design amongst them the* Cormantee Negro's, *to kill all the* Baccararoes or *White People in the Island*" (*Great Newes from the Barbadoes,* 10). Coromantines, from the so-called Gold Coast, were preferred by planters in Barbados and Jamaica in the seventeenth century (Eltis, *African Slavery,* 247, 250).
173. Thomas Tryon, *Friendly Advice to the Gentlemen-Planters of the East and West Indies* (1684), 151.
174. The third author was Aphra Behn, who used it—in the form "Backearary"—in *Oroonoko* (1688), 105.
175. Lorenzo Dow Turner, *Africanisms in the Gullah Dialect* (Chicago: University of Chicago Press, 1949), 191. Turner did not record the seventeenth-century examples.
176. See Frederic G. Cassidy and Robert LePage, *Dictionary of Jamaican English,* 2nd ed. (Cambridge: Cambridge UP, 1980), and Richard Allsopp, *Dictionary of Caribbean English Usage* (Oxford: Oxford UP, 1996). Allsopp notes that the Efik people, long established as middlemen in the slave-trading centers of eastern Nigeria, "would probably have established the item as a loan-word and spread it among slaves of other languages groups who also brought it to the New World" (61).

Chapter 9

1. For these sources, see *Clotel,* 258–62, 270–71.
2. For a full account of the myth in Brown's lifetime, see Thomas Virgil Peterson, *Ham and Japheth: The Mythic World of Whites in the Antebellum South* (Metuchen, NJ: Scarecrow Press and The American Theological Library Association, 1978), and Stephen R. Haynes, *Noah's Curse: Race, Slavery, and the Biblical Imagination in America* (New York: Oxford UP, 2002).
3. Douglass, *Narrative,* 119, 188, 163.

4. See Bernard Lewis, *Race and Color in Islam* (New York: Harper & Row, 1971); Ephraim Isaac, "Genesis, Judaism and the 'Sons of Ham,'" *Slavery and Abolition* 1 (1980): 3–17; Davis, *Progress,* 32–51; Bernard Lewis, *Race and Slavery in the Middle East: An Historical Inquiry* (New York: Oxford UP, 1990); David H. Aaron, "Early Rabbinic Exegesis on Noah's Son Ham and the so-Called 'Hamitic Myth,'" *Journal of the American Academy of Religion* 63 (1995): 721–59; Braude, "Sons of Noah," 134–35; Braude, "Cham et Noé: Race, escalavage, et exégèse entre Islam, Judaisme, et Christianisme," *Annales* 57 (2002): 93–125; Braude, "Michelangelo and the Curse of Ham: From a Typology of Jew-Hatred to a Genealogy of Racism," in *Writing Race across the Atlantic,* ed. Beidler and Taylor; Braude, "Ham and Noah: Sexuality, Servitudinism, and Ethnicity" ("Collective Degradation"); David Goldenberg, "Early Jewish and Christian Views of Blacks" ("Collective Degradation").
5. Alcuin, *Interrogationes et responsivenem in Genesin, Patrologia Latina,* vol. 100, col. 532; *The Old English Version of the Heptateuch: Aelfric's Treatise on the Old and New Testament and his Preface to Genesis,* ed. Samuel John Crawford (Early English Texts Society, 1967), 27. For *Cursor Mundi*—which assigned "Asia to sem, to cham affrik, / To Iaphet europ"—see Alfred B. Friedman, "'When Adam Delved . . . ': Contexts of an Historic Proverb," in *The Larned and the Lewed: Studies in Chaucer and Medieval Literature,* ed. Larry D. Benson (Cambridge, MA: Harvard UP, 1974), 227–29.
6. On Mandeville see Braude, "Sons of Noah," 115–20.
7. Something like Mandeville's mix can still be seen in Henry Ainsworth's *Annotations upon the First books of Moses Called Genesis* (1616), which assigns to Japhet "part of Æurope with Asia the less" (sig. I1). In *The Common Expositor: An Account of the Commentaries on Genesis 1527–1633* (Chapel Hill: University of North Carolina Press, 1948), Arnold Williams notes that "In nearly all the works on English history and antiquities, one finds fairly extensive treatment of this matter. Ralegh, Drayton, Warner, Purchas, and Heylyn all devote greater or lesser space to ascertaining which of the Gentile people sprang from which of the descendants of Japheth," and that in the Renaissance "the Gentiles . . . meant the inhabitants of Europe generally" (155).
8. *Supplement to the Fifth volume of the Athenian Gazette* (1691), 7.
9. I have searched *Luther's Works on CD-ROM,* gen. ed. Jaroslave Pelikan and Helmut T. Lehmann (Fortress Press, 2003), for uses of generic *white,* and found none.
10. *Sermons of M. Iohn Caluine vpon the Epistle of Saincte Paule to the Galathians,* tr. Arthur Golding (1574): "it is alwayes sayd that a purblind person is cleersighted, among them that are starke blind. And among the black Moores, he that is tawny will seem white. If iudgement bee giuen of a white man when he is among a dozen Moores, there will be no whiteness vnto his. But if he bee brought ageine among his owne countrymen, he will bee found to bee a farre other than he was taken to bee" (fol. 294). See also Calvin's *Commentary on Galatians,* tr. Robert Vaux (1581): "a poore blinde man among blinde men seemeth to himselfe to bee well sighted, and he that is browne among black men thinketh himself white" (M3^{v}; commentary on Galatians 6:5). Calvin's ironic remarks suggest that he was familiar with the generic idiom "white man," but did not use or endorse it himself.
11. Shuger, "White Barbarians," 520.
12. Jordan, *White Over Black,* 40–42.
13. Paul Freedman, *Images of the Medieval Peasant* (Stanford, CA: Stanford UP, 1999), 86–104.
14. *Vox Clamantis,* ed. G. C. Macauley, in *The Complete Works of John Gower,* Vol. 4 (Oxford: Clarendon, 1902), Book I.10.747–82 (42–43).
15. [Andrew Horn], *The Mirror of Justices,* ed. William Joseph Whittaker (Selden Society, 1895), 77.
16. Coke, *The First Part of the Institutes of the Lawes of England; or, a Commentarie upon Littleton* (1628), lib. 2, cap. xi, sec. 172 (sig. 2F4^{v}). Coke's marginal note cites, as his authority for this statement, "*Mirror* cap 2. S 18, Genesis 9.10.11, &c."

17. For synopses of the two positions, see Vaughan, "The Origins Debate: Slavery and Racism in Seventeenth-Century Virginia" (1989), reprinted in *Roots,* 136–74, and Barbara Jeanne Fields, "Slavery, Race and Ideology in the United States of America," *New Left Review* 181 (1990): 95–117. Fields is critiqued in Vaughan's reprint of his original article. Theodore Allen begins *The Invention of the White Race* with compelling criticisms of the logical weaknesses of both positions (1:1–24), but he is himself committed to the anticapitalist camp.
18. Williams, *Capitalism and Slavery* (Chapel Hill: University of North Carolina Press, 1944), 7.
19. For an overview of the four elements of the Williams thesis, see Barbara L. Solow and Stanley L. Engerman, "An Introduction," in *British Capitalism and Caribbean Slavery: The Legacy of Eric Williams,* ed. Solow and Engerman (Cambridge: Cambridge UP, 1987), 1–23; they regard this as less important than other aspects of his work, and it is represented in the volume by only one essay, William A. Green's "Race and Slavery: Considerations on the Williams Thesis" (25–50), which traces the history of subsequent debate, and the chronological and methodological obstacles to the race/slavery thesis.
20. O'Dair, *Class,* 43–66.
21. See the already cited works by Eldred Jones, G. K. Hunter, Winthrop Jordan, Anthony Gerard Barthelemy, Jack D'Amico, Kim Hall, Margo Hendricks, Joyce Green MacDonald, Arthur Little Jr., Virginia and Alden Vaughan, and Francesca Royster (among others).
22. Eltis, *African Slavery,* 65. Eltis demonstrates, throughout the book, the importance of "the cultural parameters within which economic decisions are made" (284).
23. See Linebaugh and Rediker, *The Many-headed Hydra,* and Allen, *Invention of the White Race,* 2:148–61.
24. Both volumes of Allen's *Invention of the White Race* are dedicated to proving his "social control" thesis; he cites six Virginia examples of "hostility directed by non-ruling-class European-Americans at non-European-Americans" between 1669 and 1694 (2:161–62). Allen dismisses his own examples of worker colorphobia on the grounds that they merely "echo" the "explicitly anti-negro tenor" of laws passed by the plantation bourgeoisie. But such laws began to be passed long before Bacon's Rebellion, and before "the invention of the white race." One part of White's causative chronology forgets another.
25. Morgan, *American Slavery,* 128.
26. See Bernard Capp, *The World of John Taylor the Water-Poet, 1578–1653* (Oxford: Clarendon, 1994).
27. Taylor, "The Author of the Verse, takes leave of the Author of the Prose," in *Master Thomas Coriat to his Friends in England . . . the last of October 1616* (1618), sig. E3.
28. Taylor, "Plutoes Proclamation concerning his Infernall pleasure for the Propagation of Tobacco," in *The Nipping or Snipping of Abuses* (1614), sig. C4^{v}-D1^{v}.
29. Taylor, *The Praise of Hemp-seed* (1620), sig. B2, C3.
30. *Taylor his Travels: from the Citty of London in England, to the Citty of Prague in Bohemia* (1620), D2-D2^{v}.
31. Taylor, "A Bear," in *Bull, Beare, and Horse, Cut, Curtaile, and Longtaile* (1638), sig. D5.
32. Best, *True Discourse,* 29–30 (sig. f3-f3^{v}); discussion of Ham follows on pp. 30–32 (sig. f3^{v}–4^{v}). In Hakluyt's 1600 reprint of Best (cited by Jordan), both discussions occur on the same page (52, sig. E2^{v}).
33. For Tabari and his sources, see Braude, "Cham et Noé."
34. See Braude's discussion of the (somewhat obscure) mid-fifteenth-century allusion to the curse by Azurara ("Sons of Noah," 127–29).
35. A Dominican friar, Fray Francisco de la Cruz, in 1575 told the Inquisition in Lima that an angel had told him that "the blacks are justly captives by reason of the sins of their forefathers, and that because of that sin God gave them that colour, and that the cause is not the reason given by philosophy, and that they are of the tribe of Aser . . ." (*que los*

negros son justamente captivos por justa sentencia de Dios por los pecados de sus padres, y que en sen-al desto les dio' Dios aquel color, y que no es la causa de ser negros la razón que dan Philosophos sino de la dicha, y que son del tribu de Aser, de quien dijo el patriarcha Jacob assinos fortes). For this testimony see Marcel Bataillon, "Le <<Clérigo Casas>> ci-devant Colon, réformateur de la colonisation," *Bulletin Hispanique* 54 (1952): 368 (citing "Procès inédit de l'Archivo Histórico Nacional de Madrid, *Inquisición,* Leg. 1650, fol. 1320). I have not seen the Inquisition manuscript itself. Bataillon glosses the friar's reference to "Philosophos" with the explanation that "les naturalistes attribuaient cette couleur à l'action du soleil," and it is not clear whether Bataillon's gloss refers to something specific from the manuscript that he has not quoted or merely reflects his own knowledge of sixteenth-century debates. As Bataillon notes, Fr. Francisco's memory evidently confused Aser with Issacar (Gen. 49: 14–15). A generation before this confession, Spain had forbidden the enslavement of Indians in its New World dominions and officially switched to imported Africans for a supply of slave labor.

36. Bodin, *Methodus ad Facilem Historiarum Cognitionem,* 94 (sig. n3[v]); *Method,* 87.
37. Guillaume Postel, *Cosmographicae disciplinae compendium* (Basle, 1561), 16–19; William J. Bouwsma, *Concordia Mundi: The Career and Thought of Guillaume Postel (1510–1581)* (Cambridge, MA: Harvard UP, 1957), 4, 252–61. Braude, "Ham and Noah," identified Postel as Bodin's source. Bouwsma documents Postel's use of Arabic and Jewish sources (37–47) and his knowledge of travel literature, including Munster, Pigafetta, Martyr, and Varthema (58). Postel claims that Chus was born black though his parents were white: "Chus niger ex albo parente" (sig. B3, p. 17), and re-named Africa "Chamesia" (14, etc), i.e., "the land of Ham."
38. Genebrardus, *Chronographiae libri quatuor* (Paris, 1580), 26–27, as cited and summarized by Don Cameron Allen, *The Legend of Noah: Renaissance Rationalism in Art, Science, and Letters* (Urbana: University of Illinois Press, 1949), 119.
39. Origen, *Homilies on Genesis and Exodus,* tr. Ronald Heine (Washington, DC: Catholic University of America Press, 1981), 215: "For the Egyptians are prone to a degenerate life and quickly sink to every slavery of the vices. Look at the origin of the race and you will discover that their father Cham, who had laughed at his father's nakedness, deserved a judgment of this kind, that his son Chanaan should be a servant to his brothers, in which case the condition of bondage would prove the wickedness of his conduct. Not without merit, therefore, does the discolored posterity [*decolor posteritas*] imitate the ignobility of the race [*generis*]." Braude, who calls attention to this passage in Origen ("Cham et Noé"), notes that *decolor* could mean "black" in classical Latin; however, Heine's introduction supplies overwhelming evidence that the translation of Origen's lost Greek originals into Latin by Rufinus (ca. 403–05) was a paraphrase rather than a literal translation, and hence the specific word *decolor* might reflect the views of Rufinus rather than those of Origen himself. The passage does not mention Chus at all. For the many intertwined meanings of the Latin noun *genus* (anachronistically translated "race" by Heine), see Taylor, *Castration,* 146–47, 154–55. For Origen's more general allegorical equation of a "black" person with sin, see Goldenberg, "Jewish and Christian Views."
40. The first printed edition, by Aldus Manutius (Venice, 1503), was followed by those of Merlin (1512), Erasmus (1536), Grinaeus (1571), and Genebrardus (1574). Braude notes that the medieval church would have had little use for Origen's theory and that slavery was instead normally explained by the curse of Esau ("Cham et Noé"). But he does not call attention to the number of sixteenth-century editions, or to Bodin and Genebrard.
41. Torniellus, *Annales sacri et profani* (Frankfurt, 1611), 133; I have checked the original (the 1611 edition, instead of the 1620, to which Allen refers), but I quote Allen's translation and summary from *Legend of Noah,* 119. (There is no other English translation.) Torniellus has a slightly different explanation of the origin and transmission of African blackness;

he argues "that Ham's wife's mind was either on something black at the time of Chus' conception or else she was afflicted with a longing for black during his gestation. The wife of Chus was white and, consequently, bore both black and white sons to her husband, who considerately assigned the hotter and more comfortable regions of the earth to his dark offspring" (Allen, 119; *Annales,* 134). The complexity of this mechanism, however, matters less than the adoption of the curse of Ham in recognition of the failure of classical geographical theory to explain the phenomenon.

42. Pory, *Description of Africa,* 1:68, 20.
43. Sandys, *A Relation of a Journey begun an: Dom: 1610* (1615), 136–37 (N2^{v}-N3).
44. Purchas, ed., *Hakluytus Posthumus,* 2:913 (book 2, chapter 8, section 3). Noted by Braude, "Sons of Noah," 137–38 (who does not discuss the 1615 text).
45. *Hakluytus Posthumus,* I.i.31 (chapter 9).
46. Heylyn, *Microcosmos,* 2nd ed. (1627), 771: "the inhabitants" of America "(though a great part of this country lieth in the same parallell with *Ethiopia, Lybia,* and *Numidia*) are of a reasonable faire complexion, and very little (if at all) inclining to blacknesse. So that the extraordinary and continuall vicinity of the Sun, is not (as some imagine) the efficient cause of blacknesse: though it may much further such a color: as wee see in our country lasses, whose faces are alwaies exposed to wind and weather. Others, more wise in their own conceite, though this conceit know no confederate; plainely conclude the gernative seed of the *Africans* to be black, but of the *Americans* to be white: a foolish supposition, and convinced not only out of experience, but naturall Philosophie. As for that foolish tale of *Cham*'s knowing his wife in the Arke, whereupon by divine curse his son *Chus* with all his posterity, (which they say are *Africans*) were all black: it is so vaine, that I will not endeavour to retell it. So that we must wholly refer it to God's peculiar will and ordinance." As Jordan noted (*White Over Black,* 19), by the 1666 third edition Heylyn was more accepting: "Possibly enough the Curse of God on *Cham* and on his posterity (though for some cause unknown to us) hath an influence on it" (Heylyn, *Cosmographie,* 1016).
47. Billings, "Transfer of English Law," 240.
48. Frederickson, *Racism: A Short History,* 19–25; Michael Adas, *Machines as the Measure of Men: Science, Technology, and Ideologies of Western Dominance* (Ithaca, NY: Cornell UP, 1989), 291.
49. Browne, *Pseudodoxia Epidemica,* ed. Robin Robbins, 2 vols. (Oxford: Clarendon, 1981), 1:508, 512 (book VI, chap. 10). As representative modern geographers Browne cites by name Ortelius, Leo Africanus, and Duarte Lopez.
50. Peter Biller has traced the belief that "white" was normative to two thirteenth-century academic texts: Vincent of Beauvais's *Speculum naturale* and Thomas of Cantimpré's *Liber de natura rerum:* see "The Black in Medieval Science: What Significance?" ("Collective Degradation"). In one of the 9,885 chapters of his work (it is so large that there are few extant copies), Vincent discusses skin, stating that "Among men it is naturally white (*alba*), except in those parts of the world where hot rays of the sun burn" (xxviii.30; col. 2012). Cantimpré agrees that "cutis alba est naturaliter in hominibus in omnibus fere partibus orbis" (i.42). Interpretation of both passages depends on how *alba* is translated; although "pale brown" may have been its meaning in classical Rome, it may have meant "white" for these thirteenth-century clerics. As Biller acknowledges, this medieval context requires further study, which might demonstrate that ideas of European whiteness had spread northward from Italy, Sicily, and Spain by the mid-thirteenth century; however, neither author was English, by birth or habitation, and the relevance of their work to a study of Anglophone whiteness is very uncertain. Biller's other medieval examples refer to women, or assume the classical geohumoral distribution, or are at best ambiguous.
51. Browne, *Pseudodoxia Epidemica,* 1:510: "faire or white people translated into hotter Countries" do not as a result become black, "as hath been observed in many Europeans

who have lived in the land of Negroes." Browne's "faire or white" is grammatically ambiguous: "faire" might represent a different category than "white" or simply be another name for the same thing. But these "Europeans" are the only humans to which Brown applies the adjective "white." In other places he notes that the inhabitants are "not black" or "not Negroes" or "faire" or "tawny," but he applies "white" only in this sentence about Europeans (and in his description of semen).

52. Browne, *Pseudodoxia Epidemica,* 1:516. Brown here develops the theory articulated by Duarte Lopez, discussed in chapter 4.
53. Christopher Hill, *The English Bible and the Seventeenth-century Revolution* (Penguin, 1994), 3, 7, 18, 23. On printing's transformation of the medieval Bible, see Braude, "Sons of Noah," 106–07. Black notes that the printing of the Bible made the "curse" explanation much more widely available to the general population (*Making of New World Slavery,* 83).
54. Jordan claims that "When the story of Ham's curse did become relatively common in the seventeenth century it was utilized almost entirely as an explanation of color rather than as justification for Negro slavery" (*White Over Black,* 18). But Sandys, Cooper, and Weemes all relate it specifically to the enslavement of Africans, and Browne insists that the curse is specifically slavery (not color), noting that many of Ham's posterity were not enslaved (*Pseudodoxia Epidemica,* 1:520). Of the English authors, only Best does not mention slavery at all, but he was surely aware of the African slave trade: Frobischer's mentor Captain John Hawkins had made the first English slaving voyages to Africa in the 1560s.
55. Bataillon, "Clérigo Casas," 368.
56. See the Reverend Samuel Sewall's *The Selling of Joseph, A Memorial* (Boston, 1700), in *The Diary of Samuel Sewall,* ed. M. Halsey Thomas, 2 vols. (New York: Farrar, Straus and Giroux, 1973): the first objection that he finds it necessary to refute is that "*These Blackamores are the Posterity of Cham, and therefore are under the Curse of Slavery*" (2:1119). Cotton Mather's *The Negro Christianized: An Essay to Excite and Assist That Good Work, The Instruction of Negro-Servants in Christianity* (Boston, 1706) begins "Suppose these Wretched negroes, to be the offspring of *Cham* (which yet is not so very certain,)" (1). He later finds it necessary to rebuke the foolish suggestion that "None but *Whites* might hope to be Favored and Accepted with God! Whereas it is well known, that the *Whites,* are the least part of mankind . . . Away with such Trifles! The God who *looks on the Heart, is not* moved by the colour of the *Skin*" (24–25).
57. Browne, *Pseudodoxia,* 1:518, 520 (Book 6, chapter 11).
58. On the implications of this chronology for early modern explanations of human diversity, see Taylor, *Time, Space, Race,* and Kidd, *British Identities Before Nationalism,* 9–33.
59. It is misleading to claim, as Jordan does, that "in the seventeenth century" the curse theory "was probably denied more often than affirmed" (*White Over Black,* 18–19). The denials came from secular intellectuals like Bodin (in Latin only, without explanation), Browne (in a book with a Latin title aimed at only the most educated of readers), and Heylyn (in another huge academic book with a Greek title)—and Heylyn by 1666 was giving in. By contrast, the affirmations came from clergymen (Generardus, Torniellus, Cooper, Purchas, Weemes) and pragmatic laymen (Best, Sandys, Taylor, Peyton, Jobson). The first extended refutation in English—Browne's—was not published until almost 70 years after Best had defended the theory (in a book shorter, and of more general interest, than Browne's).
60. See Oliver F. Emerson, "Legends of Cain, Especially in Old and Middle English," *PMLA* 21 (1906): 831–929; Ruth Mellinkoff, *The Mark of Cain* (Berkeley: University of California Press, 1981); John Block Friedman, *The Monstrous Races in Medieval Art and Thought* (Cambridge, MA: Harvard UP, 1981), 93–106; Braude, "Sons of Noah," 128–29.

61. Peyton, *Glasse of Time* (1620), sig. R4-S2. Many other lines could be quoted: for instance, "Ah cursèd Cain, the scourge of all thy race, Now thou hast got a black and murd'ring face; For God above (in *Justice*) hath ordained Thy offspring all should to this day be stained . . . No other cause the *world* could ever tell / To make them look as if they came from hell . . ."
62. *The Geneva Bible: A facsimile of the 1560 edition* (Madison: University of Wisconsin Press, 1969), fol. 4v–5.
63. Calvin, *Commentary on Genesis,* tr. Thomas Tymme (1578). The commentary was originally published in Latin (Geneva, 1554), then French (Geneva, 1564).
64. According to Wahb ibn Munabbih (d. 730), "Ham the son of Noah was a white man . . . and Almighty God changed his color and the color of his descendants in response to his father's curse. . . . They are the blacks" (quoted by Bernard Lewis in *Islam,* 2:210).
65. *Geneva Bible,* "The first table," sig. 3H4.
66. For the importance of biblical as opposed to Aristotelian justifications of slavery, see Peter Garnsey, *Ideas of Slavery from Aristotle to Augustine* (Cambridge: Cambridge UP, 1996); Jennifer A. Glancy, *Slavery in Early Christianity* (Oxford: Oxford UP, 2002); and Braude, "Ham and Noah" (who also calls attention to the "thousands of years of confusion" about exactly who was cursed).
67. According to Tabari, "Ham attacked his wife [sexually] in the ark, so Noah prayed that his seed be altered, and he produced the blacks": see Braude, "Cham et Noé," citing the original Arabic as well as *The History of al-Tabari,* gen. ed. Ehsan Yar-Shater (Albany: State University of New York Press, 1985-), vol. 1, *From the Creation to the Flood,* tr. Franz Rosenthal (1989), 347. As Braude notes, versions in the Palestinian Talmud and Genesis Rabbah almost certainly predate the Islamic period. Origen's *Homilies* does not contain the sexual explanation, which however does occur in Chrysostom and Ambrose of Milan (fourth century) and in Peter of Riga (early thirteenth). See Haynes, *Noah's Curse,* 29, 31.
68. According to Andrew Willet, *Hexapla in Genesin* (1608), Ham was "given over to all leaudnes, corrupting mankind with his evill manners: and taught them, by his owne example, approoving the same, that it was lawfull, as the wicked use was before the flood, to lie with their mothers, sisters, daughters, with the male, and brute beasts" (105–06); Ham's evil influence was not limited to Africans. But Purchas argued that "Cham, the son of Noah, was by his father banished for particular abuse of himself, and public corruption of the world, teaching and practicing . . . sodomy, incest, buggery . . . in which the Egyptians followed him": see *Purchas His Pilgrimage,* 2nd ed. (1614), 564.
69. Gamble and Hair find Jobson's belief that large penises are dangerous and cumbersome "curious" (*Discovery of River Gambra,* 114). On the medical background, see *Rare Verities. The Cabinet of Venus Unlocked and Her Secrets laid open. Being a Translation of part of Sinibaldus his Geneanthropeia* (1658): "A Mean in all things is the best thing in the world. . . . Wherefore it is not to be questioned, a too long yard [=penis] is not good." This claim is followed by advice on "*How to shorten the Yard being too long*" (40). *Rare Verities* is a translation and adaptation of *Geneanthropeiae* (Rome, 1642), by the Neapolitan physician Giovanni Sinibaldi.
70. Jobson, *Golden Trade,* 52–53 (sig. H2v-H3).
71. Purchas, *Hakluytus Posthumus,* 1/9/13, 1571.
72. John Bulwer, *Anthropometamorphosis* (1650), 260; Anonymous, *The Golden Coast* (1665), 75–76 (referring to the "extraordinary greatness" of "a *Negroes* . . . Members"); John Ogilby, *Africa* (1670), 451 ("The Men are . . . furnish'd, as most of the *Blacks* upon the *Guinee* Coast, with large Propagators").
73. On the history of comparative penis-size scholarship, see David M. Friedman, *A Mind of Its Own: A Cultural History of the Penis* (New York: Free Press, 2001), 103–06.
74. Braude, "Sons of Noah," 132. For a fuller exposition of early sexual interpretations of Genesis 9, see Braude, "Michelangelo."

75. Floyd-Wilson implies that Linschoten's testimony about African sexuality has been influenced by Leo Africanus, and more generally challenges the independence of all other witnesses by insisting that "Leo's work was available in a popular printed source *before* the earliest English travel narratives" (*English Ethnicity,* 141, 202–03). The claim that the Italian or Latin printed texts of Leo were "popular" in England stretches the definition of *popular* to include expensive imported texts in a foreign language. Whether one interprets fifteenth- and sixteenth-century African sexual customs negatively or positively, it can hardly be denied that, in many parts of Africa, they differed from the official sexual norms of western Europe.
76. Ibn Botlan, cited in Evans, "From the Land of Canaan to the Land of Guinea," 24.
77. Smith, *Acoustic World,* 147–67.
78. Bakhtin, *Rabelais and His World,* tr. Helene Iswolsky (Bloomington: Indiana UP, 1984), 368–436.
79. Calvin, *Genesis,* 9:22, 23.
80. For Bodin's revision of classical climate theory on the issue of European sexual coldness and African sexual heat, see Floyd-Wilson, *English Ethnicity,* 34–35, 45–47, 140–42.
81. I explore the social and psychological consequences of that racialized sexual ethic in a forthcoming book, tentatively titled *White Desire.*
82. Augustine, *The City of God,* Book XVI, chapters 2, 10, 11; *Reply to Faustus,* Book XII.
83. Weemes, *The Portraiture of the Image of God in Man* (1627), 279. (Subsequent quotations are from 278–79.)
84. For Luther, see *Lectures on Genesis,* 9:20–27, in *Luther's Works,* ed. Jaroslav Pelikan, Vol. 2 (St. Louis: Concordia, 1960), 166–86. Luther interprets Ham as a hypocrite, who considers himself holier than his father.
85. Calvin, *Commentary on Genesis,* chapter IX, para. 22–27.
86. Augustine, *City of God,* Book XVI, chapter 2, 10.
87. Hill, *English Bible,* 266, citing John Aylmer, *An Harborough for Faithfull and Trewe Subjects* (1559), sig. P4^v-R1^v, and *The Complete Works of John Lyly,* ed. R. W. Bond, 3 vols. (Oxford: Clarendon, 1902), 2:210.
88. Thomas Cooper, *The Blessing of Japheth, Proving the Gathering in of the Gentiles, And Finall Conversion of the Jewes. Expressed in divers profitable Sermons* (1615), 34, A2, 3, 20.
89. Herbert, *Relation,* 114, 6, 15, 196. Herbert elsewhere speculated that the inhabitants of the Cape of Good Hope "have no better Predecessors then Monkeys" (17), and in discussing Siam he notes that "The people are included within the burning Zone, therefore not faire" (195). He thus combines the curse of Ham with geographical and biological explanations for human diversity.
90. Cooper, *Blessing of Japheth,* 9, 35, 46.
91. Herbert, *Relation,* 186–87.
92. Eden, "Preface," in *Decades,* ed. Arber, 51–55.
93. See William S. Maltby, *The Black Legend in England: The Development of Anti-Spanish Sentiment, 1558–1660* (Durham, NC: Duke UP, 1971), 23–24, 29–33.
94. Las Casas, *The Spanish Colonie, or Brief Chronicle of the Actes and Gestes of the Spaniards in the West Indies,* tr. M. M. S. (1583).
95. *The Discoverer of France of the Parisians, and all other the French Nation,* tr. E. A. (1590), 8.
96. Shakespeare, *Love's Labour's Lost* 1.1.175; Spenser, *A View of the Present State of Ireland,* ed. W. L. Renwick (Scholartis Press, 1934), 43–44.
97. See for example Peter Heylyn, *Microcosmos* (1621), sig. C4, p. 23, and Pierre d'Avity, *The Estates, Empires and Principallities of the World,* tr. Edward Grimstone (1615), 116.
98. The change in map-centering was noted by Lesley B. Cormack, *Charting an Empire: Geography at the English Universities, 1580–1620* (Chicago: University of Chicago Press, 1997), 7.

99. Cooper, *Blessing of Japhet,* 9, 35, 45.
100. "What Purchas contributed to English descriptive geography was a growing Protestant bias and an increasing belief in the ability and need of the English to achieve a Protestant hegemony over the pagan and Catholic world" (Cormack, *Charting an Empire,* 140).
101. *OED white a.*7 (examples from 970s on).
102. *The Gospel of Philip,* tr. R. McL. Wilson (Mowbray, 1962), 39 (saying 54); *Das Evangelium Nach Philippos,* ed. W. C. Till (Berlin: Gruyter, 1963), 28 (111.25–28).
103. Gage, *Color and Culture,* 70.
104. S. J. Gould and E. S. Vrba, "Exaptation—A Missing Term in the Science of Form," *Paleobiology* 8 (1982): 4–15.
105. Mufwene, *Ecology,* 5, 11, 68, 160.
106. Richard Younge, *The Cause and Cure of Ignorance, Error, Enmity, Atheisme, Prophanesse, &c.* (1648), sec. 53. Similar objections had been raised by Samuel Ward in *A Coal from the Altar* (1615), 22, 39–40, 45 (the earliest example of this tendency, reprinted four times by 1626, and included in three collections, 1623–35).
107. Cooper's *The Blessing of Japheth* claims to be a collection of "*diuers profitable Sermons,*" but he does not say where they were delivered, and the dedication suggests that the occasion(s) might have been private; the book contains nine sheets.
108. On the similarity of preachers and playwrights, and of the institutions of early modern London church and early modern London theater more generally, see Martha Tuck Rozett, *The Doctrine of Election and the Emergence of Elizabethan Tragedy* (Princeton, NJ: Princeton UP, 1984), 15–25. For a massive account of the complex relationships between preachers and professional writers (of both plays and cheap pamphlets), see Peter Lake with Michael Questier, *The Antichrist's Lewd Hat: Protestants, Papists and Players in Post-Reformation England* (New Haven, CT: Yale UP, 2002).
109. [Robert? Wilkinson], *Lot's Wife. A Sermon Preached at Paules Crosse* (1607), 42. This sentence about Cham seems to have been first quoted by Vaughan (*Roots,* 6), but he does not contextualize it. The printed sermon contains eight sheets.
110. Wilkinson refers to "Cosmographers" in the very next sentence (42), and to the reports of "Late Authors . . . which are as they say eye witnesses of their own report" (43).
111. Thomas Adams, *The White Devil, or the Hypocrite Uncased: in a sermon Preached at Pauls Cross, March 7. 1612* (1613), 1–2 (B1-B1^{v}), 28 (E2^{v}). The date "1612" refers to the old calendar, where the new year began on March 21. The book was entered in the Stationers' Register on April 28, 1613, and presumably printed soon after.
112. *OED*'s earliest citations of *skin-deep* come from Sir Thomas Overbury's *A Wife* and *Characters* (both published in 1613). Its first citations of the verb *skin* in the sense "provide a superficial cover" come from 1602 and 1603. These new senses presumably reflect the gradual assimilation of the new medical knowledge provided by dissection.
113. Two editions are dated 1613, and others appeared in 1614, 1615, and 1617. For Adams himself, see the list of his printed sermons in STC; his *Works* were published in 1629.
114. The first recorded English example of the oxymoronic image of the "white devil" comes from the 1575 translation of *A Commentarie of M. Doctor Martin Luther upon the Epistle of St. Paul to the Galatians* (reprinted six times by 1635), where in the commentary on verse 4 it occurs twice (f. 21, 25^{v}), with the phrase repeated and highlighted both times by a marginal note.
115. Pierre Viret, tr. W. Chauncie, *The Worlde possessed with Deuils, conteyning three Dialogues. 1. Of the Deuill let loose. 2. Of Blacke Deuils. 3. Of White Deuils* (1583), sig. D4^{v}-e3^{v}. In explaining the "difference betweene blacke and white Deuils," Viret specifically contrasted "whyte Deuils" with "Iewes, Turkes, and Paynims" (a1–1^{v}), and specifically identified white devils as "hypocrites" (H2^{v}, c1^{v}, c3^{v}, d5^{v}). The origin of the idiom in Luther

and Viret was noted by R. W. Dent, *John Webster's Borrowing* (Berkeley: University of California Press, 1960), 69–70.

116. Adams, *White Devil,* 1–2 (B1-B1[v]), 28 (E2[v]).
117. Adams, *White Devil,* 35 (F2), 31 (E4[v]). The printed text always italicizes "white devil" and "black saint."
118. Middleton, in the preface to *Two Gates of Salvation* (1609), cited a sermon delivered the month before at Paul's Cross, so it would not be surprising if he heard or read Adams's sermon. In *The Triumphs of Truth,* Middleton's Black King appears when the pageant reaches Paul's Churchyard (352), and specifically recommends to the Mayor "Saint Paul's Cross" (450), where Adams delivered his sermon. Like the black saint in Adams, the Black King has recognized and repented the sins of his youthful "days of error" (394). The Black King, explaining his conversion, remarks that "Such benefit in good example dwells" (404), also a theme of the sermon: "that which I fasten on, is the power and force of example" (4; B2[v]). Adams congratulates the city for "your zeal" (three times repeated), which he would "put . . . into the *Chariot* of grace" (34, F1[v]); in the pageant Truth rides in a chariot, attended by Zeal. Adams says that the Pope "hath stolne *Truths* garment, and put it on *Errors* backe, turning poore *Truth* naked out of doores" (40, F4[v]); Truth and Error are the opposed protagonists of the pageant.
119. For the earliest examples of the idiom in drama, see R. W. Dent, *Proverbial Language in English Drama Exclusive of Shakespeare, 1495–1616: An Index* (Berkeley: University of California Press, 1984), D310. Dent cites Middleton's *Revenger's Tragedy* (1606): "Royal villain, white devil!" (3.5.146). Here *white* refers to the lecherous Duke's white hairs, which should signify the wisdom and reverence he so conspicuously lacks. Middleton used the idiom again in *The Widow* (1615–16): "The miller's a white devil" (4.2.42). There the whiteness is (comically) that of flour, in ironic contrast to the proverbial dishonesty of millers. Although Dent cites Elizabeth Cary's closet drama *The Tragedy of Mariam, The Fair Queen of Jewry* (published in 1613), Cary's devil is not explicitly white but simply painted. See *Mariam,* ed. Barry Weller and Margaret W. Ferguson (Berkeley: University of California Press, 1994): "Now do I know thy falsehood, painted devil, Thou white enchantress" (4.4.175–76). Here *white* is parallel to *painted,* suggesting that the "fair" Mariam is white only because she uses cosmetics to falsify her true complexion. *Mariam* does not actually contain the phrase "white devil," and the date of composition of her text remains conjectural.
120. In the earlier literary examples, the white devil is a foreigner. In all these early texts, the whiteness is something other than skin (hair, flour, starch, dyed clothing), or it refers to the conventionally white complexion of a beautiful woman of high social rank; it is not racial.
121. *The World Tossed at Tennis* also includes a male character called "Deceit the disguiser." When he appears attending a "divine," Deceit is accused of being a "horrid hypocrite" (718) and a "white-faced devil" (723). "Deceit" is "the devil's name" (605), and "the Devil with Deceit" finally enter together (812.2–3). On the original title page, the Devil is represented as a conventional figure, with cloven hooves and tail—and utterly black. All these passages are confidently attributed to Middleton. By contrast, Rowley appears to have written the scene in Middleton and Rowley's *A Fair Quarrel* (1616?) where a physician who has seemed to be a young woman's benefactor tries to blackmail her and is then called a "white devil" (3.2.137); Rowley, unlike Middleton, does not seem to play on the literal meaning of *white.*
122. For the importance of castigation (and "chaste thinking") to the ideology of whiteness, see Little, *Shakespeare Jungle Fever,* 8–21. Little there combines and applies to race the work of Stephanie H. Jed, *Chaste Thinking: The Rape of Lucretia and the Birth of Humanism* (Bloomington: Indiana UP, 1989) and Eve Kosofsky Sedgwick, "Paranoid Read-

ing and Reparative Reading; or, You're So Paranoid, You probably Think This Introduction Is About You," in *Novel Gazing: Queer Readings in Fiction,* ed. Sedgwick (Durham, NC: Duke UP, 1997), 5–28. Unlike Little, I do not think actual generic whiteness occurs anywhere in Shakespeare, but I agree with much of his diagnosis of the ethnocentric and colorphobic structure of Shakespeare's work.

123. Pieter de Marees, *Gold Kingdom of Guinea,* tr. Dantzig and Jones, 49.

124. *Hakluytus Posthumus,* 938 (VII.ii.3, chapter "Of their Apparell" in "A description and historicall declaration of the golden Kingdome of Guinea, otherwise called the golden Coast of Myna.")

125. Thomas Tryon, "A Discourse in way of Dialogue, between an *Ethiopian* or *Negro-Slave,* and a *Christian* that was his Master in *America,*" Part III of *Friendly Advice to the Gentlemen-Planters of the East and West Indies. In Three Parts* (1684), 190, 193.

126. Tryon, *Friendly Advice,* 186. See also: "This Hypocrisie of yours is notorious" (174); "Is *Hypocrisie* a Virtue?" (185); "*Christ* hath not more bitter Enemies in the World, than some of you that wear his *Livery*" (186); "justly be branded for *Hypocrites*" (219). In addition to cases like these, where Tryon actually uses the word *hypocrite,* the bulk of the treatise details the sins of the "Nominal *Christians*" (113).

127. Tryon, *Friendly Advice,* 199, 116.

128. Godwyn, *Advocate,* 14, 3, 78, 53, 26. Godwyn refers repeatedly to the curse theory: "*Cham's African* Race, and the *Curse* said to be annexed thereto" (19), "as *Natives* of *Africa* . . . believed to be Descendants from *Cham,* and under the *Curse*" (43), and spends many pages attacking it from different angles (19–23, 43–61). Remarkably, he even makes a secular and historicist argument against the Old Testament text itself, as merely an expression of Israelite self-interest: "the recording thereof by *Moses,* doth seem to have been especially done only for *Israel's* justification in *dispossessing* of them" (47).

129. Braude claims that "it was not until the eighteenth century . . . that the curse of Ham came to gain broad acceptance," and that a decisive turning point was the citation of the Arabic historian Tabari in Augustin's Calmet's enormously influential *Dictionnaire historique, critique, chronologique, géographiique et littéral de la Bible,* 2 vols. (Paris, 1722). Godwyn demonstrates that, at least in Barbados, the widespread acceptance of the theory did not depend on Tabari or Calmet, indeed did not depend on endorsement by anyone in the church establishment. Braude, himself a polylingual polymath, perhaps overestimates the importance of intellectuals.

130. Godwyn, *Advocate,* 14, 3, 4.

131. See John Stubbs's December 1671 letter to Mary Fox ("The truth is freely preached, both to white people and black people") in *The Journal of George Fox,* ed. John A. Nickalls (Cambridge: Cambridge UP, 1952), 601.

132. *Clotel,* 63. The third-person version of this incident printed in *Clotel* ends with the statement that "After giving the newly-christened freeman 'a name,' the Quaker gave him something to aid him to get 'a local habitation,'" echoing Shakespeare's *A Midsummer Night's Dream* 5.1.15–17 ("the poet's pen Turns them to shapes, and gives to airy nothing A local habitation and a name"). This sentence is not present in Wells's *Narrative,* 242–43, and the allusion has not been noted in editions of *Clotel.* By means of it, Brown defined his own previous status under slavery as "nothing," and equates the Quaker with Shakespeare: both, in their different ways, gave him his identity, as free man and writer.

133. Godwyn, *Advocate,* 27, 40, 39, 84, 83. Quite what he meant by "in a proportionable measure" is not clear; I suspect he meant "the whites may not suffer as badly, but considering that they are white, it is as bad for them as the even more brutal treatment of the negroes is for negroes."

134. Godwyn, *Advocate,* 48, 43, 41, 162, 89. "Since this Argument against the *Negro's* is drawn from holy Scripture," the slave owners lay particular stress on it, but "in other cases [they]

seem no more to believe" the Bible than the Koran (60–61). By contrast, some of the colonists themselves admit that "the *Negro's* belief in the Deity is more *simple, pure,* and *sincere* than the Christians" (107). Godwyn accuses the whites of "Sloth and Avarice" (60), "*Murthers* and *Depredations*" (129), and "other *Inhumanities,* as their emasculating and Beheading" their slaves (41); their "chief Deity" is "*Profit*" (13) and like the Dutch their "*Religion is . . . governed by their Trade*" (3). They are also particularly guilty of "Debauchery (hardly to be outdone (therein) by *Sodom,* were it standing" (36); if, as they claim, Negroes are not human but mere beasts, then "what will become of those *Debauches,* that so frequently do make use of them for their *unnatural* Pleasures and Lusts? Or of such of our People who have intermarried with them? Sure they would be loath to be indicted of *Sodomy,* as for lying with a Beast" (30).

135. John Bunyan, *The Pilgrim's Progress from this World to That which is to Come,* ed. J. B. Wharey and Roger Sharrock (Oxford: Clarendon, 1967), 133–34. This passage is present in the 1678 first edition (of what would later retrospectively be called "the first part").

136. Bunyan's marginal note also cites Proverbs 29:5 ("A man that flattereth his neighbour spreadeth a net for his feet") and Daniel 11:32 ("And such as do wickedly against the covenant shall he corrupt by flatteries"). But only 2 Corinthians is relevant to Bunyan's black/white imagery.

137. Luther's commentary on Galatians was crucial to Bunyan's conversion experience, and he later said it was more useful "for a wounded conscience" than any book but the Bible itself: see *Grace Abounding to the Chief of Sinners,* ed. W. R. Owens (Harmondsworth: Penguin, 1987), 35.

138. In the anonymous polemical pamphlet *Tyranipocrit Discovered* (1649), for instance, a "white devil" (Hypocrisy) marries a "black devil" (Tyranny). Given the immediate political referents of this allegory, neither color can have had an epidermal significance.

139. Bunyan, *Pilgrim's Progress,* 286.

140. Massing, "From Greek Proverb to Soap Advert: Washing the Ethiopian," *Journal of the Warburg and Courtauld Institutes* 58 (1995): 180–201.

141. Brome, *The English Moore,* ed. Steen, 4.4.51–54.

142. Massinger, *The Parliament of Love,* in *Plays and Poems,* ed. Edwards and Gibson, 5.1.468; Sir William Berkeley, *The Lost Lady* (1637), ed. D. F. Rowan (Oxford: Malone Society, 1987), line 2236.

143. Carolyn Prager, "'If I be Devil': English Renaissance Response to the Proverbial and Ecumenical Ethiopian," *Journal of Medieval and Renaissance Studies* 17 (1987): 257–79; Frank M. Snowden Jr., *Blacks in Antiquity: Ethiopians in the Greco-Roman Experience* (Cambridge, MA: Harvard UP, 1971), 196–215.

144. Prager demonstrates the popularity of washing-the-Ethiop tropes in early modern drama, but Middleton never quoted it. (The example at *Roaring Girl* 1.2.178 was written by Dekker, who also used it in *The Honest Whore, Part Two.*)

145. John Calvin, *Commentaries on the Book of the Prophet Jeremiah and the Lamentations,* tr. John Owen (Edinburgh, 1860), 191.

146. *White* does occur in Thomas Gataker's exegesis of Jeremiah 13:23 in *Annotations of all the Bookes of the Old and New Testament* (1651), which cites the classical proverb and explains that "assoon might a blackmoor be with washing made white, . . . as this people brought to ought that was good, and it is in vain therefore to take any further pains with them." But the racial sense is not explicit here, and again the context emphasizes anti-Jewish rather than antiblack prejudice.

147. Beedome, *Poems Divine and Humane* (1641), sig. D2^{v}.

148. *Aesop Improved, or, Above three hundred and fifty Fables, mostly Aesop's. With their Morals, paraphrased in English Verse* (1673), sig. A3: "True it is that Mr. Oglesby hath helpt the world to a Translation of some part of *Aesops Fables,*"—referring to John Ogilby's edition

of 1651—"which is incomparably good; for such as can reach the sense and price of it, but certainly to understand so lofty a Poem as that is, requires a better capacity, and more skill in Poetical phrases, and Fictions, than the generality of those who are willing to read *Aesops Fables* are endowed with. And doubtless the price of his two excellent Folios upon *Aesop,* doth as much exceed most mens purses, as the Style and language thereof doth their Capacities."

149. For a comparison between Bunyan's allegorical method and the 1673 edition of Aesop's fables, see Graham Midgley's introduction to his edition of *The Poems,* in *The Miscellaneous Works of John Bunyan,* gen. ed. Roger Sharrock, vol. 6 (Oxford: Clarendon, 1980), xl-xli.
150. *Aesop Improved,* 193; cited by Massing, 184.
151. For examples of Luther's influence on *Pilgrim's Progress,* see Richard L. Greaves, *Glimpses of Glory: John Bunyan and English Dissent* (Stanford, CA: Stanford UP, 2002), 221, 234, 236, 245, 253, 512.
152. Bunyan, *The Holy War* (1682), ed. Roger Sharrock and James F. Forrest (Oxford: Clarendon, 1980), 9, 7.
153. *An Exposition on the Ten First Chapters of Genesis, and part of the Eleventh,* posthumously published in *The Works of that Eminent Servant of Christ, Mr. John Bunyan* (1692), 1:69–74; *The Miscellaneous Works of John Bunyan,* gen. ed. Roger Sharrock, v*olume 12,* ed. W. R. Owens (Oxford: Clarendon Press, 1994), 263, 271–72, 266–67: "*Cush,* Black. Of *Ham* and *Mizraim* came the *Ethiopians,* or *Blackamores:* The Land of *Ham* was the Countrey about *Egypt;* wherefore *Israel* was first *afflicted* by them. . . . So then, the Curse came betimes upon the Sons of Ham; for he was the Father of *Cush.*" For the date of composition of this unfinished work, see Greaves, *Glimpses of Glory,* 463, 639 (who places it in 1682–83) and Owens, xxv (who suggests "Bunyan may have been working on it right up to the end of his life"). Neither Greaves nor Owens acknowledges or discusses Bunyan's acceptance of the curse of Ham theory.
154. John Eachard, *Some observations upon the Answer to an enquiry into the grounds & occasions of the contempt of the clergy* (1671), 139.
155. Bunyan, *Poems,* ed. Midgley, 236 (XXXII).
156. I quote the King James version (1611), which Bunyan certainly knew.
157. Flavius Josephus, *The Antiquities of the Jews,* 2:10–11. This Ethiopian Mosaic excursion is elaborated (chapters 71–76) in the anonymous Hebrew Book of Jashar [*Sefer ha-Yashar*], printed at Venice in 1625 but probably written in Spain in the eleventh century. Bunyan probably knew neither of these sources, or the many patristic commentators who, worried about polygamy, debated whether this wife could be equated with the Midianite Zipporah, married by Moses during his youthful exile from Egypt (Exodus 2:15b–3:1).
158. This is the translation that would have been familiar to Bunyan and his readers. Braude points out that the Hebrew word for the color white does not appear in the original, which says only "like snow," and he argues that the passage may compare snowflakes with the flaking of diseased skin ("Black Skin/White Skin"). But of course snow is white as well as flaky. Braude's more general point about the absence in ancient Hebrew of color categories for populations is not endangered by this passage, which is talking about the skin color created by God's infliction of a disease on one individual.
159. Midgley's commentary note claims that "Moses's wife in this poem is more exactly Moses's wife's handmaid, Hagar the Egyptian, who is interpreted allegorically by St. Paul in Gal. 4:22–31" (*Poems,* 338). But Hagar was never a member of the household of Moses. The theology of the poem certainly comes from Galatians, but not the Egyptian wife of Moses.
160. Bunyan, *Poems,* ed. Midgley, 254–55 (LIV).
161. F. J. Harvey Darnton, *Children's Books in England: Five Centuries of Social Life,* third ed., rev. Brian Alderson (Cambridge: Cambridge UP, 1982), 51–67.

162. For the distinction between a "book written only for children" and books intended to be shared by children and adults, or adult books that retrospectively became children's books, see William Sloane, *Children's Books in England and America in the Seventeenth Century* (New York: Columbia UP, 1955), 117.
163. Midgley, "Introduction," in Bunyan, *Poems,* xxviii-xli. Since Midgley's edition appeared, these genres of simple, widely circulated religious verse, and their importance to the seventeenth-century book trade, have been explored in Tessa Watt's *Cheap Print and Popular Piety.*
164. Bunyan, "To the Reader," in *Poems,* ed. Midgley, 190–92.
165. Mary V. Jackson, *Engines of Instruction, Mischief, and Magic: Children's Literature in England from Its Beginnings to 1839* (Lincoln: University of Nebraska Press, 1989), 16.
166. For the importance of such texts in nineteenth-century America, see Donnarae MacCann, *White Supremacy in Children's Literature: Characterizations of African Americans, 1830–1900* (New York: Routledge, 1998).
167. Georgius Hornius, *Historia philosophica libri septem* (Leyden, 1655), 1:59–61, 104, 127–30, 139 (Noah's sons) and *De originibus Americanis libri quatuor* (Leyden and Hague, 1652), 24–38 (ruling out the Ethiopians, Celts, English, and Scandinavians as progenitors of American indigenes). Horne's *Dissertatio de vera aetate mundi* (Leyden, 1659) was based on Archbishop Ussher's work and attacked the alternative chronology of Vossius. On Horne's early links to England—the subject of his first book—see A. J. van der Aa, *Biographisch Woordenboek der Nederlanden* (Haarlem, 1852), 392–93. On his pioneering contribution to the history of philosophy, see Donald R. Kelly, *The Descent of Ideas: The History of Intellectual History* (Aldershot: Ashgate, 2002), 85, 97, 165, and Jonathan Israel's "Philosophy, 'History of Philosophy', and *l'histoire de l'esprit humain:* a historiographical question *and* problem for philosophers" (2003, www.princeton.edu/values/newhistories/israel.doc). For an account of Horne's *Americanis* ("the most important book on the problem prior to the Restoration"), see Allen, *Legend of Noah,* 128. None of these recent scholars mentions *Arca Noae.*
168. Georgius Hornius, *Arca Noae, sive Historia Imperiorum et Regnorum a condito orbe ad nostra tempora* (Leyden, 1666; Leyden and Rotterdam, 1668; Frankfurt and Leipzig, 1674; Leipzig, 1675). I have not attempted to trace any editions beyond these, listed in the British Library catalog. I have also not searched other works by Horne that might reiterate the *Arca Noae* thesis—*Historiae Naturalis et Civilis, ad nostra usque tempora, libri septem* (1670, etc.), *Orbis imperans* (1668, etc.)—or his first book, *Rerum Britannicarum libri septem* (Leiden, 1648), which might clarify his connections with England.
169. "Alias pro colorum diversitate commode quoque distinxeris posteros Noachi in *albus,* qui sunt Scythae & Japhetaie, *nigros,* qui sunt Aethiopes & Chamaei, *flavos,* qui sunt Indi & Semaie" (*Arca Noae,* 37); "Japhet . . . *Asia* Septentrionales plagas & universam *Europam* una cum novo orbe sive *America* obtinuit: ita ut omnium amplissimam spatio terrarum & multitudine populorum, tum Imperiorum & regnorum majestate, cultu, literis, duratione, haereditatem acceperit, divinae benedictionis gratia. . . . Sola enim hodie Japheti familia per universum terrarum orbem dominatur, omnibus Imperiis, regnis, populisque per Europam, Asiam, Africam, & Americam in ditionem ejus ac potestatem redactis" (112).
170. Greaves, *Glimpses of Glory,* 612.
171. Bunyan, *Holy War,* ed. Sharrock and Forrest, xlvii-xlviii.
172. Bunyan, *Poems,* ed. Midgley, 189.
173. On Bunyan's complicated relationship with imperialism and contemporary American fundamentalism, see particularly Tamsin Spargo, *The Writing of John Bunyan* (Aldershot: Ashgate, 1997), 97–136.

Chapter 10

1. For the racial implications of whiteness in *Moby Dick,* see Joe Kovel, *White Racism: A Psychohistory* (Free Association, 1970), 234–46; Albert Boime, *The Art of Exclusion: Representing Blacks in the Nineteenth Century* (Washington: Smithsonian Institution Press, 1990), 4–5; Morrison, *Playing in the Dark,* 68–69; Dyer, *White,* 212.
2. In Fletcher's scene I have counted words only from the beginning of interactions between seller and buyers at 3.1.17 ("That's he") to the final purchase (3.1.142); if I included the beginning and ending of the scene, the disproportion between *Clotel* and *A Very Woman* would be even greater. In both texts I counted hyphenated compounds as a single word. In *A Very Woman* I counted only dialogue (words that would be heard onstage), not stage directions or speech prefixes; again, including these other categories would have made numbers an even smaller fraction of Fletcher's scene.
3. "Fifty chekeens" (3.1.29), "an hundred" (3.1.48, referring to a different slave), "fourscore" (3.1.54, referring to another), "for these two" (3.1.56, referring to others), "A hundred is too much" (3.1.67), "Here's one you shall have" (3.1.70, referring to another), "Offer to swear he has eaten nothing in a twelve month" (3.1.87), "Twenty chekeens for these two" (3.1.90), "five-and-twenty" (3.1.91), "She is nine year old, at ten you shall find few" virgins (3.1.95), "I have sold a hundred of 'em" (3.1.119), "His price is forty" (3.1.141).
4. Dryden, "Astrae Redux," lines 292, 320–23. The poem elsewhere plays on the whiteness of Albion; Dryden used *white* in an unmistakable generic sense in his translation of Dominique Bouhours's *Life of St. Francis Xavier* (1688), 88, 124 ("white Men").
5. Robert Brenner, *Merchants and Revolution: Commercial Change, Political Conflict, and London's Overseas Traders, 1550–1653* (Cambridge: Cambridge UP, 1993).
6. Michael J. Braddick, *The Nerves of State: Taxation and the Financing of the English State, 1558–1715* (Manchester: Manchester UP, 1996); Bernard Capp, *Cromwell's Navy: The Fleet and the English Revolution, 1638–1660* (Oxford: Oxford UP, 1989); Ian Gentles, *The New Model Army in England, Ireland and Scotland, 1645–1653* (Oxford: Blackwell, 1992); Jack P. Greene and J. R. Pole, eds., *Colonial British America: Essays in the New History of the Early Modern Era* (Baltimore: Johns Hopkins, 1984). For an overview of these interrelated developments, see Michael J. Braddick, "The English Government, War, Trade, and Settlement, 1625–1688," in *The Oxford History of the British Empire,* vol. I, *The Origins of Empire: British Overseas Enterprise to the Close of the Seventeenth Century,* ed. Nicholas Canny (Oxford: Oxford UP, 1998), 286–308.
7. Charles M. Andrews, *British Committees, Commissions, and Councils of Trade and Plantations, 1622–1675* (Baltimore: Johns Hopkins UP, 1908), 48–60; British Library Egerton MS 2395, fol. 86b (para. 13). Another version of these "Overtures" is signed by Martin Noell and Thomas Povey; in the title of that document, "the West Indias" is crossed out and replaced by the more comprehensive "a Councell to be erected for foreigne Plantations," and "his Highness" (referring to Cromwell) is crossed out and replaced by "his Majestie" (Egerton MS 2395, fol. 270–71).
8. "Overtures touching the West Indies," Add. MS. 11411, fol. 3–3^{b}, extensively quoted in Andrews, *British Committees,* 59–60.
9. See C.O. 1/14, "Instructions for the Councill appointed for Forraigne Plantations" (fol. 142b): "bringing the severall Colonies & Plantations within themselves into a more certaine civill and uniform Governm^{t}"(143a), "all of them being collected into one viewe & managem^{t}" (143a), "to order & settle such a continuall correspondencie" (143a), "to send vnto you in writing . . . What numbers of men" (143a). For a parallel text of the earlier Povey proposals and the final Instructions, see Andrews, *British Committees,* 69–70. One of Povey's brothers lived in Barbados, another in Jamaica.

10. See C.O. 1/14: "The counsell this day appointed M[r] Denham M[r] Waller M[r] Povey the Clarke of this Counsell (being wth them present) to be a committee to meete to morrow (being Tuesday) at eight of the clock in the morning at M[r] Surveyoers Lodgings in White-hall to write Letters and dispatches to Jamaica the Carybee islands Virginia &c and to adiourne as cause shall require" (145b, 7 January 1661).
11. *CSPC* 5:14. In addition to Cooper, Drax, and Colleton, the petition was signed by Sir Peter Leare, Captain Thomas Middleton (no relation to the playwright), Martin Noell, and Thomas Kendall. Noell had been trading with Montserrat and Nevis since 1650, and he owned 20,000 acres in Jamaica as well as a plantation in Barbados; Drax had made his fortune in Barbados and had been involved in the slave trade since at least 1654.
12. Andrews, *British Committees,* 76–77. On Waller, see Taylor, "White Literary Criticism."
13. This example—not noticed by previous investigators, and to my knowledge never before printed—antedates by 10 years the first example in *OED* (*white n.*[1]13), which in any case is translated from French and refers to North African Muslims (see above, chapter 2, note 143).
14. British Library MS Egerton 2395, fol. 289–90, describing the minutes of the meeting of the committee on "Jan. 10th 1660" [= 1661], "reported" to the Council "Jan. 14th." This manuscript consists of papers written or collected by Thomas Povey. However, *white* or *whites* does not appear in any of the chronologically earlier documents in the manuscript, including the many that deal with problems of labor supply in Jamaica.
15. The three manuscript copies of this report known to me are all undated. See *CSPC,* 5:229 (item 791), where one of them (C.O. 324/1, fol. 275–83) is editorially identified as "1664?" because it directly responds to a meeting of the Council on August 24, 1664 (item 790), which had postponed further consideration for a week. Eltis quotes another copy (C.O. 1/18, ff. 224–26) and dates it "c. late 1650s" (*African Slavery,* 61–62). But that date cannot be correct, because the Council of Foreign Plantations (specified in the title of the document) did not exist in the late 1650s. The third copy (Egerton MS 2395, fol. 277–278[v]) also specifies that these propositions were "reported from the Committee to the Councell of Foreigne Plantations." The order of documents in Egerton MS 2395 has been altered; in the original foliation, this document began on f. 59, but even so it followed the original 53–54 (which contains revisions postdating the Restoration). Nor does the original foliation seem a reliable indicator of chronology.
16. C.O. 1/18, fol. 268 (item 113), "Reasons proposed by the Kings command for his Ma[ties] Settling a plantation in Jamaica." Item 114 is another copy of the same memo, with the annotation "original of this paper was given to M[r] Sec: Morris Octb[r] 3:1664" (270a). No author is identified; Sir Charles Lyttleton is the author of the "account of the State of Jamaica" (item 111) which was delivered to Secretary Morris.
17. See C.O. 1/14: "a Letter intended to be sent to Barbados and to be as a Presedent for the other Plantations" (146b, 14 January 1661).
18. C.O. 1/14, fol. 149b; also in Egerton MS 2395, fol. 333–333[v] (and 335 for the same letter, sent to Virginia). For a summary of the whole letter, see *CSPC* 5:5–6 (item 24). Although the summary says "number of inhabitants," the Council in fact only asked for "numbers of men."
19. C.O. 31/1, fol. 50a (para. 5). This 1661 Barbados census contrasts with one mandated by the Governor and Council on November 8, 1654: "Ordered, that the several Constables in the Bridge Town & Bay . . . forthwith take the names of all persons, both men, women & children, freemen, & inmates, as well fforeigners as others, that are inhabitants, in & about the Indian Bridge Town; & make a Return thereof to y[e] Governor" ("Minutes," p. 68). In 1654 "white men and blacks" were not yet demographic categories, but they had become so by 1661.
20. Foucault, *History of Sexuality,* vol. I, *An Introduction,* tr. Robert Hurley (New York: Pantheon, 1978), 139–45.
21. C.O. 389/4, fol. 48b.

22. A copy of Berkeley's reply to the inquiry, now in the PRO, identifies itself as a response "to inquiries dated 29th September 1670, but not received till January 11th by his brother Culpeper" [*CSPC,* 7:232, citing Col. Papers Vol. XXVI, Nos. 77, 77I, II].
23. Hening, ed., *Statutes at Large,* 2:515. Jordan noted the use of *whites* in this document but did not quote or discuss it: see *White Over Black,* 96, n. 123. This was the earliest use of the noun *whites* known to Jordan. Asked by the Lords, "What number of planters, servants and slaves . . . are there in your plantation?" Berkeley replied that there were "two thousand *black slaves,* six thousand *Christian servants.*" Berkeley's answer equated *black* with *slaves;* that same equation had been made by the London lords themselves in another question, asking "what *blacks* or *slaves*" had been imported to the colony during the preceding seven years.
24. For this definition of "a racialized society" I am indebted to Nell Irvin Painter, quoted in "Disciplinary Misconceptions," *Chronicle of Higher Education,* July 12, 2002, B4.
25. Andrews, *British Committees,* 129. Andrews transcribes the entire text (127–32).
26. For the Leeward Islands, see *CSPC* 7:393 (no. 896.1), Governor Stapleton's reply (July 17, 1672) to the inquiries (February 16, 1672, but not extant) of the Council for Foreign Plantations: "Impossible to know how many whites or blacks have died" [Col. Papers, Vol. XXIX, No. 14.1]. For Bermuda, see Lefroy, *Memorials,* 2:428–32 (inquiries of April 10, 1676; reply July 16, 1679). For Connecticut, see *The Public Records of the Colony of Connecticut,* 15 vols. (Hartford, 1850–90), 3:291–98 (inquiry of August 1, 1679, reply of July 15, 1680): "18. What number of Whites, Blacks or Mulattos have been born and christened, for these seaven yeares last past, or any other space of time, for as many yeares as you are able to state an account of?" (293). Governor Leete's answers do not use *white,* as adjective or noun (but do use *blacks,* twice).
27. See pp. 186–88. I learned of this model only after completing my manuscript research in the PRO and British Library; I had initially assumed—based on the inaccurate summaries in the *CSPC*—that the generic noun originated in the West Indies. However, a variation of the hierarchical model recognizes that innovations (like the Beatles) sometimes originate in a secondary population center (like Liverpool) and move from there to the primary metropolis (London), from which they are dispersed outward to the whole system: see Guy Bailey et al., "Some Patterns of Linguistic Diffusion," *Language Variation and Change* 5 (1993): 359–90. If the English noun turns out (in some future search of archives I have missed) to have originated in Barbados, it would fit this variant model. For other early modern language changes that appear to have originated among metropolitan governing elites, see Matti Rissanen, "Standardization and the language of early statutes," in *The Development of Standard English, 1300–1800: Theories, Descriptions, Conflicts,* ed. Laura Wright (Cambridge: Cambridge UP, 2000), 117–130; Rissanen discusses the disappearance of multiple negation and the rise of the subordinator *provided that* in statutes between 1400 and 1700. In any case, London is crucial to its saturation of Anglophone societies.
28. Vaughan, *Roots,* 15, 259. (Vaughan quotes the English translation in the text and the Dutch original in the notes.) For the Dutch and the slave trade, see Robin Blackburn, *The Making of New World Slavery* (Verso, 1997), 193–5, 211–12.
29. All the first occurrences of the noun are plurals. Once *whites* started being treated as a noun, then like other countable nouns it could be made singular by subtracting the multiple marker -s.
30. Terence W. Hutchison, *Before Adam Smith* (Oxford: Blackwell, 1988), 40.
31. John Arbuthnot, *Essay on the Usefulness of Mathematical Learning* (1701), in *The Life and Works of John Arbuthnot,* ed. G. A. Aitken (1892), 421–22.
32. On Graunt's statistical expertise and caution, and his relationship to Petty (who was mathematically sloppy and unsystematic), see D. V. Glass, "John Graunt and His *Natural and Political Observations,*" *Proceedings of the Royal Society of London. Series B, Biological Sciences* 159 (1963): 2–32. As Glass notes, "it is generally assumed that Petty supplied the statistics for Romsey, Hampshire" (32, n. 138).

33. John Graunt, *Natural and Political Observations . . . upon the Bills of Mortality* (1662), in *The Economic Writings of Sir William Petty,* ed. C. H. Hull, 2 vols. (1899), 2:323, 378, 354, 396–97.
34. Graunt, *Observations,* 355; William Petty to Lord Anglesea (December 1672), in Edmond Fitzmaurice, *The Life of Sir William Petty* (1895), 153.
35. See Peter Buck, "Seventeenth-Century Political Arithmetic: Civil Strife and Vital Statistics," *Isis* 68 (1977): 67–84.
36. For midcentury divisions in Barbados see Larry Gragg, *Englishmen Transplanted: The English Colonization of Barbados 1627–1660* (Oxford: Oxford UP, 2003), 43–78.
37. Graunt, *Observations,* 334, 347–48.
38. *The Papers of Benjamin Franklin, Volume 4,* ed. Leonard W. Labaree and Whitfield J. Bell Jr. (New Haven, CT: Yale UP, 1961), 234.
39. *The Petty Papers: Some Unpublished Writings of Sir William Petty,* ed. Marquis of Lansdowne, 2 vols. (Constable, 1927), 2:231, 2:108. The latest figures in "Some Remarques of the people of New England" are dated 1678; Petty noted that they were "drawne from Papers sent from thence."
40. Petty, *Economic Writings,* 1:296, 267.
41. "The Scale of Animals," *Petty Papers,* 2:30–31. This seems to have been written between October 1676 and July 1678 (2:19–20).
42. "Nouvelle Division de la Terre, par les Differentes Especes ou Races d'Hommes qui l'Habitent," *Journal des Sçavans* 12 (Amsterdam, April 26, 1684): 148–55, translated in Thomas Bendyshe, "History of Anthropology," *Memoirs Read Before the Anthropological Society of London, 1863–4,* 1 (1865): 360–64. The original was published anonymously; for Bernier's authorship, see Jordan, *White Over Black,* 216–17. Hannaford dates "The First Stage in the Development of an Idea of Race" to between 1684 and 1815, choosing "1684 as the arbitrary starting point" because of the publication of Bernier's work, which "marks a significant methodological departure" (*Race,* 191).
43. William Petty, *The History of the Survey of Ireland, commonly called The Down Survey* (1655–66), ed. T. A. Larcom (Dublin: Irish Archaeological Society, 1851).
44. Buck, "Political Arithmetic," 80–81; J. H. Plumb, *The Origins of Political Stability: England 1675–1725* (Boston: Houghton Mifflin, 1967), 11–13.
45. R. E. W. Maddison, *The Life of the Honourable Robert Boyle F.R.S.* (Taylor & Francis, 1969), 71–72 (on Boyle's relationship with Petty), 101–02 (on the New England Company), 134 (on Boyle's connections with various trading companies).
46. Michael Hunter, *Science and Society in Restoration England* (Cambridge: Cambridge UP, 1981), 37. For colonial inquiries see *The Correspondence of Henry Oldenberg,* ed. A. Rupert Hall and Marie Boas Hall, 13 vols. (Madison: University of Wisconsin Press, 1965–86), 2:146–51; for more general inquiries, 2:224–6, 241 (on agriculture).
47. Thomas Birch, *The History of the Royal Society,* 4 vols. (1756), 1:407; *Correspondence,* 2:209 (Boyle missed the meeting, which therefore did not receive his queries).
48. "General Heads for a *Natural History of a Countrey,* Great or small, imparted likewise by Mr. *Boyle,*" *Philosophical Transactions* 1, no. 11 (1665): 186–89. In "The early Royal Society and the Spread of Medical Knowledge," in *The Medical Revolution of the Seventeenth Century,* ed. Roger French and Andrew Wear (Cambridge: Cambridge UP, 1989), Roy Porter interprets "countrey" to mean "county" (280). But this is surely mistaken: it would hardly be necessary to ask about the "color," and so on, of the inhabitants of English counties, and the first item asks for "longest and shortest days and night, the Climate . . . what fixt starrs are and what not seen there," again indicating distant locations.
49. Abraham Hill, "Inquiries for Guiny," *Philosophical Transactions* 2 (1666): 472.
50. Boyle had asked for accounts of "the *Inhabitants* themselves, both *Natives* and *Strangers,* that have been long settled there" ("General Heads," 188). Black slaves were the largest and most obvious category of "Strangers" who had long been "settled" in a country other

than their own; Iberian settlers in Africa and America were the other obvious group to which this might apply, and inquiries about them necessarily also involved inquiries about the blacks they lived alongside. Since the sixteenth century, investigators had reported on interbreeding between Portuguese and blacks, and Boyle—an avid reader of the literature of European exploration—almost certainly had such issues in mind. In either case, Boyle's expessed interest in long-settled strangers was an interest in blacks.

51. "The Remainder Of the *Observations* made in the formerly mention'd Voyage to *Jamaica,*" *Philosophical Transactions* 3 (July 13, 1668): 721; "Of some particulars, referring to those of *Jamaica* . . . Communicated by Mr. *Norwood* the younger, an Eye-witness," *Philosophical Transactions* 3 (1668): 825.
52. *The Works of Robert Boyle,* ed. Michael Hunter and Edward B. Davis, 16 vols. (Pickering and Chatto, 1999), 4:1–201. Probably originally written in 1655–56 (4:xi), *Colours* was in print by March 30, 1664 (xiv). For Hooke's praise, see *Micrographia: or some Physiological Descriptions of Minute Bodies made by Magnifying Glasses* (1665; but licensed on November 23, 1664), 54–55, 83. Boyle mentions Christopher Wren's praise in a letter of October 29, 1664: see *The Correspondence of Robert Boyle,* ed. Michael Hunter, Antonio Clericuzio, and Lawrence M. Principe, 6 vols. (Pickering and Chatto, 2001), 2:373. Joseph Glanville includes an adulatory account of the book in *Plus Ultra* (1668), 98. I quote other responses below.
53. See Boyle, *Colours,* 153: "though the Heat of the Sun may Darken the Colour of the Skin, by that Operation, which we in *English* call Sun-burning; yet Experience doth not Evince, that I remember, that that Heat alone can produce a Discolouring that shall amount to a true Blackness, like that of *Negroes.*" I cite *Colours* from the 1664 edition (whose page numbers are reproduced marginally in *Works,* ed. Hunter and Davis).
54. In *Colours* Boyle cited George Sandys (159) and Andrew Battel as reported by Purchas (165–67). Boyle cited travel writers, and maintained his scepticism about climatic explanations for color, throughout his career. See for instance his earlier and later references to Piso (*Works,* 3:232, 350–51), Ligon (3:351), Tulp (3:356), Duarte Lopes (4:341), Acosta (4:374, 484), and Leo Africanus (10:331). Boyle added new authorities as they became available, including (12:61) Job Ludolf the Elder's *Historia Aethiopica* (1681), translated as *A New History of Ethiopia* (1682). In his posthumously published *The General History of the Air,* edited by Locke (1692), Boyle noted that "in many Regions of Ethiopia the Summer Heats are more mild than in Portugal" (12:105) and collected references to cold nights in Morocco, Guinea, and Jamaica (12:101); discussing "the Peripatetick doctrine about the Limits and Temperaments of the three Regions, into which they divide the Air," he concluded, "I think it fitter we should wish it to be true, than that we should believe it is so" (12:100). This condemnation of wishful thinking aptly characterizes the later appeal of geohumoralism to eighteenth-century abolitionists (and some postmodern literary critics).
55. New sources identified by Boyle's editors (4:64) include—in addition to the living witnesses I discuss later—Olaus Magnus (ca. 1498–1568), Archbishop of Uppsala, *Historia de gentibus septentionalibus* (1555), and Thomas James, *The Strange and Dangerous Voyage of Captain Thomas James in his intended Discovery of the Northwest Passage into the South-sea* (1633).
56. Boyle's next book, *New Experiments and Observations touching Cold* (1665), uses the same epigraph as *Colours,* cross-references "the *History of Whiteness and Blackness*" (*Works* 4:416) and refers repeatedly to the effects of cold on "the pores of the skin." His unpublished "Dialogues concerning Heat and Flame"—which, like *Colours* and *Cold,* was written in the late 1650s—discusses the heat of the sun and its effect on the skin (13:262). See also his unpublished "Tract concerning Flame" (14:55–62).
57. Boyle, *Colours,* 153–61.
58. Compare Browne, *Pseudodoxia,* 1:522–23 ("Lastly, it is a very injurious method unto Philosophy, and a perpetual promotion to Ignorance, in points of obscurity, nor open unto

easie considerations, to fall upon a present refuge unto Miracles, or . . . lay the last and particular effects upon the first and generall cause of all things . . .") with Boyle, *Colours,* 159 ("But though I think that even a Naturalist may without disparagement believe all the Miracles attested by the Holy Scriptures, yet in this case to flye to a Supernatural Cause, will, I fear, look like Shifting off the Difficulty, instead of Resolving it; for we enquire not the First and Universal, but the Proper, Immediate, and Physical Cause of the Jetty Colour of *Negroes* . . .").

59. Given the anatomical, medical, and chemical developments analyzed in this paragraph, it is misleading for Floyd-Wilson to dismiss "empirical knowledge" as an explanation for the decline of classical climate theory or to describe the entire discourse of the emergent sciences of the seventeenth century as an effort to mystify, rather than ascertain the origins of blackness (*English Ethnicity,* 78–79, 193). The Aristotelian and Hippocratic model of the human body is fundamentally inaccurate, a fact that all of us (including Floyd-Wilson) take for granted on a daily basis.
60. Malcolm R. Oster, "The 'Beame of Diuinity': Animal Suffering in the Early Thought of Robert Boyle," *British Journal for the History of Science* 22 (1989): 151–79.
61. William Harvey, *Exercitatio anatomica de motu cordis et sanguinis in animalibus* (Frankfurt, 1628). On Boyle's admiration for Harvey, see Richard A. Hunter and Ida Macalpine, "William Harvey and Robert Boyle," *Notes and Records of the Royal Society* 13 (1958): 115–27.
62. Robert G. Frank Jr., *Harvey and the Oxford Physiologists: Scientific Ideas and Social Interaction* (Berkeley: University of California Press, 1980). Boyle is the book's central figure. The first medical textbook to accept Harvey's theory of circulation was published by Boyle's friend Nathaniel Highmore (1651).
63. John Harris, *Lexicon Technicum: or, An Universal English Dictionary of Arts and Sciences* (1704), entry for Humours; cited by Wheeler, *Complexion,* 27. Wheeler shows by many examples that the humoral theory continued to be cited throughout the eighteenth century, but that is not surprising, given the slow development of an alternative systemic theory of the body. But the classical humoral theory was increasingly residual; Boyle's anatomical body was emergent, and more and more self-evident to European intellectual elites, although the new concept took a long time to saturate community thought. Abolitionists in particular resisted it, preferring discredited climatological explanations for skin difference.
64. See Walter Pagel, *Parascelsus* (Basel: Karger, 1959); Charles Webster, *The Great Instauration: Science, Medicine and Reform 1626–1660* (New York: Holmes & Meier, 1976), and *From Paracelsus to Newton: Magic and the Making of Modern Science* (Cambridge: Cambridge UP, 1982). Characteristic of changing attitudes was the practice of Sydenham: although he generally accepted the humoral model, he abandoned it whenever empirical evidence suggested the value of a specific cure, and toward the end of his life he was inclined to jettison it completely. See Kenneth Dewhurst, *Dr Thomas Sydenham (1624–1689): His Life and Original Writings* (Wellcome Historical Medical Library, 1966), 62.
65. Noah Biggs, *Metaeotechnia Medicinae Praxeos. The Vanity of the Craft of Physick* (1651), 12. On Biggs see Allen Debus, "Paracelsian Medicine: Noah Biggs and the Problem of Medical Reform," in *Medicine in Seventeenth Century England,* ed. Debus (Berkeley: University of California Press, 1974), 33–48. For other attacks on Galenic medicine see Andrew Wear, *Knowledge and Practice in English Medicine, 1550–1680* (Cambridge: Cambridge UP, 2000), 368–69, 378–79.
66. The traditional four elements were first assigned four colors (white, black, red, yellow-green) by Empedocles of Akragas (490–435 B.C.E.): see Robert A. Crone, *A History of Color: The Evolution of Theories of Light and Color* (Dordrecht: Kluwer, 1999), 4–5.

Descartes had attacked the theory of the four elements, in the work posthumously published as *Le Monde de Mr. Descartes ou le Traité de la Lumière* (Paris, 1664): see *The World and Other Writings,* tr. Stephen Gaukroger (Cambridge: Cambridge UP, 1998), 18. Boyle could not have been influenced by that discussion, but the concurrence of Descartes and Boyle powerfully undermined the classical view.

67. Boyle, *Of the Usefulnesse of Natural Philosophy* (Oxford, 1663), Part II, Sec. I, Essay IV, in *Works,* 3:317. A misleading account of Boyle's attitude to humors is given in B. B. Kaplan's doctoral dissertation, "The Medical Writings of Robert Boyle: Medical Philosophy in Mid-Seventeenth Century England" (University of Maryland, 1979), who quotes only part of the key sentence: "And *though* I am very unwilling to meddle with medical Controversies, and am apt to think, that Chymists are wont to speak somewhat too slightingly of the humors of the humane Body, and allow them too little a share in the production of Diseases; *yet* (to skip other reasons) the strange stories related by . . . other eminent Physitians . . . together with some odde Observations of this nature, our selves have had opportunity to make, do very much incline us to believe, That the generality of former Physitians have ascrib'd too much to the Humors . . . Qualities" (italics added). In Kaplan's rendering, this becomes "Boyle remarked that *though* he was 'very unwilling to meddle with medical controversies,' he was '*yet* apt to think, that chymists are wont to speak somewhat too slightly of the humours of the human body, and to allow them too little a share in the production of diseases'" (104, italics added)—thus placing the phrase "apt . . . diseases" after, rather than before, the pivotal *yet.* Kaplan never quotes the end of the sentence (after Boyle's "yet"). Boyle clearly believed that "the Juices of the Body" were important to human physiology and medical diagnosis, but he rejected the classical division into *four* humors and promoted a more sophisticated chemical analysis of bodily fluids.
68. Boyle, *Colours,* 163–64.
69. Boyle, *Colours,* sig. A6 (analytical Table of Contents). Browne normally refers to "complexions," using the word *skin* only three times in his three chapters on Negroes: once describing a fountain that allegedly dyed "the skin" (1:513), once noting that the inhabitants of Guinea "moysten their skins with fat and oylie materials" (1:514), once referring to "the tincture of the skin as a spermaticall part traduced from father unto son" (1:516). This last statement most nearly anticipates Boyle's conclusion, but soon afterward Browne states that "men and other animalls receive different tinctures from constitution and complexionall efflorescences" (1:526), and conjectures that the blackness of Negroes might arise from the "blacke humor" described by Aristotle (1:528). Browne characteristically piles up possibilities, without articulating a single clear hypothesis.
70. For Boyle's belief that better microscopes might enable us to see the physical structures that caused color (a hope later reiterated by Newton), see *Colours,* 40–41.
71. See *The Illustrations from the Works of Andreas Vesalius of Brussels,* ed. J. B. deC. M. Saunders and Charles D. O'Malley (Cleveland: World Publishing Co., 1950), esp. 92, 172 ("I have cut away the skin . . . We have removed the skin").
72. Pusey, *History of Dermatology,* 39; Archibald Gray, "Dermatology from the Time of Harvey," *Lancet* 2 (1951): 795–802. Girolamo Mercuriale's *De morbis cutaneis* (Venice, 1572)—the first book entirely devoted to what we would now call dermatology—remains fundamentally humoral: see *Mercurialis on Diseases of the Skin,* tr. R. L. Sutton Jr. (Kansas City: Lowell Press, 1986).
73. W. S. C. Copeman, "The Royal Hospitals before 1700," in *The Evolution of Hospitals in Britain,* ed. F. N. L. Poynter (Pitman Medical Publishing, 1964), 36.
74. P. W. M. Copeman and W. S. C. Copeman, "Dermatology in Tudor and Early Stuart England," *British Journal of Dermatology* 82 (1970): 303.
75. Hooke, *Micrographia,* 212.

76. For the traditional view see for example Helkiah Crooke's *Microcosmographia* (1615): "the Cuticle, which the Greekes call *Epidermis* . . . is altogether without bloud, because it receiveth neither veine nor arterie" (71). Crooke's humoralism determines his explanation of skin color: the underlying *cutis* "is naturally white, but according to the humours that abound, or the bodyes under it, saith Hippocrates in his Booke *de succis,* it varieth the colour. For example where blood aboundeth . . . there a rosie rednesse mingleth it selfe with the white, or overcommeth it. . . . In Chollericke men the skin is pallid or yellowish: in Melancholy swarty and blackish or duskish" (72).
77. Malpighi, *Epistolae de pulmonibus* (Bologna, 1661). For his career as a whole see Howard Adelmann, *Marcello Malpighi and the Evolution of Embryology,* 5 vols. (Ithaca, NY: Cornell UP, 1966), and Domenico Bertoloni Meli, ed., *Marcello Malpighi: Anatomist and Physician* (Firenze: Olschki, 1997).
78. Malpighi, *De externo tactus organo* (Messina ["Neapoli"], 1665), reprinted in *Opera Omnia Botanico-Medico-Anatomica* (Leiden, 1687): "ex quo transeunter deduco non incongruam fort nigredinis Æthiopum causam: certum enim est, ipsis cutim albam esse, sicuti & cuticula, unde tota nigredo a subjecto mucoso, & reticulari corpore ortum trahit, & quia diverso quandoque in variis locis colore insicitur; modo enim nigrum, ut in lingua, modo album, ut in palato, modo subflavum est; ideo censeo ejusdem varietatem in hominibus contingere posse, in singulis enim cutis partibus videtur necessaria haec colligantia, & papillarum tutela, quae hoc rete habetur" (2:204).
79. Boyle, *Experiments and Considerations about the Porosity of Bodies, in two Essays* (1684): "those very numerous glandules which the excellent Anatomists *Steno* and *Malpighi* are said to have discovered beneath the *Cuticula,* and which for their smalness and shape have been called *Glandulae miliares*" (*Works,* 10:110). Boyle had been working on this text on and off since the late 1650s, so it is impossible to tell when this sentence was composed. Boyle's reference to "so great a multitude of Capillary Vessels" just underneath the cuticula must also derive from Malpighi: see *Of the Reconcileableness of Specifick Medicines to the Corpuscular Philosophy* (1685, but written ca. 1682), in *Works,* 10:394. Boyle sent a copy to Malpighi, who acknowledged its receipt in a lost letter (10:xlv). On the mutual admiration of Boyle and Malpighi see also Adelman, *Malpighi,* 1:498–99, 714–15.
80. William Cowper's *The Anatomy of Humane Bodies* (Oxford, 1698) included an illustration of "The Capillament of the little Aqueous Vessels placed between the *Papillae* according to *Bidloo*" [=Goverdus Bidloo, whose plates Cowper copied without acknowledgment, generating a subsequent scandal]. Cowper notes that "I must confess notwithstanding all the diligence I could yet use in examining this Part with the Microscope, or otherwise, I have hitherto doubted of the Existence of these Acqueous Vessels, between the *Cuticula* and *Cutis;* in which some have placed the Seat of that Tawny Tincture of the *Ægyptians,* and that Black one of the *Æthiopians*" (sig. C1). Cowper's syntax makes it unclear whether his doubts remain, and the precise organic mechanisms and processes that produce variant skin color were not definitively described until much later. But Cowper does transmit Malpighi's theory into printed English, apparently for the first time.
81. "An Essay upon the Causes of the Different Colours of People in Different Climates; by John Mitchell, M.D. Communicated to the Royal Society by Mr. Peter Collinson, F. R. S.," *Philosophical Transactions* 43 (1744): 109. Boyle and Mitchell differed from each other about the exact location and mechanism of human pigmentation, but both located it in the skin. On the larger intellectual and European context of race and the anatomical body in the late seventeenth and eighteenth centuries, see Jordan, *White Over Black,* 216–68. Jordan, however, does not mention Boyle.
82. For a convincing critique of the classical "attitude toward individuals and groups of peoples which posits a direct and linear connection between physical and mental qualities,"

see Benjamin Isaac, "Slavery and Proto-racism in Graeco-Roman Antiquity" ("Collective Degradation").

83. For two recent celebrations of geohumoralism, see Floyd-Wilson, *English Ethnicity,* and Wheeler, *Complexion.* Each cites the other.
84. This observation is reported in one of the additions Boyle made to the Latin edition of *Colours* (the text most often reprinted in the seventeenth century), transcribed and translated in *Works* 4:91. Boyle's source was "a trustworthy gentleman who, when he was in America" witnessed this effect, which "amazingly enough . . . can be removed by no amount of skill or effort; but within eight or ten days it goes away of its own accord."
85. "I look not on a Human Body, as on a Watch or a Hand-mill, *i.e.,* as a Machine made up only of Solid, or at least Consistent, Parts; but as an Hydraulical, or rather Hydraulo-pneumetical Engine": Boyle, *A Free Enquiry Into the Vulgarly Receiv'd Notion of Nature* (1686), in *Works,* 10:540.
86. Although they were not in other aspects Cartesians, Boyle, Locke, and Newton all accepted Descartes' mind/body dualism: see Laurens Laudan, "The Clock Metaphor and Probabilism: The Impact of Descartes on English Methodological Thought 1650–1665," *Annals of Science* 22 (1966): 73–104; and G. A. J. Rogers, "Descartes and the Method of English Science," *Annals of Science* 29 (1972): 237–55.
87. Wheeler, *Complexion,* 26.
88. See Boyle's *Works:* "'tis scarce possible to paint this ugly *Negro* in blacker colours than his own" (12:339) and "the French, amongst whom this Vice is grown so Epidemical (as of Blacknes amongst the Ethiopians) its commonness has removed all the deformities they would otherwise find in it" (12:317). Both phrases occur in *A Free Discourse against Customary Swearing* (1695), written in 1647; the colorphobia therefore antedates Boyle's work on whiteness. Boyle began his investigations of color with a prejudice against blackness.
89. Discussing "the effects of Seminal Impressions," Boyle noted that "even Organical parts may receive great Differences from such peculiar Impressions, upon what account soever they came to be setled in the first Individual persons, from whom they are Propagated to Posterity, as we see in the Blobber-Lips and Flat-Noses of most Nations of *Negroes*" (*Colours,* 161–62). The albino is described in one of Boyle's additions to the Latin edition (*Works,* 4:93).
90. Shakespeare, *Othello,* 2.2.64; Purchas, *Hakluytus Posthumus,* 20 vols. (Glasgow: MacLehose, 1905), 4:1–2.
91. For other examples (of many), see Ogilby, *Africa* (1670), 451 ("flat or Camosi'd Noses"), and Matthew Hale's *Primitive Origins of Mankind* (1677), ii.vii.200 ("The Ethiopian . . . flat-nosed and crisp-haired").
92. "Piso assures us, that having the opportunity in *Brasil* to Dissect many Negroes, he clearly found that their Blackness went no deeper than the very outward Skin, which *Cuticula* or *Epidermis* being remov'd, the undermost Skin or *Cutie* appear'd just as White as that of *Europæan* Bodyes. And the like has been affirmed to me by a Physician of our own, whom, hearing he had Dissected a negroe here in England, I consulted about this particular" (Boyle, *Colours,* 163–64). Boyle refers to Gulielmus Piso, *De Medicina Brasiliensis Libri Quatuor* (Leiden, 1648), published as the first four books in Georg Markgraaff, *Historia naturalis Brasiliae* (1648). As Boyle's editors note, Piso was physician to the Dutch settlement in Brazil from 1636 to 1644 (*Works,* 4:89).
93. Brown's source for this information was Theodore Dwight Weld's *American Slavery As It Is: Testimony of a Thousand Witnesses* (New York, 1839); the relevant passages are reproduced in Levine's edition of *Clotel,* 267–68. The parenthetical phrase "(their owners of course,)" is not present in the original advertisement. The prospectus quoted by Weld came from the South Carolina Medical College, and Dr. T. Stillman did not lecture there, but in another "Medical Infirmary" in Charleston. Brown suppressed the locale because

he quoted these documents in a conversation that takes place among characters located in Natchez; he made Stillman a lecturer in the college in order to stress the macabre connection between the two documents.

94. Mary Campbell interprets Sir Thomas Browne's discussion of the "sperm of Negroes" (*Pseudodoxia,* 1:516) "in light of the historical relations possible at the time between European doctors and African bodies . . . there have been few innocent 'enquiries' in Browne's day into the reproductive physiology of African men. The image of the Black patient quickly becomes the image ('species') of a specimen ('species') in the lab where Bacon wants to 'dissect it into parts'; this is the ultimate image of the overdetermined passivity and reification enforced by slavery and subsequently sustained by eugenics" (*Wonder and Science,* 91). But although Campbell points to the same destination William Wells Brown describes, she is imagining it in *Pseudodoxia Epidemica,* which does not refer to contemporary accounts, but cites Aristotle for the assertion that "all seed was white." Likewise, Bacon's image of dissection does not refer to black bodies. Unlike Boyle, Browne does not refer to European doctors dissecting the bodies of black slaves on New World plantations; Browne does not here refer to doctors at all, and does not confine the discussion of sperm to blacks. Boyle, in 1664, does what Browne, in 1646, did not do. Campbell's analysis fits Boyle, not Brown.
95. Royal Society Boyle Papers, no. 27. See Michael Hunter's *Letters and Papers of Robert Boyle: A Guide to the Manuscripts and Microfilm* (Bethesda, MD: University Publications of America, 1992), 45–46.
96. See Philip D. Curtin, ed., *Africa Remembered: Narratives by West Africans from the Era of the Slave Trade* (Madison: University of Wisconsin Press, 1967), 215; William D. Piersen, "White Cannibals, Black Martyrs: Fear, Depression, and Religious Faith as Causes of Suicide among New Slaves," *Journal of Negro History* 62 (1977): 147–58; Taylor, *Time, Space, Race.*
97. Godwyn, *Advocate,* 41.
98. Edward Littleton, *The Groans of the Plantations* (1689), 19–20.
99. Ligon, *Barbadoes,* 93.
100. See Boyle's discussion in *The Usefulness of Natural Philosophy,* II, sect. 2 (1671): "A Forreigner accidently bringing some Sugar-Canes, as Rarities, from Brasil into Europe, and happening to touch at the Barbadoes, an English Planter that was Curious, obtain'd from him a few of them . . . the Negroes, or, as they call them, Blacks, living as Slaves upon that spot of Ground, and imploy'd almost totally about the planting of Sugar-Canes and making of Sugar, amount at least to between five and twenty and thirty thousand persons . . . by divers intelligent and sober persons interested in the Barbadoes (and partly by other wayes) I have been informed . . . one of the Antient Magistrates of that Island lately assur'd me" (*Works,* 6:424–25). Boyle's testimony here about the origins of the sugar trade in Barbados does not seem to have been noted by historians.
101. Boyle, *Works,* 13:309–10 (included in unpublished sections from the original manuscript version of *The Usefulness of Natural Philosophy,* and therefore antedating *Colors*). Boyle specifically cites "(lib 4, cap i)" of Piso. In the published text of *Usefulness* he refers to "our often commended Piso" (3:421).
102. In *The Excellency of Theology, compar'd with natural Philosophy* (1674), discussing the merits of secular discoveries, Boyle notes that "many of these Improvements do rather Transfer than Increase Mankind's goods, and prejudice one sort of Men as much as they Advantage another," and he cites as an example "the Discovery of the Peruvian and other American Mines; by which (especially reckoning the multitudes of unhappy men that are made miserable, and destroyed in working them,) mankind is not put into a better condition than it was before" (*Works,* 8:62).
103. See Steven Shapin, "Pump and Circumstance: Robert Boyle's Literary Technology," *Social Studies of Science* 14 (1984): 483.

104. Boyle, *Some Considerations about the Reconcileableness of Reason and Religion* (1675), in *Works,* ed. T. Birch, 6 vols. (1772), 4:182; Sprat, *History of the Royal Society* (1667), 100.
105. Boyle, *Colours,* 22; John Josselyn, *An Account of Two Voyages to New-England* (1674), 187: "It is the opinion of many men, that the blackness of the *Negroes* proceeded from the curse upon *Cham*'s posterity, others again will have it to be the property of the climate where they live. I pass by other Philosophical reasons and skill, only render you my experimental knowledge: having a *Barbarie-Moor* under cure . . . then I perceived that the *Moor* had one skin more than *Englishmen;* the skin that is basted to the flesh is bloudy and of the same Azure colour with the veins, but deeper than the colour of our *Europeans* veins. Over this is an other skin of a tawny colour, and upon that *Epidermis* or *Cuticula,* the flower of the skin (which is that Snakes cast) and this is tawny also, the colour of the blew skin mingling with the tawny makes them appear black." Josselyn confirms that "many men" believed the Curse of Cham theory: see chapter 9.
106. See Maddison, *Boyle,* 128; Dewhurst, *Sydenham;* and Andrew Cunningham, "Thomas Sydenham: Epidemics, Experiment and the 'Good Old Cause,'" in *The Medical Revolution of the Seventeenth Century,* ed. Roger French and Andrew Wear (Cambridge: Cambridge UP, 1989), 164–90 (esp. 179–83).
107. *The Whole Works of that Excellent Practical Physician, Dr. Thomas Sydenham,* tr. John Pechey, 10th ed. (1734), 9–10.
108. Wear, *Knowledge and Practice in English Medicine,* 456.
109. Henry Oldenberg, in "The Publisher to the Reader," claims that Boyle's book gives readers "such accurate Observations and Experiments, as may afford them and their Offspring genuine Matter to raise a Masculine Philosophy upon" (*Colours,* sig. A8^{v}).
110. Boyle, *Colours,* 163–64.
111. Pepys, *Diary,* 3:63 (April 11, 1662). For a contextualization of this passage, see Taylor, *Time, Space, Race.*
112. Pepys, *Diary,* 6:215 (September 7, 1665), 8:236–37 (May 26, 1667). On June 2, he finished Boyle's *Colours,* admitting that it "is so Chymicall that I can understand but little of it, but understand enough to see that he is a most excellent man" (8:247).
113. *The Works of Sir Thomas Browne,* ed. Geoffrey Keynes, 4 vols. (Chicago: University of Chicago Press, 1964), 4:66 (July 10, 1676). Browne went on to note that "this tincture seemes not to bee deepe, for if their skinnes bee cutt the scarre becomes paler." Browne had not made this observation in *Pseudodoxia Epidemica,* and must in the interim have been influenced by Boyle or by Boyle's source, Piso.
114. Nehemiah Grew, *Musaeum Regalis Societatis: Or, A Catalogue and Description of the Natural and Artificial Rarities Belonging to the Royal Society and Preserved at Gresham Colledge* (1686), 3–8. The "skin of a moor" had been acquired by the Royal Society from the collection of Robert Hubert, described in *A Catalogue of the Many Natural Rarities* (1664), and seen by an Italian visitor in 1669: see Lorenzo Magalotti, *Travels of Cosmo III, Grand Duke of Tuscany, through England (1669)* (1821), 188.
115. Cristina Malcolmson, "'The Explication of Whiteness and Blackness': Skin Color and the Physics of Color in the Works of Robert Boyle and Margaret Cavendish," in *Fault Lines and Controversies in the Study of Seventeenth-Century Literature,* ed. Ted-Larry Pebworth and Claude J. Summers (Columbia: University of Missouri Press, 2002), 187–203.
116. Boyle argued that, by means of "some peculiar and Seminal Impression" (161), "White Parents may sometimes have Black children" (166), and thereby "that a Race of *Negroes* might be begun, though none of the Sons of *Adam* for many Precedent Generations were of that Complexion" (166).
117. The word *scientist* is first recorded in 1834; Boyle called himself (among other things) a "naturalist" (a sixteenth-century word), and if we want to avoid anachronism we should call him "the first white naturalist."

118. It is noticeable that, where sixteenth- and early seventeenth-century accounts used *white* to describe non-European peoples, Boyle in summarizing those objections to the classical climatic theory never uses the word. He describes peoples who are exceptions or contradictions to the climatic rule as "at most but Tawny" (154), "not *Negroes* . . . not so much as Tawny-Mores . . . Olive-colour'd" (156), "but Tawny" (159). He identifies only Europeans as "people of a White complexion" (160), though he acknowledges differences in degrees of whiteness among Europeans. Thus, "the *Danes* . . . and even the *English* . . . have usually Whiter faces than the *Spaniards, Portugalls* and other European Inhabitants of Hotter Climates" (153); "the *Danes* be a Whiter People than the *Spaniards*" (154); "the *Swedes* and other Inhabitants of those cold Countreys, are not usually so White as the *Danes,* nor Whiter than other Nations in proportion to their Vicinity to the Pole" (155); Moscovites are generally "far less Whitish than the *Danes,*" but the "Antient *Russians* . . . were rather White like the *Danes,* than any thing near so Brown as the present *Muscovites* whom he guesses to be descended of the *Tartars,* and to have inherited their Colour from them" (155); "the White people removing into very Hot Climates"—that is, Europeans colonizing tropical regions (161); "as white as that of *Europæan* Bodyes" (164). In considering the evidence for seminal transmission of skin color, at the very end of the essay Boyle cites Andrew Battel's evidence that "sometimes" there are "*White Children*" born in the Congo, whose "*Parents are* Negroes," but these are rare—"*The King of* Longo *hath four of them*" (166–67). These exceptions constitute examples of the skin color of individuals, and (although important for understanding the origination and transmission of skin color) they clearly differ from the wholesale attribution of whiteness to an entire European population, elsewhere in Boyle's treatise.

119. Whether we call Boyle a "white naturalist" or a "white scientist," from our perspective the adjective undermines the authority of the noun. But Boyle would not necessarily have agreed. See Lotte Muligan, "Robert Boyle, 'Right Reason,' and the Meaning of Metaphor," *Journal of the History of Ideas* 55 (1994): 235–57, for evidence that "Boyle throughout his life repeatedly presented himself as the Christian Virtuoso" (239), believing that his Christianity improved his science (and that his scientific objectivity made him a better defender of the Church of England). For Boyle as "lay theologian," see also Jan W. Wojcik, *Robert Boyle and the Limits of Reason* (Cambridge: Cambridge UP, 1997): "Boyle often conflated discussions of questions about natural philosophy with theological considerations; this tendency only emphasizes the point that for him, the two were inseparable" (152).

120. Shapin, *A Social History of Truth: Civility and Science in Seventeenth-Century England* (Chicago: University of Chicago Press, 1994), 127. See also Shapin's contrasting picture in "Who was Robert Hooke?" in *Robert Hooke: New Studies,* ed. Michael Hunter and Simon Schaffer (Woodbridge: Boydell Press, 1989), 253–86.

121. On Boyle's pallor, see Maddison, *Life,* 222; John Aubrey, *Brief Lives,* 37; John Evelyn, *Diary and Correspondence,* ed. Bray, 3:351; *Robert Boyle: by Himself and his Friends,* ed. Michael Hunter (Pickering, 1994), 89.

122. Michael Hunter, *Science and Society,* 33, 128, 132.

123. On the "truly *international* Boyle," see Lawrence M. Principe, *The Aspiring Adept: Robert Boyle and His Alchemical Quest* (Princeton, NJ: Princeton UP, 1998), 217–18.

124. Boyle, *Colours,* 152, 154, 155, 157,162, 166, 164. Boyle's editors identify some of his living sources: "Adam Olearius (1600–71), secretary to the Duke of Holstein, wrote *Relation du voyage de Moscovie, Tartarie, et de Perse* (1656) based upon his journeys for the Duke" (*Works,* 4:85). The Russian ambassadors "were received by Charles II on 29 December 1662," a spectacular occasion which Boyle witnessed (4:86). Samuel Collins (1619–70) was physician to Tsar Alexis Romanov from 1660 to 1669 (4:64).

125. See Michael Hunter, "Science and Heterodoxy: An Early Modern Problem Reconsidered," in *Reappraisals of the Scientific Revolution,* ed. David C. Lindberg and Robert S.

Westman (Cambridge: Cambridge UP, 1990), 437–60. The man who probably deserves the title of "the first *English* scientist," Thomas Hariot, was often attacked as an atheist: see R. H. Kargon, *Atomism in England from Hariot to Newton* (Oxford: Clarendon, 1966), 18–30.

126. See Steven Shapin and Simon Schaffer, *Leviathan and the Air-Pump: Hobbes, Boyle, and the Experimental Life* (Princeton, NJ: Princeton UP, 1985); Shapin, *Social History of Truth;* Adrian Johns, *The Nature of the Book: Print and Knowledge in the Making* (Chicago: University of Chicago Press, 1998).
127. In *Some Considerations of the Usefulnesse of Naturall Philosophy* (1663), Boyle equated Indians with lower-class Europeans: "Midwives, Barbers, old Women, Empiricks, and the rest of that illiterate crue, that presume to meddle with Physick among our selves; and partly by the Indians and other barbarous Nations, without excepting the People of such parts of *Europe* it self, where the generality of Men is so illiterate and poor, as to live without physicians" (*Works* 3:426).
128. Edmund Berkeley and Dorothy Smith Berkeley, *John Clayton: Pioneer of American Botany* (Chapel Hill: University of North Carolina Press, 1963), 43; Raymond Phineas Stearns, *Science in the British Colonies of America* (Urbana: University of Illinois Press, 1970), 184.
129. "A Letter from the Rev^{d}. Mr. John Clayton . . . to Dr. Grew, in Answer to several Queries relating to *Virginia,* sent to him by that learned Gentleman, A.D. 1687 . . . ," *Philosophical Transactions* 41 (1739–41): 143–45. Clayton also uses the phrase "a white Native" (157).
130. Hume, "Of National Characters" (1742, rev. 1753), in *Essays Moral, Political, and Literary,* ed. T. H. Green, 2 vols (1875), 1:252. For Hume's revisions, see Wheeler, *Complexion,* 186.
131. Jefferson, *Notes on the State of Virginia* (1785), ed. William Peden (Chapel Hill: University of North Carolina Press, 1954), 139, 142.
132. Brague, *Eccentric Culture: A Theory of Western Civilization,* tr. Samuel Lester (South Bend, IN: St. Augustine's Press, 2002).
133. Peter Dear, "*Totius in verba:* Rhetoric and Authority in the Early Royal Society," *Isis* 76 (1985): 154.
134. Maddison, *Boyle,* 4, 11, 188.
135. For the overwhelming aurality of earlier cultures, and of England even in the sixteenth and early seventeenth centuries, see Smith, *Acoustic World.*
136. For the foundational exposition of this explanation, see Elizabeth L. Eisenstein, *The Printing Press as an Agent of Change: Communications and Cultural Transformations in Early-Modern Europe,* 2 vols. (Cambridge; Cambridge UP, 1979).
137. Walter J. Ong, *Ramus, Method, and the Decay of Dialogue: From the Art of Discourse to the Art of Reason* (Cambridge, MA: Harvard UP, 1958), 9.
138. Boyle had in fact been preceded by Harriot, who—among other contributions to optics—found the sine law of refraction and measured the dispersion of white light, using a prism: see J. Lohne, "Thomas Harriott (1560–1621), the Tycho Brahe of Optics," *Centaurus* 6 (1959): 113–21, and John W. Shirley, *Thomas Harriot: A Biography* (Oxford: Clarendon, 1983), 380–88. However, Hariot's work remained unpublished and exercised no influence on subsequent investigations.
139. For a cogent explication of Boyle's theory of matter, see Frederick J. O'Toole, "Qualities and Powers in the Corpuscular Philosophy of Robert Boyle," *Journal of the History of Philosophy* 12 (1974): 295–315.
140. The first corpusucular theory of light was articulated in an unpublished thesis (Caen, 1618) by Isaac Beeckman (1588–1637), rector of the Latin school in Dordrecht. Beeckman influenced Descartes and Gassendi. See K. van Berkel, *Isaac Beeckman (1588–1637) en de mechanisering van het wereldbeeld* (Amsterdam: Rodopi, 1983) and *In het voetspoor*

van Stevin, Geschiedenis van de natuurwetenschap in Nederland 1580–1940 (Meppel-Amsterdam: Boom, 1985).

141. On Digby's experimentalism and atomism, see R. T. Peterson, *Sir Kenelm Digby: The Ornament of England, 1603–1665* (Jonathan Cape, 1956), 182–87.

142. Sir Kenelm Digby, *Two Treatises* (Paris, 1644), 262. Digby's book was printed in London in 1645.

143. Boyle repeatedly praised Digby: "The Atomicall Philosophy . . . so luckyly reviv'd & so skillfully celebrated in divers parts of Europe by the learned pens of Gassendus, Magnenus, Des Cartes & his disciple our deservedly famous Countryman Sir Kenelme Digby" (*Works,* 13:227); "I must recommend upon the authority of Sir Ken Digby" (13:241); "the eminently learned Sir Kenelme Digby" (3:165); "that great Person, *Sir Kenelm Digby*" (3:230); "my Noble Friend Sir *Kenelm Digby*" (3:348). These texts date from about 1654 to 1663. Boyle specifically referred to Digby's *Two Treatises* in *The Excellency of Theology* (published 1674, but written 1665) and *Experiments and Notes about the Mechanical Origine or Production of Electricity* (1675): see *Works,* 8:24, 511–12. There are two surviving letters from Digby to Boyle on chemical recipes (*Correspondence* 1:272–74, 283–85, May-June 1658), and Hartlib wrote to Boyle about Digby in 1654 (1:174–76). As Principe notes, "The relationship between Digby and Boyle has not been fully explored, but it is clear that they communicated regularly" (*Aspiring Adept,* 167). The lack of attention to their relationship almost certainly derives from the presumption, among earlier historians of science, that Boyle's chemistry represented a revolutionary break from the "mysticism" of an amateur and alchemist like Digby.

144. Digby's influence on *Colours* has not been noted by Boyle's modern editors or critics. But Digby—following Descartes—anticipated Boyle's conclusion that "white is that, which reflecteth most light" (*Two Treatises,* 261). Unlike Descartes, Digby—like Boyle—consistently reversed the alphabetical order of black and white, writing of "the disposition of those bodies which produce white or blacke coulours" (259) and of "the generation of these two colours (white and blacke) in bodies" (262). Like Boyle, he described black in rhetorically negative terms: "blacke reflecteth least light" (259), because when light strikes a black object it is "as it were absorpt and hidden in caves" (259) or "so entangled there (as though the winges of it were birdlimed over) that it can not fly out againe" (261).

145. When Digby claims that "white thinges are generally cold and dry; and therefore, are by nature ordained to be receptacles, and conservers of heat, and of moysture; as Physitians do note" (*Two Treatises,* 262), he is referring to Aristotelian and Galenic commonplaces. On Digby's Aristotelianism more generally, see Peterson, *Digby,* 188–92.

146. On the very different contemporary reputations of the two French atomists, see Thomas M. Lennon, *The Battle of the Gods and Giants: The Legacies of Descartes and Gassendi, 1655–1715* (Princeton, NJ: Princeton UP, 1993). Lennon, incidentally, describes Digby's *Two Treatises* as the most "significant Aristotelian work" of the century (53).

147. Boyle, *Colours,* 94–96. Boyle cited Gassendi's *De apparente Magnitudine solis humilis & sublimis epistolae quatuor* (Paris, 1642), Epistle 2, p. 45. Gassendi's Latin is translated by Boyle's modern editors thus: "I should like you to consider this: when it falls on a transparent object, light seems colourless, but when it is impeded by something opaque, it looks white, and the more so the more dense or compressed it is. Thus, water is not of itself white in colour, but the ray of light reflected by it onto the eye looks white. Again, when the surface of the water is flat this reflection happens from one side only: but if the water happens to swell up into bubbles, each bubble causes a reflection, and creates the white appearance on a certain part of its surface. Furthermore, foam formed from pure water seems to shine and look white for the very reason that it is a densely packed mass of the tiniest bubbles, each one reflecting its own ray of light, and thus creating the effect of continuous whiteness or shininess. And finally, snow seems to be nothing other than a sort of very pure foam

formed from the very tiniest and most densely packed bubbles. But to elaborate these trivialities of mine any further would lay me open to ridicule" (*Works* 4:62).

148. Boyle, *Colours,* 93. For other examples of antialphabetical ordering, see sig. a4^{v}, pp. 87, 94, 107, 120, 122, 126, 127, 128, 130, 131, 132, 133, 156, 170, 171.
149. Boyle, *Colours,* 116.
150. Descartes, "Optics: First Discourse," in *Discourse on Method, Optics, Geometry, and Meteorology,* tr. Paul J. Olscamp, rev. ed. (Indianapolis: Hackett, 2001), 73: "there are bodies which, being met by rays of light, break them up, and take away all their force, such as those which we call black, which have no more color than shadows; and that there are others which reflect these rays. . . . And that again, among the latter, some reflect these rays without causing any other change in their action, such as those which we call white". For the French, see "La Dioptrique, Discours I," in *Discours de la Methode Pour bien conduite sa raison, & chercher la verité dans les sciences. Plus La Diaoptrique. Les Meteores. Et La Geometrie. Qui sont des essais de cete Methode* (1637), in *Oeuvres de Descartes,* ed. Charles Adam and Paul Tannery, rev. ed., vol. 6: *Discours de la Méthode & Essais* (Paris: Vrin, 1982), 91–92. Boyle acknowledges early in *Colours* something that "the most ingenious *Des Cartes* hath very well observ'd" (13); Boyle's editors note that he here refers to "part I of *La dioptrique*" (*Works* 4:29). He again refers to "the *Cartesians*" and their hypotheses about light and color near the end of Part I (85). On the more general question of Cartesian influence on Boyle, see Laudan, "The Clock Metaphor," and the response by Rogers, "Descartes and the Method," esp. 248–55.
151. Digby, *Two Treatises,* 259.
152. "Of the Common Practices of Dying. By Sir WILLIAM PETTY," included in Sprat, *History,* 308.
153. Boyle, *Colours,* 96–97. For the equivalency of *body* and *object,* see the opening sentence of Boyle's analysis: "Whiteness then consider'd as a Quality in the Object, seems chiefly to depend upon this, That the Superficies of the Body that is call'd White." Elsewhere Boyle uses "White Object" where he would normally write "White Body" (106). Boyle uses the phrase "White Body" or "White Bodies" obsessively in the section on whiteness and blackness: 102 (twice), 103, 104 (twice), 107 (twice), 108 (twice), 112, 114, 115, 127, 131 (twice), 142, 171. It also shows up in the subsequent section (pp. 189, 198, etc.). See also "Whiteness of Bodies" (94), "Bodies as White" (96), "a Body White" (97), "a Body extremely White" (99), "a Body appear White" (113), "A Body that is not White, may be made White . . . the Body White" (115), "a Body White" (117), "this Body . . . made White" (141), "a Snow-white Body" (151), "Bodies are White" (170), "Bodyes . . . that are White" (174), "Whiteness of the Body" (175). Boyle also often (though less frequently), refers to "Black Bodyes," but here as elsewhere I am more concerned to track the evolution of whiteness. Boyle's use of *bodies* in the sense "objects" was anticipated by Descartes and Digby—in Digby's case, the discussion of whiteness occurs in the first of his two treatises, entitled *The Nature of Bodies.*
154. Descartes, "Description of the Human Body" (1647–48), in *The World and Other Writings,* tr. Stephen Gaukroger (Cambridge: Cambridge UP, 1998), 204–05; *Description du Corps Humain,* in *Oeuvres,* ed. Adam and Tannery, rev. ed., 11:283–86.
155. Boyle, *Colours,* 164. In the ethnographic chapter Boyle also used "body" in the human corporeal sense twice elsewhere (160, 163). Similarly, Boyle used the noun "Blacks" to refer to Negroes (154, twice) and to chemical substances (138).
156. Boyle had promised, at the beginning of *Colours,* "the delivery of matters of fact" (2); "matters of fact" recurs at the beginning of his discussion of ethnic color (152).
157. Boyle, *Colours,* 145, 96, 102, 103. Boyle offered multiple phrasings: "the Superficies of the Body that is call'd White . . . Reflect the Rays of Light that fall on them, not toward one another, but outwards towards the Specators Eye" (96). Boyle's central idea about

whiteness and reflection had been anticipated by Descartes: "a white body (i.e., a body disposed to reflect light in all other directions without changing it)" (*Discourse,* tr. Olscamp, 94).

158. See Beale's response to *Colours,* in a letter he wrote Boyle on April 25, 1664: "in mine owne narrowe thoughts I was most of all plunged at the causes, & difference of Whitenesse & blacknes" (*Correspondence* 2:269). Highmore's letter—"I have with a greate deale of pleasure reade over your booke of coloures where by youre many experiments I finde myselfe confirmed in a phansy I longe since pleased myself withall"—also immediately began by addressing Part II (2:271).

159. Marie Boas Hall, "Introduction," in *Experiments and Considerations Touching Colours . . . a Facsimile of the 1664 edition* (New York: Johnson Reprint Corporation, 1964), xiv-xv.

160. Principe, *Aspiring Adept,* 221.

161. Floyd-Wilson, *English Ethnicity,* 47.

162. Boyle, *Colours,* sig. A6, 132.

163. Sprat, *History of the Royal Society,* ed. Jackson Cope and Harold Whitmore Jones (St. Louis: Washington UP, 1959), 4; Petty, cited in Hunter, *Science and Society,* 124.

164. For an overview of preceding scholarship and a persuasive analysis of the situated centrality of Bacon, see Julie Robin Solomon, *Objectivity in the Making: Francis Bacon and the Politics of Inquiry* (Baltimore: John Hopkins UP, 1995).

165. David Lloyd, "Race under Representation," *Oxford Literary Review* 13 (1991): 62–94; Dyer, *White,* 38–39.

166. My attitude toward the truth claims of science resembles Paul Feyerabend's: that "being responds to some approaches, but not all" (*Conquest of Abundance,* xviii, etc). Individuals and societies determine *which* of the various possible approaches gets chosen and developed.

167. See the undated letter to Boyle from the physician and natural philosopher Nathaniel Highmore (1613–85): "Such objects (you say) from whence all the beames of light are reflected are white. But if the superficies be such that there is a paucity of beames reflected the object then appeares blacke. I beseech you Sir to pardon my boldness in begging your farther consideration of this description of blacke. If blackness arise from the paucity of beames reflected, how comes it that black bodies should be as perfectly seene as greene or blew. The paucity of beames must make the object less visible as in landskips where by reason of the distance many raies of light in the reflection are lost before they come to the eie, & so those things are imperfectly & faintly represented . . . I cannot understand how the loosing some beames should make the object perfectly visible & blacke" (*Correspondence,* 2:271–72). Highmore's second book, *The History of Generation* (1651), was the first work dedicated to Boyle; Boyle cites Highmore as "amongst the accuratest of our modern writers."

168. Cavendish, *Experimentall,* 54, 56.

169. Boyle, *Colours,* 106, 117.

170. Locke, *Essay,* II.i.4.

171. See for instance Peter Dear, "*Totius in Verba . . .*"; Brian Vickers, "The Royal Society and English Prose Style: A Reassessment," in *Rhetoric and the Pursuit of Truth,* ed. Vickers and Nancy Struever (Berkeley: University of California Press, 1985).

172. Lawrence M. Principe, "Virtuous Romance and Romantic Virtuoso: The Shaping of Robert Boyle's Literary Style," *Journal of the History of Ideas* 56 (1995): 377–97.

173. See Boyle, *The Christian Virtuoso* (1690), sig. A5^{v}-A6: " . . . proper Comparisons do the Imagination almost as much Service, as Microscopes do the Eye; for, *as* this Instrument gives us a distinct view of divers minute Things, which our naked Eye cannot well discern; because these Glasses represent them far more large, than by the bare Eye we judge them; *so* a skilfully chosen, and well-applied, Comparison much helps the Imagination, by illustrating Things scarce discernible, so as to represent them by Things much more familiar and easy to be apprehended."

174. Hobbes, *Leviathan* (1651), 20 (Part I, chapter v); Petty, "Preface," *A Discourse Made before the Royal Society . . . Concerning the Use of Duplicate Proportion* (1674).
175. William Petty, *The Advice of W. P. to Mr. Samuel Hartlib for The Advancement of Some Particular Parts of Learning* (1648), 12; *The Petty-Southwell Correspondence 1676–1687,* ed. Marquis of Lansdowne (Constable, 1928), 324 (November 24, 1687).
176. Petty's emphasis on motion probably derived from Hobbes, for whom it was the cause of all effects, particularly "effects one body moved worketh upon another." See Hobbes, *Elements of Philosophy concerning Body* (1656), 53 (Part I, ch. vi, art. 6), translating *Elementa philosophiae sectio de corpore* (1655), 45.
177. Paul Feyerabend, *Conquest of Abundance: A Tale of Abstraction versus the Richness of Being,* ed. Bert Terpstra (Chicago: University of Chicago Press, 1999).
178. Milton, *Paradise lost. A Poem Written in Ten Books* (1667), sig. A1 (in modern editions, I.1–3).
179. Richard S. Westfall, *Never at Rest: A Biography of Isaac Newton* (Cambridge: Cambridge UP, 1980), 154–55.
180. Sprat, *Royal Society,* 113.
181. Newton wrote, "If I have seen further it is by standing on ye sholders of Giants" in a letter to Hooke (February 5, 1676), responding to Hooke's own generous letter, attempting to heal a breach by then four years old: see *The Correspondence of Isaac Newton,* ed. H. W. Turnbull, 7 vols. (Cambridge: The Royal Society, 1959–77), 1:416. Hooke's own investigations were heavily indebted to Boyle, and Newton had leaped to his central conclusion in his undergraduate notebooks by the end of 1664, before publication of Hooke's *Micrographia* in 1665. Newton never had to concede his debt to Boyle in the way he was eventually compelled to acknowledge (privately) Hooke, because Boyle did not publicly challenge him. Boyle and Hooke had been asked to comment on Newton's initial paper, but Boyle (characteristically) did not, leaving Hooke to engage in the polemics that Boyle always detested and, wherever possible, avoided. Newton did not publish *Opticks* until just after Hooke's death, although it had been drafted some years before.
182. Westfall, *Never at Rest,* 89 (on the date of the "Quaestiones," and Newton's reading), 94–96 (on the presence in the "Quaestiones" of "the central insight to the demonstration of which his entire work in optics was directed, that ordinary light from the sun is heterogeneous, and that phenomena of colors arise, not from the modification of homogeneous light as prevailing theory had it, but from the separation or analysis of the heterogeneous mixture into its components"). Westfall's conclusions here draw on A. R. Hall, "Sir Isaac Newton's Note-book, 1661–65," *Cambridge Historical Journal* 9 (1948): 239–50, and Richard S. Westfall, "The Foundations of Newton's Philosophy of Nature," *British Journal for the History of Science* 1 (1962): 171–82. They are extended in Alan E. Shapiro's introduction to *The Optical Papers of Isaac Newton: Volume I: The Optical Lectures 1670–72,* ed. Shapiro (Cambridge: Cambridge UP, 1984), 4–7, and in A. Rupert Hall's *All Was Light: An Introduction to Newton's Opticks* (Oxford: Clarendon, 1993), 13–17.
183. Newton to Oldenburg, January 6, 1672 (*Correspondence,* 1:79).
184. Hall, *All Was Light,* 41; Dennis L. Sepper, *Newton's Optical Writings: A Guided Study* (New Brunswick, NJ: Rutgers UP, 1994), 45; Francis A. Jenkins and Harvey E. White, *Fundamentals of Optics,* 4th ed. (New York: McGraw-Hill, 1976), 249–50; Alan E. Shapiro, "The Evolving Structure of Newton's Theory of White Light and Color," *Isis* 70 (1980): 211–35.
185. Describing "the Sun and other Powerfully Lucid Bodies," Boyle suggested that "*if* any Colour be to be Ascrib'd to them as they are Lucid, *it seems it should* be Whiteness; for the Sun at Noon-day, and in Clear weather . . . appears of a Colour *more approaching to White,* than when nearer the Horizon . . . And when the Sun Shines upon that Natural

Looking-glass, a Smooth water, that part of it, which appears to this or that particular Beholder, the most Shin'd on, does to his Eye seem *far Whiter* than the rest . . . when the Sun was Veil'd over as it were, with a Thin White Cloud . . . by casting my Eyes upon a Smooth water, as we sometimes do to observes Eclipses without prejudice to our Eyes, the Sun then not far from the Meridian, appear'd to me not Red, but *so White,* that 'twas not without some Wonder, that I made the Observation" (*Colours,* 97–99; italics added). All Boyle's examples of white sunlight—introduced by hypothetical *if* and hesitant *seems*—are expressed in terms of comparative, not absolute, whiteness. He does go on to contrast the common expression "red hot" with the "White heat" found in "the Forges of Smiths, and the Furnaces of other Artificers" (99). By this reasoning the sun *should* be white, because it was hotter than any other object known to seventeenth-century science. This entire discussion must have influenced Newton, who nevertheless asserted in a few words what Boyle only suggested in a long paragraph.

186. "A Letter of Mr. Isaac Newton, Professor of the Mathematicks in the University of Cambridge; containing his New Theory about *Light* and *Colors*" (February 6, 1672), *Philosophical Transactions* 6, no. 80 (February 19, 1672): 3083.
187. Milton, *Paradise Lost* 3:572 ("golden sun"), 3:625 ("Of beaming sunny rays, a golden tiar"), 5:442 ("perfect gold"), 6:12–13 ("the Morn . . . arrayed in gold"), 6:28 (God speaking from "a golden cloud"). The idea that gold was the only "perfect" metal was traditional. Of these quotations from Milton, only the first is included in the figures I give in the text for *golden sun* (taken from searches of Literature Online).
188. Thomson, *Liberty* (1735), Book II, lines 222–25.
189. Figures for *golden light* and *white light* are from Literature Online; I have checked contexts up through 1900, and discounted phrases that do not refer to optical phenomenon. For copyright reasons the database is much less comprehensive for twentieth-century authors. A search for *white* within five words of *light* found a few anticipations of Shelley. Only one antedates Newton: in Robert Holland's *The Holie Historie of Our Lord and Saviour* (1594), rhyme prompts the simile "His clothes were white as is the light." After Newton, Benjamin Keach's *Spiritual Melody* (1691) contains "Robes so white that shine like Light" (Hymn 185); Joseph Watson's *The Eclogues and Georgics of Virgil* (1753) describes comets as "white tracks of trembling light"; Ann Radcliff's *Udolpho* (1794) refers to the "whiteness of the moon light." Moonlight also lies behind Coleridge's image in "The rime of the Ancyent Marinere" (*Lyrical Ballads,* 1798), where "the bay was white with silent light," and Erasmus Darwin's *The Botanic Garden* (1799), where "with milky light the white horizon streams". William Mason's *Elfrida* (1811) has "white-rob'd Son of Light." At about the same time, Coleridge's translation of Schiller's *The Death of Wallerstein* contains "one White stain of light" (in a dark sky).
190. David Armitage, "John Milton: Poet against Empire," in *Milton and Republicanism,* ed. Armitage, A. Himy, and Quentin Skinner (Cambridge: Cambridge UP, 1995), 206–25; Andrew Hadfield, "The English and Other Peoples," in *A Companion to Milton,* ed. Thomas N. Corns (Oxford: Blackwell, 2001), 174–90. Milton does not name Ham, but refers to "the irreverent son / Of him who built the ark, who for the shame / Done to his father, heard this heavy curse,/ *Servant of servants,* on his vicious race" (*Paradise Lost* 11:101–04). Given the later resonance of the word *race,* this looks racist to modern readers, but Milton does not give any hint that the curse fell on Africans. He does, however—like others discussed in the preceding chapter—seem to generalize the curse to *all* Ham's descendants (not just Canaan).
191. Oldenberg to Newton, February 8, 1672, *Correspondence* 1:107.
192. Thomas Kuhn, "Newton's Optical Papers," in *Isaac Newton's Papers and Letters on Natural Philosophy,* ed. I. Bernard Cohen, 2nd ed. (Cambridge: Harvard UP, 1978), 28. Neophyte Newton lacked the social or intellectual authority, within the emergent scientific com-

munity, that Boyle possessed; he also lacked Boyle's principled modesty. By refusing to acknowledge his indebtedness to others, he wounded the vanity and provoked the hostility of Robert Hooke. Moreover, where Boyle notoriously described every detail of his experiments, Newton compressed his, publishing an account much more elliptical and incomplete than his earlier Cambridge lectures on the subject.

193. Hall, *All Was Light,* 44, 62.
194. Newton to Oldenberg, June 11, 1672, *Correspondence* 1:183. The text as printed in *Philosophical Transactions* does not italicize "Paradoxical."
195. For some of the relevant weaknesses, see A. I. Sabra, *Theories of Light from Descartes to Newton* (Cambridge: Cambridge UP, 1981), ch. 11; Sepper, *Optical Writings,* 204–07; Hall, *All Was Light,* 52–54, 66.
196. Newton, "New Theory," 3083, 3085.
197. *Philosophical Transactions,* 6 (1972), no. 80, pp. 3075 ("The CONTENTS," at the top of the page on which Newton's paper begins), 3088–94. Both refer to an English-language review of Philippus Baldaeus, *Beschriving der OOST-INDISCHE KUSTEN, MALABAR, COROMNDEL, CEYLON, etc.* (Amsterdam, 1672).
198. *OED mixture* 1.e. (examples of the sexual sense 1604–1712).
199. "A Letter from Mr. Anth. Van Leeuwenhoek concerning the Seeds of Plants, with Observations on the manner of the *Propagation* of *Plants* and *Animals,*" *Philosophical Transactions,* 17 (1693): 705 (using the variant spelling "*Mestico*").
200. "Mr. Isaac Newtons Answer to some Considerations upon his Doctrine of *Light* and *Colors;* which Doctrine was printed in *Numb. 80* of these Tracts" (June 11, 1672) *Philosophical Transactions* 7, no. 88 (1672): 5090.
201. Sir Isaac Newton, *Opticks* (New York: Dover, 1953), 132 (Pro. IV, Theor. III). See also "This Unchangeableness of Colour" (121, Prop. I, Theor. I).
202. See I. Bernard Cohen's introduction to Newton's *Opticks,* xviii-xxxix; Marjorie Hope Nicolson, *Newton Demands the Muse: Newton's "Opticks" and the Eighteenth Century Poets* (Princeton, NJ: Princeton UP, 1946); and Hall, *All Was Light,* 180–236.
203. "Epitaph. Intended for Sir Isaac Newton" (1730), in *The Poems of Alexander Pope,* ed. John Butt (New Haven, CT: Yale UP, 1963), 808.
204. Sepper, *Optical Writings,* 182–83.
205. Newton, *Opticks,* 134 (in the text of Proposition V, theorem IV [Book One, part two]). "The Whiteness of the Sun's Light" recurs on p. 153 and is implied throughout, in innumerable references to "the Sun's light" collocated with white, whites, and whiteness. Newton repeats this formula despite having to admit, elsewhere, that "the Sun's Light" is not "perfectly white: But . . . inclines to yellow" (164). But even after this admission, he concludes Book One asserting that a "white light" is "perfectly and totally white like a beam of the Sun's Light" (188–89).
206. Newton, *Opticks,* 134–36, 150–52, 156, 258–59.
207. Dyer, "White" (1988), reprinted in *The Matter of Images,* 2nd ed. (Routledge, 2002), 127–28.
208. Newton, *Opticks,* 124, 151.
209. Newton, *Opticks,* 406. In the final sentence of the *Opticks,* Newton asserts that all mankind originally worshipped the one true God ("the first Cause") "under the Government of Noah and his Sons before they corrupted themselves" (406). This refers cryptically to Newton's unorthodox belief that all religious error could be traced back to the sons of Noah and to Egypt. For the nefarious role played by Egypt in Newton's chronology and theology, see Westfall, *Never at Rest,* 351–56.
210. Newton, *Opticks,* 260, 266–67, 152.
211. "Newtons Answer," 5099: "A beam of the Suns Light being transmitted into a darkned room, if you illuminate a sheet of White Paper by that Light, reflected from a body of any

colour, the paper will always appear of the colour of that body, by whose reflected light it is illuminated. If it be a red body, the paper will be red; if a green body, it will be green; and so of the other colours."

212. Newton, *Opticks,* 152–53.
213. Newton, *Opticks,* 15; Boyle, *Colours,* 102–03. Boyle's use of white paper (but not of the darkened room) had been anticipated by Digby, who described an experiment with a prism and "a sheete of white paper upon a blacke carpett" (*Two Treatises,* 263). Even earlier, Descartes had described a prism experiment involving "cloth or white paper" (*Discourse,* tr. Olscamp, 335); but the French *blanc* had other associations for an English reader. In any case, Boyle used the object and the idiom much more frequently than Descartes or Digby.
214. *OED white a.* 11e, *white paper,* examples from 1569; *blank a.*2.a ("Of paper etc. . . . not written upon, free from written or printed characters . . ."), examples from 1547.

Chapter 11

1. Mills, *The Racial Contract* (Ithaca, NY: Cornell UP, 1997), 11.
2. Locke, *Essay* III.i.1.
3. Hobbes, *Leviathan,* 1.4.23–24.
4. *Oroonoko* (1688), in *The Works of Aphra Behn,* ed. Janet Todd, 7 vols. (Columbus: Ohio State UP, 1992–96), 3:59, 63, 63, 69, 82, 90, 93, 94, 100, 104, 109, 110, 118.
5. *OED white a.*3 ("Of or in reference to the skin or complexion"). This sense is identified as "Now rare or obsolete except as in" the racial sense (*a.*4). *OED*'s examples range from about 900 to 1689. The last—"He has . . . a Skin so white—and soft as Sattin with the Grain"—comes from Nathaniel Lee's comedy *The Princess of Cleve* (2.2), based on Marie-Madeleine de la Vergue, Comtesse de La Fayette's *La Princesse de Clèves* (1678). *OED* dates the quotation from Lee "1689," the date of the play's publication. But Lee went mad and was incarcerated in Bedlam in 1684, so the play must antedate 1684 and is now tentatively dated 1681. Even in this example, the admired "white" body is male—itself a radical departure from earlier standards and clearly related to the rise of a generic sense of whiteness.
6. Behn, *Oroonoko,* 61, 105. "Blacks" is used in the paragraph before "gloomy Race," and "Whites" in the paragraph before "degenerate Race."
7. Bernier, "Nouvelle Division" (quoted and discussed on pp. 312–13, 323–4, 329, 468).
8. *OED*'s subclassifications seem to me unhelpful for the noun *race,* but they include "the offspring or posterity of a person, a set of children or descendants" (*n.*[2] 1.a, from 1570), and "limited group of persons descended from a common ancestor" (*n.*[2] 2.a, from ca. 1600); these human senses are obviously related to the animal category "a breed or stock of animals" (3.a, from 1580). These groupings in turn seem clearly to lead to "mankind," that is, "the human race," presumably regarded as descendants of Adam and Eve (5.a, from 1580), but also lead to "a tribe, nation, or people, regarded as a common stock" (2.b, from ca. 1600), and "genus, species, kind of animals" (3.c, from 1605). The movement from "nation, or people" (2.b) to "one of the great divisions of mankind" (2.d) depends, presumably, not only on the size of the population but its presumed origin: thus, Spenser's "of English race" (*Faerie Queene* 1590, I.x.60) differs from Milton's "Pygmean Race" (*Paradise Lost* 1667, I.780) in that "English race" presumes the vaguely common origin of a people defined primarily by location (with an associated culture), whereas "Pygmean race" focuses on physical difference.
9. George Guffey, "Aphra Behn's *Oroonoko:* Occasion and Accomplishment," in *Two English Novelists: Aphra Behn and Anthony Trollope* (Los Angeles: University of California Press, 1975), 3–41; Anita Pacheco, "Royalism and Honor in Aphra Behn's *Oroonoko,*" *SEL* 34 (1994): 491–506.

10. Behn, *Oroonoko,* 119.
11. Behn, *Oroonoko,* 119. I take it that Cleopatra, in Shakespeare's *Antony and Cleopatra* (1607?), was dark-complected, but that she belonged to the distinct theatrical (and social) category of "gypsy" (1.1.10, 4.13.28) rather than "Negro." Moreover, although Cleopatra may be tragic and "Beautiful," she could hardly be described as "Constant."
12. Behn, *Oroonoko,* 119, 112, 118.
13. Tryon, *Friendly Advice,* 214, 220.
14. Godwyn, *Advocate,* title page, 142, 155, 130.
15. "And it being taken into Consideration by the gouerno^{r} Councell and assembly that negroes though they are slaues and bought as goods and Chattles yett are they Reasonable Creatures and Capable of being taught the Principles of o^{r} Religion and that wee ought to Endeavo^{r} the makeing of them Christians the more to aduance the glory of god and by that Doctrine so Ciuilize and binde them more to our Seruice and interest, as wee see our neighbours the Spaniards and other nations doe who neu^{r}theless keepe them as Slaues, and findeing that being thus baptized and made Christians they serue their masters with more fedillity and Respect and are therefore treated by them with more humillity and Justice and being allsoe Further Considered that here is needfull of Extraordinary meanes to keepe the negroes Faithfull and dutifull because the Island is soe uast and hath soe many Couerts and Conueniencyes to hide themselues and gett victualls. . . . Recommend to all the inhabitants of this Island the Care and endeauour to instruct their Slaues Especially the younger Sorte in the Christian religion and doe Enact and ordaine as hereby it is enacted, and ordayned by the authority aforesd that all negroes Lawfully bought or borne slaves shall here continue to bee so, and Further bee held adjudged and taken to bee goods and chattles and ought to come to the hands of Executors and adm^{r}s as other assetts doe their Christianity or any Law Custome or Vsage in Engld or else where to the contrary notwithstanding" (C.O. 139/1, fol. 109b–110a). This paragraph is not present in the 1664 slave code in the same manuscript; in most details the two codes are identical. Notice that "all the inhabitants of this Island" means, essentially, the white free population (a usage already present in the 1623 Bermuda law regulating Negroes, discussed in chapter 2).
16. Godwyn, *Advocate,* 140: "And as to that which some would in the *fourth* place object, touching their release from servitude upon *Baptism,* tho I do not see that they here do retain any *apprehensions* thereof, their *Law* (of which I have only heard mention here"—*here* meaning Barbados, as is evident from many other passages in the text—"but do know that there is such both in *Virginia* and *Mary-land*) having carefully *barred all such Pleas.*"
17. Tryon, *Friendly Advice,* 139.
18. For these cases see Jordan, *White Over Black,* 78–79. Jordan attempts to minimize this early evidence by conjecturing that in the Davis case, "it is possible that the 'negro' may not have been female" and that "There may have been no racial feeling involved" in the Sweet case, since similar penances were imposed for extramarital fornication between whites. But if the Davis case had involved sodomy, that fact would surely have been more relevant than the skin color of his partner; sodomy was a crime recognized by English law, wheras "lying with a negro" was not. In the Sweet case, the presence of "racial feeling" is surely indicated by three facts: (1) the English gentleman is named, but the woman is not, conforming to a pattern whereby whites were given personal identities and blacks were not; (2) the English gentleman is sentenced to "penance in church according to laws of England," but the woman is "whipt," a distinction in punishment not attributable to the "laws of England," which must therefore be based on race, not gender; (3) the woman is identified as a "negro," a fact irrelevant if Sweet's crime were simple fornication.
19. Hening, ed., *Statutes,* 2:170.

20. Winthrop D. Jordan, "American Chiaroscuro: The Status and Definition of Mulattoes in the British Colonies," *William and Mary Quarterly,* III, 19 (1962): 183–200.
21. "Father Antoine Biet's Visit to Barbados in 1654," *JBMHS* 32 (1967): 56–76.
22. Godwyn, *Advocate,* 30.
23. Bernier, "Nouvelle Division," 363. I have changed the translation from the nineteenth-century English "dear" to modern "expensive."
24. Jefferson, *Notes on the State of Virginia* (1785), Query XVIII. As Jordan notes, Jefferson's "remarks about Negroes in the only book he ever wrote were more widely read, in all probability, than any others until the mid-nineteenth century," constituting "a fixed and central point of reference and influence" (*White Over Black,* 429).
25. For a critique of Locke's handling of this problem, see Susan James, *Passion and Action: The Emotions in Seventeenth-Century Philosophy* (Oxford: Clarendon, 1997), 284–8.
26. Locke, *Essay,* II.xxi.63.
27. For the origin of the image, see Aristotle, *De Anima,* tr. W. S. Hett (Cambridge: Harvard UP, 1935), 430^{a}1: "This would be in the same sense as when we say that a tablet [γραμματειω] which is empty is potentially written upon; which actually occurs in the case of the mind" (166–67). For the English currency of the image, see *OED tabula* 1.a (including a 1662 quotation from South's *Sermons,* "Aristotle . . . affirms the Mind to be at first a mere *Rasa Tabula*"). Joseph Glanvill, a champion of Boyle and the Royal Society, had written in *The Vanity of Dogmatizing* (1661) that "our initial age is like the melted wax . . . capable of any impression from the documents of our Teachers . . . and we may with equal facility write on this *rasa Tabula,* Turk, or Christian" (128). Locke himself used the phrase in early drafts: "the minde . . . at first 'tis probable to me is rasa tabula" (*Draft A,* 2), "the soule . . . at first it is perfectly rasa tabula" (*Draft B,* 17); but in the published *Essay* Locke changed the original image to "white paper" (II.i.2). I cite Locke's drafts from *Drafts for the "Essay Concerning Human Understanding," and Other Philosophical Writings: Volume I, Drafts A and B,* ed. Peter H. Nidditch and G. A. J. Rogers (Oxford: Clarendon, 1990).
28. *OED slate n.*[1] 2.a (examples from Chaucer to the nineteenth century).
29. Chaucer's Pardoner had "hair as yellow as wax" (*Canterbury Tales,* Pro. 675). Locke also described "wax" as "yellow" (*Draft A,* sec. 1). He acknowledged that the sun could "whiten" it, but this change produced a color that was not its natural unmodified color; therefore, as an image of the unaltered originary mind, the unaltered originary color of wax would be yellow.
30. Papyrus rather than a tablet is used for the metaphor in a passage in Aetius, ca. 100 C.E. See *The Hellenistic Philosophers,* ed. and tr. A. A. Long and D. N. Sedley, 2 vols. (Cambridge: Cambridge UP, 1987): "When a man is born, the Stoics say, he has the commanding part of his soul like a sheet of paper ready for writing upon. On this he inscribes each one of his conceptions. The first method of inscription is through the senses. For by perceiving something, e.g., white, they have a memory of it when it has departed" (1:238). In the original Greek text (2:240) the single word here translated as "a sheet of paper" (χάρτην) means literally "papyrus" or "papyrus roll," an inscriptible surface quite distinct from modern paper in its texture, raw material, mode of production, and—most important for our purposes—color. Bleaching was an essential part of the manufacture of paper: see Albertine Gaur, *A History of Writing,* rev. ed. (New York: Cross River Press, 1992), 44–47. In the early modern period the finest paper was made from "pure white linens": see Philip Gaskell, *A New Introduction to Bibliography* (Oxford: Oxford UP, 1972), 66. In Aetius, *white* is not associated with χάρτην, but is one of the impressions from the outside world which is recorded on the papyrus roll. (I suspect the translation "a sheet of paper" is based in part on the modern translators' familiarity with Locke's metaphor.)
31. In Locke's *Essay* the metaphor is used even earlier than the passage already quoted (II.i.2): "For such, who are careful (as they call it) to principle Children well . . . instil into the

unwary, and, as yet, unprejudiced Understanding, (for white Paper receives any Characters) those Doctrines they would have them retain and profess" (I.iii.22). Locke also used it in the Conclusion to *Some Thoughts concerning Education* (1693), ed. John W. and Jean S. Yolton (Oxford: Clarendon, 1989): "a Gentleman's Son, who being then very little, I considered only as white Paper, or Wax, to be moulded and fashioned as one pleases" (sec. 217). More generally, Locke used the image of white paper repeatedly throughout the *Essay:* "to find a difference between the white of this Paper and that of the next degree to it" (II.xvi.3); "So that if it be asked, whether it be *essential* to me or any other particular corporeal Being to have Reason? I say no; no more than it is *essential* to this white thing I write on, to have words on it" (III.vi.4); "no more than it can be a doubt to the Eye, (that can distinctly see White and Black,) Whether this Ink, and this Paper be all of a Colour. If there be Sight in the Eyes, it will at first glimpse, without Hesitation, perceive the Words printed on this Paper, different from the Colour of the Paper" (IV.ii.5), "*Instance whiteness of this Paper* . . . whilst I write this, I have, by the Paper affecting my Eyes, that *Idea* produced in my Mind, which whatever object causes, I call *White*" (IV.xi.2).

32. The comparison of white paper to an unprejudiced mind had been made first, apparently, in Richard Eden's "Preface to the Reader" (1555), when he contrasted the pagan inhabitants of the New World with the "Juws and Turkes" whose commitment to another religion made it hard to convert them to Christianity: "But these simple gentiles, lyvinge only after the lawe of nature, may well bee lykened to a smoothe and bare table unpainted, or a white paper unwritten, upon the which yow may at the fyrst paynte or wryte what yow lyste, as yow can not vppon tables alredy paynted, unlesse yow rase or blot owt the fyrste formes" (Martyr, *Decades,* ed. Arber, 57). Eden's "smooth and bare table unpainted" is clearly an English translation of tabula rasa, where "a white paper unwritten" represents his own addition of a modern image to the ancient one; Eden's metaphor may well have been encouraged by Martyr's description of some Amerindians as "white" (discussed in chapter 3, above). Unlike Locke, Eden compares the "white paper" to adult minds. The same is true of Thomas Hobbes in *The Elements of Law Natural and Politic,* ed. J. C. A. Gaskin (Oxford: Oxford UP, 1994): "if the minds of men were all of white paper, they would almost equally be disposed to acknowledge whatsoever should be in right method, and right ratiocination delivered unto them. But when men have once acquiesced in untrue opinions, and registered them as authentical records in their minds; it is no less impossible to speak intelligibly to such men, than to write legibly upon a paper already scribbled over. The immediate cause therefore of indocibility, is prejudice; and of prejudice, false opinion of our own knowledge" (chapter 10, sec. 8; p. 62) . . ."young men, who come thither [to the universities] void of prejudice, and whose minds are yet as white paper, capable of any instruction, would more easily receive the same" (chapter 28, sec. 8; p.176). Although *Elements* was completed in May 1640, it was not published (in two pirated parts) until 1650 and not published in its entirety until 1889. Locke did not own any version of the text (or Eden's *Decades*): see John Harrison and Peter Laslett, *The Library of John Locke* (Oxford: Oxford Bibliographical Society, 1965). Hobbes was not describing children, and Hobbes did not—here or elsewhere—use the word *white* in an ethnic sense. Boyle, who did use *white* in an ethnic sense in *Colour* (1664), in *The Usefulness of Experimental Philosophy* (1663) used "white paper" metaphorically: "As the Quill that a Philosopher writes with, being dipt in Ink, and then mov'd after such a manner upon White Paper" (*Works,* 3:259). In Boyle, the white paper is passive "Matter" acted upon by "an Intelligent Agent." But Boyle did not describe the mind as white paper.

33. In discussing "the power in Things to produce in the Mind . . . a Sensation," Locke uses—as his only example of "the effect of that Power"—the "Paper I write on, having the Power . . . to produce in me the Sensation, which I call White," and then reiterates that "the Sensation of White, in my Mind, being the Effect of that Power, which is in the

Paper to produce it, is perfectly *adequate* to that Power" (II.xxxi.12). I have not noticed, in any earlier text I have examined, such a repeated conjunction of *white* and *power.*

34. Jean d'Alembert, *Preliminary Discourse to the Encyclopedia of Diderot* (1751), tr. Richard N. Schwab (Indianapolis: Bobbs-Merrill, 1963), 84.
35. Locke used the word on four occasions in the *Essay:* "there being nothing more to be desired for Truth, than a fair unprejudiced Hearing" (the fourth sentence of the Epistle Dedicatory), "It would be sufficient to convince unprejudiced Readers of the falseness of this Supposition" of inate ideas (I.ii.1), "I can only *appeal* to Mens own unprejudiced *Experience,* and Observation" (I.iv.25, the final sentence of Book I), and the already-quoted description of the "unprejudiced" understanding of the child (II.i.2).
36. In the final sentence of Book I Locke appealed for "unprejudiced" readers, while describing himself as "a Man who professes no more . . . than an unbias'd enquiry after Truth" (I.iv.25); later he claims that "I with an unbiassed indifferency followed Truth" (II.xxi.72). Like *unprejudiced, unbiased* is a mid-seventeenth-century coinage: *OED* first records it in 1647.
37. Hans Aarsleff, "Locke's Influence," in *The Cambridge Companion to Locke,* ed. Vere Chappell (Cambridge: Cambridge UP, 1994), 252.
38. The passage continues: "But when I give *Cajus* the name *Husband,* I intimate some other Person: and when I give him the name *Whiter,* I intimate some other thing: in both cases my Thought is led to something beyond *Cajus,* and there are two things brought into consideration. And since any *Idea,* whether simple, or complex, may be the occasion, why the Mind thus brings two things together, and, as it were, takes a view of them at once, though still considered as distinct: therefore any of our *Ideas,* may be the foundation of Relation. As in the above-mentioned instance, the Contract, and Ceremony of Marriage with *Sempronia,* is the occasion of the Denomination, or Relation of Husband; and the colour White, the occasion why he is said whiter than Free-stone."
39. Locke's editors have not identified a specific historical referent. The only notable Sempronia in Roman history is the sister of the Gracchi, and she was not married to a Caius, but to Scipio Africanus. Probably the most famous Sempronia in seventeenth-century literature was a character in Nicolas Chorier's pornographic *Satyra Sotadica* (1660?). I hope to treat the relationship between Locke and pornography elsewhere.
40. Although some modern editions and scholarly articles read "consideration of a man" in place of "consideration of Man," Nidditch does not list any variants in this passage (Locke, *Essay,* 319). I have personally checked the editions of 1690 (both issues), 1694, 1695, and 1700, confirming Nidditch's collations: all these texts read "Man," without the indefinite article.
41. James Farr—in his influential article "'So Vile and Miserable an Estate': The Problem of Slavery in Locke's Political Thought," *Political Theory* 14 (1986): 263–89—claims that "this childish notion is patently false, and can be remedied by simple 'collection and observation' (279). But Farr's statement completely reverses the meaning of Locke's phrase. Locke denies that the child's conclusion is based on rationalist, Aristotelian or Cartesian modes of reasoning; it does not depend, he says, on any maxim or axiom or postulate or principle such as "*It is impossible for the same Thing to be, and not to be.*" Instead, "the foundation of his Certainty" is "the clear distinct Perception he hath of his own simple *Ideas* of Black and White . . . whether he knows that Maxim or no." It depends on "Perception," not "Principle." Consequently, for the child, "the Principle of *What is, is,* proves not this matter; but it depends upon Collection and Observation, by which he is to make his complex *Idea* called *Man.*" Again, Locke contrasts "Principle" with "Observation" (a synonym for "Perception"). Nowhere in this paragraph does Locke declare that the child's view is "patently false," nor does he suggest that it could be "remedied" by "Collection and Observation." Instead, "Collection and Observation" were the very methods by

which the child formed "the single complex *Idea* which he calls *Man.*" Whether Locke is endorsing the child's view or not, he unambiguously attributes it to empiricist rather than rationalist modes of inquiry.

42. Constantine Caffentzis argues—in *Clipped Coins, Abused Words and Civil Government: John Locke's Philosophy of Money* (New York: Autonomedia, 1989), 193–202—that "what Locke objected to was not so much the *conclusion* 'a negro is not a man' but its *modality, i.e.,* it is impossible for a negro to be a man. Locke finds such negative certainty impossible for any proposition involving substance terms like 'man'" (202). Differentiating himself from Caffentzis, William Uzgalis—in "'An Inconsistency Not to Be Excused': On Locke and Racism," in *Philosophers on Race: Critical Essays,* ed. Julie K. Ward and Tommy L. Lott (Oxford: Blackwell, 2002), 81–100—contends that "Locke is criticizing as inadequate a series of ideas of man," and rejects the child's view "as dangerous and absurd" (84–85). My own view is that Locke does not criticize either the modality or the conclusion. What Locke denies is the usefulness of a priori "Maxims" (the subject of the whole chapter); but he also specifies that the child does *not* base its certainty on any maxim. He concludes the chapter with the assertion that "as these Maxims are of *little use,* where we have determined *Ideas,* so they are, as I have shewed, of *dangerous use,* where our *Ideas* are not determined; and where we use Words that are not annexed to determined *Ideas,* but such as are of a loose and wandering signification sometimes standing for one, and sometimes for another *Idea*" (Iv.vii.20). But he does not characterize the child's ideas as "not determined" or "loose and wandering." If Locke were criticizing the child's conclusion or the child's reasoning, why did he not simply and directly say that it was absurd? We know that many adult English-speaking subjects, in Locke's time, would have agreed with the child, so Locke could not have assumed that the child's conclusion was so self-evidently absurd that all his readers would have recognized its absurdity.

43. Léon Poliakov briefly noted some of Locke's uses of generic *white* in *The Aryan Myth: A History of Racist and Nationalist Ideas in Europe,* tr. Edmund Howard (New York: Basic Books, 1974), 145–50. My own conclusions were reached before I discovered his, and we analyze and contextualize the passages differently, but I endorse his conclusion that they "suggest a prejudice already well rooted in English society" (145).

44. *Draft A,* sec. 27: "a child haveing framd the Idea of a man it is probable that his Ideas [*sic*] is just like that picture which a painter draws of the visible appearances, joynd togeather & such a complexion of Ideas togeather in his understanding makes up the single complex Idea which he calls Man. wherof white or flesh colour in England being one, the child can demonstrate to you that a Negro is not a man because a white colour was one of the constituent simple Ideas of the complex Idea he calls Man" (48). This is the very same section of the draft that contains the date "10 Jul. 71" (43); however much time may have been expended on composition of the draft as a whole, this section is very securely dated.

45. In the fourth edition, *complexion* (present in Draft A) was changed to *Complication,* the reading printed by Nidditch. In my quotation of the passage I have kept *complexion,* clearly a sensible reading with the then-current meaning "combination, complication" (*OED n.* 9), but also suggesting Locke's preoccupation in this passage with *complexion* in the sense "skin color" (*OED n.* 4.a).

46. Locke emphasized that the words were not his own ("I have taken care that the Reader should have the Story at large in the Authors own Words"), and in a note (Nidditch, 333) Locke identified his source as (the second edition of) Sir William Temple's *Memoires of what passed in Christendom from 1672 to 1679* (1692), 57.

47. For a defense of the logical coherence of Locke's position see Paul Guyer, "Locke's Philosophy of Language," in *Cambridge Companion to Locke,* 115–45. Guyer provides an unconscious example of this process through his own selection of quotations from Locke,

which does not include any of the examples I quote, so uncomfortable for modern liberal defenders of Locke.

48. In his gloss of the second sentence, Locke adds the word *same,* apparently linking it to the previous sentence, so that "the same thing, that has the Essence of Man" can be read as a reference to the preceding "white" man, who is not only white but rational.
49. For the traditional use of "reason" to distinguish humans from other animals (going back to Aristotle), see Keith Thomas, *Man and the Natural World: Changing Attitudes in England 1500–1800* (Allen Lane, 1983), 30–35.
50. For Locke's "consistent and unified anti-essentialist and nominalist philosophical position," as exemplified by this passage among others, see W. L. Uzgalis, "The Anti-Essential Locke and Natural Kinds," *Philosophical Quarterly* 38 (1988): 330–39.
51. For Locke's 275 books concerning geography and exploration (more than his books of philosophy), see *Library of John Locke,* 18–19.
52. On Sydenham's skepticism, his sense that the causes of disease remained "occult," see Wear, *Knowledge and Practice,* 452, 311.
53. Gates, "Critical Remarks," in *Anatomy of Racism,* ed. David Theo Goldberg (Minneapolis: University of Minnesota Press, 1990), 323.
54. Locke, *Two Treatises of Government,* ed. Peter Laslett (Cambridge: Cambridge UP, 1988), 269.
55. Arthur Lovejoy, *The Great Chain of Being* (Cambridge, MA: Harvard UP, 1966), 229–31.
56. See H. W. Hanson, *Apes and Ape Lore in the Middle Ages and the Renaissance* (Warburg Institute, 1952), 261–86.
57. Phlegon, *Book of Marvels,* tr. William Hansen (Exeter: University of Exeter Press, 1996), 22 (pp. 46, 152); Aelian, *De Natura Animalium,* tr. A. F. Scholfield, 3 vols. (Cambridge: Harvard UP, 1958), 7.19 (κυνοκεψάλους), 15.14 (πιθήκους . . .πυρρυος). Phlegon (recovered and printed in 1568) does not identify a father of the monkey-child, but a simian father would be a possible explanation, and this is the only historically specific and datable example from the classical world. In the first passage of Aelian (known in manuscript throughout the Middle Ages and early Renaissance, printed with a Latin translation in 1556 and 1611), the Greek κυνοκεψάλους means literally "dog-face" and was associated with Egyptian religion, so that it probably refers to east African baboons; in the second, the Greek πιθήκους is the general word for ape or monkey, but πυρρους (flame-colored, yellow-and-red) suggests the orangutang.
58. *OED* identifies the drill with *Mandrillus leucophaeus,* a species found from southeastern Nigeria to northwest Cameroon, and on Bioko Island, Equatorial Guinea: see C. P. Groves, *Primate Taxonomy* (Washington, DC: Smithsonian Institution Press, 2001). But the earliest scientific description of that species is by J. S. Gartlan, "Preliminary Notes on the Ecology and Behavior of the *Mandrillus leucophaeus,* Rigen, 1824," reprinted in *Old World Monkeys: Evolution, Systematics and Behavior,* ed. J. R. Napier and P. H. Napier (New York: Academic Press, 1970), 445–80. The meaning of the English word was not, before 1824, so species-specific. Another baboon, called in English the "mandrill" (*Cynocephalus maimon*), is native to Sierra Leone, and was first named in William Smith's *New Voyage to Guinea* (1744), 51. Nicolaas Tulp, a Dutch anatomist, published an engraving with the first reasonably accurate representation of one of the great apes of western Africa in *Observationes medicarum libri tres* (Amsterdam, 1641), 275; he called it "*Homo silvestrus*" [=man of the woods], or "Orang-outang" (a word that originated in Java, first recorded in 1631 by the Dutch East Indian physician Jacob Bontius). The animal in the engraving—captured in "Angola"—is clearly not an orangutang; from the description of its behavior and the engraving of its appearance, it was almost certainly a chimpanzee. Tulp's book was known to John Bulwer, who noted in his *Anthropometamorphosis* (1654) that "This relation of *Tulpius* shows this creature to have been a kind of *Ginney* Drill, for

it answers very directly the Effigies of that *Ginney* Drill, which this *Michaelmas* Terme, 1652. I saw neare Charing Crosse . . . The Keeper of it affirmes, it will grow up to the stature of five foot . . . which *Drill* is since dead, and I beleeve dissected" (439–40). Tulp's engraving does not resemble the primate now identified as a drill; an adult male chimpanzee (which may weigh up to 150 pounds) is much likelier than an adult male drill (which weighs about 45 pounds) to be plausibly identified as the sexual partner of a human female. The English word probably was initially used (by modern scienctific standards, imprecisely) to cover a number of anthropoid primates native to the West African coast from Sierra Leone to Angola.

59. III.vi.32 ("The same Convenience that made Men express several parcels of yellow Matter coming from *Guiny* and *Peru* under one name . . . Gold"), III.vi.19 ("By the Word *Gold* here, I must be understood to design a particular piece of Matter; *v.g.* the last Guinea that was coin'd"). The first passage makes it clear that the coin named "Guinea" still alluded, for Locke, to the place named "Guinea." Gold and slaves were the chief profitable commodities extracted by Europeans from West Africa.

60. *Drill* occurs in sections 22, 23, 36, and 39 of III.vi. It also occurs at III.x.21, in a reiteration of the same theme: "When a Man asks, whether this or that thing he sees, let it be a Drill, or a monstrous *Foetus,* be a *Man,* or no; 'tis evident, the Question is not, Whether that particular thing agree to his complex *Idea,* expressed by the name *Man:* But whether it has in it the real Essence of a Species of Things, which he supposes his name *Man* to stand for." Locke then proceeds to explain why that supposition is an "abuse of words."

61. *Draft A,* sec. 2: "a child unused to that sight and having had some such descriptions of the devil would call a Negro a devil rather than a man, and at the same time call a drill a man" (p. 9). Locke repeated the association in *Draft B,* sec. 84: "a child unused to the sight of a More & haveing had some such descriptions of the devill would call a negro a devill rather then a man & at the same time perhaps call a Dryll a man." In both drafts, this passage is immediately preceded by the example of "an Englishman bread in Jamaica," who had never seen ice; that example survives into the printed text (III.vi.13). But while in the drafts the confusion created by the drill was attributed to a child, in the published texts that uncertainty was Locke's own. When he wrote that "There are some Brutes, that seem to have as much Knowledge and Reason, as some that are called Men" (III.vi.12), he was almost certainly referring to primates like the drill, whose intelligence had provoked similar observations by other Europeans in the seventeenth century. He explicitly contrasted the mental abilities of a drill with those of a mentally defective human being (a "changeling," in his terminology): "Nobody will doubt, that the Wheels, or Springs (if I may so say) within, are different in a *rational Man,* and a *Changeling,* no more than that there is a difference in the frame between a *Drill* and a *Changeling.* But whether one, or both these differences be essential, or specifical, is only to be known to us, by their agreement, or disagreement with the complex *Idea* that the name *Man* stands for: For by that alone can it be determined, whether one, or both, or neither of those be a Man, or no" (III.vi.39).

62. A commendatory poem to John Bulwer's *Chirologia: or the Naturall Language of the Hand. Composed of the Speaking Motions, and Discoursing Gestures thereof* (1644), signed by "Jo: Harmarus, *Oxoniensis,*" claimed that as a result of Bulwer's analysis of the universal language of gesture "Thus may we trade with the dumb *Ginnie Drills* By Exercise: and make our secret wills Known to those rationall Brutes" (sig. a4[v]).

63. I am aware of three Portuguese sources of such reports. The earliest is André Álvares de Almada, *Brief Treatise on the Rivers of Guinea* (ca. 1594), tr. P. E. H. Hair (Liverpool: privately published, 1984), chap. 15, sec. 5: "In Serra Leoa there lives a kind of monkey not found elsewhere in Guinea; they are called *daris,* and have no tail, and if they were not hairy it would be possible to declare that they were human like ourselves, for in other respects there

is little difference. . . . They are fond of the conversation of young women, and if they meet any who have lost their way and are alone, they seize them and carry them off with them, and give them many caresses in their fashion." Another Portuguese witness was the Jesuit missionary Álvares, who lived in Sierra Leone for more than a decade; at the end of his long and detailed description of the *daris* (chimpanzee) he recorded that "There are heathen that claim to be descendants of this animal . . . they consider it the soul of their forefathers, and they think themselves of high parentage. They say they are of the animal's family, and all that believe they are descended from it call themselves *Amienu*" (*Ethiopia Minor,* tr. Hair, chap. 1, f. 51). Finally, André Donelha was, like Almada, a Portuguese trader in western Africa in the late sixteenth century, although his description of the chimpanzee was not written down until later. In *An Account of Sierra Leone and the Rivers of Guinea of Cape Verde, 1625,* ed. Avelino Teixeira da Mota, tr. P. E. H. Hair (Lisbon: Junta de Investigações Científicas do Ultramar, 1977), 93 (fol. 8), he wrote: "Also they say that if it meets with a woman alone, it makes a match with her." All these texts remained in manuscript until the twentieth century. Obviously, these witnesses were not Locke's direct source, but they do demonstrate that such rumors were picked up by the Portuguese before other Europeans began intruding in the area. They also, independently of each other, record the Temne word for the chimpanzee, *daris,* which might be the source of the English word *drills.* Although *OED* conjectures that *drill* was taken from an African word, it does not offer a candidate. If English listeners misinterpreted the Temne terminal *s* as a plural (an easy error for them to make, since they would probably be seeing more than one chimpanzee), Temne *d-ris* could be transliterated as *dri<l>s,* and then mistakenly normalized to singular *dri<l>.* See note 106, below.

64. According to the *OED* the word *chimpanzee* was first used in September 1738, when the London Magazine reported the arrival of a "creature . . . taken in a wood at Guinea . . . which the Angolans call Chimpanze" (465). Note the reference—here of the chimpanzee, as in Bulwer of the so-called drill—to both Guinea and Angola. The ship that brought the chimpanzee to London in 1738 had gone from the coast of West Africa to Carolina and then London; it was clearly involved in the triangular slave trade.

65. Bulwer, *Anthropometamorphosis,* 437–43. Bulwer cites Tulpius, and Phillipus Salmuthus, *Observationum Medicarum Centuriae Tres Posthumae* (Brunswick, 1648), 2. John Ogilby's description of Angola in *Africa* (1670) refers to the same chimpanzee Bulwer had seen ("Such a Creature was some years ago brought from hence"), noting that "This Beast in shape so much resembles a Man, that some have held opinion, that it is of humane mixture with an Ape," and that it "sets upon, and overpowers Women and Maids" (558). Likewise, "Negro-Land" contains "that monstrous Creature, which the Inhabitants call'd *Quoias-Morrou,* or *Worrou;* and the *Portugals, Salvage,* that is, *A Satyr:* It hath a great Head, a heavy Body, fleshy Arms, and strong, no Tails, and goes sometimes upright, and sometimes like an Ape on all four. The *Blacks* report it to be of humane Extract; but by the alteration and change of the Woods and the Wilderness, it is become half a Beast. . . . The *Blacks* relate strange things of them, and avere it for an infallible truth, that it not onely over-powers feeble Women, and unmarried Maids, but also dares set upon Armed Men" (386).

66. Donna Haraway, *Primate Visions: Gender, Race, and Nature in the World of Modern Science* (New York: Routledge, 1989); Londa Schiebinger, *Nature's Body: Gender in the Making of Modern Science* (Boston: Beacon Press, 1993), 75–114. Neither discusses the early examples I cite here.

67. Gernot Rotter, *Die Stellung des Negers in der islamisch-arabischen Gesellschaft bis zum XVI. Jahrhundert* (Bonn, 1967), 158–61, 182. As early as 1308, in Montpelier, the Christian Arnau de Vilanova's *Speculum introductionum medicinalium* described Africans as "in form like apes, in color black . . . frequently exercising their lust bestially, regardless of sex, age and species" (*in forma symi et in colore nigri . . . frequenter luxuriam vero bestialiter ex-*

ercent, nec seum nec etatem nec speciem attendents). See *Opera nuperrime revisa* (Lyons, 1532), cap. lxxvii, "De regionibus," fol. 26 (cited by Biller, "Black in Medieval Science," who translates the Latin less literally than I do). Does this unusually negative early caricature reflect Arab influence?

68. Herbert, *Relation of Some Yeares Travaile,* 17.
69. "The genterey heare doth liue far better then ours doue in England: they haue most of them 100 or 2 or 3 of slaues apes whou they command as they pleas. . . . This Island is inhabited with all sortes: with English, french, Duch, Scotes, Irish, Spaniards thay being Iues: with Ingones and miserabell Negors borne to perpetuall slauery thay and thayer seed" ("Extracts from Henry Whistler's Journal," 146).
70. Sir Thomas St. Serfe, *Tarugo's wiles, or, The coffee-house* (1668), 14.
71. Godwyn, *Advocate,* 82, 12, 10. See especially Godwyn's statement in relation to drills: "there wanting not *Irrational* Creatures, such as the Ape and Drill, that do carry with them some resemblances of Men. The too frequent unnatural conjunctions (as *Tavernier* discourseth in his Voyages) of some *Africans* with those Creatures (tho not so as to Unpeople that great Continent) giving occasion for such surmises as to some few *there,* tho never of any that were brought *hither"* (12). Even Godwyn seems to acknowledge the facticity of Tavernier's reports, but denies that any of the offspring of those putative drill-human unions have been transported to Barbados. Moreover, in calling the drills "Irrational," he directly contradicts the conclusions of observers like Tulp and Bulwer, who had actually seen drills, and considered them "rational Brutes," that is, rational animals, who therefore satisfied the traditional definition of "Man." For other reports by Godwyn of the Barbadian denial of Africans' status as human, see pp. 30 (where he says that some of them have, by their own account, committed sodomy, by "lying with a Beast"), 38 (a "Religious" woman complains to him that "I might as well Baptize a Puppy, as a certain young *Negro,*" and "another of the *same Sex,* upon my baptizing a *Male Negro* of hers" told him that baptism "*was to one of those no more beneficial, than to her black Bitch*"). These examples might be dismissed on the grounds that they constituted no more than "the accusation . . . that planters regarded and treated their slaves *like* beasts" (Jordan, *White Over Black,* 233). Jordan denies that "white men in the eighteenth [century] thought Negroes were beasts" (230); but Godwyn makes exactly that claim about *some* white men in the seventeenth century, and says that they buttressed that belief with a specific theory of separate Negro origins. Moreover, George Berkeley reported—after a visit to Rhode Island—that the English colonists had "an irrational contempt of the blacks as creatures of another species": "A Sermon Preached Before the Incorporated Society for the Propagation of the Gospel in Foreign Parts, 1732," in *The Works of George Berkeley,* ed. A. C. Fraser, 4 vols. (Oxford: Clarendon, 1901), iv, 403–04.
72. Trapham, *A Discourse of the State of Health in the Island of Jamaica* (1679), 113–17. Trapham lumped Amerindians with Africans, as Locke did not.
73. In I.iv.12 Locke dismissed the argument that men were born with an inate sense of God and morality by citing the existence of people who "are wholly without *Ideas of God,* and Principles of morality; or at least have but very ill ones. The reason in both cases being, that They never employ'd their Parts, Faculties, and powers, industriously that way . . ." The fault is theirs, not God's. "Had you or I been born at the Bay of *Soldania,* possibly our Thoughts, and Notions, had not exceeded those brutish ones of the *Hotentots* that inhabit there: And had the *Virginia* King *Apochancana,* been educated in *England,* he had, perhaps, been as knowing a Divine, and as good a Mathematician, as any in it. The difference between him, and a more improved *English*-man, lying barely in this, That the exercise of his Faculties was bounded within the Ways, Modes, and Notions of his own Country, and never directed to any other, or farther Enquiries: And if he had not any *Idea* of a God, it was only because he pursued not those Thoughts, that would have led him to it." Uzgalis

cites this passage as evidence that Locke believed "that all people are essentially the same biologically, and that the significant differences between Englishmen and those in other lands is purely cultural" ("Locke and Racism," 87). But Uzgalis ignores two things about this passage. First, the tentative character of Locke's assertion of equality ("perhaps . . . possibly"). Second, its asymmetry: if we had been *born* in the Bay of Soldania, we might be as brutish as the *Hottentots;* if a *native American* king had been *educated* in England, he might have become an excellent mathematician. Hottentots are born; Americans are made. It would have been more logical and more symmetrical for the second clause to assert that, if a *Hottentot* had been educated in England, that *Hottentot* might have become an excellent mathematician. Why did Locke avoid the symmetrical and logical conclusion? Presumably because he found the idea of Amerindian equality with an Englishman intrinsically more plausible than the idea of Hottentot equality. This passage displays the same asymmetry in Locke's views of (white) Indians and (black) Africans that I discuss later in this chapter. Finally, Uzgalis does not quote the earlier part of Locke's paragraph, which places the blame for the irreligious immorality of non-Europeans squarely on their failure to use the gifts God gave them. The whole passage presumes European cultural, moral, and religious superiority over all non-Europeans, including even the American Indians.

74. John Evelyn, *Numismata, a discourse of medals, ancient and modern* (1697), 311 ("A Digression concerning Physiognomy").
75. *Library of John Locke,* 244 (1677 French and 1680 English editions of Tavernier), 144 (Godwyn), 214 (*Prae-Adamitae*). La Peyrère strongly influenced Richard Simon's *Histoire Critique du Vieux Testament* (Paris, 1678), tr. as *A Critical History of the Old Testament* (1682); Locke owned all Simon's biblical criticism (13 items, 1680–99, pp. 233–34).
76. For a full account of the origin, content, and significance of the pre-Adamite theory, see Richard H. Popkin, *Isaac La Peyrère (1596–1676): His Life, Work, and Influence* (Leiden: Brill, 1987).
77. The relevant passages in Paracelsus's *Astronomia magna* (1520) are translated in *Readings in Early Anthropology,* ed. J. S. Slotkin (Chicago: Aldine, 1965), 42.
78. Bruno, *De innumerabilis immenso et infigurabili; sue de universo et mundis libri octo* (Frankfurt, 1591), bk. 7, ch. 18, in *Opera Latine Conscripta,* ed. F. Fiorentino *et al.* (Naples, 1879–91), I, part II, p. 282: "No sound thinking person will refer the Ethiopians to the same protoplast as the Jewish one."
79. For Thomas Nashe's 1592 charge against Harriot, see John W. Shirley, *Thomas Harriot: A Biography* (Oxford: Clarendon, 1983), 186–87, 318–19.
80. Vanini, *De admirandis naturae reginae Deaeq. mortalium arcanis* (Paris, 1616), lib. IV, dial. xxxvii.
81. *Men before Adam, or, A discourse upon the twelfth, thirteenth, and fourteenth verses of the fifth chapter of the Epistle of the Apostle Paul to the Romans by which are prov'd that the first men were created before Adam.,* tr. Anonymous (1656).
82. Godwyn, *Advocate,* 15. Popkin, who emphasizes the nonracist character of La Peyrère's theory, cites Godwyn at the beginning of his chapter "Pre-Adamism and Racism," but mistakenly claims that Godwyn was describing colonists "in Virginia" and attributes the sentiment only to Godwyn's "opponents," rather than emphasizing its popularity (as Godwyn does).
83. Lom D'Arce, *Nouveaux Voyages de Mr. Le Baron de Lohontan dans l'Amérique septentrionale* (Hague, 1703), 249–52 (letter dated May 10, 1693).
84. L. P., *Two Essays, Sent in a Letter from Oxford to a Nobleman in London* (1695), 26–8.
85. John Harris, *Remarks on some late Papers relating to the Universal Deluge; And to the Natural History of the Earth* (1697), preface, sig. A1.
86. For the same strategic ambiguity, see Locke's statement in *Two Treatises of Government* that "the Race of Men have now spread themselves to all the corners of the World" (2.36).

Farr quotes this phrase as evidence that Locke "remained wholly within the boundaries of Christian cosmology and accepted the Biblical account of human origins" (279). But Farr ignores the word *now:* in 1689 Europeans and other light-skinned people—the Jews and Muslims and Christians who all descended from Adam—had indeed compassed the globe. This statement of contemporary fact commits Locke to no "cosmology" at all. Farr's only other evidence for Locke's rejection of pre-Adamite theories comes from the same paragraph, where "Locke speaks of the 'first peopling of the world by the children of Adam'" (279). But Farr has to wrench that quotation from its context: "For *supposing* a Man, or Family, in the state they were, at first peopling of the World by the Children of Adam, *or Noah*" (italics added). The word *supposing* works in the same way as *if:* it commits Locke to nothing. And "Adam or Noah" is another strategic evasion, especially given contemporary interpretations of Noah's curse against Ham's descendants. Finally, Farr's claim about Locke's religious orthodoxy is special pleading. Most scholars believe—on the basis of evidence he kept private during his lifetime—that Locke was Socinian and unitarian; rejection of the Trinity was not only heretical but directly impinged on "Christian cosmology" (because whether or not Jesus was a divine coequal of God determined whether he had existed from eternity). In light of the strong evidence for Locke's religious heterodoxy, we have no intrinsic reason to credit him with orthodox views about Adam (a figure much less central to Christian thought than Jesus).

87. Richard H. Popkin, "Hume's Racism Reconsidered," in *The Third Force in Seventeenth-Century Thought* (Leiden: E. J. Brill, 1992), 64–75. Popkin does not connect Hume to Locke in this respect.
88. Locke keeps reiterating this point: "I cannot see how it can be properly said, that Nature sets the Boundaries of the *Species* of Things . . . but we ourselves divide them" (III.vi.30); "*Nature makes many particular Things, which do agree* one with another, in many sensible Qualities, and probably too, in their internal frame and Constitution; but 'tis not this real Essence that distinguishes them into *Species;* 'tis *Men,* who . . . *range them into Sorts, in order to their naming,* for the convenience of comprehensive signs" (III.vi.36); "I do not deny, but Nature, in the constant production of particular Beings, makes them not always new and various, but very much alike and of kin one to another: But I think it is nevertheless true, that *the boundaries of the Species, whereby Men sort them, are made by Men*" (III.vi.37). In every case, Locke contrasts Nature with Men, as definers of species boundaries, ignoring God.
89. Paolo Casini, "The Reception of Newton's *Opticks* in Italy," in *Renaissance and Revolution: Humanists, Scholars, Craftsmen and Natural Philosophers in Early Modern Europe,* ed. J. V. Field and Frank A. J. L. James (Cambridge: Cambridge UP, 1993), 222.
90. See Anne Goldgar, *Impolite Learning: Conduct and Community in the Republic of Letters 1680–1750* (New Haven, CT: Yale UP, 1995).
91. On Locke's relationship with Bernier, see Maurice Cranston, *John Locke: A Biography,* rev. ed. (Oxford: Oxford UP, 1985), 170 ("strange to say, all Locke's references to him in his journal deal with Bernier's knowledge of the East; none with Gassendi, or indeed with any philosophical question at all"); for the *Journal,* see *Library of John Locke,* 163. I call Bernier "corpuscularian" on the basis of his *Abrégé de la philosophie de Gassendi* (Paris, 1674–75; rev. ed. Lyon, 1684).
92. "Nouvelle Division de la Terre," 361–62.
93. *OED texture n.*4 ("The constitution, structure or substance of anything with regard to its constituents or formative elements"); under both the "organic" (4.a) and "inorganic" (4.b) categories of this usage, Boyle provides the first examples (quotations from 1660, 1663, 1665).
94. "*An Extract of a Letter of Mr.* Listers, *containing some Observations made at the* Barbado's," *Philosophical Transactions,* 10 (1675): 400.

95. Boyle, *Works,* 5:xli, 501 (November 6, 1665).
96. *Library of John Locke,* 209, 23, 91–93.
97. For Boyle's influence on Locke, see—in addition to studies cited in the next note—Richard I. Aaron, *John Locke,* 2nd ed. (Oxford: Clarendon, 1955), 12; Kenneth Dewhurst, "Locke's Contribution to Boyle's Researches on the Air and on Human Blood," *Notes and Records of the Royal Society of London* 17 (1963): 198–206; M. A. Stewart, "Locke's Professional Contacts with Robert Boyle," *Locke Newsletter* 12 (1981): 19–44.
98. See G. A. J. Rogers, "Boyle, Locke, and Reason," *Journal of the History of Ideas* 27 (1966): 205–16; David Palmer, "Boyle's Corpuscular Hypothesis and Locke's Primary-Secondary Quality Distinction," *Philosophical Studies* 29 (1976): 181–89; Peter Alexander, *Ideas, Qualities and Corpuscles: Locke and Boyle on the External World* (Cambridge: Cambridge UP, 1985); the whole book is important for understanding Locke's relation to Boyle, and in chapter 13 Alexander specifically discusses Locke's treatment of "Essences, species and kinds" (263–79).
99. Bracken, "Essence, Accident and Race," *Hermathena* 116 (1973): 81–96. In arguing for Locke's "decisive influence," Bracken noted the importance of "Locke's views about substance and quality," citing IV.vi.7, II.xxi.13, IV.vi.9, IV.iii.6. He did not discuss III.vi. He also did not recognize a distinction between Catholic and Protestant Christianity; the Protestant tendency to identify an "elect nation" was prone to less universalizing interpretations. (See chapter 9.)
100. G. W. Leibniz, *New Essays on Human Understanding,* tr. Peter Remnant and Jonathan Bennett (Cambridge: Cambridge UP, 1996), 226 (II.xxv.1), 234 (II.xxvii.8), 333 (III.viii.1), 424 (IV.vii.16); 315 ("'women have conceived by' baboons"), 234 ("an orang-utang," responding to II.xxvii.8). Although not published until 1765, Leibniz's response was completed just before Locke's death.
101. Leibniz, *New Essays,* 320, 234. Remnant and Bennett note that the quarrel over species and essences is fundamental to the difference between Locke and Leibniz (xxvi-xxix).
102. For Locke's critique of the idea "That all Things that have the outward Shape and Appearance of a Man, must necessarily" possess "a rational Soul," see IV.iv.15; for the critique of "reason" as an adequate criterion, see II.xxvii.8 (the parrot) and III.vi.22, 29. Eugene Miller, in "Locke on the Meaning of Political Language," *Political Science Reviewer* 9 (1979), could "find no basis in Locke's account of substances for criticizing someone who chooses to define the essence of man in such a way as to exclude Negroes or any other racial group" (178).
103. Stillingfleet, *The Bishop of Worcester's answer to Mr. Locke's letter, concerning some passages relating to his Essay of humane understanding* (1697), 120.
104. Stillingfleet, *The Bishop of Worcester's answer to Mr. Locke's second letter wherein his notion of ideas is prov'd to be inconsistent with itself, and with the articles of the Christian faith* (1698), 160, 170.
105. *Mr. Locke's reply to the right reverend the Lord Bishop of Worcester's answer to his second letter* (1699), 364.
106. Tyson, *Orang-Outang, sive Homo Sylvestris; or, The Anatomy of a Pygmie Compared with that of a Monkey, an Ape, and a Man* (1699), A1 [unsignatured first gathering] 4, D4; 94–95, N3^{v-r}. I conjecture that Tyson's specimen may have been a bonobo chimpanzee because he specifies that it came from Angola and that it was considerably smaller than the "darris" or "barris" (which he identifies with a "drill"). See note 63, above.
107. Uzgalis, "Anti-Essential Locke," 338.
108. Wilson, *The Invisible World: Early Modern Philosophy and the Invention of the Microscope* (Princeton, NJ: Princeton UP, 1995), 238–44 (citing Locke's 1668 "Anatomie" fragment and *Essay* II.xxviii.12 and IV.iii.29).
109. "So that if it be asked, whether it be *essential* to me, or any other particular corporeal Being to have Reason? I say no; no more than it is *essential* to this white thing I write on, to have

words in it" (III.vi.4). To prove his point Locke invokes a parallel case, in which "this white thing" (white paper) stands for, occupies the same logical space, as "me." Locke had raised the problem of the definition of "Man" as an exemplar of the problem of "the Names of Substances" in III.vi.3 and continues with that subject here. So the comparison of himself with white paper comes in his second paragraph on the definition of Man.

110. The fashion started in France, and was massively reinforced when Charles II returned to England in 1660; Pepys had one by 1663. See Richard Corson, *Fashions in Hair: The First Five Thousand Years* (Peter Owen, 1965), 205–16. Although white wigs occasionally were worn by women earlier in the century, the first English text I have found attributing one to a real or allegorical male is Nicholas Billingsley's *The Infancy of the World* (1658), where "White Periwigs adorn the bald-pate woods" (106). More literally, an anonymous *Address to the Hopeful Young Gentry of England* (1669) complained "how fashion has prevail'd against nature to perrugue all complexions with the fairest hair" (32), and John Lacy's *The Dumb Lady* (performed 1669, printed 1672) featured a "brave gallant with a fine white Periwig that cost twenty pound," whose "white Periwig" is mentioned three times (IV.i, V.i). In *The Miser* (1672?), Thomas Shadwell referred to men "of five and twenty in white Periwigs" (II.ii); "White-Wig" shows up also in the Prologue to Dryden's *Marriage a la Mode* (performed 1672).

111. Norman Kretzmann, "The Main Thesis of Locke's Semantic Theory," *Locke on Human Understanding: Selected Essays,* ed. I. C. Tipton (Oxford: Oxford UP, 1977), 135.

112. Kretzmann calls Locke's *Essay* "the first modern treatise devoted specifically to philosophy of language. No work had a greater influence over the development of philosophical semantics during the Enlightenment than did this Book Three. . . . the source of its special influence lay in the fact that Locke had expressly connected semantic inquiry with theory of knowledge" ("Locke's Semantic Theory," 123). Locke told Molyneaux (January 20, 1692/3) that "some parts" of Book III, "concerning words," had cost him "more pains to express than all the rest" of the *Essay.*

113. For the conflation of Africans and Amerindians, see for instance Richard H. Popkin's influential essay "The Philosophical Bases of Modern Racism," in *Philosophy and the Civilizing Arts: Essays Presented to Herbert W. Schneider,* ed. Craig Walton and John P. Anton (Athens: Ohio UP, 1974), 126–45. Identifying Locke as a pioneer of the "degeneracy theory," Popkin consistently conflates "the Indians and the Africans" and "Africa and America" (133). Defenders of Locke against Popkin have thus been able to use evidence of Locke's favorable attitude toward Amerindians to conceal his consistently unfavorable attitude toward Africans.

114. Browne, *Works,* 3:338. The exact date of this manuscript is not certain, but Browne repeats the idea, virtually verbatim, in a letter to his son Edward dated July 10, 1676: "A greater division of mankind is made by the skinne then by any other part of the body, that is into white skinn'd men or negro's" (4:66). For Browne's use of *tawny* to describe populations, see *Pseudodoxia Epidemica,* ed. Robbins, VI.x (1:512, twice). Even in the earlier work, Browne wrote that "the Inhabitants of America are faire" (1:512).

115. Bernier, "Nouvelle Division," 362.

116. On this distinction in Jefferson see Joyce Oldham Appleby, *Without Resolution: The Jeffersonian Tensions in American Nationalism* (Oxford: Clarendon, 1992), 20. Appleby lists "Bacon, Locke, and Newton" as Jefferson's "intellectual heroes" (14).

117. For the fledgling colony of Carolina Locke "had a hand in drafting and promulgating some 'temporary laws'" including one "declaring that 'no Indian upon any occasion or pretense whatsoever, is to be made a slave; or without his own consent to be carried out of our country'" (Farr, 266, citing C.O. 5/286/41) and another requiring that Indian settlements and large tracts of land around them be respected (Farr, 285–86, citing C.O. 5/286/46). "He was intrigued by their customs and their medical practices, fascinated by

their sexual mores, convinced of their 'native rustic reason,' and praising of their forms of government because they were founded on 'consent and persuasion, [rather] than compulsion'" (Farr 278, quoting *Essay* IV.xix.6 and Bodleian MS Locke c. 33, fol. 11). However, Farr precedes these observations with the comment that "Locke had generous or non-disparaging things to say about other *peoples of color,* especially American Indians" (278, italics added). This is a modern category, not a seventeenth-century one. Moreover, on the same manuscript page that Farr cites (Bodleian MS Locke c. 33, fol. 11, dated March 1679) Locke records that "Mr Berniers told me" about the Brahmins of India; Berniers is the author of the 1684 division of the global population into distinct races.

118. John Locke, *A Letter Concerning Toleration: Latin and English Texts* (written 1685, published 1689), ed. Mario Montuori (Hague: Martinus Nijhoff, 1963), 68–71.

119. For analysis and critique of Locke's "waste land" argument in relation to America, see James Tully, "Rediscovering America: The Two Treatises and Aboriginal Rights," in *An Approach to Political Philosophy: Locke in Context* (Cambridge: Cambridge UP, 1993), 137–76; John Douglas Bishop, "Locke's Theory of Original Appropriation and the Right of Settlement in Iroquois Territory," *Canadian Journal of Philosophy* 27 (1997): 311–37; Kathy Squadrito, "Locke and the Dispossession of the American Indian," in *Philosophers on Race,* 101–24.

120. See J. R. Wordie, "The Chronology of English Enclosure, 1500–1914," *Economic History Review,* 2nd series, 36 (1983): 483–505, and Linebaugh and Rediker, *Many-Headed Hydra,* 16–19, 52.

121. Bodleian Library Locke MS e.9, "Some of the Cheif Greivances of the present constitution of Virginia with an Essay towards the Remedies thereof" (1697–98), fol. 32–33: "At p[r]sent I should advise . . . that as many Indian Children be Educated at y[e] College as may be."

122. *Draft A,* sec. 2; *Draft B,* sec. 84.

123. *Statutes at Large of South Carolina,* 1:55 (article 110). Article 107 specifies that "religion ought to alter nothing in any man's civil estate or right . . . no slave shall hereby be exempted from that civil dominion his master hath over him, but be in all other things in the same state and condition he was in before" (1:55). The manuscript is in Locke's handwriting, and in a letter to Locke, Sir Peter Colleton referred to the Fundamental Constitutions as "that excellent form of government in the composure of which you had so great a hand": see *The Correspondence of John Locke,* ed. E. S. de Beer, 8 vols (Oxford: Oxford UP, 1976), 1:395. Of course, it is possible that Locke did not agree with everything in the document, but it is ridiculous for Uzgalis to argue against Colleton's (contemporary) testimony by citing unsubstantiated remarks by two twentieth-century defenders of Locke ("' . . . The Same Tyrannical Principle': Locke's Legacy on Slavery," in *Subjugation and Bondage: Critical Essays on Slavery and Social Philosophy,* ed. Tommy L. Lott (Lanham, MD: Rowman & Littlefield, 1998), 72–73.

124. In "Three Approaches to Locke and the Slave Trade," *Journal of the History of Ideas* 51 (1990): 199–216, William Glausser notes that "in the much later commentaries to St. Paul, [Locke] carefully restated the distinction between religious and civil freedom articulated in the Carolina constitution," describing as a "fault" the belief that slaves were "freed by Christianity" (203–04).

125. Cranston, *Locke,* 115; Davies, *Royal Africa Company,* 58, 62, 65. Glausser points out that, with so much money at stake, Locke certainly would have "looked carefully both at the company's charter . . . and at a report of its first year's activities," which both make clear the centrality of slave-trading to the company's operations ("Three Theories," 201).

126. "Trade," Locke MS c. 30 (undated, but after records of a Council meeting in May 1675), fol. 18.

127. Locke MS c. 33, fol. 5[v].

128. H. R. Fox Bourne, *The Life of John Locke,* 2 vols. (New York, 1876), 2:353.

129. Locke MS c. 30, fol. 50–50^{v}. This report was sent to the Lord Justices and to the Lords Commissioners for Trade and Plantations by the Board of Trade, from "Whitehall. August the 10th 1697," signed by Locke and three others; it asserts "the prejudice" the proposed Panama colony "would bring to his Mat$^{y's}$ Islands, and Colonies in those parts, and principally to the Island of Jamaica, by alluring away their Inhabitants . . . and especially by carrying to that place the certain advantages of Commerce with the Spaniards for Negroes and European Commodities"; for "the preventing of so grand inconveniences," they recommend that the proposed venture be stopped. These objections to the Panama colony were repeated in a letter from the Board of Trade to the House of Lords, dated "Whitehall January the 18th 1699/1700," again mentioning the disadvantages "principally to the Island of Jamaica (the most important" of "our Plantations in America," by "diverting the present course of Trade which is of the greatest advantage to England" (fol. 118^{v}).
130. Peter Laslett, "John Locke, the Great Recoinage, and the Origins of the Board of Trade: 1695–1698," *William and Mary Quarterly,* III, 14 (1957): 370–402.
131. "Instructions for Francis Nicholson," September 13, 1698, C.O. 5/1359, p. 294: "You shall *Endeavour* to gett a Law passed for the restraining of Inhumane Severities, which by ill Masters, or Overseers may be used towards their Christian Servants or Slaves, and that Provision be made therein that the willfull killing of Indians and Negro's may be punished with Death, and that a fit penalty be imposed for the maiming of them. . . . You are also with the Assistance of the councill and Assembly there to find out the best means to facilitate, and *Encourage* the Conversion of Negroes and Indians to the Christian Religion" (italics added). The Governor was ordered to try; but Locke would not have approved of the Governor overriding the legislature's authority by insisting on such a law.
132. Nicholson was ordered to send "all Laws, Statutes, and Ordinances now in force, or which at any time shall be made and enacted within his said Colony" to London for review ("Instructions," 269–70). During the years of Locke's tenure, the Virginia Assembly passed a law "That all children born in this country be bond or free, according to the condition of their mother" (*Statutes at Large,* 3:140, September 1696), another that "a negro or slave" convicted of hog stealing should "stand two hours in the pillory and have both his eares nailed thereto and at the expiration of the said two hours have his ears cutt off close by the nailes, any thing in the aforesaid act or in any other law to the contrary in any wise notwithstanding" (3:178, April 1699), a poll tax "for every negro or other slave which shall be imported into this his majesties colony" (3:193, April 1699). All these laws were forwarded to London for approval.
133. "Instructions," 291.
134. "Cheif Greivances," fol. 6: "by every forraigner y^{t} settles in ye English Plantations, ye King gains a new Subject wthout any loss whereas by every English Man settling there he gains indeed a new Subject to ye plantations but loses an old subject for him in England." Locke had earlier noted that "the Country wants ten times ye Numb^{r} of people they now have" (fol. 3). Nicholson was instructed to "send an Account unto his Majesty and to the Commissioners for Trade and Plantations of the present number of Planters, and Inhabitants Men, Women, and Children, as well Masters as Servants, free, and unfree, and of the Slaves . . ." ("Instructions," 286).
135. The entire Germantown document (February 18, 1688) is reproduced in F. Michael Higginbotham, *Race Law: Cases, Commentary, and Questions* (Durham, NC: Carolina Academic Press, 2001), 490.
136. George Keith, "An Exhortation & Caution to Friends, concerning Buying or Keeping of Negroes, 1693," reprinted in *The Pennsylvania Magazine of History and Biography* 13 (Philadelphia, 1899): 265–67.
137. Baxter, *A Christian Directory* (1673), 557–59.

138. See Colleton's discussion of curing "Gonorheas in his Negros" (*Correspondence,* 1:387, August 12, 1673), and his dissuasion of Locke from his intention to become absentee landlord of a plantation (1:380, 394). Farr notes that in October 1673 Locke read to the Council of Trade an official letter from Colleton tabulating the slave population in Barbados, including thousands of women, boys, and girls; women and children should, according to Locke's own arguments, never have been enslaved ("Slavery," 275–76, citing C.O. 1/30/99).
139. Brown, *The American Fugitive in Europe,* in *Travels,* 132.
140. For a critique of Locke's "fraternal patriarchy," see Carole Pateman, *The Sexual Contract* (Stanford, CA: Stanford UP, 1988), esp. pp. 3, 21–22, 37, 52–53, 70–71, 84–94, 104–05.
141. Gerda Lerner, *The Creation of Patriarchy* (New York: Oxford UP, 1986), 76–101; Lawrence H. Keeley, *War before Civilization* (New York: Oxford UP, 1996), 83–97; Taylor, *Castration,* 170–71. (In ancient societies castrated slaves were, like female slaves, used sexually by dominant males.)
142. Mills, *Racial Contract,* 11–12, 97.
143. Locke, *Two Treatises,* 315.
144. Welchman, "Locke on Slavery and Inalienable Rights," *Philosophy in Context* 25 (1995): 67–81. In Welchman's paraphrase, for Locke "the term *man* no longer denotes any human being, but only those human beings who are persons. Children born to non-persons are neither the children of men nor entitled to claim rights natural to men" (80).
145. Cranston, *John Locke,* 135.
146. Milgram, *Obedience to Authority: An Experimental View* (New York: Harper & Row, 1974).
147. Bauman, *Modernity and the Holocaust* (Ithaca, NY: Cornell UP, 1989), 65.
148. For the importance of oceanic distance to the rise of racism and the slave trade, see Taylor, *Time, Space, Race.* By contrast, Thomas L. Haskell has attributed the rise of sympathetic universalism to the imaginative habits required for successful long-distance investing: see "Capitalism and the Origins of the Humanitarian Sensibility," Parts I and II, collected in *The Antislavery Debate: Capitalism and Abolitionism as a Problem in Historical Interpetation,* ed. Thomas Bender (Berkeley: University of California Press, 1992), 107–60. But Eltis notices an important temporal dimension to this process: before about 1750, market behavior "could have had almost exactly the opposite effect," serving "to increase its possessor's power to intervene in the lives of others without generating any feeling of moral responsibility for the suffering that might result" (*African Slavery,* 80–81). Eltis attributes the shift to the rise of what Haskell calls "recipe knowledge," but it could also be due to the progressive "shrinking" of the Atlantic, described in *Time, Space, Race.*
149. Hancock, *Citizens of the World: London Merchants and the Integration of the British Atlantic Community, 1735–1785* (Cambridge: Cambridge UP, 1995), 387, 81, 396, 203, 18.
150. See Taylor, *Time, Space, Race.*
151. Bauman, *Modernity and the Holocaust,* 98, 102.
152. Manent, *The City of Man,* tr. Marc A. LePain (Princeton, NJ: Princeton UP, 1998), 118.
153. Bauman, *Modernity and the Holocaust,* 66.
154. On the relationships between *Utopia* and English imperialism and colonization, see Jeffrey Knapp, *An Empire Nowhere: England, America, and Literature from Utopia to The Tempest* (Berkeley: University of California Press, 1992), esp. 7, 21, 248.
155. For this larger context, see Fitzmaurice, *Humanism and America* (although he ignores the legacy of classical slavery).
156. Moses Finley identified five "slave societies" where slaves were central to economic production and the social structure: two classical (Greece, Rome) and three founded by early modern European colonists (in Brazil, the Caribbean, and the southern United States): see *The Ancient Economy* (Berkeley: University of California Press, 1973), 70–83, and Eltis, *African Slavery,* 8–9. Neither scholar notes that the link between the first two and the last three was the humanist educational revolution in Renaissance Europe.

157. Steven N. Zwicker, "England, Israel and the Triumph of Roman Virtue," in *Millenarianism and Messianism in English Literature and Thought 1650–1800,* ed. Richard H. Popkin (Leiden: E. J. Brill, 1988), 37–64. See also J. G. A. Pocock, *The Machiavellian Moment: Florentine Political Thought and the Atlantic Republican Tradition,* 2nd ed. (Princeton, NJ: Princeton UP, 2003), 401–5, and Peter Burke, "A Survey of the Popularity of Ancient Historians, 1450–1700," *History and Theory* 5 (1966): 135–52.
158. Locke was here—as usual, without acknowledgment—adapting a metaphor from Boyle: see *Selected Philosophical Papers of Robert Boyle,* ed. M. A. Stewart (Manchester: Manchester UP, 1979), frontispiece, vi, xvi, 160, 170, 174. The last three passages occur in Boyle's *Some Considerations Touching the Usefulness of Experimental Natural Philosophy. The First Part* (1663), where they refer not to the human body in particular, but to "the World" (*Works,* 3:248, 256, 259–60). Where Boyle has "some rude Indian" (3:248), Locke substitutes "a gazing Country-man" (II.vi.3).
159. "Of Time and Idleness," in *The Early Essays and Ethics of Robert Boyle,* ed. John T. Harwood (Carbondale: Southern Illinois UP, 1991), 239, 248.
160. On Boyle's neuroses, see Michael Hunter, "The Conscience of Robert Boyle: Functionalism, 'Dysfunctionalism' and the Task of Historical Understanding," in *Renaissance and Revolution: Humanists, Scholars, Craftsmen and Natural Philosophers in Early Modern Europe,* ed. J. V. Field and Frank A. J. L. James (Cambridge: Cambridge UP, 1993), and "Casuistry in Action: Robert Boyle's Confessional Interviews with Gilbert Burnet and Edward Stillingfleet, 1691," *Journal of Ecclesiastical History* 44 (1993): 80–98.
161. Browning, *Ordinary Men: Reserve Police Battalion 101 and the Final Solution in Poland* (New York: HarperCollins, 1992), 162.
162. John R. Williams, *The Life of Goethe: A Critical Biography* (Oxford: Blackwell, 1998), 52.

Epilogue

1. "The Original Jim Crow," in W. T. Lhamon, Jr., *Jump Jim Crow: Lost Plays, Lyrics, and Street Prose of the First Atlantic Popular Culture* (Cambridge: Harvard UP, 2003), 98; "White Man," in *The Collected Poems of Langston Hughes,* ed. Arnold Rampersad (New York: Knopf, 1994), 194–5.
2. This genealogy was compiled by my father, Donald Lee Taylor; it represents research completed in 2001.
3. Anthony Bozza, *Whatever You Say I Am: The Life and Times of Eminem* (New York: Crown, 2003), 84–5.
4. Eminem, "I'm Back" and "Criminal," *The Marshall Mathers LP* (Santa Monica: Aftermath/Interscope Records, 2000); "Brain Damage," *The Slim Shady LP* (Santa Monica: Aftermath/Interscope Records, 1999); "Marshall Mathers," *Marshall Mathers.*
5. Tricia Rose, *Black Noise: Rap Music and Black Culture in Contemporary America* (Hanover, NH: UP of New England, 1994), 27–61.
6. David Dalby, "The African Element in American English," in *Rappin' and Stylin' Out: Communication in Urban Black America,* ed. Thomas Kochman (Urbana: University of Illinois Press, 1972), 180–81.
7. Eminem, "If I Had," *Slim Shady LP,* and "Rabbit vs. Papa Doc," *8 Mile* (Santa Monica: Shady/Interscope, 2002); *OED trash n.*4 (first examples in 1831 and 1833).
8. Eminem, "The Way I Am," *Marshall Mathers LP.* For über-wigger, see Crispin Sartwell, "wiggers" (www.crispinsartwell.com/longwigger.htm) and the Stormfront White Nationalist Community (www.stormfront.org/archive). A Google search for "Eminem" and "wigger(s)" (June 20, 2004) produced 3217 hits.
9. David Roediger, "*Guineas, Wiggers,* and the Dramas of Racialized Culture," *American Literary History,* 7 (1995), 659–661; Clarence Major, ed., *Juba to Jive: A Dictionary of African-American Slang* (New York: Viking, 1994), 511.

10. "White America," *The Eminem Show* (Santa Monica: Aftermath, 2002). Unless otherwise attributed, quotations from Eminem refer to this song.
11. Best Album, Best Male, Best Hip Hop (MTV Europe awards, 2002); Best Album International, Best Solo Artist International (Brit awards, 2003); World's Best Pop/Rock Artist (World Music awards, 2003); Best Foreign Artist, Best Foreign Album (Rockbjörnen, Sweden, 2003). The album also won many American awards: "Without Me" won video of the year, best male video, best rap video, and best video direction (MTV Music Video awards, 2002), best album, best R&B/Hip Hop album (Billboard Music Awards), best rap album, best video (Grammy awards, 2003).
12. *Eminem "Talking": Marhsall Mathers In His Own Words,* ed. Chuck Weiner (Omnibus, 2002), 119.
13. Frank Rich, "Mr. Ambassador," in *White Noise: The Eminem Collection,* ed. Hilton Als and Darryl A. Turner (New York: Thunder's Mouth Press, 2003), 109.
14. On "mimetic desire," see René Girard, *Deceit, Desire, and the Novel: Self and Other in Literary Structure,* tr. Yvonne Freccero (Baltimore: Johns Hopkins UP, 1990), 2–47.
15. Bonnett, *White Identities,* 142–3.
16. For the erasure of non-European whites, see Bonnett, *White Identities,* 26: "The development of racial whiteness demanded the disappearance of non-European white identities. However, this is not to argue that the latter setoff identities were necessarily actively obliterated or suddenly replaced."
17. Nick Hasted, *The Dark Story of Eminem* (Omnibus Press, 2003), 18.
18. "Whether you're latino, white, black, Asian, it don't matter" (*Eminem "Talking,"* ed. Weiner, 16). Although latinos are themselves divided over whether to consider themselves white, this catalog makes it clear that Mathers does not.
19. For the mixed ancestry of minstrelsy, see William J. Mahar, *Behind the Burnt Cork Mask: Early Blackface Minstrelsy and Antebellum American Popular Culture* (Urbana: University of Illinois Press, 1999).
20. See Ray B. Browne, "Shakespeare in American Vaudeville and Negro Minstrelsy," *American Quarterly* 12 (1960): 374–91; Charles Haywood, "Negro Minstrelsy and Shakespearean Burlesque," in *Folklore and Society* (Hatboro, PA: The Folklore Association, 1966), 77–92.
21. John F. Poole, *Ye Comedie of Errours* (New York, n.d.), in *Nineteenth-Century Shakespeare Burlesques,* ed. Stanley Wells, 5 vols (Wilmington, DE: Michael Glazier, 1978), 5:59.
22. For an example of successful avoidance, see Richard W. Schoch, *Not Shakespeare: Bardolatry and Burlesque in the Nineteenth Century* (Cambridge: Cambridge UP, 2002).
23. *Nineteenth-Century Shakespeare Burlesques,* ed. Wells, xiii, 12; Lhamon, *Jump Jim Crow,* 441, 1, 4, 349, 355, 358, 383, 82, 362.
24. See Joseph Roach's magnificent *Cities of the Dead: Circum-Atlantic Performance* (New York: Columbia UP, 1996), and Taylor, *Time, Space, Race.*
25. See Herbert Marshall and Mildred Stock, *Ira Aldridge: The Negro Tragedian* (Rockliff, 1958), and—more generally—Hill, *Shakespeare in Sable.*
26. Brown, *Travels,* 203–7.
27. On the legal reasons for the 1996 change from M&M to Eminem, see Bozza, *Life and Times,* 14.
28. "My Name Is," *Slim Shady LP.*
29. *Are Italians White? How Race is Made in America,* ed. Jennifer Guglielmo and Salvatore Salerno (New York: Routledge, 2003); Noel Ignatiev, *How the Irish Became White* (New York: Routledge, 1995); Karen Brodin Sacks, "How Did Jews Become White Folks?," in *Race,* ed. Steven Gregory and Roger Sanjek (New Brunswick: Rutgers UP, 1994), 78–85; David Roediger, *The Wages of Whiteness: Race and the Making of the American Working Class* (New York: Verso, 1991).

30. Bozza, *Life and Times,* 93–95, 176–87; Armond White, "Genius—Not! Eminem Melts in Your Hands" (2003), in *White Noise,* ed. Als and Turner, 179–90.
31. Eric Lott, *Love and Theft: Blackface Minstrelsy and the American Working Class* (New York: Oxford UP, 1993), 95; "Without Me," *Eminem Show.*
32. Norman Mailer, "The White Negro" (1957) in *Advertisements for Myself* (New York: Putnam, 1959), 337–58.
33. Bozza, *Life and* Times, 199; Hasted, *Dark Story,* 35; *Eminem "Talking,"* ed. Weiner, 91.
34. For links between hip hop and sport, see Nelson George, *Hip Hop America* (New York: Viking Penguin, 1998), esp. 144–53; Bozzo, *Life and Times,* 43, 176, 179, 198; Rich, "Mr. Ambassador," 104, 107; Hasted, *Dark Story,* 70.
35. Cornel West, *Race Matters* (Boston: Beacon Press, 1993), 84.
36. Farai Chideya, *The Color of Our Future* (New York: William Morrow, 1999, 5–34).
37. "Captive Audience: Poetry is needed now more than ever," *The Times,* July 2, 2003: p. 17.
38. Ralph M. Rosen and Victoria Baines, "'I Am Whatever You Say I am . . . ': Satiric Program in Juvenal and Eminem," *Classical and Modern Literature: A Quarterly,* 22 (2002): 103–27.
39. Eminem, "Business," *Eminem Show.*
40. Michael Gonzales and Havelock Nelson, *Bring the Noise: A Guide to Rap Music and Hip-Hop Culture* (New York: Harmony, 1991); Rose, *Black Noise;* Als and Turner, ed., *White Noise.*
41. *OED white a.*1.f. The first cited example refers to x-rays and does not use the expression "white noise," which is not recorded until 1943.
42. *Journal of Aeronautical Science* 10 (1943), 129/1; P. B. and J. S. Medawar, *Life Science,* 1 (1977), 14 (both cited by *OED*).
43. *Eminem "Talking,"* ed. Weiner, 16–17.
44. "Stan," *The Marshall Mathers LP.*
45. Hasted, *Dark Story,* 111 (quoting an interview with *NME*). For Eminem's misogyny more generally see Bozza, *Life and Times,* 235–48; Richard Goldstein, "The Eminem Consensus," in *White Noise,* ed. Als and Turner, 129–33, and James Keller, "Shady Agonistes: Eminem, Abjection, and Masculine Protest," *Studies in Popular Culture* 25 (2003):13–23.
46. For early black male criticism of the misogyny of many black male rappers, see for instance Bakari Kitwana, *The Rap on Gangsta Rap* (Third World Press, 1994) and Michael Eric Dyson, *Between God and Gangsta Rap: Bearing Witness to Black Culture* (New York: Oxford UP, 1996), 178–86.
47. Joe L. Kincheloe, "The Struggle to Define and Reinvent Whiteness: A Pedagogical Analysis," *College Literature* 26 (1999), 177.
48. Eminem, "Who Knew," *Marshall Mathers.*
49. Eminem, "Bitch Please Part 2," *Marshall Mathers.*
50. Eminem, "The Way I Am," *Marshall Mathers.*
51. For a critique of assertions about Shakespeare's "universality," see my book *Reinventing Shakespeare.*
52. Johann Hari, "The President's Friend," in *White Noise,* ed. Als and Turner, 210; Bozza, *Life and* Times, 51–2; Michael Eric Dyson, *Holler if You Hear Me: Searching for Tupac Shakur* (New York: Basic/Civitas, 2001), 92.
53. Bozza, *Life and Times,* 1.
54. Michael Rogin, *Black Face, White Noise: Jewish Immigrants in the Hollywood Melting Pot* (Berkeley: University of California Press, 1996), 12.
55. William Bowers, "8 Mile," *White Noise,* ed. Als and Turner, 21.
56. Ron Grundmann, "White Man's Burden: Eminem's Movie Debut in 8 Mile," *Cineaste 28* (March 1, 2003): 30–35.

57. On Stallone's Rocky films as white recovery fantasies, see Aaron David Gresson III, *The Recovery of Race in America* (Minneapolis: University of Minnesota Press, 1995), 170; this forms part of his analysis of Vanilla Ice (167–74), which concludes in what could be a description of *8 Mile:* "The white star is thus at once purged and victorious," achieving "the heroic recovery of racial hegemony" (174).
58. Eminem, "One Good Move" (October 26, 2004); Hasted, *Dark Story,* 66.
59. *Eminem "Talking,"* ed. Weiner, 134; Hasted, *Dark Story,* 191.
60. Bakari Kitwana, *The Hip Hop Generation: Young Blacks and the Crisis in African American Culture* (New York: Basic/Civitas, 2002), 3–84.
61. Nas, "I Want to Talk to You," *I Am* (New York: Columbia, 1999).
62. *Eminem "Talking,"* ed. Weiner, 126, 18.
63. Eminem, "Cum on Everybody," *Slim Shady LP.*
64. James Baldwin, "On Being 'White' . . . and Other Lies," *Essence* (April 1984): 90–92.
65. Wimsatt, *Bomb the Suburbs* (New York: Soft Skull/Subway and Elevated, 2000), 32.
66. Bozza, *Life and Times,* 255.
67. See www.eminemweb.com/biography and www.eminem.net/biography.
68. George, *Hip Hop America,* 57.
69. Fifty Cent (featuring Eminem), "Patiently Waiting," *Get Rich or Die Tryin* (Santa Monica: Shady/Interscope, 2003).
70. Eminem, "Bully," *Straight From the Lab EP* (Santa Monica: Shady/Interscope, 2003).
71. Fred L. Pincus, *Reverse Discrimination: Dismantling the Myth* (Boulder, CO: Lynne Rienner, 2003).
72. On adoption, overpopulation, and reproduction, see the last chapter of my book *Castration.*
73. Eminem, "Bitch Please Part 2," *Marshall Mathers.*
74. Eminem, "My Name Is," *Slim Shady LP.*

Index

Compiled by Ronald A. Tumelson